Fifth Edition

MANUFACTURING
ORGANIZATION
AND MANAGEMENT

Harold T. Amrine
Professor Emeritus of Industrial Engineering
Purdue University

John A. Ritchey
President, Cardinal Consultants

Colin L. Moodie
Professor of Industrial Engineering
Purdue University

PRENTICE-HALL, INC., Englewood Cliffs, New Jersey 07632

Library of Congress Cataloging-in-Publication Data

AMRINE, HAROLD T.
   Manufacturing organization and management.

   Bibliography
   Includes index.
   1. Factory management.   I. Ritchey, John Arthur,
(date).   II. Moodie, Colin.   III. Title.
TS155.A478   1987   670.42′068   86-18641
ISBN 0-13-555814-X

Editorial/production supervision: *Denise Gannon*
Cover design: *Lundgren Graphics, Ltd.*
Manufacturing buyer: *Rhett Conklin*

Printed in the United States of America

10 9 8 7 6 5 4

ISBN 0-13-555814-X   025

PRENTICE-HALL INTERNATIONAL (UK) LIMITED, *London*
PRENTICE-HALL OF AUSTRALIA PTY. LIMITED, *Sydney*
PRENTICE-HALL CANADA INC., *Toronto*
PRENTICE-HALL HISPANOAMERICANA, S.A., *Mexico*
PRENTICE-HALL OF INDIA PRIVATE LIMITED, *New Delhi*
PRENTICE-HALL OF JAPAN, INC., *Tokyo*
PRENTICE-HALL OF SOUTHEAST ASIA PTE. LTD., *Singapore*
EDITORA PRENTICE-HALL DO BRASIL, LTDA., *Rio de Janeiro*

CONTENTS

8   WORK MEASUREMENT   134

9   MATERIALS HANDLING   160

10   PHYSICAL FACILITIES   185

Section Three   MANUFACTURING CONTROL   225

11   FUNDAMENTALS OF CONTROL   225

PREFACE

The purpose of this book is the same as it has been in the previous four editions, namely, to familiarize the reader with the principles, practices, and functions of manufacturing management. The reader in this case could be a graduate or undergraduate student, a non-engineer or an engineer, or an ordinary layman. If such persons are unfamiliar or only partially familiar with what goes on in a manufacturing organization, then this book is designed to fill in the gaps.

Manufacturing enterprises have been undergoing many changes in an attempt to produce higher quality products and to become more competitive in the markets of the world. This poses many new challenges for manufacturing managers. They must be conversant with the ever-changing technology applicable to their operations. At the same time, they can't overlook their existing buildings and machines or discard the sound practices that they built on over the years. Thus, in this edition we have tried to balance the old with the new and to cover those principles and functions that will continue to have universal application.

Of necessity, manufacturing organization and management involves many topics, but in discussing each of these we have attempted to indicate relationships with other topics. In other words, a person concerned with maintenance should have an understanding of the impact of maintenance decisions on other areas, such as production control and quality control. A lack of understanding of the total picture can easily happen when one concentrates on solutions to individual problems. In this volume we have tried to place emphasis on problems and give some attention to solutions, leaving any exhaustive treatment to others.

As in previous editions, we have tried to write this book in a simple, easily understood style. We have retained a minimum of quantification, because we don't want the reader to get lost in equations. Recognizing the increasing importance of "human resources," additional emphasis has been placed on people. New questions and case problems have been added to every chapter to enable the reader to expand on the topics covered. Any instructor involved can use these to elaborate on the assignments and perhaps use them as a means of introducing new material.

We are mainly concerned with topics dealing directly with manufacturing activities; however, it is recognized that successful manufacturing cannot exist without giving proper attention to the areas of finance, marketing, and personnel. For this reason, chapters dealing with these topics are included as a separate section at the end to be utilized in whatever way the instructor sees fit. Again, to the uninitiated, some understanding of these topics is essential to complete the total picture of manufacturing organization and management.

Many of the concepts contained herein have applicability in areas other than manufacturing, and the applications seem to be expanding every day. Hospitals, banks, warehouses, and department stores, to name a few, all have problems relating to employees, costs, inventory control, maintenance, and almost everything covered in this text. For this reason, persons dealing with these areas and others should not be alarmed by our emphasis on the words "manufacturing" and "production." The basic concepts are the important thing, and the application of many of the concepts outlined herein will lead to improved and more profitable operations.

Without losing our original flavor, we have endeavored to bring the material in this fifth edition up to date and to add new materials, in an effort to make the coverage most useful to today's generation of manufacturing managers. In doing so, we have had the benefit of comments and suggestions from many organizations and have obtained reactions and contributions from numerous students who have gone through the material presented in earlier editions. We are indeed grateful for all this interest and sincerely hope that this new treatment will continue the tradition of getting persons started satisfactorily in a very rewarding career in manufacturing management.

HTA
JAR
CLM

1

PRODUCTIVITY AND MANUFACTURING MANAGEMENT

The managing of a manufacturing firm today presents a greater challenge than ever before. Top managers of companies are presented with an endless stream of problems that arise from continuing inflation, energy, high taxes, government regulations, shortage of capital, worker dissatisfaction, high costs of inadequate productivity, and intense foreign competition. To get some idea of the magnitude of these problems, one need but pick up a daily newspaper or newsmagazine and read about efforts to offset price increases, to secure capital for plant modernization, to increase productivity, to meet foreign competition, and so forth.

It long has been recognized that high productivity has been one of the keys to the high standard of living that has existed in the United States. Further, it doesn't require extensive analysis to reveal that productivity is the backbone of a nation's economic progress—in those countries where productivity is high, the standard of living is high. In recent years, there has been increasing concern in the United States about our slowdown in productivity increases and the long-range impact that this can have on each of us and on America's ability to compete in the world's markets. Thus, increasing productivity should be a national challenge, and it behooves all managers to do their utmost to achieve ever increasing levels.

Since many of the functions that we shall be discussing in this book have a direct bearing on productivity, it seems only fitting that we devote part of the introductory chapter to an overview of this subject. At the outset, let us distinguish between *production* and *productivity*. Production is the output of the productive forces, whereas productivity is a measure of the output resulting from a given input—such as the number of lawn mowers assembled by a crew in one hour.

Productivity in the United States

For many years, the United States was looked to as the acme of high productivity. It was singled out as symbolizing the ultimate in industrial attainment, and many people visited the United States in an effort to study its manufacturing and distribution methods with a view to introducing these into their nations.

Thus, it came as somewhat of a shock to observe that as the continuing industrialization of many nations (particularly Japan, West Germany, Italy, and France) increased, their engineers were able to develop equipment and processes and to build new plants that surpassed ours. Their progress has continued unabated, and data provided by the Bureau of Labor Statistics, U.S. Department of Labor, in December 1979 show that productivity in manufacturing in the United States increased 23.6 percent from 1968 to 1978, whereas it increased 89.1 percent in Japan, 63.8 percent in West Germany, 60.1 percent in Italy, and 61.8 percent in France. More recently, in 1984 productivity rose 3.5 percent in the United States, whereas it grew by 9.5 percent in Japan, 4.7 percent in West Germany, 6.3 percent in Italy, and 5.0 percent in France. It is not surprising, then, that many Americans have become alarmed, and organizations such as the Institute of Industrial Engineers and the American Productivity Center (in Houston) have become national voices for productivity improvement. Likewise, companies such as Motorola maintain an intensive company-wide program to increase productivity and quality.

In order to visualize the impact that various factors may have on a worker's productivity, let us consider a simple example—that of washing an automobile. A man using an ordinary garden hose and a sponge might do the job at a leisurely pace in one hour. If he increased his effort, he could do the job in a shorter period of time. However, in so doing, he may do a poorer job and the quality of his work may suffer. Through an investment in a building and mechanized car washing equipment, this same man might be able to wash 20 or 30 cars per hour. Thus, it is evident that such factors as worker effort, the method used, quality of workmanship, and machines used have an effect on productivity.

One thing that many people agree on is that a significant increase in productivity in the long run cannot be achieved solely by increased worker effort. The real growth can come about only through capital investment in newer and better machines, equipment, and facilities. Incidentally, this is one way in which the aforementioned nations have been able to surpass us in recent years. Whereas many foreign plants have been built quite recently and contain the latest in equipment and manufacturing methods, large numbers of American companies haven't been able to keep pace. Some of the blame for this can be attributed to the tax breaks provided by foreign countries and to the federal depreciation schedules used in this country which tend to discourage capital investment. Further, some of the capital equipment investment currently being made in the United States is for anti-pollution, which is a good investment for the nation but probably doesn't improve productivity. Illustrative of the magnitude of some of these investments by companies was the expenditure of $25 million on pollution controls in one automotive foundry.

Lest we be left with the impression that the human element is not important, there is no question but that productivity has been affected by the level of social unrest that exists in many plants—particularly among the younger workers in mass production industries. This has given rise to much attention being focused on the behavioral sciences, on human factors, and on ways to motivate workers to produce at satisfactory levels.

Social and Economic Background of American Industry

Because of her early democratic philosophy, the United States has developed as a "classless" society composed of a "melting pot" of people. People from many foreign countries brought with them their own customs and ideas and made their unique contributions to a conglomerate society. Newcomers and their descendants became aware that in the United States the opportunity to succeed and to be judged on the basis of accomplishments was the ideal. Thus, the country's growth was built on the achievements of men such as Henry Ford, Andrew Carnegie, John D. Rockefeller, George Eastman, and many others. By and large, those who have been successful in business have been greatly respected.

In 1890, at about the time the United States was changing from being principally an agricultural nation, the Sherman Antitrust Act was passed. This law was designed to protect against monopolies by declaring that any combination in restraint of trade among the states was illegal. The rigid enforcement of this national policy prevented price-fixing, the formation of cartels, and other practices common in some European and far eastern countries. Because of the limitations imposed by this law, the managers of the businesses in the United States accepted the concept of true competition and concentrated their attention on ways in which they could increase their volume of business. The spirit of competition has continued unabated, and many people consider it to be the most important single factor leading to the development of the United States as a great industrial nation. Nonetheless, there has been growing concern in recent years that the restraints imposed on American companies place them at a severe disadvantage in competing in world markets.

As a result of its early immigration policy, the United States has experienced an ever increasing population. The result of this has been to provide an adequate supply of labor and a large internal market that has been conducive to mass production. However, a large population is not synonymous with high productivity or national prosperity, as is evidenced by India. Rather, it is the combination of a large and growing population, high real wages, and a desire for material goods that has been conducive to mass production in the United States.

Many trade-union advocates argue that the strong unions that developed in the United States have had significant influence on the level of productivity attained. They contend that the continuous pressure put on management for higher wages, shorter working hours, retirement plans, and other benefits has forced management to reduce costs and to operate businesses efficiently. There may be a considerable element of truth in this assertion, but at the same time, there has been a tendency for certain unions to resort to restrictive practices, to slow progress, and even to have an influence on the closing of plants. This is illustrated by a manufacturer of I-beam truck axles that was forced to close a plant in Cleveland because the union insisted on piecework rates that were exorbitant and priced the company out of its market. It is ironic to note that this company found that it could make these axles in one of its plants in Brazil and deliver them to its customers in the United States cheaper than it could make them in Cleveland.

Not one of the least significant factors contributing to the industrial development in the United States has been our educational system, founded on the philosophy that it is the right of everyone to have an education. This has led to a system of higher education capable of producing the great numbers of engineers, scientists, computer programmers, accountants, and others possessing the necessary skills that have been in demand by American industry.

There are many other factors that have influenced the growth of industry in the United States. Among these are the influence of installment buying and its tremendous impact on the purchasing power of the nation, and the great emphasis placed on market research.

The Changing Nature of Manufacturing in the United States

The 1970's and early 1980's brought about great changes in the distribution of manufacturing centers throughout the world. A "trade war" has developed which poses the basic issue of which nations will produce the bulk of the world's capital goods and will survive. Change is accelerating so rapidly, that the manufacturing world at the beginning of the twenty-first century will be as different from 1985 as today's tools are from those used to win World War II. In their 1985 Industry Outlook, *Business Week* said, "The decline of manufacturing America during the 1970's and early 1980's has been one of the most important economic developments in this century."

In his book, *"The Next American Frontier,"* Robert Reich states,

> The trend is becoming clear. First, America's basic steel, textile, automobile, consumer electronics, rubber, and petrochemical industries are becoming uncompetitive in the world. Secondly, now that production can be fragmented into separate, globally scattered operations, whole segments of American industries are becoming uncompetitive. Whatever the final product, those parts of U.S. produc-

tion requiring high-volume machinery and unsophisticated workers can be accomplished more cheaply in developing nations. Automation, far from halting this trend, has accelerated it. Sophisticated machinery is readily moved to low-wage countries . . . Some of the world's most automated textile plants are now found in Hong Kong and some of the most advanced steelworks are in South Korea . . . America's manufacturing base is eroding precipitously.

Since World War II, we have moved steadily from a capital-intensive industrial society based on physical resources to a diversified service economy based on human resources. In 1985, the service enterprises employed 3 out of every 4 working Americans and generated two-thirds of our gross national product. Over 95 percent of the 25 million new jobs created since 1970 were in services. In 1984, private services contributed 56.6 percent to the gross national product versus only 21.2 percent from manufacturing.

Because of the changing international climate in manufacturing, many American companies are linking up with their former rivals in a vast array of joint ventures and purchase agreements. A number of foreign companies (e.g., Honda, Mazda, Mitsubishi, Nissan, Toyota, Volkswagen, Sony, Landis and Gyr, and Kikkoman Foods), are buying American companies or building new plants in the United States. It is estimated that by the end of the 1980's Honda, Mazda, Mitsubishi, Nissan, and Toyota will be turning out a million or more cars and trucks per year in the United States. Unfortunately, these plants hold down employment potential because they get many of their parts from Japan.

Illustrative of the dilemma that can confront an entire industry is the shoe industry. Total imports of shoes in 1960 were 4% of the market. However, imports from Brazil, Taiwan, South Korea, Spain, and Italy captured 63% of the market in 1983 and 71% in 1984. Over 100 of the 600 shoe factories in the United States had been closed by 1984, leading to widespread complaints from the shoe industry and prompting the International Trade Commission to make recommendations to the President that this industry be given relief, perhaps in the form of import curbs. Increasingly, we are witnessing frantic calls from spokesmen from various industries for protection from the flood of imported goods and the tremendous disparity in the balance of payments (e.g., trade deficits of $60 billion in 1983 and $110 billion in 1984). In 1985, the U.S. Department of Commerce announced that for the first time since 1914 the United States had become a debtor nation, a status usually associated with developing countries. Many people ask, "What has happened to our vaunted American industrial might?"

A presidential Study Commission on Industrial Competitiveness,[1] headed by Hewlett-Packard's John Young, submitted a plan to the White House in 1985 which criticized U.S. performance in several key areas:

Technology. The U.S. is frittering away its lead in high tech by spending too little on civilian research and development.

---

[1]See "America's High-Tech Crisis," *Business Week*, March 11, 1985, p. 58.

Manufacturing. Even more damaging is industry's failure to master the discipline of modern manufacturing. It does little good to design state-of-the-art products if within a short time our foreign competitors can manufacture them more cheaply. But U.S. companies are hard pressed to match Japanese investments because the cost of capital here is double what it is in Japan.

Capital. The high cost of capital in the U.S. is the result of three problems: Americans save too little, the government spends too much, and the tax system is biased against investment. The Japanese can invest twice as much as we can and because of the overvalued dollar their products are 25% cheaper than they should be.

Antitrust. To determine what is or isn't anticompetitive, the Justice Department needs to consider overall world market positions, not just those of the U.S. market.

People. American workers are still mired in adversarial relationships with management that may no longer serve the best interests of both parties and the public. Furthermore, the U.S. isn't doing enough to help the workers adapt to changes in technology.

Trade policy. The U.S. hasn't kept up with the new realities of world competition. Washington responds belatedly, if at all, to damage caused by dumping or foreign policies that distort trade flow.

Despite the aforementioned unsettling developments, American manufacturing is not doomed. Some companies have had poor experience in trying to manufacture parts or complete products in foreign countries and are bringing their business back to the United States. Then, too, some products (e.g., breakfast cereals, soaps, paper products, cosmetics, and pharmaceutical products) always will be made here. In other industries, increased automation and operating efficiency will tend to neutralize lower foreign labor costs and improve America's competitive position. As stated at the outset of this chapter, the managing of a manufacturing firm presents a great challenge which can only be met by realizing that American industry is being internationalized.

Industrial Management in the United States

Over the years writers on industrial management have discovered that the factors that make for successful manufacturing operations can be described using words all beginning with the letter "M." We choose to use this sometimes overworked coincidence because it serves as an easy learning aid to the uninitiated and at the same time gives a quick overall view of manufacturing activity. Each of the "M's" will be discussed briefly, but they can be introduced by the following sentence: Profitable manufacturing comes about through the use of *money* to bring together *machines* and *materials* in such a manner that *men*[2] can employ proper *methods* to

---

[2]*Men* here should be understood to mean both male and female workers. The "M" device is not intended to discriminate, but rather to simplify.

produce products that will be acceptable to *markets;* all of these activities are coordinated by *management*.

Money is mentioned first because it is a prerequisite to any manufacturing operation. Money is necessary to provide the plant and equipment, to purchase raw materials, and to meet payrolls until such time as there is income from the sale of products. Money problems in industry usually get intertwined with problems of forms of ownership; therefore, later chapters of this book will deal both with financing and with ownership forms, with special emphasis on the corporation.

Machines, in the broad sense used here, include all production facilities such as buildings, tools, and equipment, as well as machines in the strict sense. These are the "tools of production," whether they be simple inspection benches or complex numerical-control machines. Machines cost money, but they then become fixed assets in a manufacturing establishment. They are used over again year after year, so the investment in machines can be expected to last for an appreciable time. Appropriate chapters are devoted to a consideration of providing these physical facilities for a manufacturing enterprise.

Materials, in contrast to the "fixed" investment in machines, constitute a temporary investment. Materials are those things that become a part of the finished product offered for sale or that are used in the manufacture of that product. Some material may be "raw" in the strict sense of being directly derived from our natural resources—such as iron, wheat, or crude oil. Other materials that one plant may consider raw may in reality be another plant's finished product. Examples would be sheet steel, transistors, and lubrication oil. Materials introduce problems of procurement, storage, and handling—all of which will be treated in later chapters.

Men in the sense used here are those people in the manufacturing concern who use the machines and materials provided to make the product. The day of the completely automatic factory is not yet here; and regardless of the state of mechanization a company might employ, some workers will be required—if only to press buttons. The problems of people within a company are extremely important, for without productive workers the rest of the efforts toward a profitable manufacturing activity will be in vain. For this reason, space is devoted here to handling workers, methods of wage payment, and union relationships.

Methods are integrators of machines, materials, and men. The methods used in bringing these three factors together may mean the difference between profitable operation and bankruptcy. As a result, companies are constantly searching for better ways of doing things, better materials, and improved sequences of operation. There may be "one best way" today, but the alert company does not allow any one method to be "best" for very long. The search for better methods will be described in later chapters.

Markets are the means by which a company secures income, not only to pay for the cost of the factors discussed so far, but also to provide a profit. Manufacturing may quite successfully utilize only the previous factors discussed, and a company may end up with a warehouse full of manufactured products of the highest quality. The operation does not become profitable, however, without markets for those products. Markets may be discovered or they may be developed; our discussions will give appropriate coverage to this problem.

Management may be last on the list of seven factors, but it is the keystone of the manufacturing enterprise. Although it involves men and women, we choose to give it special recognition because of its role in coordination. Management may be likened to the quarterback of a football team, with the other "M" factors playing particular positions on the team. All have their roles to play, but the quarterback must appraise the overall situation, call the right signals, and "manage" the effort to reach the goal line. Manufacturing enterprises don't always reach their goals—any more than football teams do.

The primary functions of management have often been described as those of planning, organizing, staffing, directing, and controlling. These five functions are required of anyone in a management position, whether this be the president of the company or a foreman. *Planning* connotes setting goals for the company (or department, as the case may be) and outlining the steps to be taken to reach these goals. *Organizing* is the process of dividing the overall job into its various parts so they can be assigned to individuals to carry out. *Staffing* involves the hiring, developing, and placing of qualified people in the various jobs. *Directing* is the process of issuing orders and instructions to carry out plans. *Controlling* is an appraisal step. It compares actual performance with plans, to be certain that plans are being carried out. Corrective action may be necessary in order to get performance back in line; or conceivably a change in plan may be called for. For the company as a whole, quality control is certainly a part of "controlling," but the quality-control manager will also need to plan, organize, staff, direct, and control his own quality-control operations. Thus, we see the importance of management throughout a manufacturing organization.

There are a number of general practices that *able* American managers have adhered to. Among these are the following: (1) they have maintained balanced emphasis on all phases of business activity and have tried to develop each function as a complement to the others; (2) they have demonstrated a willingness to take business risks and have evidenced much dissatisfaction with the "status quo"; (3) they have been willing to open their doors and to share information with others; (4) they have recognized the need for expert advice and have been quick to employ staff specialists or outside consultants; (5) they have recognized the need for aids in "decision-making" and have established long-range planning groups, computer facilities, and so forth; (6) they have recognized that there is no need to manufacture a product if it can't be sold, and they have put great stress on market research, advertising, and sales promotion—and on sound methods of distribution; (7) they have endeavored to establish a sound organization structure, for they have recognized that organization is one of the principal factors determining the productivity of labor, assuming capital and natural resources to be constant; (8) they have recognized that organizations must be built around "people" and not "things," and that strong emphasis must be placed on supervisory leadership; and (9) they have stressed the need for continuous training and cooperation with educational institutions.

Although these nine practices are among those that American management has generally adhered to, there is still considerable diversity in how companies are managed. In Chapter 3, we shall deal more completely with management in a manufacturing concern. In the remainder of this chapter, let us give consideration to some of the more specific characteristics of modern manufacturing.

Characteristics of Modern Manufacturing

Modern manufacturing has a number of characteristics that make for increasing success year after year. Many of these will be explained throughout this book, but a few deserve mention at this point, for they are basic to most manufacturing activity.

Perhaps the foremost characteristic of manufacturing today is a basic philosophy that *manufacturing is important*[3] and deserves primary consideration from top management. Manufacturing has come of age and requires sound planning, highly qualified engineers and other staff people, well-trained workers, and modern facilities and equipment. Only first class companies can hope to compete in the world's markets!

The second characteristic of modern manufacturing is the increasing emphasis being placed on *quality*. In today's international marketplace, quality is the only way to win! How often have you heard, "My Toyota is terrific, it is much better made than American cars." Thus, it comes as no surprise that Ford advertises that "Quality is job number 1." In the same way, Motorola advertises that it is "90,000 people in pursuit of perfection."

The third characteristic of modern manufacturing is the increasing recognition that a company's greatest asset is its *people*. More and more companies are eliminating headquarters staff specialists in order to get decisions made on the "firing line" by the people who are actually involved in producing the products. (It is of interest to note that in a recent study it was disclosed that companies plan to thin middle management positions by 30 percent.) There is the realization that if you give employees a voice in operations, they are motivated and ingenious, and will try to achieve the same goals as management. Let us look at an example that took place in a Ford assembly plant. In this plant, every person on the line was given access to a button that could be used to shut down the line. The buttons were used about 10 times per day, just in time to make a quality adjustment. After the first few months, the number of defects per car had dropped from 17.1 to 0.8 per

---

[3]Indicative of this is the fact that the American Society of Mechanical Engineers established a new Manufacturing Division in 1985.

car, the number of cars requiring rework after they came off the line fell by 97 percent, and the number of grievances plummeted.

A fourth characteristic of manufacturing today is the almost universal preoccupation with *cost control*. Whereas cost control in the United States previously was essentially an annual project, it now has become a continuum. Senior managers are questioning every function, eliminating some jobs, combining others, flattening corporate pyramids, and pushing responsibility ever lower in the hierarchy. The axe falls quickest on staff functions—planning, training, clerical services—that are deemed expensive luxuries.

A fifth characteristic of manufacturing today is that of *focus* and *specialization*. Many companies have learned that they can't be good at everything and that they need to focus on what they do best. Some manufacturers concentrate on producing a single item, and others restrict production to a line of related products. The result of such specialization is usually lowered cost of production and improved quality. Specialization also means the division of work or effort, and this operates both at the worker level and at the management level.

A sixth manufacturing characteristic today is *mechanization*. The Industrial Revolution was the application of the mechanization idea. Early inventions in spinning and weaving made machine operations of what had until then been handwork. Eli Whitney's system of interchangeable manufacture made possible the mass-production industries we now take for granted. Today, mechanization has been carried so far that we no longer consider it simply a manufacturing characteristic. The use of machines has become a part of our way of life, whether we are mowing the lawn or operating a factory.

Although people have for many years been able to transfer manual skill to machines, it has only been recently that we have been able to transfer a certain amount of intelligence to machines. In other words, some machines today can do their work without the aid of human thinking during the process. This has led to the extensive use of numerical control, to automation of an advanced variety, to flexible manufacturing systems, and to dreams of a completely automatic factory.

A seventh characteristic of modern manufacturing is the increasing use of *computers and data processing equipment*. Perhaps no other recent development has had more impact on American industry than the widespread usage of computers. It has made possible the handling of enormous amounts of data, the establishment of data bases, and the solving of complex business and engineering problems at fantastic rates of speed. The range of application of computers and data processing equipment has been extended almost as rapidly as new equipment and techniques of application have been developed, and includes computations for scientific research, control of individual machines and total manufacturing processes, production and inventory control, quality control, maintenance control, processing of payrolls, keeping of accounts, and many other functions. The continuous development of microprocessors and computer capabilities promises to be an increasingly valuable aid to production management and will make it possible to provide speedy answers to problems involving models, to eliminate much unnecessary clerical work, to control various kinds of manufacturing processes, and to provide speedy communications.

The eighth and last characteristic is the use of *simulation* and *mathematical models* to aid in decision making. The increasing development of computer software has made it possible to try different manufacturing configurations prior to installation and to select that method which best fits the planning criteria. This provides management with a valuable planning tool and helps prevent taking steps that may prove to be ill-advised and costly.

The aforementioned characteristics of modern manufacturing may not be a complete list because the setting for manufacturing in the United States is a dynamic and ever changing one. However, they are distinguishing features that may be found in the best managed and most successful companies in the United States, be they large or small.

Summary

In this chapter, we have endeavored to point out the importance of productivity and the role that industrial management plays in trying to achieve high productivity levels. Since productivity is a problem of growing importance to the United States and to all of us, we should be cognizant of those factors which have an important bearing on the subject. Therefore, you will find that most of the chapters that follow in this book will touch on topics influencing the productive output of manufacturing establishments.

QUESTIONS

1. How may increased productivity offset increases in employees' wages?
2. Discuss the likelihood that productivity both on the farm and in the factory will become so high that the average person will need to work only 20 hours a week.
3. The eight richest countries with one-tenth of the world's population possess over 50 percent of the world's wealth. What impact may increased production and productivity in the underdeveloped nations have on manufacturing in the United States?
4. Define the management functions of planning, organizing, staffing, directing, and controlling in terms of some business or organization with which you are familiar.
5. Although it wasn't always true, Japan has acquired the reputation of producing high-quality products. What influence may this have had on the productivity of that country?
6. In addition to the factors discussed in this chapter, what other factors have had influence on the attainment of a high level of industrial productivity in the United States?
7. Increasingly, the managers of American companies are college or university graduates. What are the long-range implications of this as a company policy?
8. Can specialization of effort in manufacturing be carried too far? If so, what are the consequences?

9. In the long run, what effect may the increasing use of computers and data processing equipment have on employment levels?

10. By the year 2000, how do you envision the United States will be faring in the international marketplace?

11. Some of the "free market" advocates are of the opinion that if our shoe and other industries can't compete with those of other nations, we should get out of the business. Comment on this philosophy.

12. Why do you think that manufacturers in the United States recently have become increasingly aware of the importance of manufacturing, quality, people, cost control, and other developments?

CASE PROBLEM

Graves Safe Company

Graves Safe Company is a small metal products company (300 employees) that has been engaged in making a variety of office safes for over 75 years. The company has had its ups and downs over the years and has been strongly influenced by the nation's business cycles. Despite the fluctuating state of the economy, the company has steadily moved forward and has been doing its utmost to modernize its plant and equipment. Then, too, the replacement of a 70-year-old president two years ago with a 45-year-old, dynamic, aggressive executive vice-president, Wilbur Mason, has really given the company a shot in the arm.

As a progressive president, Wilbur Mason has expressed great interest in maintaining a history of the productivity attainments of the company. He has touched on this informally in several staff meetings and has gotten favorable support. He has decided to move ahead on this matter and has appointed a committee of four people—Jonathan Smith, Manager of Industrial Engineering (to be chairman); Arthur Wilkinson, Chief Engineer; Stephen Richardson, Manufacturing Manager; and Joseph Stanford, Personnel Manager—to provide him with preliminary recommendations within six weeks.

Questions:

1. One of the initial findings of the committee was the results of a survey taken in 1981 that disclosed that less than 3% of the businesses in the United States have systems for measuring productivity. Thus, it appeared as though Graves Safe would not have a lot of companies that it could emulate. Nevertheless, they could profit from the experiences of those companies that were willing to share information. It soon became evident that if productivity equals output divided by input, the committee would have to define both output and input. How do you recommend that they do this?

2. In trying to compile a history of productivity in the company, what problems might be anticipated?

3. Of what real value would a history of productivity be? Is it worth the effort required to determine it?

2

BACKGROUND OF MANUFACTURING MANAGEMENT

Until the development of the factory system and the general concept of manufacturing, there was no such thing as management as we know it. It is true that people operated businesses of one kind or another, but for the most part these people were owners of the business and did not regard themselves as managers as well. The development and use of the management concept probably occurred for three reasons. The first has already been mentioned, namely, the development of the factory system of production. The second essentially stems from the first, namely, the development of the large corporation with many owners and the necessity to hire people to operate the business. The third reason stems from the work of many of the pioneers of scientific management who were able to demonstrate the value, from a performance and profit point of view, of some of the techniques they were developing. For the most part, the early developments were applied in manufacturing concerns, but later, and particularly today, we see these management concepts having great application in all types of businesses, including banks, department stores, farms, insurance companies, hospitals, government units, and many others.

The student of management or of manufacturing management should have some knowledge of the background of the field being studied and with that knowledge should be in a better position to contribute further to its growth and application in the world of business and industry.

Management Prior to 1800

Evidence of the development and use of management principles in antiquity is meager, but nevertheless it is present. The Babylonians made use of the minimum-wage rate principle in about 1950 B.C., and the Chinese applied the principle of division of labor about 1644 B.C. The Egyptians as far back as 1300 B.C. recognized the importance of organization and administration in the bureaucratic states. The Greeks have left us little evidence of their having insight into the principles of management, but the existence of their various councils, popular courts, and boards indicate an appreciation of the managerial function. Socrates discusses the advantages of specialization of labor in connection with the development of an ideal city in Plato's *Republic*. Finally, the Bible tells us that Moses "chose able men out of all Israel, and made them heads over the people, rulers of thousands, rulers of hundreds, rulers of fifty, and rulers of ten."

Advancing to English industry in recent centuries, we find considerable evidence of the recognition of the principles of management in relation to doing work. Standard practice instructions, employee welfare plans, and recognition of the principle of overhead charges were in use in various industries in Great Britain between 1600 and 1800. In 1776, Adam Smith, a British economist, published his *Wealth of Nations,* in which he discredited the economic policies of the past and promoted the overthrow of practices that had come down from earlier times but were unsuited to modern society. Smith dealt with such subjects as capital, freedom of trade, rent, wages, and profit, but his premise was that the annual labor of a nation is the source from which it derives its supply of the necessities and conveniences of life. He developed the concept that improvement in the productivity of labor depends largely upon its division and upon the wages paid to labor.

Adam Smith wrote during the period of time in Great Britain when the Industrial Revolution was taking place. In a certain sense, he provided some theoretical concepts that, when coupled with the practical problems forced upon industry by the Industrial Revolution, provided the basis for modern manufacturing management.

The Industrial Revolution

The beginnings of modern industry can be accurately dated and placed. The series of events that brought the factory system into being is referred to as the Industrial Revolution and occurred largely in England from 1770 to the early 1800's. These events are generally referred to as the great inventions, and these inventions brought the machine age to all civilized people. At the time, they revolutionized the character of industrial England, and somewhat later, the industrial life of the United States.

The great inventions are eight in number, with six of them having been conceived in England, one in France, and one in the United States. Most of them have to do with the spinning of yarn and the weaving of cloth. This is logical from the point of view that cloth was the principal export commodity of England at the time and was in short supply owing to the considerable expansion of England's colonial empire and its commercial trade. The inventions are discussed in their chronological order below.

Hargreaves' spinning jenny.   In 1764, James Hargreaves invented a spinning machine capable of spinning eight threads of yarn at one time in contrast to the usual single thread on the spinning wheel. His invention was not patented until 1770—the date usually associated with it.

Arkwright's water frame.   Richard Arkwright, a barber, established in 1771 the first of numerous successful mills employing his patented spinning machine driven by water power; hence its name, "water frame." Arkwright's interest in the mills themselves gained him a reputation as a promoter of efficiency and developer of the factory system.

Crompton's mule.   Samuel Crompton's invention in 1779 superseded both of the previous inventions. It was called the "mule" and combined the principles of the "jenny" and "water frame" and can be thought of as a hybrid mechanical offspring. This invention produced an enormous increase of production and did away with hand spinning.

Cartwright's power loom.   The three previous inventions increased enormously the capacity to spin raw fibers into yarn, and the next need was for a machine to weave the yarn into cloth. In 1785 Edmund Cartwright, a clergyman, patented the "power loom," a machine for weaving. It was not adopted by industry to any great extent until 1811, but the basic principle had been developed, and machine weaving became the chief factor in destroying the ancient system of domestic manufacture, or manufacture in the home.

Watt's steam engine.   Clearly, the new spinning and weaving machinery could not revolutionize industry of themselves, for power was needed to drive them, and the water power in use was insufficient and not always available. James Watt patented his steam engine in 1769, but nearly ten years passed before he was able to build a large operating machine, and it was not until 1785 that the steam engine was introduced into a factory for spinning cotton. Its advantages over water power as a prime mover were immediately apparent, and manufacturers began to adopt it.

Berthollet's chlorine bleaching discovery.   The next bottleneck in the industry turned out to be bleaching capacity. Until this time, bleaching had been accomplished by wetting the cloth with a mild alkali and spreading it in large fields where it would be exposed to the action of sunlight. The process itself was a very slow one—let alone the limitations of inconstant sunlight—so that it took at least six months for the weavers to get their "gray goods" bleached. In 1785 a French chemist, Claude Louis Berthollet, discovered the bleaching power of chlorine. The chemical bleaching agent whitened cloth in a few hours and worked as well on dull days as on sunlit days. The original process was handicapped by the hazardous fumes of the chlorine gas, but in 1798 Charles Tennant discovered the process of making bleaching powder from chlorine and lime, which eliminated this problem.

Maudslay's screw-cutting lathe.   Early machines were made largely of wood, and it was evident that metal machinery for manufacturing would be limited in application unless there were means available to build such machinery and keep it in repair. Henry Maudslay, in 1797, developed the combination of a slide rest, change gears, and power-driven lead screw, which is a distinguishing feature of many machine tools even today. The Maudslay lathe made possible machines with which to build other machines and was therefore extremely important in the development and continuation of the Industrial Revolution.

Interchangeable manufacture.   The eighth great invention of the Industrial Revolution was neither a machine nor a process, but a system of interchangeable manufacture, meaning that the parts of any assembly can be produced to so close a tolerance that they can be selected at random and assembled into a component. An American, Eli Whitney, is given credit for first establishing such an interchangeable system of manufacture in 1798, in carrying out a contract for ten thousand muskets. Simeon North did the same thing in 1799 on a contract for five hundred pistols. Interchangeable manufacture is commonplace to us today, but its origin and development played an extremely important role in the growth of mass-production techniques.

Charles Babbage

Although the practice of manufacturing management began and spread during the Industrial Revolution, it was the work of Charles Babbage that began to reveal the science of manufacturing management. His book, *On the Economy of Machinery in Manufactures* (1832), clearly indicates that he was much in advance of his time and that he influenced later manufacturing management thinking. Much of his work has application today; so a study of Babbage is of more than historical interest.

Charles Babbage (1792–1871) was a professor of mathematics at Cambridge University and spent a considerable portion of his life, his private fortune, and a grant from the British government in an attempt to build an analytical calculating machine. He never successfully completed the machine; however, he provided all the specifications necessary to build an effective automatic computer.

Babbage's problems in constructing his computer were centered around the difficulty of getting its various parts produced with sufficient accuracy to allow the computer to operate. He spent ten years visiting workshops and factories, both in England and on the Continent, in an attempt to search out means of producing his various required parts. These years offered him a unique opportunity to observe and study the various problems introduced by the developments of the Industrial Revolution and the growth of the factory. His book relates his experiences and indicates his main thoughts on the subject. Following is a brief summary of some of his main ideas.

First, Babbage took the concept of labor developed by Adam Smith and extended it, indicating that Smith had not gone far enough in his analysis. Babbage showed that the division of labor made it possible to hire workers with precisely the skills required for the various parts of the total job to be done, and that these specialized workers could be paid salaries commensurate with the skills they brought. This, he believed, would have the effect of lowering the total cost of a manufactured article. Babbbage was interested in the establishment of proper costs of manufacture, and in controlling these costs he gave attention to the problems of depreciation and obsolescence and discussed the relationship between fixed costs and volume.

Babbage also recognized the existence of management problems as distinct from the various techniques used in manufacturing. He thought that scientific methods should be applied to the management of an enterprise and even suggested a list of questions to be answered in making a systematic survey of the enterprise. He advocated an organizational pattern very similar to our line and staff type of organization today.

Babbage was also greatly interested in the problems of production and human relations. His interest in timesaving methods can be compared to that of Taylor or Gilbreth a generation or so later in the United States. He was aware of the time-study practice and of the difficulty in obtaining correct measurements, in view of the fact that workers under observation tend to be self-conscious. Control of waste and of the use of by-products also received his attention. He treated the problem of human relations at length and showed concern for the unfortunate opinion among workmen that their own interest and that of their employers were at variance. He said that the consequences of this frame of mind would be neglect, lack of participation, and possibly even sabotage.

Finally, Babbage indicated an interest in and knowledge of advertising, selling, and the development of new products. He advised the manufacturer to reduce his unit price as much as possible in order to increase his market, and to expect his profit from the volume of goods sold rather than from a wide margin of profit on each unit.

Management Beginnings in America

The Industrial Revolution in Great Britain came to the United States in 1790 in the building of the Slater Cotton Mill at Pawtucket, Rhode Island. The principles and practice of manufacture of this mill made possible the growth of the factory system in the United States. The bringing together in one location of relatively large concentrations of workers and raw materials created problems of management that had never been faced before. No one knew how such efforts should be organized, directed, or controlled. Businessmen applied their efforts more directly to problems of machines, material, and equipment, rather than to management activity as such. Workers received little attention as individuals, and management as a process involving people was largely disregarded.

It was not until after the Civil War that the basic ideas of management began to take shape in ways useful to businessmen. The ideas of Babbage had not penetrated our mind (nor England's mind either, to any great extent), and it remained for Frederick Taylor to develop the basic concepts in America and to lead the crusade toward their adoption by business and industry.

Before turning to Taylor's work, one significant development needs to be noted. At the annual meeting of the American Society of Mechanical Engineers in 1886, Henry R. Towne, president of Yale and Towne Company, presented a paper titled "The Engineer as an Economist." Towne pleaded for the recognition of management as a field distinct from the various techniques employed in industry and expressed the belief that shop management was of equal importance to engineering in the successful conduct of industrial establishments. At the same meeting, Henry C. Metcalfe, a captain in the U.S. Army Ordnance Department, presented a paper titled "The Shop Order System of Accounts." In his paper, Metcalfe suggested a plan of organization based on the fundamental division of work between the shop and the office. Frederick Taylor was present at the meeting and participated in the discussion that followed the presentation of both papers. In particular, he mentioned that at the Midvale Steel Company during the past ten years he had been organizing a system similar to that of Mr. Metcalfe.

Frederick W. Taylor

Frederick Taylor was born in 1856 and studied in France, Germany, and Italy during his youth. Impaired eyesight kept him from entering college. Instead, he served as an apprentice in a small pump works in Philadelphia. Later, after his eyesight had improved, he earned an M.E. degree at Stevens Institute. He was employed by the Midvale Steel Company from 1878 to 1889, beginning as a laborer, then progressing to clerk, machinist, gang boss, foreman, chief draftsman, and finally chief engineer; he achieved the latter position after taking his degree. He served as a consulting engineer after 1889, and one of his best-known assignments was with the Bethlehem Steel Company between 1898 and 1901. In addition to his consulting, he developed various new processes of manufacturing, taking out about a hundred patents. He retired from practice in 1901, and until his death in 1915, he devoted all of his time and effort to the cause of "scientific management."

Taylor's best-known papers are "A Piece Rate System," published in 1895; "Shop Management," published in 1903; and "On the Art of Cutting Metals," published in 1906. He later condensed his thinking and experience in a book, *The Principles of Scientific Management,* published in 1911.

Taylor is properly called "the father of scientific management." Although his basic approach followed the lead of Babbage and Towne, he was the first to advocate a science of management—or a science of doing work—the same as there was a science in other fields. Taylor had had experience in the shop, and he knew the conditions there; so he attacked the problem from the bottom up, focusing his attention upon the worker, his wages, and the methods by which wages were determined (see Chapters 7 and 8).

To overcome the problems he had observed, Taylor believed that management should accept some special responsibilities for planning, directing, and organizing work. Furthermore, he felt it essential to separate the planning of work from its execution, so that each individual would be able to work at his highest level of efficiency and could be compensated accordingly. Under this concept, management would have four new duties. First, management must develop a science for each element of a person's work, which would replace the old rule-of-thumb method. Second, management should scientifically select and train, teach, and develop the worker, whereas in the past the worker chose his own work and trained himself as best he could. Third, management must heartily cooperate with employees so as to ensure that all the work be done in accordance with the principles of science that have been developed. Fourth, although in the past the workers were doing almost all the work and also had the greater part of the responsibility, in the future management should assume the greater part of the responsibility and the work, for which they are better fitted than the workmen.

Taylor's charge to management was to have far-reaching effect on modern manufacturing. Perhaps even today we could benefit by a closer study of his basic principles. One of the more significant aspects of his influence was the "mental revolution," which he insisted was the essence of scientific management. Perhaps Taylor was guilty of overstating his case and using the word "science" somewhat loosely. He succeeded, however, in demonstrating that the philosophies, attitudes, and processes of the managers of his time were grossly inadequate. Through his efforts, rule-of-thumb methods were replaced by measurement and experimentation, and, in fact, this process continues even today.

Other Management Pioneers

Taylor had many contemporaries and associates who carried forward his ideas and who developed many divergent views. Of particular significance was the work of Henry L. Gantt, the Gilbreths, and Harrington Emerson. These people did much to extend scientific management thinking beyond the factory, where Taylor did most of his work.

Henry L. Gantt. Gantt worked with Taylor at Midvale Steel and generally held the same views that Taylor did, except that Gantt gave more attention to the man who was performing the work than to just the work itself. He appears to have had a better understanding than Taylor of the psychology of the worker and recognized the importance of morale and the use of non-financial rewards to promote morale.

In 1902 Gantt opened an office as a scientific management consultant and concentrated on the establishment of bonus systems, although he was also responsible for the reorganization of many plants. He is widely known, even today, for his development of the "Gantt Chart," which is a technique for graphically representing work to be done and work already accomplished (see Chapter 14). This chart evolved from his work for the United States government during World War I and has been widely used since that time.

Frank and Lillian Gilbreth.   Frank Gilbreth was a successful contractor who became interested in work methods while working earlier as a bricklaying apprentice. Subsequently he developed many improvements in the methods of bricklaying and in other construction trades. His new concepts of work planning and of training workers in the correct methods of work not only increased productivity but contributed to the health and safety of the workers.

Frank Gilbreth's tremendous energy and capacity for organization resulted in the development of motion study and its inclusion as a basic part of scientific management. He and his wife, Lillian, were responsible for the introduction of various special charts and the use of motion pictures to help analyze, study, and improve jobs (see Chapter 7). They were both interested in the employee as an individual and placed considerable emphasis upon the psychological factors in management. Upon the untimely death of Frank in 1924, Mrs. Gilbreth carried on their work alone with great enthusiasm and energy, serving as Professor of Management at Purdue University from 1935 to 1948.

Harrington Emerson.   Emerson got into scientific management work after having had experience as a teacher of modern languages and in banking and real-estate operations. He later started his own consulting firm and did special economic and engineering research work for the Burlington Railroad. In addition, he carried out the reorganization of the Atchison, Topeka, and Santa Fe Railroad. His background and interest in the railroads qualified him to serve as an expert witness in the I.C.C. wage hearings of 1910 and 1911. He testified that if all American railroads improved their management as much as the Santa Fe had done, the total savings would be more than a million dollars a day.

Although Emerson worked at the same time as Taylor, their methods of operation were different. Taylor was quite precise with his work and was interested in the determination of basic data. Emerson, on the other hand, was much more flexible in his approach and attempted to apply the ideas of scientific management to a broader range of organizations. Emerson was particularly interested in efficiency and wrote extensively on the subject. He further emphasized the importance of correct organization in efforts to achieve high productivity.

QUESTIONS

1.   To what extent can Frederick Taylor be considered the father of an Industrial Management Revolution in this country?

2. In the years to come, will the current age of automation be considered a "second" Industrial Revolution?

3. Explain the difference between Charles Babbage and Adam Smith in their approach to the division of labor.

4. Select a name from among the following and investigate his contribution to the scientific management movement: Frederick A. Halsey, Harry Hopf, Henry S. Dennison, Carl Barth, and James Rowan.

5. Why didn't the factory system get started before the Industrial Revolution?

6. Compare and contrast "interchangeable manufacture" with "duplicate manufacture."

7. On what basis was the word "scientific" attached to the work of the various management pioneers?

8. To what extent has the computer brought about a modern industrial revolution?

9. Looking ahead 50–100 years, what leaders of business, industry, or government of today will be considered pioneers or innovators at that time?

CASE PROBLEM

Professor Taylor

Professor Taylor had taught a course in Manufacturing Management to engineers at State University for a number of years. Although many engineers in his classes were not completely turned on by the subject matter, they still felt that as the years went by in their professional careers there would be a great likelihood that they would get into some kind of a management position and therefore some knowledge of manufacturing management would be desirable. Nevertheless, many saw a technical career ahead of them and felt that manufacturing management was an unnecessary course.

Professor Taylor had felt this dilemma for many years, but this semester he faced another problem since, for some reason, the business college sent a number of their students over to take his course. On the first day of class some of the more technically oriented engineers started giving him their usual line of objections to the course. However, they had hardly spoken their piece when the business students chimed in with their thoughts.

One business student summed up their line of reasoning this way:

> For the most part, we (business students) expect to find jobs in financial institutions, merchandising organizations, government offices, health organizations, and the like. It is very unlikely that any of us will end up in manufacturing organizations, so many of the topics you cover in this course such as processes, manufacturing controls, and research are really not relevant to anything we see in our future.

Questions:

1. Do you agree with the point of view expressed by the business student? Discuss points both for and against his argument.

2. Outline the point of view of the technically minded engineers.

3. Outline the point of view of the management-minded engineers.

3

MANAGEMENT REQUIREMENTS

In this chapter we wish to devote specific attention to the general problem of management. In other words, consideration will be given to the process of management itself with the contention that the process is applicable to all of the various components of a manufacturing enterprise. This does not minimize the importance of technical competence in the particular area in which a manager works, for any person in charge of a particular activity must bring to his job a high degree of technical competence as well as managerial competence.

Management Defined

Management has often been defined as "the accomplishment of goals through others." This may be an oversimplified definition but it leads us to some points that need to be made at the outset. The first point relates to the "accomplishment of goals." Management in the true sense involves the accomplishment of goals or objectives and is not simply a position within a business. Many people have the word "manager" in their titles, but in actuality they merely preside over an activity rather than manage it toward the accomplishment of a certain objective.

The second point in relation to our definition deals with the "through others" aspect. Management as an activity is concerned with the work of other people, namely, subordinates; and it is concerned with the direction and coordination of the effort of those people. Although every manager may have a few specific duties, which only he or she can perform, the role of a manager, strictly speaking, is based on the fact that the activities of subordinates must be coordinated and directed. In this sense a manager may be more concerned with the accomplishments of subordinates than with his or her own, for their accomplishments mean the meeting of the overall goal or objective set.

Finally, in relation to our definition, we must recognize that it applies to all levels of the organization. The lowest-level supervisor is a manager in the same way as the high-level executive. Job content varies, authority varies, and the types of problems faced vary, but nonetheless all levels of an organization hierarchy are composed of managers if they have goals set as a measure of performance, and if they have subordinates who assist in the carrying out of the objectives specified.

Management in Manufacturing

The general concept of management had its beginning in manufacturing activities, as will be recalled from our discussion in Chapter 2. Frederick Taylor's experience as an apprentice and as a worker in the factory led him to conclude that much could be gained by "managing" the operations in the factory rather than just allowing them to take place as the various workers involved thought fit. Certainly he was concerned about the practice of "soldiering," which he knew to take place, but he was also concerned by the fact that each worker was allowed to perform his task as he liked without having to conform to any standardized method or procedure. This led to his many studies in an attempt to improve operating efficiency, and these studies were of a technical and operational nature as well as of a managerial nature. However, it was his studies regarding management that essentially ushered in the general concept.

Although Taylor's background was largely in the factory, both he and his contemporaries saw the value of applying the new concepts to all phases of business life. It has been repeatedly demonstrated that success in a business activity can be insured and enhanced through the application of management principles and concepts. Admittedly, some businesses succeed *in spite* of what the management does; however, we are directing our attention toward the business that succeeds *because* of what the management does.

Management and Ownership

To sharpen our understanding of the subject at hand, we must recognize the separation of management and ownership that exists in most large manufacturing concerns today. During the hundred years prior to Taylor's time it was common for the "manager" of a concern to also be its owner. As businesses grew in size, not only with increased trade but with increased mechanization, and as more risk was involved, ownership gradually moved to the corporate form with its many owners and the spreading of risk. Of course, people invest their money and accept risk only with some hope of return, and this hope manifested itself in a demand for improved performance of the organization as a whole. Heads of corporations were almost forced to introduce new methods and concepts that were being developed and publicized, if for no other reason than to satisfy the demands of the many stockholders.

The net result of all of this was and is that there are many managers throughout industry who hold little or none of the stock of the company for whom they work, but they accept a large portion of the responsibility for achieving the results desired by the corporation. True, many modern-day managers own some shares of stock in a corporation and may even have options to buy more. In most cases, however, the amount held is not sufficient to have any direct influence on the votes taken at the stockholders' meetings. Their influence is much greater in their role as an employee or manager of the corporation.

Of course, many corporations are owned or all their stock is owned by one person or a few people, who in turn manage the concern. But for our purposes these people are simply wearing two hats, one as an owner, and one as a manager. Our attention will be directed toward the role of the manager without regard to ownership status.

Management as a Profession

With many persons becoming interested in management as a separate and identifiable field of activity, and with many persons making their living as managers, it was inevitable that there would be some tendency toward professionalization of management. Since, indeed, this trend continues today, we must give some attention to the possibility of management becoming a true profession.

Definitions vary as to what constitutes a profession, but in general a true profession has the following characteristics:

1. It is a specialized body of principles, skills, and techniques.
2. It has formalized methods of achieving training and experience in the field.
3. There is an organization composed of persons in the field with professionalization as its goal.
4. Its conduct is guided by a set of ethical codes.
5. Charging of fees is based on services rendered, but with due emphasis given to service rather than to monetary reward.

Although the field of management appears to be making progress in many of the areas stated above, it seems clear that management is still not fully a profession.

The requirements would seem to indicate that licensing of managers would be in order, much as doctors and lawyers are licensed; however, such licensing is non-existent and there is no large movement under way to promote it. There is an abundance of literature in the field filled with principles, techniques, and specialized knowledge. However, one cannot help but feel that in many cases quantity has been used to compensate for a lack of quality. Furthermore, the direct relationship between a knowledge of this literature and success in a managerial position has yet to be fully established. In the literature increasing attention is being given to the importance of ethics, so there is evidence of improvement in this regard. There is an abundance of management consulting firms throughout the United States, so it would appear that if charging for services rendered is a criterion of a profession, management would qualify as such in that area, at least.

Instead of just one organization whose aim is the professionalization of management, there are a number of management associations and associations of specialists, all with slightly different goals and attitudes toward the idea of professionalization. Some organizations, such as the American Management Association, deal with the subject generally and essentially act as information exchange groups. Many other associations are organized around a particular type of function or activity within an enterprise and are more concerned with the professionalization of that activity than they are with management in the broader sense. Typical of such organizations would be those of engineers (such as the Institute of Industrial Engineers and the American Society of Mechanical Engineers), purchasing agents, quality control people, and personnel specialists. These groups do also have an interest in management since each specialty or function must be managed, but their greater interest seems to be directed toward the specialty involved.

Management has become such a popular word in recent years, and the number of people interested in management has so increased, that it is a rare educational institution that does not offer some kind of a program to develop one's managerial skills or prepare one to enter this field. Perhaps the interest in this field of management stems more from an image of status and privilege connected with anyone holding such a position, rather than with the performance requirements attached to that position.

It is not unusual for a freshman entering college to state his preferred field of interest to his counselor as "management." It is questionable whether a student can devote his college years to a study of pure management as such and thereby qualify himself to perform any kind of managerial activity upon graduation. Such an attitude of the student indicates a failure to understand the technical competence that must be associated with any managerial position. It is better that the student achieve technical competence in some specialized field such as accounting, engineering, or law, with the study of some managerial concepts on the side. After he has proved his worth in this technical area he can then perhaps move into a position where technical skills and managerial skills can be combined. Needless to say, the person really becomes a manager by learning to "manage."

Universality of Management

Though management may lack truly professional status, the principles, skills, and techniques involved enjoy a considerable amount of transferability from one industry to another. Many examples can be cited of persons leaving high-level positions in one type of industry and going to similar high-level positions in very different types of industries. No doubt there are limitations to such transferability, for it seems improbable that a successful baseball manager would be equally successful in managing the open hearth department of a steel mill. On the other hand, Fran Tarkenton has gone from successful football quarterback to management consultant.

The point is, that to the extent a second job requires the analytical, human, and managerial skills used on the first job, a person might be successful in transferring from one to another at the managerial level. To the extent, however, that the second job involves a large number of technical skills not present in the first job, nor present in the background and training of the person involved, a successful transfer could not be made until those technical skills are achieved in some manner. To illustrate, in one instance a high-level military officer resigned and took on the position of president of a manufacturing concern. Before taking over the direction of the concern he spent almost a year touring all of its facilities and learning the many technical phases of that business. Evidently, he must have been a highly capable individual to be able to do even this, and certainly he brought to the job many managerial skills he had learned firsthand in the military. However, he must be credited for recognizing that pure management ability was inadequate in an organization where he lacked knowledge of the technical factors involved.

Responsibilities of Management

Managements of today's industrial concerns are considered to have responsibilities toward four groups: stockholders, employees, customers, and the general public.

To stockholders, management has the traditional responsibility of protection of investment plus the earning of a return on that investment. This responsibility hasn't changed over the years except in the concept of return on investment. Many managers are accused of looking only at short-run gains, when they should be looking more at the long-run return on investment.

To employees, management today has a variety of responsibilities. Management must try to provide steady jobs at good pay, hours, and working conditions, besides providing for physical security during and after working hours and economic security after retirement.

To customers, management must provide a quality product at a competitive price and render satisfactory service as required. This means keeping up to date with progress in the field so that customers always have available the latest improvements.

To the general public, management has the responsibility of always being a good citizen. This means taking an interest in the affairs of the community, complying with the spirit as well as the letter of the law, being particularly careful about nuisances such as waste disposal, noise, or odors, and in every way appearing to be an asset to the community rather than an eyesore.

It is within the framework of these four broad responsibilities that management must operate; and operation might as well take place in a goldfish bowl, for all groups and subdivisions of each group will be watching closely for evidence of failure to live up to the responsibilities prescribed. Criticism might follow and could manifest itself in proxy fights, labor unrest, loss of sales, or restrictive ordinances. Any or all of these might result in financial loss to the company, which in turn might ultimately cause bankruptcy. No doubt the trend could be stopped before it reached the bankruptcy stage; the point here is the necessity for a balanced viewpoint toward responsibilities in place of the old saw that management's responsibility is to make a profit. Profits are necessary—so necessary that they can hardly be called a responsibility. Instead profits are an *obligation:* they *must* be obtained before management can even approach the fulfillment of responsibilities. Profits may be obtained in the short run by following a short-sighted policy in regard to the responsibilities outlined. But for long-run profits and growth of the company, management must seriously consider responsibilities to all groups rather than just to stockholders.

Role of Objectives

Mention has been made earlier of the fact that some people head businesses and in so doing simply preside over them instead of managing them in the true sense. A significant feature of true management is the establishment of objectives and their use as guidelines in the direction of the enterprise. One can possibly argue that certainly every person in a managerial position has objectives toward which he is attempting to direct the enterprise; however, one can also just as forcefully argue that many such objectives so stated are not really driving forces throughout the enterprise but something fabricated on the spur of the moment to answer the question raised. It is relatively easy for managers to ignore objectives, for they often become so involved in performing tasks that they forget what it is that they are attempting to achieve. Also, many of us adopt the attitude of "let's see how it turns out," rather than "let's make it turn out the way we want it to."

To have meaning, an objective must have definiteness. It is not uncommon for companies to publish a list of objectives designed for popular consumption; and these objectives tend to read a little bit like the list of responsibilities mentioned in the previous section. Such a list may be desirable as general objectives, but they do not assist to any great extent in the operation of the business, for they are not sufficiently definite. Definiteness usually involves quantification. If an objective cannot be quantified, its interpretation is then open to question and no one can say whether or not it is accomplished. If one desires as an objective the establishment of a certain sales goal, it should be clearly established ahead of time how sales are to be measured (dollars or units, for example), where we stand currently so far as these sales measures are concerned, and what we expect to achieve or where we expect to be in relation to sales at a certain definite period in the future. Some objectives defy quantification, but nonetheless many objectives now stated in rather general and nebulous form could probably be quantified if additional efforts were made to do so.

The establishment of objectives should be carried out throughout an organization. In other words, one can visualize a hierarchy of objectives the same as a hierarchy of managerial levels. There would be a set of objectives for the company as a whole—in particular objectives to be met during a certain measured period in the future such as six months or one year. There would be another set of objectives for each of the main subdivisions of the business. These subdivisions of course would contribute to the attainment of the overall company objectives. A similar line of reasoning would be applied to all the other levels within the oganization, including the very lowest ranking supervisor in either the line or staff departments. Every person in a managerial capacity should have a complete understanding at all times of exactly the objectives he and his own unit within the business are attempting to achieve. If each supervisor has such a clear understanding of his objectives, he will be less apt to get lost in the performance of tasks to the detriment of the achievement of results.

The Functions of the Manager

The managerial functions are generally agreed to be planning, organizing, staffing, directing, and controlling. Although authors may differ slightly in their use of these terms or the order in which they are listed, there is general agreement as to the content of each function. This section discusses each of these functions and devotes some attention to the problem of coordination. Although coordination is not generally regarded as one of the basic management functions, it is extremely important to the success of any organization.

The reader must appreciate that we are discussing these functions as having almost universal application. In other words, the various activities of a manufacturing concern, such as selling, production, engineering, or purchasing, all require management, and the functions we describe here all have applicability to the management of each of these activities.

Planning

Planning, in the managerial sense, is the determination of what to do and how to do it. Planning, therefore, becomes a matter of making decisions from among many alternatives. Obviously, the manager must have knowledge of the many opportunities that present themselves and must have ability to create and develop opportunities, but in the long run he or she must be able to analyze the opportunities and to select the best one for the conditions that exist. Decisions must be made, for example, as to what product lines to offer for sale, the prices to be charged, the method of production to be used, wage levels to be paid, and the amount of research to be carried on.

It is apparent that there are two kinds of planning: long-range planning and short-range planning. Long-range planning obviously stems from the company's long-range objectives and involves steps to be taken toward meeting these objectives. For example, to get a desired foothold in a certain market it may be necessary to introduce one product this year, another product next year, and to build a new plant the third year. In the short run, however, the manager must work out precisely the steps to be taken to develop and introduce the new product. In the very short run this involves the placing of orders for certain materials and the hiring and training of workers. The shorter the time period involved, the more specific the plans must be.

Much of the planning activity of the manager may be handled by various staff groups. Later we will discuss process planning, production planning, and product planning, and although these may be the responsibility of certain designated managers, the managers may make use of staff assistants to help them work out possible alternatives and make recommendations as to the best alternatives. In recent years many techniques such a linear programming, PERT, computerized data bases, and simulation have been used by these various staff groups to aid them in making analyses of alternatives and, later, recommendations for decisions. Let us not forget, however, that these techniques do not make decisions but only indicate guidelines for decision making. Decisions are always made by managers.

Evidence of planning in a manufacturing concern may be found in the statement of objectives and in the outline of plans to achieve those objectives. Further evidence of planning is revealed by production schedules and shipping schedules, books or statements of company policies, manuals of paperwork procedures, books of manufacturing or operating procedures, and rule books. Not all companies have all of these books, and some companies may have many more, but these are typical of printed matter found in a company that is evidence that the managerial function of planning is being carried out. An example of thorough planning is the Saturn project of General Motors, whereby the corporation, in introducing a brand new car, established a separate company to produce and market it. No doubt many other companies have carried out planning just as extensively, but the Saturn project received much publicity in the press.

Organizing

Organizing will be discussed separately in the next chapter, but it is not something that can be done once and for all and then forgotten about, for organizing becomes a basic function of every manager and one to which constant attention must be given if the set objectives are to be achieved. Basically, organizing involves determining the activities required to achieve the objectives established, grouping these activities on a logical basis for handling by a subordinate manager, and finally, assigning a person to the job designed. In carrying out these steps, it is assumed that the manager will delegate the necessary authority to the person or persons involved as subordinates and that these subordinates will assume the responsibility necessary.

The organization structure should not be regarded as an end in itself, but as a tool for accomplishing the objectives of the enterprise or department within the enterprise. One type of organization is better than another only because it enables a better job to be done in accomplishing these objectives, not because it "looks better" or because it is one used by some other company. Every manager must perform the function of organizing but must also keep in mind that organizing is a dynamic thing and a means to an end rather than an end in itself.

Staffing

Staffing as a managerial function involves developing and placing qualified people in the various jobs in the organization previously designed. Like organizing, this function is not performed once and for all, but must be constantly worked at in order to have qualified people available in the future to move into vacated positions or to allow the company to expand its activities. This function, therefore, includes such things as the development of manpower requirements for all the various existing jobs, the appraisal and selection of candidates for positions, and the training and development of both candidates and incumbents on jobs in order to improve their capability and potentiality. Personnel, human resources, or training departments frequently exist as an aid in carrying out this managerial function; however, the basic responsibility for managerial development and for staffing in general rests with each individual manager, who cannot sidestep this responsibility by assuming that the training department will handle it. Good managers develop managers.

An important aspect of the staffing function is to identify those who are to be given opportunities to develop into managers. Many such people exist within the company and could be promoted. Most every company will always want to introduce new blood into the organization and will carry on active recruiting efforts by advertising, making use of consultants who specialize in "head hunting," and carrying on extensive recruiting campaigns at colleges and universities. College graduates are usually employed more on the basis of potential rather than their ability to perform on their first job. In this way, companies feel that they are introducing new blood at the entry level and thereby providing a base for the business to grow and prosper.

Direction

Direction, or supervision as it is frequently called, involves the motivation and guidance of subordinates toward the objectives. The concept is a simple one and one with which we are all familiar, for throughout our lives we are constantly being guided by or are attempting to guide others. However, it is also evident in our everyday lives that the guidance of some is more effective than that of others. The superior manager should have knowledge of the more effective techniques of supervision and use them in order to improve the performance of his subordinates.

A detailed discussion of the methods of supervision is beyond the scope of this book, but mention should be made of a few principles of direction. In general, workers perform better on a job when they know what is expected of them and are well trained in performing that job. Furthermore, workers appreciate having knowledge concerning the job to be performed and how that job fits into the total picture. To have to do a job simply because the boss says to do it does not usually lead to maximum performance on that job. Subordinates appreciate having some authority delegated to them and will normally develop within themselves a comparable amount of responsibility to go with the authority delegated. Every supervisor would do well to make a study of the psychological needs of people and appeal to these needs in attempts to motivate subordinates toward improved overall performance.

Controlling

Chapter 11 will be devoted to a discussion of the fundamentals of control, and many of our manufacturing activities have as their role in life the control of manufacturing performance. Control compels events to conform to plans. Compelling events to conform to plans invariably means determining which person or persons are responsible for the deviation from plans and taking the steps necessary to see that these persons modify their performance. Although we have many aids and tools for this process, basically things are controlled by controlling people.

Coordination

Coordination is not generally regarded as a separate function of the manager, but it is so essential to the successful performance of any manager that we wish to devote some attention to it. Basically, it is the achievement of harmony of individual effort toward the accomplishment of organizational goals. In this sense, it becomes particularly important as an aspect of the function of direction.

Communications play an extremely important role in coordination, for many breakdowns in coordinating efforts occur because people simply do not have the information or knowledge they need in order to bring about coordination. Coordination is also facilitated if the persons involved have had some part to play in the planning and policy-making phases of the management process. This does not mean that managers should abdicate the planning role, but simply that they might facilitate their own task of direction and coordination by allowing subordinates to assist them in developing plans. The plans themselves thereby become much more important to the subordinates, and they normally put forth greater effort to be certain that these plans are carried out successfully. Informal relationships within a company also tend to facilitate coordination, for workers who know each other well outside the job will normally work together better on the job.

Management Appraisal

Appraising the performance of management is of considerable importance because of the prevalence of hired managers over owner-management in industry today. Managers who are also owners can operate their business almost any way they see fit. Hired managers, on the other hand, are forced to please not only owners but other groups as well, as we have seen earlier.

Each group will appraise using its own particular sets of standards, but we will want to examine the problem without regard to satisfying the desires of any one group. Instead, our goal will be to achieve that delicate balance point where all groups are reasonably well satisfied. This is practically an impossible task, but hired management in today's world is forced to try.

Approaches to Management Appraisal

Managements have been appraised for years by simply looking at the balance sheet and profit and loss statement for a particular period. From these statements, certain ratios and indices are computed that give indication of management efficiency. Such a method of appraisal is at least partially satisfactory. It won't tell the whole story of how good an overall job management has done, but it tells some of it—provided that some standards of financial performance have been established.

Certain inadequacies of appraisal by financial statement are evident. For example, in looking at financial statements we are tempted to conclude that so much profit was made per dollar of sales. This may be true on the average, but it doesn't represent the true situation for all sales. This will be shown in our discussion of breakeven charts (see Chapter 17), which will clearly indicate losses on sales up to the breakeven point and profits on sales above that point. This comes about because of certain fixed costs that exist in a manufacturing business whether or not any products are made and sold. Knowing a company's breakeven point assists in appraisal, for it serves as a sensitive barometer in indicating the need for a change in operations to insure profits.

Another difficulty with the use of financial analyses as a sole means of management appraisal is that seldom can one obtain from such analyses any indication of future strength or prospects for a company. Financial strength can easily be ascertained from a balance sheet, but at no place on the balance sheet is there an indication of new product development that might be necessary for the future of the business, nor is there a place to indicate what is being done to train and develop managers for the future operation of the business. Almost by definition, financial analyses must simply be analyses of the past. Other methods of appraisal are usually necessary in order to measure the company's position in relation to its preparation for the future.

An approach to management appraisal is the *management audit*. A management audit is usually a subjective comparison of a rather detailed breakdown of the responsibilities of management with actual performance or with company policy in regard to each item. In this way the auditor can arrive at a general conclusion as to how well management has fulfilled its responsibilities. Management audits are not usually conducted for the purpose of arriving at a numerical answer pertaining to performance, but instead to uncover opportunities for improvement. For example, should the audit reveal a policy of giving employees only two paid holidays per year when the national average is nearer six, management has had pointed out an opportunity to improve. Without a periodic audit covering specific points of importance, management will often become lax and make inaccurate or wrong assumptions concerning its performance. The audit forces a fresh look from time to time.

Some companies attempt to audit themselves, and this procedure is satisfactory to the extent that the internal auditors can be objective in their phrasing of questions and acceptance of answers. Many companies, however, bring in outside consultants to conduct audits, feeling that these outsiders have had wider experience at the audit type of work and also will bring a fresh outside point of view to the whole procedure. In either case the audit should be regarded as a "fresh look" at the company's position and should attempt to evaluate where it is, where it is heading under present programming, and whether its present objectives and plans to meet those objectives are still valid in the light of any changes in the social, technical, or political environment. It is relatively easy for managers at all levels to become so engrossed in day-to-day activities that they overlook an evaluation of overall performance in relation to long-range objectives. The management audit, if made annually, or perhaps every two or three years, might serve to force managers at all levels to stop and consider both current goals and future ones. Frequently, even day-to-day decisions will be simplified by a clear picture of where the business is headed.

This discussion of management appraisal is largely from the point of view of management as a whole. However, appraisals can and should be made of individual components of the business and of individual managers. For example, the manager of a particular production department might be appraised on such performance factors as percent rejects, percent downtime on various machines, various cost values, employee turnover rates, and some measure of productivity such as output per man-hour expended. Measures such as these are extremely important for both line and staff departments and should receive considerable attention if a company is to achieve any kind of improvement in productivity.

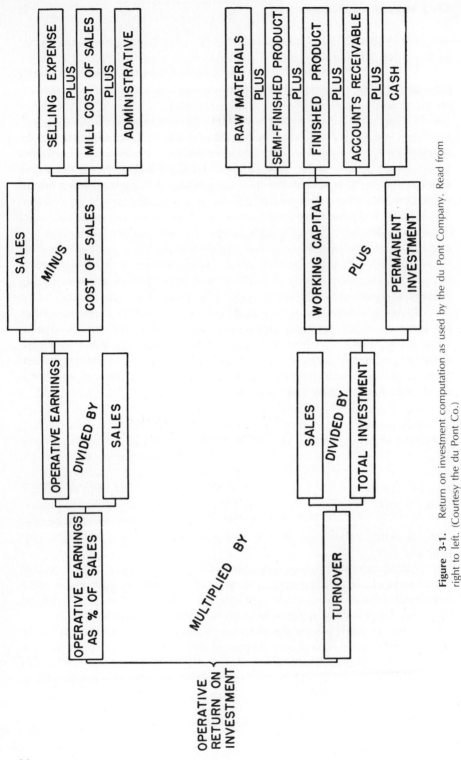

Figure 3-1. Return on investment computation as used by the du Pont Company. Read from right to left. (Courtesy the du Pont Co.)

34

Management Decentralization

For many years the du Pont Company and the General Motors Corporation have decentralized not only their manufacturing operations, but their management as well. Each division head is held directly accountable for the operation of his or her division in all respects and can operate the division more or less as a separate company. In du Pont the appraisal of each division head is based largely on "return on investment," computed as illustrated in Figure 3-1. The influence of intangible factors is recognized, but this method of decentralized management puts the division manager in "business for himself," and under these circumstances return on investment must be satisfactory in the long run.

The success of this philosophy of operation has been so great that many other large companies have adopted it, although some decentralized concerns—GMC, for example—have moved back somewhat toward centralization. Smaller companies that do not have large separable divisions can still use the same basic idea by setting up profit centers. A department, group of departments, or product can be set up on a profit-or-loss basis. Monthly reports as to profit or loss for that particular operation will have more meaning to all concerned than efficiency or labor turnover figures. Efficiency and labor turnover figures are important, but they do not have quite the impact and meaning of a report showing that on the X line of products the company lost $5000 last month. The manager of the X line can readily see that prompt action on his part is needed, for in the final analysis the success of a business is determined by whether or not it makes money.

QUESTIONS

1. Describe the coordinating role of management.
2. Select some company with which you are familiar and develop a series of statements outlining the responsibilities of the management of that company.
3. Do profits come to a company after responsibilities have been met, or must a company make a profit before it can meet its responsibilities?
4. Managerial positions are held by many people who are not in fact managers. Explain how this can be.
5. Compare the job of a plant foreman with that of a vice president of manufacturing as far as the five basic functions of management are concerned. To what extent does each apply to the two jobs?
6. Does engineering qualify as a profession according to the criteria stated?
7. How successful could a department store manager expect to be as a baseball team manager?
8. Outline a reasonable set of objectives for each of the various levels in a manufacturing concern of your acquaintance.
9. Explain how top management should "control" the work of the training department.
10. How can computers aid the appraisal task?

CASE PROBLEMS

National Products Co.

There are sixteen separate divisions of the National Products Co., each having its own head-quarters and officers. The divisions are not separate in a corporate sense but are divisions of National Products operating under a plan of decentralization—both in physical location and in management. Each division manufactures a line of products unrelated to the others. For example, one makes oil drilling equipment, another makes special metals, and a third has a line of chemicals. Total employment of National Products is over 9000, but there are no more than 225 employees at any one location, since each division has from 2 to 8 manufacturing plants. The small size of manufacturing plants occurred largely through the parent company's acquisition of small companies over the years.

The general offices of National Products are located in New York City and, in addition to corporate offices, comprise a number of staff departments, which act strictly in an advisory capacity to the divisions.

For many years the president of National Products has been concerned about the problem of developing and maintaining adequate managerial personnel throughout the company. It has been common practice to transfer managerial personnel from one division to another, but the president could never be certain that the proper choices were being made.

Recently the president hired Mr. Lewis Gilbert to study the problem and gave him the title of assistant to the president. Mr. Gilbert had worked a number of years for a management consulting firm and had specialized in management appraisal problems. The president made clear to Mr. Gilbert that his first assignment was to develop methods for appraising the worth of persons in managerial positions from foreman on up. Later on Mr. Gilbert was to study the problem of identifying people with managerial potential and to recommend management development programs.

Questions:

1. What are some approaches Mr. Gilbert might take to handle his first assignment?
2. Can the worth of a division president be determined simply by how much profit the division makes in a year? In ten years?
3. How can Mr. Gilbert expect to identify people with managerial potential?
4. What would constitute a good management development program for National Products?

Schillings Corporation

The Schillings Corporation, a producer of toilet goods for over 100 years, has been outstandingly successful. Not only have they grown to dominate the market in several product lines, but their profit and dividend record over the years has made them one of the recognized blue-chip stocks.

One reason for their success seems to be the emphasis that is placed on management and the development of competent managers at all levels of the organization. Individual training programs are worked out for all persons involved, although there are some short courses on particular topics where all trainees are assembled for periods varying from a couple of hours to a week depending upon the topics to be covered.

The president of the company watches the training programs very closely and has weekly review sessions with the training director, Jack Boyd. At a recent review session the president suggested to Jack that consideration be given to inserting in the overall training effort a short course devoted to management concepts. He pointed out that the firm's usual treatment of trainees was to expose them to all sorts of technical details, methods of operating in the company, company procedures, safety, human relations, and quality requirements, to name a few, but nowhere was there time devoted to what it means to be a manager.

Jack and the president discussed the matter for some little time before it was finally agreed that Jack would put together a proposed outline of topics to be covered, as well as a schedule to be followed. But just as Jack was leaving, the president gave him this parting thought: "Don't forget that every manager's job has technical requirements, conceptual requirements, and human requirements and that the mix of these requirements varies with the level of the manager in the organization."

Questions:

1. Make a list of suitable topics that Jack should include in his outline.
2. How much emphasis should be placed on this proposed course as compared to emphasis on the technical aspects of the business?
3. At what stage in the trainees' program should the proposed course be inserted—that is, early, in the middle, or late? State reasons for your choice.
4. What did the president mean by his last comment to Jack?

4

ORGANIZATION AND PLANNING FOR MANUFACTURING

This section of the book, comprised of Chapters 4 through 10, is concerned with the design of manufacturing systems. For the most part, these chapters deal with the various physical facilities that make up a manufacturing system. The selection and arrangement of such physical facilities is extremely important, from the point of view of both materials handling and job design. Following the discussion of these topics in this section, we will review in the next section various types of controls that are exercised in the operation of a manufacturing system.

Before turning to the design of manufacturing systems, however, it is desirable to consider the problem of organization and its relationship to manufacturing. No human group activity is ever really successful unless it is "organized." Only rarely do people achieve satisfactory results without first having organized their thoughts or organized their method of approach before tackling a problem or task. It is with this thought in mind that we take up the subject of organization of a manufacturing concern before getting into either its design or its control. The effort of every person in a manufacturing concern must be related to the common purpose and to the efforts of all other persons in the enterprise. Proper organization and planning attempts to accomplish this essential coordination.

The word "organization" is often used with various meanings. It can refer to a group of people such as a club or lodge, and it can also refer to a company, meaning both the people and the facilities that make up that company. The more strict meaning of the word will be used in this chapter, namely, the relationships among people and groups that make up a company. These relationships are usually shown on an organization chart and described in an organization manual, both of which will be discussed later.

Organization in Manufacturing

Although we are speaking largely of the manufacturing concern, it should be obvious that the points made under the heading of organization and planning apply to the non-manufacturing firm as well. Banks, hospitals, department stores, and railroads are examples of other types of enterprises, and though the functions performed in these enterprises may be considerably different from those in many manufacturing establishments, the need to coordinate and organize their functions is universal.

Need for good organization.   Irrespective of what it makes, a manufacturing organization is an association of individuals working together to obtain the goals of an enterprise. When two or more individuals cooperate in a work effort, one of them must direct the activities of the group, or else they will work as individuals at cross-purposes with each other. Direction from one source is therefore essential for the coordination and success of any group effort.

It has been clearly demonstrated that every member of a manufacturing organization performs better on the job when he or she knows what the job is, who the boss is, what the organization structure is, what authority is possessed by the job holder, what should be done in case of an emergency when the boss is not present, and how and to whom to report essential information. These factors are essential to a good organization and apply to all members of an organization, whether they be managers, supervisors, machine operators, or laborers. All will do better work if they understand their roles in the organization, both individually and collectively.

Good organization does not eliminate the need to hire good people or to train them properly after hiring them. It will never be possible to design an organization and describe the jobs in that organization in such a manner that good judgment on the part of the people comprising that organization will not be required. Nonetheless, good organization should tend to reduce the number of management problems which arise, minimize effort involved, reduce organizational friction, promote effective teamwork, and keep operating costs at a minimum.

Objectives of organization.   The overall objective of manufacturing organization is to develop teams that function as a single instrument for low-cost production. In other words, the manufacturing organization should prove the concept that the whole is greater than the sum of its parts.

Divisional and departmental activities in an enterprise are set up to obtain efficient and maximum performance. It is expected that the firm's managers will control operating results, conserve and coordinate human effort, and optimize costs and profits. From top to bottom, each member of the organization must be motivated to maximize results on the job, coordinate his or her efforts with other departments, and generally develop the necessary team spirit. Without mutual understanding and cooperation, the organization whole could easily turn out to be less than the sum of its parts.

Organization design. The preceding discussion of organization, its need and its objectives, may seem reasonable enough, but we must finally get to the point of actually designing the organization to meet the requirements specified. However, prior to the design of the organization itself, there must be a thorough understanding of the goals of that organization and the nature of the business to be conducted. This was covered more completely in Chapter 3, "Management Requirements," but at this point we must keep in mind the influence that certain goals may have on the nature of the oganization itself. Manufacturing requirements must be analyzed to determine the various types of production facilities and departments needed. The sales objectives, the types of customers to be served, the line of products to be offered, and the goals in regard to employment, payrolls, and employee standards of living may influence the organization design. These are only a few of the items dealing with business objectives that need to be thoroughly considered.

Once these goals and objectives for the business have been formulated, the next step is to determine what functions are necessary in order to achieve these goals. For a manufacturing company, typical functions include production, distribution, finance, procurement, personnel and employee relations, engineering and research, control, and general offices. These categories are obviously functional and in any particular case would undoubtedly be broken down into various subdepartments. For example, a control function might be divided between production control, quality control, and inventory control. The problem of the individual organization designer is to determine which functions for this particular business are important enough to warrant at least one person assigned to that function.

The next step in organization design is to group or relate the various functions that have been specified. The principle of *span of control* (see later discussion) tells us that there is a limit to the number of subordinates who should report to one person; so it is necessary for us to plan for different levels in our organization. Therefore, if certain functions seem logically to relate to each other, they might possibly be grouped together and report to one person who in turn would report to a higher level. The three control functions referred to earlier could logically be grouped together in this manner. After grouping and relating all of the previously specified functions, we can see a pyramid developing, as is typical of most organization charts.

Our next step in organization design is to design or describe the various jobs that will later have to be filled. We have previously identified functions that would be of sufficient importance to warrant at least one job, but conceivably some functions, in particular those dealing with actual production departments, would require many more persons. This step, then, requires the close examination of each previously identified function and the outline of the various positions that will be required. A job description for each position should be prepared that outlines the general duties and responsibilities of the incumbent, as well as the background, education, and experience deemed desirable to the person placed on that job. Job descriptions will be reviewed in Chapter 21.

Strictly speaking, our organization design is now complete. However, there is still the task of filling all of the jobs that have been specified and described, a task which falls under the managerial function of staffing. If this is a new organization, obviously an extensive recruiting program will be necessary to find persons with the necessary skills to fill the jobs described. In a going organization, people presently on the payroll must be utilized, and so the task becomes one of matching job requirements with the personal qualifications of the people available. In either case, it is highly probable that job designs must be modified somewhat in order to make use of the personal qualifications available. Or an extensive training program may be necessary in order to upgrade or otherwise qualify people for the jobs that have been designed.

Two points need to be especially emphasized about this approach to organization design. One is that this is admittedly an ideal approach. Many will say that it is so ideal that it has absolutely no practical application. This may be true in some cases. However, the procedure can be defended on the grounds that it is better to set up a tailor-made organization to fit the particular needs of the company than to allow an organization to grow and develop according to the accident of who happens to be around at the time. In other words, in practically all other aspects of modern manufacturing management we do not allow things to develop by chance; so why should we make an exception of organization?

The second point to be emphasized in regard to organization design is its great need for flexibility. The procedure discussed is not something to be done once and then left standing throughout eternity without further review or change. Flexibility is one of the most important characteristics of good organization. The objectives, policies, and procedures of the company should be constantly under review and updated as conditions and experience dictate. These changes in turn should cause the organization to be examined and modified accordingly. New jobs may be created from time to time. Other jobs may be eliminated and still others combined or rearranged in any way it is believed will lead to more effective operation of a department or the company as a whole. Further flexibility must be built into the organization design in order to provide for the development of people and their eventual promotion within the organization. Some jobs can be used mainly as training positions, and others may have their content modified from time to time in order to allow for the qualifications and/or the development of the incumbent. In summary, then, at any one time there should be ideal organization toward which the company is moving in its procurement and training of personnel. However, as time passes, the concept of flexibility in the organization design must be adopted in order to meet the changing requirements of the company. Some companies have become so flexible in their outlook toward organization design that they have been experimenting with work groups having no bosses. While this may tend to violate a principle of organization design, there can be little objection as long as the result is improved performance.

   Organization charts.   The result of an organization design is usually an organization chart that shows the formal relationships among functions and the people responsible for those functions. An example of such a chart for a large company is shown in Figure 4-1. Some companies do not make use of organization charts, feeling that they might induce a certain structural rigidity. These companies feel that loosely defined relationships among people in the organization will provide an incentive for those people to expand their spheres of interest and activity for the ulti-

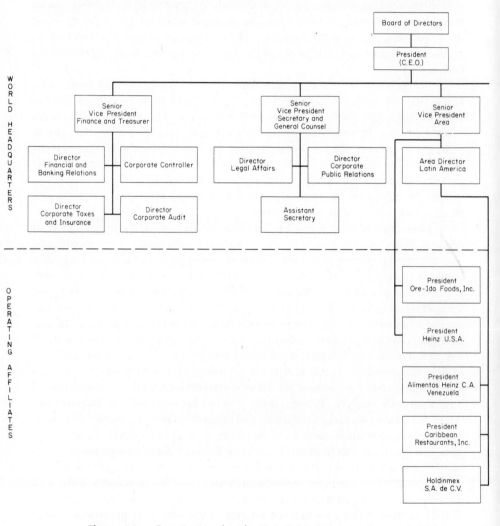

Figure 4-1.   Organization chart for H. J. Heinz Company. (By permission.)

mate good of the business. In other words, they feel that organization charts effectively place straight jackets on aggressive, energetic executives.

It is not our purpose to settle the argument as to the usefulness of organization charts. Instead, let it be emphasized that organization is not an end in itself but simply a means to an end. So the organization should not be considered an eternal arrangement, but rather a picture of the organization structure at one particular moment. If a strait jacket is then imposed, it will not be done by the organization chart, but by the executives using the chart. The chart can and should be changed as often as necessary, and in a company of any size and complexity it can be a very useful tool of coordination regardless of the frequency of changes.

Figure 4-1 shows an organization chart in the pure and simple form; that is, only the basic structure of departments and functions is displayed. Sometimes more information is desired, in which case the names of persons in charge and perhaps the number of people they supervise will be included. Duties and requirements of a job

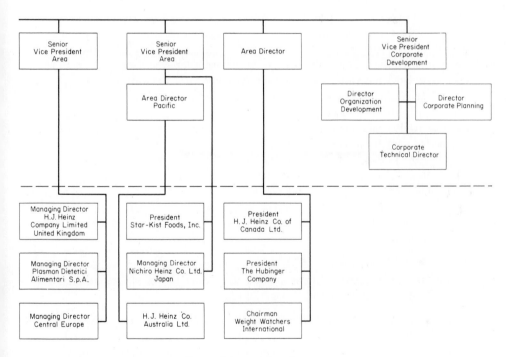

Figure 4-1. continued

may also be shown, but these are usually placed in the organization manual, which will be discussed later.

The advantages and uses of the organization chart are appreciable. First, they do show the lines of direct authority and thereby serve as a quick check on who is responsible for the various functions. Charts also show up weaknesses in an organization, such as more than one person being assigned the same work, or certain work never having been assigned to anyone. The chart can serve as a training device and as a guide in planning for expansion. It can be used to alert the public about work relationships within the company as well as to remind employees about who supervises whom.

Organization Principles

Volumes have been written about principles of organization, all of which are designed to assist in the development of an organization structure able to carry out its basic objectives. In this section we shall review a few of the more common principles and show their application to the organization design.

Span of Control

Span of control, or span of management, as it is often referred to, is one of the more widely known organization principles. Specifically, the term refers to the number of persons that report to any one supervisor or executive. A favorite point of discussion revolves around the number of subordinates who should report to any one supervisor, and various writers have concluded that the ideal span is between about four and eight. Studies in actual practice, however, indicate that in many organizations there is a much greater span than this. It is fairly common to have as many as twelve subordinates reporting to one person, and surveys have shown the number to vary from one to twenty-four.

The important point about the span-of-control principle is not so much the use of any "magic" number of subordinates, but the realization that each supervisor undoubtedly has a limitation in the number of subordinates that can be adequately supervised. The number will vary considerably from person to person and from situation to situation. Below are some of the factors to be considered in working out the proper span of control.

1. Level in the organization.   Generally speaking, executives at the top of an organization will have fewer people reporting to them than will foremen and supervisors at the bottom of the managerial hierarchy.

2. Type of problems encountered.   This factor will probably correlate closely with level in the organization, for the more difficult policy-type decisions usually rest at the top of the organization, whereas the carrying out of routine procedures is done at the lower levels. However, there are exceptions to this at both the higher and lower levels; so the factor needs separate identity. Subordinates carrying out routine work regardless of the level will require less supervision than subordinates carrying out work that requires many policy decisions and coordination with the work of others. This means that narrower spans would probably exist in maintenance and research departments, and wider spans would be suitable for assembly-line work or routine clerical operations.

3. Abilities of the persons involved. For reasons not always clearly understood, some supervisors can handle the work of more subordinates than other supervisors and do so without undue strain on themselves or reducing the efficiency of the organization. Likewise, a group of highly skilled and qualified subordinates will require less supervision, and in such a case the span could be broadened. The necessity to train subordinates in new procedures will almost always reduce the desirable span.

4. Willingness of the supervisor to delegate authority. Some supervisors find it extremely difficult to delegate authority and may even go to the extent of checking every action taken by every subordinate. For such individuals the span of control is necessarily limited. Hopefully, however, supervisors can be trained to delegate more duties and authority to their subordinates, and in fact, some companies force their supervisors to delegate more of their work through the simple expedient of assigning them more work than they can possibly get done by their usual methods of close supervision.

Organization Levels

In applying the span-of-control principle to an organization design it is easy to see that many levels will be or could be created, since the narrower the span of control, the more levels will be necessary to accomplish the same amount of work. Generally speaking, however, a large number of organizational levels between the chief executive and the lowest-level worker seems to be undesirable from a communication point of view. Information that must travel through a number of different levels in an organization in order to reach its destination almost invariably becomes distorted, if not lost. This fact is easily demonstrated by playing the parlor game in which a message is repeated from person to person around the room by whispering. The last person to receive the message states it out loud, and usually the stated message has little or no accuracy in relation to the message that was started around the room in the first place. Although such misunderstandings may be fun in the parlor, they can be catastrophic in a manufacturing organization, and for this reason many companies make it a point to keep the number of levels in the organization as few as possible, perhaps no more than four, between the chief executive and the lowest level of supervisor.

Clearly, if one attempted to impose a specific number for a span of control and another specific number for organization levels, a bind could easily result in the design of the organization. The only answer to this dilemma, within the scope of this volume, is to point out the factors mentioned above in regard to span of control, and to remind the reader that principles such as these are only guidelines to be modified as necessary to meet the situation at hand.

Subdividing Activities

The various activities and functions necessary to carry out the objectives of a manufacturing enterprise must be broken down and grouped in some manner for efficient operation and coordination. Departments and heads of departments should be assigned a homogeneous group of functions or activities, and hopefully this might be composed of one primary function together with the related secondary functions. Following are some of the common bases for subdividing activities:

Function.   The most common basis for subdividing activities is by function, such as manufacturing, engineering, and sales. This is perhaps the most basic breakdown of activities, for it allows the company to take advantage of specialists in each of the various fields. The other bases for subdividing activities have more to do with subdividing within one of these functions.

Process.   To subdivide manufacturing activities by process is quite natural. Such processes as plating, refining, distilling, bleaching, and machining all lend themselves to subdivision as separate and distinct activities.

Equipment.   Subdividing by equipment follows very closely that by process. "Equipment" refers to such items as punch presses, drill presses, milling machines, and machine tools in general. Such classes of equipment often provide a basis for separating activities, and the idea is not exclusive to the factory. For example, offices often have their word processor or computing departments, thereby indicating a subdivision by equipment.

Location.   Activities may be segregated simply on the basis of where they are physically located. This may at times mean some strange combinations, but such combinations may make possible a much more efficient organization and smoother operation.

Product.   Many times activities are separated according to the product. One department may make TV cabinets while a second department makes end tables. One group in the engineering department may work on pumps and a second group on nozzles. The same could be true for functions such as sales, purchasing, or advertising.

Classes of customers.   A sales department can divide its activities according to the classes of customers it serves. One sales group may service the retail trade and another the wholesale trade. Or, in advertising, one group may handle advertising in the popular media such as television, radio, and the popular magazines, while another group might handle advertising in trade magazines and other specialized media.

In speaking of these various bases for subdividing industrial activities, it is not implied that all would be used in every company or that no other bases exist. It is important that an organization be set up to accomplish the goal or mission of the enterprise in the most efficient manner. In setting up the organization for any particular industrial situation, one must select the bases for subdivision that will give the best results for that situation. The criterion that groups of people should comprise a workable, homogeneous, and separate field of activity should be applied. In many types of business the pattern of organization may be well established, but one must remember that although these established patterns have worked well in the past, it is still possible that a more efficient pattern may be found in the future.

Responsibility and Authority

Given a choice, most of us would prefer to possess authority rather than responsibility. This is a result of the power aspects of authority having been overemphasized. Any authority that we possess, however, comes from one or more of three sources. The first is the legal authority delegated to us from our superior and constitutes the right to command or to act in a given situation. The other two sources cannot be considered as strictly legal, but are certainly beneficial in getting things done. One is some personal characteristic of the leader involved, such as technical knowledge or a charismatic personality. The other is the consent of the persons being led. It is fairly obvious that a leader might have all kinds of legal authority to direct the actions of a group, but without the support of that group, he or she will be powerless. By the same token, some person without legal authority may turn out to be the leader of a group because of a dynamic personality, technical know-how, or an ability to somehow gain the support of the group. Ideally, of course, the leader of a group should possess all three sources of authority, and generally speaking a person is not designated the leader of a group without seeming to possess qualities that would lead to gaining the complete support of subordinates.

Quite clearly, authority is the key aspect of any managerial position. Managers working with subordinates must be in the position to get things accomplished through these subordinates using whatever means necessary, including the power to command. At the same time managers can delegate some authority to subordinates if they feel that this will assist in accomplishing the tasks at hand.

Responsibility, on the other hand, is essentially an obligation, or rather the taking on of an obligation to perform. It is this obligation to perform that often makes authority preferable to responsibility. A person may enjoy the power of authority but may not be certain that he wants to be held responsible for the results of exercising that authority.

Unlike authority, responsibility cannot be delegated, although people often speak of delegating or assigning responsibilities. Duties or activities are assigned and authority is delegated. Responsibility comes from within the subordinate himself. The superior attempts to exact responsibility from the subordinate, but it is the subordinate who must *feel* responsible. A superior with subordinates who have accepted their responsibilities, however, has not lost any of his own responsibility. His subordinates are *sharing* the responsibility. A plant manager is still responsible should one of the department managers fail to meet a schedule in spite of the fact that the department manager feels completely responsible.

Organization manuals (to be discussed later) often list, for each position, the duties, authority, and responsibilities that go with that position. It should be clear that any person taking a job so described is being *assigned* the duties listed, *delegated* the authority designated, and *requested* to assume the responsibilities outlined.

Measuring authority and responsibility is a difficult task, but it seems clear that on any job the two should be approximately equal. In other words, a manager requested to assume certain responsibilities, must be delegated sufficient authority to enable him or her to meet those responsibilities. If such authority is delegated and the manager fails to assume the equivalent responsibility, the authority will probably be withdrawn or changes will be made in job assignments.

Matching Abilities and Requirements

We have already outlined the ideal approach to organization design, whereby positions are fully worked out and described, and then persons to fill these positions are either recruited or trained. This is called an ideal approach, but it has its practical aspects. Jobs, whether they be management jobs or worker jobs, can be analyzed and a determination made as to the physical, mental, and skill requirements for each. In like manner, employees or potential employees can be evaluated through the process of interviewing, testing, checking references, and determining interests and aptitudes. A scientific approach to both job design and worker-evaluation makes it relatively easy for a company to match the abilities of its employees or prospective employees with the requirements of the various jobs it has available.

Occasionally, when a person leaves the organization it may prove impossible to find another worker who matches exactly the requirements of the open position. In such a case, the job must be modified to make it possible to staff the opening, particularly if time is a factor. This means there will be an exchange of job functions until the person available and the job open do match. The necessity to modify the ideal organization design emphasizes the desirability of flexibility in organizations. However, it should be emphasized that workers should be fitted to jobs whenever possible.

Organization Structures

The basic structure of an industrial organization depends on the size of the company, the nature of the business, and the complexity of the problems faced. The most common form of organization structure is the line and staff, but there are a number of variations of this basic form.

Line Organization

The simplest form of organization is the straight line. The significant feature, as the name implies, is that the positions listed on the organization chart are in a vertical line, as can be seen in Figure 4-2. In this organization the president handles all problems that arise, whether they have to do with production, sales, finance, or personnel. He has no "staff" to aid him and so must be a Jack-of-all-trades. Any company that starts small probably starts with a line type of organization. The owner is the general manager, and he may have one or two people working for him. As the business grows, he finds he is overburdened with details of hiring, sales, and purchasing, and so he needs a line and staff type of organization.

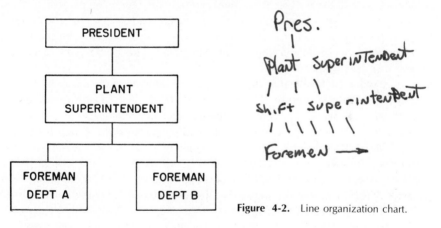

Figure 4-2. Line organization chart.

The Line and Staff Organization

The line and staff type of organization is shown in simplified form in Figure 4-3. One can see that the only difference between this and the line type of organization of Figure 4-2 is the addition of some specialists. In this case the specialists are the chief engineer and the sales manager, who were added in order to relieve the president of some of his burden. Certain responsibilities are shared by the two spe-

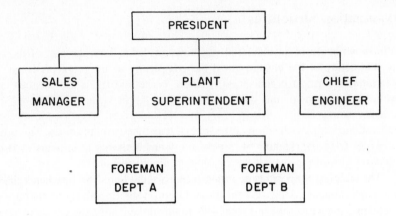

Figure 4-3. Line and staff organization chart.

cialists, but they report to the president, who retains overall responsibility for the operation of the business.

The idea of the addition of staff people can be and has been extended much further than this simple example shows. Figure 4-1 shows an organization making extensive use of the staff idea. It would be impossible for a company of any size to use a pure line type of organization, for no one person possesses the ability to manage all the various functions that must be performed in a diversified business. It may be possible in a one-man machine shop, but not in a factory employing several thousand men and women.

It was mentioned earlier that staff people should possess a certain amount of authority and responsibility. The question is: How much? Does a chief engineer make *all* decisions in regard to engineering matters and a sales manager *all* decisions in regard to sales? In a true line and staff organization the answer is "probably not." The staff person only studies a situation and makes recommendations to the superior. The superior makes the decision. Of course, the superior would be foolish to hire a specialist in a field and then never pay any attention to what he/she recommends. The function of the superior in this case is to coordinate the recommendations of all the specialists involved.

It is felt in many cases that the specialist should not just recommend, but should have full authority over his or her particular function. This principle is followed in many companies and is called a line and functional staff type of organization. It is a variation of the regular line and staff; the only difference is in the *degree* of authority that is granted the people concerned.

Frederick Taylor first developed the idea of a functional type of organization in his paper entitled "Shop Management," which was presented in 1903. Taylor suggested a pure functional organization. In his arrangement each worker would report to a speed boss, a gang boss, a repair boss, an inspector, a time and cost clerk, an instruction card clerk, a route clerk, and a disciplinarian. Each boss would have full authority over his or her particular function and would instruct the workers in that function.

It is doubtful whether this particular type of organization has ever existed in any company, for it has the obvious drawback that each person has too many bosses. Probably too high a premium is placed on coordination and cooperation among the various bosses. However, pure functional organization has the advantage of full and maximum utilization of the specialties of the various bosses. This advantage has led to the broadening of responsibility and authority of ordinary staff people without disturbing their basic relationships with the line.

The addition of people to an organization's staff should not be taken lightly. It is extremely difficult to measure the contribution of staff personnel to the business, and without good measures, people are often added for the sole reason that it seemed like a good idea at the time. Once added, however, they may be difficult to remove even when the need for their services has evaporated. On the other hand, companies in serious financial condition always seem to be able to fire much of their staff in order to cut costs. One often wonders why the staff couldn't have been kept leaner all along rather than wait for a crisis.

Types of Staff Departments

Staff departments are not all alike and are generally thought to be of four kinds: (1) advisory, (2) control, (3) service, and (4) coordinating. The four categories are not mutually exclusive, and in fact it may turn out that many staff departments have duties and responsibilities that fall into all four categories.

An advisory group has little authority in itself but is expected to serve as a group of specialists in a particular area and advise the decision-making executives as to the best course to follow in any particular instance. Typical advisory groups are legal, public relations, and labor relations departments.

Control departments include personnel, credit, budgeting, accounting, and auditing, and such departments typically have full authority to see that their particular functions are properly carried out everywhere in the organization.

Service departments are those assigned to carry out certain specific duties such as construction, purchasing, traffic, insurance, maintenance, engineering, and research. These groups seldom advise and seldom have authority; they usually are referred to as "staff" groups since they do not actually work on the product.

Coordinating departments typically give advice, but such advice is usually followed by the line groups so that essentially such departments do turn out to have authority. Typical departments might be order and distribution departments as well as a production planning department.

Use of Committees

Someone has said that a committee is a group of people who take a week to do what one good person can do in an hour. Despite the number of cases in which this is undoubtedly true, a committee in an organization quite often performs worthwhile tasks. If two heads are better than one, the use of a committee will pay off.

A committee is often found on an organization chart at a high level of management. Such a committee is usually composed of all the various heads of departments or functions and often serves to formulate and direct policy for the entire business. Other committees may exist further down in the organization. Some of these may be standing committees, while others may be formed to work on one particular problem, being dissolved once they have arrived at a solution.

The purpose served by forming a committee at any level in the organization may be one or more of the following:

To coordinate various functions.   A committee to consider new products might be composed of representatives from sales, production, and engineering in order to insure that any new development would meet the requirements of all three groups.

To secure cooperation of various personnel.   An executive issuing an order cannot always be certain the order will be carried out in the manner he desires. Talking over the proposed order with a committee gives him an oppportunity to answer questions about it, and likewise gives the people concerned a chance to air their objections. The usual result of such a session is better understanding all the way around.

To solve a problem.   This is where the "two heads are better than one" idea can demonstrate its effectiveness. An individual faced with a problem may not have the ability to come up with a solution; or perhaps he may become stagnant in his thinking. The stimulation brought about by discussing the problem with others often brings about a solution.

To train younger executives.   Committee meetings may be called to give the younger executives a keener insight into the operation of the business. Or a young executive may be given an assignment and asked to explain the results to the committee, thereby demonstrating her capabilities. Her superiors can then appraise her performance and plan her future training.

One other use of a committee should be mentioned in passing: it may rubber-stamp the ideas of the executive who forms it. This use, of course, is undesirable and quite wasteful, but committees are often formed for this purpose by the executive who is afraid to stand behind his own decisions. He wants others to share the responsibility, so he uses a rubber-stamp committee.

A committee will be more successful if the following requirements are met:

1. There must be a real need for the committee.
2. There should be as few individuals on the committee as possible.
3. The chairman must conduct meetings as efficiently as possible, having the agenda prepared in advance and prohibiting discussions not relating to the matter at hand.
4. Meetings must begin and end on time.
5. Any item that can be more effectively handled by an individual rather than by the committee should not be included on the committee agenda.
6. The duties, responsibilities, and authority of the committee should be clearly defined.
7. Committees should be disbanded upon completion of the objectives for which they were formed.

One can see that what underlies the above list is the avoidance of wasted time and the cost that goes with it. Committees enjoy a certain degree of unpopularity in many companies because everyone associates wasted or lost time with a committee meeting. This can be avoided to a great extent by following the requirements listed.

Matrix Organization

Further examination of the use of committees, and in particular the purposes to be served by committees, has led a number of companies to adopt what is known as a matrix structure in organization. Basically, this structure is an elaboration of the use of committees and is shown in outline form in Figure 4-4.

Figure 4-4 indicates the typical type of organization across the top, with functional departments reporting directly to the general manager. Each employee has a superior within his or her functional department, as in conventional organization charts. The additional feature is the formation of project teams and the designation of program managers as indicated on the left of Figure 4-4. Each team for any particular project is made up of experts from the various functional departments as required. The persons assigned to a project team may work with that group for some months or even years, after which they are released and sent back to the functional department or possibly assigned to some other project team. Conceivably, persons could also be assigned to more than one project at a time depending on project requirements.

Obviously, this type of organization structure has most use in those

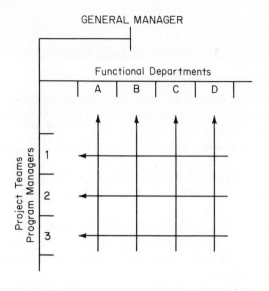

GENERAL MANAGER

Figure 4-4. Matrix structure.

companies or departments within companies that perform many of their activities as projects rather than continuous production. It offers the advantage of an organized team for any particular project while each member of the team still has a home back in the functional department. The disadvantage of the matrix is that the organization principle of unity of command is violated inasmuch as each employee appears to have two bosses, namely, the functional department head and the project manager. Companies making use of this type of organization feel that the advantages overcome the disadvantages, particularly as time goes on and greater experience is gained with this type of structure.

The Informal Organization

The discussion in the preceding paragraphs concerned what might be termed the "formal organization," in which the precise relationships among the various jobs in the company are set down on paper in terms of a formal organization chart. The need for such an arrangement has been emphasized. We must return to the facts of organizational life, however, and realize that these jobs are held by people and not by robots. As a result, some informal relationships exist that are not shown on any chart.

Superimposed on the formal organization chart of Figure 4-5 is an informal organization that might exist. The informal organization is shown by the dotted lines. Disregarding for the moment the cause of these informal relationships, the effect could be something with which to reckon. Executive 3 has some relationship with Employee 211, which could easily bypass the formal relationship through Em-

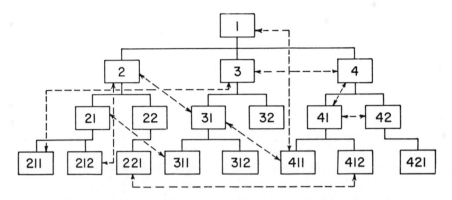

Figure 4-5. Informal relationships indicated on top of a formal organization chart.

ployees 2 and 21. In a similar manner, Employee 31 has a special relationship with Employee 411 that could mean a disruption of the normal channels. And so on for the rest of the informal relationships shown.

Such informal relationships come about for a variety of reasons. Some people are natural leaders wherever they are placed in an organization, and other people will go to them for advice regardless of the formal organization structure. Social activities are probably the largest cause of informal relationships, for if Employee 21 and Employee 311 bowl on the same team every Monday night, inevitably there will be created a strong bond between them that no formal organization chart can break. Looking at the darker side of the picture, if Employee 41 and Employee 42 are both running for the same political office, a very special relationship may exist between them. Extreme friendship may create favoritism to the detriment of overall employee relations, and animosity may make for inefficiency and breakdown of respect for superiors. On the other hand, many times these special relationships result in things being done more efficiently. The important point is that special relationships exist in every organization, and they do not necessarily follow the lines shown on the formal organization chart.

An organization purist may wish to stamp out any evidence of the informal organization, suspecting that its net effect would be harmful. Let such a purist be reminded, however, that horizontal communications are enhanced by the informal organization, thereby improving cooperation and coordination between departments. If all communications had to be vertical and conform strictly to an organization chart, efficiency would soon be reduced to zero.

Tools of Coordination

Coordination is of prime importance in an organization, for without proper coordination the efforts and the purposes of the people employed by a company are not unified. To achieve coordination, companies make use of certain tools. One of these is the organization chart, which has already been discussed in some detail. Two others are the *organization manual* and the *standard practice instructions.*

Organization Manual

The organization chart is usually an outline or skeleton of a company's organization, showing only job titles and their relationship to each other. It is the organization manual that provides substance for the chart. The manual will normally outline in detail all the duties and responsibilities that go with each job the chart shows. In addition, some manuals include for each job an outline of relationships with other jobs, the public, other companies, and the government.

Such written information about the positions in an organization helps work to progress much more smoothly. First of all, all personnel know exactly what they are to do and what the scope of their authority is. Secondly, overlap of duties and responsibilities can be avoided, thereby making for a more efficient organization. Thirdly, such a manual assists in training, for new staff members taking over a job can tell exactly what is required of them; they don't depend on their predecessors to remember all the various aspects of their jobs.

An organization manual can be useful only if it is kept up to date; and it is this burden of keeping it up to date that causes many companies not to use them or to discard them once they are started. The same can be said of the organization chart. This tendency can be minimized by refraining from making the chart and manual too elaborate to start with and by designing both so that they will be easy to change. Manuals in loose-leaf form can be changed readily. Charts made using some of the special tapes developed for this purpose are equally flexible. The use of such time-saving devices will give the maximum incentive to keep the chart and manual up to date and thereby insure their usefulness.

Standard Practice Instructions

Although the organization manual outlines who has what responsibilities, it does not say *how* these various operations are to be carried out. This is the purpose of the standard practice instructions.

Such instructions cover a great variety of procedures. Examples might be requisitioning supplies, issuing employee passes, computing vacation pay, and receiving material from a vendor. Standard practice instructions may also include material on how to perform the manufacturing processes, although these instructions are more likely to be in another booklet sometimes called "manufacturing standards."

Of course it is assumed that the method of performing a job as outlined in the standard practice instructions is the best one available. Even more important, perhaps, is that the SPI will insure the use of the *same* method throughout the company. In other words, consistency in performing tasks is achieved. Certainly it would be undesirable, for example, if various departments were computing vacation pay using different formulas. The possibility of such an occurrence is minimized with use of up-to-date standard practice instructions.

The remarks made earlier about keeping the organization manual up to date also apply to the standard practice instructions. Nothing can be more exasperating than to be following a procedure outlined in the SPI and then be told that the procedure is out of date. Unless the booklet can be kept current, it is probably better to have none at all.

When the organization chart, the organization manual, and the standard practice instructions have been prepared, they become tools to facilitate coordination in the enterprise. The organization chart tells who is to perform a function and how that function is geared into the organization. The organization manual explains what the person's responsibilities and duties are. Finally, the standard practice instructions describe how the various tasks are to be performed.

Organization Planning

We have tried to emphasize the importance of proper organization to successful operation of a manufacturing concern and to give some indication of what makes for proper organization. Two other points have also been emphasized. One is that organization is a dynamic sort of thing. It changes and needs to be changed. It is not something to be worked out on a chart and then filed away. Secondly, organization is given consideration in a business only because such consideration contributes to the good of the business. Organization is not a goal in itself—it *assists* in arriving at the goal. This assistance is felt in some companies to be so important that separate departments of organization have been established. Such departments are charged with the responsibility of organization planning, of continually defining and grouping the separate activities of the enterprise so that each can better contribute to company objectives. Giving this responsibility to a person or department insures that it will not be overlooked. Of course, separate organization departments can be justified only in the fairly large companies; so some companies have made organization planning the responsibility of an industrial engineer. This has worked out satisfactorily; industrial engineers can seek out improvements in organization as well as improvements in methods, materials handling or production control.

Basically, the work of organization planning is to establish an "ideal" organization and to engineer and plan so as to approach that ideal. We must recognize that the ideal itself won't remain static. Conditions change, objectives change, and management concepts change, but at any one time there should be a common understanding of what organization would be ideal.

Working the company's actual organization toward the ideal is the main task of organization planning. Many factors keep the company from announcing that "tomorrow morning we will start operating using the ideal organization." One of the more important factors is the informal organization, which we have discussed earlier. Informal organizations cannot be overlooked; so it is the job of organization planning to reconcile the informal relationships with the formal ones. Another factor is that there may not be people available who are capable of taking over the responsibilities called for in the ideal organization. Long-range management development programs may be called for to insure a source of competent executives. A third factor is the natural resistance to change possessed by people presently in the organization. Once people get accustomed to associating with a certain group of co-workers, they don't want to change. They can be forced to change, but the consequences may be resentment and inefficiency.

These factors may deter us from making organizational changes in the short run, but they should not deter us in the long run. We can also make changes at certain opportune times. There are always retirements, people quitting for better jobs, or other eventualities that force change. Changes can then be made in the direction of the ideal organization plan. In the course of time a rational plan of organization can be achieved without seriously disturbing the people involved.

We see, then, that organization planning involves the patient changing of an organization structure and accompanying job descriptions toward an ideal or ultimate plan of organization that most effectively meets the requirements of the business.

Some advantages of organization planning are as follows:

1. Provides for succession.   Analyzing the retirement dates of executives will alert the company to the need to groom replacements. Having a plan of replacements for all jobs will minimize the emergency should someone quit or die unexpectedly.

2. Facilitates promotion from within and the improvement in morale that accompanies the adoption of such a policy.   Looking at organization requirements ahead of time makes it feasible to train some good prospect for a top job, rather than depending on bringing someone in from the outside.

3. All will have a better understanding of what is required on their jobs and consequently will perform better.   Organization planning means that each job must be carefully studied as to duties, responsibilities, objectives, limits of authority, and relationships with other parts of the organization. These facts become part of the organization manual and will eliminate any uncertainty in the minds of job incumbents. Friction will be reduced, and executives can spend time on policy matters rather than in settling differences.

4. Provides a long-range plan for the handling of special problems.   In any organization there are certain people who don't fit in. These people and their problems can't be eliminated all at once, but a plan will indicate a more desirable course of action than simply "waiting for something to happen."

5. Provides for the long-run strength of the business. The strength of any manufacturing enterprise depends upon the dynamics of its organization. By planning its organization, a business can be assured of a strong position not only today but also tomorrow.

QUESTIONS

1. Does a partnership have any organization problems?
2. How does a manager go about getting his subordinates to assume responsibilities that are considered a part of their jobs?
3. Explain the principles of responsibility and authority.
4. On what bases are the activities listed on the organization chart in Figure 4-1 divided? How might the other bases for subdividing activities be used on this chart?
5. Explain the development of the informal organization in a company and outline the desirable and undesirable features of such a development.
6. What are the strengths and weaknesses of the line type of organization?
7. What are the strengths and weaknesses of the functional type of organization?
8. Explain how the organization chart, the organization manual, and standard practice instructions are tools of coordination.
9. Would a small company, say of 200 employees, have need for the tools of coordination?
10. What is an "ideal" organization and how is it useful in organization planning?

CASE PROBLEMS

Pearson Punch Presses, Inc.

The management of Pearson Punch Presses, Inc., consists of seven men: Mr. Eli Pearson, the company president, and, reporting directly to him, six supervisors who in turn head divisions of the manufacturing operations. The six divisions are machining, casting, small parts, assembly, die shop, and forge shop. Eight types of standard punch presses are produced by the company, and each division is thoroughly familiar with the requirements for each of the types. Little difficulty is experienced in coordinating the work of the various divisions.

All sales are handled through manufacturers' agents, and Mr. Pearson himself spends considerable time working with the various agents and promoting sales through them. He also handles the purchasing activity since he maintains outside contacts. Ten clerks in the office handle all paper work connected with sales, purchasing, and payrolls. In addition to the ten clerks, there are 145 factory employees.

The division supervisors are called upon to handle a variety of activities. Each operates his division more or less as a separate factory, hiring and firing his own employees, handling grievances, making out purchase requisitions, setting pay rates, inspecting materials and parts, figuring time cards, and maintaining equipment. All supervisors are capable, and although kept busy, they enjoy the broad responsibility and authority granted them by Mr. Pearson.

Through his contacts with other companies, Mr. Pearson realizes that the machine tool industry is growing and that his company must grow with it or be left behind. The market for his eight standard presses will probably contract in the future unless he can reduce costs. In addition, new and improved presses with automatic controls must be developed.

Mr. Pearson can see many problems ahead of him in trying to get his company in line with the times. One of these involves his company's organization structure. He has expressed the feeling that "a more modern organization" would be needed before the company could progress very far toward expansion.

Questions:

1. Draw an organization chart of Pearson Punch Presses, Inc., as it now stands.
2. Draw a recommended organization structure for this company.
3. Outline and explain the particular points or features of your recommended structure.

Hansen Electronics, Inc.

Both Teds recognized that something had to be done and done fast. Profits for the past year had been non-existent, and the first loss in the company's history is projected for this year. The electronics business just wasn't what it used to be, and Hansen was suffering from increased competition the same as most of the rest of the industry. The profit margins that meant rapid growth and success for Hansen over the past decade were simply not there.

Both Ted Williams, Vice President for Manufacturing, and Ted Lang, Vice President for Personnel, had been discussing the problem for many months and in fact had set up regular monthly meetings to which they invited certain of the staff to make presentations regarding various analytical studies relating to the problem at hand.

At today's meeting Fred Videon of the Personnel Department staff presented the results and conclusions from a study that he had initiated on his own. The study related to the proportion of line personnel to staff personnel in the company as it had varied over the years.

Fred's data indicated that the first full year of operation after the company's founding produced a profit of 27% on investment and the ratio of line workers to staff workers stood at 18 to one. Ten years later profits had decreased to 24% and the line-to-staff ratio was reduced to 12-to-one. Today, 30 years after the company's founding, the profit ratio is down to essentially zero, but the line-to-staff ratio is almost down to one-to-one. In other words, for every worker that is occupied producing a product that is to be sold and generate income, there is another worker making some study (such as this one), doing some research, typing up invoices, or some such thing, all in the name of helping but not really contributing to the company's income.

Fred's presentation went on for some time, since both Teds thought they saw all sorts of holes in Fred's argument and dwelled at some length on the necessity of many of the staff activities that were involved. For example, where would the company be today without the research that was conducted some ten years ago, and which now is the heart of the current product line?

Fred couldn't deny the validity of this argument, but he went on to cite instances of many other companies which during good times tended to let their staffs grow and become fat cats only to be faced with wholesale layoffs when times became bad. He was careful to point out that he didn't know for certain how much Hansen had been subject to this syndrome, but the data he had collected seemed to indicate that the possibility was worth further investigation by those with authority to do something about the situation.

When it finally came time to go home, the meeting broke up with both Teds shaking their heads from side to side and wondering to themselves, "Have I really been a party to this?"

Questions:

1. Consider and evaluate the ratio of line to staff personnel as a measure of organization efficiency. Should the ratio be strictly a body count or perhaps of salaries and wages paid to each group?

2. Fred mentions just the word ''staff,'' while the text points out that there are four types of staff. Should distinctions be made among the types of staff when trying to develop ratios? In other words, are some staffs more important than others?

3. If top management should decree that half the staff must be let go, what types of things would have to be done to insure that the company can continue to operate without these staff people?

4. To what extent are the two Teds responsible for what has happened, and what should they have done to prevent it from developing?

5

DESIGN OF MANUFACTURING PROCESSES

One of the activities that can have considerable impact on the success of an industrial enterprise is the careful planning of manufacturing processes in advance of the actual production of goods.

Design of manufacturing processes is not restricted to the new firm or the new product. To meet competition, manufacturing organizations are continually reviewing their operations with the objective of increased production at lower manufacturing costs. The introduction of new products, product improvements, and model changes make it mandatory that adequate organization and procedures be provided for the planning of manufacturing methods. Many techniques and procedures are involved, such as methods engineering, plant layout, and others. A close interrelationship of all is prerequisite to optimum results.

Before beginning to discuss the factors that have a bearing on process design, let us consider the relationship that the design of a product has to its manufacture. There usually are several ways in which a product or part can be made based on its end use and the quality desired. Thus, the control knob shaft for an automobile light switch might be made on an automatic screw machine, in a die casting machine, in a cold forming press, or by some other process. It is highly desirable for the product designer and the process engineer to collaborate on the design of the product (or part) to insure that realistic specifications (on materials and quality) are set and that the product has been designed to be produced by the most economical method.

Scope of Process Design

Industry employs a pattern of activity in the design of manufacturing processes. Generally speaking, this activity starts with the receipt of the product specifications and ends with the final plans for the manufacture of the product. In a broad sense this pattern of activity is uniform, regardless of the kind of product or the type of manufacturing involved. The steps are as follows:

1. A careful review of the product design and specifications to make sure that economical manufacture is feasible.
2. Determination of the methods of manufacture that will result in the optimum manufacturing cost.
3. Selection—or development—and procurement of all machines, tools, and other equipment required for the manufacture of the product at the required quality and rate of production.
4. Layout of the production area and auxiliary spaces, and installation of the manufacturing facilities.
5. Planning for and establishing the necessary control of materials, machines, and manpower to insure the effective utilization of the manufacturing facility for the economical production of the product.

The above steps may be identified as functions of various activities, such as manufacturing engineering, process engineering, methods engineering, or tool engineering. No matter what the group or groups involved are called, the scope of process-design activity can be identified as all work that is necessary to arrange for the manufacture of the product by the most economical means and in compliance with all safety regulations.[1]

Basic Factors Affecting Process Design

There are three basic factors that affect the design of a manufacturing process, namely:

1. The volume or quantity of the product to be manufactured.
2. The required quality of the product.
3. The equipment that is available, or that can be procured, for the manufacture of the product.

---

[1]The Occupational Safety and Health Act of 1970 (to be discussed in Chapter 18) established many regulations pertaining to occupational safety and health that employers must adhere to. In some cases, the required guidelines may impose considerable challenge to process designers.

Volume

The volume to be manufactured must always be considered as the volume to be produced within a given period—i.e., as the rate of production. In this manner it can be related to the capacity of the manufacturing equipment under consideration and the best methods selected accordingly.

The anticipated volume should be based also upon a sales forecast. This is of particular importance in the introduction of a new product. Funds should be expended for the improvement of processes only when the forecast indicates such a volume of sales that an appropriate return on the investment can be realized.

Generally speaking, the greater the volume of the product to be produced, the greater is the opportunity to incorporate advanced methods of manufacture into the design of the manufacturing process.

The number of identical units to be produced vitally affects the selection of manufacturing methods. When multiplied by the total volume to be produced, the savings per unit of product or per component part may be applied to the purchase of more modern equipment. It may justify new and better machine tools, the use of numerically controlled machines, robotic devices, or other major items. More often, however, it will justify better auxiliary equipment, such as jigs, fixtures, or dies, which will in turn increase the productive capacity of the existing equipment in the plant.

Methods of manufacture vary widely with the volume to be produced. The production of heavy industrial apparatus and ships involves very few units of product, requires skilled machinists or other craftsmen using general-purpose machines and tools, and demands assembly by skilled labor. On the other hand, the mass production of washing machines, refrigerators, radios, automobiles, and similar goods is accomplished with a large proportion of automatic machinery and on a planned assembly line that requires a minimum of skill (see Chapter 6).

Product explosion and standardization.   Many concerns are engaged in multi-product operations; that is, they make more than one product or product line. Most products are assembled and can be "exploded"—or broken down—into assemblies, subassemblies, and component parts. Where more than one product is involved, there is usually standardization of subassemblies or component parts among the different products.

The process engineer must design processes at all levels of fabrication—that is, for producing assemblies, subassemblies, and component parts. When considering the volume to be produced, particularly of component parts, he or she must plan on the total requirements. Thus, standardization of component parts and product explosion are of primary importance to the process engineer.

Economic manufacturing lot size.   A major portion of the activity of the process engineer deals with the individual component parts of the assembled product. For many parts the productive capacity of the machines used exceeds by far the planned daily use of these parts in assemblies. As a result, these parts are produced intermittently, or in "lots." There are a number of ways available for determining the most cost-effective lot size. (A more detailed discussion of this topic is presented in Chapter 12.) One of the consequences of producing parts in "batches" or "lots" is that work-in-process (WIP) inventory will result. Current production management thinking is opposed to accumulating inventories of raw materials or WIP. Rather than having a minimum amount of stock on hand at all times, in case of emergencies, it is desired to have the work pieces only when needed and "just in time." (The "just in time" inventory concept will be discussed in more detail, also in Chapter 12.)

Quality of the Product

The required quality of the product has a definite effect on the design of the manufacturing process. When the quality level is determined, it is the responsibility of the product or design engineer to stipulate it in the drawings and specifications. Such documents as bills of materials, parts lists, assembly and detail drawings, and engineering releases can give the process engineer a clear understanding of the quality requirements for all assemblies, subassemblies, and component parts. Then, methods and equipment must be selected that assure the production of parts of the required quality at the lowest manufacturing cost.

The dimensional requirements, types of surfaces to be produced, and other characteristics of parts to be manufactured must be matched to the capabilities of different types of machines and methods. The mechanical condition of equipment should be checked carefully to determine whether it will produce parts in accordance with its rated performance. Capability studies have been developed that, by the use of applied statistics, will predetermine the quality level for an operation by the machine that has been selected by either the planning or routing group.

Generally speaking, the higher the required quality level of a product, the higher is the cost to manufacture it. Quality problems, as well as statistical quality control (SQC) methods, will be discussed in greater detail in the chapter on quality control (Chapter 15).

Equipment

In the majority of situations the process engineer must attempt to design manufacturing processes that are adaptable to and will balance the productive load of available existing equipment. In the case of a new plant and a new product this does not apply; however, this latter condition is the exception rather than the rule in industry.

Adapting methods to types of available equipment is a principal factor when manufacturing in economic lots. At times the number of machines available of a given type or size may influence the design of the process. The process as designed may overload the productive capacity of a certain machine group. In such a case an alternative method may be planned using other types of equipment, even though this plan results in an increase in the manufacturing cost. Close liaison must be established with the production control function where current machine loads are maintained.

That only existing types of equipment can be used by the process engineer should not be stipulated. This would stifle any progressive ingenuity on his part. Often new methods may be devised, the use of which will justify the purchase of new and more productive equipment. In considering a new machine, its adaptability for use in the manufacture of all parts of the product should be carefully reviewed; the volume of production of one component part might not indicate sufficient savings to warrant the purchase, whereas additional changes in processes of other parts might justify the new equipment and result in an overall reduction in the cost of manufacture.

Process engineers must be constantly alert to new improvements in machine tools and equipment that may be used in the manufacture of the product.

Types of Manufacturing

Based on a careful consideration of volume, quality, and equipment, the process engineer can determine the type of manufacturing best suited for any production situation. The type to be employed is generally determined by the manufacturing process design. For the most part, the various types of manufacturing involve either *continuous* or *intermittent* production of goods.

Continuous Manufacture

Continuous manufacture is the production of goods on a flow basis at a predetermined rate. Flow methods require that the product move constantly—or approach constant movement—from operation to operation without a controlled storage at any point in the process. Continuous manufacture is typical of large food-processing plants and many chemical industries.

The assembly operation in a manufacturing environment is often a continuous operation. Examples of this are the assembly-line techniques used by manufacturers of automobiles, radios, refrigerators, and similar products (see Figure 5-1). Usually a constantly moving conveyor is employed, the base frame of the product starting at the head of the line and other component parts or subassemblies being added as the "growing product" moves along, the final finished assembly being taken off the conveyor at the end of the line. Another example of continuous manufacture would be that of a transfer machine, as illustrated in Figure 5-2.

Continuous manufacture also may be employed in the manufacture of component parts, such as a transmission housing. In this situation a "balanced line" of

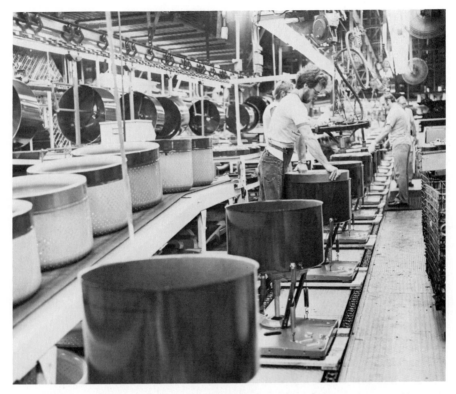

Figure 5-1. Washing machines being assembled on a drag-chain type conveyor. Note the belt conveyor on the left, which delivers the porcelain inner tub to the operator station for placement into the outer tub. Also shown in the upper left is the overhead porcelain parts delivery conveyor. (Courtesy The Maytag Company.)

machine tools or operations is planned. For example, the operator of the first machine will take a rough casting from a stockpile and perform the first operation. The partly processed part is then passed on, usually by placing it on some type of conveyor, to the next operator, who performs the next operation. Thus, operation by operation, the casting is processed until a completely machined part has been produced.

Balancing lines. To be economical, each operation in a continuous line must require approximately the same length of time—or else two or more machines working simultaneously must be provided for the "slow" operations. The design of a continuous process line to equalize the time required at each work station is called *balancing the line*. The balancing of an assembly line involving manual labor is not as difficult as the balancing of a line of machine tools, because once the operation time of a machine is established it becomes fixed. On the other hand, manual labor can be redistributed to gain an effective steady flow by changing the job content for each operator on the line.

Figure 5-2. All machine operations and the assembly of two bushings and three studs for washing machine gear cases and gear case covers are automatically completed on this Buhr Transfer Machine. Two operators control the process, including loading and unloading, tool change, monitoring the machine, and controlling the quality. Note the combination storage–delivery conveyer overhead. (Courtesy The Maytag Company.)

Recent advances in line balancing have been made possible through the use of computers. For example, in one company a program was developed that enables the computer to determine 1000 complete manpower combinations and then pick the 10 best. The final choice among the 10 is then up to the industrial engineer.

Group technology.   A manufacturing concept that has gained acceptance in U.S. industry is called *group technology*. Group technology (GT) is an approach to manufacturing in which similar parts are identified and then grouped together to take advantage of their similarities in design and manufacture. The similar parts are grouped into *part families* on the basis of geometric size or shape or because similar steps are required in their manufacture. As an example, a plant producing literally thousands of different parts might be able to group them into significantly less than a hundred families. Since each family would possess similar design and manufacturing characteristics each part in a family could be processed in a similar manner. This system makes it possible to arrange machines and equipment in groups, which facilitates continuous manufacturing of part families almost as if they were identical parts.

An inseparable adjunct to GT is the development of a parts classification and coding system. Such a system aids in the identification of each existing part as a member of a family and the addition of new parts to the appropriate family. Design engineers can use coding schemes to facilitate the design process by easily searching a data base to see whether there are old, existing part designs that are similar to a new part which must be designed. This is almost a case of the engineer protecting himself from "reinventing the wheel." In addition to their design retrieval capabilities, group technology classification and coding methods lend themselves to computer-aided process planning.

Mechanization and automation. Current trends toward mechanization and automation indicate the potential of continuous manufacturing in industry. The development of loading, unloading, and transfer devices is resulting in mechanized production lines. Also, the further addition of measuring and feedback mechanisms for the full control of the process results in automation. This subject will be discussed in further detail in Chapter 6.

Intermittent Manufacture

When continuous manufacture is not feasible, for either large or small quantities of product, intermittent manufacture is employed. In this type of manufacture the product is processed in lots rather than on a continuous flow basis. It is a function of the process engineer to determine the economic manufacturing lot size for each component part, subassembly, and assembly.

For example, the economic lot size for the production of a gear to be used on a power lawn mower might be 1500 pieces, and production of another 1500 gears of this type may not be planned for another three months. In this case 1500 blanks might be cut from steel bar stock and tagged for a specific job number. The 1500 blanks would then travel from work station to work station. At each work station the operation would be completed on all of the 1500 parts before the lot was moved to the next work station.

Ideally, there would be no waiting time as each lot arrived at the next work station. Realistically, this objective is hard to attain. In an intermittent manufacturing plant there are usually one or more lots ahead of each work station awaiting processing. This is one reason why intermittent manufacturing requires a larger inventory of goods in process than continuous manufacturing.

Intermittent manufacture is particularly adaptable to concerns making product lines, such as several sizes of the same basic design of water pump. In situations such as this it is good practice to standardize component parts for use in many different products or sizes of products. Accumulation of the many product requirements results in optimum economic manufacturing lot sizes.

Job-lot manufacture. Intermittent manufacture is often referred to as job-lot production when manufacturing to a customer's purchase order or specification. Job-lot production is characteristic of concerns manufacturing large or expensive machines or equipment. A customer may order one, two, or more units of the product; a manufacturing order is entered for that lot only, material is procured, the units produced and shipped. The product may be considered standard so far as the manufacturer is concerned, but units are produced only after they are sold.

Although in some instances repeat orders may be received, the possibility of such is discounted in the design of the manufacturing processes and in the computation of the production costs. On the other hand, the special tools, patterns, and dies are usually stored for such a contingency. This practice presents a difficult storage problem for the job-lot manufacturer.

Mixed Types of Manufacture

Most industries use both continuous and intermittent manufacture in the production of goods. While continuous assembly operations are not uncommon, continuous production of all the component parts of a product—the objective of the automatic factory—is not as common as might be expected. The reason is the difficulty of balancing the unit manufacturing times for all component part requirements. For example, the productive capacity of a plant making a line of electric motors might be such that a year's requirement for a small special pin could be produced on an automatic screw machine in two days. On the other hand, the power presses producing the stampings used in the stators and rotors might have to work to capacity to keep the assembly line supplied with parts. Thus the power presses producing these stampings could be placed in a continuous process line, which in turn would flow into the motor assembly line. To attempt to "tie-in" the production of the special pin on a continuous manufacturing basis obviously is out of the question.

Many factories are classified as continuous manufacturing plants even though they may use both continuous and intermittent manufacturing techniques. This classification is justified by the fact that each plant is designed to utilize its full capacity in the production of assembled products at a planned rate of production.

The real challenge is to increase the flexibility of mechanized or automated equipment so that its use is possible for more than one size of part or so that different parts may be processed on the same mechanized line. The successful solution of this problem will result in a greater degree of integration of continuous manufacturing techniques in a normal intermittent manufacturing situation.

Manufacturing Equipment Configuration

It should be noted that the physical arrangement of the manufacturing facilities within the production environment will depend on whether it is continuous, intermittent, or mixed type of manufacturing that is being undertaken. For example, continuous production systems tend to have the different, required manufacturing facilities arranged sequentially in what might be viewed as a line. On the other hand, intermittent, batch-type manufacturing systems normally have like facilities (punch presses, for example) grouped together in a production department or work center. A batch of parts will move from department to department as directed by the process routing. Generally, work pieces in an intermittent manufacturing system will be required to move a longer distance while progressing through their required processes than will work pieces within a continuous manufacturing system.

Mixed-type manufacturing systems will have physical arrangements that are a combination of the other two types. The material flow distance will be longer than that in a strict continuous system, but will generally be shorter than that in an intermittent system. A much more thorough coverage of the facilities design problem will be presented in Chapter 10.

Computer-Aided Design and Computer-Aided Manufacturing[2]

One of the most significant trends in manufacturing in recent years is the increasing use of the digital computer in the design and manufacture of products. The common term used to refer to this trend is CAD/CAM, which stands for computer-aided design and computer-aided manufacturing. Computer-aided design (CAD) involves the use of computers in creating or modifying the product design. In CAD, the product designer makes full use of computer interactive graphics. Thus, the designer is able to take advantage of a system in which the computer is employed to display pictures, symbols, or data. In so doing, the designer is able to sit at the console of a computer terminal (see Figure 5-3) and make any additions to or changes in the design that are desired. The details of the design are stored in the computer's memory and can be withdrawn at any time in a copy of the design. It is possible that in future CAD/CAM systems the traditional engineering drawing may become obsolete. Further, the design contained in the computer's memory will be linked directly to the computer-controlled (CAM) machine tools.

Computer-aided manufacturing (CAM) has been defined by Computer Aided Manufacturing-International (CAM-I) as

> The effective utilization of computer technology in the management, control, and operations of the manufacturing facility through either direct or indirect computer interfaced with the physical and human resources of the company.

---

[2]Much of the material in this section is adapted from Mikell P. Groover, *Automation, Production Systems and Computer-Aided Manufacturing;* Englewood Cliffs, N.J.: Prentice-Hall, Inc., 1980, pp. 261–270, by permission.

Figure 5-3. Designer using a computer graphics terminal of the type that may be used in a CAD/CAM system. (Reprinted by permission from "Computer-Graphics Augmented Design and Manufacturing." © 1979 by International Business Machines Corporation.)

Applications of CAM involve the monitoring or controlling of manufacturing operations as well as any indirect applications where the computer is used (e.g., in production and inventory control—to be discussed in later chapters).

As one reviews the significant trend toward the use of computers in all phases of manufacturing, it is evident that we are only a few years away from the time when entire plants will be automated and under the control of a single computer. Sizeable segments of some plants are already operating in this fashion. For example, in one plant an integrated machining system uses a computer containing programs for 140 parts. The computer is used to run machine tools and to direct parts automatically from one machine to another. Further, process controlling mini- and micro-computers and programmable controllers are being used (sometimes in conjunction with a large main-line computer) increasingly to control time, quantity, and quality, and to monitor tool life. The use of equipment of this type can affect productivity significantly.

A manufacturing environment where processes are interconnected for digital computer control purposes is often referred to as a *computer-integrated* manufacturing system, and the term CIM is currently as popular as CAM.

Relation of Process Design to Types of Manufacturing

There is a definite relationship between the design of the manufacturing process and the type of manufacture that is adopted. For continuous manufacture the methods and processes must be determined before the line is set up. The manufacturing process is built into the line. Once processing lines are established, any further changes in methods should be held to a minimum owing to the dependency of each operation on all preceding operations. Changes usually require that the line be shut down with the resultant loss of the productive capacity of the entire plant. Changes in the line for improvement of methods are usually held up until a model change is made in the product. For continuous manufacture the design of the manufacturing process must be thorough and accurate.

Although the volume to be produced is not the only factor in the selection of the type of manufacturing, continuous manufacturing usually means that the volume of production is large. Large volume usually justifies the use of highly specialized tools and equipment; thus the machine tool may be built to fit the methods (see Figure 5-4). In this case the methods would control the selection of tools and equipment.

For intermittent production no lines are set up. The process engineer is usually required to adapt the methods and processes to the types of equipment available or

Figure 5-4. Special-purpose machine used to drill, ream, and tap holes simultaneously on two diesel engine blocks. (Courtesy Navistar.)

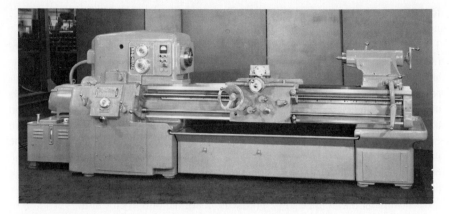

Figure 5-5.   Standard engine lathe. (Courtesy Monarch Machine Company.)

to be procured. General-purpose machine tools and equipment are employed, as each machine may be used for varying operations on many different component parts of the product (see Figure 5-5). One advantage of intermittent manufacture over continuous manufacture is that changes in methods can be made more readily and seldom will interfere with the overall productive capacity of the plant.

The Design of Manufacturing Processes

Although the fundamentals of process engineering are the same for all types of manufacturing and all kinds of products, the procedures and techniques will vary among different industries. The design of manufacturing processes by a large chemical or food-processing plant will involve different procedures and techniques from those used in designing processes for the manufacture of heavy industrial equipment by a job-lot industry. Each, however, will follow the same basic pattern.

None of the steps in the design of a manufacturing process can be eliminated. It is simply a matter of when certain things are done and by whom they are accomplished. What characterizes modern industry is the careful planning of manufacturing methods by technically qualified personnel as opposed to the early attitude of ''let the shop make it''—where the final plans for making the part were often left to the operator actually doing the operation.

Process Design Procedures

A typical industry that presents all phases of process design in a logical order might be a manufacturer of home appliances such as refrigerators, ranges, and washing machines. Such plants usually employ both continuous and intermittent manufacturing techniques and, in the total, are usually planned as continuous manufacturing plants.

To the layman the design of manufacturing processes for such a plant presents a complicated picture. Actually the procedure is simple; it looks complex only because the layman looks at the product as a whole. The process engineer, on the other hand, usually starts with the consideration of a single component part and performs an operation analysis. A basic procedure in this type of plant might be as follows:

1. The product designer and the process engineer work in close cooperation during the design of the part to insure that all possible manufacturing problems are taken into consideration as the component part design is developed. As pointed out at the beginning of the chapter, close cooperation between the process engineer and the product engineer is of major importance to the economical manufacture of a product. Best results can be obtained when these two join forces in the early design stages of the product. Consideration should be given to the detailed design of each component part to insure the best manufacturing methods for the product as a whole. Such a procedure will insure the minimum of design changes that may be required at a later date to accommodate the manufacturing process.

2. Completion of the design of the part makes it possible to proceed with the determination of the three basic factors of volume, quality, and the manufacturing equipment available. In many cases the purchase or development of new and more modern equipment enters into the considerations.

3. The next step is the decision to "make or buy." Because of the wide range the impact of this decision has on the plant, the final decision is normally made at an organizational level higher than the process engineer. Comparison of the price of the finished part delivered to the plant can be made with the estimated manufacturing or shop cost as determined by the process engineer. Many rather intangible factors, such as maintenance of level of employment, optimum utilization of plant facilities, and trade relations with sources of supply, are involved. The decision to make or buy must be considered in all manufacturing situations.

4. Assuming that the part is to be made, the next step is to consider all the work that is necessary to bring the part from the raw material state to the completely machined or processed part ready for assembly. Whether or not an actual list of the work to be done is prepared will depend to a large extent on the experience of the process engineer. In any event, this step will translate the designer's blueprint of the part into a complete understanding of what has to be done by the manufacturing group.

5. The process engineer next groups the work to be done into operations. The basic factors of volume to be produced, required quality of the product, and capabilities of the equipment available are carefully considered in this step. Each operation is assigned to the type and size of machine—or work station—that will perform the job most economically. The number of operations required to complete the part is established at the optimum point that will keep the manufacturing costs at a minimum. Quantitative measurement is somewhat easier in this step than the step

of "make or buy." The various techniques of methods engineering and work measurement—including the use of standardized time values—are employed in this phase of manufacturing process design. Also, it is evident that suitable computer programs can be very useful in this step.

A typical part is shown in Figure 5-6; the work involved is listed in Figure

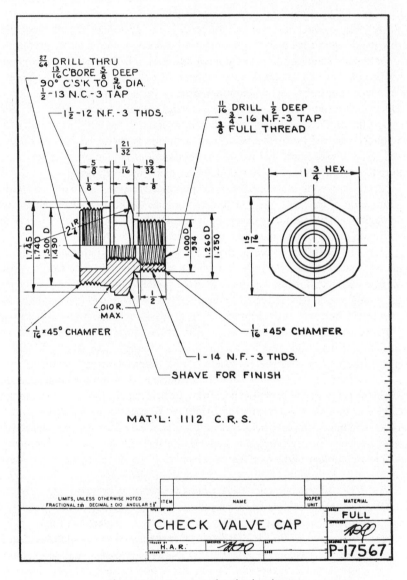

Figure 5-6.   Drawing of a check valve cap.

a. Turn $1\frac{15}{16}$ D

b. Turn 1.745–1.740 D

c. Turn 1.500–1.490 D

d. Turn 1.000–0.934 D

e. Form $2\frac{1}{4}$ R

f. Shave $2\frac{1}{4}$ R

g. Thread $1\frac{1}{2}$–12 NF-3

h. Thread 1–14 NF-3

i. Chamfer $\frac{1}{16}$ × 45 degrees–1.500 D

j. Chamfer $\frac{1}{16}$ × 45 degrees–1.000 D

k. Drill $\frac{27}{64}$ thru

l. Counterbore $\frac{13}{16}$ × $\frac{5}{8}$ deep

m. Countersink 90 degrees to $\frac{9}{16}$ D

n. Tap $\frac{1}{2}$ —13 NC-3

o. Drill $\frac{11}{16}$ × $\frac{1}{2}$ deep

p. Tap $\frac{3}{4}$ —16 NF-3 × $\frac{3}{8}$ full thread

Figure 5-7. List of work to be done on check valve cap P-17567.

5-7. This particular part can be processed in two operations on a turret lathe if the operations are as shown in Figure 5-8.

6. The last step in operation analysis is to arrange the operations in the proper sequence for the most economical manufacture.

STANDARD PROCESS SHEET							
Material Specs. _1112 CRS_ Purchased Stock Size _1¾″ hex. × 16′_ Pcs. Per Pur. Size _107_ Weight _1.35 # per unit_		Part Name _Check Valve Cap_ Usage _Speed Control Valve_ Assy. No. _P8015_ Assy. Sub. Assy. No. _P17570_			Part No. _P17567_ Date Issued _____ Date Sup'd. _____ Issued By _T.E.C._		
Oper. No.	Operation Description			Dept.	Machine	Set up	Rate	Tools
10	Turn 1.745 D, turn 1.500 D and chamfer; form turn 1.000 D, 2¼ R and 1½ D, shave 2¼ R; Drill 27/64 thru, c'bore 13/16 × 5/8 deep, ctsk. 90° to 9/16 D; thread 1½-12 and tap ½-13; cutoff.			K	Turret lathe WS 2 AW equal	1.50 hr	¹⁰/hr	Lot P #210
20	Chamfer 1.000 D; drill 11/16 × ½ deep tap ¾-16 × ⅜ full thread; thread 1-14.			K	"	0.50 hr	³⁵/hr	Lot P #211

Figure 5-8. Standard process sheet for making a check valve cap.

It is apparent that if a computerized system were being used, the process engineer could use a keyboard terminal and a CRT (cathode ray tube) display to plan the process. Then a final document for the shop could be printed (see Figure 5-9) automatically, and the plan could be stored in computer memory for future retrieval.

Computer-aided process planning. Much of what the process planner does can be quantified so that it is susceptible to computer generation. There has been much activity by software firms in recent years to develop computer-aided

```
PLANT ID-97    MICLASS NO.:     -    -    -    -    -    -    -

PART,TYPE: B99999-A999     I   SO#   I   QTY   I  DUE DATE I REVIEWED I BY: I
PART NAME: COVER PLATE     I-------I-------I-----------I-----------I-----I
DWG. REV.: 11-25-46        I       I       I           I           I     I
PART CODE: 30              I       I       I           I           I     I
PLN.CLASS: 422             I       I       I           I           I     I
MATERIAL : C1018           I       I       I           I           I     I
MAT.SIZE : .5 RD.          I       I       I           I           I     I
QTY.LIMIT: MIN- 1   MAX-100 I      I       I           I           I     I
   PLANNER: F. ZSALUDKO    I       I       I           I           I     I
      DATE: 2-4-80         I       I       I           I           I     I
                           I 95062 I  50   I 8-14-80 I 2-5-80    I FZ  I

OP  W/S                                            TOOLS/   S/U   HRS  PL
NO  IDEN        OPER. INSTRUCTIONS       RPM   FEED FIXTURES  HRS   EA.  CL
--  ----  -----------------------------  ----  ---- --------  ---   ---  --


10 1100 C/O TO REQ'D. LOT LEN.                              .100    -


20 3500 FACE, TURN 1-63/64 DIA.                            1.170  .142
        DRILL, C'BORE 1.00 DIA.
        FORM 15 DEG. ANGLE, HOLD FLAT
          TO .115 FMP
        CHAMFER, C/O, DEBURR


30 5300 DRILL, C'BORE 1/4 DP.                               .330   .012


40 8000 DEBURR COMPLETE                                     .100   .046


50 6100 GANG GRIND FACE, HOLD 1/8 FLAT                      .550   .011


60 1500 FINAL INSPECT                                       .500    -
```

Figure 5-9. Computer printout of a process plan. (Courtesy *American Machinist.*)

process planning (CAPP) packages. Groover[3] defines CAPP as "the automatic generation of a process plan (or route sheet) to manufacture the part. The process routing is developed by recognizing the specific attributes of the part in question and relating these attributes to the corresponding manufacturing operations." Group technology concepts are used extensively in most CAPP software packages. In advanced computer-aided manufacturing (CAM) systems, the process plan can be automatically generated as the part is designed.

Use of process analysis charts.   The process analysis chart is a useful technique for accumulating and summarizing the work of the process engineer. This technique presents a complete, graphical picture of the process planned for the manufacture of the product. Careful analysis of such charts by experienced process engineers will often indicate opportunities for improvement—or possible "bottlenecks"—in the manufacturing process.

Process charts and their preparation will be covered in the chapter on methods engineering (Chapter 7).

Pilot processes.   Many manufacturing process designs, particularly in the chemical industry, are prechecked by first doing a computer simulation and then building and operating a "pilot plant." A pilot plant is a small-scale operation of the total manufacturing plan—in regard to either the size of the equipment or the productive capacity of the experimental setup. In many cases only parts of the manufacturing process are checked by this technique. In any event, the objective of the pilot-plant operation is to verify whether the process design will produce the required results at the anticipated manufacturing costs.

Process Design Communications and Records

In designing the manufacturing process, the process engineer determines the work methods, the type of machines to be used, and the operation sequence for each part, subassembly, and final assembly of the product. To be of value to the manufacturing organization, this information must be presented in a clearly understandable and systematic manner. Sound communications between the process engineer and the operating departments is most essential. Information must be accurate and up-to-date at all times. It is obvious that the use of a computer can greatly reduce the time required to process information.

---

[3]*Automation, Production Systems and Computer-Aided Manufacturing,* pp. 559 and 560.

Standard Process Sheets

To be usable, the final design of the manufacturing process must be recorded. The actual forms of these records vary; however, they all carry essentially the same basic information and are prepared for the same purpose. These records have many names: master route sheet, process sheet, process plans, process and tooling record, and master plan. A typical form is shown in Figure 5-8.

Regardless of the name or type of form used, the information recorded represents a plan for a standard way of making the part. The term most descriptive of this objective is *standard process sheet*.

The importance of clearly stated and complete standard process sheets cannot be overemphasized. A master copy should be maintained in the process engineering department at all times, if possible. The master file of standard process sheets represents the "know-how" in the manufacture of the product and is probably one of the most valuable assets of the manufacturing concern.

It is emphasized that operation descriptions should be brief, concise and clear, and leave no room for misinterpretation. Also, it should be noted that the process engineer selects the *type* of machine or equipment to be used—not a specific machine by its shop number. Selection of machines by shop number restricts the flexibility of the routing function of production control and should be avoided in the design of the manufacturing process. Routing, which determines *where* an operation is to be performed, is discussed more fully in Chapter 14.

Preparation and Use of Standard Process Sheets

All work done in the processing of a product should be planned and recorded on standard process sheets or some other suitable form. As a rule, a standard process sheet is prepared for each part produced in the plant. (A "process" is the set of all operations that take place on any component part, subassembly, or assembly between controlled storages; or the set of all operations that are performed on a continuous process or assembly line.) Standard process sheets are not normally prepared for purchased parts that require no work before their use at assembly.

A principal problem in the distribution of standard process sheets is the necessity of keeping them up-to-date. Thus, the process engineer must be alert to an engineering design change that might be initiated after the part has been released for production. The trouble that might result from the production of a lot of goods from an obsolete standard process sheet is obvious. It is to avoid this possibility that some plants issue the standard process sheet only with the manufacturing order for the production of a specific quantity of parts. In these cases it is common practice to duplicate the information from the standard process sheet on the route sheet that accompanies the work through the plant. The combination of these forms with the addition of the manufacturing order number constitutes the manufacturing order. In most cases, these orders are destroyed after the production has been completed. This practice is particularly adaptable to intermittent or job-lot production. Various duplicating systems are available by which the master record of the standard process sheet can be used to duplicate information directly to the route sheet or manufacturing order copies.

Job-lot plants furnish manufacturing orders or route sheets based on the design of the manufacturing process. The master standard process sheets are then filed so that they may be available if a repeat order is received. In some industries this presents quite a problem. For example, the manufacture of airplanes has been plagued with an almost constant change in product specifications and methods of manufacture. As a result, the microfilm recording of manufacturing records has been adopted by many manufacturers.

In contrast, in a continuous manufacturing industry the use of the standard process sheet in the operating departments may be so limited that it is almost non-existent. This does not mean that the process was not carefully designed. As a matter of fact, the manufacturing process was designed into the process and assembly lines—thus requiring much greater care in the planning than in the case of intermittent manufacture. Once the process is designed into the line, the operating personnel have little, if any, need for reference to the standard process sheet.

Improvement of Product Design for Manufacturing

Often the product—or its component parts—is so designed that economical production is not possible. The logical solution is to modify or redesign the product in order to permit manufacture at a lower cost. Another situation that may call for the redesign of a product is the lack of suitable machines or equipment.

In such situations the process engineer has four possible solutions:

1. The part may be purchased from a concern having the proper equipment.
2. The necessary equipment may be procured.
3. Existing equipment may be modified to produce the part.
4. The part may be redesigned so that it can be produced on available equipment.

In many instances the fourth solution will prove the most feasible.

It is not the prerogative of the process engineer arbitrarily to make changes in the design of the product. It is, however, his responsibility to recommend to the product designer such changes as might result in cost reductions. All changes in product design and specifications must originate from the product-engineering group to insure that no change made will materially affect the functional requirements of the product.

Evaluation of the Design of Manufacturing Processes

The objective in designing the manufacturing process is to insure the production of a quality product at the optimum cost. A major problem confronting the process engineer is determining when this objective has been attained.

Manufacturing methods is a dynamic and changing area of activity. Better tools and equipment are constantly being developed. New materials are being introduced and new uses for old materials discovered. Every process engineer must be alert to changes in the basic factors of volume, product quality level, and equipment availability. Any of these changes may affect the design of the manufacturing process.

A basic tenet of the process engineer should be that there is always a better way to make the product. Cost-reduction and value analysis programs (to be discussed in Chapter 7) sponsored by management are common in industry. Competition makes such policies prerequisite to success in manufacturing.

The improvement of manufacturing plans cannot go on indefinitely to the exclusion of the production of the product. Production schedules must be met. Plant facilities may also limit the extent of the improvements that can be made within the current manufacturing plan. All of these problems are best solved by the cooperative efforts of all functions involved. Any solution, however, should be accepted as only one bench mark in the continuing improvement of the manufacturing process.

Many intangibles must be considered from time to time. Among these are the cost of larger inventories caused by the leveling of production to prevent labor turnover, the more common problems of overhead distribution, and the value of the customers' goodwill that may be lost through late deliveries or a poor quality product. These and many other intangible values enter into the total evaluation of the manufacturing process design.

QUESTIONS

1. The Welch Manufacturing Company is a new firm being started to manufacture power lawn mowers. What information would be needed to make a decision as to whether or not it should be planned for continuous or intermittent manufacture?

2. Why does a higher quality level of product usually result in higher manufacturing costs?

3. Select some common object—a cigarette lighter, a pencil sharpener, a pair of pliers—and sketch a new design that you feel would, cost less to manufacture.

4. What are the long-run implications of CAD/CAM on the employment of machine operators? On increases in productivity?

5. Discuss the necessity of close cooperation between the product engineer and the process engineer.

6. What is the function of the standard process sheet?

7. Describe any limitations you see in the group technology approach to machine arrangement.

8. Explain the meaning and application of "balancing out the line."
9. What is the best measure of success of the work of the process engineer?
10. Discuss the ways in which computers might be used to facilitate the process engineer's duties.

CASE PROBLEM

The Howard Company

The Howard Company is a relatively small firm that makes gears and gear assemblies such as speed reducers and tractor transmissions. The firm was started 30 years ago by the present owner, John Howard. Mr. Howard has seen his firm grow slowly from a small five-machine workshop to its present size of 35 employees and 27 machine tools. The manufacturing facilities are quite traditional and are arranged in a job-shop type configuration. The firm's customers are all within a 150-mile radius of the plant and continue to give Howard business because of its high quality and dependable delivery dates. Most orders are for small quantities; twenty-five of a specific product or component would be a large order.

Two of Howard's customers have expanded their production of certain product lines extensively, and as a result Howard has been given the opportunity for long-term contracts for large quantities of a certain type of speed reducer and a specific transmission for a small garden tractor. Mr. Howard knows that his present shop processes and arrangement are inadequate for the expanded business. Mr. Howard and his supervisors are very enthusiastic about the potential new business and wish to do whatever is necessary to make their manufacturing processes equal to the new demands that will be placed on them. However, Howard management does not want the changes that will result from these two products to completely change the character of their manufacturing environment and possibly jeopardize their relationships with other customers.

Questions:

1. In general, how should Howard integrate the new orders with the old business?
2. Is this situation an opportunity for group technology concepts?
3. Would computer-aided manufacturing (CAM) be appropriate here?
4. Do you think situations like this happen often in industry?
5. Would you use continuous or intermittent manufacturing for the new products? Why? If continuous, how would you integrate this with the intermittent character of the other work?

6

INDUSTRIAL EQUIPMENT

As was pointed out in the preceding chapter, there are a number of situations that prompt a company to consider the purchase or lease of new equipment or machines. This invariably leads to the same kind of questions that many people face in buying a new car—what kind should they get? how much can they afford to spend for it? how much will it cost to operate? what kind of service can they get on it? how long will it last? Further, we know that the function for which it is going to be used will influence their decision—Volkswagens aren't designed to pull heavy trailers. In this chapter, we wish to discuss some of the many factors that have a bearing on the selection of suitable machines and equipment.

Processing Equipment

Processing equipment includes all of the machine tools, auxiliary tooling and equipment, and other manufacturing items that are directly employed in the working, treatment, inspection, or packaging of the workpiece or product. Such items of equipment as turret lathes, sewing machines, inspection devices, chemical tanks, meatcutters, sand molders, and polishing tools fall into this classification.

Basic Manufacturing Processes

There are hundreds of types of processing equipment in use in today's manufacturing plants. Some means of classifying such equipment is needed to clarify the relationship between machines and the particular process or processes for which they are best suited. One common method of such classification is in terms of the type of work performed on the workpiece while in (or on) the unit of processing equipment. Broaching, turning, coining, drawing, milling, forging, welding, sewing, shearing, mixing, stamping, and mortising are examples of basic manufacturing operations. It should be noted that there may be one or many different machines that can perform any particular basic process. For instance, gear shaping is somewhat limited to a specific type of equipment; drilling, however, can be done on drilling, boring, and tapping machines, as well as on any of the machines in the lathe family.

The basic manufacturing process can be subdivided, in many cases, into more detailed elements of work, and these are sometimes known as *work units,* or steps in the manufacturing process. The work unit is simply the smallest subdivision of processing and is usually accomplished without intentional interruption. For the basic process of drilling, for instance, the work unit would specify the specific diameter and depth of the hole to be formed. Work-unit names such as coredrill, centerdrill, tapdrill, and drill are applied for specific types of work on the workpiece. It should be noted that one or more work units make up an *operation,* which has been defined as all of the work that is performed on a part at essentially one location, or in one unit of processing equipment.

Some of the basic processes are associated with specific types of workpiece material; for instance, mortising is primarily a woodworking process. Likewise, the associated equipment may be classified by type of material, such as metal working, woodworking, plasticworking, and so on. Thus, processing equipment can be classified to some extent by the particular industries in which it is used.

Types of Processing Equipment

Processing equipment may also be classified by the construction and mounting of the unit: fixed power tools and equipment, portable power tools and equipment, portable hand tools and equipment, and auxiliary tools and equipment. *Fixed power tools and equipment* include all of the machines and other power-operated processing units that are floor- or bench-mounted or supported, such as drill presses or wood shapers. *Portable power tools and equipment* are those that can be picked up in the hand or hands for use, such as electric hand drills. *Portable hand tools* include the many types of wrenches, screwdrivers, chisels, measuring rules, and so forth, which are used in the hands and are not power-operated. *Auxiliary tools and equipment* are the cutting tool bits, cutters, press dies, jigs, fixtures, gages and so forth, which are needed by industry to adapt the basic manufacturing equipment to specific products and processes. Such items as benches, tables, desks, and chairs are usually classified as plant equipment, along with service facilities, dust collectors, lockers, and others.

Processing equipment may also be classified as general purpose or special. *General-purpose equipment* is designed for maximum flexibility, so that many different products and processes can be performed on each unit. The common engine lathe, shaper, wood lathe, and drill press are examples of such equipment; skilled operators are required to set up and use such equipment in order to produce the specific products desired. These machines are adapted to various products and processes by the attachment of auxiliary tooling and equipment, and by the application of operator skills. They are used extensively in intermittent manufacture, where a unit of production equipment may be employed on several different products or operations within a short time. General-purpose equipment is often arranged in the plant in groups or departments of identical or similar machines. The distinct advantage of general-purpose equipment is its adaptability to many products and basic processes.

Special-purpose equipment, on the other hand, is designed and used to produce one or a few specific products, and it does not have the flexibility of the general-purpose unit. Automatic controls are commonly built into these machines to minimize the need for skilled operators and to eliminate as far as is practical the possibilities for human error. Higher production rates and lower unit manufacturing costs are the chief advantages claimed for such equipment. Special-purpose equipment is often arranged in the plant into product lines, permitting direct flow of the product from machine to machine in a nearly straight line and offering much more opportunity for conveyorization of materials. This equipment is commonly designed with integral automatic handling devices and automatic or semi-automatic controls. The various equipment types will be discussed in more detail in the following section.

Trends in Machine Design

Because of industrial competition (particularly foreign competition), unit manufacturing cost (the cost to manufacture one complete unit of product) has become increasingly important as a measure of operating success. Consequently, many manufacturers are finding it desirable to concentrate their production facilities on one or a few products that they can make and sell in large quantities, thus permitting the installation of high-production, low-unit-cost manufacturing lines. This type of specialization is a strong incentive for manufacturers to obtain processing equipment that can produce specific products rapidly and accurately. Technological developments in cutting-tool materials, machine construction, and automatic handling and control devices have stepped up the movement toward more specialized equipment. Carbide and ceramic-oxide cutting tools, combined with automatic, high-horsepower machines, can work materials at rates considered to be out of all reason only a few years ago.

The majority of machine tools are built by the many manufacturers who specialize in this field. Often, however, companies that require special equipment either make it themselves or contract it out to small job shops. As an example, the General Electric Company has designed, developed, and built the first models of many of the machines used in the lamp industry.

Transfer machines have been developed to move the part, sometimes mounted in a holding fixture, from station to station. Transfer machines lend themselves particularly to drilling, boring, reaming, tapping, end milling, and similar processes. These machines are sequence controlled through the use of limit switches, cams, and control devices (e.g., programmable controllers and minicomputers). All of the processing work and the movement of the product from the feed end of the machine to the discharge end is done automatically. Transfer machines have been used most commonly on castings and large forgings. Their primary advantage is in mechanizing the production process, eliminating the necessity for heavy manual work, and expediting the manufacture of the product. An 11-station Le Maire Transfer Machine for processing diesel engine cylinder blocks is illustrated in Figure 6-1.

Figure 6-1. A transfer machine composed of four individual machines, each with a numerical control system, arranged to operate separately or linked together to function as a complete unit. (Courtesy Navistar.)

Figure 6-2. Rotary transfer machine that will drill, tap, mill, trepan, rough bore, finish bore, and counterbore a family of 29 different parts. It should be noted that the guards were removed for photographing. (Courtesy Kingsbury Machine Tool Corporation.)

Another type of machine that incorporates material handling is the rotary indexing machine. This machine is built around a cylindrical base casting topped by a rotary indexing table to which fixtures are attached for holding and positioning the parts. The processing tools are mounted over the rotary table at the index positions. Each part receives a progressive series of operations as it indexes from station to station through one complete (or partial) revolution of the table. Illustrated in Figure 6-2 is a Kingsbury machine capable of turning out a large number of parts per hour.

One of the highly significant developments that is beginning to change the industrial scene is the increasing use of robots.[1] Robots have been used in plants since the early 60's, but the first models were huge machines designed for heavy, hazardous jobs. The new breed of robots is smaller and more mobile, and can perform more functions because of the advances in microcomputers. A typical model can be fitted with a variety of artificial hands, e.g., a mechanical gripper that enables it to move parts from one location to another, a spray head that converts it into a painter, or an arc that turns it into a welder (see Figure 6-3). In one of the automotive companies, auto bodies are indexed through a series of robots performing hundreds of spot welds. Various body styles are identified by a central control system which selects the correct welding sequence from each robot's memory. As robot evolution continues, the robots are increasingly being used for a wide variety of jobs formerly performed by workers, e.g., assembly operations, inspection of parts, and planing, shaping, and finishing wood. One of the great advantages gained from the

---

[1] See "Robots Join the Labor Force," *Business Week,* No. 2640, June 9, 1980, pp. 62–76.

Figure 6-3. An industrial robot shown spot welding moving automobile bodies. (Courtesy Cincinnati Milacron.)

use of robots is that the machines can be programmed to repeat a variety of functions accurately, without any risk of human accidents, and at considerably less cost per hour than a human operator. As the development of sensory robots continues, it is evident that robots will be one of the keys to the development of the automatic factory. For example, robots available in the mid-1980's can be equipped with artificial intelligence software in their computer controllers and made to interact with the work environment through computer-controlled vision systems.

Another far-reaching trend that has been taking place in industry is the use of numerically controlled machines (see Figures 6-4, 6-5, 6-6, 6-7, and 6-8). Numerical control (NC) has been defined by Groover[2] as "a form of programmable automation in which the process is controlled by numbers, letters, and symbols." NC equipment is being widely used throughout industry today, and it has been estimated that by the turn of the century at least 75% of all parts that are not mass produced will be made on numerical control equipment. The technological breakthroughs in the development of microprocessor chips have had tremendous impact on the increasing use of NC equipment. For example, as recently as 1971 the

---

[2]*Automation, Production Systems, and Computer Aided Manufacturing*, p. 64.

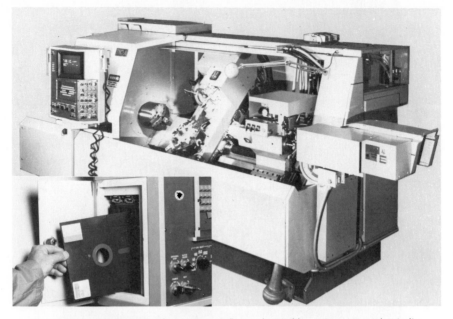

Figure 6-4. Slant bed lathe that uses new "floppy discs" (like a 45-rpm record as indicated in the insert) to store programs. A program editor is built right into the machine, so that it is capable of on-line editing and entering programs directly into the machine. (Courtesy Jones and Lamson, Waterbury Farrel Division of Textron, Inc.)

various elements that together compose the central processing unit of a digital computer were first made available in the form of a single integrated circuit chip, which has become known as a *microprocessor*.[3] Within a digital computer the central processing unit (which constitutes the heart of the computer) usually consists of an arithmetic/logic unit, an accumulator, an instruction register, instruction decoding logic, a program counter, general-purpose registers, and control and timing logic. As you can see, the central processing unit is capable of performing a variety of highly complex activities. The incorporation of all of these functions into a single silicon chip (that would easily fit on a fingernail) has made the development of microcomputers a reality. Further, it has made possible small, relatively inexpensive controls on machines. Thus, all but the simplest new NC machines are being equipped with computer-numerical control (CNC) utilizing microcomputers based on microprocessors. One of the latest developments in numerical control is the computerized manufacturing system in which a group of NC machines, inspection ma-

---

[3]See Joseph M. McKenzie, "Microcomputer Fundamentals," *The Western Electric Engineer*, Vol. XXI, No. 3, July 1977, p. 3.

Figure 6-5. A six-spindle tape-controlled drill press capable of performing the functions of drilling, boring, tapping, reaming, counterboring, and spot facing. (Courtesy Collins Radio Company.)

chines, and automatic material handling devices are used to link a series of operations under the control of a computer. Facilities such as this are referred to as *Flexible Manufacturing Systems* (FMS).

One of the essential features of NC machines is that information can be stored in a "memory" system in a coded form such that the information can be withdrawn in the sequence needed. The information stored includes operations to be performed on the workpiece while it is in the machine. Once the program has been made, the machine will operate to make parts according to the program for as long as desired. Thus, a high degree of mechanization can be obtained with what is essentially a general-purpose machine, since any number of different programs for different parts can be fed to the machine.

There is some indication that processing equipment of the future may be designed to make better use of the vertical space in a plant as a means of saving on floor space, for equipment is tending to become larger. Transfer machines may one day move the product up and down as well as back and forth. Volume utilization of space may replace present-day linear utilization considerations.

Figure 6-6. A numerically controlled machine that provides for random selection of tools from the tool storage magazine. (Courtesy Kearney & Trecker Corporation.)

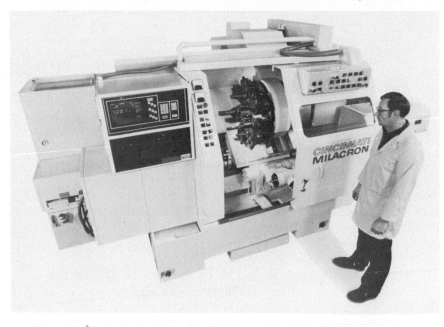

Figure 6-7. A turning center (shown with guard open) capable of holding 14 tools and containing a computer numerical control panel. (Courtesy Cincinnati Milacron.)

Figure 6-8. CNC control with solid-state mass storage that can be used on various numerical control machines. (Courtesy Controls and Data Systems Division, White-Sundstrand Machine Tool Company.)

Mechanization and Automation

For centuries people have been seeking to replace or reduce manual work with tools and other devices that either provide leverage for human effort or supplement human power with another power source. Automation is the continued effort to mechanize work, by replacing manual activity with machine activity. It is difficult to distinguish between mechanization and automation, since the two terms are used interchangeably throughout industry. However, automation would seem to encompass more than is generally accepted as a definition for mechanization. This distinguishing feature is the inclusion of feedback control in automation, which makes it possible for machines to operate entirely automatically and to correct or adjust for variations from preset conditions or criteria. The use of automation necessitates serious consideration of its far-reaching effects upon the economic and social relationships in the world, since the ultimate aim would appear to be the complete freeing of many from physical work in industry. Obviously, however, automation increases considerably the need for skilled setup men and operators and for maintenance and planning personnel.

One of the first examples of automation was a flour-processing mill constructed by Oliver Evans in Philadelphia in 1784. In this mill, grain was handled entirely by powered conveyors from the receiving bin through to the finished sacks of flour. Another early example was an automatic loom, operated from punched paper cards, which was developed by Joseph Jacquard in Paris in 1801. Of the larger American companies, the A. O. Smith Corporation and the General Electric Company mechanized some of their operations at an early date. The word *automation* dates back to about 1947, when the Ford Motor Company set up a section in one of its plants to design automatic handling equipment for its operations. Since that time, the term has spread widely to represent many different things.

The unit-operations industries, such as refineries and chemical processing plants, have seen much more development of mechanized handling and automatic control than have the industries that manufacture discrete product units, which often require individualized handling from operation to operation. In the past few years, however, there has been accelerated development and use of automatic handling and control equipment in these latter industries. As an illustration of this advancing technology, the Kitchens of Sara Lee has an automated bakery in which a digital computer directs the entire maufacturing operation—from the receiving dock to the shipping platform. The computer will perform such multitudinous operations as monitoring the bulk storage status and use of liquid and dry ingredients; monitoring batch blending and mixing operations; computing and monitoring oven zone temperatures and speeds of oven conveyors; monitoring product change-overs automatically on many different selections of cakes; directing the random storage of palletized products in a holding freezer; directing order picking, and assembling loads of mixed products onto pallets.

Automatic production involves essentially four elements:

1.   Automatic handling of the product between processing units.   This is accomplished primarily by conveyorization; by the use of power-operated materials handling equipment that provides continuous or intermittent movement of the product or materials on belts, chains, and slats; or by oscillation or pneumatic pressure. With the increasing use of industrial robots, these machines will gain widespread use in moving workparts from one location to another. They will be particularly popular where workparts are heavy or very hot, or where hazardous conditions exist.

2.   Automatic infeeding of processing units.   There are many different types of automatic infeeding equipment; however, most of the currently available equipment can be classified into six categories: (1) bar feed mechanisms, (2) mechanical transfer arms, (3) hopper feeders, (4) magazine feeds, (5) dial feeds and indexing tables, and (6) roll grip feeds. All of these devices serve to transfer materials from storage racks, hoppers, stock reels, or directly from conveyors into the processing position in the machine. In some cases, a progression of two or more such mechanisms may be employed. The selection of an infeed unit depends upon the particular machine to be fed, the physical characteristics of the part to be handled, and the production rate desired. Feeding equipment may be built in by the machine tool builder, or it may be added separately by the user.

As indicated in the preceding section, industrial robots are achieving increasing popularity as machine loading and unloading devices. They are particularly useful in loading and unloading machines such as stamping presses, injection molding machines, and metal cutting machines.

3. Automatic control of processing units during the cycle of operation. Automatic control equipment also comes in many varieties, ranging from the simple cam or tracer attachment to complex computer and electronic systems. An *automatic controller* has been defined by the American Society of Mechanical Engineers as

> A mechanism which measures the value of a variable quantity or condition and operates to correct or limit deviation of this measured variable from a selected reference. It includes both the measuring and the controlling means.

This definition applies to feedback or closed-loop control providing automatic corrective action for physical changes in the process value or condition under control. However, automatic control is considered by many to include *sequence control,* or the timing of occurrences in an operating cycle through the use of cams, counters, gears, and so forth. Automatic screw machines and transfer machines, for instance, are time- or sequence-controlled—there is no feedback or corrective action involved. Closed-loop or feedback[4] control circuits, which have been used for many years in the unit-operations industries, have only recently begun to be applied to discrete-item equipment. This is often referred to as *adaptive control,* and it can be applied to the operation of cutting tools on NC machines.

4. Automatic discharge of the product from the processing unit. Removal of the product from a processing unit may be accomplished by conveyor, chute, transfer arm, pneumatic ejectors, or similar devices. This element is usually the least difficult to provide.

Automation of processing equipment offers great promise for the elevation of human work in industry to a level requiring the further development and application of the human mind, while machines perform the physical work.

---

[4]Feedback control is used today on time-sequencing operations for varying conveyor or indexing speeds, numerically controlling machines, and automatic weighing, counting, packaging, inspecting, and so forth.

Portable Tools

Portable tools must not be neglected in any consideration of the processing equipment used in industry. These tools, which include both power-operated and non-power equipment, are usually supported in the hand or hands while in use. Such tools as screwdrivers, wrenches, and so on are non-power portable tools; those that have electric or pneumatic motors are power-operated. Electric power tools may be used anywhere in the plant where there is a suitable outlet. But many industrial plants use pneumatic tools because they do not require as much maintenance, have a longer life, and are not as subject to petty theft.

Auxiliary Tools and Equipment

Machine tools, presses, and certain other types of processing equipment must be adapted with auxiliary tooling before they can be used. Auxiliary tooling includes the cutting tools, press dies, jigs and fixtures, gages, and other auxiliary devices that are used on or with the basic processing units.

Cutting tools do the actual work in modifying the workpiece or product. They are mounted onto the machine tool either on an arbor or in a tool holder. During the cutting process, heat is created by the action of the chip rubbing on the face of the tool, and this heat tends to destroy or break down the cutting edge. The suitability of a tool for cutting a particular material, therefore, depends upon the ability of the tool material to retain its hardness at elevated temperatures, as well as on the ratio of the hardness of the tool material to the hardness of the partpiece material.

There are five primary cutting tool materials in use today: carbon steel, high-speed steel, cast alloys, cemented carbides, and ceramic oxides. Diamonds, carborundum, aluminum oxide, and other abrasive materials are also used in grinding wheels and other special cutting tools.

Press dies make up another classification of auxiliary tooling. The more common types of dies are (1) cutting dies, (2) forming dies, (3) drawing dies, (4) extrusion dies, and (5) forging dies. Dies are used to adapt power presses to perform specific work units.

Jigs and fixtures are the auxiliary tools used to support and locate the workpiece on units of processing equipment. There is a technical distinction between a *jig* and a *fixture,* even though the two terms are often used interchangeably. A fixture is simply a holding device, and the workpiece is positioned to the tools by controls on the machine (see Figure 6-9). A jig, however, not only holds the workpiece but also guides the tools to it. Fixtures are used in milling, planing, shaping, assembly, and similar operations. Jigs are employed in drilling, boring, reaming, and certain welding operations.

Gages and other types of inspection equipment make up another classification of tooling. Gages are of two different types: *measurement gages,* which provide a specific reading or value for any measurable characteristic of the workpiece, and

Figure 6-9. Fixture used on the numerically controlled machine illustrated in Figure 6-6. (Courtesy Kearney & Trecker Corporation.)

attribute gages, which only indicate whether a measurable characteristic is within or beyond set limits. A comparator is an example of a measurement gage; a plug gage is an example of the attribute type. Figure 6-10 illustrates these two types of gages.

In the chemical and food-processing industries, as well as others, such items as mixers, molding forms, patterns, and attachments are examples of auxiliary equipment. Certainly sewing-machine attachments in the textile industry fall into this general category.

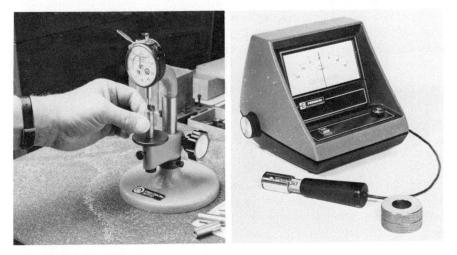

Figure 6-10. Dial measurement gage (Courtesy Precision Brand) and dimentron plug gage featuring interchangeable plug gages and meter scales. (Courtesy Federal Products Company.)

Economics is an important factor in all tool-selection considerations. The higher cost of more durable materials, closer tolerances, finer workmanship, and more rugged construction must always be weighed against the benefit to be gained. In many cases the expected usage for a tool in terms of the number of applications expected for it will be a determining factor in tool selection. Other factors include the workpiece material, weight, shape, and size. In many cases, the use of commercially available standard tools or tool components will be more economically justifiable than the design and building of special auxiliary tooling and equipment.

Tool control. Because so many auxiliary tools are used in an industrial plant, a control system of some type is essential to avoid excessive duplication and loss or misplacement. In such a system of control, each tool is classified according to type and uses and is assigned a tool inventory number. These tools are kept in one or more cribs until needed on the production floor. Tool control promotes standardization of tools and assures that the tools will be kept in good condition and ready for use when needed. Computer database management systems are often used for this purpose.

Computer integrated manufacturing systems. An extension of the FMS concept is a computer integrated manufacturing system (CIMS). In a system such as this, the computer control equipment will be placed in a hierarchical configuration with one host computer acting as the master planner which communicates with the other control computers or programmable controllers. These digital devices are physically separated and communicate through a network of communication channels. This is often referred to as a *local area network* (LAN).

The programmable controller that might be used in a CIMS is a type of computer that expands the flexibility potential of manufacturing systems. It was initially developed as a replacement for hard-wired control relays. The PC (sometimes referred to as PLC, for programmable logic controller) can have its control duties rapidly changed merely by changing its program (see Figure 6-11).

Determination of Equipment Requirements

There are many facets to the problem of selecting the best possible equipment for any particular manufacturing enterprise. It has already been indicated that the basic manufacturing processes at least limit the choice of equipment for making a particular product. In many manufacturing plants the process engineer is responsible for indicating the type of equipment to be used for each operation as she develops the routing or sequence of operations for a product. Therefore, she should conscientiously familiarize herself with improvements in equipment and with new processes. She may specify either a specific machine, or (preferably) only a general type of machine—the latter so that there may be some flexibility in scheduling and routing

Figure 6-11. Programmable controller. (Courtesy Material Flow Control Laboratory, Purdue University.)

the product to specific machines in the plant. Such flexibility is also desirable for plant-layout and materials-handling considerations.

Human factors in machine selection.   An important consideration in the selection of a new unit of equipment for a plant should be the type and degree of operator skill required in relation to the skills presently available within the organization. The ease with which the equipment can be operated and the safety features provided are equally important selection factors. So far as possible, machines should be fitted to the plant labor force. As a step in this direction, those companies using participative management take advantage of operators' recommendations in selecting new equipment. There is real payoff in such a practice.

Standardization of equipment.   It is also economically desirable to standardize on processing equipment, provided that such standardization does not take from an operation the equipment best suited to meet quantity and quality requirements. Standardization reduces the cost of maintenance; a smaller number of repair parts need to be stocked, and the maintenance crews grow more familiar with the equipment. Standardization may also permit better utilization of equipment, since various product schedules can be superimposed on the available standardized machines. Where specialized equipment is economically desirable, some attempt should be made to standardize at least on service parts within the company.

Equipment purchase vs. rental. For the plant that has been making products and has equipment available, it is logical to use this equipment to the fullest extent before leasing or buying new equipment, as long as a new or different machine is not significantly better. When it is desired to add equipment in the plant, there are three possibilities: (1) the equipment can be purchased new or used, (2) the equipment can be leased or rented, and (3) the equipment can be fabricated within the plant. Companies can lease almost any kind of equipment through the machine tool builders or through machinery-rental concerns. Leasing is becoming an increasingly important means of procuring equipment. It follows, then, that thorough economic analyses should be conducted for the plant for which additional equipment is being considered before deciding whether to lease or buy.

Determination of the Number of Machines Required

The number of pieces of each type of equipment needed to produce a part is contingent upon the quantity of parts to be made within any given time period, the number of working hours in the plant within this same time period, and the various production rates on the operations to be performed, as well as the setup time for each operation, the number of setups per machine for the time period, the operating efficiency of the plant (i.e., the per cent of effective utilization of equipment), and finally, the scrap loss at each operation. All of these factors must be either known or estimated before a reasonably accurate determination of machine requirements can be made. Since scrap loss is cumulative, it is usually necessary to calculate equipment requirements starting at the last operation to be performed on the product and working backward toward the first operations. To find the requirements for any particular piece of equipment in a process, the total number of hours per month (or other time period) that the equipment is required to produce the desired quantity is divided by the total number of hours per month that the equipment is available, taking plant efficiency into account. Then the total requirements for all operations to be performed on each unit of equipment are considered in terms of the number of setups involved and the time required per setup. In a product-line layout of equipment, where each machine is set up to perform only one operation, the setup time can be neglected, but the problem of line balancing becomes important. For the process-type layout, where machines are commonly used on several different parts and/or operations, setup and scheduling time losses must be carefully considered; however, balancing is not a serious problem.

In balancing the capacities of various machines in a product-line layout, it may be desirable to buy more than enough machines when the equipment is not too expensive, if this will avoid possible shutdown or restriction of the entire manufacturing line. However, when such equipment is quite expensive, it may be necessary to provide only the minimum number of machines and rely upon overtime or extra shifts to meet production requirements when breakdowns occur.

Machine capacities can thus be stretched by increasing the available hours per month, by decreasing the required hours through an increase in operating efficiencies, or by decreasing scrap losses and setup times.

Much of this analysis requires only simple mathematics; however, for manufacturing environments in which there are many parts and different machine tool types to consider, the volume of calculations can be extensive. For this reason it is not uncommon for industrial engineers to use electronic spreadsheet software on microcomputers to perform the analysis. Whitehouse[5] describes some applicable methods.

Equipment Investment

The purchasing of equipment involves capital expenditures, so there are several important economic elements to be considered in deciding what equipment to buy and when to buy it. New equipment is purchased either to meet specific requirements of a process or to improve upon a process as performed on an existing or available unit of equipment. Greater productivity, reduced unit-manufacturing costs, and higher quality are the primary objectives in equipment replacement.

Equipment replacement policies.   In recent years manufacturing management has given serious consideration to policies for replacement of equipment. There are some who feel that any piece of equipment that is over ten years old is obsolete and should be replaced. To some extent this is certainly true, since many types of industrial equipment are being continually improved upon year after year. The move toward higher-horsepower machines to use the capabilities of the newer cutting-tool materiais is a clear indication of the need for replacing equipment that is not operating as productively as possible. The developments in numerically controlled equipment, in equipment that will hold tighter tolerances, and in equipment that is better designed from a methods standpoint, are all good reasons for replacing old equipment. The question, of course, is *when* should the replacement be made and *what* is the best replacement unit.

A well-designed equipment replacement policy must consider all of the comparisons between an existing unit of equipment and its possible replacement or replacements. In order to make a sound economic comparison, all of the factors must be converted into cost considerations. One method for evaluating replacement alter-

---

[5]"Electronic Spreadsheets Evaluated for IE Applications," *Industrial Engineering*, Vol. 17, No. 2 (1985), pp. 17–28.

natives was developed for the Machinery and Allied Products Institute by George Terborgh and is known simply as the MAPI formula.[6] In this method the terms *defender* and *challenger* are used to represent, respectively, the presently owned or available equipment and the proposed equipment.

In some cases, there may be two or more challengers to one defender for purposes of selecting the best replacement equipment if replacement is indicated. The MAPI method is a special type of cost analysis in which the defender and the challenger or challengers are compared for a period of *one year* after the assumed replacement of the defender by the challenger. The *operating inferiority* of the defender is compared to the *additional costs* of the challenger. From this comparison, the next year's gain from replacement can be determined, and an estimate can be made of the investment recovery period. While the specific formulas and evaluation forms suggested in the original MAPI document are no longer completely valid in today's industrial environment, the concepts proposed by Terborgh are still valid.

One of the limitations of many replacement policies is that only the particular units of equipment involved are considered, whereas on a plant-wide cost basis the effect of replacement upon other operating costs may be highly significant. However, new methods are being applied to replacement studies. Both direct and indirect costs should be considered in any replacement study, since one may be affected by the other. Overhead costs are increasing quite rapidly in many of today's mechanized factories; therefore, machine utilization, materials handling, quality, and other factors are important considerations. As industry continues toward more highly mechanized and automated plants, the selection and evaluation of new and replacement equipment will be an increasingly important function of industrial management.

Machine selection decisions.   Anytime a company decides to purchase a new machine or piece of equipment, a decision must be made as to what to do with the displaced equipment (e.g., sell, trade in, keep for standby) and which make and model to buy. Many factors will influence this decision, including such items as the initial cost, trade-in allowance, operating expenses, service policy, delivery dates, and reputation of the manufacturer. Assuming that everything else is equal, the problem tends to become essentially one of economic selection and picking the machine that minimizes cost or maximizes profit. There is a slight controversy among engineering economists over which of the two criteria (cost minimization or profit maximization) is the superior analysis criterion. For some situations they will provide different answers; the analyst should understand the nature of the data he or she is using.

In endeavoring to make a decision among alternative machines, a problem arises in trying to decide what costs should be included and how they should be

---

[6]The *MAPI Replacement Manual* can be obtained from the Machinery and Allied Products Institute in Washington, D.C.

determined. These costs will usually include the initial cost of the machine and the costs of operating the machine, as, for example, direct and indirect labor, direct and indirect materials, power, maintenance, replacement parts, insurance, and interest on invested capital. The service life and expected salvage value at the end of the service life must also be predicted. With this information available, two alternative machines may be compared as illustrated in the following example:

	Machine A	Machine B
Initial cost	$10,000	$15,000
Annual operating cost	2,000	1,500
Expected years of life	10	10
Salvage value	1,000	2,000
Total cost for 10 years	$29,000	$28,000

On the basis of this total cost comparison, Machine B would be favored.

One of the deficiencies of the foregoing analysis is the failure to take into consideration interest and the time value of money. Interest is an important factor to be taken into account in investment decisions and should be given consideration as a part of the total economic analysis. Thus, the different initial investments in and operating costs of the two machines illustrated in the previous example will influence the interest costs associated with each of them.

Several mathematically based procedures which can be considered to fall under the category of engineering economics are available for machine replacement studies in which the time value of money is to be analyzed.

Depreciation and obsolescence.   The concepts of *depreciation* and *obsolescence* must be examined in order to evaluate various replacement policies that have been developed.

The term depreciation has several different meanings that depend upon the point of reference. Depreciation may be thought of as a piece of equipment's loss in value over a period of time. This common concept is used in everyday speech—"my car depreciated $2000 the first year." Another concept of depreciation, one that we shall refer to in the sections that follow, is the accounting concept. The accounting concept is based on the view that over the years the useful life of a piece of equipment wastes away. Since the piece of equipment's useful life has been exhausted in the service of the business, it follows that the cost of the equipment is a business expense for the life of that asset. Thus depreciation accounting aims to distribute the cost of an asset, less salvage value, over the estimated useful life of the asset. It is a systematic and rational method of *allocating* a yearly charge for the loss in value of the asset. On the other hand, depreciation accounting may not follow the market value change in an asset.

Another aim in depreciation accounting is to have some measure of the monetary value of each of the assets in a business. Thus, the accountant makes use of the common term *book value* to refer to the difference between the cost of an asset and the total of the depreciation charges made to date against the asset.

According to the Internal Revenue Service, "Any reasonable method that is consistently applied may be used in computing depreciation."[7] Prior to the Economic Recovery Tax Act (ERTA) of 1981, the three methods most generally used were (1) the straight line method, (2) the declining balance method, and (3) the sum-of-the-years'-digits method. The depreciation concept can be explained best by an example.

The *straight line method* is the simplest method for computing depreciation. Under this method, the cost of the equipment less its salvage value is generally deducted in equal annual amounts over its period of estimated useful life. The method of calculating this amount may be illustrated by the following example. For an engine lathe that cost $6000 and is estimated to have a service life of 5 years and a salvage value after 5 years of $1000, the annual depreciaton would be

$$D = \frac{\$6000 - \$1000}{5} = \$1000$$

The annual depreciation and book value under the straight line method are illustrated in the following table.

	The Straight Line Method	
End of Year	*Depreciation Charge During Year*	*Book Value at End of Year*
0	—	$6,000
1	$1,000	5,000
2	1,000	4,000
3	1,000	3,000
4	1,000	2,000
5	1,000	1,000

Other depreciation methods, such as declining balance or sum of the years' digits, will have non-linear yearly allocation rates. Some of the mathematical formulations of these methods can be complex. Most of the methods are thoroughly examined in engineering economy texts.

The Economic Recovery Act of 1981 set up a new, standardized depreciation methodology that is easier to use than older methods. Known as the *Accelerated Cost Recovery System* (ACRS) method of depreciation, it classifies property as belonging to one of four established classes (see Table 6-1). Each class specifies the

---

[7]See "Tax Information on Depreciation," U.S. Treasury Department, Internal Revenue Service Publication 534, pp. 10–72.

Table 6-1.   Class of Depreciable Property under ACRS

Yearly Property Class	Examples
Three-Year	Automobiles and light-duty trucks
	Machinery and equipment used in connection with research and experiments
Five-Year	Heavy-duty trucks
	Office equipment
	Machinery and equipment
Ten-Year	Public utility property
Fifteen-Year	Includes public utility property except 3-year property or 15- or 18-year real property that has mid-point class life of more than 25 years

number of years the equipment is to be depreciated. Table 6-2 shows the specific yearly rates of depreciation for various classes of property. Whichever depreciation method is used, the amount of depreciation written off each year affects the cost of doing business because it affects profits, which in turn affect taxes. The ACRS method is easiest to use and is preferred by the IRS, which allows the use of other methods as well.

A company wishing to show good earnings records will undoubtedly depreciate its equipment as little as possible. On the other hand, if a company wishes to avoid high income taxes, it will try to depreciate its equipment as much as possible. The Internal Revenue Service's regulations provide some encouragement for this procedure because an organization may utilize some specific rules which, under cer-

Table 6-2.   Depreciation Schedule under ACRS

Recovery Year	Property Class			
	Three-Year	Five-Year	Ten-Year	Fifteen-Year
1	33%	20%	10%	7%
2	45	32	18	12
3	22	24	16	12
4		16	14	11
5		8	12	10
6			10	9
7			8	8
8			6	7
9			4	6
10			2	5
11				4
12				3
13				3
14				2
15				1

tain circumstances, will allow extra deductions for some years of the life of the asset. Since the tax code is subject to periodic change, it is important for manufacturing management to be aware of the current law.

Depreciation rates and depreciation policies cannot be determined in a completely arbitrary manner. Since depreciation is a cost of doing business, it has an effect on the profits of the business. As profits vary, so does the federal income tax paid by the concern. The result is that the Internal Revenue Service takes considerable interest in a company's depreciation policies just in case there is an attempt to "manipulate" the amount of income tax due. In general, the IRS will go along with any reasonable method of depreciation as long as it is consistently applied and meets legal restrictions.

Let us remind ourselves that this discussion on how fast or how slow equipment is depreciated has nothing to do with the performance or maintenance of the equipment. Instead, this is only a bookkeeping operation. It should also be pointed out that the depreciation process, which on a company's books shows a depreciation reserve account, does not set aside money with which to buy new equipment as the old wears out. It simply charges off the cost of equipment to each year's operation. The company still has to dig up cash somewhere in order to purchase new equipment.

Obsolescence causes loss in value of equipment, but in this case the loss comes about because of the development and introduction of a new and better machine or process. Our first machine may produce at 100 percent efficiency and be in first-class condition, but it may be capable of producing at a rate of only ten pieces an hour. If someone comes out with another machine that is capable of producing at a rate of 130 pieces an hour, then our first machine is rendered obsolete in spite of its first-class mechanical condition. And this may have happened during the second year of its life! The first machine certainly can still be operated, but the cost per piece produced will be so much higher than the cost for those produced from the second machine that the product may be priced out of the market.

QUESTIONS

1. Of concern in equipment selection are *processes, operations,* and *work units.* Briefly define these three terms, telling how they differ.
2. What type of equipment would usually be found in a metal-working job shop? List the types of machines, auxiliary tooling, and other processing equipment you would expect to find in such a shop.
3. What technological developments within recent years have contributed to the development of more special-purpose equipment in industry?
4. You are a member of a planning group in a manufacturing plant making automotive transmission housings. What type or types of mechanized equipment would you propose for this plant?

5. Describe the operation of a typical "programmed" machine tool.

6. What impact may industrial robots be anticipated to have on manufacturing operations in the future? Discuss their impact on the use of personnel.

7. What are *forming dies* used for in press operations?

8. Discuss the long-range effects that microprocessors and other digital devices may have on manufacturing.

9. How does the "human factor" enter into equipment selection?

10. The "hardening" operation in a certain production line is a "bottleneck" operation. If the cost of additional equipment is prohibitive, how can the capacity of the present hardening equipment be "stretched" when necessary?

11. Which of the depreciation classes will manufacturing equipment be in under ACRS, and which year gives the largest deduction?

CASE PROBLEMS

Shay-Moore Company

The Shay-Moore Company plans to manufacture four new products in the following quantities: Product A—5000 per month, Product B—700 per month, Product C—1300 per month, and Product D—25,000 per month. Loren Todd, the process engineer, has been asked to determine the machine requirements for manufacturing these products. General-purpose machines are to be used, arranged in departments of like machines.

Loren finds that all of the products require engine lathe processing. Production standards for the operations to be performed in the engine lathe department are as follows: Product A—8 pcs./hour, Product B—17 pcs./hour, Product C—26 pcs./hour, and Product D—55 pcs./hour. As has been the company's practice, he decides to base machine requirements upon the optimum scheduling of products to the machines, and estimates that an overall efficiency of 80%, including downtime for setups, can be obtained in the engine lathe department. The plant will operate on one 8-hour shift, 5 days per week, and 48 weeks per year— less 6 paid holidays.

Questions:

1. Neglecting scrap loss, what is the minimum number of engine lathes required to produce the specified monthly schedules in the lathe department? (Use estimated efficiency and compute requirements to the nearest tenth of a machine. You may assume that all the engine lathes are interchangeable.)

2. If each product requires a different type of engine lathe, how many machines will be required for each of the four products if an overall efficiency of 90% can be obtained with specific machines assigned to specific products? (Specify the number of whole machines without decimal remainder.)

3. How many engine lathes would be required to produce the schedule for Product A only, if a scrap loss of 5% is taken into account? (Use 94% efficiency.)

4. Under what circumstances would it be desirable to purchase special-purpose machines to fill orders such as these?

The Acme Digital Company

Acme Digital produces programmable controllers for the industrial control market. Acme did not invent the programmable controller; however, shortly after that product obtained industrial acceptance for controlling components in manufacturing systems, they came out with a controller line which achieved customer acceptance from the beginning. Acme currently has several sizes of programmable controllers and related equipment which they market nationally. Since there are a number of large, well-known competitors in this industry, Acme must have very efficient manufacturing processes and procedures in order to achieve customer recognition in this marketplace. Toward this end, Acme has installed computer and numerically controlled manufacturing equipment wherever it can be justified.

Recently, Acme invested large sums of money in automatic insertion machines. This equipment will insert electronic (digital) components into a card which will eventually be placed in the programmable controller. The automatic component insertion equipment is very productive (in comparison with manual insertion); however, Acme has been experiencing some difficulty in achieving anywhere near the productive output from these machines that their manufacturers say is possible. What has happened is that the very fast insertion machines have exposed a less than adequate material supply system. The main cause for unproductive insertion machines is untimely delivery of components to be inserted. Acme is concerned about this and is investigating methods for improving the situation. The decision to purchase the very productive insertion machinery was based on achieving the high production capacity which the machinery vendor promised.

Questions:

1. List all the problems that you can think of which the entire programmable controller manufacturing plant will experience because of the bottleneck insertion machines.
2. Would better material handling equipment aid the situation here? Why? If your answer is yes, what type of material handling equipment is needed?
3. Would there be any gain by having very large inventories of parts just before the insertion machine stations? Discuss the advantages and disadvantages.
4. Is this a case of "islands of automation"? Discuss.

7

METHODS ENGINEERING

The history of American industry has been one of a never-ending search for more efficient manufacturing methods. The highly competitive nature of business forces management to give constant heed to ways in which production per man-hour and productivity in general can be increased. Methods engineering has contributed immeasurably to the search for better methods, and the effective utilization of this management tool has helped in the accomplishment of these objectives.

Methods engineering is that body of knowledge concerned with the analysis of the methods and the equipment used in performing a job, the design of an optimum method, and the standardization of the proposed methods. This field is frequently referred to as "motion study," "methods design," "operation analysis," "work study," or "job design." It is closely affiliated with the function of "work measurement" or "time study," which will be discussed in the next chapter.

Areas of Application

The application of methods engineering may be required in a variety of circumstances. It ranges from the design of a new plant, to the design of a new process, to the improvement of an existing process, to the improvement of an existing workplace. Wherever work is being done, methods engineering is a desirable function to insure that the work is being done in the easiest, safest, and most productive way. Following are examples of methods improvements in a variety of circumstances:

A pneumatic nut driver saves over 70 percent of the time needed to install phenolic fuse holders in electronic chassis made by Altec Lansing Corporation, Whittier, California. Also, it tightens fuse nuts to the right degree of tension and eliminates stripping the fine phenolic threads. The women assemblers find powered nut driving less fatiguing than manual tightening.[1]

A revolving assembly line linked with a new welding technique has sliced production cost more than 50 percent at the General Electric Company, Air Conditioning and Heating Division, Trenton, New Jersey. An added benefit was a 90 percent reduction of down time. Advantages of the new setup are many: it reduces the size of the working area, provides better quality and inventory control, cuts maintenance downtime, creates cleaner and less noisy work stations, increases plant capacity, and cuts the number of production steps from six to four.[2]

Two complete new overhead systems in the firm's electroplating department enable Custom Processing Company, High Point, N.C., to plate more parts with four men on one shift per day than were done previously with seven men on each of two shifts per day. At the heart of the operation are eight compressed-air load-balancing units that let the operator "feel" the load while the devices do all the work of lifting and lowering. With the load-balancing devices, the operators no longer have to manually lift heavy bars from which metal tubular furniture parts are hung, and move them through a series of tanks. Now, operators can more easily handle heavier loads, so the tanks are larger and accommodate more parts per pass.[3]

A Wisconsin furniture maker has turned to hanging its inventory from the roof to put a ceiling on unnecessary labor and storage costs and gain space without expanding his facilities. In turning out nearly 6000 pieces of furniture each week at its plant in Jefferson, Wisconsin, Schweiger Industries has been plagued by the problem of storing furniture frames. The plant floor was cluttered by hundreds of frames in various stages of production, resulting in the loss of valuable working space. The firm decided to get its production off the ground by suspending the frames from a magnetically controlled conveyor system attached to the ceiling. The idea worked so well that the magnetic memory escort system now controls the entire production schedule at the plant, turning the ceiling into a huge furniture vending machine.[4]

[1]"Airpower Tightens Nuts Just Right," *Factory*, Vol. 122, No. 1, January 1964, p. 207.

[2]"Assembly Line Welding Cuts Costs and Downtime," *Factory*, Vol. 122, No. 2, February 1964, p. 168.

[3]"Pneumatic Load Control Units Boost Plating Productivity," *Modern Materials Handling*, Vol. 28, No. 6, June 1973, p. 53.

[4]"Magnet-Controlled Conveyor Hangs Parts from Ceiling," *Modern Materials Handling*, Vol. 28, No. 6, June 1973, p. 51.

By switching to corrugated packaging Monroe Tube Company, Monroe, NY, was able to reduce labor, material, and shipping costs and deliver products in a neater, more attractive package. It is also easier to store and dispose of than the wooden pallet boxes formerly used.[5]

In the Ford Motor Company, there had traditionally been difficulties with seat-cover installations. A line employee worked up a method using Saran Wrap in appropriate places to increase slipperiness and thus make it easier to set covers. He did the entire experiment on his own at home. He then brought the results to work and shared them with his colleagues.[6]

The foregoing examples illustrate the universal need for methods design and the tremendous benefits to be derived from sound applications. Because of the economies that result from continuous methods improvement programs, industry has long considered this one of the best avenues to manufacturing cost reduction and increased productivity.

Origin of Methods Engineering

Methods engineering grew out of the pioneering developments of the Gilbreths (Frank B. and his wife Lillian M.), who developed many of the tools of "motion study" as a part of formulating a systematic approach to the analysis of work methods. Frank B. Gilbreth first became interested in methods analysis as an outgrowth of his observations of bricklaying. Gilbreth, who in 1885 was employed as an apprentice bricklayer, soon observed that a journeyman bricklayer used one set of motions when laying bricks slowly, another set when working at average speed, and still a different set when working at rapid speed. As a result of his observations, he invented an adjustable scaffold and developed a set of motions that greatly increased the number of bricks that could be laid in a day.

Gilbreth eventually became so engrossed in motion study that he discontinued the successful contracting business he had established in order to concentrate his full attention on the development of motion study. His wife, Lillian Gilbreth, who was a psychologist, proved to be a capable partner in the development of the many motion study techniques credited to them. Prior to his death in 1924, the Gilbreths had developed many of the analysis techniques in use today. In their quest for the "one best way" the Gilbreths made use of the process chart, the right- and left-hand operation chart, micromotion study, therbligs, and the chronocylegraph. These will be discussed later in this chapter.

---

[5]"Corrugated Packaging Improves Manufacturer's Bottom Line," *Industrial Engineering,* Vol. 12, No. 4, April 1980, p. 62.

[6]*Fortune,* May 13, 1985, p. 26.

Organization for Methods Engineering

As indicated previously, methods engineering is a necessary function to insure that the most efficient methods are being used. This activity is most frequently performed by industrial engineers. These engineers may be assigned to a central methods engineering or industrial engineering department or may be assigned on a decentralized basis to specific operating departments. Some multi-plant companies maintain both a central industrial engineering group to work on problems common to many plants and also assign industrial engineers to each plant to work on projects pertinent only to that plant.

It is readily apparent that methods design may be either "before the fact" or "after the fact." That is, it may consist of designing a new process or system not previously used in the organization, or it may consist of the improvement of an existing process or workplace. In attempting to determine how much engineering time and effort can be justified on a methods project, the following factors should be taken into account: (1) the volume of production to be scheduled on the job, (2) the anticipated life of the job, (3) the current investment in machines, tools, and equipment, and (4) the personnel considerations (union requirements, retraining time, and so forth).

As specialists in methods design, methods engineers must work with and secure information from many persons. Thus, they come in close contact with product engineers, quality control engineers, maufacturing engineers, production planning engineers, plant engineers, production supervisors, and many others. On major projects, methods engineers frequently serve as chairmen of planning committees composed of such persons as product engineers, manufacturing engineers, quality control engineers, production supervisors, and others.

Approach to Methods Design

Charles E. Geisel states[7] that in order to design a system (method) thoroughly there are eight elements that must be considered, namely:

1. Purpose. The function, mission, aim, or need for the system.
2. Input. The physical items, people, and/or information that enter the system to be processed into the output.
3. Output. That which the system produces to accomplish its purpose, such as finished steel, assembled toasters, boxes, and so forth.
4. Sequence. The steps required to convert, transform, or process the input to the output.

---

[7]In Gavriel Salvendy, Ed., *Handbook of Industrial Engineering;* New York, N.Y.: John Wiley & Sons, 1982, p. 3.1.2.

5. Environment. [The] condition under which the system operates, including physical, attitudinal, organizational, contractual, cultural, political, and legal [environments].

6. Human Agents (Workers). The people who aid in the steps of the sequence without becoming a part of the output.

7. Physical Catalysts (Equipment). The equipment and physical resources that aid in the steps of the sequence without becoming part of the output.

8. Information aids. Knowledge and information resources that aid in the steps of the sequence without becoming part of the output.

Good jobs, the same as good machines, must be designed. An inviolate principle should be to insure that jobs are structured around the needs of the worker as well as the needs of the company. The worker should be capable of doing the job and doing it well. Further, as will be pointed out later, he or she should have an opportunity to contribute to the design.

In order to insure that the optimum method[8] is found, a systematic approach to methods design, far superior to the use of a "hit or miss" method, is used. Stated in its simplest form, this approach consists of the following steps:[9]

1. Analyze the problem. Identify the problem and then secure all known information about it through the use of appropriate analysis techniques.

2. Question the present method. If a method presently exists, question the details of the known information to determine the principles violated.

3. Synthesize a proposed method. Formulate a proposed method for performing the work, embodying all the principles of sound methods engineering.

4. Apply the proposed method. Standardize and apply the new method.

To assist in the first two steps of the procedure outlined above, a number of analysis techniques have been developed, and suitable questions have been prepared in the form of checklists. Several of these analysis techniques and their accompanying questions will be discussed in the sections that follow.

Tools for Methods Analysis

Process Chart

In analyzing the movement of a product, person, or paper work, the *flow process chart* is invaluable in providing a graphical representation of the step-by-

---

[8]The search for the best methods is a never-ending one, and the optimum method today will be superseded by a better method in the future.

[9]For a discussion of a more detailed approach, see M. E. Mundel, *Motion and Time Study;* 5th ed. Englewood Cliffs, N.J.: Prentice-Hall, Inc., 1978, p. 37.

Symbol	Name	Activities Represented
◯	Operation	Modification of object at one workplace. Object may be changed in any of its physical or chemical characteristics, assembled or disassembled, or arranged for another operation, transportation, inspection, or storage.
⇨	Transportation	Change in location of object from one place to another.
☐	Inspection	Examination of object to check on quality or quantity characteristics.
◻	Delay	Retention of object in a location awaiting next activity. No authorization is required to perform the next activity.
▽	Storage	Retention of object in location in which it is protected against unauthorized removal.

Figure 7-1. Symbols used for process charting.

step sequence that takes place. The American National Standard Industrial Engineering Terminology[10] defines a flow process chart as follows:

A flow process chart is a graphic symbolic representation of the work performed or to be performed on a product as it passes through some or all of the stages of a process. Typically, the information included in the chart is quantity, distance moved, type of work done (by symbol with explanation), and equipment used. Work times may also be included.

To facilitate the charting of a process, it is common practice to make use of symbols such as those illustrated in Figure 7-1.

The use of these symbols is illustrated in Figure 7-2, which shows a flow process chart for the present method of manufacturing a steel collar. Examination of this chart will show that it outlines the various operations, transportations, inspections, delays, and storages that take place on that part as it moves from one stage of completion to another.

The proposed method illustrated in Figure 7-3 resulted from questioning each of the steps in the present method and synthesizing a result. Typical questions that may be raised about each of the steps on a process chart include the following:

1. Can an operation be eliminated?
2. Can an operation be combined with another operation?
3. Can the production sequence be changed?
4. Can an operation or inspection be simplified?
5. Can a movement be eliminated or shortened?
6. Can a delay or storage be eliminated?
7. Can this step be eliminated by redesigning the product or using different material?

---

[10]See "Work Measurement and Methods," American National Standard Industrial Engineering Terminology (ANSI Z94.12–1972); New York: The American Society of Mechanical Engineers, 1973, p. 5.

		SUMMARY						FLOW PROCESS CHART	NO. *326*

		PRESENT		PROPOSED		DIFFERENCE	
		NO.	TIME	NO.	TIME	NO.	TIME
○	OPERATIONS	5					
⇨	TRANSPORTATIONS	4					
☐	INSPECTIONS	0					
D	DELAYS	5					
▽	STORAGES	0					
	DISTANCE TRAVELLED	200 FT.		FT.		FT.	

FLOW PROCESS CHART PAGE *1* OF *1*

DEPARTMENT *127*
OPERATION *Machining collar*

ITEM CHARTED *Collar* NO. *RO-352*
CHARTED BY *E. S. T.* DATE _____

	DETAILS OF (PRESENT / PROPOSED) METHOD	OPERATION / TRANSPORT / INSPECTION / DELAY / STORAGE	DISTANCE IN FEET	QUANTITY	TIME	ANALYSIS WHY? (WHAT? WHERE? WHEN? WHO? HOW?)	NOTES	ACTION CHANGE (ELIMINATE / COMBINE / SEQUE. / PLACE / PERSON / IMPROVE)
1	In storage rack	○⇨☐D▽				✓	Can rack be located nearer saw ?	✓
2	Attached to hoist	○⇨☐D▽		1		✓		✓
3	Moved to saw	○⇨☐D▽	15	1				
4	Unloaded from hoist	○⇨☐D▽		1		✓		✓
5	Cut to length	○⇨☐D▽		1				
6	Await move man	○⇨☐D▽					Can conveyor be used ?	✓
7	To lathe # 16	○⇨☐D▽	35	36				
8	Await lathe operator	○⇨☐D▽						✓
9	Face end, turn seat & thr'd	○⇨☐D▽		1				
10	Await move man	○⇨☐D▽						✓
11	To lathe # 17	○⇨☐D▽	20	36				
12	Face end & turn shoulder	○⇨☐D▽		1			Is shoulder necessary ?	✓
13	Await move man	○⇨☐D▽						✓
14	To assembly dept.	○⇨☐D▽	130	36				
15		○⇨☐D▽						
16		○⇨☐D▽						
17		○⇨☐D▽						
18		○⇨☐D▽						
19		○⇨☐D▽						
20		○⇨☐D▽						
21		○⇨☐D▽						
22		○⇨☐D▽						
23		○⇨☐D▽						
24		○⇨☐D▽						
25		○⇨☐D▽						

Figure 7-2. Flow process chart for present method of manufacturing a steel collar.

Right- and Left-Hand Operation Chart

The right- and left-hand operation chart provides a suitable means of analyzing activity when a person is working at essentially one location. This type of

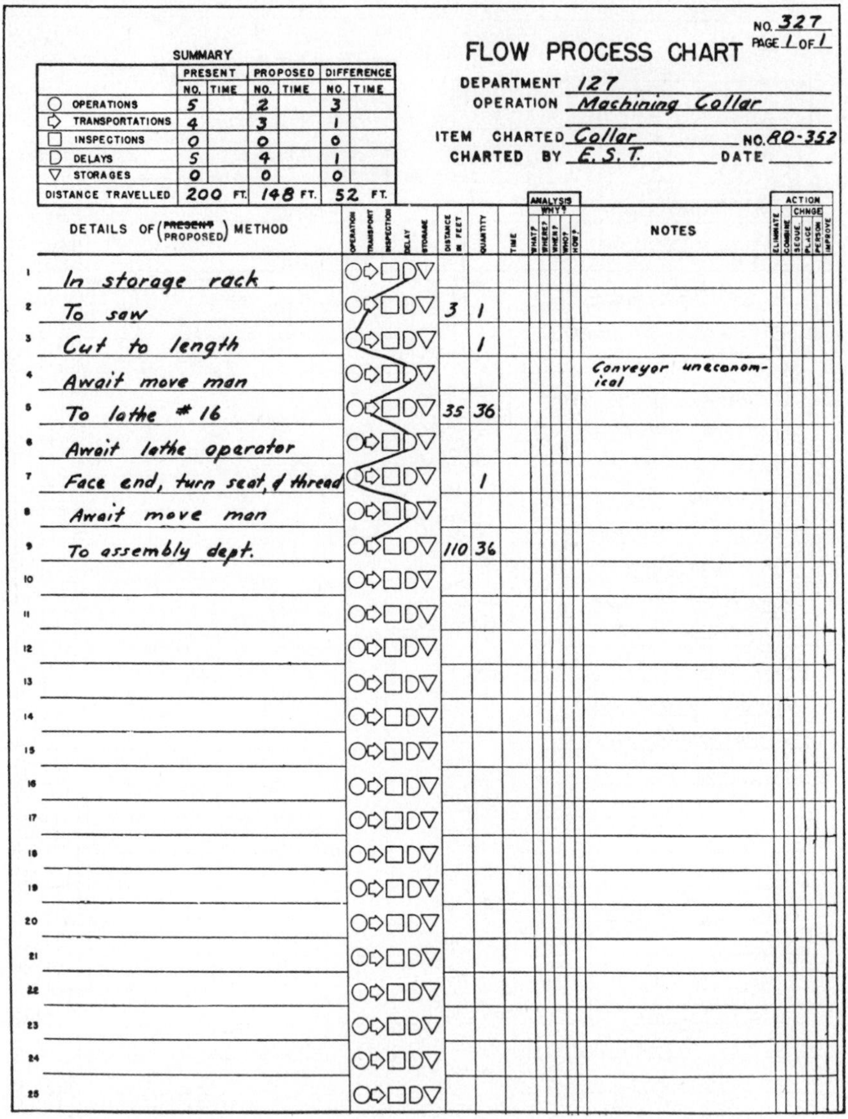

FLOW PROCESS CHART   NO. _327_   PAGE _1_ OF _1_

SUMMARY

	PRESENT NO.	PRESENT TIME	PROPOSED NO.	PROPOSED TIME	DIFFERENCE NO.	DIFFERENCE TIME
○ OPERATIONS	5		2		3	
⇨ TRANSPORTATIONS	4		3		1	
□ INSPECTIONS	0		0		0	
D DELAYS	5		4		1	
▽ STORAGES	0		0		0	
DISTANCE TRAVELLED	200 FT.		148 FT.		52 FT.	

DEPARTMENT _127_
OPERATION _Machining Collar_
ITEM CHARTED _Collar_   NO. _RO-352_
CHARTED BY _E.S.T._   DATE ____

#	DETAILS OF (PRESENT/PROPOSED) METHOD	Symbols	DISTANCE IN FEET	QUANTITY	TIME	ANALYSIS WHY?	NOTES
1	In storage rack	○⇨□D▽					
2	To saw	○⇨□D▽	3	1			
3	Cut to length	○⇨□D▽		1			
4	Await move man	○⇨□D▽					Conveyor uneconomical
5	To lathe # 16	○⇨□D▽	35	36			
6	Await lathe operator	○⇨□D▽					
7	Face end, turn seat, & thread	○⇨□D▽		1			
8	Await move man	○⇨□D▽					
9	To assembly dept.	○⇨□D▽	110	36			
10		○⇨□D▽					
11		○⇨□D▽					
12		○⇨□D▽					
13		○⇨□D▽					
14		○⇨□D▽					
15		○⇨□D▽					
16		○⇨□D▽					
17		○⇨□D▽					
18		○⇨□D▽					
19		○⇨□D▽					
20		○⇨□D▽					
21		○⇨□D▽					
22		○⇨□D▽					
23		○⇨□D▽					
24		○⇨□D▽					
25		○⇨□D▽					

Figure 7-3. Flow process chart for proposed method of manufacturing a steel collar.

analysis is particularly suitable for operations involving assembly work and inspection where no machine is involved.

Figure 7-4 illustrates a right- and left-hand operation chart for assembling a ball-point pen. Examination of this chart discloses that the operation is broken down into a series of simultaneous actions (suboperations, transportations, delays, and

OPERATION CHART

SUMMARY	PER _1_ PIECES						COMPANY	_A.C. Wright Corp._

	PRESENT		PROPOSED		DIFFERENCE	
	LH	RH	LH	RH	LH	RH
○ OPERATIONS	2	6				
⇨ TRANSPORTS	3	6				
▽ HOLDS	9	0				
D DELAYS	0	2				
TOTAL	14	14				

DEPARTMENT _Assembly_
OPERATION _Assemble ball point pen_
_No. RT45_
OPERATOR _R.O. Jenkins_
CHARTED BY _S.O.J._ DATE _____
PRESENT } METHOD
~~PROPOSED~~   SHEET _1_ OF _1_

LEFT HAND	OPER. TRANS. HOLD DELAY	No.	OPER. TRANS. HOLD DELAY	RIGHT HAND
To barrel	○⇨▽D	1	○⇨▽D	To ink cartridge
Grasp "	○⇨▽D	2	○⇨▽D	Grasp " "
To assembly area	○⇨▽D	3	○⇨▽D	To assembly area
Hold barrel	○⇨▽D	4	○⇨▽D	Insert cartridge in barrel
" "	○⇨▽D	5	○⇨▽D	To spring
" "	○⇨▽D	6	○⇨▽D	Grasp "
" "	○⇨▽D	7	○⇨▽D	To assembly area
" "	○⇨▽D	8	○⇨▽D	Assemble spring on cart'ge
" "	○⇨▽D	9	○⇨▽D	To cap
" "	○⇨▽D	10	○⇨▽D	Grasp cap
" "	○⇨▽D	11	○⇨▽D	To assembly area
" "	○⇨▽D	12	○⇨▽D	Assemble cap to barrel
To rack	○⇨▽D	13	○⇨▽D	Wait for left hand
Place in rack	○⇨▽D	14	○⇨▽D	" " " "
	○⇨▽D	15	○⇨▽D	
	○⇨▽D	16	○⇨▽D	
	○⇨▽D	17	○⇨▽D	
	○⇨▽D	18	○⇨▽D	
	○⇨▽D	19	○⇨▽D	
	○⇨▽D	20	○⇨▽D	
	○⇨▽D	21	○⇨▽D	
	○⇨▽D	22	○⇨▽D	
	○⇨▽D	23	○⇨▽D	

Figure 7-4. Operation chart for right and left hand in assembling a ball point pen.

holds) performed by the two hands. In performing Step 2 (questioning) of the systematic approach, each of the steps of the original method should be questioned by means of a series of questions such as the following:

1. Can a suboperation be eliminated or combined?
2. Can a transportation be eliminated or shortened?
3. Can the sequence of motions be changed to facilitate the operation?
4. Can a delay be eliminated?
5. Can a hold be eliminated through the use of a jig or fixture?

Multiple Activity Chart

In those operations involving the combination of a person and a machine, a person and several machines, or any combination of people and machines where delays are prevalent, the multiple activity chart provides a convenient technique for analyzing the combined activity. Very often the objectives of this type of analysis are to attain the maximum utilization of a machine, to attain the optimum person to machine relationship, or to bring about the best balance of crew activity. For this reason, the time factor is an important consideration and necessitates the use of a graphical representation involving time. Figure 7-5 contains a chart illustrating the present method of performing the operation "drill cleat." Use of this chart is very similar to that of the right- and left-hand operation chart except that the symbols are used in column form in order that the time factor may be represented, and an additional column is used to represent the machine. Where more than one person and one machine are analyzed, it is common practice to use a column to represent each person and each machine.

The formulation of a proposed method will result from a questioning approach and synthesis similar to that used for the right- and left-hand operation chart.

Use of Motion Pictures and Videotape

The experienced methods engineer finds that one of the most important aids is the use of motion pictures. There are many situations in which it is difficult to observe all of the action taking place because of the high speed of activities or the complexity of the operation. Having observed slow-motion motion pictures, we are familiar with the fact that one can take motion pictures at high speed and then, by projecting them at normal speed, slow the action down. By the same token, we can take the pictures at slow speed and project them at what appears to be high speed.

In the use of motion pictures, methods engineers may have several objectives in mind. First and foremost, they may want a permanent record of the work as it was being performed. Or, they may wish to use the film for analysis purposes commonly referred to as "micromotion" or "memomotion" studies to be discussed in some detail in the sections that follow.

In much the same way that motion pictures have been used for methods analysis, a recent innovation has been to make use of videotape. The development of improved, relatively low-cost equipment has made this technique increasingly at-

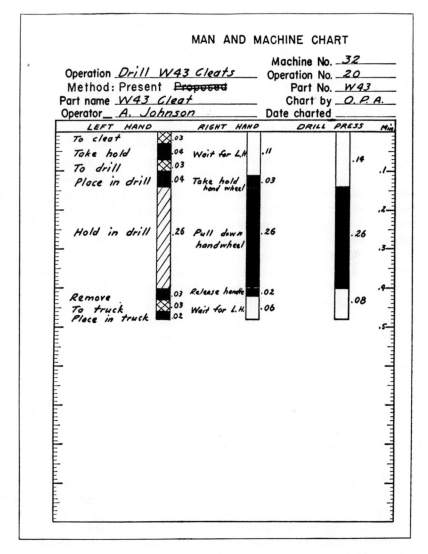

Figure 7-5. Person and machine chart for drilling wood cleats. (Adapted from M. E. Mundel, *Motion and Time Study*, 5th ed.; Englewood Cliffs, N.J.: Prentice-Hall, Inc., 1978.)

tractive. A videotape has a number of advantages over motion pictures. One of these is credibility. The fact that it is much harder to edit than film and is immediately available for playback makes it less suspect on the part of the employee and his or her supervisor. Further, videotape is a real people-involvement tool, because people are so familiar with television.

Micromotion Study

Micromotion study, which was originated by Frank B. Gilbreth, is one of the most exacting forms of work analysis available for job improvement. It is an analysis technique making use of motion pictures taken at a constant and known speed. The film becomes a permanent record of both the method being used and the time consumed in doing the work.

Although micromotion study was originally employed primarily for job analysis work, in recent years several new uses have been found for this analysis tool. For example, it may be used to study the interrelationships among the members of a work group, to study the relationship between an operator and his machine, to obtain the time for an operation, to establish a permanent record of a job method, and similar activities. Even though micromotion study is a valuable analysis tool, it has not been used extensively in industry because it is expensive, time-consuming, and frequently meets with union resistance (because of the motion pictures).

Micromotion study provides a valuable technique for making minute analyses of those operations that are short in cycle, contain rapid movements, and involve high production over a long period of time. Thus, it is very useful in analyzing operations such as the sewing of garments, assembly of small parts, and similar activities.

The usual procedure for performing micromotion study is to take motion pictures of the operations, analyze the resulting film, and prepare a *simo* (simultaneous motion cycle) chart from the results of the film analysis. In analyzing the film, very accurate time values (commonly 1/2000 minute) may be obtained by reading a clock (microchronometer) that appears in each frame of the motion picture. Most persons prefer not to use the clock and instead use a camera driven by a constant-speed motor, making possible a constant time interval (such as 1/200 minute, 1/10 minute, 1 second) between adjacent frames of the film (see Figure 7-6).

The film is analyzed by breaking the job cycle down into *therbligs*,[11] or basic body motions. Although the 17 therbligs are not the smallest subdivisions into which human activity can be subdivided, they are widely known and can be conveniently applied.

Figure 7-8 shows the therbligs with their symbols, colors, and definitions.

In analyzing the motion-picture film, it is common practice first to record the description on a *film analysis sheet;* from this information a simo-chart may be prepared. Examination of the simo-chart illustrated in Figure 7-9 discloses that the simultaneous action of either hand may be determined by reading horizontally across the chart and that the duration of each therblig is illustrated by the time column.

After the simo-chart of the operation has been made, the chart should be stud-

---

[11]Therblig (an anagram of Gilbreth) is a term coined by Frank Gilbreth to describe the 17 basic subdivisions of human activity.

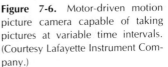

Figure 7-6. Motor-driven motion picture camera capable of taking pictures at variable time intervals. (Courtesy Lafayette Instrument Company.)

Figure 7-7. A video camera suitable for motion study. (Courtesy Lafayette Instrument Company.)

ied and subjected to question in order to find a better way of doing the work. Every attempt should be made to eliminate those therbligs that are non-productive (hold, avoidable delay, unavoidable delay, plan, rest, select, search), as well as to shorten those that are productive.

Name of Symbol	Symbol	Color	Activity Represented
Search	Sh	Black	Occurs when hand or eyes are hunting or groping for something. *Example:* Trying to find or pick a part from a pile.
Select	St	Gray	Occurs when one object is being picked from among several. *Example:* Locating a particular bolt from among several.
Grasp	G	Lake red	Consists of taking hold of an object. *Example:* Closing the fingers around a pencil.
Transport empty	TE	Olive green	Refers to moving the empty hand while reaching for something. *Example:* Reaching for a desk pen.
Transport loaded	TL	Grass green	Refers to moving an object from one place to another. *Example:* Carrying a desk pen from the holder to the paper.
Hold	H	Gold ochre	Refers to the retention of an object in a fixed location. *Example:* Retaining a fountain pen barrel in one hand while assembling the cap to it with the other.
Release load	RL	Carmine red	Occurs when the hand lets go of an object. *Example:* Letting go of a desk pen when it is placed in a holder.
Position	P	Blue	Consists of aligning or orienting an object preparatory to fitting it into some location. *Example:* Aligning a plug preparatory to inserting it into an electrical outlet.
Pre-position	PP	Sky-blue	Consists of locating an object in a predetermined manner and in the correct position for some subsequent motion. *Example:* Lining up a desk pen for insertion into its holder.
Inspect	I	Burnt ochre	Examination of an object to determine some quality such as size, shape, or color. *Example:* Visual examination of finish of a desk.
Assemble	A	Violet, heavy	Consists of combining one object with another. *Example:* Putting a nut on a bolt.
Disassemble	DA	Violet, light	Consists of separating two objects which were combined. *Example:* Removing a nut from a bolt.
Use	U	Purple	Consists of applying or manipulating a tool, control or device for the purpose for which intended. *Example:* Tightening a bolt with a crescent wrench.
Unavoidable delay	UD	Yellow ochre	Refers to a delay by body member which is beyond the control of the operator. *Example:* Right hand pauses during the operation of assembling a mechanical pencil while the left hand asides a completed pencil.

Figure 7-8. Therblig symbols and definitions.

Avoidable delay	AD	Lemon yellow	Refers to a delay by body member which is within the control of the operator. *Example:* An operator pauses or deviates from the normal motion pattern.
Plan	Pn	Brown	Refers to a delay in a motion pattern while the operator decides how to proceed. *Example:* An operator assembling a complex valve pauses to decide which part should be next.
Rest for overcoming fatigue	R	Orange	Occurs when a worker pauses to overcome the fatigue from the previous work. *Example:* An operator pauses to rest after having lifted several heavy castings into a metal truck.

Figure 7-8.   (continued)

Videotape Analysis

The use of videotape in motion study is becoming increasingly common because of the advancements in equipment. (See video camera in use in Figure 7-7.) Videocassette recorder and playback equipment are available that enables the engineer to play the tapes in various forward slow-motion modes as well as in reverse. This enables the engineer to study the tape recording in the same way that was described previously for film analysis. Videotape has the additional advantage over photographic film in that it is available for immediate analysis. Moreover, frame count display is an integral part of the equipment, and the engineer can incorporate sound recordings with the visual recording.

Memomotion Study

Before leaving the general area of micromotion study, let us touch briefly on memomotion study. Memomotion study, which was originated by M. E. Mundel, is a special form of micromotion study in which the motion pictures are taken at slow speeds. Sixty frames per minute and one hundred frames per minute are most common.

Memomotion study has been used frequently to study the flow and handling of materials, crew activities, multi-person-and-machine relationships, stockroom activities, department store clerks, and a variety of other jobs. It is particularly valuable on long-cycle jobs or jobs involving many interrelationships. In addition to having all of the advantages of micromotion study, it can be used at relatively low film cost (about 6 percent of the film cost at normal camera speeds) and permits rapid visual review of long sequences of activities.

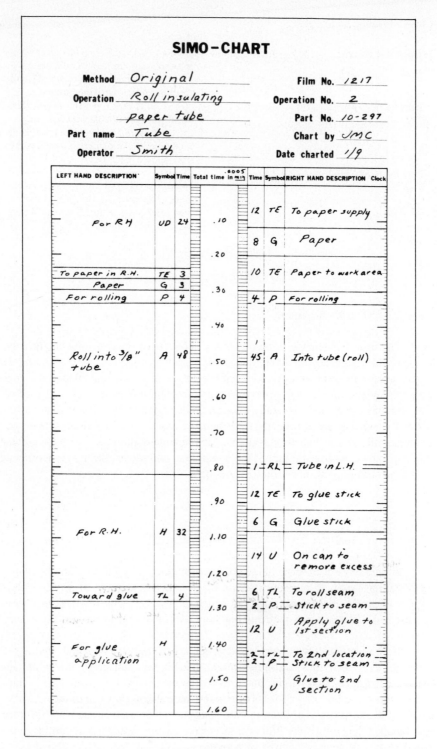

SIMO-CHART

Method _Original_   Film No. _1217_

Operation _Roll insulating_   Operation No. _2_

paper tube   Part No. _10-297_

Part name _Tube_   Chart by _JMC_

Operator _Smith_   Date charted _1/9_

LEFT HAND DESCRIPTION	Symbol	Time	Total time in .0005 min	Time	Symbol	RIGHT HAND DESCRIPTION Clock
				12	TE	To paper supply
For RH	UD	24	.10			
				8	G	Paper
			.20			
To paper in R.H.	TE	3		10	TE	Paper to work area
Paper	G	3				
For rolling	P	4	.30	4	P	For rolling
			.40			
Roll into 3/8" tube	A	48	.50	45	A	Into tube (roll)
			.60			
			.70			
			.80	1	RL	Tube in L.H.
			.90	12	TE	To glue stick
For R.H.	H	32	1.10	6	G	Glue stick
				14	U	On can to remove excess
			1.20			
Toward glue	TL	4	1.30	6	TL	To roll seam
				2	P	Stick to seam
				12	U	Apply glue to 1st section
For glue application	H		1.40	2	TL	To 2nd location
				2	P	Stick to seam
			1.50		U	Glue to 2nd section
			1.60			

Figure 7-9. Simo-chart for making insulated sleeves. (From M. E. Mundel, *Motion and Time Study,* 5th ed.; Englewood Cliffs, N.J.: Prentice-Hall, Inc., 1978. Reprinted by permission.)

Principles of Motion Economy

Through the pioneer work of Gilbreth, Ralph M. Barnes, and other investigators, certain rules for motion economy and efficiency have been developed. Some of the most important of these principles are the following:

1. The movements of the two hands should be balanced and the two hands should begin and end their motions simultaneously.
2. The hands should be doing productive work and should not be idle at the same time except during rest periods.
3. Motions of the hands should be made in opposite and symmetrical directions and at the same time.
4. The work should be arranged to permit it to be performed with an easy and natural rhythm.
5. Momentum and ballistic-type movements should be employed wherever possible in order to reduce muscular effort.
6. There should be a definite location for all tools and materials, and they should be located in front of and close to the worker.
7. Bins or other devices should be used to deliver the materials close to the point of use.
8. The workplace should be designed to insure adequate illumination, proper workplace height, and provision for alternate standing and sitting by the operator.
9. Wherever possible, jigs, fixtures, or other mechanical devices should be used to relieve the hands of unnecessary work.
10. Tools should be pre-positioned wherever possible in order to facilitate grasping them.
11. Objects should be handled, and information recorded, only once.

Through the application of these principles, it is possible to greatly increase the output of manual labor with a minimum of fatigue.

Human Factors Engineering

It is clear from the discussion of the principles of motion economy that human beings are a major consideration in the design of job methods. Further, it is apparent that there is a person–machine relationship that exists in many work situations. It is for this reason that we should like to dwell for a few moments on some of the human elements of work methods design.

In recent years, a body of knowledge has developed pertinent to the design of work situations which has come to be known as *human factors engineering*. This field is sometimes referred to as *biomechanics, ergonomics,* or *engineering psychology*. The principal focus of human factors engineering has been on the development of principles and data to be used in adapting equipment and working environments for human use. This information encompasses such areas as sensory and motor processes, human information processes, physical stresses placed on various elements of the body, illumination, noise, vibration, atmospheric conditions, controls, and instrument panels.

In considering the application of human factors principles to the design of a workplace layout, typical questions that one might raise are: is the workplace designed for proper lifting of objects? has adequate consideration been given to illumination and the elimination of glare? is the workplace the right height for the worker? has proper seating been provided to ensure comfort? have suitable footrests and armrests been provided? are dials and controls designed properly and located in suitable areas? are hand tools designed so that they do not require undue stress or discomfort?

Although the human body can endure much discomfort and stress and can perform many unnatural motions over a limited period of time, prolonged exposure to such circumstances may eventually raise problems. Illustrative of this was the use of ordinary needle-nose pliers by employees on a wiring operation in a large company. The operators were using their index fingers to open the pliers after each closing motion with the result that some operators developed sore fingers and wrists. Through a complete redesign of the pliers the problem was alleviated.

In considering a person in a work situation, we recognize that he or she has physiological, psychological, and sociological characteristics. The engineer designing work methods should have sufficient familiarity with each of these to be able to design work situations suited to the workers. One of the first things that the engineer must be aware of is the fact that people are different. Thus, if a workplace arrangement is designed for the "average" worker, it is likely that the company may not employ an "average" worker to do that job. It follows, then, that the engineer must consider differences in such things as body measurements and not attempt to provide facilities suited for the "mythical average."

Work Simplification Programs

For many years, it has been common practice to conduct *work simplification, methods improvement,* or *cost reduction* programs in industry. These programs usually have as their objective the reduction of manufacturing costs through the participation of many persons. For example, in a work simplification program conducted by a large electrical manufacturing company, anticipated annual savings contributed by some 3000 supervisors was estimated to approach $7,500,000.

The concept of work simplication was introduced by Allen H. Mogensen in the 1930's and emphasized worker participation as a means of achieving maximum cost reduction. In the widespread adoption of these programs throughout industry, government agencies, and elsewhere, there has been recognition of the need to acquaint many people with the aims and objectives of methods improvement programs. This orientation should take place at all levels, not only to bring about greater acceptance of methods improvement programs, but also to provide the knowledge of good methods design to all persons who may benefit from such information. Thus, it has been found profitable to present the programs to members of management (including the president of the company), product engineers, manufacturing engineers, foremen, group leaders, and key operators. Frequently, the company suggestion system may be incorporated into the work simplification program.

It is customary for the methods engineers to conduct a training program as a basis for implementing the work simplification programs. These programs may be given in one continuous session, but more often are limited to a series of two- or three-hour sessions held once or twice each week. In one large company, the course consists of twenty hours and covers the following topics:

1. General economics.
2. Problem-solving approach.
3. Process charts.
4. Operation charts.
5. Multiple-activity charts.
6. Principles of motion economy.

Usually, the participants in the program are asked to apply the principles that they have learned to one or more operations being performed in their respective departments. Through the discussion of these problems, they are able to appreciate the benefits to be derived from a methods improvement program. Also, these people, being closer to their jobs than the methods engineers, can often suggest methods improvements that would escape the trained methods engineer.

One of the factors commonly cited as a reason for the high productivity in Japanese plants is the use of small production, product-, and customer-oriented teams that have a major influence on production methods. General Motors plans to use this concept in its Saturn plant and expects to have no more than 15 workers to a team. These team members will talk over ideas and problems. Further discussion of the team approach will be covered in Chapter 15 under "quality circles."

Job Enlargement and Enrichment

Most of the principles that are applied in methods improvement have the tendency to reduce the content of a job method. Though this sometimes may be done to reduce the skills required to do the job, it may result in jobs that are boring and monotonous and lead to little worker satisfaction. Many workers employed on automotive-type assembly lines contend that their jobs are too dull and monotonous, and the pressure is too intense. This has led to the contention of a number of social scientists that jobs need to be enlarged or enriched. Frederick Herzberg,[12] one proponent of job enrichment, feels that the purpose of job enrichment should be to eliminate the undesirable characteristics of highly repetitive, specialized work by enlarging it to include

1. Greater variety of knowledge and skill.
2. Giving a person a complete natural unit of work (module, division, area, and so on).
3. More complex utilization of the important cognitive and motor abilities possessed by the worker.
4. More freedom and responsibility in the performance of the tasks at hand.

Both in the United States and in Europe, a number of well-known companies have initiated programs to try to overcome some of the objectionable features of jobs. Illustrative of this is the team approach being used in one Swedish automotive plant in which each group of workers does a variety of tasks and decides among its members how the work is to be allocated. In an American pet-food plant all production tasks are assigned to teams of 8 to 12 members, each worker learns every job, and there are no supervisors. It is noteworthy that in this plant each worker learns every job, fewer workers are required than initially planned, and productivity is estimated to be about 40 percent higher than in comparable plants which use traditional methods. Among the principles that commonly are applied in job enrichment programs, the following are adhered to by one large company:

1. Insure that there is variety in the job content.
2. Include in the work situation an opportunity for the worker to grow and learn.
3. Provide an opportunity for each worker to have knowledge of the part that his or her job plays in the total manufacturing process required to produce the product.
4. Design the work so that it has meaning to the worker and provides pride in performance to the worker.
5. Insure that the work is reasonably demanding and functionally inclusive. Provide for self-direction of the work and for the checking of quality of output.

In an attempt to get some measure of the importance of job enrichment in the minds of female production workers in the sewn products industry, a survey[13] dis-

---

[12]"One More Time: How Do You Motivate Employees?" *Harvard Business Review*, January–February 1968, p. 59.

[13]Emanuel Weintraub, "Has Job Enrichment Been Oversold?" Technical Papers, American Institute of Industrial Engineers, Norcross, Georgia, 1973, p. 346.

closed that an overwhelming majority like the work they do; they prefer a simple job that they can learn thoroughly and stick with, and they resent being switched around. Factors which appeared to be uppermost to these workers were their wages and job security. Thus, on the basis of this study, it appears as though job enrichment is not the key to all workers' job satisfaction.

Though there still is considerable debate as to the desirability of job enrichment programs, there is growing evidence that the enrichment of some kinds of jobs (particularly in new plants) may be both desirable and profitable. Thus, it makes good sense for companies to consider this route as a possible approach to higher productivity and higher quality products.

Value Analysis

As a part of the approach to methods improvement, the methods engineer should question the impact of the design of the parts, the materials used, and the equipment used on the productivity of operations. That is, the methods engineer should be thoroughly familiar with *value analysis,* an activity that is closely related both to methods improvement programs and to purchasing and that is being used extensively in industry and the government. "Value analysis is an objective study of every item of cost in every component part, subassembly, or piece of equipment. This includes a study of the design, the material, and the process in a continual search for other possible materials and new processes."[14] Value analysis involves the evaluation of an item's function and relates its effect to the end product. The purpose of it is to attempt to insure that every element of cost contributes proportionately to the function of the item.

Just as in the work simplification approach, value analysis uses a questioning attitude and asks some key questions:

1. What is it?
2. What does it do?
3. What does it cost?
4. What is it worth?
5. What else will do the job?
6. How much will it cost?

It is obvious from the questions that value analysis is concerned with function, cost, and value and is of utmost importance in the purchasing function (see Chapter 13). It probably tends to put more emphasis on materials than the traditional methods analysis or work simplification programs. At the same time, it is an important ingredient of a total methods improvement and cost-reduction program.

---

[14]Frank J. Johnson, "Value Analysis-Engineering-Function Oriented Cost Reduction," Proceedings Fourteenth Annual Conference, American Institute of Industrial Engineers, Denver, May 1963, p. 144.

Suggestion Systems

An important source of ideas for cost-saving improvements is the suggestion system. Suggestion systems are based on the premise that oftentimes the workers performing jobs day in and day out have an insight into methods improvements that the engineer may not possess. The purpose of the suggestion system is to motivate workers to present any ideas they may have on ways in which the company can be operated better. As a reward for submitting their suggestions, it is common practice to pay workers a percentage of the annual savings that will result.

Some companies have found it difficult to administer suggestion systems successfully and have discontinued them. On the other hand, many companies have found them to be an invaluable source of cost-saving ideas and are happy to pay out large sums of money each year in order to encourage the continuance of this stream of potential savings.

Social and Economic Effects of Methods Study

As was pointed out at the beginning of this chapter, modern industry is constantly searching for better methods. When a business ceases to move forward, it will lose ground and may eventually fail. It is for this reason that the major companies have organized industrial engineering groups, work simplification and value analysis programs, suggestion systems, quality circles, and other methods of achieving reduced costs of manufacturing their products. One of the consequences of these programs has been increased mechanization, which, in turn, has led to the production of more and more goods per man-hour. Among the long-range benefits derived from this increased output have been higher real wages, an improved standard of living, a shorter work week, and a reduction of the physical rigors of the job.

Besides the long-run effects, many short-run effects may have a marked effect on the worker and are probably uppermost in his or her mind. It is obvious that in order to have methods improvement, there must be continual changes in the status quo. This will invariably lead to worker resistance because it is normal to resist change. Any worker who is "laid off" as a result of methods changes probably will be bitter about the change, as might his or her fellow workers. In order to avoid this situation, some companies have adopted the policy that no employee will be "laid off" as a result of methods changes.

QUESTIONS

1. Based upon your observations, how extensively do you think methods design has been applied to industry and to the home?
2. Why is it desirable to use a systematic procedure in methods design?

3. Describe some job you have witnessed recently in which the person obviously was using a poor method. How would you suggest improving the method?

4. How do you account for the fact that only a small percentage of companies use suggestion plans?

5. In seeking an improvement, what are some of the questions you might ask about each of the therbligs required in the operation of removing your pen from your pocket and writing your name on a sheet of paper?

6. Why do workers resist change? How might this resistance be reduced?

7. Is job enrichment inconsistent with the goals of a methods improvement program? Why?

8. Is it possible for a company to be using good methods even though it does not have a methods improvement program?

9. Observe a waitress or other person performing a job and chart the activities on a flow process chart.

10. Who should be responsible for and involved in a value analysis program?

11. Would the use of small production teams eliminate the need for methods engineers? Why?

CASE PROBLEMS

Illinois Machine Company

The Illinois Machine Company manufactures tremendous quantities of automatic screw machine parts for use in its line of handcraft tools. When the parts are discharged from the machine, they roll down chutes and into a tote box. The length of the drop has caused nicks and scratches on some parts that couldn't take this kind of handling. This has led to an excessive number of rejects.

Arthur Erickson, the foreman, has just completed the company's work simplification training program and has decided to analyze this operation for improvement. As suggested by his instructor, he decides to use a logical procedure in tackling this problem.

Questions:

1. Perform each of the steps of the procedure as they might be performed by Arthur Erickson.

2. Suggest ways in which the rejects could be eliminated.

Allegheny Paper Company

The Allegheny Paper Company manufactures a variety of paper products. Recently, it has experienced an increasing demand for cut-to-size flakeboard.

A workman who had previously worked in a brick-making plant noticed that cut-to-size flakeboard was being stacked and banded together on the floor in an awkward fashion. He suggested that Signode Corporation's brickstacking jig could be used to do the job better. He pointed out that the stacking jig has an L-shaped side which forms a right angle. The jig contains multiple "U-type" channels or slots through which steel strapping can be fed; the choice of channels depends on the size of the bundle. Where extra-long bundles need to be stacked and strapped, two jigs could be positioned side-by-side.

By stacking the sheets of flakeboard on the jig, the strap-channels in the jig would permit one person to feed strapping around a bundle easily and then tension and seal the strapping. The jigs also would save strapping, because the operator could work directly from the strapping coil, unwinding only as much strap as needed. As it is now done, the operators have to pre-cut lengths of strapping and lay them on the floor. This involves guesswork as to how long the pieces of strapping should be, and because a too short piece of strapping is useless, the workers naturaly tend to overestimate.

Questions:

1. Assume that you are an engineer employed in the company's Methods Engineering Department and have been asked to evaluate this idea as a beneficial suggestion. How do you appraise the idea? Why?
2. What other possibilities appear as feasible solutions to the problem?
3. In gathering information for a problem such as this, what sources would you use?

Harvey Electric Company

Harvey Electric Company makes a large variety of electronic controls for use with heating and air conditioning equipment. The company has made extensive use of industrial engineers for many years and has an outstanding reputation for the progressive, pioneering achievements of these engineers. Thomas Fitzgerald, Manager of Industrial Engineering, is a strong believer in sending his engineers to any conferences, workshops, or training programs which may prove beneficial to the company. Two of his engineers have just returned from attending the Annual Conference of the Institute of Industrial Engineers. As a result of attending a session on the use of videotape, they became completely sold on the use of videotape studies in carrying out their projects. They suggested to Tom Fitzgerald that he should purchase videotape equipment and that it would be of great use in the department in performing cost reduction studies, machine utilization studies, work measurement studies, and in countless other ways. Further, they pointed out that the ITT Company had purchased all of the equipment that they needed for approximately $3500.

Questions:

1. Of what value might videotapes be in performing methods analysis studies?
2. What problems might arise from the use of video equipment?
3. What additional information should Thomas Fitzgerald secure in trying to decide whether or not to purchase the video equipment?

Forbes Instrument Company

Forbes Instrument Company, a manufacturer of electronic measuring devices, was organized in California in 1975 and has experienced a compounded annual growth rate in excess of 45 percent. Because of its excellent growth record, the company is planning to build a new facility for 500 employees in North Carolina to supply its eastern customers. Since the company attributes much of its success to participative management, Henry Robertson, President, insists that the new facility must provide an attractive, ergonomically sound environment, must be conducive to maintaining a high level of quality, must facilitate the employees' productive ability, and must provide for a high degree of flexibility.

As the chief industrial engineer responsible for planning the work stations in the new facility, you are constantly reminded of the traditional work benches used in your present facility and how inefficient they are. You have read (see Evelyn Brown, "Flexible Work Stations Offer Improved Cost-Effective Alternative for Factory," *Industrial Engineering* June 1985, p. 50–59.) about the growing use of modular work stations and the glowing reports about how they have increased employee satisfaction and productivity. Thus, you have decided to assign Bill Perkins, one of your junior engineers, to secure information on the use of modular work stations.

Questions:

1. Where should Bill Perkins seek information on this assignment?
2. What cost, productivity, and other benefits might be gained from installing such equipment?
3. Should Bill Perkins favor using such equipment? Why?

8

WORK MEASUREMENT

Work measurement (commonly referred to as "time study") is concerned with the determination of the amount of time required to perform a unit of work. For many years, its principal use was for wage-incentive purposes; however, present-day industry finds many uses for work measurement, and it has become one of management's most important tools. Increasingly, it has been used to measure indirect labor (e.g., maintenance workers and materials handlers) and office work.

Work measurement is used to determine the amount of time required by a qualified worker, using a standard method and working at a standard work pace, to perform a specified task. The time required for this task is commonly referred to as the "standard" or "allowed" time.

Origin of Work Measurement

Frederick W. Taylor is credited with having introduced work measurement, or time study, as an essential part of scientific management, in the Midvale Steel Company in 1881. While serving with Midvale as a gang boss and foreman, Taylor was confronted by questions such as "What is the best way to do the job?" "What equipment should be used?" and "What is a fair day's work?" In attempting to answer these questions, he studied each of the various jobs for the purpose of finding the best method. He taught the worker how to use the new method, maintained the working conditions so the worker could do the job properly, established a time standard for accomplishing the work, and then paid the worker a premium for doing the work in the prescribed time and manner. As one source says,[1] "With Taylor, as with the factory manager today, time study was a tool to be used in increasing the overall efficiency of the plant, making possible higher wages for labor, and lower prices of the finished products to the consumer."

Uses of Work Measurement Data

Analysis of the many manufacturing and control functions required in the fabrication of a product will disclose that most of them depend upon time. Without using some unit of time, it would be virtually impossible to plan and schedule production, to make cost estimates on new work, to balance production lines, or to control labor costs. If standard or allowed times are to be used, they should, for greatest accuracy, be obtained by a formal system of work measurement.

The standard or allowed time values are usually determined for each of the operations required in the manufacture of a product and are commonly expressed in hours per piece or per 100 pieces. Standard times may be used for any of the following purposes:

1. The balancing of production lines for new models or new products.
2. The balancing of crew activities on those jobs requiring several workers.
3. Planning and scheduling the flow of production through the plant.
4. Making cost estimates on new products or new models.
5. Providing a basis for cost determination.
6. Providing a basis for wage-incentive plans.
7. Establishing supervisory objectives and providing a basis for measuring supervisory efficiency.

Work Measurement Equipment

Following its introduction by Taylor, the stopwatch was for many years the most common tool for determining time standards. Although used less frequently today, it still is in common use for measuring certain jobs. Figure 8-1 shows a decimal minute stopwatch of the type that has been used extensively in industry. This watch

---

[1]R. M. Barnes, *Motion and Time Study: Design and Measurement of Work;* New York: John Wiley & Sons, Inc., 1980, p. 16.

Figure 8-1.   Decimal-minute
stopwatch.

has a sweep hand that makes one revolution per minute; therefore, each division on the large dial represents one one-hundredth of a minute.

The miniaturization of electronic circuits has led to the development of a number of digital timing devices. One of these is a battery-operated digital stopwatch of the type illustrated in Figure 8-2. This stopwatch is easy to read and can be used in the same manner as the spring-driven stopwatch shown in Figure 8-1. Another electronic device is a digital time study board (see Figure 8-3) that features a visual display like those found on hand calculators. The board can be operated by pushing a button and may be operated for many hours on a single battery. Another unique device, the Datamyte data collector (see Figure 8-4), has been designed to make computer-aided time studies possible and records observations on a computer-readable cassette cartridge. As the observer makes entries on the keyboard, the record is automatically recorded on magnetic tape. This tape can be computer-processed immediately or stored for retrieval later.

For those situations in which monitoring the performance of a machine or group of machines is desired, electronic recording systems have been developed which will automatically count the number of stops, accumulate machine downtime, calculate production rates, calculate machine efficiency, and so forth.

Other timing devices that have been used somewhat infrequently in industry are the motion-picture camera and the video camera. When the motion-picture camera is used, it most frequently is driven by a synchronous motor drive (see Figure 7-6) at a speed of 1000, 100, or 60 frames per minute. This permits measurement of time in either thousandths or hundredths of a minute or in seconds.

Figure 8-2. Electronic digital stopwatch. (Courtesy Meylan Corporation.)

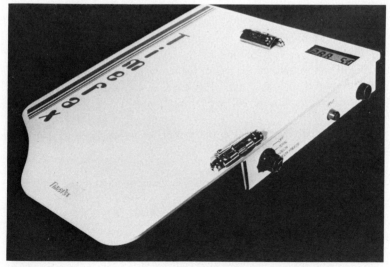

Figure 8-3. A digital time study board. (Courtesy Timefax Division of Logic 1 Electronics.)

Figure 8-4. Datamyte Data Collector. (Courtesy Electro General Corporation.)

Work Measurement by Stopwatch or Other Timing Devices

In this section, we shall discuss the common procedure used in setting a time standard using a stopwatch or one of the other timing devices. Most of our discussion will concentrate on the use of the stopwatch, since its usage in industry has been widespread over the years. However, it should be readily apparent that essentially the same procedure will prevail no matter which of the various timing devices is being used.

The steps usually performed in the making of a stopwatch time study are as follows:

1. Securing permission from the supervisor for making the study and explaining to the operator the purpose of the observations.
2. Checking the job method for improvements, standardizing the job method, and recording on the observation sheet complete information about the job and operator.
3. Breaking the job down into elements and recording these elements in detail on the observation sheet.
4. Determining and recording the times for each of the elements.
5. Rating or leveling the operator's performance.

6. Providing allowances for personal time, fatigue, machine delays, and so forth.
7. Calculating the standard or allowed time.

Standardizing the Job Method

It is important that the work measurement analyst give consideration to the current job method prior to determining the time. Oftentimes the methods being used are poor, and obvious improvements are in order. Whenever possible, the job methods should be altered prior to the taking of the time study in order to insure that the analyst's efforts are not being wasted on a job that may soon undergo change.

The significance of the analysis of work methods was recognized by the Department of Defense when Military Standard (MIL-STD) 1567, Work Measurement, was published in 1975. (Not all services accepted this standard until 1983, and even then, the Navy excluded all shipbuilding programs from it.) The standard, which is applied to all major system production contracts in excess of $100 million annually, sets criteria for the work measurement systems in those companies providing the goods or services. It stipulates that job methods be analyzed before time standards are set and that the standards meet a specific degree of statistical accuracy.

The importance of standardized job conditions should not be underestimated, since any variation in job conditions or methods will have a marked influence on the time required to perform the task. For this reason, it is difficult to set accurate time standards on those jobs that are undergoing frequent change, involve large fluctuations in materials, or contain other variables greatly influencing the production time.

It is evident that it will take time for a new operator to learn a given job. On simple jobs, the time required may be very short, whereas on complex jobs it may take weeks or months. Thus, the time study analyst should be familiar with "learning curves" and insure either that the operator's learning curve has flattened out before the study is taken, or that appropriate adjustments are made in the time values.

When there is a choice of operators whose work performance may be studied, it is common practice to choose an operator who is neither the best nor the poorest worker. Before approaching the operator, the analyst should secure the supervisor's permission and, where applicable, clear the matter with the union. The supervisor should inform the operator in advance that a work measurement study is to be made, explaining the purpose of the study. At no time should the study be made without the operator's knowledge—and never in secret.

The information on the observation sheet should be accurately recorded. It is important that all information that may be used to identify the operation and describe the conditions prevalent at the time of the study be put down carefully. Also, it is essential that a dimensioned sketch of the workplace, showing all tools, machines, and materials, be included on or attached to the observation sheet.

Recording the Job Method

When an operation is being timed, the job should be broken down into separable parts and each of the parts timed. These parts are called *elements* and each contains a series of motions that can be identified, described, and recorded. (As an illustration, elements are listed on the observation sheet shown in Figure 8-5a.) In

TIME STUDY SHEET

OPERATION _Drill oil hole in shaft_ OPER. NO. _30_

MACH.TYPE _Delta drill press_ MACH.NO. _214_ DEPT. _A17_

PART NAME _Shaft_ PART NO. _PL 138_ OPERATOR _B. Alden_

STUDY NO. _A-112-56_ ANALYST _T. F. Jones_ DATE ___

WRITTEN STANDARD PRACTICE

ELEM. NO.	LEFT HAND DESCRIPTION	RIGHT HAND DESCRIPTION	MACHINE ELEMENT	SPEED	FEED	STD. TIME
1	Get shaft from tote box and place in jig	Wait for left hand				.111
2	Grasp jig handle and close jig	Advance drill to part				.203
3	Hold jig closed while drilling	Advance drill 1½" during drilling	Drill ⅛"x1¼ deep hole	920		.747
4	Open jig	Raise drill				.058
5	Remove shaft from jig and place in tote box	Wait for left hand				.110
6	Remove chips once every 20 pieces	Assist left hand				.012

STANDARD PRODUCTION— PCS./ HR.	48.34	STANDARD TIME—MINUTES / PC.	1.241

SKETCH OF WORKPLACE

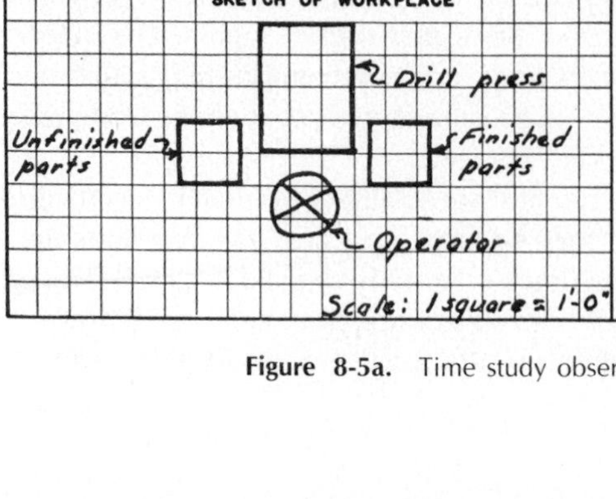

SET-UP, TOOLS, JIGS, FIXTURES, GAGES—

Jig. No. DJ-532

⅛" high speed drill

Drill press

Unfinished parts

Finished parts

Operator

Scale: 1 square = 1'-0"

Figure 8-5a. Time study observation sheet (front).

separating an operation into elements, it is recommended that (1) the elements be as short as can be conveniently timed, (2) man-time be separated from machine-time, (3) constant elements be separated from variable elements, and (4) the elements have clear-cut beginning and end points.

Each element should be recorded in sufficient detail so that the job method is completely described and can be duplicated in identical fashion at a later date.

Determining the Time

After the operation has been divided into elements, the next step is to determine the time for each element. The two most commonly used methods of timing with the stopwatch are known as *continuous* and *snapback,* or repetitive, timing. In continuous timing, the analyst starts the watch at the beginning of the first element and allows it to run for the duration of the study. At the end of each element, the watch reading is recorded in the proper place on the observation sheet. At the conclusion of the study, the time for each element is determined by subtracting the time at the beginning of the element from the time at the end.

In snapback or repetitive timing, the watch is started at the beginning of each element, and at the end of the element it is read and snapped back to zero, and the time is recorded on the observation sheet. This process is repeated for each element for as many cycles as desired in the study.

Each of the methods described above has obvious advantages over the other and in the hands of experienced work measurement analysts probably results in about the same degree of accuracy. However, the continuous method is generally considered best because it includes the overall time for the study and eliminates the possibility of leaving out delays and the necessity for snapping the watch back to zero. The observation sheet shown in Figure 8-5b illustrates the use of the continuous method. (Note that readings are listed under the R column and subtracted times under the T column.)

Although the foregoing discussion has touched on using a spring-driven stopwatch, one of the other timing devices could be used in essentially the same way. For example, the electronic stopwatch illustrated in Figure 8-2 allows the analyst to use either the continuous or the snap-back mode of timing.

The time required to perform a job may be expected to vary slightly from cycle to cycle. Even if the operator works at a constant pace, some variation may be anticipated because of such things as the difference in exact positioning of materials or tools, difference in exact locations in which parts are disposed of, and variations in watch readings. Since work measurement is a sampling process, the analyst must insure that a sufficient number of cycles are timed in order to give an adequate sample from the statistical population or universe from which the values have been drawn. It follows that the greater the number of cycles timed, the more nearly the results will be representative of the activity being measured. The greater the inconsistency of the time values for an element, the larger the number of observations that

STUDY NO. A-34-56 — STOP WATCH OBSERVATIONS

TIME BEGAN 9:10 TIME ENDED 9:33
PRODUCTION DURING STUDY 20

ELEMENTS		CYCLES																								
		1		2		3		4		5		6		7		8		9		10		AVE. ELEM. TIME	RATING	NORMAL TIME	ALLOW.	STD. TIME
NO.	DESCRIPTION	R	T	R	T	R	T	R	T	R	T	R	T	R	T	R	T	R	T	R	T					
1	Release shaft	10	10	13	09	25	10	36	08	49	09	64	12	75	10	85	10	99	09	12	10	.095	110	.105	5%	.110
2	Close jig	19	(09)	31	18	42	17	52	16	67	18	81	17	91	16	04	19	15	16	30	18	.176	110	.193	5%	.203
3	Back-off drill	90	71	02	71	14	72	24	72	37	70	51	70	61	70	75	71	87	72	03	73	.717	100	.717	5%	.753
4	Release jig	95	05	06	04	18	04	29	05	43	06	56	05	65	04	80	05	92	05	07	04	.046	110	.051	5%	.053
5	" shaft	04	09	15	09	28	10	40	11	52	09	65	09	75	10	90	10	102	10	16	09	.095	110	.105	5%	.110
																						.010	105	.011	5%	.012
1		25	09	36	09	55	08	66	08	81	09	92	10	05	10	20	11	30	09	41	10					
2		43	18	54	18	74	19	85	19	98	17	10	18	24	19	37	17	46	16	59	18					
3		13	70	34	80	46	72	57	72	67	69	80	70	94	70	08	71	18	72	31	72					
4		18	05	38	04	50	04	61	04	72	05	85	05	00	06	12	04	22	04	35	04					
5		27	09	47	09	58	08	72	11	82	10	95	10	09	09	21	09	31	09	45	10	STANDARD TIME—MINUTES/PC				1.241
6	Remove chips																			65	20	FOREIGN ELEMENTS—				

Note: circled reading faulty

DETAILS OF ALLOWANCES—
5% personal only

Figure 8-5b. Time study observation sheet (back).

will have to be taken to assure a desired accuracy. To help in the determination of the number of observations required to provide the desired level of accuracy, Mundel[2] suggests the use of formulas such as

$$N' = \left(\frac{40 \ \sqrt{N \ \Sigma X^2 - (\Sigma X)^2}}{\Sigma X} \right)^2$$

where N' = required number of observations to predict the true time
within ± 5% precision and 95% confidence level[3]

N = actual number of observations of the element

X = each individual time (T) for the element

Σ = sum of individual times

If a 95% confidence level and a precision of ± 10% were desired, then the formula becomes:

$$N' = \left(\frac{20 \ \sqrt{N \ \Sigma X^2 - (\Sigma X)^2}}{\Sigma X} \right)^2$$

In addition to these formulas, Mundel, Barnes, and others have prepared tables and nomograms that may be used to determine the number of observations required to give the desired level of accuracy.

After securing the time values, the representative time for each element must be calculated. Most organizations use the arithmetic average, but some prefer to use the modal, or most frequently occurring, time. This representative time is then multiplied by a rating or leveling factor to get the normal time.

Rating the Operator's Performance

During the process of taking a time study, the analyst may observe that the operator is working either faster or slower than the analyst's concept of what should be normal work tempo. It is obvious that if the operator is working faster than normal, then the time required to do the work will be smaller than if he or she is working at a normal or slower than normal pace. In order to adjust the time values, it is common practice to use a process called *rating* or *leveling*. In essence, rating is the process in which the time study analyst compares the performance of the operator being observed with the analyst's own concept of normal performance.

A number of systems of rating have been devised in industry. Some organizations rate pace or tempo of movement only; others take into account skill and effort.

---

[2]*Motion and Time Study*, 5th ed.; Englewood Cliffs, N.J.: Prentice-Hall, Inc., 1978, p. 625.

[3]This means that the probability is that 95% of the time N' will provide a sufficient number of readings to cover the chance variables and to provide a time value within ±5% of the true mean time value.

No matter what system is used, the judgment of the work measurement analyst is required, and this allows room for possible error. The magnitude of this error, however, is surprisingly small for well-qualified analysts.

The majority of work measurement analysts rate each element of a time study, although many prefer to rate the overall study. The rating factor is most frequently expressed as a percentage of normal performance (normal performance = 100 percent), and normal time for each element may be calculated as

$$\text{Normal time} = \text{Average time} \times \frac{\text{Percent rating}}{100}$$

The normal time is not the time allowed for the job, because it must be increased by any additional time allowed for interruptions, the operator's personal needs, and delays beyond his or her control.

Determining Allowances

The normal time for an operation represents the amount of time the average operator would require when working at the normal pace and disregarding any additional time for personal needs, rest, and other delays beyond the operator's control. Obviously, an operator cannot be expected to maintain this pace throughout the workday, and additional time in the form of allowances is usually provided to cover such items as personal needs, rest for overcoming fatigue, machine delays, materials delays, or other unavoidable delays.

The allowance for personal needs varies from about 2 percent to 5 percent for light work. For more rigorous work this allowance may be increased to as much as 50 percent.

Inasmuch as modern industry has taken many steps to eliminate the causes of fatigue, and "fatigue" is a vague phenomenon that is difficult to measure, many companies do not make an allowance for it. Other companies have worked out satisfactory figures by trial and error. In many cases these figures are based upon the total weight lifted or moved by the worker and may amount to as much as 30 percent or more.

An additional reason for adding an allowance occurs when an operator is tending more than one machine. So-called "machine interference" allows for the time a machine must wait or be delayed while the operator completes work on another machine. It is the job of the analyst to determine a suitable machine interference allowance that can be added to the other allowances to get a valid standard time.

Special allowances for machine delays, material delays, materials variations, and similar events beyond the control of the operator are usually determined by means of all-day time studies or delay studies. The *ratio-delay* or *work sampling* study is a particularly useful method of determining these allowances and will be discussed later. This method, which is a statistical sampling technique utilizing a large number of random observations by an analyst, may be used to determine the percentage of time a machine is down and the reasons why it isn't operating.

The standard or allowed time is determined by increasing the normal time by the total amount of the allowance as follows:

$$\text{Standard time} = \text{Normal time} \times \frac{(100 + \text{allowance in percent})}{100}$$

One of the ways that a time study analyst can increase his or her productivity is through the use of a microcomputer to determine the standard time. When using a computer, the analyst performs the normal stopwatch measurement and then inputs the data into the computer.[4] It is evident that both hardware and software are required. One of the most popular software packages is the electronic spreadsheet program. This program makes it possible to develop a computerized matrix or worksheet to record and manipulate the input data. The spreadsheet can then be viewed through the video monitor of the computer or printed out on a printer. There are a number of spreadsheet software packages that are useful under different conditions.

Work Sampling

In 1934 L. H. C. Tippett[5] described a statistical approach that he had used in the English textile industry to measure operator and machine delays. He found this method to be quite effective for determining the cause of loom stoppages in the factories he was studying.

R. L. Morrow,[6] who was one of the first persons in this country to use Tippett's method, called it "ratio-delay." The ratio-delay method began to find gradual use in American industry and was given great impetus in 1952 when it was featured in an article by C. L. Brisley[7] and renamed "work sampling." Since 1952 work sampling has gained widespread usage in the following ways:

1. To measure the working and non-working time of people and machines to use in estimating delay allowances.

---

[4]See Kevin J. McDermott, "Microcomputer and Spreadsheet Software Make Time Studies Less Tedious, More Accurate," *Industrial Engineering,* Vol. 16, No. 7, July 1984, p. 78.

[5]"Statistical Methods in Textile Research. Uses of the Binomial and Poisson Distributions. A Snap-Reading Method of Making Time Studies of Machines and Operatives in Factory Surveys," *Shirley Institute Memoirs,* Vol. 13, November 1934, pp. 35–93.

[6]*Time Study and Motion Economy;* New York: Ronald Press Co., 1946.

[7]"How You Can Put Work Sampling to Work," *Factory,* July 1952, pp. 84–89.

2. To estimate the percent of utilization time of machines and equipment, such as machine tools, fork-lift trucks, elevators, overhead cranes, and so forth.
3. To estimate the percent of time devoted to each of the duties included in the jobs performed by such people as maintenance personnel, office workers, managers, and nurses.
4. To measure a task for the purpose of establishing a time standard on it.

Work sampling has become a popular tool for use in areas such as those listed because it is easy and convenient to use, possesses known reliability that can be established at the outset, and operates without the use of the stopwatch or other timing devices.

Work sampling, as the name implies, is a sampling technique based upon the laws of probability. It is founded on the statistical premise that the occurrences in an adequate, random sample of observations of an activity will follow the same distribution pattern that might be found in a lengthy, continuous study of the same activity. This may be represented by the following proportion:

$$p = \frac{x}{N} = \frac{\text{Number of observations of the activity}}{\text{Total number of observations}}$$

Thus, the work sampling method consists of taking a number of intermittent, randomly spaced,[8] instantaneous observations of the activity being studied, and from this, determining the percent of time devoted to each aspect of the operation. To illustrate the manner in which this may be done, let us consider a woman operating a fork-lift truck. By means of 50 instantaneous observations taken at randomly spaced times, the operator was observed and the following tally marks were noted to indicate whether she was working or idle (definitions have to be predetermined to establish what constitutes "working"):

Operator's Status	Tally	Total
Working	𝖳𝖧𝖫 𝖳𝖧𝖫 𝖳𝖧𝖫 𝖳𝖧𝖫 𝖳𝖧𝖫 𝖳𝖧𝖫 𝖳𝖧𝖫 𝖳𝖧𝖫	40
Idle	𝖳𝖧𝖫 𝖳𝖧𝖫	10
	Total No. of Observations	50

(It should be noted that the 50 observations used in this example is a much smaller number than normally would be required, and in actual practice hundreds of observations may be necessary.)

---

[8]In a method referred to as multi-minute measurement (MMM), work sampling observations are taken at predetermined periods of time rather than at random times. When properly applied, MMM meets the need for relative accuracy and may be useful in setting standards in group situations such as in an office or indirect work environment.

It follows, then, that (based on the observation) we have an estimate indicating that the operator was working 40/50 of the total, or 80 percent of the time, and was idle 10/50 of the total, or 20 percent of the time.

This simple approach illustrates the manner in which work sampling may be used. The key to the accuracy of the technique is in the number of observations. A greater number of observations provides a higher degree of accuracy. The question of how many observations are necessary to insure a certain level of accuracy may be calculated through the use of standard formulas based on the binomial distribution.[9] The use of such formulas would disclose that more than 50 observations should be taken in the fork-lift study.

The procedure for making a work sampling study consists of essentially the following steps:

1. Determine the objectives of the study, including definitions of the states of activity to be observed.
2. Plan the sampling procedure, including:
   a. An estimate of the percentage of time being devoted to each phase of the activity.
   b. The setting of the accuracy limits desired.
   c. An estimation of the number of observations required.
   d. The selection of the length of the study period and the programming of the number of readings over this period.
   e. The establishment of the mechanics of making the observations, the route to follow, and the recording of data.
3. Collect the data as planned.
4. Process the data and present the results.

As indicated earlier, work sampling has a number of advantages over conventional work measurement methods. Among these are the following:

1. It is economical to use and usually costs considerably less than a continuous time study.
2. It can be used to measure many activities that are impractical to measure by time study.
3. It isn't necessary to use a trained work measurement analyst to make the observations.
4. Work sampling measurements may be made with a pre-assigned degree of reliability.
5. It measures the utilization of people and equipment directly.
6. It eliminates the necessity of using the stopwatch for measurements.
7. It provides observation over a sufficiently long period of time to decrease the chance of day-to-day variations affecting the results.

---

[9]See Albert H. Bowker and Gerald J. Lieberman, *Engineering Statistics*, 2nd ed.; Englewood Cliffs, N.J.: Prentice-Hall, Inc., 1972, p. 123.

Even though work sampling is a valuable tool, it has limitations, namely:

1. Normally, it is not economical for studying work at a single location or work that is highly standardized and can be studied by conventional work measurement methods.
2. It is of little value in helping to improve work methods and doesn't offer some of the opportunity for methods analysis that accompanies time study methods.
3. Management and the workers may not understand statistical work sampling.
4. Some of the observers may not adhere to the fundamental principles of sampling and may bias the results.

Predetermined Time Systems

In recent years there has been increasing usage of elemental- or basic-motion time systems for establishing time standards. These systems, which have been devised by several large companies and management consulting firms, are based on the premise that the average time for a person to perform a basic motion or therblig should be relatively constant. Most of the systems ("methods time measurement," "work factor," "basic motion times," "method time analysis," "basic time survey," "elemental time system," and so on) consist of tables of standard time values for performing various types of basic motions—move, reach, position, and so forth. The time values may be applied to any type of operation that may be resolved to the basic motions, eliminating the necessity for using the stopwatch. Figure 8-6 illustrates some of the time values used in one system, methods time measurement. This system is said to be the foremost system, due to the excellent organization and support of the MTM Association. (Information on MTM systems is available from the MTM Association.)

The MTM-1 data illustrated in the figure has been combined into other versions, and one of these, MTM-4, is a computer-aided system. The MTM-4 system has built into it the capability of retrieving elements from previous studies, rearranging the elements in any order, and adding additional elements to complete a job method. The retrieval process is automatic and requires only the input of suitable code numbers.

In 1974 H. B. Maynard and Company introduced the Maynard Operation Sequence Technique (MOST), a predetermined-motion time system that was developed in Sweden and is faster than the MTM system on which it is based. This system, which was computerized in 1977, assumes that manual work tends to be performed with the standard set [Action distance (A), Body motion (B), Gain control (C), Placement (P)] of activities and that motion times for each of these activities can be predetermined and assigned to a sequence model. As an example, many jobs consist of walking a short distance, picking up a part, carrying it to the workplace, and placing it on the workplace. MOST defines each of these activities by a letter and a number indicating the degree of complexity. (See the General Move Model in Figure 8-7.)

To express the method variation for each of the activities, a fixed scale of index numbers is used—0, 1, 3, 6, 10, 16, etc. Each index number stands for a multiple of 10 TMU's. (1 TMU = .00001 hour.)

The procedure for setting a time standard using a system such as MTM is to break the job method down into basic motions and then apply the appropriate time values for each motion. The sum of these time values becomes the standard time for the job. (See Figures 8-8 and 8-9.) Additional time for allowances may have to be added in some cases depending upon the job being analyzed and the system being used.

The advocates of the elemental-motion time systems claim the following advantages to their use:

1. Time standards may be set in advance of the performance of the job.
2. They make the analyst motion-conscious and facilitate obvious improvements in methods.
3. Production lines may be balanced in advance.
4. Cost estimates may be made in advance of making the product.
5. The use of standard data is facilitated.
6. They facilitate choosing between alternative methods.
7. They facilitate training supervisors to be methods-conscious.

Standard Data

A study of the elemental breakdown of many different jobs reveals that many of the elements are similar. For example, in machining operations, such as on a drill press, all elements may be virtually the same except for the cutting time. Thus, in setting time standards on drilling operations, it is desirable to consider all jobs as a "family" of operations and try to select elements that may appear to occur continually on that type of work. This frequently is referred to as the accumulation of *standard data*. The standard data, for the most part, consist of elemental time standards that have been taken from previous studies. These time values may have been obtained from stopwatch time studies or from predetermined time systems.

The application of standard data is essentially the same process as that used in conducting a stopwatch or other time study. The operation is broken down into elements, appropriate time values (in the form of tables, curves, equations, and so forth) are selected from the data file, suitable allowances are added, and the allowed time is determined. The advantages of this method are that it is possible to set a new standard in advance of performance of the operation and to set it more quickly, cheaply, and consistently than by an individual study.

TABLE I – REACH – R

Distance Moved Inches	Time TMU				Hand In Motion		CASE AND DESCRIPTION
	A	B	C or D	E	A	B	
3/4 or less	2.0	2.0	2.0	2.0	1.6	1.6	A Reach to object in fixed location, or to object in other hand or on which other hand rests.
1	2.5	2.5	3.6	2.4	2.3	2.3	
2	4.0	4.0	5.9	3.8	3.5	2.7	
3	5.3	5.3	7.3	5.3	4.5	3.6	B Reach to single object in location which may vary slightly from cycle to cycle.
4	6.1	6.4	8.4	6.8	4.9	4.3	
5	6.5	7.8	9.4	7.4	5.3	5.0	
6	7.0	8.6	10.1	8.0	5.7	5.7	
7	7.4	9.3	10.8	8.7	6.1	6.5	
8	7.9	10.1	11.5	9.3	6.5	7.2	C Reach to object jumbled with other objects in a group so that search and select occur.
9	8.3	10.8	12.2	9.9	6.9	7.9	
10	8.7	11.5	12.9	10.5	7.3	8.6	
12	9.6	12.9	14.2	11.8	8.1	10.1	
14	10.5	14.4	15.6	13.0	8.9	11.5	D Reach to a very small object or where accurate grasp is required.
16	11.4	15.8	17.0	14.2	9.7	12.9	
18	12.3	17.2	18.4	15.5	10.5	14.4	
20	13.1	18.6	19.8	16.7	11.3	15.8	
22	14.0	20.1	21.2	18.0	12.1	17.3	E Reach to indefinite location to get hand in position for body balance or next motion or out of way.
24	14.9	21.5	22.5	19.2	12.9	18.8	
26	15.8	22.9	23.9	20.4	13.7	20.2	
28	16.7	24.4	25.3	21.7	14.5	21.7	
30	17.5	25.8	26.7	22.9	15.3	23.2	
Additional	0.4	0.7	0.7	0.6	0.4	0.75	TMU per inch over 30 inches

TABLE II – MOVE – M

Distance Moved Inches	Time TMU			Hand In Motion B	Wt. Allowance			CASE AND DESCRIPTION
	A	B	C		Wt. (lb.) Up to	Dynamic Factor	Static Constant TMU	
3/4 or less	2.0	2.0	2.0	1.7				
1	2.5	2.9	3.4	2.3	2.5	1.00	0	
2	3.6	4.6	5.2	2.9				A Move object to other hand or against stop.
3	4.9	5.7	6.7	3.6	7.5	1.06	2.2	
4	6.1	6.9	8.0	4.3				
5	7.3	8.0	9.2	5.0	12.5	1.11	3.9	
6	8.1	8.9	10.3	5.7				
7	8.9	9.7	11.1	6.5	17.5	1.17	5.6	
8	9.7	10.6	11.8	7.2				B Move object to approximate or indefinite location.
9	10.5	11.5	12.7	7.9	22.5	1.22	7.4	
10	11.3	12.2	13.5	8.6				
12	12.9	13.4	15.2	10.0	27.5	1.28	9.1	
14	14.4	14.6	16.9	11.4				
16	16.0	15.8	18.7	12.8	32.5	1.33	10.8	
18	17.6	17.0	20.4	14.2				
20	19.2	18.2	22.1	15.6	37.5	1.39	12.5	
22	20.8	19.4	23.8	17.0				
24	22.4	20.6	25.5	18.4	42.5	1.44	14.3	C Move object to exact location.
26	24.0	21.8	27.3	19.8				
28	25.5	23.1	29.0	21.2	47.5	1.50	16.0	
30	27.1	24.3	30.7	22.7				
Additional	0.8	0.6	0.85	0.75	TMU per inch over 30 inches			

EFFECTIVE NET WEIGHT

Effective Net Weight (ENW)	No. of Hands	Spatial	Sliding
	1	W	W x F_C
	2	W/2	W/2 x F_C

W = Weight in pounds
F_C = Coefficient of Friction

Figure 8-6. Methods Time Measurement Tables. (Copyrighted by the MTM Association for Standards and Research. No reprint without written consent from MTM Association, 16-01 Broadway, Fair Lawn, New Jersey 07410.)

TABLE III A – TURN – T

Weight	Time TMU for Degrees Turned										
	30°	45°	60°	75°	90°	105°	120°	135°	150°	165°	180°
Small – 0 to 2 Pounds	2.8	3.5	4.1	4.8	5.4	6.1	6.8	7.4	8.1	8.7	9.4
Medium – 2.1 to 10 Pounds	4.4	5.5	6.5	7.5	8.5	9.6	10.6	11.6	12.7	13.7	14.8
Large – 10.1 to 35 Pounds	8.4	10.5	12.3	14.4	16.2	18.3	20.4	22.2	24.3	26.1	28.2

TABLE III B – APPLY PRESSURE – AP

FULL CYCLE			COMPONENTS		
SYMBOL	TMU	DESCRIPTION	SYMBOL	TMU	DESCRIPTION
APA	10.6	AF + DM + RLF	AF	3.4	Apply Force
			DM	4.2	Dwell, Minimum
APB	16.2	APA + G2	RLF	3.0	Release Force

TABLE IV – GRASP – G

TYPE OF GRASP	Case	Time TMU	DESCRIPTION		
PICK-UP	1A	2.0	Any size object by itself, easily grasped		
	1B	3.5	Object very small or lying close against a flat surface		
	1C1	7.3	Diameter larger than 1/2"	Interference with Grasp on bottom and one side of nearly cylindrical object.	
	1C2	8.7	Diameter 1/4" to 1/2"		
	1C3	10.8	Diameter less than 1/4"		
REGRASP	2	5.6	Change grasp without relinquishing control		
TRANSFER	3	5.6	Control transferred from one hand to the other.		
SELECT	4A	7.3	Larger than 1" x 1" x 1"	Object jumbled with other objects so that search and select occur.	
	4B	9.1	1/4" x 1/4" x 1/8" to 1" x 1" x 1"		
	4C	12.9	Smaller than 1/4" x 1/4" x 1/8"		
CONTACT	5	0	Contact, Sliding, or Hook Grasp.		

TABLE V – POSITION* – P

CLASS OF FIT		Symmetry	Easy To Handle	Difficult To Handle
1–Loose	No pressure required	S	5.6	11.2
		SS	9.1	14.7
		NS	10.4	16.0
2–Close	Light pressure required	S	16.2	21.8
		SS	19.7	25.3
		NS	21.0	26.6
3–Exact	Heavy pressure required.	S	43.0	48.6
		SS	46.5	52.1
		NS	47.8	53.4

*Distance moved to engage–1" or less.

METHODS-TIME MEASUREMENT
M T M-I APPLICATION DATA

1 TMU	= .00001 hour
	= .0006 minute
	= .036 seconds

Figure 8-6. (continued)

m⟩⟩	A B G A B P A		GENERAL MOVE SEQUENCE MODEL		
INDEX **X 10**	**A** ACTION DISTANCE	**B** BODY MOTION	**G** GAIN CONTROL	**P** PLACEMENT	**INDEX** **X 10**
0	≤ 2 IN. ≤ 5 CM			HOLD TOSS	**0**
1	WITHIN REACH		LIGHT OBJECT LIGHT OBJECTS SIMO	LAY ASIDE LOOSE FIT	**1**
3	1 - 2 STEPS	BEND AND ARISE 50% OCC	NON SIMO HEAVY OR BULKY BLIND OR OBSTRUCTED DISENGAGE INTERLOCKED COLLECT	ADJUSTMENTS LIGHT PRESSURE DOUBLE	**3**
6	3 - 4 STEPS	BEND AND ARISE		CARE OR PRECISION HEAVY PRESSURE BLIND OR OBSTRUCTED INTERMEDIATE MOVES	**6**
10	5 - 7 STEPS	SIT OR STAND			**10**
16	8 - 10 STEPS	THROUGH DOOR CLIMB ON OR OFF			**16**

Figure 8-7. General Move Table for MOST. (Courtesy H. B. Maynard and Company.)

In establishing standard data, the following steps are commonly taken:

1. The range of items to be covered is determined.
2. A trial breakdown of elements common to all items is established.
3. Time studies are made of the entire range of items to be covered.
4. A master list of elements is prepared and listed on a master summary sheet.
5. The individual element times for each time study are posted on the master summary sheet.
6. The constant elements are separated from the variable elements and the results are shown in the form of curves, nomograms, tables, or formulas.

As is indicated in step 6, the data may be shown in several ways. Figure 8-10 illustrates a chart expressing the time required for one element of a grinding

MTM ELEMENT ANALYSIS   File [   ]

Part Name __Transfer Link_____   Part No. __079219__

Oper. Name __Stake Two Studs to Link_____   Oper. No. __020__

Operator _____ No. _____ Analyst __DJR__   Date __10/4/__

DESCRIPTION – LEFT HAND	F	MOTION	TMU	MOTION	F	DESCRIPTION – RIGHT HAND
Reach to Stud		R12C	14.2	R12C		Reach to Stud
Grasp Stud		G4B	9.1			
			9.1	G4B		Grasp Stud
Move to Fixture		M12C	15.2	M12B		Move to Fixture
		G2		G2		
Place Stud to Fixture		P2SE	16.2			
			2.0	MfC		
			16.2	P2SE		Place Stud to Fixture
Release Stud		RL1	2.0	RL1		Release Stud
Reach to Link		R6C	10.1			
Grasp Link		G4A	7.3			
Move to Right Hand		M6A	8.1			
		G2				
			2.0	G1A		Grasp Link
Move to Studs		M3C	6.7			Assist Left Hand
Place to First Stud		P1SE	5.6			⸮
Assist Right Hand			2.0	MfC		Move to Stud
⸮			5.6	P1SE		Place to Second Stud
Reach to Button		R4A	6.1	R4A		Reach to Button
Grasp Button		G5	0.0	G5		Grasp Button
Activate Press		APA	10.6	APA		Activate Press
			0.0	RL2		Release Button
			6.1	R4A		Reach to Fixture
			0.0	G5		Grasp Fixture
			6.1	M4A		Slide Fixture
			0.0	RL2		Release Fixture
			6.1	R4A		Reach to Button
			0.0	G5		Grasp Button
Activate Press		APA	10.6	APA		Activate Press
Release Button		RL2	0.0	RL2		Release Button
Reach to Link		R4D	8.4	R4D		Reach to Link
Grasp Link		G1B	3.5			
			3.5	G1B		Grasp Link
Disengage Link From Fixture		D2E	7.5	D2E		Disengage Link From Fixture
Release Link		RL1	8.9	M6B		Aside Link to Box
			2.0	RL1		Release Link
			———			
			210.8			

Figure 8-8. An MTM study using MTM-1 data. (Courtesy MTM Association for Standards and Research.)

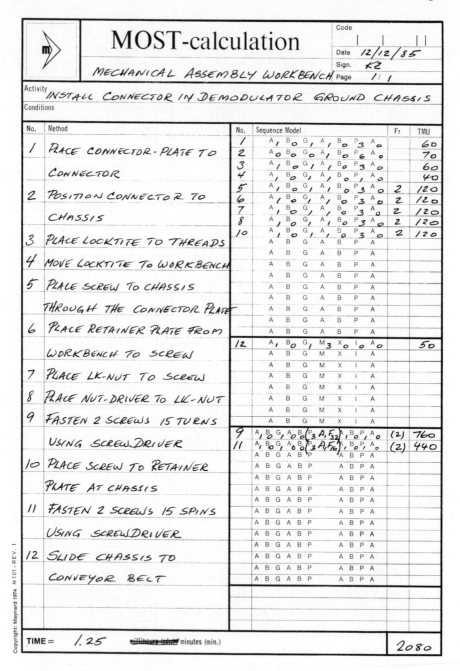

Figure 8-9. Calculations for an application of MOST. (Courtesy H. B. Maynard and Company.)

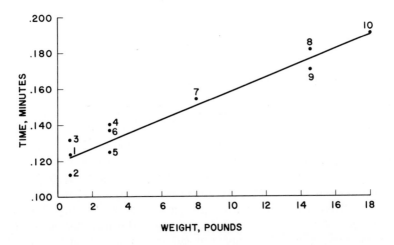

Figure 8-10. Time required to transfer piece from tote pan to centers and engage feed.

operation—take piece from tote pan, place in centers, and engage feed on the grinder. Each point on this chart represents a different time study, and ten different studies were used in compiling the data for this curve. In plotting a curve for a variable element such as this, the form of the independent variable must be determined. For example, prior to selecting the curve shown in the figure, the time-study analyst had determined the major factor (i.e., weight) which appeared to have the greatest effect on the time. He found that a closer and more consistent relationship existed between the time values and weights than existed for such other factors as length or diameter of the journals being ground. One final word on this curve is that the best fitting line may be determined mathematically by using the least squares method.

Increasingly, companies are using computers as a means of storing and retrieving standard data. These systems may be relatively simple or quite complex, depending on the desires of the users. However, most of the systems involve storing time standards for different elements of operations and then providing a coding system for storing and retrieving the data. In some of the more elaborate systems, part information, workplace layouts, and other data may be included. One system[10] is built around the concept that many parts have the same basic configuration and processing requirements. The system takes into consideration the part family number, material, the dimensions of the part, and other pertinent information and then

---

[10]See Thomas J. O'Neill, Ashwin G. Shah, Alfred N. Heymin, Cecil C. Holmes, "System 18—A Programmable Computer System for Standard Data Application," Proceedings, 1977 Spring Annual Conference, Institute of Industrial Engineers, Norcross, Georgia, pp. 34–41.

calculates the standard times for each routed operation and prints out a calculation sheet and an operator instruction sheet.

Administration of Work Measurement

One of the major problems encountered in administering time standards is that of maintaining accurate standards. The work measurement department must provide a continuous check on the job method, materials, and tools to make sure there have been no changes that will affect the time values. This can be accomplished only by continuous review of job methods with complete cooperation of the supervisors.

Inasmuch as a great deal of judgment enters into the setting of a time standard, many work measurement analysts are subjected to frequent training sessions on rating and other phases of the time study procedure. This helps maintain reasonable consistency among the persons involved and helps to provide uniform time standards throughout the plant.

In those companies having wage incentive plans, management has frequently been accused of "rate cutting" and "speedup" and must guard against gaining this reputation. Most companies guarantee that unless there is a change in the job method the time standard will remain in effect no matter how high the incentive earnings of the workers may be. Oftentimes, this allows a worker on whose job there is a "loose" standard to work at a slow pace and still get high incentive earnings. This presents a difficult problem and sometimes is solved only through collective bargaining.

Inasmuch as there have been several references to the interrelationship between work measurement and wage incentives, let us discuss this subject briefly. Basic to the installation of a wage incentive plan (to be discussed in Chapter 20) there should be a managerial decision as to the earning potential under such a plan. It is quite common in industry to expect that the worker should be able to earn a 25 to 35 percent bonus if he or she works at a good incentive pace. However, it is obvious that the amount the worker can earn is influenced by how hard he or she works, the job method used, and the concept of normal work pace (for rating purposes) that was used in establishing the allowed time. Here, then, we see the great influence that the rating or leveling step involved in setting a time standard can have on the operator's ability to earn a bonus. If the operator being observed during the setting of a stopwatch time study is rated erroneously and is judged to be working at a slower pace than the time study analyst's concept of normal, then the allowed time will be less than if the operator were judged to be working faster than normal. It follows, then, that if an organization is to have an effective wage incentive program, there must be a well defined "normal" time (which may vary from plant to plant) and time standards must be set accurately. Failure to adhere to this will lead either to the workers' loss of incentive to attain bonuses or to "runaway" bonuses based on too "loose" time standards.

Criticisms of Work Measurement

Individual workers' reactions to work measurement are based largely on how it affects them and their fellow workers. If employees are working on a job where they can maintain a work pace that they don't consider too fast, or where they are able to receive sizable incentive earnings, then they will probably be in favor of work measurement. On the other hand, if they feel they are forced to "speed up" and have difficulty in keeping up or making a bonus, then they will probably be opposed to it. At the same time, their attitude will be greatly influenced by the attitude expressed by their union leaders.

Unions historically have opposed the use of time study, piecework, and wage incentive plans. In actuality, union officials' attitudes towards work measurement probably have ranged from complete opposition, to toleration, to acceptance. In some companies, the unions tolerate the setting of time standards but reserve the right to accept or reject them (and rejection is a major cause of the presentation of labor grievances). Some labor-management agreements contain clauses that allow a union to use their own analysts to study questionable standards. Further, some national unions employ their own industrial engineers or industrial engineering technicians to assist their local unions in any disputes that arise.

In spite of the progress made by many companies in improving their work measurement practices, innumerable companies maintain an inadequate staff of qualified analysts and may be condemned for faulty practice.

QUESTIONS

1. How does work measurement contribute to the operation of a modern industrial concern?
2. How do you account for the fact that the stopwatch has been the most commonly used timing device?
3. Comment on the suitability of work sampling to set time standards on maintenance operations.
4. Why is it desirable always to secure permission before starting a stopwatch time study?
5. Why are job descriptions timed as a series of elements rather than as unit jobs?
6. Why is it desirable to rate or level a time study?
7. Are standard data a suitable substitute for an elemental-motion time system? Why?
8. How would you recommend training work measurement analysts to insure consistency of their rating ability?
9. Discuss the various ways in which work measurement might be computerized.
10. Will the use of work measurement be eliminated in the factories of the future? Why?
11. Discuss the manner in which videotape might be used in work measurement.
12. Utilizing the MTM data illustrated in Figure 8-6, determine an allowed time for the operation contained in Figure 7-4. Make a sketch showing locations of parts and distances.

CASE PROBLEMS

Keller Manufacturing Company

The Keller Manufacturing Company is a small company employing about 150 persons in the manufacture of aluminum windows. The company has made extensive use of time study for its wage incentive plan, production scheduling, and cost estimating for the past 10 years.

Last year Roger Bellows, a highly experienced time-study man, quit the company. This left the company without a trained time-study analyst. Mr. Davidson, the general manager, decided that the company could get along without replacing Roger Bellows and that Robert Musgrave, the timekeeper, could set time standards in addition to his other duties.

Robert Musgrave is a personable and conscientious employee, and he endeavored to do a good job of setting accurate standards. However, during the past year great inconsistency has crept into the time standards—some are much too "tight" and others too "loose." Several persons in the shop who appear to be loafing are able to make bonuses of 100% whereas others who are working hard are barely able to make a 10% bonus. Since the company has the policy of guaranteeing time standards against cutting, Mr. Davidson has stated that the standards that are too "loose" can't be altered. However, Mr. Davidson has decided that something must be done about the situation.

Questions:

1. Comment on the circumstances that led to the time-study predicament.
2. What can Mr. Davidson do to correct the situation existing in his company?
3. What stand will the union probably take in regard to any changes in the status quo?

Triton Company

The Triton Company has completed plans to establish a new plant in Indiana to manufacture diesel engines and parts. The plant will be located in a new building, and there is no readily available pool of skilled workers. Since the company anticipates growing to a work force of about 1000, it has decided to embark on an intensive recruitment, selection, and training program. Further, the company has decided to introduce a new concept of management in which each new employee will be assigned to a team upon completion of the training program. Each team will have a team leader who will be selected by the team members for one year. Team leaders may come from any age group.

In the plant, it is planned that the teams will serve as basic units on which the whole plant organization structure will be based. The teams' spheres of activity will be as extensive as management can make them and will include such functions as housekeeping, scheduling, quality control, selection of additional members, and establishing production standards. Team members will be thoroughly indoctrinated in the importance of all of these activities in the production process. It is proposed that team members will meet daily to discuss production problems, schedules, and material requirements. As the occasion demands, the teams will meet with section managers to discuss any special problems.

Questions:

1. How do you anticipate that the proposed organization structure will work from an operational point of view?
2. Do you think that it is a good idea for the teams to establish their own production standards?

3.   Discuss the strengths and weaknesses of setting production standards in this way.

MRA Incorporated

MRA Incorporated is one of the country's foremost producers of steel office equipment, and the company has enjoyed outstanding success. Because of its high-quality products and the maintenance of a sound marketing policy, the company is looked to as a leader in its field. Much of MRA's success is due to an enlightened personnel philosophy of trying to treat its employees right; this has led to highly satisfied employees and the reputation of MRA's being a good place to work.

Through the years, MRA has maintained a sizable industrial engineering staff, responsible for a variety of functions in the manufacturing areas, namely, time standards, wage incentives, job methods, plant layout, materials handling, cost reduction, and process engineering. The Manager of Industrial Engineering has long felt that productivity in the administrative offices was significantly below that of the shop. He finally sold the Vice President of Operations and the Sales Manager on letting his staff conduct a preliminary work study in the Sales Department to determine whether more intensive analysis would be fruitful.

Questions:

1.   How should the industrial engineers proceed on the preliminary study?
2.   How can they get the cooperation of the employees?
3.   Would MMM (see page 146) be a useful tool for the analysts to use? Explain.

9

MATERIALS HANDLING

In order to manufacture any product, it is necessary either that materials move from one step of the manufacturing process to another or that operators move to the materials. The most common practice, of course, is to move the materials. This movement of materials from one processing area to another and from department to department necessitates the use of much manpower and equipment and the handling of tremendous tonnages of materials. It has been estimated[1] that one out of ten in the labor force is involved in handling, and, in a specific plant, 50 tons of materials must be handled to produce one ton of finished products.

The handling of materials, which is an integral part of facilities design, has always been an important factor in manufacturing. But only recently has much attention been focused on this problem with a view toward the improvement of equipment and methods and the reduction of manufacturing costs. There has been growing realization of the magnitude of the problem and recognition of the high ratio of materials handling costs to other costs of manufacturing. For example, one survey showed an average of 22 percent of the cost of manufacture was for the handling of materials; other estimates run as high as 60 to 80 percent. This trend may increase as greater degrees of mechanization appear in industry with the resultant decrease in labor cost.

Recently, the materials handling function has been undergoing significant

---

[1]See James M. Apple, *Material Handling Systems Design;* New York: Ronald Press Co., 1972, p. 15.

changes in concept and implementation. Management has been changing its view of materials handling as the routine transfer of materials from place to place and is beginning to think of it as part of a total *materials flow system.* This change in thinking has come about largely as a result of new automatic handling and storage equipment and systems that are integrated closely with automatic processing and sophisticated management information and control systems. Through the installation of such systems, companies are recognizing that they may benefit from economies in production and distribution, space savings, improved shop control, decreased parts shortages, fewer late deliveries, and improved quality. It is not surprising, then, that materials handling is one of the principal areas in which industry's equipment investment is markedly on the increase.

As noted earlier, materials handling is an integral part of facilities design. The most common objective in contemporary facilities design (plant layout) is to develop a layout which has a machine (or department or machining center) configuration that will minimize the sum of the result of multiplying the weights of the materials moved by the distances moved. In other words, manufacturing facilities are designed, for the most part, to minimize the materials handling effort. We have chosen to discuss materials handling prior to the treatment of plant layout (to be covered in Chapter 10) in order to acquaint the reader with background information that will be useful in considering the design of production facilities.

Definition of Materials Handling

In a broad sense, *materials handling* includes all movement of materials in a manufacturing situation. It has been defined by the Materials Handling Division, American Society of Mechanical Engineers as follows: "Materials Handling is the art and science involving the moving, packing, and storing of substances in any form." This is an all-inclusive definition and can include fluids and semi-fluids, as well as discrete items. For the sake of simplicity, we shall limit our discussion in this chapter to the movement of discrete items, such as gears, tires, castings, and boxes. Likewise, we shall consider only the movement of materials within the plant or storage areas. Movement of materials between plants—particularly when common carriers are used—is generally considered a problem in *traffic* and is frequently handled by a separate traffic department.

Based on the somewhat restricted concept that we have established for discussing the subject of materials handling, we shall be concerned only with the storage and movement of goods that have been received by the manufacturer. This will include the handling of materials through various storages and operations from the raw materials state to the final completion stage and shipment of the product. Much of our discussion will revolve around the use of equipment, but we shall also take into consideration *people* as materials handlers.

Although the handling of materials as individual pieces or parts is common practice by the worker at the machine or bench, parts are usually assembled into unit

Figure 9-1. A palletized load of boxes being handled by a lift truck. (Courtesy Eaton Corporation, Industrial Truck Division.)

loads for transport between work stations. *Unit load* refers to tote pans, boxes, pallets, or skids, which are designed to carry more than one part, package, or product at a time. Figure 9-1 illustrates a unit load.

Much has been done in the mechanization of materials handling. As the automatic factory of the future is developed, the time may come when the handling of materials will be so closely integrated with the manufacturing process that the handling and processing of the product will be identified as one activity.

Objectives of Materials Handling

The simplest solution to the materials handling problem—"No movement, no cost"—is hardly practicable for a complete manufacturing process. It is a basically sound approach when one is attempting to improve a complete production cycle and when the number of handlings can be reduced. It is also a good solution in the making of heavy industrial equipment. In this latter situation it is often more feasible to bring the tools and workers to the product than to transport the product to the machine or work area.

In addition to the objective of reducing the overall costs of materials handling by reducing the number of handlings involved, the following may be considered as objectives of the engineer in his approach to this problem:

1. Lower the unit materials handling costs.   It is obvious that if the overall materials handling costs are reduced the unit costs will be reduced. This approach requires the costs of handling be allocated to or identified with the units of product, or its component parts that are moved. In many manufacturing situations this allocation is not too easy. For example, in a plant making many different products, a shop truck may be used to move a load that has 12 tote pans, each pan containing different numbers of different parts. The breakdown of this cost of movement to the cost for each part handled (a unit handling cost) is not practicable. Considerable judgment is required to determine the detail into which materials handling costs are to be analyzed. However, where feasible, a unit-cost analysis may be very effective in determining which handlings involve excessive costs.

2. Reduce the manufacturing-cycle time.   The total time required to make a product from the receipt of raw materials to the finished goods can be reduced through effective materials handling. Movement of materials can be speeded up or handled over shorter distances. Successful reduction of the manufacturing-cycle time will reduce inventory costs and other production costs incident thereto.

3. Contribute toward a better control of the flow of goods.   A principal way in which good materials handling practice can effect savings is by making the control of goods easier—particularly in continuous manufacturing, where all operations are "tied together" by the materials handling plan. In this situation the problem of production control (to be discussed in Chapter 14) is reduced to control at the starting point of the process and to the watching of the rate of flow at selected control points throughout the process. On many assembly lines the conveyor actually controls the rate of output. In intermittent manufacturing, the integration of the materials handling plan with a comprehensive management information and control system can make a great contribution to the control of materials flow.

4. Provide for improved working conditions and greater safety in the movement of materials.   Many of the provisions of the Occupational Safety and Health Act require adherence to safe handling practices. These must be followed. In addition, it is evident that the safe handling of materials will be reflected in a better industrial accident record. This is both a tangible saving in reduced insurance rates and an intangible saving in improved employee morale resulting from safer working conditions.

5. Provide for fewer rejects.   Care in the handling of the product will contribute to a better quality level of the goods produced. Products damaged by inefficient handling are all too often a major cost to manufacturers.

6. Achieve decreased storage requirement. Better movement and storage of materials should increase the utilization of storage space.

7. Gain higher productivity at lower manufacturing cost. Any materials handling system, if it is worth its investment, is designed to improve productivity. This improvement should be achieved by moving materials in the fastest, most efficient and economical way possible.

Principles of Materials Handling

A good materials handling engineer will generally have several years of experience that can be brought to bear on the solution of materials handling problems or the design of materials handling systems. While materials handling analysis is to a large extent an experience-based endeavor, the current increased availability of digital computers makes materials handling analysis susceptible to extensive mathematical analysis. However, where a strong quantitative analysis is not possible, a number of guiding principles have evolved over the years to aid materials handling engineers in solving problems. Like all principles, they need to be applied judiciously and may prove to be more helpful in analysis than in finding solutions to problems.

Over the years, discussions of principles of materials handling have been published by many experts in the field. The following list has been adapted from a number of these sources:[2]

1. Eliminate wasteful methods by:
    a. Reducing to a minimum the number of handlings of materials.
    b. Eliminating unnecessary mixing and subsequent sorting.
    c. Using mechanical aids to eliminate the use of hand labor in movement of materials.
    d. Avoiding the unnecessary transfer of materials from floor to workplace or from container to container.
    e. Increasing the speed of handling.
    f. Utilizing containers and unit loads.
    g. Utilizing gravity as a moving force wherever practicable.
    h. Introducing automaticity into the materials handling plan.

---

[2]See Harry B. Stocker, *Materials Handling,* 2nd ed., Englewood Cliffs, N. J.: Prentice-Hall, Inc., 1951; Gordon B. Carson (ed.), *Production Handbook,* New York: The Ronald Press Company, 1972; The Material Handling Institute, Inc., *An Introduction to Material Handling,* Pittsburgh: 1966; James M. Apple, *Material Handling Systems Design,* New York: The Ronald Press Company, 1972; W. Grant Ireson and Eugene L. Grant (eds.), *Handbook of Industrial Engineering and Management,* 2nd ed., Englewood Cliffs, N. J.: Prentice-Hall, Inc., 1971; James Tompkins and John White, *Facilities Planning,* John Wiley & Sons, 1984; and G. Salvendy, *Handbook of Industrial Engineering,* New York: Wiley Interscience, 1984.

2. In laying out the plant:
   a. Plan a system for materials flow and combine handling with processing wherever possible.
   b. Provide for continuous or appropriate intermittent flow of materials.
   c. Provide for the optimal flow of materials between operations and with a minimum of retrograde movement.
   d. Plan the layout of the work-station area for a minimum of handling of the product.
   e. Maximize the quantity and size of weight handled.
   f. Coordinate the overall materials handling throughout the entire plant.
   g. Provide for safe handling and safe equipment and integrate with the management information and control system.
   h. Plan for adequate receiving, storage, and shipping facilities.
   i. Make optimum use of building cubage.
   j. Design adequate aisle and access areas.
3. In the selection and application of materials handling equipment:
   a. Plan activities and analyze equipment needs before considering the purchase of new equipment.
   b. Insure that the existing equipment is being used effectively.
   c. Use the simplest equipment that is adaptable to the problem; avoid the use of complicated mechanisms and controls.
   d. Adopt standard equipment if possible; insure that the purchase of special equipment is economically justified.
   e. Select equipment that is flexible in its application.
   f. Select equipment that will minimize the ratio of mobile equipment deadweights to pay loads.
   g. Determine comparative costs of equipment before purchasing.
   h. Recognize the need for different equipment for different jobs.
   i. Recognize the need to provide suitable building conditions for the equipment.
   j. Provide for alternative methods for use in emergencies.
   k. Give consideration to the maintenance of the equipment.
   l. Replace obsolete methods and equipment with more efficient ones.

Under certain circumstances the approach to the materials handling problem may be reduced to a checklist. In such cases care should be exercised to insure that the checklist does not become a crutch on which the materials handling personnel lean exclusively. Checklists, although very useful, may tend to limit the ingenuity and creativeness of individuals who are so essential to industrial progress. The ability to approach any problem with an abstract and totally uninhibited attitude is invaluable to the engineer in materials handling, as it is in any other field of activity. An engineer who has several years of experience in the materials handling area is a valuable resource to a firm.

Analysis of Materials Handling Problems

In Chapter 7, we discussed a systematic approach to the solution of methods problems. The same procedure will work equally well in solving materials handling problems. It requires establishing an objective, collecting as much factual data as possible, analyzing the data, applying known principles, and formulating a solution. In collecting the data, careful attention should be given to the effects of handling on the product, the present method, and cost factors.

Too often the materials handling engineer does a superficial job of analyzing the problem and thinks only, "What equipment can be purchased to do this job?" A better approach would be to analyze the problem thoroughly, formulate a solution, and only then give consideration to any equipment that may be required. An approach of this type led one company, a maker of collapsible wire containers, to discover that it could solve most of its materials handling problems by using its own product instead of purchasing outside equipment.

Increasingly, companies are taking advantage of their computer facilities to aid in the planning and designing of materials handling systems. The computer can be used to store and prepare data needed in the planning stages. Further, there has been growing use of simulation to study the behavior of systems under different conditons and under different strategies and to test various alternatives against each other prior to costly implementation. A number of computer languages have been developed (e.g., SLAM, GEMS, SIMAN, GPSS, etc.) which may be used to simulate a variety of different situations. The SIMAN (SIMulation ANalysis)[3] software, for example, contains subroutines that were included specifically to facilitate the inclusion of materials handling equipment (e.g., conveyors, carousels, fork trucks) in the analysis.

General Types of Materials Handling Equipment

A detailed discussion of the many types of materials handling equipment and of the capabilities and characteristics of each is beyond the scope of this book. Such details, however, are important to the engineer developing the materials handling plan for a manufacturing plant. Extensive information covering specifications of various equipment is available, particularly from the materials handling equipment manufacturers.

Inasmuch as there are estimated[4] to be about 570 types of equipment devel-

---

[3]C. D. Pegdon, *Introduction to Siman;* Systems Modeling Corp., State College, Pennsylvania, 1982.

[4]James M. Apple, *Material Handling Systems Design;* New York, Ronald Press, 1972, p. 129.

oped or being developed for the handling of materials, classification may also be quite confusing. Tompkins and White[5] divide materials handling equipment into five classifications. They give the following list but note that numerous variations can exist within each category:

1. conveyors
2. monorails, hoists, and cranes
3. industrial trucks
4. containers and supports
5. auxiliary and other equipment

A less discriminating classification scheme would define materials handling equipment as being of the fixed-path (e.g., conveyor), fixed-area (e.g., crane), or wide-area (e.g., industrial truck) variety. Several examples of materials handling equipment commonly found in industry are shown in Figures 9-2 through 9-4.

Figures 9-5 and 9-6 illustrate specialized installations of materials handling equipment. In selecting equipment, considerable attention should be given to the flexibility of the equipment. The greater the degree of flexibility designed into a piece of materials handling equipment, the easier it is for the planner to integrate the application of the equipment into the manufacturing situation.

As indicated previously, there is a growing trend to use a systems approach in the planning and designing of materials handling systems. Increasingly, microprocessors and minicomputers are being used in all aspects of materials handling. As Hill points out,

> The growth, diversity, and economics of electronics during the past decade [have] had greater impact on the development and composition of the U. S. material handling industry than any other single factor. Low cost circuitry and solid state electronics have fostered the development of a host of new products such as keyboards, terminals, automatic code readers, and real time controllers, while improving existing products through integration of high performance machine controls, maintenance, and diagnostic tools.[6]

Illustrative of this growing use of computers and controls is an innovative system[7] installed in a tractor plant which uses large computer-controlled carriers in assembling the tractors. The system uses wire-guided carriers, called automatic guided vehicles, to move the tractors between assembly bays. The brain of the system is a computer that controls all carrier functions, including the speed, direction of travel,

[5]*Facilities Planning;* New York, John Wiley & Sons, 1984, p. 142.

[6]John M. Hill, "Computers and AS/RS Revolutionize Warehousing," *Industrial Engineering,* Vol. 12, No. 6, June 1980, p. 37.

[7]See "Innovative Assembly Line Uses Computer-Controlled Carriers," *Industrial Engineering,* Vol. 11, No. 5, May 1979, p. 44.

Figure 9-2. A 10-ton floor-controlled overhead crane being used to move coils of steel. (Courtesy Harnischfeger.)

Figure 9-3. Chain-monorail conveyor used to deliver parts to work stations. (Courtesy Richards-Wilcox Manufacturing Company.)

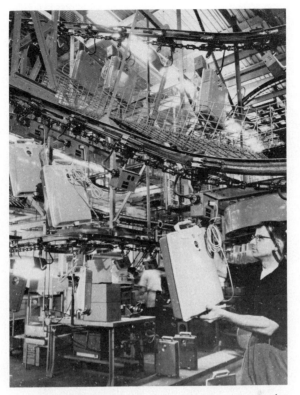

Figure 9-4. Vacuum cleaners being placed on conveyor from the final assembly area. Note that the cleaners are plugged in while being moved. (Courtesy Mechanical Handling Systems Inc.)

and motions of the jacks that lift and lower the tractors on and off stands in the assembly area.

Factors Affecting the Selection of Materials Handling Equipment

The selection of materials handling equipment requires the attaining of proper balance between the production problem, the capabilities of the equipment available, and the human element involved. The ultimate aim is to arrive at the lowest cost per unit of material handled.

The production-problem factors that enter into this consideration are the volume of production to be attained (in terms of the rate of production), the class of materials to be handled, and the layout of the plant and building facilities. The equipment that can be economically justified for the manufacture of 1000 television

Figure 9-5. A high-stacking electrical truck capable of operating in five-foot aisles and stacking one-ton loads thirty feet high. (Courtesy The Raymond Corporation.)

sets a day would be entirely different from the equipment used in a plant manufacturing 20 steam turbine generators a year; in this comparison both the production rate and the weight and class of the materials are different. Likewise, the equipment in a flour mill or food processing factory would present a quite different problem.

It might well be assumed that in the design of a new plant the layout and building facilities could be adapted to the best materials handling plan. However, in

Figure 9-6. Industrial automatic guided vehicle. (Courtesy Clark Equipment Company.)

this most favorable situation some compromise may still have to be made owing to other factors, such as future plant expansion, flexibility of layout, or restrictions that may be placed on the type of building to be constructed. It is obvious that in the case of an existing plant the layout and building facilities affect the selection of materials handling equipment.

Equipment factors to be taken into consideration may well include the following:

1. Adaptability. The load-carrying and movement characteristics of the equipment should fit the materials handling problem.

2. Flexibility. Where possible, the equipment should have flexibility to handle more than one material, referring either to class or size.

3. Load capacity. Equipment selected should have great enough load-carrying characteristics to do the job effectively, yet should not be too large and result in excessive operating costs.

4. Power. Enough power should be available to do the job.

5. Speed. Rapidity of movement of material, within the limits of the production process or plant safety, should be considered.

6. Space requirements.   The space required to install or operate materials handling equipment is an important factor in its selection.

7. Supervision required.   As applied to equipment selection, this refers to the degree of automaticity designed into the equipment.

8. Ease of maintenance.   Equipment selected should be easily maintained at reasonable cost.

9. Environment.   Equipment selected must conform to any environmental regulations.

10. Cost.   The consideration of the cost of the equipment is an obvious factor in its selection.

Figure 9-7 shows an equipment-selection chart applying many of the above factors to specific items of equipment. There are other equipment factors that may enter a problem in materials handling equipment selection. These also may be important, even as the relative importance of the preceding factors is not indicated by the order in which they are listed.

In considering the cost of purchasing new equipment, the materials handling engineer confronts more than the mere purchase price. As pointed out in the discussion in Chapter 6, he faces a problem in engineering economics. He should consider not only the initial purchase price but the direct and indirect labor required in operating the equipment, installation costs, maintenance costs, power requirements, insurance requirements, space requirements, depreciation charges, salvage value, time value of the money invested, and any other costs that can be foreseen. It is obvious that anticipated annual savings should exceed the total annual costs if the investment is to prove to be a sound one. Equipment leasing is an alternative to be considered.

In the selection of equipment for movement of materials on the floor, battery-operated equipment is gaining in popularity. This has come about because of the continuous improvement in batteries, the energy situation, the economics of operation, and environmental considerations. Likewise, robots are becoming increasingly popular, as are systems using driverless tractors and automatic product identification devices.

The human element cannot be overlooked in the selection of materials handling equipment. The consideration of materials handling might bring to mind the laborer who is "all brawn and few brains," but modern materials handling equipment may in some instances require both intelligence and skill for its effective operation. Hence, the capabilities of the available manpower enter into the equipment selection.

Safety of personnel is an important human factor. The equipment selected must result in safe working conditions, must meet all of the requirements of the Occupational Safety and Health Act, and finally, must be accepted by the union and the workers. The eccentricities of labor in this respect must always be anticipated as

MATERIALS HANDLING EQUIPMENT SELECTION CHART

	Materials		Movement			Supervision Required			Path			Speed			Power				Load			Space		
	Bulk	Packaged	Vertical	Horizontal	Combination of Vert. & Horiz.	Close Supervision & Detailed Dispatch	Little Supervision & Detailed Dispatch	Automatic or Semi-Automatic	Completely Variable	Fixed Path	Fixed Area	Variable	Fixed	Either Fixed or Variable	Electricity - Line	Electricity - Bat.	Internal Combustion	Gravity	Unit Load with Limit	Continuous Loading Max. Load per Unit	Fixed Units by Spacing of Carriers	Minimum Width Aisles	Constant Utilization of Fixed Area	No Floor Space
Trucks - Industrial																								
Manual																								
4 wheeled platform	X	X		X		X			X			X			manual power				X			X		
2 wheeled platform	X	X		X		X			X			X			manual power				X			X		
2 wheeled special (barrel, etc.)		X		X		X			X			X			manual power				X			X		
Dollies		X		X		X			X			X			manual power				X			X		
Pallet Lift		X		X		X			X			X			manual power				X			X		
Powered																								
Driver-walk																								
Pallet Lift		X		X		X			X			X			X	X			X			X		
Platform		X		X		X			X			X			X	X			X			X		
High Lift Fork	X[1]	X	X	X	X	X			X			X			X	X			X			X		
Driver-ride																								
Pallet Lift		X		X		X			X			X			X	X			X			X		
Platform		X		X		X			X			X			X	X			X			X		
Low Lift Platform	X[1]	X		X		X			X			X			X	X			X			X		
High Lift Platform	X[1]	X	X	X	X	X			X			X			X	X			X			X		
Telescoping Fork Lift	X[1]	X	X	X	X	X			X			X			X	X			X			X		
Tractors and Trailers																								
Industrial Tractor																								
3 wheeled																								
4 wheeled																								
Industrial Trailer																								
According to wheel arrangement	X[1]	X		X		X			X			X				X	X					X	X	
Cranes, Hoists, and Monorails																								
Crane																								
Overhead bridge, travelling	X[1]	X		X	X						X			X	X				X					X
Gantry	X[1]	X		X	X						X			X	X				X					X
Jib		X		X	X						X			X	X				X					X
Hoists																								
Chain, manual	X[1]	X	X			X					X	X			manual power				X					X
Elec. motor drive	X	X	X			X					X	X			X				X					X
Pneumatic	X	X	X			X					X	X			X				X					X
Monorail																								
Carrier	X[1]	X		X	X		X		X						X				X				X	
Trolley		X		X	X				X						X						X		X	
Chain Trolley		X		X	X		X		X						X						X	X	X	
Conveyors																								
Roller, Gravity																								
Spiral		X	X		X			X	X			X						X	X					X
Portable		X		X	X			X	X			X						X	X					X
Fixed		X		X	X			X	X			X						X	X					X
Roller, Live																								
Chain Drive		X		X	X			X	X						X	X			X					X
Belt Drive		X		X	X			X	X						X	X			X					X
Wheel, Gravity																								
Portable		X		X	X			X	X			X						X	X					X
Fixed		X		X	X			X	X			X						X	X					X
Belt																								
Flat	X	X	X	X	X			X	X			X			X	X	X		X					X
Troughed	X		X	X	X			X	X			X			X	X	X		X					X
Portable	X	X	X	X	X			X	X			X			X	X	X		X					X
Fixed	X	X	X	X	X			X	X			X			X	X	X		X					X
Drag																								
Pusher Bar	X		X	X	X			X	X				X		X				X					X
Screw	X			X	X			X	X				X		X				X			X	X	X
Floor Chain	X[1]	X		X	X		X		X				X		X						X	X	X	
Overhead Chain	X[1]	X		X	X		X		X				X		X						X	X	X	X
Apron																								
Wood Slat	X	X	X	X	X			X	X			X			X	X	X		X					X
Steel Slat	X	X	X	X	X			X	X			X			X	X	X		X					X
Ball Transfer		X		X	X	X			X			X	X		manual power				X					X
Bucket Conveyor	X		X		X				X				X		X					X				X
Continuous Chain Trolley	X[1]	X		X	X		X		X				X	X	X						X			X
Slides and Chutes																								
Spiral or Straight																								
Wood	X	X	X		X			X	X			X						X	X					X
Steel	X	X	X		X			X	X			X						X	X					X
Vibrating	X		X	X			X	X	X			X		X	X				X					X
Pneumatic Systems																								
Rigid Tube and Nozzle																								
Bulk loaders	X			X	X				X			X			X					X				X
Bulk unloaders	X			X	X				X			X			X					X				X
Rigid Tube																								
Cylindrical Carrier		X		X	X				X			X			X				X					X
Oval Carrier		X		X	X				X			X			X				X					X
Elevators																								
Freight																								
Electric	X[1]	X	X			X			X			X			X				X				X	
Hand	X[1]	X	X			X			X		X		X		manual power				X				X	
Hydraulic	X[1]	X	X			X			X				X		X				X				X	
Dumb waiter	X		X																					
Continuous Lifts																								
Arm		X	X				X	X	X			X			X						X		X	
Tray		X	X				X	X	X			X			X						X		X	

(1) with scoop, bucket, etc.

Figure 9-7. Equipment selection chart. (From W. G. Ireson and Eugene L. Grant, *Handbook of Industrial Engineering and Management;* Englewood Cliffs, N. J.: Prentice-Hall, Inc., 1971. Reprinted by permission.)

closely as possible and steps taken to "sell" the new equipment to those who will operate or come into contact with it. This is an area where participative management and the use of *methods circles* will be of great importance.

Accounting for Materials Handling Costs

The cost of materials handling arises from two sources: the cost of owning and maintaining equipment and the cost of operating the system. General cost-accounting practice classifies the cost of handling materials as an indirect cost or overhead. This classification is based on the position that the movement of the materials does not contribute to their physical change or add value to them as a product or as a component part thereof. In some manufacturing situations, such as a carbon black plant where the material is constantly moving during the production process, this contention of the cost accountants might be challenged. However, the problem of classification of unit handling costs in most situations is more of an academic than a practical nature. In many instances the clerical costs to determine unit materials handling costs, either to apply them as a direct cost value or to use them as standard costs for the control of the operations, may exceed any savings that might be effected through such control or analysis.

Furthermore, as discussed above, the determination of a unit handling cost is at times quite difficult. But as the rate of production or flow of material is increased, and the different types or kinds of part and product are reduced, it becomes much easier to determine and allocate materials handling unit costs accurately. When feasible, costs should be determined on a unit cost basis for the proper evaluation of the materials handling problem. Such analyses will indicate those costs that are excessive, thus pointing out those areas where improvement of the materials handling system may pay the greatest dividends.

In any case, the expense of accumulating and determining unit costs must be justified through the use of such costs as a continuing control and guide for the reduction of the expense of handling materials.

It is evident that the current trend toward integrating materials handling with the actual operations required in the processing of the product will result in losing the identity of materials handling costs as such—these costs being included in the direct labor or machine costs for the manufacture of the goods.

Relation of Materials Handling to Flow of Material and Plant Layout

The pattern of flow of materials in a plant definitely affects the materials handling costs. The production process should be so planned and the machines and benches so arranged that the handlings of materials are reduced to a minimum with as little backtracking of goods as possible. The type of manufacturing is a major factor in this respect.

In the layout of a plant for continuous manufacture the pattern of flow is planned well in advance; because of balanced machine and assembly lines, it lends itself to a well-planned flow of component parts, subassemblies, and assemblies. This makes it possible to plan the handling of materials in advance, procure and install the best equipment for the job, and design for a minimum materials handling cost. However, once installed, the plan lacks flexibility—usually it cannot be changed without major expense.

The layout of a plant for intermittent manufacture may be much more flexible. Backtracking of materials should be minimized, but the nature of this type of layout makes this a more difficult problem to solve. Equipment selected will in most cases be more general purpose in nature, and as a result it may be changed for improved materials handling methods without incurring major expense. A further discussion will be included in Chapter 10.

The use of flow process charts is most helpful in planning processes and identifying the materials handling elements. This technique of methods analysis can be used not only as a designing tool but also for critical analysis of existing movements and handlings of materials. Instructional literature and forms are prepared by equipment manufacturers to assist their prospective customers in analyzing their materials handling problems.

In the same manner that good flow of materials should be planned for the plant layout as a whole, the layout of each work station—each machine location or workbench—should be carefully planned to insure the minimum handling of materials by the most effective means. As has been previously pointed out, this activity is really a part of operations analysis of the work to be done and the equipment to be used. Processing and materials handling must be closely coordinated for best results.

Another important materials handling factor in plant layout is the space required by the equipment to be used for moving goods. Factory trucks require certain turning radii, floor and overhead conveyors require space for installation, and cranes and hoists must be carefully laid out in the factory plan for maximum utilization. Note again Figure 9-5, where a narrow-aisle material stacking truck enabled the construction of storage facilities which utilize less factory space than standard-size stacking devices would require. Further, it should be noted that the Occupational Safety and Health Act imposes quite rigid regulations on aisle widths, conveyor guarding, overhead clearances, and similar safety requirements. All of this presents to the engineer a problem in compromising between building availability and the space requirements of the materials handling equipment to be used. It is seldom that the materials handling equipment can be planned first and the building planned around the equipment. Of course, the possible modification of the building structure or layout must be considered when contemplating a change for the improvement of materials handling methods by the adoption of new equipment.

On assembly lines that involve manual labor, the length of the line to be planned depends on attaining a proper balance between the work to be done by each assembler and the speed at which the line is to be operated. The work station for each man or woman on the line must be planned; the sum total of these stations affects both the floor space required and the design of the conveyor.

It is obvious that with the current trend towards automation the entire problem of space requirements for materials handling equipment will be gradually integrated with the processing-space requirements. As a matter of fact, such integration exists today in large automobile factories and in plants producing large volumes of household appliances.

Storage

Material in storage is generally thought to be stationary or idle. But the use of conveyors as storage devices is quite popular. These conveyors may be overhead and constantly moving, yet utilizing ceiling-space storage. Such an installation is pictured in Figure 9-8. Other storage installations may be like the skate conveyors shown in Figure 9-9b. In one midwestern furniture plant the complete floor of the

Figure 9-8. Overhead storage conveyors. (Courtesy General Electric Company.)

Figure 9-9a. View of control console in automatic warehouse. The operator at the console can determine the conditions at the truck dock by noting the light panel above the belt conveyor. To complete an order, he inserts a "begin order" punched card in a card reader on the console. (Courtesy The Alvey-Ferguson Company.)

Figure 9-9b. View of automatic warehouse showing automatic pick racks. Cartons are released from these racks onto the belt conveyor. (Courtesy The Alvey-Ferguson Company.)

Figure 9-9c. View of automatic warehouse showing the merging point where the belt conveyors serving the automatic pick racks are brought together in a single line. (Courtesy The Alvey-Ferguson Company.)

Figure 9-9d. View of automatic warehouse showing truck dock area. Five feeder lines convey assembled orders to preselected docks, and each feeder line serves either of two adjacent docks. (Courtesy The Alvey-Ferguson Company.)

finish drying room is covered by a large slat conveyor that moves very slowly; pieces placed on this "floor" at one side of the room are dry when they reach the other side.

Storage facilities and plants are also closely related to the unit loading plan for the product. It is very common to make use of high-rise storage racks as illustrated in Figure 9-5. Permanent racks and bins may be eliminated in a warehouse if goods are palletized in such a manner that the pallets can be stacked, or if the product is so packaged that the package can be used as a stacking unit (see Figure 9-10). Stackable tote boxes and bins also make the utilization of storage space quite flexible.

In order to make maximum use of cubage, high-rise, rack-supported, totally dedicated buildings are increasing in favor. In these buildings, the racks support both the roof and the sidewalls, and this greatly decreases the cost.

Increasing interest in the automation of storage warehouses is taking place

Figure 9-10. Modern industrial fork truck. (Courtesy Clark Equipment Company.)

Figure 9-11. An automatic warehouse system. (Courtesy Hartman Engineering Manu-facturing.)

(see Figures 9-9a, b, c, d). One such warehouse[8] constructed in the midwest handles cartons of toilet articles in a broad range of sizes and varieties. It can fill up to 800 average orders per day in a normal 8-hour shift. Up to 90 different items can be picked automatically from special racks and merged with previously hand-picked, low-demand items at speeds up to 400 fpm. An order assembled in this manner can be routed automatically to any of five truck dock feeder lines in less than a minute. The five feeder lines can receive and/or accumulate orders simultaneously.

One of the interesting developments recently has been the installation of what might be referred to as a "warehouse machine" as illustrated in Figure 9-11. This is an automatic warehousing system that permits unit loads of materials to be automatically moved into or out of storage by a series of conveyors and stacker–retriever devices operating between the stacks. The entire system can be operated by one person, who can control the warehouse from a remote or computer control room.

[8]See "Punched Cards Control Carton Order Picking," *Automation*, June 1963.

It is evident that materials handling and storage problems can be jointly solved to the mutual advantage of both functions. Likewise, the common solution directly affects the layout of the plant facilities, or is itself influenced by the existing floor plan and building construction.

Packaging

Whether packaging is or is not a phase of materials handling is to some degree an academic question. The unit load is in itself a "package." Generally speaking, however, the term *packaging* is used to cover the preparation of the final product for shipment, particularly if the product is a consumer good.

From the viewpoint of a materials handling problem, packaging of the incoming materials as well as of the outgoing product directly affects materials handling methods and equipment—and the resultant materials handling costs. The designing of the package for a product, although usually identified as a separate activity or function, is closely interrelated with materials handling, methods of production, and marketing. Attractively packaged goods on the shelves and counters of the store, as well as the identification of large shipments on trucks and railroad cars, are effective advertising and sales promotion.

The package of today is a far cry from the crate and box formerly used for shipment. Lumber may now be shipped in palletized loads instead of being piled in a boxcar wherein each individual board must be handled when unloading. Furniture, which used to be carefully enclosed in wooden crates—the cost of which often equaled the value of the product being crated—is now boxed in fiberboard cartons. Delicate precision instruments that formerly required cushioned containers are now suspended in plastic envelopes in rigid boxes. These are just a few examples of the fairly recent improvements in the field of packaging.

Modern packages are also designed for efficient storage, not only from the standpoint of rigidity for stacking, but also for effective protection of the product from deterioration. The use of plastics, particularly in the packaging of foods, has contributed to the latter objective of sound packaging.

Mechanization has had important influence on the field of packaging. This is particularly true in the food processing industry, where special machinery has been developed that provides for the handling and packaging of the product without the use of the human hand. Looking into the future, a large manufacturer of electric refrigerators is now packaging the complete unit in a large fiberboard container on a completely automatic machine. In this case it is particularly interesting to note that the first step in this development was the redesign of the package. This first step was put into effect in the shipping room in advance of the availability of the special machine; and with the use of manual labor it still resulted in outstanding savings.

Thus, the package in which the material is handled is an important part of the total materials handling problem in a manufacturing situation.

Organization for Effective Materials Handling

Good materials handling practice is the responsibility of all members of the manufacturing team, from the top management down to the trucker working in the aisle
of the plant. Very few other elements of manufacturing activity must be so carefully
considered by each function in the manufacturing organization. Optimum effectiveness of materials handling procedures can only be attained if each individual
recognizes and plays his part. Education and training in materials handling are prerequisite to minimum materials handling costs.

Although the responsibilities and duties involved in materials handling must
of necessity become a part of each individual's job, the coordination of the total
materials handling problem can be assigned to one individual or group. Large manufacturing organizations can well afford to organize specialists in materials handling
into one of the staff or advisory groups reporting to the manager of manufacturing.

Responsibilities assigned such a staff group may well include:

1. Determining all new methods for the handling of new materials or
   products and selecting the equipment to be utilized.
2. Conducting research in materials handling methods and equipment.
3. Conducting education and training for all manufacturing personnel in
   good materials handling practices.
4. Establishing controls of current materials handling costs by analysis of
   costs and comparison to budgets of either unit or total materials
   handling costs.
5. Initiating and conducting a continuing materials handling cost-
   reduction or cost-improvement program.
6. Determining measurements for effectiveness of materials handling that
   can become the yardsticks for progress in this activity.
7. Developing and conducting a preventive maintenance program for all
   materials handling equipment.

Each of the above activities will contribute to lower materials handling costs.
In smaller plants these responsibilities must be assumed as part-time jobs by members of the manufacturing line organization. However, maximum effectiveness
might be attained by assigning the principal coordinating responsibility for all materials handling activities to one individual or to a committee of several from the manufacturing group.

QUESTIONS

1. Make a list of the materials handling devices that you might find in a modern home.
   Can any of these be improved? Are there any other new devices that might be feasible?
2. Discuss the need for standardizing wooden pallets (such as that illustrated in Figure
   9-1).
3. What benefits may result from planning a system for materials handling?

4. In what ways has the large, modern supermarket improved materials handling as compared to the small neighborhood grocery?

5. A large manufacturer of bulbs for flashlights is now shipping them in bulk, that is, loose in cartons of 500 to 1000. Make a list of the cost factors that were considered in the adoption of this method of packaging and shipping.

6. Outline instances where product handling and processing either are combined or (as you see it) could be combined.

7. Should materials handling labor cost be a direct cost or an indirect one? Give reasons.

8. Do you see any particular role for the purchasing department to play in reducing materials handling costs?

9. To what extent does low materials handling cost depend upon efficient materials handling equipment?

10. Discuss the benefits that can be gained from using simulation in planning materials handling systems.

11. What type of package would you suggest for a clock radio that measures 10'' x 8'' x 5''? Defend your selection.

12. List the reasons for considering plant layout at the same time materials handling requirements are determined.

CASE PROBLEMS

Grover Cotton Mills

Grover Cotton Mills in Atlanta is a large producer of denim fabric. The company has long recognized that its handling and storing of baled denim is inefficient but has found the problem difficult to solve.

The large steel-strapped bales of denim are hauled from the end of the production line to the finished goods warehouse by means of two-wheeled hand trucks. Because of their weight, the bales are usually placed on the floor or, at best, stacked two high. This has resulted in little usage of the cubage in the warehouse and excessive warehousing costs.

Grover's warehouse is a long (300 ft.), narrow (60 ft.) building with an arched-truss roof. The height is 22 feet in the center and about 12 feet along the walls. All material feeds into the warehouse from one side and out one end.

An increase in production has led to increased need for warehouse space, but the general manager refuses to authorize the building or renting of additional space. His contention is that adequate space is available if used efficiently. He has requested that the industrial engineering department analyze the warehouse situation and make recommendations for increasing its utilization.

Questions:

1. What recommendations should be made for improving the use of the warehouse?
2. Can manual handling be reduced? How?
3. Should new equipment be purchased? Why?
4. If new equipment is purchased, what is a reasonable time period in which to repay the investment?

Acme Closure Company

The Acme Closure Company is one of the country's largest producers of metal closures for glass bottles.

The high-speed machines used by Acme enable it to meet its production demands, but have created a materials handling problem. This problem arises from the necessity to handle, move, and store the tremendous daily output of a battery of screw cap machines. Some of the machines turn out as many as 100,000 screw cap shells per hour. These must be moved either to a final manufacturing operation on a lower floor or to a storage area for future use.

James Elrod, the materials handling engineer, worked on the above problem for several weeks and has recommended that special box-type (30" x 48 " x 36") trucks be purchased. These trucks come equipped with casters and can be easily moved by hand. A special feature of these trucks is a hinged door, which opens when the box is tilted forward. This would allow the caps to slide out and down a chute to the floor below, where final manufacturing is completed.

James Elrod has also recommended the purchase of storage racks on which the trucks can be stored in the storage area. By means of a fork-lift truck, the box trucks can be stored three trucks high.

Questions:

1. Do you consider James Elrod's recommendation a good one? Why?
2. What other possibilities appear as feasible solutions to this problem?
3. In considering solutions to problems such as this, where would you secure further information?

Kay Marie Cosmetic Company

John Bobson, the production manager of Kay Marie Cosmetics, has noticed that during the past eighteen months there has been an increasing number of problems associated with lost material, lack of storage space for incoming raw materials and completed products awaiting shipping, and general clutter of work in-process materials on the shop floor. These problems have been manifested in delayed deliveries to customers, idle processes and workers, and lack of space for the increased production which the marketing department requested for several product lines that are currently selling well.

Mr. Bobson recently attended a regional meeting of the production management society to which he belongs, and one of the talks he heard had the title "Utilize Your Storage Cube!". At the talk, Mr. Bobson found out that the goal of utilizing a storage cube is to plan your storage areas such that materials are stored (stacked) high and dense. This arrangement will enable more material to be stored in a given area. Mr. Bobson noticed that the Kay Marie Co. did not store their materials very high at all. He asked Tom Rexson, manager of industrial engineering, to look into the problem. He suggested that he speak with a vendor of storage racks to get advice on the type of racks that would be good for the type of materials that would be stored.

Questions:

1. If Kay Marie now has standard lift trucks, what advantage might they realize if Mr. Bobson considers the use of narrow-aisle fork trucks for the new storage area?
2. Discuss the implications of one centralized storage area vs. several decentralized storage areas at Kay Marie.
3. Discuss the concept of manual vs. automatic materials handling in a high-rise, dense storage environment.
4. What might be the utility of conveyors in a storage environment such as this?

10

PHYSICAL FACILITIES

The many manufacturing establishments that dot our countryside are not something that spring up overnight, but represent the culmination of many man-hours of planning. Countless decisions, such as the products to be made in the plant, the equipment required, the type of structure needed, and the location of the plant, had to be made before the ground could be broken to build the plant. In this chapter we shall be giving consideration to the various problems associated with the location and design of the physical facilities for manufacturing concerns.

Plant Location

The immensity of the plant-location problem is attested to by the fact that billions of dollars are spent each year on new manufacturing buildings in the United States, not to mention the ever increasing investment in foreign subsidiaries. For each of these plants, someone had to make a decision as to where to put it, and many plants have ended up in somewhat surprising locations. Indeed, the widespread dispersion of our factories has done much to alter the industrial landscape. Examples of this can be seen in the recent decisions of General Motors to locate their Saturn auto assembly plant in Tennessee, the Chrysler Mitsubishi consortium to locate their new auto assembly plant in the Bloomington–Normal area of Illinois, and Toyota to locate its new plant in Kentucky.

Three situations require an answer to the question of plant location: (1) a new plant just being started, (2) a new branch of an existing plant, or (3) a new location for an existing plant.

Analysis of the reasons why many companies were started in their present locations will reveal that they were located in the community that was the home of the founder. For example, one of the country's leading fountain pen companies was started in a Midwest city because the founder owned a jewelry store in that community, and a prominent pharmaceutical company was started in its present location by a former druggist in that city. These and countless other examples lead us to believe that, in general, the exact location of an existing industrial plant is probably not too important. On the other hand, locating a new plant or a branch in a suitable place is significant because factory organizations tend to be quite immobile and, once established in a community, will tend to remain there. Then too, where a plant is located may have considerable influence on operating costs and profits. For these reasons, the location of a plant necessitates thorough analysis.

Location Planning

Before a location for a plant is sought, long-range forecasts should be made anticipating the future needs of the company. These should be based upon the company's expansion policy, the anticipated diversification of products, the changing market, the changing source of raw materials, and any other foreseeable influences. Careful attention should be given to all the economic factors that influence the need for the new plant and the size and location of the plant.

The selection of an appropriate plant location usually results from a three-step process involving, first, the region (e.g., Pacific Coast, New England, Midwest, Southeast, or Southwest) in which the factory should be situated; second, the community in which it should be placed; and, finally, the exact site in the city or countryside. The location study is frequently performed by a special committee composed of representatives from such groups as manufacturing, industrial engineering, industrial relations, product engineering, public relations, and other groups as may be necessary within the organization, although it is not uncommon to use an outside consulting firm that specializes in location studies. The purpose of the location study is to find an optimum location—one that will result in the greatest advantage to the organization.

One large company follows seven basic steps in locating and building every new plant:

1. Establish the need for a new plant.
2. Determine the best geographical area for the plant on the basis of the company's business needs.
3. Establish the requirements, i.e., product to be made, equipment and buildings needed, utilities and transportation necessary, number of employees, etc.

4. Screen many communities within the general area decided on.
5. Pinpoint a few communities for detailed studies.
6. Select the best location.
7. Build the plant.

The benefits to be gained from the relocation of an existing plant may best be shown by the example illustrated in Figure 10–1. These figures were compiled by an office-equipment manufacturer in an eastern city. This company was planning to expand in its existing location but found that big savings could be achieved with a new plant located in any of four sites in the Midwest. Note the significant savings estimated at Site A.

	Present Factory in East	Site A Midwest	Site B Midwest	Site C Midwest	Site D Midwest
Labor	$13,106,000	$11,054,000	$11,548,000	$11,934,000	$12,092,000
Overhead (Including local taxes)	1,190,000	618,000	602,000	636,000	662,000
Freight costs	507,000	432,000	366,000	360,000	338,000
Utilities	204,000	248,000	214,000	236,000	246,000
Total	$15,007,000	$12,352,000	$12,730,000	$13,166,000	$13,338,000
Estimated yearly savings at new plant:		$ 2,655,000	$ 2,277,000	$ 1,841,000	$ 1,669,000
Savings as per cent of costs at present factory:		17.7%	15.2%	12.3%	11.1%

Figure 10-1. Comparison of costs of operating an office-equipment manufacturing plant in an eastern city and in four sites in the midwest.

Factors Influencing Location

If one were to conduct a survey on why companies have chosen their present plant locations, many reasons would be cited: proximity to a good highway network, abundant labor supply, proximity to markets, adequate water supply, and so on. How important each factor is will vary from one company to another. Figure 10–2 contains a summary of those factors that are commonly considered in selecting the general region, the community, and the exact site.

Since, as is illustrated in Figure 10–2, several of the factors have a bearing on both the region and the community in which the plant is to be located, we shall discuss these without regard to which of the two is under consideration.

Factors	Region	Community	Site
Proximity to good highways	×	×	×
Labor supply	×	×	
Nearness to market	×		
Nearness to raw materials	×		
Nearness to an existing plant	×	×	
Suitable land and land costs		×	
Transportation	×	×	
Water supply	×	×	
Power supply	×	×	
Pollution control		×	
Taxes		×	
Climate	×		
National defense	×		
Community administration and attitude		×	
Schools, churches, and residential areas		×	
Zoning restrictions......................		×	×
Space for expansion			×

Figure 10-2. Factors commonly considered in locating a plant. Note that some of them are important in selecting both the region and the community.

Proximity to good highways. In one survey of 4100 firms, the most frequent factor that prompted the companies to build where they did was the quality of the highway system, particularly its relationship to markets, raw materials, and labor supply. The existence of excellent highways, such as the interstate superhighways, makes the suburbs, small communities, and country as readily accessible as the cities.

Labor supply. Obviously, a company can't operate without employees, and the nature of the labor market should be investigated to insure that an adequate supply of qualified employees is available in the area. It is necessary in some organizations that skilled craftsmen be hired to fill many of the positions, and it is desirable to locate the plant in an area where a sufficient number are available.

The level of wages paid the workers in a community is a vital factor for those companies whose labor costs represent a high percentage of the manufacturing cost. Also, the productivity level attained by the workers and the history of labor relations in the community are being given increasingly serious consideration. It has been particularly noteworthy in recent years to observe the large number of light industries that have moved into small communities where they could get the advantage of rural labor at lower hourly rates and higher productivity.

An interesting development that has begun to take place in some metropolitan areas (e.g., Chicago) is that an abundant labor supply cannot always be taken for granted in the suburbs. In addition, a factor that companies must take into account is the government requirements for "affirmative action" on minority hiring and the fact that the largest number of the minority population live in the central city—not in the suburbs.

Nearness to market. The cost of and time required for transporting the product to the customer is a major consideration for many companies. For this reason, it is desirable that the company be located near the center of its market. This is particularly true when the manufacturing process increases the bulk of the products. Examples are the automobile assembly plants situated in various parts of the country and the regional tire plants built by the major rubber companies.

When locations are chosen for branch plants, the market to be served may be the determining factor. For example, a branch plant of a California shoe company was located in Ohio in order to be nearer the midwestern, eastern, and southeastern market for ladies' shoes. Other examples include the many cement, brick, roofing, and gypsum board plants scattered across the United States.

If a plant has already been established in some community, its present location may tend to restrict its market to the area in which it is located. But for those companies producing items such as fountain pens, jewelry, and watches, in which the costs of materials and labor are high, shipping costs are of secondary importance, and the location of the plant with reference to its market is not too important.

Nearness to raw materials. Companies using bulky or perishable materials find it desirable to be near a readily available source of their materials. The food industry has this problem with its canning factories, meatpacking plants, and creameries. Other examples include steel mills, sawmills, papermills, and cement manufacturers. In these industries, the guiding principle is what the economists refer to as "weight losing." If the raw material loses a lot of weight in processing, then the plant should be located near the source of raw materials.

The relative cost of transporting raw materials must be weighed against the cost of shipping the finished product so that, ideally, the plant may be situated in that location where the costs are at a minimum. This is sometimes referred to as "weight balancing" and involves the reaching of a low-cost equilibrium between the costs of shipping raw materials and fuels and that of shipping the product to the market. The two factors of "weight losing" and "weight balancing" govern nearly all plant locations in the extractive industries. The steel industry, a prime example, has tended to locate near the coal supply because this is near the major markets for steel. Thus, the Fairless Works of U.S. Steel was located near Morrisville, Pennsylvania, where it can receive coal from Pennsylvania or West Virginia and iron ore by ship, and where it is closer to the New York market than one of its competitors, Bethlehem Steel Company.

A company may find it desirable to be near another plant for which it is manufacturing component parts, shipping crates, or similar items. This reduces the transportation time and cost and facilitates coordination between the two plants.

Nearness to an existing plant.   Oftentimes, one of the principal factors in the location of a new branch plant is that of keeping it reasonably close to the parent plant. The National Industrial Conference Board found in a survey of 476 new plant locations that the sites were chosen in 42 percent of the cases because they were near an existing plant or warehouse. That so high a percentage would select sites for this reason indicates its importance. For many companies it is important that new plants be located in an area where executive supervision and staff consultations will be facilitated. This, of course, conserves the executive's time and allows closer supervision of those activities under his or her jurisdiction.

In considering nearby communities, caution should be exercised to insure that the plants do not compete in the same labor market.

Availability of land and land costs.   The cost of land is usually a minor factor in the choice of a location. However, the availability of an adequate site sometimes presents a problem. In communities that are interested in attracting new industries, land may be offered at a considerably reduced price or at no cost, and this may influence some companies to locate there. However, a company should not be misled into accepting a site that might later prove to be a serious handicap.

Transportation.   The company should be located in an area where adequate transportation facilities of the desired type are available. Some companies find it desirable to be located at an ocean port or on the inland waterways to take advantage of the lower cost of transporting materials by boat or barge. This is particularly true for bulk materials such as coal, iron ore, and petroleum products. For other companies, access to railroad and/or trucking facilities is adequate.

The costs of shipping the product or bringing in raw materials are significant factors for many companies, and the reduced freight rates available in some areas should be weighed against other operating costs to determine the predominant consideration.

Water supply.   For those companies requiring large quantities of water in processing their products, the water supply must be given serious attention in choosing a plant location. This was a major consideration in locating a plant of a pharmaceutical company requiring tremendous quantities of water. The underground supply of water is gradually being depleted in some areas and presents a matter of critical importance to the companies already situated there. In some cases, it may force these companies to relocate their plants.

Consideration should be given to any pollution of the water, which might cause processing difficulties. Although the federal government and most states have antipollution laws, the waste materials dumped into the rivers or streams may create problems for new companies requiring a supply of fresh, pure water.

Power supply.   Every company has need for electric power, but only to those companies using tremendous quantities is this item of major importance in choosing the plant site. An adequate supply of power at low rates is available in most areas; seldom is it necessary for the company to develop its own. However, some companies prefer to maintain a power station in a standby condition to take care of any emergencies that may arise.

Pollution control.   During recent years, there has been a wave of public sentiment in regard to pollution control. This led to the establishment of the Federal Environmental Protection Agency and the setting of deadlines on air and water controls to protect the public health. The combination of new laws and social pressure has had great impact on many companies—particularly the heavily polluting industries (e.g., public utilities, steel, oil, paper, chemicals). As pointed out in Chapter 1, industry has been forced to invest tremendous sums in air pollution and waste disposal equipment. Thus, it becomes evident that those companies that may have air pollution or waste disposal problems must give major consideration to locating new plants on sites that will enable them to meet all legislative restrictions.

Taxes.   The kinds and amounts of taxes levied by a state or community should be considered in locating a plant. Taxes become one of the operating costs; the kinds of taxes and the basis for fixing them should be thoroughly investigated. As an enticement to get plants to locate there, some states and territories (particularly Puerto Rico) offer companies tax exemptions for a stipulated period of time. This has influenced many companies to locate in these areas.

Climate.   Seldom does the climate influence the location of a plant. In those companies requiring controlled temperature, humidity, and ventilation, it is possible to install equipment to maintain the required conditions.

Sometimes the personal preferences of the company executives, who will be working in the plant, influence the location of a plant in a particular climate: for example, in the early 1980's there was a trend toward locating plants in southwestern United States.

Community administration and attitude.   Since all industries have a social responsibility to the communities in which they are located, it is important that the local authorities and the populace of the community be eager to have the plant located there. Likewise, it is essential that the community be able to provide the necessary municipal services in the way of police and fire protection, maintenance of streets, refuse disposal, and so forth.

Schools, churches, parks, and residential areas.   Finding the best town for a new plant is not solely an impersonal search for lowest transportation costs, low tax rates, and an adequate water supply, but is also a search for a community in which the employees will have excellent schools, churches, parks, and residential areas available to them. Since every new plant affects a number of employees and their families, many companies feel that it makes good sense to pick a town which will provide good services and a pleasant atmosphere for their employees.

Local Sites

After the community for a plant has been selected, the problem still exists of selecting the exact site on which the plant is to be built. The final choice of site will usually result from considering the relative merits of each of the available sites.

In weighing these sites against one another, the following questions should be asked about each of the factors that should be considered:

Transportation facilities.   Is the location easily accessible to the main highways? Are the railroad facilities adequate to insure prompt receipt and shipment of goods? Can a railroad siding be made available?

Availability of water, electric power, gas, and sewers.   Is water available in sufficient quantities? Is adequate electric power available? Is adequate gas available? Is the sewer system adequate to take care of the plant's needs?

Zoning restrictions.   Will the zoning restrictions interfere with the company's building plans or operations?

Soil characteristics.   Are the soil bearing characteristics suitable for supporting the building and equipment? Will the soil provide adequate drainage?

Drainage.   Will the area drain away all surface water so that the buildings will not become an island in the middle of a flooded area?

Parking areas.   Is adequate space available to provide for employee and visitor parking?

Space for expansion.   Is sufficient space available to take care of expansion of the plant within the foreseeable future?

Accessibility by workers.   Can the site be reached by public transportation? Is the road and street network leading to the site adequate to allow speedy entrance and exit of employees during rush periods?

Cost of land.   Can the site be secured at a reasonable price?

Existing buildings.   Are existing buildings available that might be suitable for the company's operation, and can they be rented or purchased at reasonable prices?

Sources of Information

There are a number of excellent sources of information pertaining to plant locations. These include the United States Department of Commerce, state industrial development groups, state employment agencies, railroad promotion departments, power companies, city industrial development areas, and chambers of commerce. Brief information about different states and communities is contained in advertisements sponsored by these agencies in many of the leading magazines and newspapers. Complete facts and figures about the growth of the area, availability of labor, transportation facilities, wage levels, and similar information can be obtained from one or more of these groups.

Evaluation of Plant Locations

It is very difficult to make a final decision as to the choice for a plant location. One location may have the advantage from a market standpoint, another may be closer to the materials supply, and a third may provide a better labor supply. In attempting to weigh these and other factors against one another, two methods are commonly used: *rating plans* and *cost analyses*.

Rating plan.   In the rating plan, weights are assigned to each of the factors that should be considered. The factor deemed most important is given the highest weight (see Figure 10–3) and each of the other factors a lesser amount. For example, nearness to raw materials might be weighted at 400 points, nearness to market at 300, the labor supply at 275, and the other factors at lesser amounts. The total

Factor	Maximum Possible Points	Location City A	City B	City C
Nearness to raw materials	400	300	250	150
Nearness to market	300	150	200	250
Labor supply	275	150	225	175
Transportation	125	125	100	125
Water supply	200	100	150	175
Power	200	150	150	100
Waste disposal	100	50	75	75
Land and construction costs	70	60	50	50
Climate	40	35	25	40
Taxes and laws	40	35	25	40
Local site	40	40	30	35
Total	1800	1185	1295	1210

Figure 10-3.   Rating chart for three alternative plant locations.

Costs	Location		
	City A	City B	City C
Operating Costs per Year:			
Transportation Costs:			
Incoming materials	$ 100,000	$ 90,000	$ 85,000
Outgoing materials	160,000	165,000	170,000
Labor	200,000	225,000	250,000
Utilities:			
Power	60,000	65,000	65,000
Water	30,000	28,000	32,000
Fuel	60,000	70,000	65,000
Plant overhead:			
Rent or carrying costs	60,000	55,000	64,000
Taxes	10,000	12,000	14,000
Insurance	5,000	5,000	5,500
Miscellaneous	5,000	8,000	8,500
Total	$ 690,000	$ 723,000	$ 759,000
Construction Costs:			
Land	$ 100,000	$ 50,000	$ 75,000
Building	1,500,000	1,250,000	1,600,000
Special requirements	40,000	——	——
Total	$1,640,000	$1,300,000	$1,675,000

Figure 10-4. Cost comparison chart for three alternative plant locations.

number of points for each of the alternative locations is determined and is used to assist in making a decision. In most cases this rating should be supplemented with a cost analysis.

Cost analysis. As an aid in evaluating alternative plant locations, estimates should be made for all costs entering into the operation of the plant in each of the locations. These estimates should cover the initial cost of the physical facilities, the cost of raw materials, the cost of manufacture, and the cost of distribution (see Figure 10–4). After the determination of each of these costs, the unit cost for manufacturing the product in each of the locations can be reckoned and may be used to aid in deciding on the optimum location.

Trends in Plant Location

There has been a definite trend in the location of industrial plants. More and more companies have been decentralizing their operations and locating plants in small towns or suburban areas—particularly the large companies that require extensive space for buildings, parking lots, and other facilities. Also, many companies have chosen local sites that are in the country. This has allowed them to secure ample space and freed them from paying the higher tax rate usually found in the city. Often a number of advantages can be gained by locating a plant in a small town. Inexpensive building sites with ample space for expansion are usually available, and the community will probably welcome the increased revenue the company will bring into the area; a friendly atmosphere should prevail. In addition, labor is commonly available at a lower rate than in cities, more harmonious relations with the workers may be possible, and higher productivity may be attained.

Despite the apparent advantages of the suburbs, there are signs that the rush of offices and factories out of the cities may be slowing down. The suburbs present such problems as a lack of potential workers, employee transportation problems, lack of housing for lower-level workers, lack of business services, and need for managers to visit the city on many business matters.

Plant Buildings

When the company has chosen the community in which it will locate, consideration must be given to providing physical facilities. If the company is small, it may be able to rent or buy an existing building. Seldom, however, will a company requiring extensive space be able to find suitable facilities available for rent or purchase. This necessitates, then, the design and construction of new buildings.

When the construction of additional buildings or new buildings is planned for the relocation of the company, the responsibility for this function is commonly given to the plant-engineering group. This group will work closely with the architect and contractor in designing and constructing the buildings. If the company prefers, it can employ one of the large industrial construction firms, which will handle all the details of planning and constructing the buildings. Figure 10–5 illustrates a factory building built by such an organization.

In planning a building for the manufacturing facilities, a number of factors must be given consideration, including

1. Nature of the manufacturing process.
2. Plant layout and space requirements.
3. Lighting, heating, ventilating, and air conditioning.
4. Service facilities.
5. Future expansion.
6. Appearance.

Each of these will be discussed briefly in the sections that follow.

Figure 10-5. Engineering Building, Penn Controls, Inc., Goshen, Indiana. (Design and construction by the Austin Company.)

Nature of Manufacturing Process

One of the chief determinants of the kind of building required will be the type of manufacturing process. The various machines and equipment used in the manufacture of steel plate, glass bottles, rubber tires, metal castings, food products, and other items dictate the type of building to be constructed. A building must allow sufficient floor loading, head space, bay size, and ventilation, as well as providing for the storage and flow of materials and adequate loading docks and railroad sidings.

Some manufacturing processes require considerable ventilation or controlled temperature and humidity.

Plant Layout and Space Requirements

All the factors influencing the internal arrangement of a manufacturing plant will be discussed later in this chapter. Suffice it to say at this point that the location of the machines, service centers, and offices, the size of the bays required, and the degree of flexibility desired all will have considerable influence on the kind of building created. Ideally, the optimum plant layout should be determined, and the building should be just a shell around this design. However, a building that may prove to be ideal at the outset may lead to great inflexibility in the future. Thus, most new factory buildings are a compromise between the present ideal and the need to insure the necessary flexibility to meet future needs.

Lighting, Heating and Ventilating, and Air Conditioning

During recent years, industry has placed less and less reliance on natural light and has made increasing use of artificial illumination (see Figure 10–6). One of the greatest changes in the way in which plants are making use of power is through improved lighting. The Illuminating Engineering Society has recommended 100 ft.-c as an accepted level for general office work and 50 ft.-c to 100 ft.-c as an accepted level for most production areas. Many new plants have been designed to meet or to exceed these standards. This has had considerable impact on the power system design. For one thing, the main substation capacities are greater, and the distribution voltages are more frequently mated to optimum lighting economies (i.e., 480/277 volts and no lighting transformers) rather than to convenience levels (240 or 120 volts) as was formerly practiced.

Despite the Illuminating Engineering Society's recommendations for lighting levels, the high cost of energy has caused many organizations to reduce the level of

Figure 10-6. Interior view of factory building. Controlled conditions are maintained throughout this plant. Note the excellent lighting and lack of windows. (Courtesy Collins Radio Company.)

illumination—particularly in offices. One of the ways in which savings have been achieved has been by reducing the overhead general illumination and providing ample lighting at each of the working surfaces—oftentimes built into the furniture. Whereas the conventional rule-of-thumb allowance for lighting has grown to be about 5 watts per square foot in modern offices, lighting systems are now being installed that require no more than about 1.7 watts per square foot. These new concepts have led the General Services Administration to use this energy-saving approach in all new federal office space.

It is quite common in larger plants to provide separate buildings for housing high-pressure boilers for heating purposes. The sizes of these will depend on the heating requirements and the need for steam and hot water for production purposes. In several plants built recently, the boilers had the following capacities: 600-hp high pressure (250 psi) at 30,000 lbs. per hour, 465-hp, and a 200-hp Scotch marine boiler for a hot-water heating system at 30-lb. pressure. Whereas larger plants may use boilers for heating purposes, many smaller plants use individual gas-fired infrared heaters.

Most modern plants provide ample ventilation by means of roof ventilators and exhaust fans. In some areas of the plant, these may change the air as often as every three minutes. Although more and more plants are being air conditioned, such installations tend to be limited largely to those requiring controlled conditions, such as in the electronics industry. On the other hand, most of the office facilities are being air conditioned—frequently through the use of combination heating and cooling units.

Since lighting, heating, and air-conditioning are dependent on some form of energy (e.g., gas, coal, fuel oil) and the costs of energy keep increasing at a steep rate, companies are giving much attention to ways in which they can decrease these costs. This had led to the use of increased insulation in buildings, a reduction in the number of windows, new lighting systems, and other measures planned to decrease the use of energy.

Service Facilities

In addition to the heating, ventilating, and air conditioning facilities, many companies maintain other service facilities, such as fire fighting equipment, incinerators, sewage-treating systems, emergency power equipment, cooling towers, and compressed-air equipment. Some of these may be housed in separate buildings, the construction of which may be quite different from that of the main plant building.

Future Expansion

The expansion of industry has made management aware of the importance of planning for future expansion. Most companies erecting new buildings give consideration to this problem. If widespread expansion is anticipated, this may dictate the type of building to be constructed. Usually, single-story plants can be added onto much easier than multi-story plants, and in many cases a false wall is left in that side of the building to which a new addition is to be connected.

If the multi-story buildings are to be enlarged by the erection of additional floors, this must be planned in advance so that the original structure will possess sufficient footings and supporting members to carry the added weight.

Appearance

Appearance is being given considerable attention in choosing the style of architecture and building materials for modern plants. Modern factories are no longer ugly, smoke-spewing clusters, but are rapidly becoming attractive structures in well-landscaped surroundings (see Figure 10–7).

Figure 10-7. Exterior view of an attractive factory building. (Courtesy Woodward Governor Company.)

Single- vs. Multi-Story Buildings

In planning factory buildings, the advantages of single-story vs. multi-story arrangements must be weighed and that type of building selected that will best meet the needs of the company. The advantages of the single-story building are as follows:

1. Low construction cost per square foot of space.
2. Requires less time to erect.
3. Easy to expand.
4. Will take high floor loads.
5. Suitable for assembly of heavy or bulky products.
6. Allows high ceilings.
7. No space lost for elevators and stairs.
8. Fewer columns.
9. Easier to handle materials.
10. Allows flexibility in layout.
11. Rest rooms and servicing equipment may be located in overhead trusses.
12. Maximum use of daylight and natural ventilation is possible.
13. Easier to isolate obnoxious or hazardous areas.
14. Easier supervision.

And the advantages of the multi-story building are:

1. Requires less land.
2. Allows use of gravity for materials and movement.
3. Allows more compact layouts.
4. Allows vertical arrangement of production and storage space.
5. Lower heating cost.
6. Top stories may be used for departments requiring special conditions.

Trends in Building Construction

The trend appears to be to build a single-story plant connected to a single- or multi-story office located in a spacious area (see Figure 10–8). Plants are being located on large tracts of land to allow space for parking lots and future expansion.

Bay sizes are being increased to as much as 40 feet by 60 feet or more in order to allow unrestricted processing areas and to facilitate flexibility. Increased use is being made of rigid or semi-rigid frames; the size of structural members is thereby reduced and framing problems are simplified. Precast concrete units are being used more widely.

Increased use is being made of the overhead space among the roof supporting members as an area in which to locate service equipment. This space is accessible for installation and maintenance.

For some types of product manufacturing, say, electronics or digital computer devices, it has been found practical to build modular plants. Such a plant is illustrated in Figure 10–9.

Modern plant buildings are being designed to add to the beauty of the community. Through the combination of attractive designs and building materials and

Figure 10-8. Aerial view of a modern factory building. (Courtesy Link-Belt Company. Building design and construction by the Austin Company.)

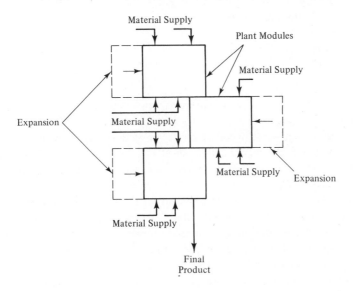

Figure 10-9. Modular factory design. (Adapted from H.J. Bullinger, H.J. Warnecke, and H.P. Lentes, "Toward the Factory of the Future," *Proceedings of the Eighth International Conference of Production Research*, Stuttgart, West Germany, Aug. 20–22, 1985.

beautifully landscaped grounds, factory buildings may become a feature of which the community is proud.

Plant Layout

Plant layout is a plan of the most effective arrangement of the physical facilities and manpower for the manufacture of the product. It brings together and fully integrates all the work that has been done by the architect, the product engineer, the process engineer, the plant engineer, and the management in their careful planning for the production of goods in an optimum manner. Plant layout, which is often referred to as *facilities design*, encompasses much more than the mere planning of the arrangement of the production equipment and should include a careful study of the following:

1. External transportation facilities.
2. Receiving operations (unloading, inspection, stores).
3. Production activities.
4. Materials handling.
5. Service and auxiliary operations.
6. Quality control and inspection areas.
7. Packaging operations.
8. Storage operations.
9. Shipping operations.
10. Offices.

Plant layout is a valuable tool of management not only for the building of new plants, but also in planning for changes in existing facilities. New products, new processes, or an increase or decrease in rates of production may require a rearrangement of production equipment. Of greatest importance is the adaptability of the plant layout to the forward planning of the company. The maintenance of the layout of a plant for historical purposes only is of little real value.

We must not confuse plant layout with the design of industrial buildings. Obviously the two problems are closely related and in reality often require a compromise between the best design in each area. Seldom can a building be constructed around an "ideal" plant layout, and many times a layout must be changed to meet the requirements of the building.

Plant layout covers the planning of space requirements for all activities in an industrial firm—offices, warehouses, rooms, and all other facilities associated with the total manufacturing plant.

Objectives of Plant Layout

The primary goal of plant layout is to maximize profits by the arrangement of all plant facilities to the best advantage of the total "manufacturing equation"—people, materials, machines, and money. If a finished layout is to fulfill this goal, it should be planned with the following objectives[1] clearly in mind.

1. Facilitate the manufacturing process.
2. Minimize materials handling.
3. Maintain flexibility of arrangement and of operation.
4. Maintain high turnover of work-in-process.
5. Hold down investment in equipment.
6. Make economical use of building cube.
7. Promote effective utilization of manpower.
8. Provide for employee convenience, safety, and comfort in doing the work.

All of these objectives might be summarized as *the planning of the plant for the best relationship between output, space, and manufacturing cost*. Output might be measured in dollar volume or in units of product. Space might be measured in square feet of floor or in cubic feet in the building structure. Manufacturing cost is obviously in money. In all manufacturing situations there is an optimum balance between these three, the attainment of which is made possible through effective plant layout.

Factors Affecting Plant Layout

Many of the basic factors that affect the design of the product, the design of the manufacturing process, the selection of tools and equipment, and the planning for materials handling carry over to influence the plant layout. We shall discuss some of these in the following paragraphs.

Product.   The type of product affects plant layout in many ways. Large and heavy equipment requires assembly bays. Also, in these cases it is often more economical to move the men and machines to the product than it is to move the product to the work area. Small and light products can be moved effectively; thus, more attention can be given to machine locations and the handling of materials. Bulk products, such as cereals, flour, or cement, more or less dictate a multi-story layout

---

[1]See James M. Apple, *Plant Layout and Material Handling*; New York: John Wiley and Sons, 1977, p. 7.

in order that the advantage of gravity can be utilized in the movement of the material.

Volume or rate of production.   This is a key factor in all manufacturing planning. In plant layout it is reflected in the total size of the operation to be planned as well as being the principal factor in the determination of the type of manufacture to be employed.

Quality.   The meeting of quality requirements in a product can be aided through effective plant layout. Soundproof rooms, "white" rooms, and air-conditioned factories are often needed to meet product specifications. In other cases the handling and storage of products—particularly if they may deteriorate—may contribute to the maintenance of the proper quality level.

Equipment.   Adequate space must be provided for all equipment—manufacturing, materials handling, and service. Equipment specifications are of major importance to the plant-layout engineer.

Type of manufacture.   It is obvious that a plant laid out for a continuous manufacturing process will be quite different from a factory operating as an intermittent plant. However, it should be pointed out that the advantages of continuous manufacture are such that it should be employed by the plant-layout engineer at every feasible opportunity. It is not uncommon in intermittent plants to set up temporary continuous lines whenever the rate of production warrants.

Building.   Ideally, a building should be built to suit the best plant layout. This ideal is seldom attained. Adapting a factory layout to an old building presents a real challenge to the plant-layout engineer. All proposals for modification of the existing structure must be economically justified. Even when a new building is to be constructed, some compromise usually is required.

Plant site.   The plant site is the connecting link between the factory and the surrounding community. Services such as railroad sidings, highways, and utilities may easily affect not only the positioning of the buildings on the plot but the internal arrangement of the departments as well.

Personnel.   Comfort and safety of personnel must always be carefully considered when laying out a plant. A single operation, or work station, may within its own boundaries be safe yet endanger other workers in the general area. This calls for protective screens or possible relocation of the process. Comfort is considered in the location of rest rooms, drinking fountains, and other personnel services.

Materials handling plan.   Basic to economical production is good materials flow and a soundly conceived materials handling system. Since materials handling is the skeleton on which the plant layout fits, it is inseparably tied in with the layout function. Thus, plant layout ties together the manufacturing plan and, in this way, dictates the specifications of the materials handling equipment. This plan also includes the provision for adequate aisles for movement of materials and the allocation of space for storage—not only in stock rooms but at the work stations.

Each of the above factors presents a problem to the plant-layout engineer. We must realize that a solution that is completely favorable in all ways is seldom reached. As in most design situations, a compromise must be made to attain an optimum solution.

The Basic Plans for Plant Layout

Before discussing how plant layouts are made, we should identify the three basic plans for the arrangement of manufacturing equipment. These basic plans are the *process layout*, the *product layout*, and the *group layout*. Selection of the basic plan to be used depends upon many factors; however, of these, the type of product and the type of manufacture are of the greatest influence.

Process layout.   In a process layout the type and operational characteristics of the manufacturing equipment are the determining factors in the arrangement of the factory. This basic plan can be readily identified, as such plants will have machine departments, heat-treating departments, finishing rooms, and assembly floors. Even within such departments, machines of similar work characteristics, (lathes, milling machines, drill presses, and so on) are commonly grouped together.

The product is fabricated by moving it from department to department according to the sequence of operations to be performed on it. The operations performed in each department are assigned to particular machines on the basis of the capability of the machine to perform that operation, the capacity required, the precision required, the availability of the machine, and so forth. Process layout may be thought of as a general-purpose type of layout that provides for great flexibility in output, design of products, and methods of fabrication.

The process layout is of particular value when production involves many types or styles of products; relatively low volume on individual items; the need to use the same machine for two or more operations; a high proportion of very heavy machines; problems in maintaining good labor and equipment balance; and many inspections required during a sequence of operations. This type of layout generally may be thought to lead to the following conditions: (1) need for a skilled labor force capable of doing a variety of operations on a machine, (2) many production orders in process at anytime, (3) frequent movement of materials between operations and departments, (4) extensive storage space in departments for unprocessed materials, (5) considerable storage space around machines, (6) high inventories of in-process materials, (7) general-purpose materials handling equipment, (8) much scheduling and careful control of materials in process, and (9) lack of mechanical pacing of work.

Product layout.   In product layout the work to be performed on the product is the determining factor in the positioning of manufacturing equipment. The aim is to arrange machines, regardless of type, in the order of the operations that are performed on the many component parts, on subassemblies, and on the final assembly of the item being manufactured. Thus, each work station—either machine or workbench—does whatever operation on the product that follows the work done at the preceding work station and then passes the product to the next work station in the line, where the next operation is performed (see Figure 5–1).

The product layout is the type that we commonly associate with the mass production of goods. It is typical of the assembly lines for automobiles, refrigerators, washing machines, and so forth. It is of particular value when production involves one or a few standard products in high volume over a relatively long period of time.

This type of layout usually has the following characteristics: (1) conveyorized movement of materials, (2) relatively small in-process inventory of parts, with most of them in temporary storage on the materials handling system, (3) mechanical pacing, either partially or completely, of movement, (4) semiskilled operators, often tending two or more machines, (5) the utilization of highly specialized machines, jigs, and fixtures, (6) little need for detailed scheduling of production control, (7) integration of inspection points into the line, and (8) high investment in specialized machines having little flexibility.

Generally speaking, the *process layout* is characteristic of intermittent manufacturing, and the *product layout* is most common in continuous manufacturing. Process layout is probably the most common in industry today. However, with current trends towards automation, the future may lead to more and more product layout in factories.

Both types present real challenges to the plant-layout engineer. In a process-type layout he or she must arrange departments—and subdepartments—so that the material is moved with the least effort over minimum distances. This problem also holds true for product layout; however, it is complicated by the problem of "balancing out the line."

Group layout.   A group layout is one for which some of the advantages of a product layout are achieved for relatively low production volumes. This is achievable when the items to be produced can be grouped into families based on the manufacturing processes required. In this way, it is possible to create a production quantity for a family which cannot be created for individual parts. A group layout can consist of several miniproduct lines, one devoted to each family. Burbidge[2] has developed a procedure, called *production flow analysis* (PFA), which enables an ana-

---

[2] J.L. Burbidge, "Production Flow Analysis," *Proceedings of the Eighth International Conference on Production Research*, Stuttgart, West Germany, Aug. 20–22, 1985.

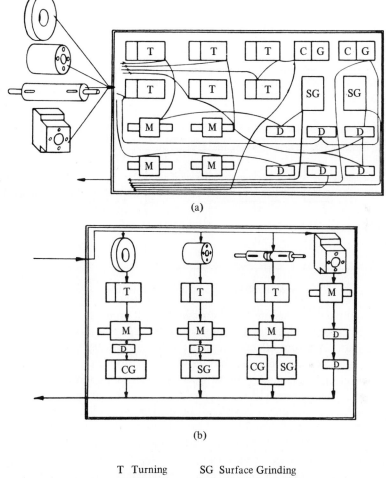

(a)

(b)

T Turning	SG Surface Grinding
M Milling	CG Cylindrical Grinding
D Drilling	

Figure 10-10. Functional and group layouts (Courtesy of Butterworths.)

lyst to group parts into families which can be effectively manufactured in a group layout configuration. The several small product (family) layouts may sometimes be referred to as manufacturing cells. Tompkins and White refer to this as a layout for a product family.

Figure 10–10, from Gallagher and Knight,[3] graphically shows the different material flow patterns that result from a process (functional) layout and a group layout.

---

[3]C.C. Gallagher, and W.A. Knight, *Group Technology Production Methods in Manufacture*, Chichester: Halstead Press, 1986.

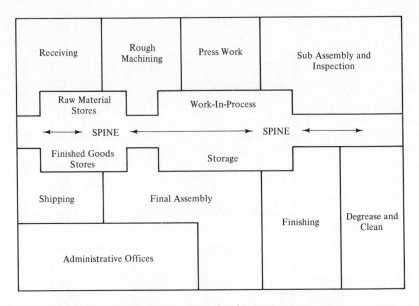

Figure 10-11. Example of Spine Layout.

Not all plant layouts are based on the classical product, process, and group formats. A type of facilities configuration know as the "spine concept" has evolved in recent years. A layout of this type is good for an industry which is subject to occasional product and processing changes which necessitate changes in the facility design. The electronics industry might be an example. In the spine concept the permanent part of the layout will be a central artery (aisle, storage area, etc.) from which all other departments will radiate. In this type of environment an extensive (and permanent) materials handling and storage system which would not be subject to change could be installed. The departments served by the facilities in the spine could periodically undergo change without causing problems with the important spine. Figure 10–11 shows a diagram of a spine-type layout which includes the features just mentioned. Tompkins and Spain[4] give other examples of spine layout configurations.

Organization for Plant Layout

If the plant-layout activity in a manufacturing plant is to be effective there must be a well defined responsibility for its accomplishment. Large concerns have special plant-layout departments; smaller firms may designate the job as a part-time

[4]J.A. Tompkins, and J.D. Spain, "Utilization of Spine Concept Maximizes Modularity in Facilities Planning," *Industrial Engineering*, Vol. 13, No. 3, March 1981, pp. 34–42.

responsibility of one of the members of the manufacturing staff or line. When a plant layout is required as a project—that is, to meet a particular need and not to be maintained on a continuing basis—a consulting firm may be engaged.

Plant layout is a *planning* activity. In determining the need for such an organization, management must consider the dynamic aspects of the manufacturing problem. If change is anticipated, owing to model changes, new products, technological improvements, or other causes, a plant-layout group will probably pay dividends.

A plant-layout group is usually a part of the industrial engineering activity. However, it may report to the plant engineer, other department heads, or possibly directly to the plant management. In any event, in performing its activities the plant-layout group will have close contact with practically every group engaged in manufacturing planning.

Plant-Layout Procedure

As in most industrial activities, there is a sound approach to the plant-layout problem. First, let us list the steps briefly, and then discuss each in detail. In solving a plant-layout problem:

1. Accumulate all the basic data that will be needed.
2. Analyze and coordinate these basic data.
3. Determine a general flow pattern for the materials in process.
4. Design the individual work stations or production centers.
5. "Assemble" the individual layouts into the total layout in accordance with the general flow pattern and the building facilities.
6. Coordinate this plan with the plan for the handling of materials.
7. Complete the plant layout.
8. Prepare an appropriation request indicating the funds needed and justifying the expenditure of these funds.
9. Convert the plant layout into floor plans that can be used by the plant engineer in the location and installation of the equipment.

This is the general pattern of attack. But from time to time the sequence may be changed to advantage.

Basic data.   Basic data must be procured from practically every other function in the manufacturing organization. Standard process sheets from the process engineering group are needed to show how the product is to be made and the tools and equipment required. If the time standards are not already posted on this form, they will have to be obtained in order to determine the anticipated rates of production for each operation. In some companies this information is consolidated on a flow process chart, which coordinates all operations into the complete process required for the manufacture of the product. Equipment lists and the specifications of the equipment must be obtained to determine the space requirements and the productive capacity of the machines involved. The plant engineer is the source of information as to the building plans and specifications. From these plans, the available space can be determined. From the production planning and control group, information must be obtained regarding the required volume and rate of production. And, finally, from the product engineer, complete specifications of the product and bills of materials should be procured.

Analysis and coordination.   Careful analysis and coordination of the basic data by the plant-layout engineer is needed to determine:

1. The kind, size, and number of every piece of equipment that must be accommodated in the layout.
2. The total number of work stations that must be planned for.
3. Total space requirements for storage of inventories, including raw materials, work-in-process, and finished goods.
4. The total number of employees that will be required.

Each part of the solution gained through this analysis should be questioned by the plant-layout engineer. All answers should be coordinated and carefully evaluated. When it is apparent that revisions in earlier planning can be made to good advantage, such changes should be recommended to the proper planning group. This is the initial compromise point in plant layout.

Flow pattern.   Analysis and evaluation of the basic data will indicate the basic plan for the layout—process, product, or group. After the selection of a basic plan, a general pattern of flow for the product should be determined. For a process layout, this results in a tentative arrangement of the various functional departments involved in the manufacturing process. In the product layout, it is a general plan for the location of the many processing and assembly lines. These general flow patterns are indicated in the block layout shown in Figure 10–12. We should again remind ourselves that most industrial plants are actually a "mix" of these two basic types of layout plan.

One of the more versatile tools that can be used to help determine the flow of materials between departments or work centers is the "Travel Chart" (see Figure 10–13), sometimes referred to as a "Cross Chart" or "From-To Chart." This chart is very useful in highlighting the distance, the volume, or the distance–volume that materials have to be moved among the various work centers. This information is of value to the engineer in trying to determine the best arrangement of facilities to optimize the materials flow.

Work stations.   The individual work station or production center is the key in plant layout. Each station should be laid out for the most effective performance of the operation, taking into account space for storage of tools and materials, ease of

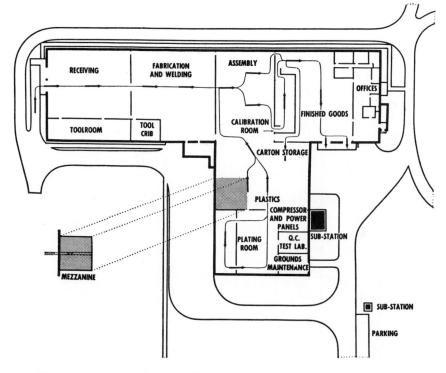

Figure 10-12.   A two-dimensional block layout. (Courtesy General Electric Company.)

maintenance of equipment, and worker safety and comfort. A typical work station layout is shown in Figure 10–14.

Prepare plant layout.   Now the parts of the jigsaw puzzle must be fitted together within the frame of the picture. Work stations are arranged in accordance with the flow pattern and within the space limitations of the building structure. Also, at this point allowances must be made for aisles, storage areas, materials handling devices, offices, services, and all other such facilities. Again, each individual location should be evaluated and all possible solutions to the problem considered. This is another point for many compromises. However, every possibility should be considered and the best combination selected—it is much easier to move templates and models than it is to rearrange machines and equipment on the factory floor!

Materials handling.   The final solution of the materials handling problem is concurrent with the arrangement of the plant layout. A good plant layout makes for efficient handling of materials. Likewise, the selection of the most adaptable materials handling equipment contributes toward arriving at the optimum layout of the manufacturing facilities.

TO DEPT. → / FROM DEPT. ↓	32	45	47	53	55	59
32		6		2	2	4
45			6	4	3	
47		6		6	4	4
53			6		2	4
55				1		2
59		3	4			
TOTAL	0	15	16	13	11	14

Figure 10-13. Travel chart illustrating the number of skid loads of materials moved daily among several departments. (It is apparent that this chart is very similar to the common mileage chart found on a road map.)

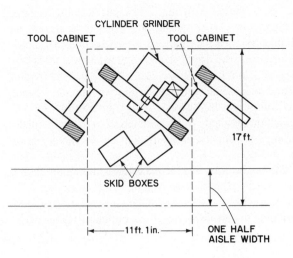

CYLINDER GRINDER
TOOL CABINET   TOOL CABINET

17 ft.

SKID BOXES

11 ft. 1 in.   ONE HALF AISLE WIDTH

Figure 10-14. A typical work station or production center, showing space allocation for machines, tool storage, materials, maintenance, and aisles. (From W. G. Ireson and Eugene L. Grant, *Handbook of Industrial Engineering and Management*; Englewood Cliffs, N.J.: Prentice-Hall, Inc., 1971. Reprinted with permission.)

Appropriation request.   The work of the plant-layout engineer seldom ends with the completion of the arrangement of the plant on paper. At every point in the making of the layout, costs must be considered. This cost is a total cost—it takes into consideration all factors involved. One of these factors is the cost of installing and arranging the equipment in accordance with the layout plan. These installation costs must now be assembled in the form of an appropriation request for the money required to convert the plan into actuality.

Floor plans.   After the plant layout has been approved, the final step is to arrange the physical facilities. In some instances this can be done directly from the layout, in others it is necessary to interpret the layout in the form of floor plans that can be used by the plant-engineering group, building contractor, and others. When such plans are required, their preparation is generally the last step taken by the plant-layout group in completing their job. However, close liaison with all parties involved is usually necessary until the last machine or piece of equipment is installed and the plant is put into operation.

We might well ask if this completes the useful life of the plant layout. This is, of course, a question of the stability of the manufacturing process. If changes can be anticipated, it is much easier to work them out by advance planning on an "active" plant layout. The maintenance of an up-to-date layout of a factory requires effective communications between the plant-layout group and all other manufacturing functions (see Figure 10–15). Too often, moves may be made in the shop without either

Figure 10-15. An industrial engineer discusses a new layout with other engineers and supervisory personnel. (Courtesy of Packard Electric Division, General Motors Corporation.)

consulting the plant-layout engineer or advising him of the change. If this condition is permitted to continue, the effectiveness of keeping the actual layout is lost.

Plant-Layout Techniques

A detailed discussion of the exact methods whereby plant layouts are made is beyond the scope of this book. In recent years, however, rapid strides have been made in this field. Materials and procedures have been developed that result not only in better looking layouts but in a reduction of the time required for their preparation.

Materials. The common base materials[5] on which layouts are constructed consist of (1) plastic sheets or boards on which grid lines have been printed or scribed, (2) metal-faced plywood with an appropriate finish on the metal, (3) sheet metal, plywood, or composition board with an appropriate finish, and (4) drawing paper or tracing paper. Many two- and three-dimensional templates are available commercially and can be procured. Self-adhering transparent tapes are available showing standard aisles, conveyors, arrows for indicating materials flow, walls and partitions, as well as other parts of the layout that used to be inked in by a draftsman. In many concerns standard templates and models are available, saving the time the plant-layout engineer would spend making measurements on the shop floor. Templates can be readily reproduced on foil either by photographic means or by Bruning or Ozalid processes. If the templates don't have adhesive preapplied, double-coated self-adhering tape or rubber cement may be used for mounting both templates and models. With these methods, moves can be made easily during the planning of the layout.

Types of layouts. Three principal types of plant-layout modeling procedures and materials are in use in modern industry: block layouts, two-dimensional transparent template layouts, and three-dimensional model layouts. Prior to the preparation of either a template or a model layout, it is common practice to make a block layout.

Block layouts. A block layout is shown in Figure 10–12. This type of layout is usually prepared to a scale of ⅛ inch equals one foot. It is a preliminary layout for study of material flow patterns. By use of this technique, a decision can be made as to the general arrangement of the plant before proceeding with the more detailed layout.

Block layouts are usually two-dimensional.

---

[5]Apple, *Plant Layout & Material Handling*, New York: Ronald Press, 1977.

Template layouts.   These are probably the most common type of plant lay-out. Modern techniques are characterized by the fact that the layouts are transparent and copies can be duplicated directly from these layouts for use in the plant or for recording purposes. A template layout is commonly prepared to a scale of ¼ inch equals one foot. Figure 10–16 shows a transparent layout and Figure 10–17 shows a print duplicated from this transparency.

Some of the advantages of the two-dimensional layout are:

1. It is the least costly.
2. It can be readily interpreted by technical personnel.
3. Duplicate copies can be made.

On the other hand the disadvantages of the two-dimensional layout are:

1. It is hard to visualize overhead equipment and possible conflicts that it may create.
2. Interpretation by non-technical personnel is difficult.

Model layouts.   These layouts are not so common, probably owing to the expense involved. However, for the construction of new plants using any overhead equipment in the way of conveyors, cranes, or mezzanine installations, this type of layout should receive serious consideration. Model layouts are prepared to the same

Figure 10-16. Preparing a two-dimensional transparent layout. (Courtesy General Electric Company.)

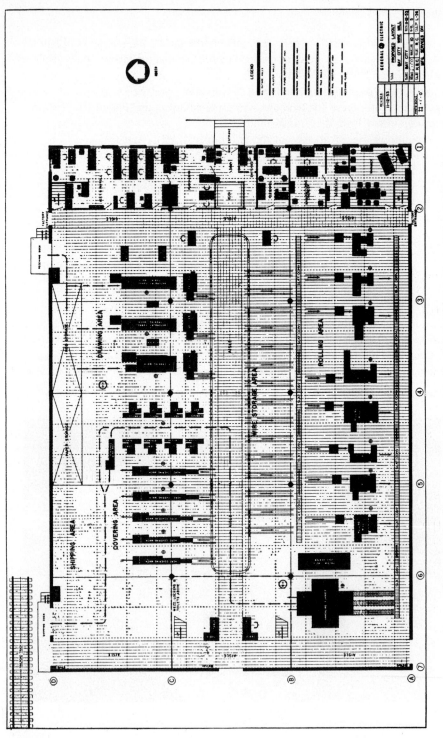

Figure 10-17. Print made from the layout in Fig. 10-16. (Courtesy General Electric Company.)

216

scale as template layouts—¼ inch equals one foot. A model or three-dimensional layout is shown in Figure 10–18. The relative advantages of this type of layout are:

1. Helps ''sell'' the layout to management.
2. Aids the visualization of the layout by non-technical personnel.
3. Facilitates the work of the plant-layout engineer in making the layout; models can be shifted quickly for study of optional arrangements.
4. Different arrangements can be photographed for comparative purposes.
5. Provides means for checking overhead structures.

Disadvantages of the three-dimensional layout are:

1. High cost.
2. Requires storage area.
3. Cannot be taken down to the shop floor for reference purposes.
4. For full effectiveness, a two-dimensional layout has to be prepared from the model layout for informational purposes.

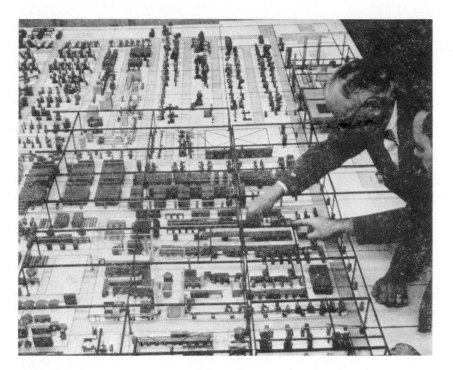

Figure 10-18. Preparing a three-dimensional plant layout using models. (Courtesy General Electric Company.)

Use of Computer Programs in Plant Layout

Over the years many principles have been developed for the guidance of the plant-layout engineer. In spite of this, there is considerable art still involved in plant layout. Application of these principles is based more on a "trial and error" approach than on quantitative measurements. On the other hand, considerable research has been conducted and is being continued to achieve a more scientific approach to the solution of plant-layout problems.

One example of such research is the attempt to balance assembly lines by mathematical models. Most assembly-line balancing has been done by trial-and-error methods. Recent research has resulted in several computer-oriented computational methods which are now being used in industry. These methods usually direct the computer to investigate all possible groupings of the assembly tasks and then to obtain the best grouping for a given set of conditions.

One of the early computer programs that was developed to assist in laying out plant facilities is called CRAFT (Computerized Relative Allocation of Facilities Technique).[6] This computer program handles up to 40 activity centers. The information that is fed into CRAFT includes the interdepartmental flow per unit of time, the unit load materials handling cost per unit distance, and an initial block diagram. The computer processes these data until it can find no improvements in locations and then prints out a block-type layout of the locations of each of the activities or departments.

Although the development of software for plant layout has not been revolutionary, continuous development has taken place to endeavor to extend CRAFT and to provide more realistic models. Apple[7] discusses several of the more widely used programs as follows:

CORELAP (Computerized Relationship Layout Planning)—locates the most-related activity, and then progressively adds other activities, based on rated closeness desired, and in required size, until all activities have been placed.

ALDEP (Automated Layout Design Program)—selects at random and locates the first activity. Subsequent activities, in required size, are selected and placed: (a) according to closeness desired, or (b) at random, if no significant relationships are found. Alternative layouts are generated and scored.

PLANET (Computerized Plant Layout and Evaluation Technique)—utilizing interdepartment flow data, computes the "penalty" cost associated with separating departments. Three heuristic algorithms are available for generating alternative configurations to be manually evaluated and adjusted.

---

[6]G.C. Armour and E.S. Buffa, "A Heuristic Algorithm and Computer Simulation Approach to Relative Location of Facilities," *Management Science*, 9(2), January 1963.

[7]*Plant Layout & Material Handling*, p. 328.

Figure 10-19. Plant layout computer graphics. (Courtesy Purdue University Laboratory for Interactive Decision Systems.)

Other programs, such as COFAD (Computerized Facilities Design), have been developed which have endeavored to combine CRAFT-based layouts with materials handling selection based on various criteria. Work continues to be done in industry and universities along this line to develop programs that will eventually lead to integrated computer-aided manufacturing systems. One of the most recent developments has been CAN-Q (Computer Analysis of Network of Queues),[8] a program for analyzing the work flow in a production system. According to its originator, "it is quite easy to use, is very efficient, and is sufficiently versatile to handle virtually any kind of production system."

CAD systems.   One often hears of computer-aided design systems for the design of physical parts such as shafts or gears; there are also a number of commercially available software packages that can be used for the design of plant layouts (see Figure 10–19). The initial offerings in this area were essentially drafting packages which made the drawing of layouts easier. Drafting and symbol placement software is becoming widely available for microcomputers also. An example of this is the MacDraw software for Apple's Macintosh computer. Three-dimensional drafting software is also available.

---

[8] See James J. Solberg, "Instructional Manual for Use of CAN-Q as an Analysis Tool for Plant Layout and Material Handling," Purdue University, West Lafayette, Indiana, January 1980.

Hales[9] reports that the new CAD graphics software which is becoming available has increased plant layout capability. He lists the following capabilities of current CAD software that is available for plant layout:

1. Two- and three-dimensional drafting.
2. Symbol libraries.
3. Bill of materials.
4. Report generation.
5. Area calculations.
6. Dynamic simulation.
7. Robotic simulation.
8. Interface with civil and structural analysis.

General Principles of Plant Layout

Some of the general principles of plant layout that have proven sound are:

1. Move materials minimum distances.   This principle brings out the concept of "straight-line" production. However, in many instances it is more practical to take circular paths such as those found in "merry-go-rounds" used in many production foundries.

2. Avoid or minimize the backtracking of materials.   Backtracking not only will increase the distance of movement but can result in congestion of the channels of materials handling.

3. Plan for a minimum of materials handling.   The advantage here has been dicussed earlier in this book. It is an overlapping principle, because the effectiveness of the plant layout will make a major contribution to this end.

4. Use manufacturing space economically.   This applies not only to the production areas but to the storage areas as well. In the past it has been common practice to regard this principle in terms of square feet of floor space only. The current trend is to consider the cubic space in the building. In many plants, overhead conveyors are now being utilized as a storage device.

5. Permit all flexibility possible.   The chance of change should always be considered and the equipment arranged so that changes can be made at minimal cost or disturbance to the manufacturing process. This is especially a problem in the automotive industry, where model changes are involved.

---

[9]H.L. Hales, "Computerized Facilities Planning and Design: Sorting out the Options Available Now," *Industrial Engineering*, Vol. 16, No. 5, 1984.

6. Allow for possible plant expansion. The plant-layout engineer should always consider potential increases in production when planning the arrangement of a factory.

In many industries there are other "rules of thumb" that have been established by experience in plant layout. For example, it is not considered good practice to place large and expensive installations such as heat-treating equipment or drying ovens for finishes centrally—preferred practice is to locate them along an outer wall. However, such practices are not yet generally accepted as fundamentals of plant layout.

Evaluation of Plant Layouts

Evaluation as to which—if any—plan represents the best plant layout is difficult. As we have noted, one objective is to get optimum output of product with a minimum of manufacturing space. There are, however, so many other factors that influence the productive efficiency of a plant, that to measure the effectiveness of the layout by space alone can hardly be accepted as conclusive.

Analysis of the materials handling involved is another possible measure of layout effectiveness. It might well be assumed that the layout that results in minimum handling of materials is the best. On the other hand, this layout might be much more costly in equipment and installation.

As pointed out previously, new quantitative tools are continually being developed that should assist in optimizing plant layouts. Based on current developments, the most effective method of evaluating alternative designs appears to be through the use of simulation, as noted previously.

QUESTIONS

1. Analyze why some company you know of may have located where it did.
2. A candy company, now located in the New York City area, plans to relocate in a small community of about 5000 persons about 45 miles away. What reasons might this company have for changing its location?
3. One large manufacturer prefers not to use more than about 10 to 15 percent of the available labor supply in any of its many new branch plants. Is this a good policy? Why?
4. Devise a plan for rating plant locations for some company with which you are familiar.
5. Why are so many companies locating their plants in the country rather than in cities?
6. Describe in your own words the typical factory building being constructed today, and comment on how it might be built more cheaply.
7. Since the air conditioning of plants is very expensive, what justification does a company have for doing it?

8. Discuss the application of the principles of plant layout to the kitchen in your home or place of residence. How about the living room and dining room?

9. Make a template for a sewing machine, range, or refrigerator. Indicate the additional space that you should allow beyond the actual dimensions of the equipment. Discuss how you arrived at these dimensions.

10. List some appropriate criteria for use in determining whether a process layout or product layout should be employed in any layout problem.

11. What restrictions does the plant building place on the plant layout? Can any of these be modified or eliminated?

12. What type of layout materials do you suggest for use when laying out (a) a machine shop, (b) an oil refinery, (c) a warehouse, (d) an office, (e) an aircraft carrier? State your reasons. Would the "spine" layout be applicable for any of these? Why?

13. If you were developing a computer program to evaluate alternative layouts, what variables would you include in it? Why?

CASE PROBLEMS

Wright Radio Company

The Wright Radio Company was started in a midwestern city by John Wright in 1935. As a result of the development of an outstanding radio transmitter and excellent management, the company experienced steady growth. During World War II it became the largest industry in the community and employed over 4000 persons.

By 1969 John Wright decided to diversify the company's line of products and to develop several new items in the electronics field. The new products were well engineered and received widespread acceptance in the aircraft and electronics industries. It became obvious that, in order to meet the demand for them, the company must expand its production facilities.

After much consideration, Mr. Wright recommended to the board of directors that the company build a new plant in another community. Further, he recommended that the new plant be located on the Pacific Coast so that it would be near the aircraft and electronics companies. Among the sites that were proposed were Seattle, San Francisco, and Los Angeles. Mr. Wright and the board finally decided to locate the plant in one of the Los Angeles suburbs.

Questions:

1. What factors should Mr. Wright and the board have considered in selecting the new plant location?

2. Do you consider Los Angeles a good choice? Why?

Rhinehart Products Company

Mr. T. J. Rhinehart, President of the Rhinehart Products Company, has developed a new injection molding machine for making small plastic parts. He feels there is a real future for such a machine and would like to begin manufacturing it. However, Rhinehart Products Company, which manufactures plastic household items, doesn't possess the necessary space or equipment to manufacture a machine of this type.

During the course of shopping for a suitable building, Mr. Rhinehart learned about a small plant in Illinois that had been used by a furniture manufacturing company that had gone bankrupt. This plant, which is located in a small town of about 1000 population, can be purchased for about $80,000, including the wood-working equipment.

Mr. Rhinehart decided to visit the plant and found it to possess the following features: (1) single-story, concrete-block construction, rectangular shape (40 ft. x 250 ft.), (2) woodtruss roof with wood deck, (3) concrete floor, (4) building built three years ago, (5) heat supplied by unit gas heaters in the shop and hot-air furnace in the offices, (6) three offices and a reception room that take up approximately 1200 square feet at the front of the building, (7) located on a railroad siding, (8) adequate truck and railroad docks, and (9) parking space for about 40 cars.

Mr. Rhinehart decided to buy the building and to convert it into a job-lot, metal-working plant for manufacturing plastic molding machines and for producing tools and dies.

Questions:

1. Do you think Mr. Rhinehart made a wise decision? Why?
2. Will this building be suitable for the purpose for which he purchased it? Why?
3. What additional information should be considered before buying a building to be used for this purpose?

Shaw Company

The Shaw Company, which is located in a large eastern city, employs about 300 people in the manufacture of pharmaceutical products. The plant is located near the center of the city, and most of the employees either carry their lunch or eat in nearby restaurants. This has led to considerable dissatisfaction on the part of the employees, and they have repeatedly expressed the desire to have a company cafeteria.

The president of the company has decided that the employees' request is reasonable and that a cafeteria should be included in a new wing of a building that is being planned. He decides that Donald Jones, the chief industrial engineer, should be responsible for planning this cafeteria and that it should be capable of feeding at least a 300-person work force.

Questions:

1. In planning this cafeteria, from whom can Donald Jones get the information he will need?
2. In what ways is the layout of a cafeteria similar to the layout of a production department?
3. What special problems may be encountered in laying out a cafeteria?

Thompson Specialty Machining, Inc., Part 1

Thompson Machining is a New England based firm which produces high-quality metal components. Because of their large variety of specialized and general-purpose machine tools, Thompson has a thriving business of making components for their customers' products which the customers could not themselves produce cost effectively. In some ways Thompson is a very large job shop. The orders they receive are usually for small quantities; seventy-five would be a large quantity for an order.

Donald Kuhn, general manager of operations for Thompson, feels that productivity could be increased if the company acquired more numerically controlled machine tools. These would have higher production rates and be more versatile than the manually operated machine tools they would replace. Mr. Kuhn also believes that additional floor space could be achieved by such a capital acquisition program because any numerically controlled machine will be more productive than its manual counterpart.

Thompson Specialty has one industrial engineer: Douglas Beck. Mr. Beck has been assigned the task of developing a plant layout design that will facilitate the integration of several NC machine tools into the existing machine tool configuration at the firm. Currently, the conventional machines are arranged in a process layout; each process function (drilling, milling, turning, etc.) is assigned to a specific department or cost center. Since some NC machine tools can perform several distinct processes within the same setup, a workpiece that ordinarily would move through several departments to complete its processing on the existing machine tools could conceivably have all operations completed with one or two setups in an NC machine tool environment. Mr. Beck is wondering what would be the best way to integrate the NC machines with the existing machine tools.

Questions:

1. If you were Mr. Beck, how would you begin this layout analysis? Why?
2. What is your feeling about placing high-productive NC machine tools together with standard machine tools? List any advantages or disadvantages you can think of.
3. If, as is anticipated, the proposed NC machine tools will replace a larger number of conventional machine tools, how should the resultant extra manufacturing floor space be utilized?
4. Will the newly acquired machine tools create "islands of automation"? If so, comment on how the problem might be handled.

Thompson Specialty Machining, Inc., Part 2

Don Kuhn, manager of operations for Thompson Machining, feels that the productivity of his industrial engineer, Doug Beck, could be improved if he acquired a personal computer with software which could aid him in plant layout and other industrial engineering activities. Personal computers such as the Apple Macintosh or IBM PC (or some other compatible computer) have database and drafting software which could aid in layout work. Mr. Beck would be able to create drawings of existing layouts and templates of machine tools and equipment used by Thompson, and these could be stored in the computer's memory. Currently available PC's have extensive main memory and hard disk capabilities which make all this possible.

Questions:

1. What is your feeling about Mr. Kuhn's proposal?
2. What about making hard copies of large or small layouts? How about color?
3. Do you think there might be a problem in training Mr. Beck or some other person if they have not been used to computers?

11

FUNDAMENTALS OF CONTROL

Planned control of all activity is a basic characteristic of modern industry. Effective control of people, materials, machines, and money contributes toward the making of profits so essential to the free-enterprise system. In the next few chapters of Section 3 we shall discuss primarily the control of materials—their procurement and storage—and the processing of these materials by workers and machines. First, however, let us study the fundamentals and principles that are common to all control procedures.

Control Fundamentals

When one hears of manufacturing control, it is usually in terms of automatic control of industrial manufacturing processes. The principles of process control are well established and there are many very successful applications of automatically controlled production processes in industry. It should be realized, however, that the same basic principles that work well for controlling processes can be applied to the manufacturing management process. It will be instructive to look at some of the concepts of process control before showing their use in management control.

Nof and Williams[1] describe automatic control as

---

[1]S.Y. Nof, and T.J. Williams, ''Control Models,'' Chapter 13, *Handbook of Industrial Engineering*; New York: John Wiley and Sons, Inc., 1982, p. 13.10.2.

self-correcting or feedback control; that is, some control instrument is continuously monitoring certain output variables of a controlled process and is comparing this output with some preestablished desired value. The instrument then compares the actual and desired values of the output variable. Any resulting error obtained from this comparison is used to compute the required correction to the control setting of the equipment being controlled. As a result, the value of the output variable will be adjusted to its desired level and maintained there.

Figure 11–1, also from Nof and Williams, presents a block diagram of a simple, single control loop of a process control. More complex control schemes are in use; however, the basic principles are the same. We can generalize the system even more and show how feedback and error correction concepts work in non-mechanical systems.

No matter which of the elements of manufacturing you plan to control, either singly or in combination, there must be four basic phases in the control system. All these basic control steps are interdependent and dynamic in all manufacturing situations. The breaking down of any control problem into these four phases, and the determination of the effective operation of each step, will materially assist in the attainment of a satisfactory solution. These four basic control phases are:

1.   There must be a *plan*.
2.   A record of *actual performance* must be maintained.
3.   Actual performance must be continually *compared* to and *evaluated* with the plan.
4.   Provisions must be made for *corrective action* in manufacturing operations when the results of the evaluation indicate the need for such action.

Let us briefly investigate why each of these steps is essential.

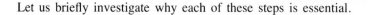

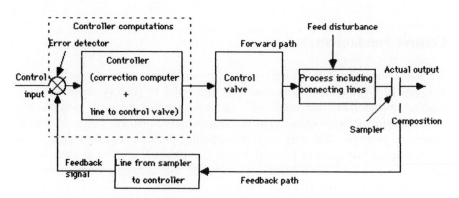

Figure 11-1.   Block diagram of a typical simple, single control loop of a process control system. (From *Handbook of Industrial Engineering*, G. Salvendy, editor, © 1982. Reprinted by permission of John Wiley and Sons, Inc.)

Plan.   A state of control can never exist unless some sort of a plan has been made.

One characteristic of today's industrial enterprise is the formulation of long-range plans, covering periods of from 5 to 15 years, or possibly longer. These plans involve all functions of the business—marketing, manufacturing, personnel, finance—and are based upon the policies and decisions of top management.

It should be pointed out that long-range planning has become increasingly difficult because of the increasing age of the population, greatly intensified world competition, the growth of government regulation and its effects on business, and the continuing inflationary spiral.

Manufacturing, on the other hand, is more often concerned with short-range plans that are made within the structure of the long-range plan. These short-range plans are made to cover that period of time during which the activities of manufacturing are fairly certain or "firm," for example, a 30-day production schedule showing daily output during that period. The establishment of a monthly or yearly budget—either in money or number of personnel—to be used for the maintenance of equipment is another short-range plan.

Day-to-day planning may be necessary for the effective implementation of the short-range plan. The planning of daily work assignments to meet the requirements of the 30-day schedule also may be necessary.

Plans can be identified with workers, materials, machines, or money, or with any combination of these elements of manufacturing. However, in making a plan, a "common yardstick" for measurement must be established. Any one of these elements may be used as a basis for measurement, but the most common base for measurement—and as a result the foundation for most planning—is either money or time.

Time is the common denominator to which practically all manufacturing elements can be resolved.

Actual performance.   All effort used in making plans is a total loss unless attempts are made to follow these plans in the manufacturing activity. Keeping records of actual performance on the same basis of measurement as the plan is an activity that is prerequisite to any system of control.

Comparison and evaluation.   The comparison of the records of actual performance to the plan and the evaluation of the results tell us how well the plan was made and how well it is being followed. When the actual performance meets the planned performance, the manufacturing situation is said to be "in control."

When performance fails to meet the plan, the situation is considered "out of control." It is possible to be "in control" and still not be operating at optimum efficiency; such a situation should be evident in the broad evaluation of performance.

Another aspect of evaluation is the prediction of possible failures in the manufacturing activity by a study of trends in performance. Anticipation of possible production bottlenecks or materials shortages by careful study of performance is one of the most valuable tools of management.

Corrective action.   Ideally, no corrective action should ever be necessary. Realistically, corrective action is the most important aspect in a control situation. Modern manufacturing is too complex to anticipate all possibilities of delays and failures when making the plan; and at the same time the allowance of too much time or money in anticipation of such problems is not good planning. As a result, corrective action is often necessary and should be taken without hesitation.

There is a difference between *correction* and *replanning*. Corrective action does not recognize any change in the original plan, for the objective of the corrective action is to get operations back on the original schedule or budget. Generally speaking, schedules and budgets should not be changed to meet failures in performance. When such changes are made, the performance of the plant is the controlling element—not the plan. It is because of this that a state of control seldom exists except where effective corrective action is being taken.

Replanning.   Replanning has its place in modern control situations. However, it is most effective when used to improve the making of plans in the future. The key to successful manufacturing controls is the constant improvement of all plans for the manufacture and distribution of goods. The use of a "re-plan" to compensate for failure to meet an original plan should be made only when one is aware of all the circumstances involved. There may be external circumstances beyond the control of the planner—for example, a market demand change or an economic downturn.

Common Characteristics of Good Control Procedures

For optimum results, there must be a clearly defined objective for every manufacturing control situation. This objective should state what is to be controlled and the degree of control that is to be maintained. Control is a tool of management that requires careful study and analysis in order to avoid the establishment of controls for the sake of control only. Too often many controls are planned that contribute little, if anything, to the efficient operation of the factory.

The objective of the control system must receive careful and continuing consideration when establishing the goals of plans. In a sense the objectives control the plans, which in turn are used for the control of manufacturing. In like manner, any change in the ultimate plan—or replanning—automatically affects the objective. Replanning should be permitted only when the objectives of the control situation can be changed without excessive loss.

"Degree of control" means how close a control needs to be maintained. Is it necessary to record production every hour, day, or week? Must an accurate inventory count be made of all parts at all stages in their processing? It is obvious that there is a point of diminishing returns where the value of such records no longer justifies the cost of their accumulation. If possible, the desired degree of control should be clearly stated in terms of the objective of the system of control.

The design and installation of control systems present a challenging problem to the industrial engineer. Some "bench marks" of good control procedures for the analysis or design of control systems are discussed in the following paragraphs.

Simplicity. Control systems should be made as simple as possible. The fewer the forms, records, or instruments that must be maintained, the easier the system is to operate, and the fewer opportunities for error. Simple systems are also easily understood by the personnel involved.

Low cost. This is an obvious "bench mark." As we shall see in later discussion of the many manufacturing controls, the savings that those controls make are often intangible. This makes the justification of high-cost systems difficult.

Adequate and timely information. This is a principal characteristic of the second phase in a control system: the recording of actual performance. Determination of the *adequacy* of information the system will obtain requires considerable judgment. Enough information must be gathered for the making of decisions; however, in many cases the accumulation of all the information that might seem desirable is too costly. An economic balance must be struck between record costs and the value of the information obtained. Information must also be *timely*. If trouble spots are to be anticipated and corrective action taken, all records must be up-to-date. Learning of the failure to meet a production schedule a week or month ago does not permit taking steps to avoid such failure. Timely information predicts *before* the completion date that the schedule will not be met—this is the indication that corrective action is necessary. As the chapters that follow point out, there is widespread use of computers in recording and processing data.

Flexibility. Although it is generally agreed that replanning should be held to a minimum, a certain amount is almost always necessary. This requires changes in plans, with the resultant changes in the control records. In much the same manner, corrective action will require adjustments in plans and schedules. A good control system permits the making of such changes without "upsetting the apple cart" and with a minimum of confusion and expense.

Permit management by exception. The system of reporting actual performance and comparing and evaluating it with the control plan should be such that only situations that require corrective action are brought to the immediate attention of management or supervisory personnel. This is, of course, the basic principle of management by exception. However, procedures should be so established that corrective decisions can be made at the lowest level possible in the management structure.

Force planning and corrective action. A control system can be so designed that management and the personnel operating the system are continually forced to look ahead. Manufacturing control is dynamic in every aspect; it is not a static or "one-shot" affair. Good control plans should foster better planning for future operations. Also, good control plans force corrective action by signaling failures to the next higher level of management.

Manufacturing Controls and People

One other area is common to all manufacturing management control problems: people. In all cases, people are involved—both management and labor. It makes little difference whether the industrial engineer is planning a new system of control or is concerned with the continuing effectiveness of an existing plan of control. At all times the personal factor must be considered. All personnel must first recognize the advantages of and the need for effective control of the manufacturing activity. Next, they must be "sold" on the system of control to be used, and finally they must be educated and trained for its effective operation.

Recognition of need. A definite recognition of the need for the control must be established. In many cases, as we shall see later, this is not too hard to do. Losses owing to ineffective controls can be identified and savings that will result from better controls predicted. The biggest obstacle here is the natural human tendency to resist change. It is often difficult to sell a new control plan to a management that is currently making good profits with the present system. The need for control must be clearly defined and constantly kept before all people involved.

Selling the system. A successful control procedure requires the full cooperation of all manufacturing personnel—from the operator on the machine or assembly line to the top management. Effective control is everybody's job. Many a plan has failed because not everyone involved believed in the need for the control or in the procedure planned for the system.

Education and training. A sound program of education and training will materially influence the success of any control program. This means the education and training of all, from top management personnel on down to the worker. Of course, more detailed education and training are indicated for those personnel who will actually operate the system. Again, this also is not necessarily a one-time affair. Control systems maintain their optimum effectiveness only when a continuing program of education and training is conducted.

Basic Causes of Control Failure

Many well-designed control systems fail to produce the anticipated results. It is not possible to enumerate all the factors contributing to such failures. However, we can briefly consider a few of the principal reasons why a control system or procedure does not function properly.

Any control system can be likened to a chain: it is as strong or effective as its weakest link. Most control procedures are in reality a system of industrial communications consisting of many steps. At each of these steps information is fed into the system, drawn from the system, or accumulated and compared with the goals of the plan. A failure at any point in the procedure "contaminates" all subsequent results that are recorded or observed by control personnel. All information up to the point of failure is valid; after the point of failure all information is inaccurate and may contribute to inefficient operation of the plant.

An entire system of control should not be condemned when in all probability failure can be isolated to only one—or at most a few—steps in the procedure. There are two basic sources of trouble: operating personnel and basic data.

Operating personnel. It is obvious that incompetent personnel who continually make mistakes should be relieved of their assignments. This, however, may be only a short-range correction of the problem. The failure of a clerk may be due to lack of proper training. He or she did not understand the "what," "how," and "why" of the duties or their importance. In the preceding paragraphs we discussed the importance of education and training of personnel if the control procedure is to be effective. Also, we pointed out that personnel who are thoroughly competent must be "sold" on the system.

Sometimes a system fails because a single person does not do the job properly.

Basic data. The results obtained from any control procedure are no better than the accuracy of the information fed into the system. Inaccurate costs, standard times, inventory counts, or any one of the other items of basic data upon which the system operates will result in poor performance. One grossly inaccurate estimate as to either cost or production time for a large component of a product may result in a poor plan for the control of production. The reporting of an inaccurate count of materials in a mass-production plant may result in a complete shutdown of the lines. Basic data must be as accurate as the degree of control demands.

Degree of control determines the degree of accuracy required in basic data. In a highly competitive market of consumer goods, costs must be controlled to tenths of one cent or possibly closer. For custom manufacture of heavy apparatus, control need not be so close. In an inventory some items must be accurately accounted for; others may be counted in hundreds and this count made monthly or possibly only once a year. Basic data must be accurate within the units of measure that are dictated by the degree of control.

Control as a Tool of Management

Any control procedure is a tool of management and not an end in itself. Maintenance of control communications and records must be justified by savings resulting either from their use in planning future operations or from the improved efficiency of day-to-day manufacture.

Every system of control has its limitations. Control procedures, for example, do not make decisions; they simply indicate when decisions are necessary and possibly what decisions should be made. Effective use of manufacturing controls depends upon the considered judgment of the people involved. There must be a thorough understanding of the control system and of the extent and validity of the information resulting from the communication procedures in the system.

The objective of the system must be in evidence at all times. *The least control that accomplishes the objective is the best control.* The fewer the records, reports, and steps in the control procedure, the simpler and less costly the system. This is a simple principle; however, the realization of this overall objective is difficult.

QUESTIONS

1. How would you apply the fundamentals of control to one of your own activities?
2. Prepare a plan covering your activities for the coming week.
3. What corrective actions might you take if you got behind in your own work schedule?
4. What units of measure might be used in setting up controls for
   (a) The baking of bread in a bakery?
   (b) A community fund drive?
   (c) An insurance company?
5. By June 15th a gasoline service station has pumped 650,000 gallons. The sales budget for June is 1,800,000 gallons. Is corrective action necessary? If so, what are some of the steps that should be taken?
6. A print shop promised to deliver 5000 special envelopes to you last Friday. When you went for them, they were not ready; you were asked to come back the following Tuesday. Make a list of the possible causes for this delay.
7. Outline a scheme for controlling sales. What types of corrective action would be appropriate in this scheme?
8. Apply the control fundamentals to a typical problem faced by a company president. Do the same for a department foreman. What basic differences are there between the two?
9. Discuss the ways computers may be of use in performing the various steps of control that can be applied to production management.
10. Draw an organization chart for any system with which you are familiar. Describe how control principles could facilitate the flow of information throughout the organization.

CASE PROBLEMS

Midwest Electric, Inc.

Thomas Sadowski, manager of operations for Midwest Electric Company, has a very time-consuming job. Midwest, a large producer of watt-hour meters and other devices for measuring electrical consumption, employs approximately nine hundred people at its Illinois plant. Twelve production foremen report to Mr. Sadowski, in addition to the managers of production control, maintenance, and industrial engineering. Mr Sadowski's day is often filled with conferences and meetings with these individuals in order to solve production problems that arise from time to time. Many times Mr. Sadowski does not leave the plant until late at night, and he always arrives at 7:00 a.m. each morning.

Recently, Mr. Sadowski has felt that he is not "managing" as he should be, but is continuously helping his subordinates to "fight fires." He feels that this is not his job; the foremen and others should do this. He really wishes to delegate authority and give responsibility to completely solve problems which occur at lower levels. To this end, he has studied the elements of control theory and feels that the four fundamentals of control, if properly applied to this situation, would allow him to delegate authority to his first-line managers and still get feedback to enable him to exercise his authority only when needed.

Questions:

1. Describe how each of the four levels of control should be applied to enable Mr. Sadowski to achieve his goal of delegation of authority while still retaining control.
2. If Midwest had a distributed computer system within their plant which had the capability for electronic mail, would this help in the implementation of a control system? Explain.
3. Differentiate between how the first-line production supervisors, the maintenance manager, the industrial engineering manager, and the manager of production control would perform under such a control system.

Meldrum Manufacturing Co.

At a meeting with all his department heads, Mr. Wilson Waterman, the factory manager of Meldrum Manufacturing Co., was discussing the use of automation in the plant. He expressed the opinion that the word had been overused and misused a great deal and that the true meaning related to a process that makes use of the fundamentals of control. He said a good example of automation is the temperature regulating system on home furnaces.

Mr. Balsa, the chief engineer, questioned this concept of automation and pointed out that a $100,000 machine recently installed by the company to produce plastic moldings automatically looked like automation to him. He emphasized the fact that this machine replaced a battery of six older machines and could be operated by one person while each of the older machines required two workers.

Questions:

1. Does automation include all four fundamentals of control? Explain.
2. Does a temperature regulating device on a home furnace employ the four fundamentals of control? Explain.
3. Outline Mr. Balsa's concept of automation in general terms.
4. What general features would have to be included on the $100,000 machine to make it conform to Mr. Waterman's concept of automation?

12

INVENTORY MANAGEMENT AND CONTROL

For the next few chapters we shall be primarily interested in the control of material in manufacturing. Actually, we are concerned with the control of the "flow" of material from a "raw" state to a finished product. Most industries buy material, transport it to the plant, change the material into parts, assemble parts into finished products, and sell and transport the product to the customer.

In our discussion of manufacturing controls, we will consider the planning for optimum quantities of material at all stages in the above-mentioned cycle, and the design and establishment of systems of control to attain this objective, as *inventory management*. We will refer to the actual steps taken to maintain proper stock levels in "raw" materials and finished goods as *inventory control*. Control of the material as it is being processed will be covered in a later chapter on *production control;* however, it should be noted that inventory control and production control are related.

If we add to the above the activity of *purchasing*—or procurement—and *traffic*, which is generally considered to cover the movement of material to and from the plant, we complete our coverage of the entire flow cycle from the buying of raw materials to the delivery of the product to the customer.

With the continuous development of industry, the importance of this total field of activity in material is steadily increasing. Improved methods and mechanization have contributed to the trend of a greater material dollar content in each product and a reduced labor or machine dollar content. As a result, in some concerns the functions of material control—inventory management, purchasing, inventory control, production control, and traffic—have been grouped under one function called *material management*.

Objectives of Inventory Management and Control

The ultimate objective of all manufacturing controls is to realize a profit through the operation of the business. A more restricted objective of the control of material is to satisfy the customer by meeting the schedule for deliveries. Failure to deliver orders on time is one principal cause of loss of business and customers. Effective control of the material throughout the manufacturing cycle reduces the chance of this problem arising.

In any consideration of the nature of discrete part manufacturing it is plain that as material flows through the system, it is subjected to starts and stops. Material must wait for machines or materials handling equipment to become available and must be ordered in advance of production and stored in a warehouse or storage area. Inventories are thus a necessary part of the contemporary manufacturing environment, and they must be managed if profits are to accrue. It should be noted, however, that the introduction of elements of computer-integrated manufacturing have reduced, to some extent, manufacturing management's dependence on some types of inventories. Also, the Japanese concept of "just-in-time" production scheduling may reduce manufacturing's dependence on inventories.

Specific objectives of the inventory management and control group are to maintain optimum inventory levels and inventory turnover for operation of the business at maximum profit and, through the control of inventories, to insure that the right material, in the right quantity, and of the right quality, is made available at the right place at the right time.

Inventory Classifications

In the same manner as we identify the various functions in material management with the flow of goods, we can identify the different types of inventories or stocks of material maintained in a manufacturing plant. All plants use the same general classification of inventories, including raw material, purchased parts, work-in-process, finished goods, and supplies.

Raw material.   A raw material inventory includes all items that, after being received at the plant, require additional processing before becoming an identifiable part of the finished product. It is obvious that the finished product of one plant—such as roll, bar, and sheet steel—may be the raw material for the next industrial purchaser.

Purchased parts.   This classification of inventory is applied to component parts of a product that need no additional processing before being assembled into the finished product. In some cases this material may be classified as raw material inventory. More times than not, however, a separate classification is justified. The TV picture tube that is the finished product of one manufacturer becomes a purchased part to the television set manufacturer.

Work-in-process.   This classification of inventory is self-explanatory. All material that leaves either raw material stores or puchased parts stores enters the work-in-process inventory until the product is completed and placed in finished goods. Work-in-process is the inventory of material, the flow of which is controlled by production control procedures to be discussed in a later chapter.

Finished goods.   Again, this is self-explanatory—it is the stock of finished products. Generally speaking, this classification applies to the quantities of finished goods that are held at the factory awaiting shipment. In many instances, however, it will include stocks held in warehouses owned and operated by the manufacturer, or stocks held on dealers' floors on consignment. In this latter case the value of the finished goods inventory is usually very high and a principal factor in the financial management of the company. A typical example of this is the piston ring manufacturer, who, in addition to supplying the original car manufacturer, also maintains large stocks of many different sizes of piston rings in automotive supply houses for quick service to the auto repairman. Usually, these stocks are on consignment; that is, the piston ring manufacturer does not receive any payment for the goods until they have been sold by the distributor.

Supplies.   All the materials needed for the operation of the plant that are not used as parts of the finished product are classified as supplies. The chapter on cost accounting identifies this inventory classification as "indirect material." On the other hand, the material that becomes part of the finished product is called "direct material." Lubricating oils, sweeping compound, light bulbs, and many other items fall into the supply category.

Optimum Inventories

The complex relationship between modern industry and its market presents a real problem in the size of inventories that should be maintained. Large inventories in the face of declining sales mean lower profits. Small and inadequate inventories in the face of an increasing market demand may result in the loss of sales to competitors—and a decreased profit. Recognition of these conditions should indicate that the optimum inventory is not necessarily either the minimum or the maximum level of inventory; nor is it operation at a maximum inventory turnover.

Inventory turnover. A very common index of inventory control, inventory turnover is the ratio of the value of the product shipped to the average investment in inventory for the same period:

$$\text{Inventory turnover} = \frac{\text{Value of product shipped}}{\text{Value of average inventory}}$$

Obviously, the higher this index, the lower the inventory levels and the lower the cost of maintaining the inventories. Also, it is obvious that a high index indicates a shorter manufacturing cycle with all the saving inherent therein.

Inventories represent a financial investment: the purchase price paid for the material, the cost of labor applied to goods that are in process or finished, and the cost of handling and storage. A determination of the proper ratio of this investment to operating profits can be used to establish optimum inventory levels for all classes of inventory. This may be done on a historical basis or by empirical means. On the other hand, it has been one of the most popular fields for investigation by use of the tools of operations research.

The planning of optimum inventory levels by inventory management requires close cooperation with the marketing function. Market trends must be predicted accurately and inventory levels adjusted—increased when increased sales are anticipated, and decreased when a lower sales volume can be foreseen. This is a problem in both marketing and manufacturing communications and again presents an opportunity for research and development of scientific means for determination of the proper solutions.

Economic lot size concept. Throughout this century management scientists have devoted considerable effort to the mathematical formulation of inventory models. An elementary building block of this analysis has been the so-called economic lot size model. Through the years it has been used to determine manufacturing batch quantities for in-plant production orders and also for determination of ''optimum'' inventory levels.

An example of a non-complex lot size model is presented later. It should be noted that many variables can be shown to affect inventory levels and most models cannot include all of them. However, even the simpler models have been shown to give good approximations. The following are considered to be basic governing factors:

Rate of usage. The anticipated rate of usage of the part must be considered together with the time required to produce a replacement lot. Quantities should be established such that at all times stock will be available to the assembly departments. This principle is used by the materials control group in determining inventory levels.

Ordering cost. Next in importance is the cost to acquire the item. In a manufacturing situation this would be a setup cost. If the part is purchased, an ordering cost would be incurred. For a cost such as this, the quantity purchased or made is important; the larger the quantity, the lower the per-piece cost. For example, if it costs $40 to set up a machine—that is, to mount the tools and get them properly set—and if only 10 pieces were to be made, the unit distribution of this cost would be $4. If 1000 pieces were to be produced, setup costs would be only 4 cents per unit. A similar example could be made for a purchased part.

Deterioration or obsolescence.   Another factor to be considered is the posdeterioration or obsolescence of a large stock of parts.

All these factors must be weighed by management and an economic lot sizedetermined that will result in the acquisition of parts at an optimum cost per unit.Availability of productive capacity for such lot sizes must be determined and included in the considerations.

Economic manufacturing lot sizes must be checked periodically, as they are subject to revision owing to sales trends and variations in the factors mentioned above.

An elementary lot size model.   The use of economic lot size models has been in effect for many years, and the literature abounds with the many formulations that have been proposed. One of the problems that arises in the use of mathematical models is the fact that many factors have a bearing on optimum lot sizes,and one can't weigh all of them in a simple formula. On the other hand, a number ofthe factors that appear in many of the complex formulas that have been developed have so little effect on the final answer that they may be left out. Also, one finds thatthe unit costs obtained for an economic lot size will vary only slightly for quantitiesa little above or below the exact economic lot size.

In considering economic manufacturing lot sizes, two opposing sets of costscome into play—the carrying costs per unit and the setup costs per unit. It is evidentthat the carrying costs per unit will increase as the size of the lot increases; likewise,the setup costs will decrease as the lot size increases. This relationship may be represented mathematically by the classic lot size model,

$$\text{Total cost} = \frac{QI}{2} + \frac{RS}{Q}$$

where the first term defines the carrying cost and the second the setup cost. If the relationship were depicted graphically, the point at which the two curves cross would be minimum economic lot size Q_0 defined by

$$Q_0 = \sqrt{\frac{2RS}{I}}$$

where

$$Q_o = \text{Economic lot size}$$

$$R = \text{Annual use of the item in units per year}$$

$$S = \text{Cost each time a new lot is ordered (setup cost)}$$

$$I = \text{Carrying cost per unit per year}$$

As an example of the use of this model, let us consider the following numbers:

$$R = 1000 \text{ units per year}$$
$$S = \$20.00 \text{ per order}$$
$$I = \$0.20 \text{ per piece per year}$$

Then

$$Q_o = \sqrt{\frac{2(1000)(20.00)}{0.20}} = \sqrt{200,000} = 447 \text{ units}$$

A note of caution should be mentioned regarding the use of this model: it is a simplified account and may not fit the conditions in many real-life situations. For example, it does not take into account variable demand, variable inventory carrying costs, the planning time per piece, and other factors. Thus, if this model doesn't fit the situation, then a model must be tailored to fit the problem.

The use of lot size models for the many different products that have to be made on a production line can frequently lead to highly unbalanced production in the manufacturing facility. This has led many companies to use computers to do the necessary computations and to provide for the "smoothing" or "leveling" of the total production output.

Computer assistance. A full description of the possible and actual use of computers as an aid in the management and control of inventories is beyond the scope of this book. Obviously, however, when large quantities of numbers have to be kept readily available and be changed from time to time, the computer is the direction to go for assistance if its use can be justified. One can do much posting of numbers by hand for the rental or purchase price of a computer, but there will be a point in almost every company's operation when the inventory problem can best be handled by computer, most often using a database management system.

A common application is for all inventory records to be kept in the computer, with inputs concerning sales and purchases or production being constantly fed in so that the computer makes the necessary adjustments. Order points have also previously been made a part of the record for each inventory item, and the computer is programmed to automatically print out a purchase or production order for the item when the inventory reaches the reorder point. This application of the computer is similar to all other applications, namely, that the computer will do exactly and *only* what it is told to do. In one such instance the users were not keeping the economic order quantities up-to-date, and as a result the company ended up with excessive inventories in items that were not selling well. The lesson regarding the need for human intervention at appropriate times is obvious.

A much more sophisticated use of computer assistance involves a company that produces some 850 product types from over 20,000 parts and components. The company has about 350 sales outlets and maintains 35 regional supply centers throughout the country. An on-line computer system is used to knit all these operations together at the factory, and a half-dozen display terminals are available throughout the plant whereby any interested person can learn through pressing a few buttons the status of any part, component, or product. Production managers can shift schedules to meet current demands, sales managers can learn the status of any order, inventory managers can determine the necessity to shift products from one storage area to another, and all can be done making use of instantaneous and up-to-the-minute information.

Inventory costs.   Typical sales personnel wish their company to stock large quantities of all items in the product line so they can meet even the most unreasonable demands of their customers. Typical production personnel wish to keep large quantities of parts on hand so there is never any danger of a production line having to shut down for lack of parts. Inventory people themselves often get carried away with descriptions of computer systems such as those just described and urge the adoption of such systems often just for the sake of proving that it can be done. The point to make here is that all these things cost money, and these costs go beyond the money cost of the parts or products themselves. Since such costs are often lost in overhead cost calculations (see Chapter 17), it is easy for managers to overlook them.

Many companies estimate that it costs as much as 25 to 30 percent per year to carry inventories; that is, each $1 million in inventory costs $250,000 to $300,000 per year to maintain. The main items of such costs are storage costs, obsolescence, damage to stocks, insurance, and the cost of capital tied up in the inventory. It is common for companies to maintain safety stocks in various items, meaning generally that they will *always* have a certain quantity of an item on hand for emergencies. Such safety stocks may well be justified in certain circumstances, but the point here is that the investment in safety stocks would by definition be a fixed investment, almost the same as an investment in a building. Often, better scheduling procedures will reduce the need for safety stocks.

Of course, *some* inventories are necessary in order for manufacturing to be carried out efficiently and in order for customers to be served properly, but there must be an ever present attempt to keep these inventories at the lowest level possible and still provide good service. It is hard to determine just when an optimum has been achieved, but one common measure is the inventory turnover ratio mentioned earlier. The ratio can be increased either by increasing sales or by reducing inventory, but either way earnings on investment are boosted. Carefully checking and controlling the various costs of inventory as individual items of overhead is another way of working toward optimum inventories. Close policing of economic order quantities has already been mentioned, and the plant industrial engineer can often come up with many other suggestions. But the mathematical model will also cost money the same as computer time; so the inventory manager must optimize system costs the same as inventory costs.

Factors Influencing Inventory Management and Control

Many factors influence inventory management and control. The principal effects of these factors are reflected most strongly in the levels of inventory and the degree of control planned in the inventory control system.

Type of product. If the materials used in the manufacture of the product have a high unit value when purchased, a much closer control is usually in order. Jewelers are much more careful with their stock of diamonds than they are with display cases full of low-priced costume jewelry. This same principle holds in manufacturing.

If the raw material used in the product is available only in a short or controlled market, this may easily influence the purchase of this material and the level of inventories maintained. In the past this has been true in the tin can industry. Purchasing agents had to watch the world tin market very closely and buy large stocks of tin at the right time as controlled by the price rather than by the production demand of the factory producing the cans.

The manufacture of standard products as compared to production of custom items will influence the inventory problem. Standard products are usually made in greater quantities and at higher rates of production; also, it is good practice to use raw material and purchased components that are standard items of the supplier. As a result, material is easier to obtain and the control of the inventory need not be so close. In addition, there is greater chance of getting back the investment in the case of overages in stock.

Custom production is more of a "one-shot" affair. Close control is required to insure that special material and parts are not lost during manufacture. A special item worth only a few dollars may hold up the production of an order worth several thousands to the manufacturer. This situation occurs particularly when producing heavy equipment, such as special machine tools, large steam turbine generator sets, buildings, or ships. On the other hand, expensive items, like motors and controls or other major components that represent a large investment, should not be received too far in advance of the date on which they are required. Inventory planning in such cases extends to include careful analysis of the delivery of material.

Type of manufacture.   The close relationship between the type of product and the type of manufacture makes an analysis of the effect on inventory controls somewhat repetitious. Continuous manufacture is common to the manufacture of standard products. However, some standard products are made in batches. Where continuous manufacture is employed, the rate of production is the key factor. Here, as a matter of fact, inventory control is of major importance and in reality controls the production of the product. The economic advantage of this type of manufacture is the uninterrupted operation of the machines and assembly lines in the plant. It is a major offense on the part of the inventory control personnel to have the plant shut down for lack of material. Intermittent manufacture, on the other hand, permits greater flexibility in the control of material.

Volume.   The volume of product to be made, as represented by the rate of production, may have little effect on the complexity of the inventory problem. Literally millions of brass bases for light bulbs are manufactured each month involving the control of only two principal items of raw material inventory. On the other hand, the manufacture of a large locomotive involves the planning and control of thousands of items of inventory. Both the inventory problem and the difficulty of controlling production increase in complexity with the number of component parts in the product and not with the quantity of products to be made.

Inventory Management

The planning of the control of inventory can be divided into two phases, *inventory management* and *inventory control*. Inventory management accomplishes the first phase, consisting of:

1.   Determination of optimum inventory levels and procedures for their review and adjustment.
2.   Determination of the degree of control that is required for the best results.
3.   Planning and design of the inventory control system.
4.   Planning of the inventory control organization.

The second phase of planning, which is the day-to-day planning required to meet production requirements, we shall discuss later as inventory control.

Optimum inventory levels.   Earlier, we discussed how inventory management is responsible for determining the inventory level that will result in the best profit. We have already pointed out that the trend of sales must be watched closely and inventories adjusted *in advance* of the change in rate of production as determined by actual sales. But this is not the only factor that must be considered by inventory management when determining inventory levels. The planning for the actual production of the product may involve problems of leveling production, that is, producing at a constant rate even though sales may fluctuate. In slack times products are built to stock; the finished goods inventory is increased to offset the demand anticipated when future sales surpass the production rate of the plant. The proper evaluation of this factor requires close cooperation with the manufacturing function.

The actual level of the inventory may also be improved by a close study of the manufacturing cycle. How long does it take a shipment of steel to pass from the raw material inventory to its appearance in the finished goods inventory as a part of the product? A study—in cooperation with the manufacturing function—of the ratio of actual processing time to waiting time may be most revealing; and when unnecessary delays are eliminated, the level of the work-in-process inventory may be materially reduced.

All these factors must be considered when inventory management seeks to establish the best inventory levels in all the different inventory classifications. It is easily recognized that this is a complex problem, which might be reduced to a mathematical model.

The interesting part of this problem is that it is not static. The picture is constantly changing; hence inventory management must plan for the review of the results as often as is necessary. Determination of what is "necessary" is in itself a problem. Some industries with consumer goods products such as food, soaps and detergents, and clothes have built up records such that reviews are needed only when major economic trends are apparent. There is considerably more risk in high inventory levels in industries manufacturing items such as the automobile or household appliances. In concerns with a multi-product line, trends of sales of each product must be watched; this is the case in furniture. Suffice it to say that, once solved, the problem of optimum inventory levels has just started!

Degree of control.   Inventory management must decide just how much control is needed to accomplish the objective. The least control—as evidenced by systems, records, and personnel—that is required to perform the function efficiently is the best control. This problem of the degree of control can be approached from the viewpoint of quantity, location, and time.

Economic purchase and manufacturing lot sizes are *quantity* considerations. These, however, are based largely on the economics of the supplier—the vendor in the first case and the manufacturing function in the second—and do not consider quantity from the viewpoint of the user. The user is concerned with the problem of optimum inventory quantities and the degree of control required for the maintenance of the planned inventory level. One approach that is gaining wide acceptance is the analysis of inventory requirements based upon the value of each item. Each item in the inventory is analyzed in relation to its yearly investment value. Almost inevitably, it is found that a small percentage of the parts in the product represents a large portion of the inventory investment, while a large percentage of the parts actually requires little investment of funds. For the "high-cost" items, plans are made to keep close control of this inventory by accurate records of receipts and issues and by close coordination of incoming shipments with production requirements. On the other hand, the items that are "low-cost" may simply be ordered in larger quantities covering several months' need, no record being made of their issue to manufacturing. More stock is simply requested when the existing stock reaches a reorder point. The intermediate-value items may be established on a perpetual inventory, but without the close control used for the high-value items.

From the standpoint of *location*, the degree of control is the number of controlled storages or control points that are to be established in the flow of the material. It has been generally recognized that inventories can be accurately controlled only if placed in locked storerooms and if written records are made for each change in the amount of each item. A full and strict compliance with such instructions often results in the inventory control being a burden instead of a tool to facilitate efficient production. One manufacturer of small radios has found that an accurate count of incoming material is the only control point needed in the operation of the plant until the assembled radios are accounted for in the shipping department. This, however, is an extreme case. How much inventory, what classification of inventory requires controlled storage areas, and how often during the manufacturing cycle a record should be made of usage, is the problem of inventory management. The greater the number of controlled storages and control points, the greater are both the degree of control and the cost of maintaining it. (Again, we should point out that the control of inventories in storerooms is referred to as *inventory control*, and the control of inventories during manufacturing processes is *production control*.)

The preceding paragraphs have to do with the adequacy of inventory control information. *Time*, or frequency, is another factor in degree of control. How often should inventory reports be made? One large plant makes a record of movement of all items in inventory every day, which, through the use of computer records, makes it possible to give management an accurate summary of the inventory each week or on a few hours' notice if requested. Is such control necessary? This is a problem of inventory management. In many large assembly plants movements of material through production control procedures are reported hourly in order that any possible delays on the assembly lines can be anticipated. Communications such as we have pointed out here are essential if a comparison of performance to plan—an essential step in any control procedure—is to be accomplished. The degree of timing planned for in any manufacturing situation must be justified by the prevention of losses that might be incurred if such communications were not in operation.

Much publicity has been given during the early 1980's to the Japanese-style "just-in-time" inventory concepts. Entire books have been written on this subject; we will just briefly describe it here. The goal of JIT is simple enough: get the material to its next processing point just at the time it is needed. Theoretically, then, no inventory will be needed. JIT can be implemented with manufacturing work-in-process or with material purchased from outside vendors. The latter will require coordination with these vendors. Generally, they will cooperate if it is a case of getting the order or not. In fact, it may turn out that the vendor will carry the inventory. One truck transportation company obtains much of its business by catering to companies that must deliver parts to other companies ''just in time.'' The Toyota company in Japan has developed a scheduling discipline for internal control of in-process material movement, called Kan Ban, which substantially reduces WIP inventories, and hence reduces the associated costs.

Having determined optimum inventory levels and the degree of control to be established to maintain such levels, it is then the problem of inventory management to design the required inventory control system and plan the organization for its effective operation. This team of system and personnel comprises the function of *inventory control* in a manufacturing organization.

Inventory Control

The inventory control group puts the plans of inventory management into operation. These plans are seldom complete in every detail. The day-to-day planning required to meet production requirements—the second phase of planning for inventory control—is the responsibility of this group.

Another responsibility is the recording and reporting of transactions involving movement of material and of the effect on the different inventories. This is the picture of actual accomplishment by the plant of the flow of material. The comparison of this performance to the existing inventory plan, and the evaluation of the current material control situation, together comprise the next step in inventory control.

The most important step, however, is the initiation of corrective actions. As we have indicated before, modern manufacturing requires careful planning. When applied, these plans often go astray; manufacturing activities can be controlled only when such variations from the original plans are detected early enough to permit emergency measures that will bring production back into accord with the original schedule.

Figure 12-1 is a simplified inventory model showing key points and quantities. Actual inventory variations in any particular situation will undoubtedly look different from that shown, but the terms will have relevance in any inventory control situation, and the numbers attached to the terms will provide the basis for corrective action in the control of any particular item.

Inventory Control Systems

Control of manufacturing inventories is basically a problem in industrial communications. Earlier, we indicated that the complexity of these systems is directly proportional to the number of items in the inventories and to the number of transactions that have to be recorded to keep abreast of the movement of the material (thus maintaining the degree of control needed to meet the objectives). It should be emphasized here that a great many of the inventory control systems in use in industry

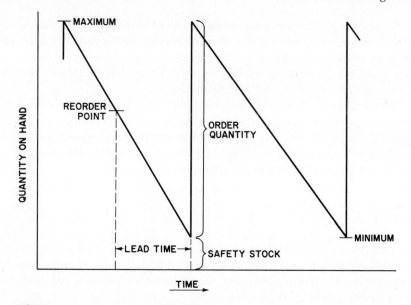

Figure 12-1. Inventory model assuming constant usage and instant replacement.

today are computer-oriented systems; however, the initial part of the discussion in this section will be concerned with basic concepts and data associated with inventory control procedures in general, without reference to capabilities of computer systems. When inventory forms are discussed, it is implied that these could also be records associated with a file in a database management system.

When a close control of inventory items is needed, some form of perpetual inventory is usually employed. A sample perpetual inventory record is shown in Figure 12-2. This type of record is called a "perpetual" inventory because a new inventory figure is determined after each transaction, so that at any time the quantity in inventory can be determined. It is evident that keeping such records for low-cost items may often cost more than the stock of items is worth.

The basic information normally carried on perpetual inventory records includes:

1. On order. This part of the record shows the quantity of material ordered but not received. New orders are added in this column and receipts subtracted.

2. Received. All receipts are posted here; there is no balance quantity in this column.

3. On hand. This balance figure represents the quantity of the item that should be in the stock room. Receipts are added to this column and issues subtracted.

4. Issued. A record of all quantities issued to the factory is entered in this column.

5. *Allocated.* In this column are entered the quantities to be reserved for later issue for specific orders. Reserving of materials still in the stock room will insure their availability when they are needed on the manufacturing floor.

6. *Available.* This is the quantity of material "on hand" that is still available for assignment to future orders.

The foregoing is fundamentally the information that can be obtained from any perpetual inventory record. In essence, it shows at any given time the quantity of material that can be assigned to incoming orders, the quantity that is being held for orders already received and in process, and the quantity of material that has been ordered from the vendor or the shop and has not yet been received by the stockroom.

Actual control of inventories is by the comparison of these levels of inventory to the planned level. Perpetual inventories are operated with a planned *minimum available* and generally with a *reorder quantity* that is greater than this value. When the availability reaches this reorder point, a purchase requisition or shop order is originated and a record made in the "on order" column. Properly operated, a perpetual inventory system should never result in an oversupply of the item. However, a *maximum* is established, and if this value is approached by the availability quantity, the situation should be investigated.

In some cases a value of the inventory is also recorded. This presents a problem in determining values.

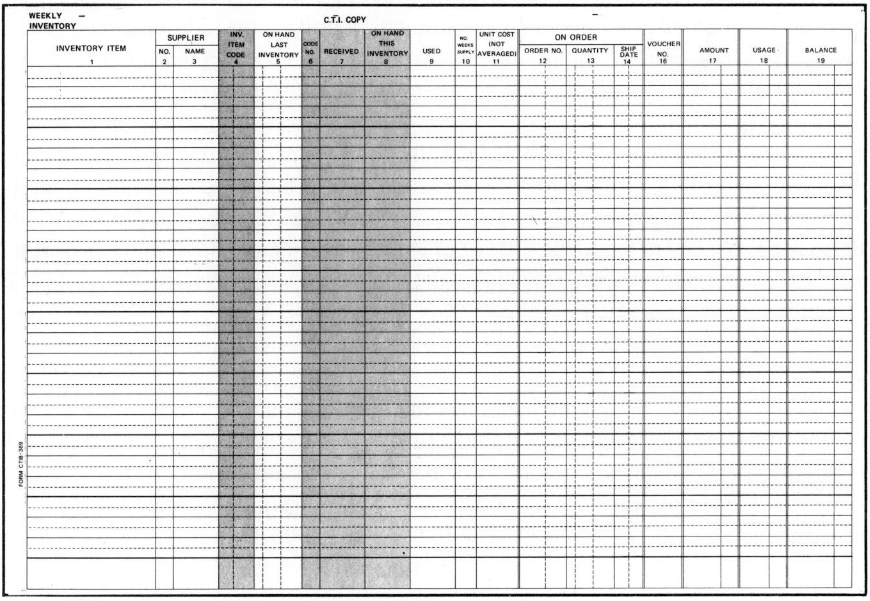

WEEKLY INVENTORY — C.T.I. COPY

INVENTORY ITEM 1	SUPPLIER NO. 2	SUPPLIER NAME 3	INV. ITEM CODE 4	ON HAND LAST INVENTORY 5	CODE NO. 6	RECEIVED 7	ON HAND THIS INVENTORY 8	USED 9	NO. WEEKS SUPPLY 10	UNIT COST (NOT AVERAGED) 11	ON ORDER ORDER NO. 12	ON ORDER QUANTITY 13	ON ORDER SHIP DATE 14	VOUCHER NO. 16	AMOUNT 17	USAGE 18	BALANCE 19

FORM CT18-369

Figure 12-2. A typical perpetual inventory record. Note that it contains order status information on the right as well as inventory status on the left. (Courtesy Moore—Business Forms & Systems Division, Glenview, Illinois.)

Pricing inventories.   There are four basic ways to price inventories for accounting purposes:

1. First in–first out (FIFO).   Under this procedure, all issues are priced at the cost of the oldest lot until that lot is used up. Then the price of the next oldest lot is used, and so on. In other words, the first price into the inventory is the first price out of the inventory when issuing materials.

2. Last in–first out (LIFO).   Under this procedure, all issues are priced at the cost of the newest lot until that lot is used up. Then the price of the next to newest lot is used, and so on. If, in the meantime, another lot comes in, the price of this even newer lot is used when issuing material until the entire quantity involved is issued, at which time the price reverts to the next newest unused quantity.

3. Average value.   Under this system, the values of issues are computed by using the weighted average cost of the material in stock. As new material is received at slightly different prices, a new computation must be made as to the weighted average cost of the total material on hand.

4. Standard costs.   A standard cost is established for each material, and all disbursements are charged out at this standard value regardless of the price actually paid for the material. The standard cost is a calculation based upon either possible replacement cost of the item or an average of past purchase prices for that item. At any rate, the standard cost should be a good estimate of what the material in question should or will cost. As the price of new material varies from lot to lot, a difference between actual purchase price and disbursing price to the factory will be generated. This difference is charged to an inventory variation account and is finally cleared out at the end of the year to the profit-and-loss account.

Two general points need to be made in connection with these pricing systems. The first is that all systems deal with the problem of pricing and have nothing to do with the physical items themselves. A different set of policies will govern which items are being disbursed to the factory upon request. For example, if one is dealing with perishable items or with items that deteriorate with age, obviously one should issue these items on a first in–first out basis. On the other hand, an inventory of lead slabs will undoubtedly be issued on the basis of last in–first out, from a practical point of view.

The second general point is the fact that these systems of pricing have only to do with the accurate costing of a manufacturing process. In the end, all such inventory accounts must balance out to zero, for one is not attempting to make or lose money at this point. Profit in a concern is made by charging a price for the final product over and above the cost of producing that product. In properly pricing inventories, we are simply attempting to accurately determine the cost of production.

The FIFO and LIFO systems of pricing inventories have greatest application in businesses that deal with fairly large inventories of items held for long periods of time. Items where these systems come into use would include commodities such as corn, wheat, hides, and soybean oil; and perhaps steel bars and other units, more or less standard, which may be stockpiled over a period of time. In general, the preference is to use the LIFO system during a period of inflation and the FIFO system during a period of deflation. In following such a guide, the businessman is attempting to get rid of his highest-priced items first and thereby place himself in a more favorable position in the future. Shifting from one system to another, however, can only be done with the permission of the Internal Revenue Service.

For a great many inventory items the choice in pricing seems to be largely between the average system and the standard cost system. Many items are used up during an accounting period and so it becomes unnecessary to consider either a LIFO- or FIFO-type system. In addition, many items are not necessarily affected to any large extent by inflation or deflation, and any fluctuation in price that takes place is relatively minor. In these cases the average system is quite satisfactory, although it has the drawback of having to perform repeated mathematical manipulations each time a new shipment is received. This is one of the reasons why many companies follow the standard cost system even though it results in a variation in inventory value that must be charged off at the end of the year.

Basic communication forms.   The basic communication forms used in perpetual inventory control are:

1. Purchase requisition.   This form is prepared by inventory control when new quantities of material should be ordered.

2. Shop order.   This form is prepared by inventory control when quantities of material need to be made by the shop for stock.

3. Receiving reports.   These are the records of material received by the stock room.

4. Stores requisition.   This form authorizes the issuance of any class of inventory material from a controlled storage to the shop. These requisitions may be prepared by the production planner (as we will discuss under production control) or by foremen, supervisors, or other authorized personnel.

These four forms are the principal sources of basic data in inventory control. Their names, although in common use, are not standardized. The name given to the form is not important; it is the function or purpose of the form that should be recognized at all times when evaluating its part in the inventory control procedure. Samples of these forms are shown in Figures 12-3 to 12-6.

In many inventory control systems other forms may be used. One of these will be an inspection report. This report will record the quality of the material, which may be raw material received from a vendor, or else component parts, subassemblies, or assemblies produced by the factory. It is this form that ties inventory control in with quality control. (The latter manufacturing control will be discussed in Chapter 15.)

PURCHASE REQUISITION   /QUOTATION CHART

| PART NUMBER | | | | | PART NAME | | | PREVIOUS PART NO | | PCN NUMBER AND /OR B /P DATE CHG LTR | | VEHICLE(S) LINE |

| COMMODITY CODE | PART CLASS | FINISH SPECIFICATION | DATES SAMPLES REQ D | DAILY VOLUME | ANNUAL VOLUME | MODEL YEAR | DATE OF INQUIRY | REPLY REQUESTED BY | BUYER |
| REMARKS AND CLAUSES | | | | | | | | CODE | |

| PREVIOUS SOURCE(S) NAME | PRICE | PERCENTAGE | REMARKS | GENERAL COMMENTS |

NAME

CODE

DATE PREP. BY SUPP / DATE REC. BY BUYER	/	/	/	/
FOB & /OR SHIP POINT				
U.S. /FOREIGN & CONVERSION				
PIECE PRICE FOB SHIPPING PLT	$	$	$	$
PIECE PRICE FOB OUR PLT	$	$	$	$
ANNUAL PIECE PRICE OUR PLT SHIPPING PLT	$	$	$	$
TOOLS (INCLUDING APPLICABLE TAXES / DUTIES)	$	$	$	$
TOTAL ANNUAL COST FOB SHIPPING PLT	$	$	$	$
TOTAL ANNUAL COST FOB OUR PLT	$	$	$	$
GROSS /WT -NET /WT	/	/	/	/
TOOL /SAMPLE PROMISE	/	/	/	/
TOOL CAPACITY PCS -SHIFTS -HRS PER SHIFT	/ /	/ /	/ /	/ /
LABOR CONTRACT EXPIRATION DATE				CLAUSES ETC

| ECONOMIC LEVEL DATES | LABOR |
| | MATERIAL |

PKG COST INCLUDED IN PIECE PRICE	$	$	$	$
PERCENT OF BUSINESS RECOMMENDED				
PART PURCHASE ORDER NO				
TOOL PURCHASE ORDER NO				

TYPE OF BUY		TARGET	PURCHASE PRICE
TARGET NOT AVAILABLE ☐		OLD OBJECTIVE	OLD PRICE
BLACK BOX ☐		NEW OBJECTIVE	NEW PRICE
KEY PART ☐ NON-KEY PART ☐		DIFFERENCE	DIFFERENCE

| APPROVALS | BUYER | DATE | P A | DATE | G P A | DATE | DIRECTOR | DATE | DIRECTOR | DATE | V P | DATE | PART NUMBER |

Figure 12-3. A typical purchase requisition. (Courtesy Moore—Business Forms & Systems Division, Glenview, Illinois.)

One fundamental principle is that the *purchase requisition* is the *key to material control.* The careful study of the procedures originating this form, as well as of the personnel authorized to sign the requisition, will result in control of inventory at its very beginning. Inventory cannot exist in the plant unless raw material or purchased parts are ordered.

Inventory control records and procedures.   A detailed discussion of the many records and procedures that are used for control of inventories is beyond the scope of this text. There are many commercial systems, such as Ditto, McCaskey Register, Remington Rand, International Business Machines (IBM), and others too numerous to mention. Inventory records may be posted in ledgers or on cards, with each entry made by hand. Basic data of inventory transactions may be typed into a computer terminal and the many calculations or reports can be prepared by computer; however, the use of bar codes and bar code scanners for point-of-transaction recording of data is fast becoming an accepted way of collecting inventory data. One can see this every day at grocery and department stores, but it is also quite extensively used in industry. Bar codes, similar to those appearing on consumer goods, are seen in warehouses and production lines. Hand-held scanner/readers are interfaced with personal computers and are quite flexible for inventory control purposes.

Currently, computers are being used extensively for perpetual inventory records. Airlines maintain a record of available spaces on flights by such means, and mail order houses have immediate information available concerning the status of all their items in inventory. Grocery stores and fast food chains have computers tied in with their cash registers so that both sales status and inventories of items are kept up-to-date. Manufacturers make extensive use of computers for inventory purposes and even have the computer print out a purchase order or manufacturing order when the inventory of an item reaches the reorder point.

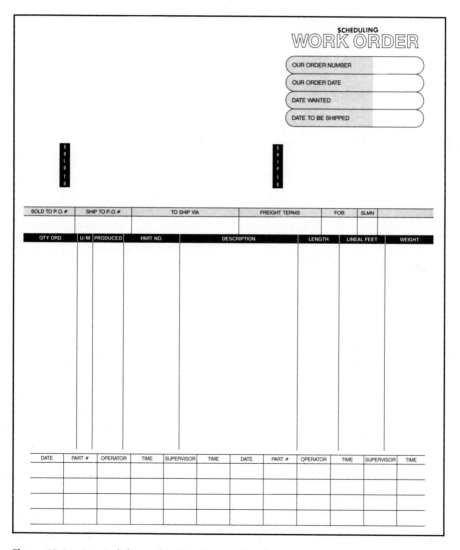

Figure 12-4. A typical shop order. Note the provision for entering information easily. (Courtesy Moore—Business Forms & Systems Division, Glenview, Illinois.)

RECEIVING REPORT

TYPE ▶	RAW MATERIAL		PURCHASED	FINISHED GOODS	CUSTOMER RETURNED GOODS
	1	2	3	4	5	6

REMARKS: IMPORTANT — RECORD ALL VENDOR LOT NUMBERS & UNITS PER LOT ON ALL RAW MATERIALS · OR · ORIGINAL LOT NUMBERS AND UNITS PER LOT ON ALL CUSTOMER RETURNED GOODS IN THIS AREA.

P.O. DATE   VENDOR NUMBER   P.O. NUMBER

SHIPPER NUMBER   PLANT CODE   DATE RECEIVED   DATE UNLOADED

DELIVERED BY:
1 TRK.   2 T.T.   3 B.C.   4 T.C.   5 BARGE   6 OTHER

RECEIVING LOCATION:
LEASE RAIL OW   KK   ZZ   Q   CD   DIRECT DEPT. CHARGE   GEN'L STG.   PREPAID P   COLLECT C

REASON CODE · RETURNED GOODS
1   2   3   4   5   6   7   8   9

CAR INITIALS AND NUMBER   1 COMPLETE SHIPMENT

DEPT. C.C. AND NUMBER · IF DIRECT CHARGE OR CUSTOMER RETURN   2 PARTIAL SHIPMENT

PRODUCT C.C. AND NBR. IF PURCH. F.G.   3 REJECTED

DEPT. NUMBER   HEEL REMAINING   ANALYST   DATE SAMPLED   LOT NUMBER ASSIGNED FOR ANALYSIS   VOUCHER NUMBER   ARRANGEMENT NO.

F.O.B. AND FREIGHT   ROUTE   TERMS   CARRIER

VENDOR   SHIP TO   AMOUNT OF FREIGHT

PRO NUMBER

CARRIER CODE NO.

RAW MATERIAL CODE NO. OR PURCH. F.G. LOT NBRS.	QUANTITY	UNIT	DESCRIPTION	TOTAL LBS. RECEIVED
				(GROSS)
				(TARE)
				(NET)
			GAL. X (LBS./GAL.)	
				(ASSAY)
				(100%)

EXCEPTIONS ON DELIVERY

LOSS AND DAMAGE REPORT NO.   SIGNATURE   ACCOUNTING KEYPUNCH FILE

53	ACCOUNT				AMOUNT	C R	TAX CODE	N D I	MATERIAL	QUANTITY	OTHER	
DIV.	LOC	MAIN	SUB	CLASS							TYPE	DETAIL
02	01	151	00	310							RR	

Q1079 (REV. 6-80)

Figure 12-5. This typical receiving report is designed for reporting each receipt of goods. Note the check list in the upper right-hand corner to simplify work. (Courtesy Moore—Business Forms & Systems Division, Glenview, Illinois.)

The industrial engineer planning an inventory control system has many methods open for consideration, and can also ask expert advice from the systems engineers employed by the manufacturers of the equipment that we have discussed above. In the final analysis, however, whatever system or method is adopted, the economics of the situation must govern the choice—hand posting versus machine records, clerical payroll versus machine investment or rental.

Bin control. We have discussed perpetual inventories at length. Again, they are applicable to what we have previously designated as high- or intermediate-value inventory items. It is still evident that such procedures as we have touched on briefly are costly. For those items in which the cost of keeping such records cannot be justified, a *bin control* is usually adopted.

In its simplest form, the bin control is based on the minimum inventory quantity, reorder point, and maximum inventory quantity determined by the study of the numbers of items required to meet the production plans of the plant. When the material is stored in the bin, the quantity equal to the reorder quantity is boxed or sealed. Material is issued from the bin without any record being made of the quantities issued. At the point where the "reserve" stock is required to fill the stores requisition, a purchase requisition is prepared and forwarded to the purchasing department. Material will then be purchased to bring the quantity of stock up to the maximum. The minimum stock may also be sealed or boxed with the reserve or reorder quantity. If this second seal is broken, the material previously ordered should be expedited.

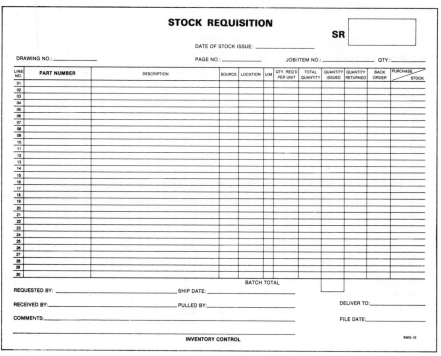

Figure 12-6. A typical stores requisition. Note the provision for the cost of the material withdrawn from the inventory. (Courtesy Moore—Business Forms & Systems Division, Glenview, Illinois.)

Bin control is a simple inventory control system. On the other hand, it should be realized that the minimums, as well as the reorder points, must be reviewed periodically in order that the stock of the item being controlled be maintained at an optimum level.

Storerooms.   Storerooms (or stock rooms) are areas in which material is held in controlled storage. All material received in the area is counted and recorded; none is issued without the proper stores requisition. Controlling materials in such a manner costs money in terms of space, personnel, and handling. These costs must be offset by better service to the factory and reduced loss of materials.

Proper location of storerooms must be related to the whole manufacturing process and considered when laying out the plant and deciding on the materials handling methods. Central storerooms require less personnel; decentralized storerooms, located with material near its point of use in the factory, require more personnel but usually cost less in the handling of material.

Space allocated to storerooms is non-productive. As a result, the general tendency is to reduce such space to a minimum, often crowding receiving and issuing areas until inefficiency results. There is a trend toward evaluating storerooms on a cubic-foot basis rather than a square-foot basis—thus forcing the planner to utilize overhead space to a maximum.

In modern production plants storerooms are often replaced by overhead conveyors that are used for storage. This point was discussed in the chapter on physical facilities. However, in again considering the entire situation, perhaps the problem in storerooms is whether or not they are needed at all. In many plants material is simply stored near the point of usage, without any controlled storage.

If storerooms are employed, the storekeeper should be held responsible for the material in this area. This can be accomplished if the room is properly enclosed and locked and if only authorized personnel are permitted to handle the material being received or issued.

Physical inventories.   A physical inventory is used to verify the balances shown on the perpetual inventory records and to obtain a correct count on all items of inventory that may be on a bin control system. Physical inventories may be taken in two different ways.

Using the first method, plans may be made for a complete shutdown of manufacturing activity. During this period teams will count all material in storerooms and on the shop floor. Material in process must be identified as to the stage it has reached in the manufacturing process. After a complete physical count has been made, operation can be resumed. The effect of this procedure on production is self-evident.

The second method, a continuous physical inventory, offsets this problem. Under this system, a certain number of items of inventory are counted each day or week and the perpetual inventory records adjusted accordingly. With careful planning the entire inventory can be checked with a minimum number of inventory teams and the entire job accomplished without disrupting production.

In addition to adjusting possible errors in the perpetual inventory, the physical inventory is utilized to adjust the inventory accounts in the accounting department. This requires that the perpetual inventory be priced and extended. Again, the policy for this procedure must be established. First in–first out, last in–first out, average value, or some other procedure for pricing inventories must be decided upon. Once decided the policy must generally be adhered to–it cannot be changed from year to year.

In computerized inventory planning and control procedures, like the MRP methodology to be described below, it is essential that inventory counts be as accurate as possible, all of the time. Production and inventory replenishment orders are automatically made (or not made) on the basis of the inventory balance currently in the computer record. Since it is impossible to physically count all inventory items everyday, especially when there are thousands of different stockkeeping items in inventory, another, statistical sampling-like method called *cycle counting* is used. In this procedure, a very small fraction of the different items is physically counted each day and the quantity found is checked with the quantity recorded in computer memory. It can be shown statistically that this method can insure that the total inventory count will be very accurate. Landvater[1] describes how this can be achieved.

Materials Requirement Planning

Earlier sections of this chapter have presented what might be called a classical approach to inventory management and control. A somewhat more elaborate and improved approach called *materials requirement planning* (MRP) has been developed in recent years and is gaining popularity in industry.

The previous system placed considerable emphasis on the ''when'' and ''how much'' questions of inventory management. The ''when'' was answered by the determination of order points, and ''how much'' was determined by calculations of economic order quantities (EOQ) or economic manufacturing quantities (EMQ). The literature abounds with formulations of these two determinations under various sets of conditions.

The order point and EOQ system assumes that each item in inventory is independent of all other items and can be ordered independently. This may be true in some instances, but certainly not with assembled products. In such cases items are definitely dependent upon each other, and MRP permits the calculation of future demands coordinated in time according to when they are required on the production line.

---

[1] See Darryl Landvater, ''How to Achieve 95% Accuracy in Your Stockroom,'' *Modern Materials Handling,* February 1981, pp. 42–45.

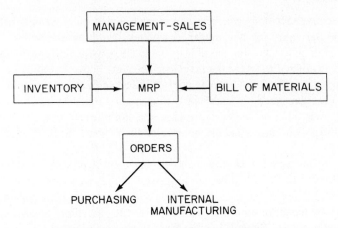

Figure 12-7. The coordinating role of MRP.

The coordinating role of MRP is shown in Figure 12-7. Inputs from management and sales would be customer orders and orders to produce products for stock. Basic inventory information would be provided by regular inventory records.

MRP would then coordinate the above information with a *bill of material*, usually prepared by production engineers. The bill of material is not simply a list of parts but is "structured," meaning that it indicates the manner in which a product is put together from parts into subassemblies and then into final assemblies. The assemblies listed can then be time phased and made into a *master schedule* which becomes the prime tool of MRP. The master schedule can be thought of as a "production forecast" which in turn can generate material and capacity requirements over a period of time, taking into account the interdependency of these requirements. As shown in Figure 12-7, MRP then issues orders for materials either through purchasing or through the internal manufacturing facility.

The apparent complexity of the MRP system can be handled easily through proper computer programming, with the result that managers can devote their time to managing production rather than tracing material. Emphasis is placed not only on having the right quantity of an item, but on having it at the right time as needed in the production cycle.

Quite clearly, then, MRP is concerned not only with inventory levels but is tied in closely with the function of production planning and control, a subject discussed in Chapter 14. Production planning and control deals with the flow of materials through the actual production process. MRP offers the opportunity for closer coordination between inventory control and production control, with attendant savings in costs as well as improvements in meeting customer shipping dates.

QUESTIONS

1. Under what circumstances might it be practicable to classify such items as nails, screws, paint, and glue as raw (direct) materials? As supplies (indirect materials)?

2. Assume that you are operating a corner popcorn stand. How would you go about deciding how much raw material (unpopped corn, popcorn oil, salt, and boxes) you should always have on hand—your optimum inventory of each item?

3. Select some product with which you are fairly familiar. Make a list of the parts or materials used in making this item and classify them into:
   (a) High-value items
   (b) Intermediate-value items
   (c) Low-value items
   What percentage of the total number of parts do you find in each classification?

4. What are the advantages of purchasing a week's supply of groceries at one time? In what way is this a form of inventory management and control? What factors affect the quantities that you purchase?

5. A manufacturer of small drill presses receives a rush order for two special machines. The base plate needed to build these machines is the standard base plate, K461. On checking the raw material of this item (K461) you find only 45 pieces in stock—all allocated to stock order 4563. Explain what you would do.

6. You are setting up an inventory control system for a plant. One of the items is a small metal bracket purchased from a local source at $0.04 each. Your annual requirements are for 10,000 parts. Explain whether or not you would put this item on a perpetual inventory. A bin control?

7. Does inventory control increase the profits of the business? Explain your answer.

8. Explain in general terms "when" an item in inventory should be reordered.

9. One company has eliminated all storerooms as such, and instead stores all material on the factory floor near the point of usage. Discuss the advantages and disadvantages of such a system.

10. Develop an inventory control system for a new product just starting production when the following information is given:
    (a) Production economic lot size is 1000 units
    (b) Production rate (supplied daily to inventory) is 50 units per day
    (c) Usage rate is 20 units per day
    (d) Production startup takes 10 ± 5 days after an order is placed
    (e) Annual cost of storing 1 unit is $5.00
    (f) Production cost of product is $15
    (g) 240 production and sales days per year

    Determine the following:
    (a) Expected maximum inventory
    (b) Expected minimum inventory
    (c) Order point
    (d) Annual inventory cost for this system
    (e) Inventory turnover

11. What advantage does MRP offer as compared to "order point" control?

12. Compare MRP with "just-in-time".

CASE PROBLEMS

The Morrell Machinery Company

The Morrell Machinery Company is a producer of specialized pulverizing equipment. Almost all of its products are made to customers' special order and vary from small units suitable for making face powder to huge machines used to pulverize rocks.

The company uses in its machines a number of bearings that are relatively expensive and that must be ordered from three to six months before the date they are needed. Because of the required lead time, it has been the practice to keep a considerable inventory of bearings on hand. Under the circumstances it is almost impossible to predict future usage, but the general intent is to keep a six months' supply of bearings on hand at all times. This considerable investment in bearings, however, still has not prevented the delay of a number of orders as a result of an inadequate supply of the right kind of bearing for a specific job.

One difficulty seems to stem from the fact that frequently, when the storeroom clerk is busy with other work, the machine assemblers help themselves to the bearings needed. The assemblers, being more interested in machine assembly than in paper work, will seldom leave requisitions for the bearings they take.

Questions:

1. What steps can be taken to insure that bearings will be on hand when needed?
2. Is there any way the investment in bearing inventory can be reduced?

Mithoeffer Manufacturing Company

The Mithoeffer Manufacturing Company has been producing major home appliances, such as ranges and refrigerators, for many years and has established a reputation for quality and durability in their products. Recently, however, the firm has been under strong price competition from other producers who also make quality products. Mithoeffer management feels that the company ties up a considerable amount of money in work-in-process inventory in order to protect its assembly lines from costly stoppages. Jim Jenson, production manager, recently suggested that the "just-in-time" inventory concept might work very well in the Mithoeffer plant.

Mr. Jenson's idea is to initially have Mithoeffer's parts vendors deliver ordered components, which are needed on the assembly line, at (or very close to) the time they will be needed on the assembly line. A number of advantages should come from this scheme: less space needed for storage, less materials handling, etc. However, all of this depends on the reliability of the vendors: one late delivery could have adverse consequences for the assembly line. Cooperation with the vendors would be a necessity.

After the vendor portion of just-in-time is established (if it *can* be established), Mr. Jenson would like Mithoeffer's fabrication departments to be placed under the just-in-time discipline. This may not be as easy as the vendor problem since many components are produced and they involve a number of manufacturing departments. One concept Mr. Jenson emphasized is that of a well-planned assembly schedule, established for several weeks (or months) in advance, which will "pull" components from the Mithoeffer departments.

Questions:

1. What problems, if any, do you think the vendors will have in achieving the just-in-time requirements for Mithoeffer?
2. Do you think the vendors will be justified in raising their prices to Mithoeffer? Why?
3. Assuming the vendor portion of the just-in-time discipline works, what problems do you anticipate to emerge during the implementation of the in-plant portion of the changeover? Can you suggest any cures for these problems?
4. If, and this might be a big "if," the just-in-time concept works, what benefits do you feel the Mithoeffer firm will achieve? Estimate the cost savings the company will realize.

The Jonesboro Corporation

The Jonesboro Corporation produces space heating units in a number of types and sizes. Most of the parts for these units are made by the company and stored for later use during assembly of the heaters.

Since many different items are made and stored, the company wishes to be certain to manufacture these items in the most economical lot size. The formula used to make this determination is

$$\text{Economic lot} = \sqrt{\frac{2 \times \text{quantity used per year} \times \text{total setup cost}}{\text{manufacturing cost per piece} \times \text{interest rate}}}$$

The company recognizes that the formula gives only approximate results, but its use has been justified because of its simplicity.

Model BY space heater has enjoyed steady sales over the years, and an assembly line operating at a fairly uniform rate of 30 units a day has been set up to produce this heater. This model takes a special nozzle that is not used on any other model. The nozzle is produced on a turret lathe that can be set up for the job at a cost of $30. The combined labor, material, and overhead cost of producing the nozzle once the machine is set up is $6.10 each. The company regularly computes inventory carrying charges at 20% of the average investment in the inventory. The plant operates regularly 5 days a week for 50 weeks of the year.

Questions:

1. What is the economic manufacturing lot size of nozzles for Model BY?
2. What other factors might influence the manufacturing lot size?
3. What types of charges are included in the 20% inventory carrying charge?
4. Comment on the suitability of the formula used.

13

PURCHASING

Purchasing is one of the key functions in the success of a modern manufacturing concern. As we indicated in the preceding chapter, no inventories are created until either raw material or purchased components are bought. This is true in most industrial enterprises, the exceptions being those primary industries that draw upon our natural resources such as coal, iron ore, and crude oil. Manufacturers' profits are affected by good purchasing practices based upon sound principles.

It has already been pointed out that the *purchase requisition* is the "key to material control" since it initiates the purchasing activity. Later, we will discuss in greater detail how the judicious use of this form will contribute to better operating profits.

Purchasing and the Control of Material

Purchasing is an important phase in the control of the flow of materials into the manufacturing plant from the vendor or supplier. The classes of inventory thus controlled are *purchased parts* and *raw material*. In addition, the inventory of *supplies* is controlled by the purchasing activity. We have already pointed out the importance of having material available when required for manufacturing operations, as well as the additional costs incurred if large quantities or expensive items are received too far in advance of the required date. Control of the flow of incoming material is an important responsibility of the purchasing group, particularly when just-in-time delivery of goods takes place.

Objectives of Good Purchasing

As a part of the overall material control activity, the statement of the objectives of the purchasing group will include most of the objectives of inventory management and control given in the preceding chapter. However, let us review them and then discuss these objectives from the viewpoint of the purchasing function.

The primary objective is to contribute toward the profits of the manufacturing activity. Another important objective is to insure the availability of materials so that delivery schedules can be maintained, thus keeping the customer satisfied. Specific objectives that support these goals are:

1. Procurement of the right material, in the right quantity, and of the right quality.
2. Receipt or delivery of this material at the right place at the right time.
3. Purchase of the material from the right source at the right price.

In most organizations the purchasing department is not responsible for determining either what material is to be bought or its quantity and quality, except for routine items such as paper and pencils. Also, other manufacturing personnel may designate the time and place for delivery. However, for effective buying, the purchasing group must be assigned the full responsibility and authority for the determination of the *source of supply* and the *price to be paid*. Each of these factors will be covered in more detail when we discuss the purchasing procedure.

Purchasing Procedure

The complete purchasing cycle consists of the following steps:

1. Receipt and analysis of the *purchase requisition*.
2. Selection of potential sources of supply.
3. Issuance of *requests for quotations*.
4. Receipt and analysis of quotations.
5. Selection of the right source.
6. Determination of the right price.
7. Issuance of the *purchase order*.
8. Follow-up to insure scheduled delivery.
9. Analysis of *receiving reports*.
10. Analysis and approval of vendor's *invoice* for payment.

It will be evident as we discuss each of these steps that in many instances some of the steps will be bypassed. For example, when purchasing a standard item from an old and established source, it is often assumed that the price and terms of purchase are right and the purchase order will be placed upon receipt of the purchase

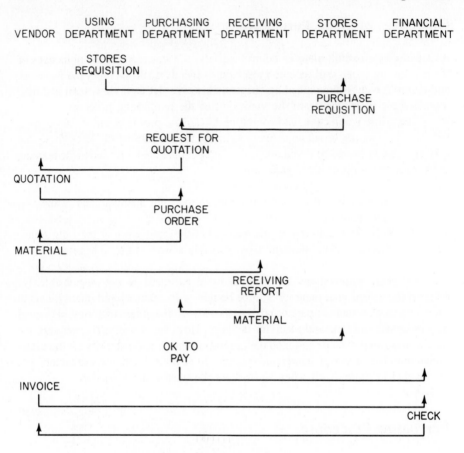

Figure 13-1. Chart of purchasing procedure.

requisition. However, periodic review of such terms and prices is often warranted and may result in substantial savings in the cost of purchased material.

Figure 13-1 charts a typical but rather simple purchasing procedure showing the origination of forms and the flow of forms to various departments. Some of the more important forms are discussed later.

Purchase requisition. Purchase requisitions (see Figure 12-3) normally originate with the inventory control group. Regardless of the type of inventory—perpetual or bin—a reorder point is established. When existing stock reaches this level, a purchase requisition is usually prepared and forwarded to the purchasing group. Minimum basic data that should be on a purchase requisition are:

1. Material. Specifications for material are usually established by the product engineer. If they are not on file in the purchasing department, copies may have to be procured from engineering. In any event, the purchase requisition must indicate clearly just what material is wanted and the required quality.

2. Quantity. The quantity is normally the amount that will bring the inventory back up to the maximum allowable as indicated on the inventory record. In the case of the purchase of raw material for processing, this maximum may or may not be the equivalent of the economic manufacturing lot size. Larger quantities may be purchased if the economic purchase lot is greater. We will discuss this a little later.

3. Delivery date. Sound inventory planning will usually result in the requesting of dates of delivery that can be readily met by the vendor. However, when the date cannot be met it is the responsibility of the purchasing group to notify the requisitioning group at once.

4. Place. Clear instructions as to the location for delivery are most essential, especially in larger plants where the receiving department may be decentralized. In any event, the requisition is not "filled" until the material is actually placed in the inventory where the request was initiated.

Purchase requisitions should be carefully analyzed by the purchasing group to see that they are complete and understandable. In well-planned inventory control all material in purchased parts and raw material inventories will have been "accumulated" on the inventory record; thus, the current total requirement for the item will be indicated by the purchase requisition. However, for miscellaneous supplies— particularly if they are not too well controlled—the purchasing group may accumulate requisitions until an economic purchase lot or quantity has been reached.

Sources of supply. A purchasing group must constantly keep itself informed as to the best places to buy all items of material required. This is no small task. Effective purchasing cannot be accomplished on a status quo basis. It is true that in a going situation old established sources will in all probability be the best sources; however, new sources should be investigated from time to time and the performance of old sources reevaluated periodically. If the purchase requisition is for a new item, then a selection should be made for inquiry from the list of potential sources by use of the *request for quotation.*

Request for quotation. The title of this form is self-explanatory (see Figure 13-2). It is sent by the purchasing group to all the selected possible sources of supply. It should be as complete as a purchase order except for the statement of the price to be paid. It is up to the vendor to submit the price; this is the vendor's quotation. Because this form is so nearly like the purchase order form, it is common practice to print THIS IS NOT AN ORDER in bold type across the form.

Selection of the right source. Upon receipt of the many quotations from the vendors, it then becomes the job of the purchasing group to select the right source. A comprehensive discussion of all the factors that enter into this decision is beyond the scope of this book. Briefly, the purchasing group is interested in the reliability of the prospective source of supply. Questions such as these might well

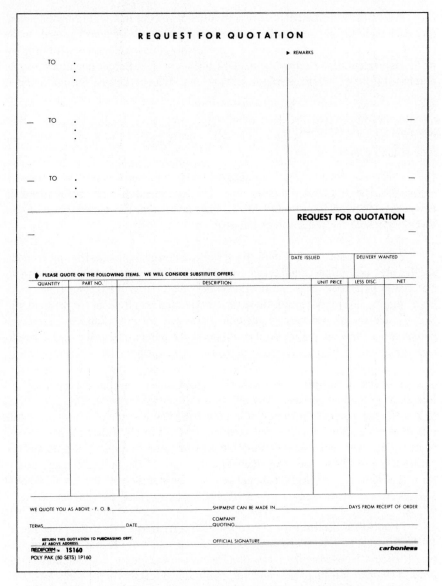

Figure 13-2. A typical request for quotation. (Courtesy Moore—Business Forms & Systems Division, Glenview, Illinois.)

be posed: Will quality be maintained and shipments made on schedule? Does the vendor have adequate tools and equipment, trained personnel, and finances to handle the contract? What is the location of the vendor's plant in relation to the purchaser's plant? What means of transportation are available between these two points? These are just a few of the points that must be considered in the selection of the right source. Obviously, another major consideration is the price quoted. However, the lowest bid may not be from the best source in light of the factors mentioned above.

Determination of the right price.   This is a major responsibility of the purchasing group. Many factors influence what is a ''right price'' and, again, a comprehensive discussion is hardly possible. In a broad sense, a right price is one that is ''right'' for all concerned—the purchaser, the vendor, the buyer's customer, and the public. Obviously, the purchaser must be able to buy material at a price that makes it possible to sell the product at a profit—but profits are also essential to the vendor. Modern industry is too complex and interrelated to permit sharp buying tactics that drive prices to a level at which the supplier cannot make a profit. Profits are essential to our economic system and, as such, essential to the public. In addition, the buyer must consider the reliability of the vendor and in some instances be willing to pay a little more for better service in quality and delivery. The final agreed-upon price may or may not be the quoted price; in some instances, when all factors are considered, it is conceivable that it may be higher. In any event, when the price is agreed upon, the purchase order is issued.

Purchase order.   Once accepted by the vendor, a purchase order (see Figure 13-3) constitutes a contract for the delivery of the goods in accordance with the terms of the purchase agreement. This constitutes a legal document, and it usually

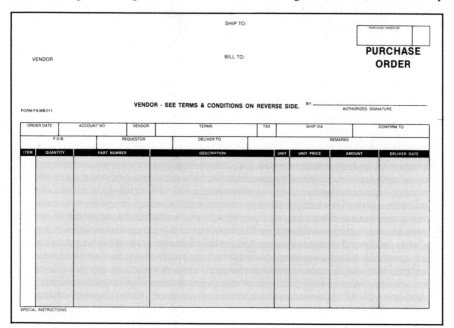

Figure 13-3.   On a typical purchase order such as this, detailed terms of the purchase contract may be printed on the reverse side of the original copy that is sent to the vendor. (Courtesy Moore—Business Forms & Systems Division, Glenview, Illinois.)

contains many other terms of agreement in addition to the quantity, quality, delivery, and price. Both state and federal laws influence purchase contracts, and as a consequence, most firms have printed purchase order forms that comply with the laws under which they operate. Once the purchase order has been placed, it is usually the practice to notify the requisitioning source so that they can enter the quantity in the "on order" column of the inventory record.

Follow-up and delivery.   The plan for the flow of material into a manufacturing plant is established by the purchasing procedure. Determination of the actual performance and comparison and evaluation of this performance with respect to the purchasing plan can only be accomplished by effective follow-up of purchase orders.

The actual production and shipment of the purchased material and component parts are, of course, the responsibility of the vendor. It is in turn the responsibility of the purchasing group to make sure that the vendor is fulfilling these responsibilities. This assurance must be had far enough in advance of the actual specified delivery date so that corrective action can be taken when necessary to get materials into the plant as originally planned. This is usually accomplished by periodic follow-up of all purchase orders, requesting the vendor to reconfirm his ability to ship the goods on schedule.

For a "tight schedule" it also may be necessary to follow the shipment or, if it is delayed, have the carrier—that is, the railroad, trucking line, or air freight service—trace the shipment and expedite its handling. This action is one of the most common tools of "corrective action." However, it should be realized that increased delivery costs are often involved. Other ways in which a purchasing group can take corrective action include transferring some of the orders to other sources of supply and assisting the vendor in his production problems. Docile acceptance of delayed delivery of material shifts control from the purchaser to the vendor. Corrective action—the final element in control—is often necessary to avoid this condition.

Receiving reports.   Careful inspection of all incoming material and parts is essential to effective material control. The purchase order is the basic source of reference. Of course, it is often supplemented by engineering specifications and blueprints. The receiving report (see Figure 12-5) is a record of what is actually received; by comparing it to the purchase order, variations in quantity can be determined. In passing, it might be well to note that a variation in quantity is often agreed upon in the purchase contract; that is, in large quantity production plus or minus 5 percent is often acceptable. If the shipment is "short," it simply means that the reorder point will be reached sooner. "Over" shipments delay the placing of the next order with the vendor. Shortages in excess of the allowed limit are usually placed on a *back order* by the supplier. Accumulations of back orders must be watched carefully by the purchasing group. Too often they are forgotten and all of a sudden stocks start building up beyond the planned maximum.

Inspection reports may be a component part of the receiving report, or they may supplement it. In any event, a report on the quality of the purchased goods is necessary. Discrepancies either in quantity or quality should be called promptly to the vendor's attention. This is normally a function of the purchasing group, but it may be a joint activity of purchasing and inspection. It is an important function of purchasing because, in addition to providing purchasing with a valid measure of vendor capabilities, it insures that proper shipments are received. Control is effective only if quantity and quality of incoming goods are maintained.

Payment of invoices. Invoices received from vendors for goods shipped should receive the approval of the purchasing group. This is the final control step in the purchasing procedure. Invoices should be checked to insure that quantities billed conform with the quantities accepted by the receiving and inspection departments. It is also good practice to check the unit prices on the invoice and the extension of these prices to the total bill. Finally, all discounts and other terms of the original purchase contract should be checked against the invoice. By this final control step, payment is made only for the value of goods received.

Although the above description of the purchasing procedure is brief, we want to point out again that not all the steps are followed in every purchasing situation. However, purchasing procedures should be reviewed often to insure that the correct steps are being included.

Purchasing work simplification. The size and complexity of industry make the job of purchasing correspondingly difficult. Like any procedure, purchasing work can be analyzed, simplified, and improved by work simplification techniques. Study and the reduction of the number of forms used, as well as the use of flow charts of the purchasing procedure, will not only increase the efficiency of the system but should reduce the cost of the purchasing operation. As with inventory control, the magnitude of the purchasing job and of all the records involved is determined by the number of parts or items for which records have to be maintained. In a large company manufacturing a multi-product line of goods, many thousands of separate purchase records must be maintained. Current trends are toward mechanization of these records by the use of computers where justification is possible.

Value Analysis

Although value analysis has been discussed in the methods engineering chapter, it requires further amplification here inasmuch as the value analysis function is commonly thought of as a part of the purchasing activity. The basic idea of value analysis is simply that of a cost-reduction technique, and as such, it might logically be treated as a part of methods engineering and of purchase simplification as discussed in the previous section. However, as it is frequently used, purchasing people have a very definite role to play; so perhaps it is logical for value analysis to be under their general direction.

The objective of value analysis is to get more value from an item in terms of function. This can and should be done whether the item is manufactured within the plant or purchased from the outside. Outside purchases make it relatively easy to evaluate savings since there is often a difference in quoted prices for the items, and the difference is a real savings to the company. The General Electric Company pioneered value analysis work, and we cite one or two of their experiences to illustrate what is meant by this process.

One of their parts was a push button that had been made as a screw machine part. Investigation among suppliers resulted in a push button that could be cold-headed from aluminum wire. Cost of the item dropped from nineteen cents to two cents. Another part was a steel "J" bolt with threads on the long end. The drawing simply said, "cut thread." A rolled thread specialist studied the part and suggested that the words "cut thread" be removed from the drawing, thereby making it possible to roll the thread. This was done and the part could then be purchased at 1.5 cents as compared to 11.7 cents formerly. The company saved eighty thousand dollars.

In both of the cases cited the function of the part remained the same, and the new part could perform this function as well as the old. The difference was the tremendous savings in cost of purchase; hence, the value of the parts increased enormously.

Value Analysis Approaches

A number of approaches have been suggested and used to facilitate the development of value analysis, and many of these approaches have been used in methods work for years. The reader is reminded, however, that any special techniques developed for value analysis should be applied to parts produced *by* the plant as well as to those purchased *for* the plant.

Asking questions is probably the simplest and most effective approach. The General Electric Company has worked out ten particular questions they feel are useful in value analysis work, and they submit each part to the ten questions. Typical questions are: Does it contribute value? Does it need all of its features? Can a standard product be found that will be usable? If a part fails any of these questions, the analyst makes a more detailed investigation. However, much depends upon the knowledge and ability of the analyst, and a part may not fail one of the test questions until after the analyst has thought of another possible solution to the function being performed by the part in question.

Frequently, a lucrative source of cost reduction can be found by asking questions of designers and others who may indicate specifications on blueprints and on bills of material. Designers who specify tolerances for a part much closer than those actually required in the application will obviously cost the company more money either in producing the quality specified or in purchasing that quality. The "J" bolt example mentioned earlier is a case in point. The designer most likely indicated "cut thread" for this part because he was unaware of any other way to produce the thread.

Making a comparative analysis is another approach used by value analysts. Investigation of all similar-type parts purchased by the company might reveal some opportunities to cut the costs of some of those parts. One analyst reviewed all the die castings purchased by his company and obtained clues as to how expensive features might be eliminated on some of the castings. Some analysts plot the weight of similar parts purchased against their cost per pound. If most parts seem to fall on a smooth line, but a few parts fall away from the line, these few might present opportunities for special investigation.

Supplier contacts are a technique of value analysis that may be of considerable help to the purchasing department. Any alert purchasing group is constantly looking for improvement and cost-reduction ideas from the various suppliers with whom they deal, and, likewise, suppliers are normally quick to make suggestions to their customers as to how they can save money. Some companies, however, have arranged supplier seminars to which they invite representatives from all their main suppliers and show special product displays in which every detailed part of their product is spread out on a table or attached to a display board. Suggestions for improvements are solicited from the supplier even if the supplier does not make the part in question. The point is that undoubtedly the supplier knows more about his particular specialty than any of the customers do, and therefore would constitute a valuable source of cost-reduction ideas.

Standardization is another approach of value analysis although, as such, it has been employed by industry for many years. To the extent that a value analysis of various parts and components suggests the possibility of standardization when it has been overlooked previously, value analysis must be given credit. One company reviewed 1447 items in its stock and found it could eliminate 794 of them through standardization. The savings were estimated at $102,000 over a two-year period. Value analysis programs are designed to reduce the cost of an item, but standardization programs may eliminate the item entirely. Certainly costs cannot be reduced any lower than that!

Factors Affecting Purchasing

In the following sections we will attempt to list the many factors that influence both purchasing practices and the results of the work of the purchasing group.

Requisitioning authority.   No purchases should be made without a properly signed purchase requisition. The first and most important step in the control of material is control of the authority to sign purchase requisitions. If "every Tom, Dick, and Harry'' can requisition material, then the control of material is to all practical purposes lost before it starts. Authority to sign purchase requisitions should be limited to as few individuals as possible. In turn, within this group there may be limitations as to the type or value of the requisition that can be signed. In an office one of the stenographers might be authorized to requisition all office supplies to a monthly limit of $250 total. On the other hand, the requisition for a $10,000 machine probably would require the signature of a member of top management.

Type of manufacture.   The type of manufacture influences the purchasing activity. Continuous manufacturing industries, such as those that produce radios and automobiles, normally operate extensive assembly lines. Material is scheduled to these lines with a minimum of stock inventory, and the majority of the control of material becomes the responsibility of the purchasing group. Also, in this case there is a tendency to have a higher dollar content of purchased parts in the product. On the other hand, in an intermittent custom building situation the dollar content of purchased parts may be low; thus, raw materials are then the principal problem of the purchasing group. There is more flexibility in schedules for incoming material. However, for large machine tools and heavy apparatus, delivery of major items is scheduled closely.

Subcontracting.   Items purchased on subcontracts are actually purchased parts or components. However, subcontracting generally takes place when it is not possible to produce the parts in the local plant. In placing this type of purchase order, the vendor is in competition with the purchaser. Care must be exercised to insure that a valid comparison is made between the price quoted and the local manufacturing cost. Close cooperation between product engineering, manufacturing, and purchasing is prerequisite to a successful subcontracting program.

Standardization of product.   In the chapter on manufacturing processes we discussed the advantages of the standardization of products and their component parts. Often it is overlooked that suppliers also attempt to standardize the items that they sell. One of the principal activities of the purchasing group is to encourage the inclusion of vendors' standards in the product design of the purchaser's product. Material and labor costs can often be reduced by the purchase of standard sizes of items such as cold rolled bar steel if the product designer accepts the finished surfaces and dimensions of the raw material as the finished specifications of the product that is being designed. This is only one example of the type of savings that can be effected through standardization. Another approach to standardization for the purchasing group is to analyze the standard stock items (such as screws, bolts, and nails) and request a reduction in the number of sizes required. Minor product-design changes can often be made to accomplish this end.

Economic purchase lot.   Earlier, we mentioned the economic purchase lot. It is similar to the economic manufacturing lot that has been discussed in Chapters 5 and 12; only the cost factors are different. Larger quantities of goods can usually be purchased for lower unit costs. These savings must be balanced against the increased costs for the carrying charges, the same as in the manufacturing lot. In manufacturing we saved in setup costs; here we save in the cost of preparing the purchase order and on all the other steps in the purchasing procedure. Owing to the cost factors involved, it is easier to calculate economic purchase lot quantities.

Short and controlled markets. We have already said that purchasing people have to know where to buy the required items of material. Even if we know the purchasing source, it is not always easy to buy. Some markets are "short"; that is, there is not enough material to meet the demand. Other markets are "controlled"; material is available but total sales are restricted. This is particularly true in times of war; material is allocated to industries, and many items are virtually non-available for the production of civilian goods. Both of these situations present real problems to purchasing.

Cancellations. Cancellation of purchase orders cannot be totally avoided. If work has been started by the vendor, or he has made other commitments on the strength of the order, he may lose considerable money. It is the problem of the purchasing group to keep this loss at a minimum. Most purchase orders have standard clauses covering the liability of the purchaser as well as the supplier. Close cooperation between marketing, engineering, manufacturing, and purchasing is required to anticipate a situation that may result in order cancellations. The sooner purchasing knows of such a possibility, the better are the chances for making the cancellation with a minimum cost to all involved.

Trade relations. Industry is so specialized and extensive that many purchases are made from vendors who in turn buy back their material in the form of the purchaser's product. This is termed *reciprocal buying*. Too often this presents a real problem to the purchasing group. Vendors who are also customers may expect advantages in price, terms, or other things. This detracts from the possibility of arriving at a "right" price. The maintenance of good trade relations under these situations is a real test of a good purchasing group. To be able to give the business to another source and still retain the goodwill of the customer-supplier is the objective of trade relations.

Purchasing Organization

The law of agency. Purchase orders and contracts are signed by individuals, each of whom acts as an agent of the company or corporation. As *agents,* they have been given either *specific* or *implied authority* to act for their employer in the purchase of material, supplies, and services, or in any other type of agreement constituting a purchase. As a consequence, the individual is known as a *purchasing* *agent.* If the purchasing agent is an officer of the company or corporation, the authority is probably specific; however, as the position is usually appointive, most purchasing agents have implied authority. In either event, they act for the concern in the procurement of the necessary material and services.

Organization structure.   There is no set pattern of purchasing organization. The same sound principles of organization apply to purchasing as to all the other functions in the manufacturing enterprise. The position of the purchasing group in the overall organization is largely dependent on the importance of the function. As we have already indicated, in cases where a large portion of the manufacturing dollar is represented by purchased material the senior purchasing agent may have vice-presidential status—and a large purchasing organization to perform the purchasing activities. In a small operation, on the other hand, we may find a single purchasing agent handling all the duties and reporting to anyone from the shop superintendent to the owner of the enterprise.

Centralization and decentralization.   In large organizations—particularly in multi-plant industries—there is a problem of centralization or decentralization of purchasing activities. A full discussion of the advantages and disadvantages of each is beyond the scope of this book. However, decentralized operations are more flexible, and the trend toward increased decentralization of large corporations indicates that this method of organization is currently the most popular. Major purchase contracts for principal materials may be retained on a centralized basis to gain bargaining advantage.

Purchasing group.   The purchasing group in larger organizations usually consists of several purchasing agents, buyers, expediters, and the necessary clerical and stenographic personnel. Organization of this group may be on the basis of product line or purchased material. If the latter, one agent may specialize in the purchase of steel, another in plastics, another in supplies, and so on, the entire organization being developed along these lines. In a multi-product manufacturing plant the purchasing organization may be divided so that certain groups do all the buying for a specific product and other groups for the other products.

Regardless of the basis of the organization pattern, its success will lie in the application of sound organizational procedure and in clear-cut understanding by all personnel of their duties and responsibilities.

Purchasing Practices

It might be well to discuss a few of the many practices of the purchasing function.

Salesperson relations.   Both purchasing and selling are rapidly gaining professional recognition. The continuing technological advance in both materials and processes requires that purchasing and sales personnel be more than "glad-hand artists"—they have to know what they are selling and what they are buying. "Sharp trading" is no longer accepted practice. As we indicated earlier in the chapter, purchases should be made at the *right price;* this can be done only if the buyer and seller each respect the knowledge and integrity of the other. Courteous treatment of the salesperson is prerequisite to sound purchasing practice. Unnecessary waiting can be avoided by giving appointments. It should always be remembered by the buyer that the salesperson is one of the principal sources of current information as to markets, products, processes, and all developments in the field in which they are both interested.

Discounts.   Industrial purchases are usually subject to cash, trade, and quantity discounts. Purchasing agents and buyers must be thoroughly acquainted with these discounts as they apply to the purchases that they are making—and with the legal aspects of the same. To promote fair trade, free from restraint and undue favoritism, laws such as the Robinson-Patman Act, Sherman Act, and Clayton Act must be common knowledge of purchasing personnel, and their requirements must be observed. However, by the use of discounts within the legal limitations, the buyer can effect substantial savings in money expended for material and services. Quantity discounts are allowed for the purchase of increased quantities of goods and are the determining factor in the establishment of economic purchase lots. Cash discounts are made for prompt payment of invoices, and it is often the practice to make an additional charge for late payment. Trade discounts are applied to material that has a fixed list price, the discount being allowed to the trade or related activity of the purchaser.

Blanket purchase order.   With many more or less standard items, companies will often negotiate blanket purchase orders for a period of time with an agreed-upon price. As the items are required in the plant, a request for shipment against the purchase order is made to the vendor without any additional paperwork. Reductions in purchasing costs could be considerable with this procedure.

The blanket purchase order can also reduce inventory costs by procuring materials only as they are required on the production line rather than storing several months' supply. This philosophy of purchasing ties in with just-in-time manufacturing discussed in Chapter 12.

Multiple sources.   It seldom is advisable to "put all your eggs in one basket." Where large quantities are involved, a good purchasing practice is to develop more than one source of supply and divide requirements between these sources. This takes considerable tact on the part of the buyer but insures against the loss of delivery that may result from fire, flood, labor troubles, or other causes that may interfere with production at a single source of supply.

Forward buying.   Although quantities to be purchased are normally determined by inventory management and control, it is often advantageous to purchase quantities in excess of the normal operating requirements of the manufacturing plant. If operational considerations or supply conditions indicate the need for such an inventory reserve, these purchases are termed *forward buying*. Forward buying is done to build up a reserve stock and thereby avoid possible shutdowns; to increase purchase quantities and thereby take advantage of quantity discounts; to purchase in economical transportation units such as a carload or shipload; to protect against risk of material shortages; and, in a short market, to insure the procurement of material of the proper quality. Successful forward buying requires good judgment on the part of the purchasing agent and management.

Speculative buying.   This is not forward buying. In speculative buying materials are bought and held for resale, the hope being to gain the advantage of a rise in prices.

Gifts.   A real problem to the purchasing organization is the practice of vendors of making gifts to purchasing personnel, particularly at Christmas. Although such gifts are not intended as bribes, it is hardly realistic to assume that they will not influence the considerations of the buyer. Many concerns now prohibit their buyers from accepting such gifts. Good purchasing practice, of course, would not consider the acceptance of favors a valid reason for deciding where to buy.

Evaluation of Purchasing

It is difficult to make a valid evaluation of purchasing as an overall activity. General measures such as the ratio of the cost of purchasing to the value of material purchased, or to the value of sales, may provide a useful index within a given organization. It is easier, however, to set up measures related to the more specific objectives of the purchasing group: Is the right material of the right quality and in the right quantity being procured from the right source at the right price and delivered at the right place at the right time? Continuous rating of the accomplishment of these objectives will indicate the success of the function, if not the total efficiency. Insofar as these objectives might be accomplished at excessive cost by the purchasing organization, it might be well to consider the ratio of purchasing costs to the profits of the concern—but again, so many other factors affect these profits that a valid measurement is highly doubtful. Continued research in the field of purchasing will no doubt result in effective ways of measuring this principal activity in the control of material in manufacturing.

Traffic

Because it is normally the prerogative of the purchaser to designate the route and method of shipment of material, in smaller manufacturing operations the function of traffic management is included in the purchasing operation. However, in larger companies traffic departments are charged with traffic responsibilities.

Traffic functions include:

1. Planning of routes for incoming material, including the selection of the method of transportation.
2. Preparation of rate charts for delivery of material.
3. Tracing of shipments to insure prompt delivery.
4. Auditing and approval of incoming freight and other transportation bills.
5. Coordinating the receipt of large shipments to avoid demurrage charges.
6. Handling the adjustment of claims for goods damaged or lost in transit.

Traffic functions need not be restricted to incoming material. In many instances manufacturers accept the responsibility for delivery of their product to the customer. It is interesting to note that one of the first steps in the design of a large steam turbine generator unit is careful planning of the route of shipment. Traffic restrictions along the route, such as the dimensions of an underpass, often must be taken into consideration in the initial design stages. In such cases as these, traffic works closely with sales, engineering, and any other functions of the organization concerned with the delivery of the product to the customer.

QUESTIONS

1. What are the advantages and disadvantages to the homemaker in purchasing a whole side of beef and keeping it in a freezer? Discuss in relation to the principles of purchasing.
2. Assume you are the salesperson for a lumber mill. Prepare a brief statement to justify the price you are asking for your lumber.
3. What is the "right price" for an automobile? Outline all considerations involved.
4. Look at the pen or pencil that you are using. If you were buying this item in large quantities for a school or an office, what would you want to know before placing your order?
5. The advantages and disadvantages of centralized and decentralized purchasing were not covered in the text of the chapter. However, prepare such a list, basing it on your own judgment. Justify each advantage and disadvantage.
6. As a purchasing agent, you are considering placing an order for 5000 wastebaskets.

One quotation is $1.07 per basket, another $1.18, and a third $1.56. What additional information do you want before placing your order? Explain your answer.

7. On what basis could a purchasing agent justify purchasing a standard item from one vendor at a higher price than the identical item could be purchased from another vendor?

8. Discuss the importance of the purchase requisition.

9. Using normal procedures, how does the inventory control department know that an item has been ordered? That it has been received?

10. Is it always good practice to have more than one source of supply? Explain.

11. Outline a plan to bring about just-in-time purchasing, tying it in with just-in-time manufacturing.

CASE PROBLEMS

Midway Products, Inc.

The maintenance department of Midway Products sent a purchase requisition to the purchasing department for 75 heavy-duty push brooms. The purchasing department asked for quotations from three distributors and received the following bids:

    Distributor A: $5.00 each list, less discount of 30%
    Distributor B: $5.40 each list
       Discount schedule:
           10 or more—20%
           50 or more—30%
          100 or more—35%
       Terms: 2%—10: net 30
    Distributor C: $5.00 each list, less 20% and 10%

Questions:

1. Assuming the quality is the same for all three, with which distributor should the purchasing department place the order?

2. Would your answer have been the same if the item had been bearings for a special production order, rather than brooms? Explain.

Bassett Soap Company

The Bassett Soap Company manufactures and sells soap powders for both household and industrial uses. During the production and packing processes a quantity of fine dust is created; this dust is removed by means of a vacuum dust collecting system. Inserted in the air stream for the purpose of trapping the fine dust particles are filters composed of several hundred cotton bags. If any of the filter bags break, dust is blown into the atmosphere; the result is a loss of soap as well as an annoyance to the community surrounding the plant.

Over the years, plant personnel have learned that the bags last for a little over a year, after which small holes begin to appear. It has therefore been the regular practice of the plant to install a complete new set of filter bags each year during the two-week vacation shutdown.

The plant regularly placed a purchase requisition for the replacement bags about 3 months ahead of the scheduled shutdown, and the same quality of bag from the same supplier had been ordered and used for a number of years. To fill the last requisition, however, the purchasing department placed the order with another supplier. It did this on the claim of the second supplier that their bag possessed the same quality characteristics but cost 22 cents less per bag.

The new bags were installed as usual during the last shutdown. Two weeks later some of the new bags began leaking dust as the result of holes that had developed. Four weeks later an emergency order was placed with the former supplier for a whole new set of bags, and a crew of six men was brought in on a weekend at overtime rates to install the new set of filter bags.

Questions:

1. What was wrong with the procedure followed by the purchasing department? What should they have done?
2. Should the plant personnel have accepted the substitute bags since they were not what had been specified on the requisition?
3. What are the extra costs involved as a result of the incident?
4. Who should be charged with these extra costs?

John Sears Corporation

The John Sears organization has always been known to quickly adopt and make use of the latest in technology as soon as it became available. It was one of the first companies in its area to buy a computer even though it had to struggle a little at the beginning to find ways to keep it busy.

The philosophy made it easy for the software salesman that came along one day to sell his package designed for inventory control. A sale was further facilitated by the fact that John Sears' business involved some 25,000 inventory items and presented terrible problems related to costs, stockouts, and obsolescence. Contact with the salesman seemed a godsend for all concerned, and Larry Berg, manager of materials, wasted no time in installing the system.

The system itself was fairly straightforward, for with the proper forms that indicated shipments and also receipts, the computer could tell anyone who desired the exact status of any item including any orders that had as yet not been shipped. An elaboration was the computation, for each item, of the minimum desired level of inventory, the reorder point, and the economic lot size to be ordered when the reorder point would be reached. The computer monitored inventory levels, and when the level of any item reached the reorder point, it would automatically print out an order form for the economic lot quantity that had been stored in its memory.

Many items in the inventory were manufactured by John Sears, while others were ordered from vendors. The order form produced by the computer was therefore made into either a shop order for the plant or a purchase order to be sent to a vendor.

The system was installed gradually, but it proved so successful for the items initially covered, that Larry got permission to spend some overtime money in order to speed up the process and thereby managed to get all inventory items covered at the end of 18 months of effort. At this point everyone sat back and waited to see the results, which would manifest themselves in lower inventory levels and higher inventory turnovers as well as fewer stockouts.

For two years after installation Larry was certain that he saw improvement in all measures of inventory performance. Stockouts were noticeably down and inventory turnover had shown some improvement, although not as much as expected. Total inventory level rose somewhat, but Larry was so anxious for positive results that he tended to overlook this factor.

After two more years Larry knew he was in trouble. Stockouts, inventory levels, and inventory turnover all seemed to have gone almost out of control. Larry's boss gave him a hard time about it all and, since the company had some other problems at the time, decided to call in a consultant to look over the situation.

After several days of study the consultant filed her report. Her conclusion regarding the inventory control system contained the following observations:

> The inventory control system being used is quite satisfactory for this company's operation and is doing the job for which it was designed. However, company personnel are not doing their job in monitoring the system. The computer does not think; people have to do the thinking. Economic lot sizes were entered in the computer some five years ago and have not been changed since to reflect changes in product demands. The result is that some order quantities are too small and result in stockouts, while others are too large and result in ordering a 10-year supply of some items rather than a few month's supply.

Larry was aghast to be told something that he should have figured out for himself and promptly set about to devise some system to monitor demand and thereby keep his economic lot sizes for both internal manufacturing and purchases more up-to-date.

Questions:

1. Review the typical economic lot size formula and show how a change in demand for an item could make the order quantity too low or too high.
2. Discuss the three measures of inventory performance mentioned and tell how they would give the manager some indication of efficient performance.
3. Develop some method of monitoring demand for an inventory item and providing a basis for updating economic lot sizes. Could your system be adapted to computer usage?
4. What differences, if any, exist between economic lot size for manufacturing within the company and economic lot size for purchases from a vendor?

14

PRODUCTION PLANNING AND CONTROL

In any manufacturing enterprise production is the driving force to which most other functions react. This is particularly true with inventories: they exist because of the needs of production. Because inventories are important, we chose to give them separate coverage in Chapters 12 and 13, in which we tried to stress the importance of inventories to production. In this chapter the relationship of production planning and control to work-in-process inventories will be stressed.

Inventory management and control, as well as control of purchasing, is a control of material. The scope of production planning and control is broader. To control work-in-process effectively, it becomes necessary to control not only the flow of material but also the utilization of people and machines. Material requirements planning, discussed in Chapter 12, is a relatively new procedure which attempts to coordinate more closely all those functions dealing with materials. In what follows, we stress production planning and control concepts, the principles of which are basic to either manual or computer-oriented systems.

Objectives of Production Planning and Control

The ultimate objective of production planning and control, like that of all other manufacturing controls, is to contribute to the profits of the enterprise. As with inventory management and control, this is accomplished by keeping the customers satisfied through the meeting of delivery schedules. Specific objectives of production planning and control are to establish routes and schedules for work that will insure the optimum utilization of materials, workers, and machines and to provide the means for insuring the operation of the plant in accordance with these plans.

Production Planning and Control Functions

All of the four basic phases of control of manufacture are easily identified in production planning and control. The *plan* for the processing of materials through the plant is established by the functions of *process planning, loading,* and *scheduling.* The function of *dispatching* puts the plan into effect; that is, operations are started in accordance with the plan. *Actual performance* is observed and recorded by the function of *reporting* or *follow-up.* Actual performance is then compared to the planned performance, and, when required, *corrective action* is taken. In some instances *replanning* is necessary to insure the effective utilization of the manufacturing facilities and personnel. Let us examine more closely each of these functions.

Process planning (routing).   The determination of *where* each operation on a component part, subassembly, or assembly is to be performed results in a *route* for the movement of a manufacturing lot through the factory. Prior determination of these routes is the job of the manufacturing engineering function.

Process planning may be generalized or detailed. In a large manufacturing works area a *general route* may be established by buildings. More commonly, it is established by departments, such as machine shop, assembly, finishing, inspection, or others. *Detailed routing* would indicate the specific work station or machine to be used for each operation. Regardless of the detail in which the routing is initially planned, a precisely detailed route eventually has to be determined. For example, if a lot of parts is routed to the machine shop for processing, and there are three separate operations to be performed in that department, the decision by the foreman or dispatcher as to the three machines to be used for the job determines the detailed route of this lot of goods through the machine shop. However, this is too often a last-minute decision, depending only on the availability of the machines instead of being guided by an effective degree of planning. On the other hand, in continuous manufacturing, when a processing line of machines is used or an assembly line is installed, the route of the materials must conform to the line: the process plans of the parts or assemblies to be produced in the departments were incorporated in the design of the original layout of the plant. The source of basic information for the process planning function is the standard process sheet, which indicates the type of machine or work station required for each operation in the process. In computer-oriented production planning systems, such as MRP, the process plans of all parts to be produced constitute an important file in the database.

Loading.   Once the route has been established, the work required can be *loaded* against the selected machine or work station. The total time required to perform the operation is computed by multiplying the unit operation times given on the standard process sheet by the number of parts to be processed. This total time is then added to the work already planned for the work station. This is the function of *loading,* and it results in a tabulated list or chart showing the planned utilization of the machines or work stations in the plant.

One of the problems in loading is the amount of utilization that can be planned for a given workshift, such as an 8-hour day. For example, owing to factors such as maintenance, repair, and setup, 85 percent utilization is considered a good average for machine tools. Under these conditions, only 6.8 hours of productive work should be loaded for an 8-hour shift. But if workers are on an incentive system and can be expected to earn an average of 20 percent bonus—and the 6.8 hours is based on standard times—a total of 8.16 standard hours can be loaded against an 8-hour shift.

Thus far we have indicated that loading is by work station or machine. This is called *detailed loading.* Loading may be generalized, like routing; that is, groups of machines or departments may be loaded as a single unit. For example, all lathe work may be loaded against the lathe department, or all milling to be done simply charged to the group of milling machines in the plant. The objective of the loading function is to maintain an up-to-date picture of the available capacity in the plant. If a general type of loading is adequate, it should be used and no further breakdown of loads made. Often it is sufficient to keep load charts on only the critical productive units or departments and assume that all other departments have adequate capacity to keep abreast of the production rate.

Obviously, load charts would be referred to when determining routes of orders through an intermittent manufacturing plant. In this case the route is influenced by the availability of department, machine group, or work-station capacity.

Scheduling.   Scheduling is the last of the planning functions. It determines *when* an operation is to be performed, or *when* work is to be completed; the difference lies in the detail of the scheduling procedure. In a centralized control situation—where all process planning, loading, and scheduling for the plant are done in a central office—the detail of the schedule may specify the starting and finishing time for an operation. On the other hand, the central schedule may simply give a completion time for the work in a given department (as in the machine department situation mentioned above). Here the foreman would be held responsible for having all three operations completed by a given date. The detailed schedule for the completion of each of the three operations in the machine department would have to be determined by the foreman or the dispatcher. Again, this is more than likely to be an after-the-fact determination rather than a result of sound planning. However, as with routing, all general schedules eventually become detailed schedules.

Prior determination of *when* work is to be done is the function of scheduling.

Combining functions.   While it is easy to define "where" as *process planning,* "how much work" as *loading,* and "when" as *scheduling,* in actual operations these three functions are often combined and performed concurrently. How far in advance routes, loads, and schedules should be established always presents an interesting problem. Obviously, it is desirable that a minimum of changes be made after schedules are established. This objective can be approached if the amount of work scheduled for the factory or department is equal to or slightly greater than the manufacturing cycle. For optimum control, it should never be less than the manufacturing cycle.

If it normally takes three days for work to pass through a department, the work load should never be scheduled less than three days in advance. The total work load ahead of the department might be three or six months. Obviously, scheduling all of the work load in advance would not be necessary for the effective day-to-day operation and would present a problem if changes in schedule were necessary.

Scheduling too far in advance of operating requirements introduces a degree of inflexibility in the control of production. Load charts may be maintained in addition to the schedule charts showing the total load ahead. This is justified only if it is necessary to identify critical shortages of productive capacity in advance of the normal scheduling procedure. Work can be loaded against a work station or department without being scheduled—but it cannot be scheduled without being loaded.

Dispatching.   Authorizing the start of an operation on the shop floor is the function of dispatching. This function may be centralized or decentralized. Again using our machine-shop example, the departmental dispatcher would authorize the start of each of the three machine operations—three dispatch actions based on the foreman's routing and scheduling of the work through his department. This is decentralized dispatching. Another case of decentralized dispatching would be where the departmental dispatcher dispatched work based upon plans of a central control office, advising them only when the work had been started. In a centralized dispatch situation, when a job had been completed on a machine or at a work station, the departmental dispatcher would call a central dispatcher and ask what job should now be started; the actual assignment of work would thus remain at a central point.

Reporting or follow-up.   The manufacturing activity of a plant is said to be "in control" when the actual performance is within the objectives of the planned performance. When jobs are started and completed on schedule, there should be very little, if any, concern about the meeting of commitments. Optimum operation of the plant, however, is attained only if the original plan has been carefully prepared to utilize the manufacturing facilities fully and effectively.

The effectiveness of any production control system is dependent on timely and adequate information regarding actual performance. This basic information normally originates with the dispatcher. Although the reporting of jobs completed is important, it is of even greater importance that delays in production be anticipated and work that is lagging behind the anticipated production rate be reported promptly to the production planning and control function. A good production control procedure makes this reporting, and a system of counter-checks by follow-up, automatic.

By its very procedures, the system will call attention immediately to danger points in the manufacturing activity.

Effective corrective action is based on these reports. Realistically, some jobs will always be running behind schedule while others may be ahead of schedule. Careful analysis of the situation may indicate how a few changes can bring the late work back on schedule by using productive capacity made available by the jobs that are running ahead of schedule.

Corrective action. This is the keystone of any production planning and control activity. A plant in which all manufacturing activity runs on schedule in all probability is not being scheduled to its optimum productive capacity. With an optimum schedule, manufacturing delays are the rule, not the exception. However, if these delays are accepted without concern and schedules revised, then the actual output of the plant, not the management, is controlling the production. It is by corrective action that management maintains full control. Means are found to get the work back on the original schedule. Jobs are shifted to other machines or work stations, overtime is authorized, and extra help is put on the job. There are many ways in which production emergencies can be met.

Replanning. Replanning is not corrective action. Replanning revises routes, loads, and schedules; a new plan is developed. In manufacturing this is often required. Changes in market conditions, manufacturing methods, or many other factors affecting the plant will often indicate that a new manufacturing plan is needed.

In summation: production planning and control plans, in advance, the route of work through the plant, determines the amount of productive capacity required to do the work, and—based upon the availability of this capacity—schedules all phases of the work so that the plant will be effectively utilized. Once these plans are established, production control provides the means to keep track of manufacturing activity and, when necessary, take corrective action or replan. It is simple: "Make your plan, then work your plan!"

We have discussed each of the production planning and control functions, emphasizing that their application in manufacturing is not uniform. However, it should be remembered that at no time can any function be eliminated. Process planning, loading, scheduling, dispatching, reporting, and corrective action are component parts of any effectively managed manufacturing operation. This is just as true of a basement wood-working shop operated by one man, as it is of a large concern employing many thousands and producing a wide line of products. Production planning and control of itself is a simple procedure; it becomes complex only in its application to a manufacturing situation. Decisions must be made as to the degree of control necessary, centralization or decentralization of the production control procedures, and when the various functions are to be performed.

Let us now discuss some of the factors that affect the application of production planning and control procedures and techniques.

Factors Affecting Production Planning and Control

The factors that affect the application of production planning and control to manufacturing are the same as the factors we have already discussed that affect inventory management and control. Let us briefly review these in relation to production planning and control.

Type of product.   Again, it is the complexity of the product that is important, not what the product is, except as this may in turn relate to the market being served. Production control procedures are much more complex and involve many more records in the manufacture of large steam turbine generator sets or locomotives to customer orders than in the production of large quantities of a standard product involving only a few component parts, such as electric blankets, steam irons, or similar small appliances. Of secondary importance is the type of market being served. A seasonal market may require careful planning of production for maximum output during a limited period of time (this is particularly true in the canning industry). On the other hand, a seasonal market in rubbers and boots may be offset by planning to manufacture to stock during the slack seasons. Manufacturing to stock, as opposed to producing only to the customer order, presents an entirely different situation.

Type of manufacturing.   This is probably the most influential factor in the control situation. For a large continuous manufacturing plant producing a standard product, we have already indicated that the routing was included in the planning of the plant layout. Also, the detailed scheduling of work between operations was accomplished when the many production lines were balanced. As a result, about all that is left for the function of production planning and control in the operation of the plant is to set up key control points in the lines and, once manufacturing is started, to make sure that all the many feeder lines are producing adequate stock so that no shutdown occurs owing to a lack of partially completed component parts or subassemblies. As we have mentioned previously, this situation is for all practical purposes a control of materials at the start of the lines.

Intermittent manufacture of multi-product lines presents quite a different problem. Optimum operation of the factory is dependent upon the effective use of all of the functions of production planning and control. All production planning and control functions occur after the manufacturing order is approved; this cannot be avoided. Depending upon the degree of control desired, the length of the manufacturing cycle, and the decentralization or centralization of control wanted, a production planning and control system must be developed that will result in the optimum operation of the intermittent plant.

Once more, the volume produced, or the size of the factory, is not a factor directly affecting the problem of the design of the control system.

Production Planning and Control Procedures

A detailed discussion of all the techniques and procedures of production planning and control is beyond the scope of this text; many complete texts exist on the subject. We have already indicated that planning and control practices will vary widely from plant to plant. Further, the many ways in which each of the functions might be carried out in practice were indicated earlier in this chapter.

It might be well, however, to point out again that any production planning and control procedure should meet the bench marks of good control practice that were outlined in Chapter 11. Though no production control function can be entirely eliminated, the least control that results in effective operation of the factory is the best control. It must be remembered that production planning and control systems should be tools of management. The objective is not an elaborate and detailed system of controls and records, but rather, the optimum operation of the plant for maximum profits.

Production Planning and Control Systems

Because production planning and control places an emphasis on the control of work-in-process, the system will in effect tie together all previous records and forms developed in all planning for the manufacture of the product. In like manner, this activity brings together all the other functions of the enterprise—marketing, engineering, personnel administration, finance, and manufacturing. Later, in our brief discussion of organization, we will point out that the production planning and control group is most generally a subgroup of the manufacturing function.

Basically, production planning and control systems are industrial communications established to insure proper relationship between market forecasts, customers' orders, manufacturing capacity and rates of production, and shipments.

Let us take a quick look at some of the records or forms that enter into the consideration of the production planning and control group in the performance of its duties. Those records and forms prepared by other functions are said to be sources of basic data—of information that is needed by production planning and control for the effective use of its own records and forms. Note again that these forms or records could be based on records in computer files.

Market forecast. The market forecast will be discussed in the chapter on marketing. Its value to production planning and control is that it will indicate future trends in manufacturing requirements. Workshift policies, plans for an increase or decrease in manufacturing activity, or possible plant expansions may often be based upon the market forecasts and in turn affect the planning of the production planning and control group.

Customer order.   These are received initially by the sales department. This is the *first* of five types of orders involved in a manufacturing situation. Although there is no uniform terminology for all five of these classes of orders, each can be readily identified by what is ordered or authorized by the form. By a *customer order* we mean an agreement to purchase the product; the agreement becomes a legal contract once the order is accepted by the manufacturer. It is really the customer's purchase order (see Figure 13–3). Such orders are usually forwarded to production planning for confirmation of the delivery date requested by the customer. This delivery date—or shipping date—must be carefully considered and agreed upon, often without an analysis of the order and its integration into load or schedule charts. If the request for delivery cannot be met, the matter should be promptly referred back to the sales group for further discussion with the customer before accepting the order.

Sales order.   This is the *second* of the five classes of orders. It is a rewrite of the customer's order specifying what has been purchased—product and quantity—and authorizing shipment of the goods to the customer. Multiple copies are prepared and all interested functions are furnished a copy. Sales orders may be written by marketing, inventory control, or production control. In any event, they are processed through the finished goods inventory (if one is maintained). In a custom manufacturing situation these orders are the base upon which all activity in preparation for manufacture is made. If items are to be shipped from stock, the shipping department will use this order as a requisition to draw the products from finished goods and to package and ship the order. In the other cases these orders are accumulated until economical manufacturing lots are reached and a stock order placed with the plant to manufacture the goods, shipment then being made as the material is received in the shipping department. In all cases, however, the production planning and control group must use these orders as the basic data for the shipping promises to which they are committed.

Stock order.   This *third* class of order is not always used. In the preceding paragraph we indicated how it may be used after sales orders accumulate to an economical manufacturing lot. It is, of course, the principal order when manufacturing to stock. It will authorize production in anticipation of future sales. It may be issued by inventory control or by marketing, but should always be confirmed by the marketing function to insure that surpluses of products are not made that will result in loss owing to obsolescence. As with the sales order, the production planning and control group will determine a completion date for stock orders and from this file will keep track of the dates for which they have commitments.

Shop order.   This *fourth* class of order deals with the manufacture of component parts. Customer orders, sales orders, and stock orders are for the finished product. In the preceding chapters we discussed how, by product explosion, the requirements are established for component parts to build assembled products.

Based upon the shortages that appear in the component parts inventory, shop orders are prepared by inventory control. When passed on to the production planning and control group, this order (see Figure 12-4) becomes the basis for the majority of the routing, loading, and scheduling performed by the plant.

Standard process sheet.   This form, which is prepared by process engineering, has been discussed in detail in Chapter 5. Also, in discussing the function of process planning, we pointed out that it is the source of basic data as to the type of machine to be used, the time required for processing, and the sequence of operations in the manufacture of the product. Routing and scheduling of shop orders, as well as loading of work stations in advance of scheduling, depend upon up-to-date standard process sheets being available to the production planning and control group.

Engineering specifications.   Blueprints and bills of materials are used by production planning and control when they become a component part of the packaged instructions issued to the shop through the control office. One good planning procedure is to accumulate all necessary data for a shop order in a single package— the standard process sheet, the blueprint, the bill of material (if an assembly operation is involved), the route sheet, and possibly the schedule for the production of the order. This complete package is then held pending the dispatching of the work to the shop.

This completes a brief review of the basic-data forms used by production planning and control. The following forms and records are prepared by the production planning and control group.

Route sheet.   This is the form upon which the route of a shop order is indicated. In practice, this form is generally combined with one of the other forms in the system. For example, the shop order, the standard process sheet, and the route sheet are often one piece of paper—usually called the *shop order* or the *manufacturing order* (see Figures 5–8 and 5–9).

Load charts.   These are prepared to show the productive capacity that has been ''sold''—and at the same time the available productive capacity (see Figure 14-1). As we pointed out when discussing the function of loading, these charts may be prepared for each work station or machine in the plant, or they may be for groups of machines or departments. One large manufacturer of heavy apparatus actually loads the entire plant, using as the scale the kilowatt capacity of the equipment being produced. Load charts, as such, are not too common. Their function is usually combined with scheduling, and only one set of charts is maintained: the schedule charts. Computer-oriented production planning and control systems can have capacity planning modules that allow a production planner to interact with the computer to plan an effective allocation of available capacity.

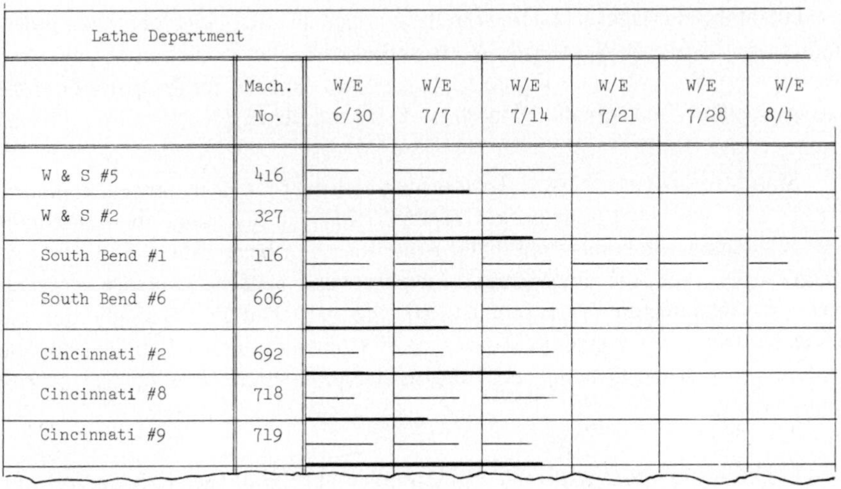

Lathe Department							
	Mach. No.	W/E 6/30	W/E 7/7	W/E 7/14	W/E 7/21	W/E 7/28	W/E 8/4
W & S #5	416						
W & S #2	327						
South Bend #1	116						
South Bend #6	606						
Cincinnati #2	692						
Cincinnati #8	718						
Cincinnati #9	719						

Figure 14-1. A load planning chart showing, for each machine, the work available each week (light lines) and the total backlog (heavy lines).

Schedule charts. Schedule charts are prepared to show the planned utilization of departments, groups of machines, work stations, or machines in the plant. These charts show not only what work is ahead of each productive unit, but also when it is planned that the work shall be done. They are usually a graphical representation—such as the Gantt charts shown in Figures 14-2 and 14-3.

In discussing scheduling, we pointed out that "firm" schedules (schedules not subject to change) should never be less than the manufacturing cycle and, for flexibility, should also not be too much greater than this period of time. A usual solution is to prepare these schedule charts for a three-month period, the first month on the chart being a firm schedule, the last two months being tentative.

In a large shop it becomes quite a problem to transmit schedule information to the many departments involved. We have indicated that it might be included in the shop order package. This solution has the disadvantage that if changes in schedules have to be made there is a lot of paper floating around the shop that has to be located and changed. Another solution is to furnish each department with the portion of the schedule chart that applies to that manufacturing unit. Finally, the schedule clerk might draw off the chart a job priority list for each unit or work station and furnish only these lists to the shop; this has the disadvantage that the departmental dispatcher will not be as apt to anticipate work running behind schedule.

Another problem in schedule charts is the matter of keeping them up-to-date. At least, it is often believed to be a problem. But if we accept the concept that, once firm, schedules should not be changed, then the incomplete work indicated on the chart will show us a *true* "late" condition of our manufacturing activity. The chart will then be most valuable in planning for corrective action. Once an order is late, it should remain late until brought back to the original planned schedule. Some of the above-cited disadvantages would be eliminated in a computer-based system.

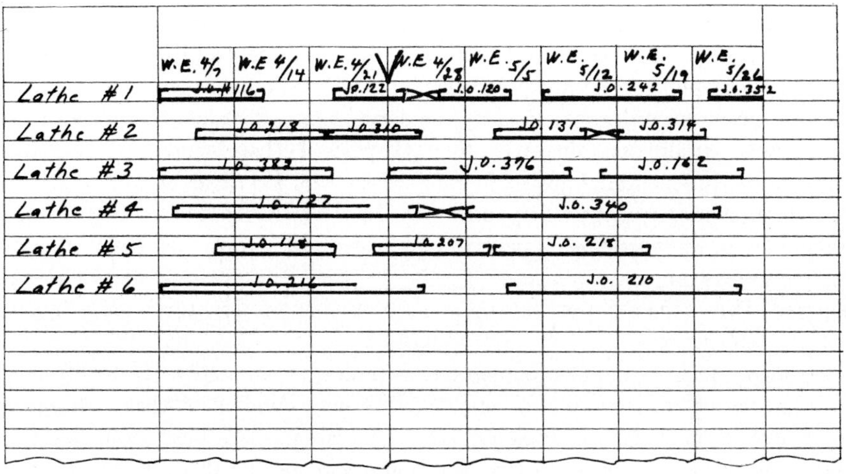

Figure 14-2. A Gantt-type machine scheduling chart showing planned starting and completion time for each job scheduled to each machine. The job order number is indicated, as well as reserved time for maintenance ($\bowtie$). In planning, the horizontal distance corresponds to time, while in posting performance, horizontal distance corresponds to percent completion. Performance has been indicated as of the week ending 4/21, as shown by the V-shaped mark (V), and the chart shows that Lathe number 1 is behind schedule while numbers 2 and 3 are ahead of schedule.

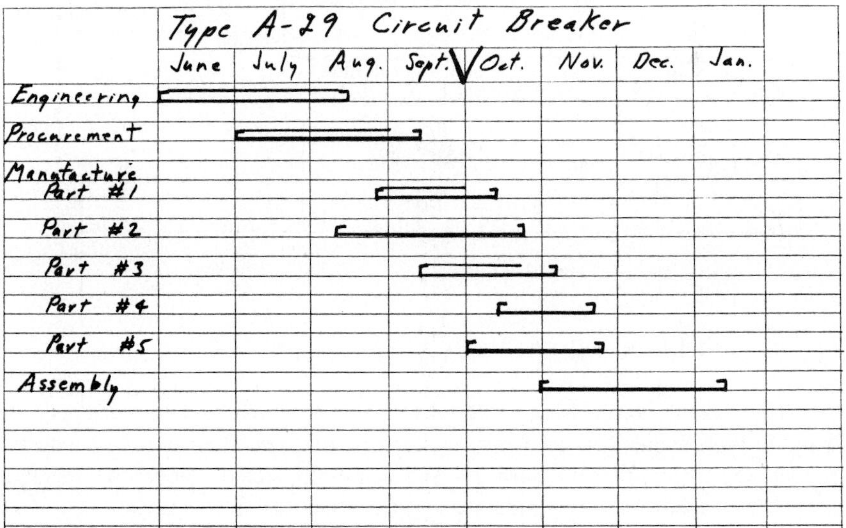

Figure 14-3. A Gantt-type chart for scheduling and showing progress on a complex task where various steps or parts must be coordinated. Status has been indicated as of the end of September, showing that the incomplete procurement program has delayed the start of production of part number 2.

Job tickets. This is the *fifth* and last type of order in a manufacturing situation. Job tickets (see Figure 14-4) authorize the performance of individual operations in the manufacturing process. Whether they should be prewritten by the production control group or made out by the departmental dispatcher when needed is not of great importance. However, they are probably one of the most important forms in the production control system. Initially, the job ticket simply authorizes that a particular operation is to be performed. However, when finally filled out upon completion of the operation, it becomes the "feedback" form that shows not only that the job is complete but also the number of parts processed and the actual time required. This is the principal form in the reporting and follow-up steps in the control of production.

Again, let us remember that there is no uniform terminology for the forms we have just discussed. However, if we get a clear understanding of what each form is being used for in the control situation, we can readily identify these forms in a manufacturing plant regardless of what title appears at the top of the sheet or card.

JOB NO. | NAME AND NUMBER OF PART | W RATE
OPERATION NO. | OPERATION | MACHINE | PCS. FINISHED
OPERATOR'S NO. | NAME | PCS. WANTED | PCS. SCRAPPED
REMARKS | ELAPSED TIME | STOPPED | STARTED
COST DEPT. OPER. LABOR TO-DATE | PRODUCTION DEPT. ACCUMULATIONS: TOTAL SCRAPPED | PIECES FINISHED | DIRECT HOURS
F-62 PIECE-WORK: PIECES | P. W. AMT. | DIRECT LABOR: HRS. | AMT. | INDIRECT LABOR: HRS. | AMT.

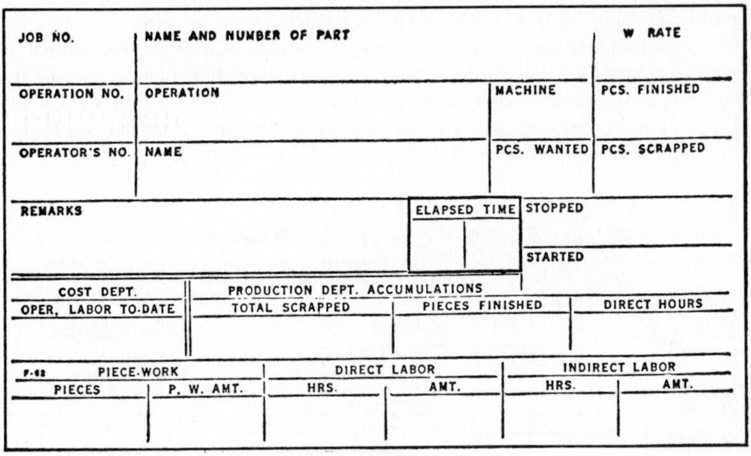

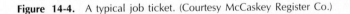

Figure 14-4. A typical job ticket. (Courtesy McCaskey Register Co.)

Project Planning Methods

The production planning and control methods which have thus far been discussed in this chapter deal primarily with the production of consumer or industrial products which could be considered to fall within the area of "repetitive manufacturing." The products to be produced are often manufactured in quantities of more than one, and their total processing time can be measured in hours, or at most, days. There does exist, however, a class of what could be considered production situations where planning and control must occur, but the product (or project) has a very long operation time and the planning and control needed are different from that which would be appropriate for repetitive manufacturing. Consider, for example, the construction of an ocean-going ship, or a prototype version of a new aircraft, or, for that matter, a college laboratory. These tasks are usually considered to fall within the domain of project planning, and a number of effective planning and control procedures have been developed for their type of environment.

The best-known methods that have been developed are CPM (for Critical Path Methods) and PERT (for Program Evaluation and Review Technique). The original PERT technique is now considered, more accurately, PERT TIME, whereas a later development is known as PERT COST.

PERT was developed in 1958 by the U.S. Navy Special Projects Office in conjunction with the consulting firm of Booz, Allen, and Hamilton. The Navy's interest at the time was to accelerate the Polaris missile and submarine project, and through the use of the PERT technique they were able to complete the project two years ahead of schedule with a savings of millions of dollars. PERT and PERT COST are becoming almost standard procedures for companies dealing with large development projects, particularly those that have contracts with the Department of Defense and/or the National Aeronautics and Space Administration.

CPM was developed by the DuPont Company and Remington Rand at about the same time as PERT. Its purpose at the time was to plan the construction of a plant, and it is used extensively by construction people today, although it lends itself very well to other types of projects also.

The use of these tools requires first of all that all elements, steps, activities, jobs, and so forth, required for a project be completely identified and detailed. Further, a sequencing order must be determined, which is based upon any technological or administrative dependencies of one part of the project upon another. Finally, the time and cost to perform each task or activity must also be estimated. At this point one is prepared to construct a network or arrow diagram that illustrates the information collected. Figure 14-5 illustrates such a diagram for a simple project. On the diagram, each arrow represents a single activity, each circle an event. An event is the completion of one or more activities. Arrows originating at a circle (event) indicate activities that can begin only after all activities (arrows) terminating at that circle have been completed. In this way, precedents for the various activities are indicated.

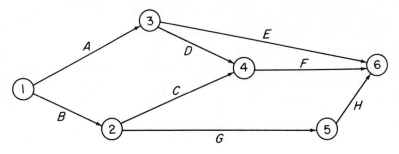

Figure 14-5. A critical path network diagram. Numbers correspond to events, and letters correspond to activities and the time taken to complete the activity.

Events are differentiated by numbers within the event circles. Each event should have a higher number than the immediately preceding event, and no two events should have the same number. Figure 14-5 makes use of letters to identify the arrows. In practice, the letters would be replaced by word descriptions of the particular activities involved. This would be particularly true when initially setting up the project and identifying all of the various steps and their precedents.

Systems Analysis

As with other manufacturing control systems and procedures, production planning and control lends itself to modern techniques such as machine accounting and use of computers. Careful study of the control system through procedure analysis will indicate the savings that may be effected by the utilization of modern equipment. These savings may be in the clerical help required in the administration of the system or in the advantages of quick compilation of data, which in turn results in up-to-date control data.

Many mechanical aids have been in use for some time. These are, in effect, mechanical Gantt charts, or adaptations thereof. Two of these devices are shown in Figures 14-6 and 14-7.

In recent years the computer has become the device which is being used more and more to improve production planning and control procedures and hopefully reduce costs. The power of the computer has also made possible extensive system analyses which in turn lead to the development of management information systems. These systems would tie all operations of the company together on an instantaneous up-to-the-minute basis. Timeliness and cost reduction are obvious advantages, but beyond that is the fact that information is available to the manager, aiding him in making much better decisions.

Figure 14-6. Demonstration setup of a visible margin leaf schedule board. (Courtesy Remington Rand, Inc.)

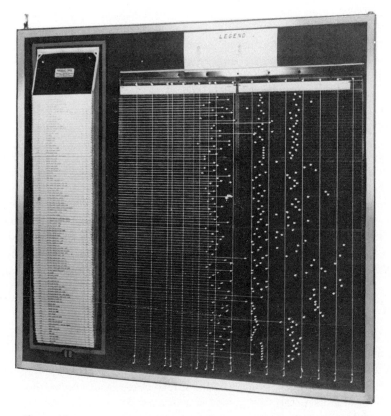

Figure 14-7. A 100-item "Produc-Trol" peg board. (Courtesy The Wassel Organization, Inc.)

Some companies have data input systems installed at various key positions throughout the plant, thereby enabling workers to report the completion of various jobs directly to a computer which in turn is capable of giving a status report whenever requested on any job or schedule. Basically, the computer performs the tasks of reporting and posting which are indicated on the various simple and hand-operated charts and devices shown in Figures 14-1, 14-2, 14-3, 14-6, and 14-7.

However, systems analysis is not the business of trying to find ways to use the computer. Instead, it is the business of trying to find improved ways of accomplishing any task. In production planning and control we are seeking control systems that allow production to proceed smoothly, efficiently, and at lower cost. The system itself will entail some cost, and so it must be constantly under examination and review. The maintenance of any record or form or the use of any computer program can only be justified if it actually contributes to the current and future planning and control of the manufacturing activity.

While many computer-directed production planning and control systems have been installed in manufacturing firms in the mid-1980's, computerization must be undertaken only after a thorough study.[1] These systems can be costly, with initial costs of $300,000 to $600,000 not uncommon. The conversion of manual records for computer use is a lengthy process, and another, often more difficult problem is the training of personnel who are familiar with a manual system to utilize the new, computerized one.[2]

Production Planning and Control Organization

It should be obvious that there is no single pattern for the organization of the production planning and control activity. In many small plants the routing, loading, and scheduling functions may well be included in the duties of the operating line: the shop manager, superintendent, and foremen. But it is difficult to combine day-to-day work with adequate planning, and as a result it is often more feasible to break away the production planning and control functions and assign them to qualified specialists. These groups should be organized as staff sections normally reporting to the top manufacturing executive.

Centralized Production Planning and Control

Centralization or decentralization of duties of the production control staff depends upon the design of the production planning and control system. In a completely centralized setup, determination of shipping promises; analysis of sales, stock, and shop orders; preparation of routes, load charts, and schedule charts; and dispatching of work to the shop complete with job tickets and all other necessary paper would be accomplished by a central production planning and control unit. In addition, as work is completed, a careful analysis of the actual performance would be made, and if corrective action were required, it would be initiated by this group.

Fully centralized production planning and control presents a real problem in industrial communications. Often some portions of the job are decentralized to the various departments in the plant. The most common practice is to assign a departmental dispatcher to each foreman. In this situation the central office will dispatch work by the day, week, or some longer period. The final dispatch is then made by the dispatcher in each department.

Decentralized Production Planning and Control

We have discussed at great length that no matter how general the planning may be in a central office, the plan must eventually be developed into a detailed plan

---

[1]See William S. Donelson, "MRP, Who Needs It?" *Datamation*, May 1979, pp. 187–191.

[2]R. G. Schroeder, J. C. Anderson, S. E. Tupy, and E. M. White, "A Study of MRP Benefits and Costs," *Journal of Operations Management*, Vol. 2, No. 1, October 1981, pp. 1–9.

on the shop floor. Some companies are now endeavoring to make each foreman a manager of his own departmental operation. In these cases the foreman is furnished with a complete staff for the production planning and control of the activities in the department.

Regardless of the degree of centralization or decentralization of these duties, the activities can be readily divided into the *planning phase* and the *control phase*. Also, there can seldom be complete decentralization. Some general production planning and control will have to be retained in a central office in order that the efforts of the various departments be coordinated in the whole.

Planning phase. We have already indicated in some detail the duties involved in the production planning phase. Working from the basic data mentioned earlier in this chapter, the personnel in this part of the activity prepare routes and load and schedule charts.

Control phase. The completed job ticket is the key to this phase of the production planning and control system. It is the means of reporting back from the shop floor that indicates that a job is completed; or if daily job tickets are turned in, the daily progress of a job can be determined. These tickets should be compared to the schedule chart and the progress of work indicated. The schedule chart is the point at which the status of the work in the shop should be presented in concise and readable form. Again, however, all of the record-keeping in the world will not control a shop. Production control records are a tool only. Alert personnel must see where orders are running late and have the initiative to take corrective action.

Relation to Other Functions

Good relationships with all the other functions in the enterprise are essential to effective production planning and control. Full cooperation with the marketing group is necessary, particularly in view of the importance of market conditions and the goodwill of customers. Both product engineering and process engineering must keep production planning and control informed as to their plans to avoid the manufacture of goods either to incorrect specifications or by an improper method. Cost control depends upon production control for essential cost information: the actual time that was required to process the material. This is just another effective use of the completed job ticket.

Measurements of Effectiveness

In determining the effectiveness of a production planning and control system, there are quite a few problems.

The key criterion might well be whether or not shipping promises are being kept—the percentage of the orders shipped on time. This, however, would not be a true criterion if excessive overtime or expediting costs were involved in getting any of these orders shipped.

The cost of the control system in relation to the value of goods shipped is another possibility. Again, however, this may not be sound: if markets slump, a bad ratio will develop. Many good production planning and control systems have been discontinued because of "high costs" under these conditions—and have never revived after business picked up.

In a study of benefits and costs of computerized production planning and control systems, Schroeder et al.[3] list the following performance criteria by which production planning and control systems might be judged:

1. Inventory turnover
2. Delivery lead time (days)
3. Percent of time meeting delivery promises (%)
4. Percent of orders requiring "splits" because of unavailable material
5. Number of expeditors (# people)
6. Average unit cost

QUESTIONS

1. A West Coast plant constantly failed to get its product to its customers when they needed the material. An investigation of the plant's production control charts indicated that all work was progressing according to schedule. What was wrong? What would you do to correct this situation?
2. In what way are the principles of production planning and control applicable to the
    a. home?
    b. supermarket?
    c. school?
3. Prepare a detailed schedule chart for your own activities next week. How could you use this chart to advantage?
4. Discuss in greater detail why the volume to be produced has little effect on the design and operation of a system of production planning and control.
5. Assume you are organizing a small plant for the manufacture of flashlights. How many of the different types of orders would you use? Explain your use of each type.
6. Compare the advantages of centralized dispatching with those of decentralized dispatching.
7. How do production planning and control contribute to the profits of the business?
8. Outline how a production foreman makes use of production planning and control concepts even though there is no such department in the plant.

---

[3]"A Study of MRP Benefits and Costs," p. 2.

9. Distinguish between production planning and production control. Should these be organized separately within a plant?

10. What are the advantages of MRP? Can you see any disadvantages?

CASE PROBLEMS

Atwater Pen Company

The Atwater Pen Company manufactures a line of fountain pens, which it sells through its salesmen directly to dealers located in cities throughout the United States. In addition to maintaining its standard line, it has always been the company's policy to try to furnish special items a customer might want. For example, it has furnished gold pens containing a one-half carat diamond in the clip, platinum pens, and white pens for nurses.

In an attempt to give the foremen as much authority as possible, the company uses a system of decentralized production control. Production orders, containing the routing and scheduling for each part, are submitted to the production departments once each week. The foremen are given considerable leeway on the production schedule, and the only requirement is that the operation must be completed by the date scheduled. Thus, if a foreman wants to dispatch a lot of parts to a machine two days before the deadline scheduled for that lot, he is free to do so.

Recently, the production control department has been plagued with frequent rush orders for special pens. This has necessitated sending a number of special manufacturing orders to Department 32, where the caps and barrels are made. Clifford White, foreman of Department 32, has been complaining about all the rush orders and maintains that he can no longer plan the work in his department so as to operate most efficiently. Bert Akers, head of the Production Planning and Control Department, understands Mr. White's problem and feels that there must be a way that would enable Atwater to adequately handle both standard and special orders for their products. Mr. Akers feels that good control starts with a firm plan that is based on actual customer orders or a reliable sales forecast. He contends that by studying the history of special orders during the past several years a forecasting method for them can be developed. In this way, a plan may be developed for integrating standard and special ("rush") orders.

Questions:

1. Do you feel that a firm that has a solid "standard item" business should go after special items that might put a strain on their production capacity?

2. What ideas do you have for forecasting these special items?

3. Present some methods for scheduling standard items with special items.

4. Would the situation at Atwater be improved by centralizing all production control? Why?

5. What benefits can be gained from giving some of the production control responsibility to foremen such as Clifford White?

Digital Components Company

Ben Benoit is production manager for Digital Components Company, and he is very concerned about the way DCC currently controls its production. The method used is a manual one in which job order tickets are written and production progress is followed through the shop by production expediters. A number of scheduling and load charts are used to enable the production control people to record and visually observe order progress. This method worked fine during the early years of the firm, when there were very few employees and the production manager could keep information about the few in-process jobs in his head. Mr. Benoit is one of the original employees of DCC and can remember their original "shop" in the garage of George Nardi, company founder and current president. Mr. Nardi had designed several unique digital control devices for the petroleum industry during the late 1960's, and these systems were the first products of the company.

Because of DCC's continuing success, the firm has had to move twice to larger production facilities during the past fifteen years. The company now has an extensive product line and many customers for digital control devices, which are used in both the continuous process and discrete product industries. In-process inventory is extensive and raw material storage has been enlarged twice during the past five years. Mr. Benoit feels that his current production control methods are just not adequate for the existing manufacturing environment. He feels that a database production planning and control method, like MRP, is needed, and he has discussed this with other production management personnel.

Mr. Benoit has been surprised at the reaction of other members of the DCC management when he discusses MRP with them: some are for it and others against it. The arguments against MRP go along the following lines: (1) Production clerks are comfortable with the current system; (2) Most part numbers will have to be changed; (3) People will have to adapt themselves to a computer-directed discipline; (4) Extensive retraining of production clerks will be required; and (5) Small errors in work-in-process or material storage quantities will be magnified by a computer program. The arguments for MRP are along the following lines: (1) Production plans can be made and updated much more rapidly; (2) The computer programs will enable production management to evaluate different production schedules before they are implemented in the shop; (3) Production capacity can be better utilized; (4) Work-in-process and raw material inventories can be reduced; and (5) Fewer production clerks and expediters will be required.

Questions:

1. Decide whether you would be for or against an MRP installation in this situation, and expand the appropriate list of reasons.
2. Should a consultant be brought in to help DCC here? Why?
3. If you do not favor the computerized production control approach, what would you suggest for DCC?

15

QUALITY CONTROL

Quality control refers to all of those functions or activities that must be performed to fulfill the company's quality objectives. These functions are very broad in some companies and encompass many employees, whereas they are limited only to inspection and a few employees in other companies.

Quality begins with the design of a product in accordance with the customer's specifications. Further, it involves the establishment of measurement standards, the use of proper materials, the selection of a suitable manufacturing process and the necessary tooling to make the product, the performance of the necessary manufacturing operations, and the inspection of the product to check on conformance with the specifications. All of this is followed by the use of the product by the customer and the feedback of information from the customer to use in any necessary redesign of the product. It is evident that control of quality is the responsibility of many people.

Before going further, let us discuss the term *quality*. Confusion arises in the use of this term because it is used indiscriminately to refer to three things: (1) quality of design, (2) quality of conformance with specifications, and (3) quality of performance.

We commonly associate quality with cost and think that a Rolls Royce is superior to a Ford, that a Waterford crystal glass is superior to an ordinary water glass, and that a hammer purchased at a discount store for $7.98 is inferior to a $16.98 hammer from the local hardware store. It is obvious that this conception of higher quality begins on the drawing board and with the establishment of rigid design specifications. As a rule, high quality of design results in high cost of manufacture and usually in high performance value. Recognizing this, the manufacturer usually thinks of the quality of the product in a different sense than does the layman. The manufacturer is concerned with how the product meets the customer's specifications and how it compares with the competitor's in the same price class. To the manufacturer, then, quality is not absolute but is relative to other factors such as the selling price of the item, the use for which it is intended, the adherence to measurable quality standards, and the degree of customer satisfaction.

Ironically, we customers are somewhat fickle in what we want in our products. Our standards of quality today may not be acceptable tomorrow. For example, the past tendency for some car bodies to rust through in three or four years is no longer tolerable among most customers.

Quality control is a staff function concerned with the prevention of defects in manufacturing so that items may be made right the first time and not have to be rejected. In order to achieve this end, several activities need to be performed. There must be inspection and/or control of incoming raw materials to insure that they meet specifications; there must be planning and control of manufacturing processes to insure that suitable methods are being used and that machines and equipment are performing satisfactorily; there must be in-process inspection to insure that items being fabricated meet specifications; and there must be final inspection and testing for product performance. In the pursuit of these activities, several techniques to be discussed later (e.g., statistical quality control) are of utmost value.

It is frequently stated that *quality is free*—that is, what costs money are all of the costs that are associated with not doing the job right in the first place: inspection, tests, reworking, scrapping, warranties, service calls, and so forth. In most manufacturing companies, these costs are estimated to be fifteen to twenty percent of the sales cost.

Organization for Quality Control

As pointed out previously, quality control is a staff function, the purpose of which is to coordinate the elements of production to fabricate a product at the desired quality level.

The organization structure for quality control varies from company to company depending on the nature of the business, the type of products manufactured, and the policy of top management. Thus, a single operator may be the most important element in manufacturing a product such as men's shirts, whereas many people would be necessary in manufacturing an airplane. In most companies it is considered essential to have someone assigned to coordinate the functions included in the quality control program. This person commonly carries the title of Manager of Quality Control, Manager of Quality Assurance, or Chief Inspector.

The level of quality control in an organization is influenced by several factors, namely, the quality level significance (of the utmost importance in the aircraft industry), the extent to which high quality represents the company to customers, the seriousness of quality system failures (e.g., in food and pharmaceutical industries), the complexity of manufacturing, and the policies of customers. Thus, each company must establish that type of organization which will best fulfill its needs. Frequently, the Quality Control Department is composed of a quality engineering function, an inspection function, and a laboratory function. Recently, some companies have changed the names of their departments that deal with quality control to Quality Assurance and have added the function of reliability engineering.

In considering organization for quality control, it becomes readily apparent that quality control is a responsibility shared by many members of the enterprise. It involves the members of management who set the quality policies, the salesmen who contract to sell products of a certain quality, the design engineers who set the product specifications, the buyers who purchase raw materials of the right quality, and the manufacturing personnel who are responsible for making the product according to prescribed specifications. It is only through the wholehearted cooperation of all these persons that a sound quality control program can be maintained.

Quality Standards

In the final analysis the quality standards for a product are established by the customer. The decision to buy or not to buy for a given price will be based on his or her satisfaction with the product. Of course, in order to secure the customer's business, the vendor must give consideration to ways of maintaining quality levels that will meet or exceed the customer's needs. Thus, it becomes necessary for management to decide what characteristics the product shall possess and then design and produce a product that embodies all the preselected characteristics.

As an example of the kinds of problems that companies can encounter, let us consider the situation that arose in Grand Haven Stamped Products.[1] Two of their customers developed indices to measure the quality performance of their suppliers, and their purchasing decisions were made on a demerit system. Grand Haven found that it was supplying inadequate quality and lost one of its contracts. This prompted the company to analyze its quality control program and to install a new statistical process control program in order to maintain an adequate quality level. (This topic will be discussed further later in the chapter.)

Many companies have established long-standing reputations for manufacturing high-quality products, and their customers rely upon them always to exceed the minimum specifications established. To illustrate this point, a large manufacturer of diesel truck engines has established a reputation for producing high-quality engines and guarantees the various components for 100,000 to 300,000 miles of operation. The manufacturer is proud of this reputation and maintains an extensive quality control program in order to insure the fulfillment of the quality standards.

---

[1]See Mark Andrews, "Statistical Process Control," *Production,* Vol. 95, No. 4, April 1985, p. 56.

Responsibility for Quality

If we ask ourselves the question, "Who is the most important person in the quality program in a company?" it immediately becomes evident that it is top management. The type of quality program maintained in the company will be based on the philosophy, policies, and methods of implementation ascribed to by the chief executive. There must be a climate for quality, and every employee should be given the encouragement, education, support, and opportunity to contribute. All of us who have seen the Maytag Company's advertisements for laundry equipment on television are left with the impression that the company aspires to produce high-quality, error-free products. And a visit to their plant in Newton, Iowa, would in fact reveal that their quality control program is designed and operated to insure the production of appliances that will meet their customers' expectations over long periods of time.

In discussing responsibility for quality, we wish to reemphasize that the quality control department is a staff department and should not attempt to assume the individual quality responsibilities of other staff or line personnel. Thus, as we shall point out, many other groups perform vital roles in achieving the company's quality standards.

The product engineers, working with the sales department, are responsible for initiating the standards to be maintained in manufacturing the product. In designing the product, the engineers determine the degree of precision to be adhered to in manufacturing the component parts and set forth the necessary materials, dimensions, and other specifications on the design drawings. In considering the standards of quality to be adhered to, the design engineers should take into account (1) the end use of the item, (2) the value of the item, (3) the relationship of the item to other components, (4) the establishment of design standards that can be attained and maintained by the shop, and (5) the chance and assignable variables that may enter into the manufacture of the item. It is important that the design engineers be familiar with the manufacturing processes so that realistic and maintainable standards can be established. If the standards (tolerances) established for the product are beyond the capabilities of the manufacturing equipment, then the item cannot meet the minimum acceptance level and will have to be rejected.

An interesting historical note pertaining to process quality illustrates the last point. In the 1950's and early 1960's two well-known American quality management consultants, Joseph M. Juran and W. Edwards Deming, spent a great deal of time in Japan training their managers, engineers, and scientists in the use of statistics and the management of quality improvement. The Japanese became familiar with the variation inherent in processing and the use of statistics as a problem-solving tool. Whereas American companies had relied on inspection and rework areas to catch and repair defective parts, the Japanese tried to eliminate waste and defects before they occurred by controlling the manufacturing process. Juran estimates that Japanese quality began to surpass American and Western product quality in the 1970's. It is ironic to note that what two Americans taught the Japanese about quality management is now finding its way back to the United States.

Recognizing the importance of designing for economic and high-quality production, many companies now have process engineers and quality control engineers work closely with design engineers to facilitate the design of products of attainable standards and to insure economical production.

As pointed out previously, the engineering department, in consultation with the sales department and manufacturing engineers, is responsible for setting the standards to be maintained in producing the product. For items such as producer goods, the sales engineer will be instrumental in conveying the customer's requirements to the engineering department. Obviously, if the product is being purchased by the customer to meet certain performance standards, it is imperative that it meet or exceed his or her needs.

All persons associated with production play a vital role in maintaining quality. The process engineer is responsible for planning the necessary steps in the manufacturing process that will allow the product to be made according to the specifications. Failure to route the product through the right machines or other production centers may result in a rejected item.

The production supervisors are at an interface between the desired quality goals and the achievement of the program. Likewise, the individual workers performing the various operations on the product are key persons in maintaining high-quality standards. There are varying levels of acceptability of the product; if the operator just barely meets the acceptance standards, the product may tend to be a borderline product. On the other hand, if the workers always try to exceed the minimum level of acceptability, then there is a strong likelihood that the level of quality will be high. In order to insure that the caliber of workmanship is kept at acceptable levels, some companies have established quality incentives. Also, it is accepted practice to pay operators working on incentive-wage plans only for the good parts they produce. Thus, they must correct any reject before they will be paid for producing the part.

There is a saying that *you can't inspect quality into the product,* and wise management recognizes the soundness of this statement. To illustrate the logic of this axiom, let us consider a situation witnessed by one of the authors in a small plant. This plant was experiencing a high percentage of rejects on its product, and the customer was returning them by the truckload. The president of the company witnessed the return of one truckload of the items and commented, "We just have to hire another inspector." However, after further consideration, he became aware of the fact that the company didn't need another inspector; it simply needed greater adherence to the quality standards by the manufacturing departments. The supervisors and workers lacked a spirit of quality-mindedness, and the company was suffering from their failure to worry about anything but production quotas.

U.S. companies mean business about quality and have come to recognize that if they are going to compete globally, quality is absolutely essential. This has prompted industry to give a great deal of thought to the establishment of more effective quality control programs to help prevent needless waste of labor and materials.

Control of Quality in Manufacturing

Basically, the control of quality in manufacturing may be said to start with the attitude of each employee being "Let's make it right." Such an attitude is not easy to attain and maintain in many plants. This has led a number of companies to initiate formal programs in an attempt to create quality-mindedness. Usually, such programs deal with inspiration, measurement, and communication. Inspiration probably has its greatest value early in a program. Programs must be planned well in order for inspiration to have a continuing effect. Measurement may be somewhat difficult to achieve. The unit of measurement should be designed to give weight to that which is important on the job—for example, the consecutive number of defect-free units or mean production hours between defects. Perhaps communication is the most important phase of the program because it is the means whereby workers can be praised for their successes.

Since people are such a vital ingredient of quality programs, there have been concerted efforts to give them training pertinent to various levels of responsibility. One way that small machine shops can improve quality is through the use of a series of videotape programs on quality based on the National Tooling and Machinery Foundation's "Doing Things Right" seminar and book.

One quality program that had its origin in Japan in the early 1960's has had tremendous impact on Japan's reputation for turning out high-quality products. This program is of a type commonly referred to as *QC Circles* or *Q Circles*. The use of QC Circles has become a genuine movement throughout the industrialized world. A QC Circle is based on the philosophy that quality can be improved through the participation of employees in the solving of quality problems. QC Circles are usually composed of 3 to 25 worker volunteers (7 is an ideal size) from the same group, with the supervisor serving as the leader. The Circles usually meet for one hour per week to discuss their quality problems, to investigate causes, to recommend action, and to take corrective action when it is within their authority. In a recent installation of QC Circles in an American company, all of the participants (who were volunteers) received training in problem analysis, brainstorming, information collection, and information display techniques. The groups generally concentrate on problems that they can solve themselves. The goals of QC Circles are improved quality, increased productivity, and increased motivation. As an example of the results of QC Circles, one company reported a 60% decline in rejects, a 10–20% increase in productivity, and strong support from the employees.

Let us now turn our attention to other aspects of the control of quality in manufacturing. The basic function of manufacturing is to convert the raw materials received by the company into finished products and to package the products for delivery. The production of a particular product will involve various types of processing equipment, tools, jigs and fixtures, and operating personnel. It is essential that all of these elements be capable of performing functions that will meet the design specifications.

It is desirable to evaluate the process prior to initiation of production. The purpose of this evaluation is to determine the capability of each element in the production process to perform as required by the specifications. Information from studies of this type may be fed back to the design engineers to assist them in establishing realistic tolerances based on the process capabilities. In manufacturing, this same information may be used for selecting specific equipment or people for a particular operation.

On page 301, we touched on the problem that Grand Haven Stamped Products had in producing parts of adequate quality. To overcome this problem, the company developed a statistical process control (SPC) program embodying four levels:

1. *Mathematics*—some people on the staff had to understand statistics.
2. *Principles*—the department supervisors had to be familiar with control charts and the principles on which they were based.
3. *Objectives and Uses*—top management had to understand and support the program.
4. *Techniques*—all employees had to have familiarity with control charts.

The company found Pareto analysis to be particularly helpful in pinpointing problem areas. Pareto analysis is the technique of arranging problems or data according to priority or importance and tying them to a problem-solving framework. Analysts have shown by Pareto analysis that 20 percent of potential problems produce 80 percent of defects. In using Pareto analysis, the company had line inspectors look at those product characteristics that could cause customer complaints and note the number of occurrences of rejections for each characteristic. They then directed their statistical control efforts at the highest percent of defects.

In some cases where it is extremely difficult to evaluate all the variables entering into the production process, it may be desirable to establish mandatory process evaluation points. These points are usually checked and approved by quality control personnel prior to or concurrently with the processing of initial units. Typical of those points that may be checked are certain operator skills, critical processes (e.g., plating), certain jigs and fixtures, and critical testing operations. Strategic use of such evaluation points can be very helpful in reducing deficiencies in products.

Although the quality of many items can be detected by one of the human senses, frequently this cannot be done. The use of suitable instruments and testing equipment is then required to make the desired measurements. One of the functions performed by quality control engineers is selecting suitable measuring devices, establishing testing procedures, and then determining the most desirable locations in which to measure. Further, there must be frequent checking of this equipment to insure that it is measuring properly. Some companies maintain laboratories for checking such equipment and also for performing those tests which are unable to be performed in the production departments.

It is an accepted fact that no manufacturing process can produce identical units time after time. If one examines the units produced with sufficiently sensitive instruments, one will find that there will be slight variations in the product. There may be several reasons for such variations: slight variations in materials, gradual dulling of tools, variation in operator's attention. Control over this variability in manufacturing can be accomplished in two different ways. First, one can maintain continuing checks on production processes and make necessary adjustments in time to prevent the production of more than a minimum of bad parts. As an illustration of this point, in one of General Motors' new assembly plants in Detroit/Hamtramck, Michigan, new technologies have been incorporated into the assembly lines to guarantee that quality standards are met. The line passes through a Perceptron visual unit, a bank of 121 cameras that measure every body opening to within a half-millimeter's tolerance. From this machine, information is fed to a computer that automatically makes any necessary adjustments in welding robots, to insure that all of the body parts fit exactly.

The second way of controlling quality is to control the outgoing quality level to keep the number of defective units within certain allowable limits. This is the basis for *acceptance sampling,* to be discussed later. It is apparent from the previous discussion of these two methods that process control attempts to control the quality being produced whereas acceptance sampling attempts to control the quality that passes an inspection point after the item has been produced.

As just discussed, inspection and process control are two of the vital ingredients of a program to control quality in manufacturing. We shall discuss each of these in some detail in the sections on inspection and statistical quality control that follow.

Inspection

Inspection is the component of the quality control program that is concerned with checking on the conformance of the item to the specifications set for it. It may be likened to the policing action necessary to force compliance with our laws. In the same way that communities need police officers, companies also need inspectors. Naturally, if everyone is doing the job of meeting the quality standards, then the need for inspection is reduced. However, even in the best-managed companies there are still many needs for inspection. People (including inspectors) are not infallible and make mistakes, materials may be faulty, and machines and tools are subject to wear and tend to get out of adjustment. Because of the many variables that enter into manufacturing, inspection is a never-ending function.

The inspection function commonly fulfills four primary responsibilities: (1) it checks the quality of incoming materials, (2) it checks on all finished goods to insure that only acceptable products reach the customer, (3) it aids in maintaining process control and attempts to locate the flaws in manufacturing that would cause subsequent difficulties, and (4) it serves in an advisory capacity in attempting to correct or prevent quality control problems.

Inspection includes all types of activities, such as testing and gaging that are required to determine whether the product meets the prescribed standards. For the most part, our discussion of inspection will refer to that performed by qualified inspectors who are members of the inspection group and whose responsibility is to check on the attainment of the minimum standards of quality.

Items That Need Inspection

In general, we may say that purchased materials, goods in process, and finished products should be inspected. This very general statement needs amplification. It will be discussed in greater detail in the sections that follow.

Purchased materials inspection.   Purchased materials should be inspected at the time they are received and before they are stocked or sent to assembly. The receiving department personnel should make at least an identifying inspection of all incoming items and note obvious damage. In some cases they may need to do more extensive checking or route the material to qualified inspectors for checking. Faulty parts, of course, should be returned.

It is not uncommon to find inspectors working in or adjacent to the receiving department. For example, in one large aircraft engine plant there is a sizable inspection department next to the receiving department. Owing to the critical nature of all purchased parts, most of them are inspected in this department as soon as received. Following this inspection, the parts are then sent to either the stock room or assembly lines. Through this procedure the company is assured that operations will not be performed on faulty materials.

Receiving inspection should always be located in such a place that all incoming materials must pass through the receiving and inspection room. The nature of the inspection will vary with the nature of the items being purchased. The inspection may be very complex, using many measuring devices, or it may be little more than a visual inspection. It may be performed on 100 percent of the items or it may be merely a sampling inspection on each lot received. In some cases operational tests may be run on purchased items such as electric motors, pumps, and similar items.

In recent years, some companies have established quality certification programs with some of their vendors that have eliminated the necessity of inspecting that vendors' products. Such programs are particularly desirable in those companies using JIT materials deliveries. For example, in one diesel engine company, the goal is to have suppliers do the inspection and to be able to use parts without any receiving inspection or warehousing at all.

In-process inspection.   Because of the many variables that permeate every phase of manufacturing, it is essential that in-process materials be given an optimum amount of inspection. The term "optimum" is used because it is possible either to over-inspect or under-inspect an item. Either practice will prove to be costly.

In nearly every manufacturing process two types of inspection will prevail. A considerable amount of *informal* inspection will be performed by the production workers. The *formal* inspection will be performed by qualified inspectors from the inspection department. As a part of the informal inspection, the workers will usually subject the piecepart to visual inspection. In addition, they may do some gaging or testing, and they will reject parts containing faulty materials.

A number of general principles apply to the determination of what, when, and where to inspect. When a new operation such as a stamping operation is being set up, the first parts produced on the machine should be inspected to insure that they meet the specifications. When a piecepart will be subjected to several successive operations, it is usually uneconomical to inspect after each operation. For the most part, only a patrol-type inspection (to be discussed later in this chapter) can be justified. In some cases the operator may be equipped with the necessary gages or measuring devices to provide a running check on the item.

It is frequently desirable to inspect a piecepart just before moving on to a very expensive operation. By rejecting the part before the expensive operation, the additional cost increment is not added to an item that will probably have to be scrapped.

It is common to inspect items after a series of manufacturing operations have been performed. Also, it is sound practice to inspect parts or assemblies when they have been completed in one department and are to be moved to another department. In general, an item that will become a component part of an assembly and will be difficult to replace or may result in damage to other parts should be thoroughly inspected before assembly. Items should be inspected before going to an operation in which the defects might be covered up, as in painting or plating.

In the highly mechanized processing that exists today, the designers of automatic machines frequently design automatic gaging devices into the machines. These devices check the critical dimensions or other characteristics and either reject the faulty items or signal the operator that satisfactory items are not being produced. In some cases a feedback system automatically resets the machine to correct for the error. Illustrative of this type of application is a CNC machine used to turn precision tubular parts for oil-well installations. By means of sensing probes on the parts being turned, any deviations from the tolerances are sensed and corrections are made automatically. Further, the system allows the incorporation of statistical quality control techniques directly into the machine control system.

In-process inspection may be performed at any of several locations: on the line or at the machine by a full-time inspector, at the machine by a roving or patrol inspector who calls periodically for parts to inspect, in an inspection crib or an air-conditioned room, or at centralized inspection points.

Finished goods inspection.   Finished goods inspection should be made by qualified inspectors. The items should be checked by measurements, operating tests, or other means to insure compliance with the specifications. Failure to provide a thorough check at this point may allow a faulty product to be sent to the customer.

Inspection Responsibility and Practices

The inspection department possesses the authority to reject those items that fail to meet the standards. Thus, as pointed out previously, it must pass on purchased materials, the processing of materials, and finished products. Also, it may be responsible for the inspection of all jigs, fixtures, dies, gages, and measuring devices used by both the inspectors and production workers. Supervision of the procedure for the disposal or rework of rejected items may be another responsibility assigned to the inspection department.

To carry out its responsibilities, the inspection department will need to establish a number of policies and procedures. It must decide what to inspect, where to inspect, how to inspect, and many other pertinent matters. Some of these have already been discussed in the preceding section; still others will be treated in the sections that follow.

Location for inspection. In most cases operators will inspect their work as they perform it. They should catch most of the obvious errors. However, this informal inspection is not sufficient. Even if they are conscientious, their checks will not be infallible and may allow faulty parts to be forwarded to the next operation. Then, too, production workers, particularly if working on a piecework incentive plan, are primarily concerned with getting out production; they place less emphasis on quality. It therefore becomes necessary to provide an additional check by inspectors.

Inspection points should be planned carefully and should be located where they will produce the most economical end results. In locating the inspection points, consideration must be given to whether the materials are to be inspected at a machine or work station or checked at a centralized inspection point. If the inspection is made at the work station, it is called "floor" inspection. Some floor inspection is done by inspectors who go from machine to machine and perform sampling inspection of the parts produced. This type of inspection is frequently referred to as "patrolling" or "traveling" inspection. In contrast to floor inspection is "centralized" inspection. This type of inspection takes place in a centralized location and necessitates taking the items to be inspected to the inspection station.

Each of the above types of inspection has advantages and disadvantages. Floor inspection allows a minimum of materials handling, reduced storage and reduced delay of material in process, close contact between the inspectors and work stations, and prompt communications and correction of processing difficulties. On the other hand, it may not occupy the full time of the inspectors. Then, too, some items require special inspection devices that may be available only in a central inspection or test station.

Centralized inspection allows the items to be inspected where the various inspection devices may be located. In addition, it facilitates the full use of the inspectors' time and is conducive to increased output per inspector. Supervision of the inspectors and adherence to standard inspection procedure is also improved. Counter to the advantages, are increased material handling, delays, additional space required at inspection stations, and communication problems.

Amount to inspect.   One of the important phases of any quality control program is the determination of the frequency of inspection and of the percentage of items to inspect. It is neither practical nor economical to expect that every item should be inspected for every specification. Therefore, it is essential that the most critical specifications be determined and that maximum concentration be placed upon adherence to these standards. We should never lose sight of the fact that inspection costs money and that *the amount of inspection should be reduced to the minimum required to maintain the degree of control desired.*

In some cases 100 percent inspection of each of the items may be necessary to attain the control desired. For example, a company that manufactures automobile horns or headlight switches will probably subject each of these items to performance tests before shipping them to the customer. The Maytag Company functionally tests every product they build. On the other hand, a company manufacturing sheet steel will not subject each sheet to chemical and tensile tests before shipping to the customer.

Reference is frequently made to "100 percent" inspection or to "sampling" inspection. In 100 percent inspection all of the items are checked for the characteristic being measured. Sampling inspection, on the other hand, does not involve a check of each item. It is based upon the statistical probability (to be discussed later in this chapter) that the characteristics of a sample will be the same as those of all items in the lot. We should not assume that 100 percent inspection is necessarily more exacting than sampling inspection. It doesn't guarantee that all faulty items will be detected. Inspectors are subject to all the frailties of the human being and may fail to catch many items that should be rejected. If, on the other hand, accurate, automatic inspection is used, the probability that there will be no defects is greatly increased.

Many factors will influence the decision on the amount of inspection to be used—for example, the type of product being made, the variability of the manufacturing process, and the variability of the materials. Items made on automatic machines (such as an automatic screw machine) are usually subject to much less variability than the same items made on a manually operated engine lathe. For this reason, these parts would usually be subjected to only a sampling inspection.

Inspection procedures and records.   It is essential that each item be analyzed to determine its inspection needs and that an adequate inspection procedure be planned for it. Likewise, every inspector should be thoroughly acquainted with the procedure to be followed and the characteristics to be measured. They should be equipped with adequate inspection devices and know exactly what to do about items that fail to meet the standards.

An important component of a quality control program is the maintenance of a sound system of records. The inspection plan for each part or assembly should be specified on a suitable form, and the nature of the inspection, the equipment required, and the inspection procedure should be stipulated. Also, each of the inspection points for each item should be indicated as one of the routing steps on the standard process sheet. Suitable inspection and quality control records and reports should be maintained. These may consist of scrap and rework tags, receiving inspection forms, sampling inspection records, patrol inspection logs, final inspection reports, and similar items. Through the maintenance and analysis of these records, it is possible to accomplish the third step of our control procedure—to detect those points in the manufacturing process where control is falling down. This, then, provides the basis for accomplishing the final step—corrective action. As will be pointed out later in this chapter, statistical quality control procedures provide a means of keeping quality in bounds and do not require the same degree of "after-the-fact" correction.

Inspection Devices

The specification sets forth certain characteristics that are to be attained in manufacturing the product. In many cases it is impossible to judge these characteristics by human senses. For example, to determine the diameter of a shaft to the dimension of $2.00000 \pm .00005$ without the aid of some measuring device would be virtually impossible. Thus, inspection must be accomplished by means of devices capable of measuring the characteristics desired. These characteristics may involve dimensions, surface finish, hardness, ductility, color, shrinkage, plasticity, viscosity, efficiency, operating characteristics, and many others. Inspection procedures must include equipment that gives the inspector an answer on the acceptability of the item. A few of the inspection devices in current use will be discussed in the paragraphs that follow.

Many of the inspection devices are referred to as *gages*. These may be used for checking the actual dimensions against the standard. Among the most common of these are the *fixed gages* (such as go–no–go gages, ring gages, and plug gages) and the *indicating gages* (such as micrometers and dial indicators) (See Figure 6-10.) The fixed gages merely tell whether a part is undersize, within limits, or oversize. The indicating gages give a measure of the actual state of affairs and how much variation is occurring. With the increasing trend toward process control and the avoidance of defects, the indicating gage is becoming increasingly important.

A device frequently used to check on profiles or contours of objects is the contour projector or comparator (see Figure 15-1). This instrument casts an enlarged shadow of the profile being checked onto a screen on which the specified contour may be marked. Failure to get coincidence of the shadow with the fixed model will reveal a defect. This device is particularly good for inspecting items such as threads and the small gears in a watch.

Figure 15-1. A contour measuring projector of the type used to check on profiles or contours of objects. (Courtesy Optical Gaging Products.)

An example of a precision coordinate measuring machine that is used frequently is illustrated in Figure 15-2. A machine like this is used in Grand Haven Stamped products Company (see pp. 301 and 305.) In using this machine, the part can be put in the machine, clamped down, and not touched again until all checks are made. The device will make all checks in about 3 minutes as against 5 minutes for conventional measuring methods.

Vision systems are finding increasing use in industry because of their speed, accuracy, flexibility, and repeatability. On page 306, we mentioned the installation of a 121 camera system in one of the General Motors Company's plants. A machine vision system can identify parts by shape, color, or texture, or read alphanumeric or bar code symbols on parts. One system has been developed for robots that is capable of making precision movements during aerospace manufacturing operations. The system is capable of extremely accurate three-dimensional measurements that enable a robot to accomplish a task like drilling without a fixture.

Illustrated in Figure 15-3 is a unique optical measuring system that uses two theodolites and triangulation to determine X, Y, and Z spatial coordinates. The system is mobile and measures by comparison with known angles and contours to an accuracy of better than a thousandth of an inch. The total system, which consists of two theodolites, a computer, a CRT with keyboard, and a printer, may be used on a large variety of industrial applications.

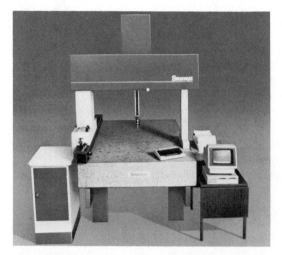

Figure 15-2. A coordinate machine capable of making multiple checks on a workplace clamped in it. (Courtesy L. S. Starrett Company.)

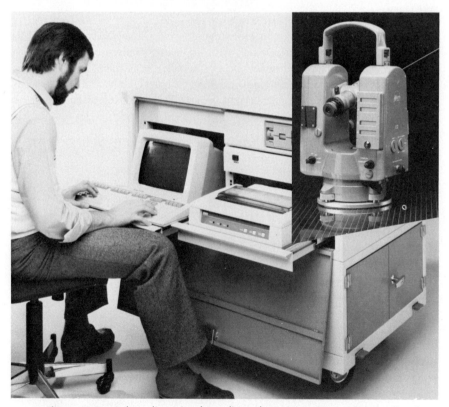

Figure 15-3. A three-dimensional coordinate determining system. (Courtesy Kern Instruments, Inc.) Illustrated in the insert is one of the theodolites.

In order to attain in-process control of quality and to keep pace with the automation of industry, instruments must be designed that can be integrated with the manufacturing process. Examples of the numerous automatic inspection devices that have been developed include the continuous monitoring of sheet steel thickness by means of beta rays or gap sensors (linked to a computer) and the monitoring of enamel thickness by means of a magnetic circuit.

Figure 15-4 shows a complex gaging system that may be used to help maintain statistical process control. This gaging system consists of five major components: a gage fixture and probes; a computer for storing, manipulating, and communicating data; a programmable controller to control all gage functions; a complete set of masters (with minimum, maximum, and average) to work with the computer and zero the data; and a 200-gallon hydraulic system to actuate various movements of the gages. Also included in the system is a robot for loading and unloading the system. The robot takes five consecutive parts off the production line for the sample, stores them, and then loads them one at a time into the gage. The type of part that can be gaged is shown in the gage as well as in the insert to the figure.

Great advances have been made in the development of instruments for checking surface finish, color, internal structure, and similar characteristics. The surface analyzer and profilometer are two instruments widely used for measuring surface smoothness. The spectrophotometer is finding extensive use in the paint and other industries concerned with close matching of colors. Industrial radiography, ultrasonics, and magnetic particle suspension are all recent developments that have

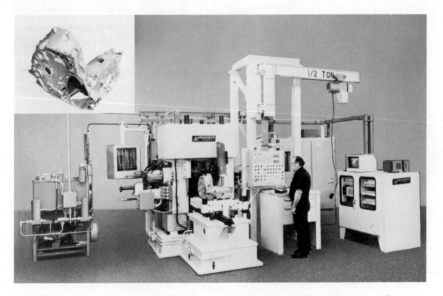

Figure 15-4. A computerized gaging system. (Courtesy Air Gage Company.) The part being gaged is shown in the insert in the upper left of the figure. Note its irregular shape.

found extensive applications in the inspection of defects in the interior or surface of metals.

Modern manufacturing makes use of many other tests to measure physical or chemical characteristics. Sizable laboratories are maintained to accomplish these tests. Also, extensive use is made of performance testing to insure the attainment of the desired standards.

Gage Inspection and Control

As pointed out previously, gages are frequently under the supervision of the inspection department. It is essential, then, that a system be established for controlling the issuance, accuracy, and maintenance of all inspection devices. Gages should be subjected to the same inventory control procedures as other devices. For the more complex instruments, suitable maintenance records should be established. Most instruments are subject to wear and should be calibrated periodically against master gages. This checking should be done under carefully controlled conditions and as often as is necessary to maintain the degree of accuracy desired. In many cases gages have to be checked daily.

Statistical Quality Control

Statistical quality control (SQC) is one of the scientific tools that modern management is using to an increasing extent in the maintenance of quality standards. It is based on the laws of probability and may be described as a system for controlling the quality of production within specified limits by means of a sampling procedure and continuing analysis of inspection results.

When used at key points, statistical quality control makes it possible to determine whether or not a given manufacturing process is capable of turning out products with prescribed specifications. In addition, it also provides control limits at which an operation can be stopped before poor work is produced. Thus, statistical quality control makes it possible to determine the capabilities of a manufacturing process at the outset, and it establishes the necessary controls so that the operations may be corrected for excessive tool wear, excessive variations in raw materials, and similar variations.

Advantages of Statistical Quality Control

The proper applicaton of statistical quality control should result in the following benefits:

1. Results in a more uniform quality of product.
2. Provides a means of catching errors at inception.

3. Reduces inspection costs.
4. Reduces the number of rejects and saves the cost of material.
5. Promotes an understanding and appreciation of quality control.
6. Improves the relationship with the customer.
7. Points out trouble spots.
8. Provides a basis for attainable specifications.
9. Provides a means of determining the capability of the manufacturing process.

Tools of Statistical Quality Control

Statistical quality control starts with the idea that variability is to be expected in manufacturing. It recognizes that the dimension of a part produced on a machine or process is not constant, but variable. Thus, if we were accurately to measure the diameter of cylindrical parts coming off an automatic screw machine, we would find that these parts would vary somewhat in their dimensions. A typical distribution of one hundred of these parts might be as illustrated in Figure 15-5. In this or any other manufacturing situation we can expect to find a certain amount of variation that is due to *chance*. This chance variation is inherent in the manufacturing process and is the result of many small and more or less independent influences that affect each of

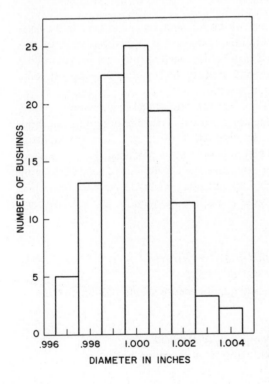

Figure 15-5. Frequency distribution of the diameters of 100 bushings.

the pieces. So long as no other, or *assignable,* causes are operating in the system, it is said to be in *statistical control.* When the minute assignable causes, such as tool wear or faulty materials, begin to influence the system, then it gets out of statistical control.

In using statistical quality control, information about the variability of a manufacturing process comes from a sampling procedure. Rarely do quality control engineers know what the true distribution of the variables in a process is. Thus, they tend to establish control limits on the basis of sampling the distribution of the measurable variables. This will be discussed in somewhat greater detail later in this chapter.

One of the advantages of statistical quality control is that it deals with samples and hence doesn't necessitate 100 percent inspection. In using samples, there is no guarantee that the sample will have the same characteristics as the entire lot; however, through proper *random* sampling[2] it is possible to determine the probability of the accuracy of the samples and to know what risks are being taken.

Sampling inspection is of two kinds: lot-by-lot sampling inspection and continuous sampling inspection. In *lot-by-lot sampling inspection,* the sample is drawn from the lot, and the lot is either accepted or rejected on the basis of the number of rejects in the sample. This is referred to as *acceptance sampling* and will be discussed in detail later. In *continuous sampling inspection,* the current sampling results are used to determine whether sampling inspection or 100 percent inspection is to be used for the next items inspected. A further classification of sampling plans is whether the sampling is for the purpose of determining a measurement expressed in numbers, i.e., *variables* inspection; or whether the sampling is for the purpose of determining whether the articles are defective or non-defective, i.e., *attribute* inspection.

The tools of statistical quality control include (1) frequency distribution, (2) control charts, and (3) acceptance sampling. These will be discussed briefly in the sections that follow.

Frequency distribution. One of the basic tools used by the statistician is the frequency distribution. The frequency distribution is essentially a list of the magnitudes of a variable and the number of times these magnitudes occur. It may be represented in a number of ways. One such distribution is presented in the form of a histogram in Figure 15-5. As pointed out previously, statistical quality control is based upon the assumption that there is inherent chance variability in the manufacture of items and that these items will fall into a frequency pattern. This was illustrated in Figure 15-5. If a curve is fitted to the frequency distribution illustrated in that figure, a bell-shaped curve called a *probability curve* will result (see Figure 15-6). If sufficient items were manufactured and measured, this curve would probably assume the shape of a symmetrical bell-shaped curve. This curve would then

---

[2]Random sampling refers to obtaining a representative sample, i.e., selecting the sample so that every item has an equal chance of being selected.

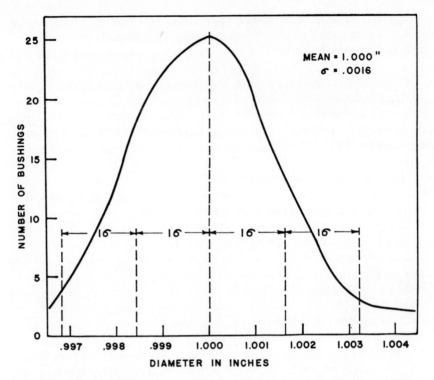

Figure 15.6. Probability curve for the bushings' diameters illustrated in Fig. 15-5.

resemble the *normal distribution curve* about which we have considerable knowledge.

The normal distribution curve is described by a specific mathematical function and is the most important of all frequency distributions. Many data in real life (e.g., heights of women, lengths of life of electric light bulbs, intelligence test scores) appear to follow the normal curve closely. There are statistical tests that can be used to determine how closely a distribution of values approximates normality. An examination of the normal curve will reveal several apparent characteristics: (1) the curve has only a single peak or *node;* (2) the values tend to cluster around the center of the distribution; (3) there are several measures of central tendency (*mean* or arithmetic average, *median* or midpoint value, and *mode* or most frequently occurring value) that fall at the same value; and (4) the curve is symmetrical around the center and the distances from the central value to the extreme values on each side are equal. In addition to the normal distribution, there are a number of other important distributions that are useful in quality control, namely, the binomial, hyper-geometric, and poisson distributions.[3]

[3]See Albert H. Bowker and Gerald J. Lieberman, *Engineering Statistics,* 2nd ed.; Englewood Cliffs, N. J.: Prentice-Hall, Inc., 1972, p. 128.

Two measures of variability that can be obtained from the frequency distribution are of great importance in statistical quality control: the *range* and the *standard deviation*. The range is the simplest measure of variability and is the difference between the highest and lowest values in the distribution. The standard deviation (σ) is the most frequently used measure of variability in statistics and may be defined as the square root of the average squared deviation from the mean; i.e.,

$$\sigma = \sqrt{\frac{\Sigma(x - \bar{x})^2}{N}}$$

Also,

$$\sigma = \frac{1}{N} \sqrt{N\Sigma x^2 - (\Sigma x)^2}$$

where N equals the number of items and x represents each measurement. For a normal distribution curve, we know that the mean (average) plus or minus one standard deviation will encompass 68.3 percent of the area or probability. In the same way, the mean plus or minus two standard deviations will include 95.5 percent; and three standard deviations will include 99.7 percent of the cases (see Figure 15-6). These mathematical relationships provide the basis for statistical quality control.

Control charts.   Earlier in this chapter, it was pointed out that no manufacturing process is completely consistent and that variability enters into the output of every product. Process control is one way to keep this variability in check by separating the variability that is due to "chance," or normal causes in the process, from those that are due to "assignable" causes. Assignable causes are those that might arise from such factors as faulty tools, differences in materials, faulty machines, operator errors, and so forth. Process control is usually accomplished through control charts, and a process is said to be in control if all the observed variations in performance are from chance causes only.

A control chart is a statistical tool that may be used to disclose those variations in the quality of output that are due to chance and those that are due to assignable causes. Control charts are valuable devices in that they tell the appropriate parties when and when not to take action on a process. The commonly used charts are the Mean ($\bar{X}$) Chart, Range (R) Chart, Defective (p) Chart, and Defects-per-Unit (c) Chart.

Control charts may be used whether the inspection is for attributes or variables. In using control charts for variables, the most commonly used charts are the $\bar{X}$ and R charts. Examples of these charts are illustrated in Figure 15-7. Examination of the charts reveals several interesting features, namely: (1) the $\bar{X}$ values that are plotted are the mean values obtained from samples of five measurements; (2) the R values are the differences between the maximum and minimum values for each sample; (3) the control limits have been established well inside the product specification limits; and (4) the trend of the points indicates when the process begins

	Time	9 am	1 pm	9 am	11 am	2 am	9 am	3 pm	7 am	9 pm	10 pm
	Sample	1	2	3	4	5	6	7	8	9	10
Measurement	1	10.0	10.01	10.01	10.01	10.02	10.01	10.01	10.01	10.0	10.02
	2	9.99	10.04	10.0	10.02	10.04	9.99	10.01	10.03	10.01	9.98
	3	10.0	10.0	9.99	10.03	10.0	10.0	10.0	10.05	10.01	10.0
	4	9.97	10.02	10.02	10.01	10.02	10.01	10.01	10.02	9.99	10.02
	5	10.01	10.01	10.01	10.01	10.03	10.01	10.03	10.01	10.01	10.01
	Total	49.97	50.08	50.03	50.08	50.11	50.02	50.06	50.12	50.02	50.03
Average ($\overline{X}$)		9.99	10.02	10.01	10.02	10.02	10.0	10.01	10.02	10.0	10.01
Range (R)		.04	.04	.03	.02	.04	.02	.03	.04	.02	.04

$\overline{\overline{X}} = 10.01$
$\overline{R} = .032$
Upper Control Limit for $(\overline{X}) = 10.03$
Lower Control Limit for $(\overline{X}) = 9.99$
Upper Control Limit for $(\overline{R}) = .07$

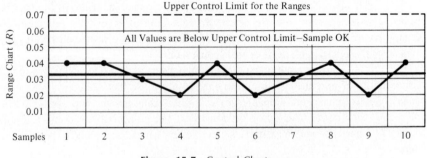

Figure 15-7 Control Charts.

to get out of control. Before proceeding farther, let us consider the manner in which the upper and lower control limits may be established. Based on our previous discussion of the normal distribution, it is only natural to expect that we would use the standard deviation of the samples as the basis for establishing the control limits. This could of course be done. However, it is common practice to use a short-cut method, based on the range, for calculating the control limits. The procedure is to calculate the range for each of the subsamples and then to determine the mean $(\bar{R})$ of the ranges. The three sigma control limits[4] are then determined by $\bar{\bar{X}} \pm 3\bar{R}/\sqrt{n}d_2$. Values of

$$\frac{3}{\sqrt{n}d_2} = A_2$$

are given in Table 15-1. Just as for the $\bar{X}$ chart, a table of factors (see also Table 15-1) is available for calculating the upper and lower control limits for the R chart. These three sigma control limits may be determined from

$$UCL_R = D_4\bar{R} \text{ and } LCL_R = D_3\bar{R}$$

Table 15-1. Factors for computing control line charts[1]

Number of observations in sample, n	Chart for averages — Factors for control limits			Chart for standard deviations — Factors for central line		Chart for standard deviations — Factors for control limits				Chart for ranges — Factors for central line		Chart for ranges — Factors for control limits				
	A	A_1	A_2	c_2	$1/c_2$	B_1	B_2	B_3	B_4	d_2	$1/d_2$	d_3	D_1	D_2	D_3	D_4
2	2.121	3.760	1.880	0.5642	1.7725	0	1.843	0	3.267	1.128	0.8865	0.853	0	3.686	0	3.267
3	1.732	2.394	1.023	0.7236	1.3820	0	1.858	0	2.568	1.693	0.5907	0.888	0	4.358	0	2.575
4	1.500	1.880	0.729	0.7979	1.2533	0	1.808	0	2.266	2.059	0.4857	0.880	0	4.698	0	2.282
5	1.342	1.596	0.577	0.8407	1.1894	0	1.756	0	2.089	2.326	0.4299	0.864	0	4.918	0	2.115
6	1.225	1.410	0.483	0.8686	1.1512	0.026	1.711	0.030	1.970	2.534	0.3946	0.848	0	5.078	0	2.004
7	1.134	1.277	0.419	0.8882	1.1259	0.105	1.672	0.118	1.882	2.704	0.3698	0.833	0.205	5.203	0.076	1.924
8	1.061	1.175	0.373	0.9027	1.1078	0.167	1.638	0.185	1.815	2.847	0.3512	0.820	0.387	5.307	0.136	1.864
9	1.000	1.094	0.337	0.9139	1.0942	0.219	1.609	0.239	1.761	2.970	0.3367	0.808	0.546	5.394	0.184	1.816
10	0.949	1.028	0.308	0.9227	1.0837	0.262	1.584	0.284	1.716	3.078	0.3249	0.797	0.687	5.469	0.223	1.777
11	0.905	0.973	0.285	0.9300	1.0753	0.299	1.561	0.321	1.679	3.173	0.3152	0.787	0.812	5.534	0.256	1.744
12	0.866	0.925	0.266	0.9359	1.0684	0.331	1.541	0.354	1.646	3.258	0.3069	0.778	0.924	5.592	0.284	1.716
13	0.832	0.884	0.249	0.9410	1.0627	0.359	1.523	0.382	1.618	3.336	0.2998	0.770	1.026	5.646	0.308	1.692
14	0.802	0.848	0.235	0.9453	1.0579	0.384	1.507	0.406	1.594	3.407	0.2935	0.762	1.121	5.693	0.329	1.671
15	0.775	0.816	0.223	0.9490	1.0537	0.406	1.492	0.428	1.572	3.472	0.2880	0.755	1.207	5.737	0.348	1.652
16	0.750	0.788	0.212	0.9523	1.0501	0.427	1.478	0.448	1.552	3.532	0.2831	0.749	1.285	5.779	0.364	1.636
17	0.728	0.762	0.203	0.9551	1.0470	0.445	1.465	0.466	1.534	3.588	0.2787	0.743	1.359	5.817	0.379	1.621
18	0.707	0.738	0.194	0.9576	1.0442	0.461	1.454	0.482	1.518	3.640	0.2747	0.738	1.426	5.854	0.392	1.608
19	0.688	0.717	0.187	0.9599	1.0418	0.477	1.443	0.497	1.503	3.689	0.2711	0.733	1.490	5.888	0.404	1.596
20	0.671	0.697	0.180	0.9619	1.0396	0.491	1.433	0.510	1.490	3.735	0.2677	0.729	1.548	5.922	0.414	1.586
21	0.655	0.679	0.173	0.9638	1.0376	0.504	1.424	0.523	1.477	3.778	0.2647	0.724	1.606	5.950	0.425	1.575
22	0.640	0.662	0.167	0.9655	1.0358	0.516	1.415	0.534	1.466	3.819	0.2618	0.720	1.659	5.979	0.434	1.566
23	0.626	0.647	0.162	0.9670	1.0342	0.527	1.407	0.545	1.455	3.858	0.2592	0.716	1.710	6.006	0.443	1.557
24	0.612	0.632	0.157	0.9684	1.0327	0.538	1.399	0.555	1.445	3.895	0.2567	0.712	1.759	6.031	0.452	1.548
25	0.600	0.619	0.153	0.9696	1.0313	0.548	1.392	0.565	1.435	3.931	0.2544	0.709	1.804	6.058	0.459	1.541
Over 25	$\frac{3}{\sqrt{n}}$	$\frac{3}{\sqrt{n}}$	.....	......	......	*	**	*	**	.....	.....	.....	.....	.....	.....	.....

$$*1 - \frac{3}{\sqrt{2n}} \qquad **1 + \frac{3}{\sqrt{2n}}$$

[1] This table has been reproduced by permission from Albert H. Bowker and Gerald J. Lieberman, *Engineering Statistics*, p. 477.

---

[4]Albert H. Bowker and Gerald J. Lieberman, *Engineering Statistics*, p. 383.

It is usual for control charts for variables to be based on averages of small samples rather than on individual measurements. The principal reason for this is that even though the population may differ somewhat from a normal distribution, the distribution of the means of random samples can be treated as approximately normal because of the central limit theorem.

Attribute control charts are necessarily somewhat different from those for variables, but the same statistical basis applies. If you will recall, attribute inspection is an absolute type of inspection for the purpose of determining whether the item should be accepted or rejected. Control charts for attributes, then, are based upon the percentage of rejections. The p chart and the c chart are frequently used for controlling attributes.

The basic statistic that we are concerned with in fraction defective charts is

$$p = \frac{d}{n}$$

where p is a fraction and d is the number of defective parts found in a sample of n pieces inspected. Since the characteristic being plotted is p, the chart is frequently referred to as a p chart. The probability distribution that is applicable in this type of situation is the binomial distribution. For the binomial distribution, the standard deviation (σ_p) is

$$\sigma_p = \sqrt{\frac{p(1 - p)}{n}}$$

where n = the size of the sample. In setting up control limits, industrial engineers have concluded that $\pm 3\sigma$ limits around the mean ($\bar{p}$) work very well. Thus, it is common practice to set the control limits on a p chart with the upper control limit (UCL) $= \bar{p} + 3\sigma_p$ and lower control limit (LCL) $= \bar{p} - 3\sigma_p$. The use of a p chart is illustrated in Figure 15-8. This chart is based on checking 100 transistors daily against the electrical specifications and determining the percent of defective parts.

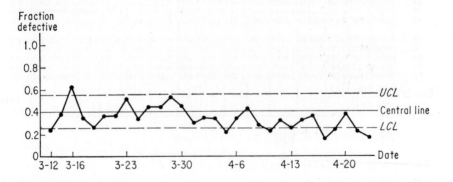

Figure 15-8 p-chart for transistors. (Reproduced by permission from Irwin Miller and John Freund, *Probability and Statistics for Engineers;* Englewood Cliffs, N. J.: Prentice-Hall, Inc., 1965, p. 344.)

Note that there is only 1 point out of control on the high side but 7 out of control on the low side. Since, in this case, it was the aim of the production line to turn out at least 60 percent of satisfactory transistors, it appears as though the process is potentially capable of doing better than that if it can be properly stabilized.

There are situations where it is essential that the number of defects in a product be controlled, such as the number of defects per hundred yards of wallpaper or the number of paint defects per automobile. A c chart may be used to control this type of process. If c may be taken as the number of defects per manufactured unit, it is the value of a random variable having the poisson distribution. If K is the number of units of product available for checking the defects, then

$$\bar{c} = \frac{1}{K} \sum_{i=1}^{k} c_i$$

and the control-chart limits for the c chart are

$$\text{UCL} = \bar{c} + \sqrt{3\bar{c}}$$
$$\text{LCL} = \bar{c} - \sqrt{3\bar{c}}$$

For an illustration of the use of this chart, see Figure 15-9, which pertains to the number of rivets missing from an aircraft.

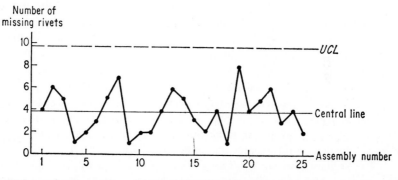

Figure 15-9. c-chart for number of rivets missing. (Reproduced by permission from Irwin Miller and John Freund, *Probability and Statistics for Engineers;* Englewood Cliffs, N. J.: Prentice-Hall, Inc., 1965, p. 345.)

Control charts are often set up at the machine, where they may be maintained by either the operator or a roving inspector. By having the chart in this location, emphasis on quality is ever present and the opportunity for corrective action is facilitated.

The trend of using computers for many manufacturing functions has led to the computerization of the functions included in a quality control charting system. For example, at the Reading Works of Western Electric Company[5] a computerized sys-

[5]See Howard J. Blomquist and Earl L. Brown, Jr., "Computerized Statistical Quality Control," *The Western Electric Engineer,* Vol. XXII, No. 1, January 1978, pp. 8–13.

tem was developed to facilitate control chart maintenance. The system also provided a data base for engineering studies, statistical analysis techniques for evaluating the data, and systematic status reports for better control and management of the chart system. The system had the versatility to be able to produce typical $\overline{X}$ and R charts, status messages, histograms, scatter plots, and so forth.

Acceptance sampling. Acceptance sampling is a sampling technique widely used for attribute inspection. In using this system, samples of a lot are inspected and the number of rejects in the sample determines whether the lot is to be accepted or rejected. When rejected, the balance of the lot is usually screened to separate the defective parts from the acceptable ones.

Acceptance-sampling plans are of most value when the nature of the process used to manufacture the product remains relatively homogeneous. Under such circumstances, it has been common for purchaser and supplier to enter into an agreement whereby the lot will be accepted or rejected according to the proportion of rejects found in the sample inspected. It is obvious that both buyer and seller assume some risk in using this procedure. However, the savings in inspection cost will usually more than offset the risk involved.

The acceptance-sampling plans in common usage are single, double, and sequential sampling. Among the best-known and most generally applicable plans are those based upon the Dodge and Romig[6] Single and Double Sampling Inspection Tables and those based upon Mil-Std-105.[7] In using these plans it is necessary first to decide the acceptable quality level (AQL) to be used. This value is usually expressed in terms of the percent of defective parts.

The Dodge and Romig Tables may be used for providing specified consumer protection at a minimum total inspection cost for a fixed-incoming quality level. Thus, if we know the percent defective for a process for a previous run of parts, we can pick a plan out of the Tables that gives this assurance on a minimum amount of inspection. The type of quality protection may be either for lot tolerance percent defective (LTPD) or for average-outgoing quality limit (AOQL).

The Military Standard 105 Tables place primary emphasis on the maintenance of a specified AQL. The Tables provide a choice of single, double, or multiple sampling plans and a choice of inspection levels. These tables are the most popular in use and have become the standard for this type of inspection for all of industry.

Following are examples[8] taken from Table VI-K of Mil-Std 105 that illustrate the use of each type of sampling using an AQL of 1.0 and normal inspection for percent defective:

---

[6]H. F. Dodge and H. G. Romig, *Sampling Inspection Tables;* New York: John Wiley and Sons, Inc., 1944, pp. 70–71.

[7]Military Standard 105D, "Sampling Procedures and Tables for Inspection by Attributes," Superintendent of Documents, Washington, D. C.: U. S. Government Printing Office, 1963.

[8]Adapted from Bartrand L. Hansen, *Quality Control Theory and Applications,* Englewood Cliffs, N.J.: Prentice-Hall,Inc., 1963, pp. 133-135. Reprinted with permission.

Single sampling plan. Based on the data in the table, select at random and examine 110 units. If three or fewer defectives are found, accept the lot. If four or more are found, reject the lot.

Double sampling plan. Select at random and examine 75 units. If no more than one defective is found, accept the lot. If six or more defectives are found, reject the lot. If two, three, four, or five defectives are found, select and examine 150 additional units. If in the total sample (225 units), five or fewer defectives are found, accept the lot. If six or more defectives are found, reject the lot.

Multiple sampling plan. Select at random and examine 30 units. If three or more are defective, reject the lot. Acceptance is not possible with first sample. If two or fewer are found defective, select and examine 30 additional units. If, in the two samples (60 units), none are defective, accept the lot. If three or more are defective, reject the lot. If one or two are defective, take a third sample of 30 units and so on. The process is continued until a decision to accept or reject the lot is complete. A final decision on acceptance or rejection must be made after the seventh sample (a total of 210 units) has been taken.

Whereas single sampling bases the acceptance or rejection of a lot on a single sample, and double sampling may use two samples, sequential sampling may use one, two, three, or more samples.

Reliability

One of the outgrowths of the electronic and space ages has been the tremendous emphasis placed on the capability of a product not to break down in operation. This has led to a concept referred to as reliability. Reliability has been defined as "the probability of performing without failure a specified function under given conditions for a specified period of time."[9] In contrast to quality control, reliability is associated with quality over a length of time, whereas quality control is primarily concerned with the relatively short time required to manufacture the product.

Reliability has come into great prominence because of the increasing complexity of aircraft, space vehicles, and electronic equipment. Whereas the designer used to be able to use a high safety factor and redundancy to offset possible breakdowns, weight and space limitations on many products have tended to make this impossible. The causes of unreliability are many, one of the major ones being the sizable number of components contained in many products. The difficulty of successfully combining many parts is clearly illustrated by the multiplication law of probability which Pieruschka[10] states as follows:

---

[9]AGREE Report, *Reliability of Military Electronic Equipment,* Washington, D. C.: U. S. Government Printing Office, June 1957.

[10]See Erich Pieruschka, *Principles of Reliability;* Englewood Cliffs, N. J.: Prentice-Hall, Inc., 1963, pp. 45–47.

The reliability of an item of equipment equals the product of the individual reliabilities of all its components when they are connected in series.

If P represents the product reliability, P_i represents the ith component, and n represents the total series of connected components, then the above definition becomes:

$$P = p_1 p_2 p_3 \ldots p_n$$

Based on this formula, given an assembly of 10 parts, each of which has a reliability of 0.99, the reliability of the equipment would be only about 0.90. A unit of equipment with 100 components, each with 0.99 reliability, would have the surprisingly low reliability of only about 0.368. It does not take too much imagination to realize the level of reliability that components must have on a complex assembly (such as a missile with about 40,000 parts) in order to function satisfactorily.

In order to turn out a reliable product, there are five key areas that must be given consideration: design of the product, production, measurement and testing, maintenance, and field operation. A number of companies have established reliability engineering groups to plan, coordinate, and integrate all phases of a complete reliability program.

QUESTIONS

1. A nationally advertised shirt sells at department stores for $25.00, whereas a comparable shirt sold by a mail-order house sells for $16.98. How would the relative quality of these two shirts be determined?
2. Are the quality standards for products always established by the customer? Explain.
3. Are chance variables always prevalent in a process? Why?
4. If a quality control program were operating perfectly, would it be necessary to have inspectors in a plant? Why?
5. Discuss the manner in which a company's quality control program may be influenced by government regulations.
6. Is it desirable for a company to inspect all incoming materials? Discuss.
7. There was a time when products made in Japan were considered inferior to ours. How did the Japanese turn this around and become well known for producing high-quality products?
8. Discuss a manufacturing situation in which centralized inspection would be particularly desirable.
9. In what ways may the use of data processing equipment and computers be of value in the quality control program?
10. In what way can statistical quality control aid in promoting the understanding and appreciation of quality control?
11. If a company maintains a good quality control program, will this insure high reliability of their products? Why?
12. How do you account for the success of QC Circles?
13. Why have vision systems become increasingly popular in quality control programs?

CASE PROBLEMS

James A. Coleman Manufacturing Company

James A. Coleman Manufacturing Company is a producer of lawn water-sprinkling equipment and systems. The company fabricates a large variety of items ranging from automatic in-ground electronic water controllers and sprinkling heads to surface sprinklers that can be attached to garden hoses. The company has experienced 30% annual growth for the past 10 years because of well-designed products and favorable acceptance by its customers. The lawn watering companies that install the in-ground systems and the hardware stores selling Coleman's products vouch for the high quality of the products. This is particularly important to Coleman's future because they design their products to last (brass nozzles instead of plastic, die castings instead of plastic, and so forth), and they sell them at a premium price.

James Coleman, the founder and president of the company, is concerned about the perpetuation of the company's reputation for high-quality products and has mentioned this to the Manager of Manufacturing, the Chief Engineer, and the Sales Manager on frequent occasions. One of the things that came out in these discussions was that "management must create incentives for excellence."

Questions:

1. How can James Coleman create such incentives?
2. To what else do you think Mr. Coleman should give consideration?

Robertson Bearing Company

The Robertson Bearing Company is a large manufacturer of precision ball bearings. It has experienced difficulty in maintaining quality standards on some operations, and its executives have become interested in using statistical quality control. To assist them in establishing this program, they have retained Professor C. G. Scitamehtam from the local university.

Professor Scitamehtam decided to illustrate some of the tools of statistical quality control by using actual data from one of the company's operations. A grinding operation, used to finish the outside diameter of a No. 2-1-26 bearing, was selected for securing samples. Ten samples, with 5 bearings in each sample, were taken at 30-minute intervals, and the results were as indicated on the following table:

	Measurements on Each of Five Items in Sample						
Series No.	A	B	C	D	E	$\bar{X}$ or Ave.	R or Range
1	1.849	1.842	1.844	1.845	1.843	1.845	.007
2	1.845	1.846	1.841	1.845	1.843	1.844	.005
3	1.846	1.849	1.847	1.841	1.847	1.846	.008
4	1.847	1.850	1.848	1.850	1.850	1.849	.003
5	1.844	1.846	1.844	1.845	1.846	1.845	.002
6	1.840	1.842	1.840	1.839	1.842	1.841	.003
7	1.845	1.844	1.843	1.844	1.844	1.844	.002
8	1.848	1.844	1.847	1.846	1.845	1.846	.004
9	1.846	1.846	1.847	1.846	1.845	1.846	.002
10	1.844	1.845	1.847	1.848	1.846	1.846	.004

Note: $\bar{\bar{X}} = 1.8450$

$\bar{R} = 0.0040$

Questions:

1.   Show the measurements in the table on a "frequency" or "histogram" type chart.
     (a)   Sketch a normal curve on the chart.
     (b)   Estimate 3σ limits—(99.7% of all cases).
     (c)   Indicate mean $(\bar{\bar{X}})$.
     (d)   Show specification tolerances ($1.845 \pm .005$).
2.   Using the data in the table, construct an $\bar{X}$ chart. Show on the chart:
     (a)   A line for the average of all samples $(\bar{\bar{X}})$.
     (b)   A point for the average of each sample.
     (c)   UCL and LCL.
3.   Construct a range chart and locate it directly beneath the above $\bar{X}$ chart. Show the control limit.
4.   Can this process be used for producing the part? Why?

Gibson-Moore Company

The Gibson-Moore Company is a large midwestern manufacturer of toiletries. One of the company's principal products is toothpaste. The company manufactures both the toothpaste and the flexible tubes in which the toothpaste is contained. Highly mechanized filling lines are used in filling the tubes and the packaging of the product.

The plastic caps that fit on the tubes are made in a separate building in lots of 100,000 and placed in large cylindrical containers. Typical defects that occur in the caps result from inadequate material being fed into the molding machine or damage that may occur in the tumbling processes used for removing sharp edges and for cleaning. Since the cost of one cap (following all operations) is $0.003 and the cost of inspecting a cap is $0.004, there has been only superficial visual inspection of caps by the tumbling machine operators.

When the caps are completed, they are stored in the cylindrical containers until such time as required to be moved to the filling department. At the filling line, the caps are dumped (as required) into a hopper which automatically feeds the caps into the production line.

A persistent problem that has been arising on the filling line is the failure of the plastic caps to fit on the tubes after the tubes are filled. Failure of the cap to fit properly on the tube results in frequent shattering of the cap or tube and the jamming of the production line. Because of the high speed of the line, as many as 30 tubes may be damaged in the process. Since filled tubes cost $0.10 each, it has become essential to find a way to control the number of defective caps fed into the production line.

Questions:

1.   What quality control plan would you recommend for overcoming this problem?
2.   Discuss any inspection procedures that you propose to include in the plan.
3.   How do the costs entering into this situation influence your plan?

16

MAINTENANCE ENGINEERING

Anyone who has been delayed on a trip because of a breakdown in an airplane, a train, or a bus can vouch for the inconvenience and frustration that it caused. Although it is doubtful whether most people give it much thought, this same breakdown may have indicated a weakness in the transportation company's maintenance program. It is on this general subject of keeping equipment in operating condition that we shall be dwelling in this chapter.

Maintenance engineering is that function of manufacturing management that is concerned with the day-to-day problem of keeping the physical plant in good operating condition. It is an essential activity in every manufacturing establishment, because it is necessary to insure the availability of the machines, buildings, and services needed by other parts of the organization for the performance of their functions at an optimum return on the investment, whether this investment is in machinery, materials, or employees.

The widespread mechanization of industry is adding to the complexity of industrial maintenance programs and is making it increasingly important that equipment be kept operating and production rolling. Industry keeps its wheels turning at a sizable maintenance cost estimated to be in excess of $14 billion per year. This tremendous cost is becoming an increasing part of the total cost of manufacturing.

As we discuss the various phases of maintenance engineering in the sections that follow, it should be evident that it is closely related to many of the other functions that have been discussed previously. We have chosen to discuss maintenance engineering along with other areas of control because many of the phases of a well-conceived maintenance engineering program are an essential part of manufacturing control.

Scope of Maintenance

Maintenance is necessary in all manufacturing establishments because machines break down, parts wear out, and buildings deteriorate. All of the many segments that comprise the industrial enterprise require attention, including the buildings, grounds, machinery, equipment, materials handling equipment, heating and generating equipment, waste disposal systems, air-conditioning equipment, washrooms, cafeterias, and so forth.

The *Maintenance Engineering Handbook*[1] classifies maintenance engineering into the following primary and secondary functions:

Primary Functions:

1. Maintenance of existing plant equipment.
2. Maintenance of existing plant buildings and grounds.
3. Equipment inspection and lubrication.
4. Utilities generation and distribution.
5. Alterations to existing equipment and buildings.
6. New installations of equipment and buildings.

Secondary Functions:

1. Storekeeping.
2. Plant protection, including fire.
3. Waste disposal.
4. Salvage.
5. Insurance administration.
6. Janitorial service.
7. Property accounting.
8. Pollution and noise abatement.
9. Any other service delegated to maintenance engineering by plant management.

Many activities are of such a specialized nature that they frequently can be done cheaper by outside contractors. Thus, many companies contract with outside firms to maintain their elevators, power plants, burned-out motors, computers, and office equipment. Washing windows and care of grounds are two other activities that are commonly performed by outside companies.

---

[1] Edited by L. C. Morrow, New York: McGraw-Hill Book Company, 1957, pp. 1–4.

Much of the housekeeping is commonly assigned to the individual production departments. Each worker may be given the responsibility for keeping his or her work area clean and free from chips, shavings, oil, or other such items. It is the departmental foreman's responsibility to insure that tidy conditions are maintained in the department. Isn't it of interest to note that one of the frequent comments made about Japanese plants is that they are "clean"?

Organization for Maintenance

There is no one best maintenance organization that can be used in all cases. The organization should be tailored to fit the particular technical, geographical, and personnel situations involved. In establishing the maintenance organization, it should be recognized that the basic necessity is to maintain a plant at a level consistent with low cost and high productivity.

Considerable debate takes place among maintenance engineers as to the level to which they should report. Some are of the opinion that they should be under production whereas others think that they should be on equal footing with the production people. In general, it is probably sound practice to have the director of the maintenance function report to the level that is responsible for most of the other plant groups that the maintenance engineers serve.

The nature of the industry, that is, whether it is primarily electrical, chemical, or mechanical, will have considerable influence on the maintenance organization. Also, the size of the plant and the scope of activities to be performed are significant factors that will affect the organization. In a small plant utilizing a minimum of mechanical equipment, the maintenance department might consist of an all-around mechanic and a helper or two. In larger companies the maintenance group would be much more lavish and contain a variety of craftsmen. A typical organization chart for a medium-size plant is illustrated in Figure 16-1. Close scrutiny of this chart will reveal a number of features worthy of discussion.

The person in charge of the maintenance engineering activities is usually an engineer and most frequently carries the title of *plant engineer*. Other titles in use include maintenance superintendent, superintendent of maintenance, and manager of maintenance. Engineers may be used elsewhere in the maintenance organization to perform such functions as supervision of the power plant operation, design of special pieces of equipment, checking of installation specifications, and planning and scheduling of major projects.

One of the noteworthy features of most maintenance organizations is the large number of crafts represented in the group. This number will vary considerably depending on the variety of manufacturing processes present and the amount of work involved. Another factor that will influence the number of craftsmen required is the availability of skilled outside contractors and management's policy regarding the use of outside maintenance organizations. It is difficult to present any basis for determining exactly how many people are necessary in each craft in the mainte-

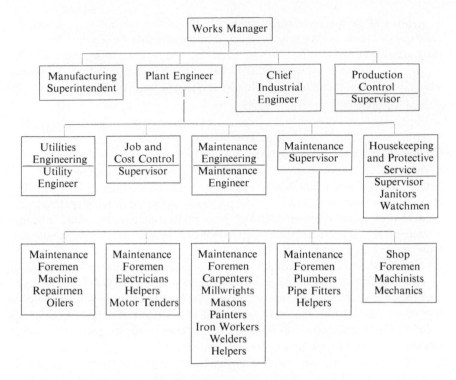

Figure 16-1. Structure of a maintenance organization.

nance organization. The ratio of maintenance to production employees will vary with the level of machinery and capital investment per operating employee and the efficiency of the maintenance organization.

An important part of the organization structure, as illustrated in Figure 16-1, is the job and cost control section. This section is responsible for scheduling work for the maintenance personnel and for maintaining cost figures on all jobs. It makes possible the efficient utilization of the craftsmen anywhere in the plant but, at the same time, does not prevent localized routine daily assignments.

Machine and repair shops and storerooms provide essential supporting sections within many maintenance organizations. The shops commonly contain machinists, mechanics, and electronics technicians capable of repairing equipment, making new parts (otherwise not available), and rebuilding equipment. The storerooms maintain a supply of spare parts (bearings, shafts, electric motors, pumps) and general maintenance materials (pipe fittings, standard hardware, light bulbs, switches, lubricants) needed by the maintenance force.

Other service groups that are commonly under the supervision of the plant engineer are the utilities engineering section and the housekeeping and protective service groups. The former is responsible for the operation of the power and heating and air-conditioning plant, the latter for keeping the plant clean and protecting the premises.

Economics of Maintenance

As pointed out earlier in this chapter, maintenance is a costly activity. When a machine or conveyor is down and people are standing idle, it costs the company dearly and greatly reduces productivity. Although maintenance methods are being improved constantly, the costs of maintaining equipment keep going up because the level and pay of the maintenance personnel keep improving and there is more equipment to service—and most plants are willing to pay a high price to get stalled machinery back on line. Then too, industry tends to spend too little for replacement of obsolete production equipment, and old equipment poses many maintenance problems.

Since maintenance is such a costly undertaking, management should give consideration to all of the pertinent economic factors in establishing the company's maintenance policy. Much thought must be given to answering such questions as (1) How much maintenance is needed? (2) What size maintenance crews should be used? (3) How can the maintenance crew be kept up-to-date and capable of servicing increasingly complex equipment? (4) Is centralized maintenance desirable? (5) Should maintenance be done by outside contractors? (6) Should a preventive maintenance system be established? (7) Should maintenance work be scheduled? (8) Should maintenance jobs be covered by a suitable work measurement system? (9) Should maintenance workers be covered by a wage-incentive system? (10) Is adequate use being made of work simplification, work sampling, waiting line theory, simulation, critical path method, and other techniques in analyzing work methods and crew sizes? and (11) Can effective use be made of computers for gathering and analyzing data and scheduling activities?

Maintenance policies. Fundamentally, maintenance policy must answer the question of the size and extent of the maintenance facilities. Foremen and manufacturing people will naturally want maintenance crews large enough so that every job can be done on a moment's notice. What mechanics do when they are not working on a maintenance job is not the concern of a production foreman. Management must look at the long-range picture and establish policies that will make possible the completion of necessary maintenance work and at the same time keep costs at a reasonable level. Skilled mechanics and electronics technicians are not easy to come by, and of course they are expensive to employ and train. Management therefore wants the "right" number on hand.

Points worthy of consideration in establishing maintenance policy are:

1. Contract out some work during peak periods to avoid getting too far behind and also to avoid hiring temporary extra help.
2. Contract with outside organizations to provide skilled service on special machines or equipment. This may prove to be highly useful on office equipment and computers.
3. Defer some maintenance work until slack periods so as to keep the

work force intact during such periods. Overhaul work and painting projects are often handled on this basis.

4. Replace machines and equipment at the optimum time. This time is difficult to determine, but many machine tool manufacturers stand willing and able to assist in such determination. The point is to replace machines before they get too old and require too much repair work. (See Chapter 6 on equipment replacement.)

Maintenance Work Assignments and Procedures

All too often maintenance work is initiated by a frenzied call from a production foreman informing the maintenance department that a machine has broken down, a conveyor has stopped, or something else has happened to stop production. Such calls usually result in immediate action in order to get production rolling again. Not all maintenance work will be this urgent, and most companies utilize a maintenance work order form to initiate the maintenance work. This form may be as elaborate or as simple as the company's accounting system demands.

If control is to be maintained on maintenance activities (as will be discussed later), no work should be done by any members of the maintenance department without a work order authorized by a responsible supervisor. The work order (see Figure 16-2) authorizes the maintenance craftsman to perform the work. Also, it provides a record of what was done, the date on which it was done, the cost of the job, the department to which it is to be charged, the materials and parts used, and similar information. Work orders may originate in the following ways:

1. Operating departments may request work to be done.
2. Regular inspections performed by the maintenance department may disclose work to be done.
3. Changes may be initiated by engineering, management, or production departments.

Such maintenance work as lubrication and inspections that are done on a regularly scheduled basis are usually covered by a patrol or blanket work order. Large maintenance jobs involving new machine or equipment installations or major machine or building repairs generally require the approval of some higher level of management before the work order can be initiated. One of the first steps on large jobs, such as installing a new conveyor, is to secure a cost estimate from the maintenance department. If the cost is such that the departmental foreman does not have the authority to approve the work, then he has to submit a proposal to the proper level of management requesting approval of the project. On large projects considerable time may elapse between the time the estimate is received and the actual performance of the work because of the necessity to plan the work, to make any necessary blueprints, to secure materials and parts, and to plan work schedules.

Received		Maintenance Repair Order	
Completed			
		CLASSIFICATION	MRO #
IN	MAN	Emergency _____	Account #
OUT	TIME	Machine Down _____	Time Paid
IN	MAN	Preventative _____	Mat'l Cost
OUT	TIME	Start On _____	Ordered By
IN	MAN	Complete By _____	Date
OUT	TIME		
IN	MAN	Mach. _____ No. _____ Inv. No. _____	
OUT	TIME	PRELIMINARY ESTIMATE OF TROUBLE	
IN	MAN		
OUT	TIME		
IN	MAN	ESTIMATE OF WORK AND ALLOWED TIME	
OUT	TIME		
IN	MAN		
OUT	TIME		
IN	MAN		
OUT	TIME		
IN	MAN		
OUT	TIME		
IN	MAN		
OUT	TIME	MATERIAL AND COST	
IN	MAN		
OUT	TIME		
IN	MAN		
OUT	TIME		
IN	MAN		
OUT	TIME		
IN	MAN		
OUT	TIME		
	Total Time		
Form 788		TOTAL COST _____	

Figure 16-2. Maintenance work order. (Courtesy Fairfield Manufacturing Company.)

The manner in which work assignments are made to the maintenance personnel will vary with the craftsman involved and whether the job is an emergency or routine one. Many small jobs are rush jobs that are initiated by a telephone call from the production supervisor. The maintenance clerk will record the request and, if the job is small, may be authorized to contact an appropriate craftsman to do the job. If the job is a large one, the clerk probably will contact a maintenance foreman to confirm the nature of the work to be done. The maintenance foreman, in turn, may pull workers off lower priority jobs to do the necessary work.

Since maintenance personnel are used all over the plant, and the foreman must travel throughout the plant to check on jobs and inspect work in progress, communication presents a big problem. As an example of the magnitude of this problem, consider an automobile assembly plant in California where there were 13.6 miles of conveyors and hundreds of process units and service equipment to keep running. To facilitate the maintenance communications in this plant, the company used seven citizen band radios and coded light panels located at strategic locations. When there was an equipment failure, the correct panel section would flash on, indicating by code the correct location of the stoppage. Contact with the appropriate maintenance group could then be made by means of radio or telephone.

Control of maintenance. Maintenance control necessarily involves paper work and records. Adequate records are necessary to a successful maintenance program almost regardless of the size of the plant. Even in our own homes, more successful operation of our many gadgets could be achieved if we set up a simple schedule of inspection for obvious defects, recorded dates and findings, and took appropriate action before breakdowns occurred.

Some of the control measures used and forms that assist are as follows:

1. Work authorization. As indicated previously, a work authorization or work order is usually required before any maintenance work can be started. The form is made out by the operating foreman concerned or by someone who has direct responsibility for operation of equipment. The order includes information concerning the location of the work, the nature of the work that is to be done, and the date the work should or could start. Approval by others in authority is usually required, not only as a control measure to be sure the work is necessary, but also to be certain that materials and labor are available, to work the order into the overall schedule, and to be sure that this order doesn't call for a violation of company policy, safety rules, or building codes.

2. Work schedule. One of the more difficult phases of maintenance control is the working out of a satisfactory schedule when a group of authorized work orders are on hand. As a first step, the maintenance foreman or job control supervisor must estimate the number of workers and the time required for each work order. Then, knowing the number of people available on the crews, he or she can derive some kind of schedule estimate. Emphasis needs to be placed on the word "estimate," for any maintenance schedule is just that. Even in the best plant an emergency call will frequently come in that disturbs the carefully worked out schedule.

3. Material costs. Costs of maintenance jobs are usually figured by keeping track of the materials used and the labor hours expended on any one job. Material costs are determined by the use of storeroom requisitions. A mechanic needing a new bearing to repair a machine checks the bearing out of the storeroom, indicating on the requisition that it is to be used on a machine on Work Order No. 246. All charges to Work Order No. 246 can then be accumulated to show a total material cost for that particular job.

4. Labor costs. Labor hours spent on any one job may be recorded in various ways. Some companies have each mechanic turn in a special card at the end of each day indicating how much time was spent on each job assigned.

The dollars charged to any hour of a mechanic's time spent on a maintenance job may be the actual dollars paid that mechanic, an average wage figure for all mechanics, or a figure representing not only average wage dollars but also the overhead of the maintenance department itself. This latter charge would include such things as maintenance foreman's salary, storeroom upkeep, and power used in the shop.

5. Budgets. Although maintenance costs fluctuate, some estimates must be made for budget purposes. Here, experience is the best guide. Next year's maintenance costs will not vary too much from last year's, assuming that the production schedule is about the same and that the management does not permit (or is planning not to permit) the general level of maintenance to go up or down. Budgets are frequently set on a percentage basis or on the basis of so many dollars of maintenance for so many units of production output. Again, experience is the guide. If actual maintenance required over the past several years worked out this way, then it is feasible to plan that way for future budgets.

In budgets, a distinction is usually made between repair jobs and improvements. Repair jobs simply put the equipment back into its original condition. Improvement jobs, on the other hand, make the equipment more useful or valuable to the company than it was originally. The repair job is charged as an operating expense while the improvement job must be capitalized and shown on the books as an asset. The income tax situation, then, makes it attractive to some of the more unscrupulous companies to designate improvements jobs as repair jobs.

6. Equipment records. Records of equipment such as that shown in Figure 16-3 are a necessary part of every good maintenance program. Such records include all the pertinent data concerning the equipment itself, such as the serial number, supplier, and initial cost. Such information is of course necessary when ordering parts or when seeking information about that equipment from the supplier. A record card might also contain a record of repair work performed, the schedule for inspections, and the costs of inspection and repair. Repair cost information is especially valuable, for with such information one can determine when costs are running much higher than normal—possibly calling for replacement.

Some companies are now making excellent use of data processing equipment and computers to assist in maintaining maintenance records. One aircraft company feeds data into the system and can get almost immediate answers to such questions as who received the service, when and where did they receive service, what kind of service was performed, how much time did the maintenance man spend, what was accomplished, how much did it cost, and where are excessive maintenance costs being incurred. Also, this system is of tremendous assistance in making decisions on what to do when, in forecasting equipment-replacement schedules, and so forth.

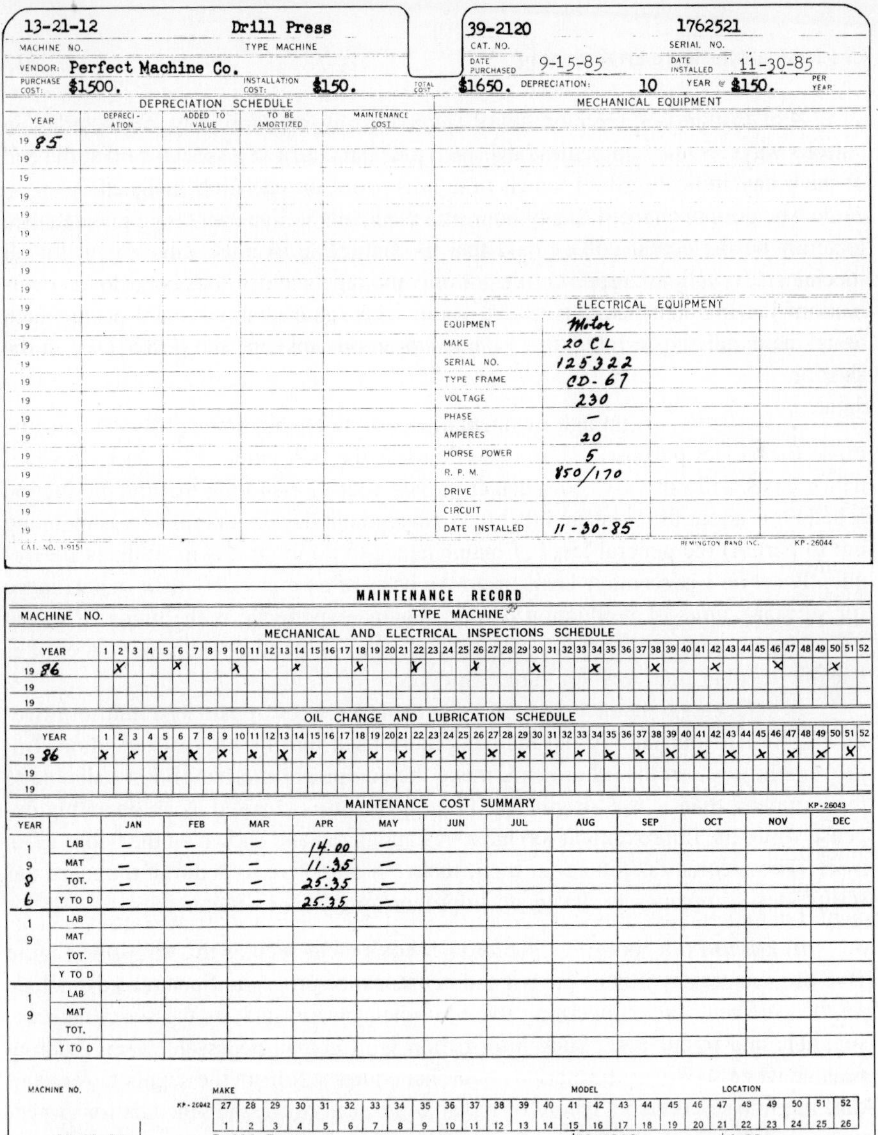

Figure 16-3. Equipment record that incorporates both a preventive maintenance schedule and a maintenance cost summary in one record. (Courtesy Remington Rand, Inc.)

Planning and Scheduling Maintenance Activities

It has been said that the tools of good maintenance are planning, scheduling, and cost accounting. The planning and scheduling section of the maintenance department has the basic responsibility for establishing job priorities, for insuring that necessary tools and materials are available, and for preparing and issuing written schedules of jobs to be done.

The size and organization of the planning and scheduling group will depend on the size and complexity of the maintenance organization. In a small company, all of the planning and scheduling may be performed by the maintenance supervisor. Under such circumstances, the planning and scheduling will probably be handled on quite an informal basis. Larger companies, as indicated in Figure 16-1, utilize a special group to plan and schedule jobs. Although much of the work done in this section is clerical in nature, the supervisor of the group should be a person with broad experience in maintenance methods. Such knowledge frequently is necessary to coordinate the scheduling of the various craftsmen in the maintenance department.

In order to do the necessary day-to-day and long-range planning required to make the most effective utilization of the maintenance personnel, suitable routines are necessary. These will involve (1) the securing of any necessary approval from the plant engineer for any projects that are of sufficient magnitude to require his attention; (2) the securing of information from equipment records, work orders, work measurement data, craft and shops' work force reports, storekeepers' procurement reports, the plant production schedule, and other pertinent sources; and (3) reference to existing master schedules. As is true of all scheduling activities, basic to maintenance scheduling and control is an estimate of the time required for each work order prior to doing the work.

The scheduling of maintenance work involves essentially two steps: a master plan of all jobs that can be predicted in advance, and a daily adjustment of this plan necessitated by emergencies. In most plants there are a number of machines and other items of equipment that need to be taken out of service periodically for inspection and overhaul. The frequency of these occurrences will vary with the equipment, but experiential figures subjected to suitable mathematical and statistical analysis will indicate the optimum time for the minimum overall costs. After these times have been established, they can be incorporated into the master maintenance schedule.

The master maintenance schedules may be broken down into weekly or daily maintenance schedules. The weekly work schedule will provide information to each craft and shop concerning the work to be done on each job for each day in the following week. This schedule would normally be issued every Thursday or Friday and would be the basis for each maintenance foreman to issue daily work assignments to the workers. Some maintenance departments prefer to centralize this function and have daily work assignments issued directly by a dispatcher in the job control section. Whatever system is used, it is good practice to issue work assignments for the next day to each craftsman prior to the end of the workday.

As a means of decreasing costs, many companies are computerizing their maintenance activities. Illustrative of this is the Newhaven plant of Parker Pen Company,[2] which produces about 30 million pens and pencils and other writing in-

---

[2] See "Comac System Reduces Downtime," *Production Engineering,* Vol. 64, No. 6, June 1985, p. 46.

struments per year. The plant has installed a computerized maintenance system that schedules routine maintenance for about 300 items of plant equipment. The system schedules lubrication and prepares a weekly maintenance plan for the week ahead for the maintenance workers. When the workers finish each job, information is fed into the system to create plant historical files. The system is also used to plan new projects. It not only enables maintenance to be carried out more thoroughly and efficiently than on the old manual system, but also has proven to be beneficial in disclosing problems that could be corrected before serious downtime occurred.

Accurate information on the number of hours of labor spent on each job and any materials used are essential items for cost-accounting purposes. These charges are made against the pertinent departments and become one of the costs of manufacturing. Further, the costs provide a check on the operating effectiveness of the departments concerned.

Types of Maintenance

Maintenance may be classified into three general categories: corrective, preventive, and predictive. Each of these will be discussed in the sections that follow.

Corrective maintenance.   Corrective maintenance is the fix-it variety, the kind most of us think of when the word "maintenance" is mentioned. In this sense maintenance becomes repair work. Repairs are made after the equipment is out of order—an electric motor will not start, a conveyor belt is ripped, or a shaft has broken. In cases such as these, the maintenance department checks into the difficulty and makes the necessary repairs. Theoretically, if the maintenance department does only corrective work, it is idle except when equipment has broken down and repairs are required.

Preventive maintenance.   In marked contrast to corrective maintenance is preventive maintenance, which is undertaken before the need for repair arises and aims to minimize the possibility of unanticipated production interruptions or major breakdowns. Preventive maintenance consists of (1) proper design and installation of equipment, (2) periodic inspection of plant and equipment to prevent breakdowns before they occur, (3) repetitive servicing, upkeep, and overhaul of equipment, and (4) adequate lubrication, cleaning, and painting of buildings and equipment.

Preventive maintenance starts on the drawing board with those design features included in a product to minimize maintenance. As an example, one of the large rubber companies had considerable difficulty with a metal-lined pump that was used to pump liquid latex. The metal pump curdled the latex and kept clogging the line. The firm installed glass-lined centrifugal pumps that decreased the friction of flow and reduced their maintenance cost by 75 percent. Not only did they reduce the maintenance cost, but the new pumps were cheaper.

Even though preventive maintenance is practiced to some extent in about 75 percent of all manufacturing companies, every preventive maintenance program has to be tailored to an individual plant. The key to all good preventive maintenance programs, however, is inspection. This inspection should cover virtually everything, including production machinery, motors, controls, materials handling equipment, process equipment, lighting, buildings, and plant services. Some plants inspect only items costing $500 or more, but others go lower. As a general rule, if a failure in upkeep may harm an employee, stop production, or waste plant assets, then consideration should be given to including such upkeep in the preventive maintenance program. Suitable statistical techniques have been developed for determining how often to inspect. Suffice it to say that too much inspection is false economy.

A well-conceived preventive maintenance program should contain the following features:

1. Proper identification of all items to be included in the program.
2. Adequate records covering volume of work, cost, and so forth.
3. Inspections on a definite schedule—with standing orders on specific assignments.
4. Use of checklists by inspectors.
5. An inspection frequency schedule—may vary from as often as once every 6 hours to as little as once a year.
6. Well-qualified inspectors—have craftsmen familiar with items being inspected and capable of making simple repairs at the time trouble is observed.
7. Use of repair budgets for major items of equipment.
8. Administrative procedures that provide necessary fulfillment and follow-up on the program.

There are many returns to the users of preventive maintenance programs: greater safety for workers, decreased production downtime, fewer large-scale and repetitive repairs, less cost for simple repairs made before breakdown, less standby equipment required, better spare parts control, identification of items with high maintenance costs, and lower unit cost of manufacture. As industry becomes more highly automated, it becomes more in need of the advantages of preventive maintenance. The costs of modern equipment are high, and so are the costs of production breakdowns. Downtime in excess of one percent is considered critical in one highly mechanized auto plant and is justification for its elaborate preventive maintenance program.

Predictive maintenance.   One of the newer types of maintenance that may be anticipated to gain increasing attention is called predictive maintenance. It is a preventive type of maintenance that involves the use of sensitive instruments (e.g., vibration analyzers, amplitude meters, audio gauges, optical tooling, and pressure, temperature, and resistance gages) to predict trouble. Conditions can be measured periodically or on a continuous basis, and this enables the maintenance people to establish the imminence of need for overhaul. Such overhaul will allow an extension to the service life without fear of failure. In an example cited by Quinn,[3] "some large turbo-generators were being dismantled for inspection every year, and more recently every three years. Now under predictive maintenance they have been operating continuously—and satisfactorily—without dismantling for over five years."

Systems of Maintenance Management

It has been estimated that as many as 75 percent of maintenance problems could be prevented by machine operators at an early stage. This has led companies to initiate job enrichment programs to try to motivate workers to provide improved surveilance of their work stations. Also, companies have organized operator–maintenance worker teams to try to improve operator–maintenance skills. Further, in some companies in which small production teams are used, members of the group have been trained to handle routine maintenance problems, such as lubrication, cleaning, making simple adjustments, and so forth.

Despite the efforts of companies to improve on the human element of maintenance, further steps have been felt to be desirable. This has prompted an increasing number of companies to install maintenance diagnostic systems for diagnosing the condition of equipment while it is operating. Muramatsu, Tanaka, and Nakajima[4] suggest the following approach that has been applied to complicated precision equipment used in process industries such as steel and chemical plants:

1. Divide the equipment and facilities into rational clusters according to the diagnostic characteristics.
2. Analyze the failures and characteristics of each cluster (classifying by importance and using a statistical analysis, etc.)
3. Develop and determine sensing, measuring, and discrimination methods and signal processing techniques taking into account the object of diagnosis, the characteristics of equipment and facilities, and the observability, reliability, and economy of diagnosis.
4. Equipment and facilities testers are made according to the diagnostic techniques developed for each cluster; these should preferably be portable.
5. A computer-aided maintenance diagnostic system is made in order to detect unusual equipment and facility conditions in the early stage and to indicate the location and the cause for failure together with the remedy, automatically.

---

[3]James D. Quinn, "The Real Goal of Maintenance Engineering," *Factory*, June 1963, pp. 90–93.

[4]Gavriel Salvendy, ed., *Handbook of Industrial Engineering*; New York, N.Y.: John Wiley & Sons, 1982, p. 11.7.7.

Maintenance systems such as that in Chrysler's Windsor, Ontario assembly plant are being integrated into highly sophisticated factory information systems[5] as a part of plant-wide data gathering and report-generating communications between manufacturing and maintenance. The heart of the system is a computer linked to a pair of programmable controllers that act as data concentrators. The factory information system is linked to all major plant systems, including robots, conveyors, transfer stations, and paint ovens. The system's computer stores detailed preventive maintenance information, pinpoints critical machine faults as they occur, and provides early warning of potential machine-related problems. The system gathers historical machine performance data to assist in the plant's preventive maintenance program. Other data that it provides include downtime and reason for downtime, number of rejects, alarm notification, diagnostics, and maintenance dispatch information.

Another example of a plant with a highly sophisticated computerized maintenance monitoring system is the IBM typewriter plant in Lexington, Kentucky. This plant has 4.7 miles of power-and-free conveyor, approximately 20 robots, and 65 manual work stations. The system is run by a network of programmable controllers and IBM computers.

Whether companies operate large, sophisticated systems, such as those just described, or have far less complex operations, machine diagnostics is becoming increasingly important in discrete parts industries. Machine diagnostic installations encompass devices for sending and receiving signals from a machine's controller (which, in turn, has its own diagnostic circuitry). The purpose of machine diagnostics is to detect and to locate unacceptable variations, communicate the problem (e.g., through a CRT terminal or other display device), and lead the operator or maintenance worker quickly to the source of the problem.

Housekeeping and Protection Service

Many of the housekeeping chores in a plant start in each employee's work area. As pointed out previously, this has led many companies to hold each worker responsible for keeping his or her machine or work area free from chips, shavings, excess oil, and similar items. Some equipment and areas are not in direct personal use by individual workers, and no one is directly responsible for them. Thus, the aisles, the washrooms, the windows, and the warehouses need to be tended by someone else. The plant engineering and maintenance department, by its very nature, is called on to maintain so much of the plant that it is quite logical to make all housekeeping a part of its duties.

It is common practice to divide the plant and offices into cleaning zones and to assign a janitor to each zone. The janitors sweep and scrub the floors, clean lavatories, clean drinking fountains, and perform other similar duties. Power sweepers

---

[5] See "Controls Integrate the Factory," *Production*, Vol. 95, No. 12, June 1985, p. 60.

have replaced manual sweeping in most plants and are used to patrol the entire plant area.

Plant security and fire protection pose continual problems in every manufacturing plant, and these two functions are frequently included as part of the plant engineer's responsibility. It is common to use guards at all of the plant entrances to insure that only authorized persons are allowed on the company's property. Watchmen are also needed to patrol the plant during non-working hours to guard against theft and fire. Some companies that are confronted with considerable fire hazard employ full-time firefighters and maintain their own fire fighting equipment.

Trends in Maintenance Engineering

Several significant trends are taking place in maintenance engineering. Increasing attention is being given to the design of buildings, facilities, and processes to eliminate as much maintenance as possible. There is increasing emphasis on manufacturing system reliability and procurement of equipment with a prescribed level of quality assurance. From an operational point of view, the maintenance engineers will be making more effective use of statistical tools to analyze the service life of the components of a manufacturing system and will be able to pinpoint problem areas and provide justification for improvement of component reliability or for periodic replacement to maintain system availability. Increasingly, maintenance will be tied into plant information systems.

The increasing complexity of manufacturing processes will necessitate the continuous upgrading and training of maintenance personnel. One plant engineer, in response to a query about the problem of maintaining a highly automated production line, stated that he virtually needed maintenance men with the technical knowledge of electrical engineers to cope with all of the controls on the line. His statement may not be too farfetched, and some maintenance experts have predicted the need for a diagnostic engineer who would troubleshoot the complex equipment and instruct less skilled mechanics in repair.

Predictive and diagnostic maintenance will get increasing attention as better instrumentation and systems are developed to detect flaws in operating conditions.

QUESTIONS

1. Make up a preventive maintenance checklist for your house, car, or some appliance with which you are familiar. Would your list be practical to put into use? Explain your answer.
2. Outline at least three types of situations in a manufacturing plant that would justify a program of preventive maintenance.
3. Through what procedure does a company keep track of the cost of a repair job?
4. What advantages does the use of a work authorization form have over the simple use of person-to-person communication concerning repair work? What disadvantages?

5.   What is the distinction between a "repair job" and an "improvement"? Is this distinction important?

6.   What role in safety work is played by maintenance engineering?

7.   Some maintenance engineers contend that preventive maintenance on many items is absolutely unnecessary. Comment on this opinion.

8.   How can the effectiveness of a maintenance department be evaluated?

9.   Is it likely that an equipment record form, such as that shown in Figure 16-3, will become obsolete? Why?

10. What appears to be the trend in maintenance programs?

CASE PROBLEMS

Akron Forgings Company

Bill Barnes had reason to be proud of the Akron Forgings Company's maintenance record for the past six months. Not once during that time had there been a production holdup because of machinery breakdowns. As maintenance supervisor, Bill had been striving for six years to achieve this goal. He knew the record probably couldn't hold for another six months; but nevertheless he appreciated that the plant manager, Stephen Cross, was predicting that it would. Mr. Cross had made this prediction when he made it a point to come out to the shop and commend Bill.

A few days later the cost records for the past six months reached Mr. Cross's desk and he noticed that maintenance costs for the period were considerably higher than they had been for similar periods during the past two years. Production levels for all three years were roughly the same.

Questions:

1.   How do you account for the high maintenance costs?

2.   Was Bill's record really a good one?

3.   What action should Mr. Cross take?

Sherman Aluminum Company

The Sherman Aluminum Company is one of the nation's leading producers of extruded aluminum products. The various manufacturing processes are located in three very large adjacent buildings. Because of the immensity of the plant, it has become traditional for the maintenance personnel to use three-wheeled motorized vehicles to move their tools and parts to the work locations.

During a recent vacation in Florida, one of the maintenance men, George Olson, observed a number of older people riding tricycles to stores in a neighborhood shopping center. Upon returning from vacation, George submitted a suggestion that tricycles be used by the maintenance men on light jobs instead of the motorized carts. He pointed out that these tricycles could be 26 inches high, heavy duty, and have a tool box mounted between the back wheels. The vehicles probably could be purchased for about $300. The advantages gained by using such tricycles would be that they could be purchased much cheaper than the present carts, would save energy, and would eliminate any environmental problems. Further, it would be a good way for the maintenance people to get exercise.

Questions:

1. If you were the Manager of Plant Maintenance, how would you proceed in evaluating this suggestion?

2. If you decide to implement the suggestion, how would you go about countering any resistance that may arise from the other maintenance personnel?

Clinton Manufacturing Company

While waiting for the service manager of Willenbrock Buick/Cadillac to check in his Cadillac for servicing, Robert Sayres, Vice President of Manufacturing for Clinton Manufacturing Company, was glancing at some of the "Mr. Goodwrench" signs. What particularly attracted his attention, however, was a framed list of the names of the mechanics and the service schools they had attended. Likewise, he noted the names of the mechanics and their specialties posted in each of the service bays.

The visit to the garage impelled Robert Sayres to compare the situation in his company with that in the garage. As his company had become increasingly automated, the maintenance problems were becoming awesome and it was difficult to keep the maintenance crew abreast of developments. But he ruminated, "Isn't the repair of automobiles similar to our problem?"

Questions:

1. Do you consider the maintenance and repair of the latest models of automobiles similar to that of maintaining production equipment such as that illustrated in Chapters 5, 6, 9, and 15? Explain.

2. Would maintenance service schools similar to those operated by General Motors be feasible? Who would run them?

3. What other alternatives do companies like Clinton Manufacturing have for providing sound maintenance of their machines and equipment in the future?

17

COST CONTROL

In a manufacturing concern accounting activities are usually divided into two parts: financial accounting and cost accounting. Financial accounting deals with the business as a whole, and at the end of a designated accounting period it produces information about the current financial status of the business, as well as the amount of profit or loss incurred during the period in question. This information is in the form of balance sheets and profit and loss statements, both of which are discussed in some detail in Chapter 24. Cost accounting, on the other hand, may be thought of as that part of the accounting procedure that deals with the determination and analysis of the costs of particular processes, jobs, or departments within the company. Such cost accounting becomes the basis of cost-control systems and budgetary control plans. Cost control and budgetary control are both essential in the operation of a modern industrial enterprise, for they permit management to plan ahead and to know when to make changes in order to fulfill the plan.

Role of Cost Accounting

Balance sheets and profit and loss statements do not reveal how profitable one product is versus another, or whether one plant produces more efficiently than another. Although the stockholder or investment analyst may care little about details of efficiency and cost, since to them the overall profit of the business is sufficient, management must take a different point of view. Naturally management is interested in maintaining the overall position of the company, but in order to insure the overall position it must have some indication of costs and profits as the accounting period goes along. In today's industrial world a company cannot afford to wait and see how profits turn out at the end of the year. Management must know at any point during the year the approximate position of costs and profits so that it may take corrective action before it is too late. This function is called cost control, and to achieve it cost accounting is necessary.

In cost accounting the total expenditures in operating a business are broken down on a per item or per unit basis, as for example the cost of producing a gallon of gasoline, a ton of coal, a dozen shirts, or a refrigerator. The same idea can be extended to cost per production order, as when a special product is made for a customer, or further extended to cost per activity or operation, such as the cost of drilling half-inch holes, or plating sheet metal of a certain size and quality. In other words, cost accounting is the job of taking overall business costs and separating them into greater detail according to unit of product produced, operation performed, or orders. For a company that manufactures only one product and only one size and style, cost accounting is no special problem, for the cost per unit can easily be determined by dividing the total cost figure by the number of units produced. In a more typical situation, however, a company may manufacture more than one product, and each product may be of a varying size and style. In that case the company must know how much of the total production cost was due to the manufacture of one product, and how much was due to the manufacture of another. Even in the company that manufactures only one product in one size and style, there would be a need to know the cost of one operation versus another for purposes of controlling these costs as time goes on.

Specifically, cost accounting provides information for the following purposes:

1. Cost determination. The costs and expenses of a business are recorded, classified, and allocated to various jobs, departments, products, or services.

2. Costs for pricing. Once costs are determined, the information also serves as a guide regarding prices to be quoted to customers. Even though selling prices are only partly governed by the costs of production, in the long run the selling price must at least equal the costs of production, or there will be serious consequences to the profit-and-loss statement.

3. Cost for managerial decision. In a sense, both the above items of cost determination and cost for pricing provide bases for managerial decisions. Although managerial decision-making actually becomes much more complex than the above statement implies, cost information may be helpful in making decisions that have to do with (a) whether to add a new product, or to drop one that is now being produced, (b) whether to manufacture a certain unit, or buy it on the outside, and (c) whether to add certain sales territories and drop others.

4. Cost control. One of the more essential purposes of cost accounting is control of expenditures. Such control leads to efficiency in use of labor, materials, machines, and plants. Although to a large extent selling prices are determined by competition, the profit-making capacity of a business is guided by the efficiency with which costs are controlled.

Basic Cost Elements

There are three basic cost elements with which we shall deal in this section: direct material cost, direct labor cost, and overhead. Overhead will be further subdivided as to whether it results from factory operation, sales effort, or general administration. Figure 17-1 shows in chart form the derivation of basic cost elements.

Direct material cost is the cost of the material that can be directly identified with the product and is delivered to the customer. In practice, any scrap or waste of material is still charged as direct material even though it is not delivered to the customer. Also, one must take a practical point of view when applying this strict definition of direct material and arriving at direct material costs. Some direct material may cost so little that it is not worth-while to identify and charge it as direct material. Paint is a good example. Each unit of product may be delivered carrying a coat of paint, but the dollar value of the cost of paint is usually so small compared to the value of the product that it would be more reasonable to charge the paint simply as indirect material or overhead.

Indirect material in general may be thought of as those items used in the manufacture of a product that do not become an integral part of it. Costs of these materials become overhead costs. Good examples of indirect material would be light bulbs to light the area, cleaning rags, sandpaper, and hand tools.

The concept of *direct labor cost* is very similar to that just described for direct material costs. The direct labor costs are the costs of labor that can be identified directly with the manufacture of the product and is delivered to the customer. As

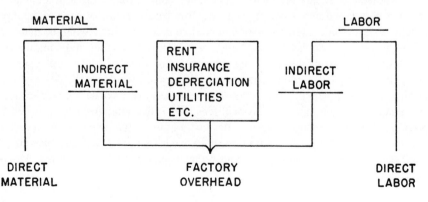

Figure 17-1. Derivation of basic cost elements.

before, if an item of direct labor becomes so small as to have little dollar value, it may be more feasible to consider it as indirect labor and treat it as overhead. Good examples of indirect labor in manufacturing operations are maintenance work, cleaning operations, and clerical work.

When added together for any one product, the direct material and direct labor costs are called *prime cost*. Prime cost, then, represents the total *direct* cost of producing a product and is usually a figure relatively easy to determine with reasonable accuracy. Overhead costs present a different kind of problem.

Overhead costs are often defined as all manufacturing costs other than direct material and direct labor, or other than prime costs. This may seem like a backward definition, but it turns out to be as useful a definition as one can devise. In practice, overhead costs are arrived at in essentially this manner. If a cost item isn't either direct labor or direct material, it must be overhead.

We have mentioned two common types of overhead: indirect material and indirect labor. Other items that usually fall into the overhead category are heat, light, power, insurance, rent, depreciation, taxes, and telephone. Often it is possible to identify overhead expense with a particular product, as when a special lubricant is used only in the manufacture of one product. In such a case one may be tempted to charge the entire cost of the lubricant to that product, instead of putting it in overhead to be apportioned later among all products; but this is seldom done because the additional accuracy obtained would not be worth the cost of the extra bookkeeping. Exceptions might be in cases where expensive dies or tools are required for one product or where readily identifiable and separable departments or buildings are used on only one product.

We have been discussing overhead costs that are incurred by the factory. When added to prime cost, these overhead costs yield what is commonly known as *factory cost*. Factory cost can be thought of as the total unit cost of manufacture. There are other costs of the business, however, and these are generally thought of as additional overhead costs, namely, the cost of selling and the cost of general administration.

The idea of separating factory, sales, and administrative costs in a company can best be grasped by visualizing separate physical locations for each of the three functions (not an uncommon situation in modern industry). In viewing the matter in this light, one can see that sales expenses would include salaries and commissions of salespeople, advertising, traveling expenses, rent on sales offices, clerical help, and general supplies. General administration expenses would be the costs of supporting the "front office," including such items as salaries of executives, clerical assistance, legal and other professional fees, and office rent. As before, it will be possible at times to identify certain sales and administrative expenses with certain specific products, but such handling of these expenses is rare. Instead, they are totaled and apportioned among the various products in a manner to be discussed in the next section.

Obtaining Unit Costs

The previous section has been largely concerned with defining cost elements. Let us consider how these cost figures are obtained, particularly on a per-unit or a per-product basis.

Direct material and direct labor present little difficulty. One can generally measure the amount of direct material used, and total cost is available from invoices. Product yields being known, the direct material dollars per unit can be easily obtained. Most factories require their employees to keep time records, and from these records the number of direct labor hours spent on any product or order can be determined. Knowing hourly rates and units of output, one can easily compute direct labor dollar cost per unit.

Getting overhead costs on a per-unit basis presents a different kind of problem. We have a total dollar figure for overhead for perhaps a month's operation. Part of this money was spent just in keeping the building and equipment intact, part was spent on providing supervisory, clerical, maintenance, and cleanup help for all departments and products, and part was spent on each of the various products produced or orders filled during that month. The question is, how much of the total should one charge to each product produced during that month?

This question can never be answered to the complete satisfaction of all, and it usually becomes necessary to compromise in some respect. In theory, overhead costs should be allocated to the various products manufactured on the basis of each product's responsibility for that cost. In practice, however, this is either impossible or too costly; so the theoretical ideal is approached as closely as possible by selecting one of the commonly used systems of allocation that best fits the situation. Common bases for the allocation of overhead costs are:[1]

1. Number of employees.
2. Direct labor costs.
3. Direct labor hours.
4. Direct material costs.
5. Machine hours.
6. Floor area.
7. Prime costs.

---

[1]This treatment oversimplifies the problem of overhead distribution as faced in most companies. Overhead usually is distributed to *all* departments first before being distributed to those departments that produce products. For example, the personnel department would be allocated its share of costs (heat, light, wages, and so on). Total personnel department costs would then be allocated to producing departments on some basis. This two-step process is necessary since the personnel department (like many others in a factory) has no "product" to which its services can be charged.

A simple example of a company making but two products will serve to illustrate the allocation procedure. Let us assume this company wished to allocate factory overhead on the basis of direct labor hours, for it appears that there is a close relationship between direct labor hours and factory overhead incurred. If overhead to be allocated for the month is $20,000, and Product A required 400 direct labor hours and Product B 600 direct labor hours, the total overhead chargeable to each product would be as follows:

$$\text{Product A } \frac{400}{1000} \times \$20,000 = \$8,000$$

$$\text{Product A } \frac{600}{1000} \times \$20,000 = \$12,000$$

Knowing the number of units of each product produced during the month, one could determine the overhead cost per unit.

The same type of allocation will be necessary for sales expense and administration expense, except that the basis of distribution will generally be even more arbitrary than that used for factory overhead. When sales and administrative expenses on a unit basis are added to unit factory costs, the result is total cost. This is summarized in Figure 17-2.

The concept of *contributed value* or *value added* should be mentioned at this point. Contributed value is factory cost minus direct material cost and is commonly used as a measure of the effectiveness of a manufacturing operation. In a sense, a company has little control over the cost of direct materials it purchases, but it does have control of all of the costs after the purchase of that direct material and so may find it useful to know what these contributed costs are and how much they vary from time to time.

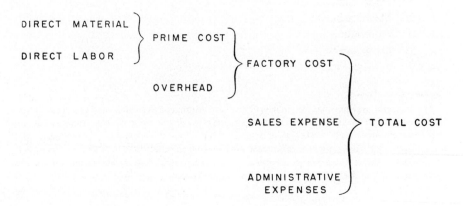

Figure 17-2. Development of the total cost of a product.

Past Versus Future Costs

We have been speaking of cost determination and cost allocation strictly in the historical sense. In other words, our discussion so far has looked at costs *after* the accounting period is over and products have been stored in the warehouse; and we have then tried to determine costs on a per-unit basis. Such figures are interesting and helpful to some extent, but they are not completely adequate. In managing operations, we need sufficient information about what future costs should be so that bids may be placed on jobs, selling prices may be estimated ahead of time, and a basis for corrective action may be provided. The use of standard costs is helpful both in predictive work as well as in control.

Standard costs are carefully worked-out estimates of what the various cost elements should be. Such estimates can usually be made only after much study and considerable experience. Even then, it may become necessary to alter them because some factors were overlooked or changed considerably. Nevertheless, actual historical costs can be compared with standard costs from time to time and thereby indicate to management where cost-reduction efforts would be most fruitful. This is the heart of cost-control work, as it is in any control system: comparison of actual with standard.

In a standard cost system the comparison of actual with standard is facilitated by setting up a number of variance accounts. Typical variance accounts are material price variance, material usage variance, labor rate variance, labor efficiency variance, and burden variance. At the end of any accounting period, usually a month, the variance accounts indicate the amount of money that actual costs exceeded or were less than standard costs. In the case of purchased materials, differences between actual costs and standard costs could occur either because more or less material was used than should have been used, or because the price paid for the material was more or less than standard. This accounts for the two material variance accounts mentioned earlier.

The determination of the standard costs for a product is a complex operation, but is similar in nature to the process of obtaining unit costs, which was discussed earlier in this chapter. As before, the determination of a direct material cost can be made in a fairly straightforward manner by studying blueprints and bills for material, and by having knowledge of yields from the various processes or machines used. Scrap factors may also have to be taken into account, but if one has had very much experience in producing the product whose cost is being standardized, the determination of direct material cost will be relatively easy and relatively accurate. Direct labor cost also will prove to be straightforward if one has had experience in manufacturing the product and has accurate time records for the employees involved. Direct labor cost determination on a standard basis is made considerably easier if the company makes use of time standards as discussed in Chapter 8. If time standards are available for all jobs, the data for any particular product need only be added in order to determine the standard labor cost for that product.

As with the allocation of overhead discussed earlier, the determination of standard overhead rates is a rather arbitrary procedure. To determine estimated overhead rate, one divides the estimated overhead for the period by the estimated production for the period in units, hours, or dollars, depending upon the previously determined base. Estimated overhead for the period may be developed from an actual study of costs to be expected, or may be based on past costs at a similar level of production and similar product mix. A typical overhead rate would be 225 percent of prime cost. To estimate overhead cost per unit, then, one simply takes 225 percent of the prime cost per unit. Of course, as with standard costs in general, overhead rates should be computed and used only after thorough study and experience.

It should be recognized that the differences or variances that occur between standard costs and actual costs will not have any real effect on the profit or loss of the business for the period in question. Variances are charged out to the profit-and-loss account so that the actual profit for the period turns out to be the same as though books had been kept on a purely historical basis. On the other hand, incorrect standard costs may have an influence on the business if one uses them as a basis for bidding on new business. For example, if a standard cost for a product is quite high in comparison to actual historical cost, and one uses the standard cost as the basis for a bid, the bid may be lost because of its high price. Likewise, a "low" standard used as a basis for a bid may serve to secure the job, but cause the company to lose money on the job. The point is to make as certain as possible that standard costs are correct costs and that operations are controlled so that actual costs then coincide as closely as possible with the standard.

Job Order Costs and Process Costs

Whether one is developing standard costs or historical costs, the problems involved will vary depending on whether one follows the job-order cost method or the process-cost method. Sometimes it is necessary to combine the two methods, but for the most part the method one uses depends upon the type of manufacture.

The job-order cost method collects the cost of jobs that are kept separate during the manufacture or construction period. The cost unit is the job, the order, or the contract; and the accounts show the cost of each order. This method assumes that the jobs can be physically identified and separated from each other. A variation of the job-order cost method is the costing of orders by lots. In many shops it is much more convenient and economical to consider a product in lots of a dozen or a hundred rather than individually.

The process-cost method consists of computing an average unit cost by dividing the total manufacturing cost by the total number of units produced in the factory over a given period of time. In particular, this would apply in those plants where the product could not be physically separated into units and would be applicable to industries such as flour mills, chemical plants, textile factories, and breweries. Because of the multiple output, it is necessary to compute a unit cost at the end of each process. Furthermore, the plan is used to cost production when the product of one process becomes the material of the next and when different products or by-products are produced by the same process.

A variation of the process-cost method is the method of costing by operations. Operations constitute the labor or the machine performances that are necessary in the manufacture of a commodity. Several different products may go through the same process, and the cost of that process would have to be divided among the various products going through it.

Cost Reduction and Cost Control

At some time or other almost every company has had some kind of program of cost reduction. The precise reason for any particular program of cost reduction may vary considerable from time to time and from company to company, but all such programs have in common the basic need to reduce costs of operations below their present level. Specific reasons could be the softening of the economy generally, particularly rough competition in a specific product line, or a wish to reduce the selling price of a particular product and thereby broaden its market.

We have been emphasizing throughout this chapter and indeed throughout this section of the book the desirability of planning and controlling operations. Specifically, in regard to costs, this means it is necessary to establish what costs should be for operations, and then to make certain that these cost goals are met by careful follow-up and control of all aspects of the production process. If this plan were followed religiously, the need for cost-reduction programs would be considerably reduced. Unfortunately, however, many companies do not follow such a plan of standardizing and controlling costs, and other companies may have such a plan but are not strict in adhering to it. In other words, their variances may always be on the high side, and in time they have a tendency to increase their standard costs rather than to decrease their actual costs. There follows a gradual upcreep in costs of operation, and one wonders why the company should have the standard cost system in the first place if it does not really make it work. This upcreep in costs is most likely to happen during periods of prosperity, when profits are relatively easy to come by and managers see no particular harm in overspending their standard costs or overspending their budget. The facts of economic life often catch up with such attitudes, however, with the result that cost-reduction programs must then be instituted and are often of the variety of an arbitrary percentage cut of all costs across the board.

It should be noted that, even with good and tight control of costs, many companies find ''fat'' creeping into their costs of operation. This ''fat'' may not be any one person's fault, but may simply follow in the wake of a gradual introduction of new processes or new systems without a corresponding reduction in other costs. Sometimes the elimination of old products and old systems is not done thoroughly enough to eliminate all the costs involved with that old product or system. This means that even in the very well-run company, a cost-reduction program of a relatively short duration may be desirable from time to time. If for no other reason, the program could serve to re-educate everyone in the necessity to hold costs down and also provide an opportunity to trim off the "fat," which may have been developing over the months.

Finally, we must mention the regular and continuing cost reduction efforts that should be a routine part of every manufacturing activity. Some parts of engineering departments essentially have a full-time job devoted to cost reduction, although they may not always regard it in that light. Methods engineers, process engineers, and product engineers almost always measure their accomplishments in terms of cost reductions they are able to bring about. All of the control functions mentioned earlier in this section should have as a part of their regular duties the reduction of the cost of carrying out that particular function. As an example, the quality control function not only attempts to reduce the cost of manufacture by improving the quality level produced, but also should attempt to reduce the cost of performing the quality control function. In other words, it should attempt to find better and cheaper methods for controlling the quality of the product.

Budgetary Control

The previous sections outlined the use of cost standards as a device for controlling manufacturing operations. Cost accounting, although not a control device itself, provided the necessary information for setting up cost standards. Budgets are also used for cost-control purposes and will be discussed in that role in the pages that follow.

Budgets and Their Use

We normally think of budgets in terms of a number of dollars and a list of items on which those dollars will be spent. A business budget differs somewhat from this common concept inasmuch as it must be more detailed. It will specify units to be produced, broken down into sizes and styles, as well as costs of production. In fact, a considerable part of the budget comes from the use of the estimated cost breakdown figures discussed earlier. The budget can then be thought of as an overall plan for the operation of the business in terms of sales, production, and expenditures. One can see that it thereby acts as a coordinating device among the various functions of the business. If the overall budget is to have any meaning or any usefulness, executives in charge of the various functions are going to have to work together in developing their plans for the year ahead.

Another useful purpose of the budget is to facilitate planning within the company. A budget prepared without adequate planning is hardly worth the paper it is written on. Executives must have a good idea of what lies ahead before they can develop adequate budget estimates.

A third purpose of budgets has already been mentioned, namely, that of control. After having made plans for the year ahead and coordinated all plans in a consolidated company budget, we can then use the budget figures to control operations during the year. "Control" here is used in the usual sense of noting when expenditures fall outside the budget estimates, tracing down the cause of such variation, and taking corrective action as necessary.

Fixed and Flexible Budgets

The preparation of a budget begins with an estimate of sales for the year ahead. Techniques for making such forecasts are discussed in Chapter 25. From sales forecasts production requirements can be determined, taking into account the inventory situation. The production estimate then becomes the basis for determining material, personnel, plant, and equipment requirements and the costs allied with each (see Chapter 24).

A budget made up in this manner, based on one level of production output, is called a *fixed budget*. There is one budget figure for each item of cost, and this figure becomes a ceiling on the cost of that item. Fixed budgets are very satisfactory for stable businesses, but should a business be subject to fluctuating sales or varying rates of output, the rigidity of a fixed budget imposes hardship. To overcome this, some companies make use of *flexible budgets*, or budgets made up for different levels of production. For example, budgets might be made up for 80 percent, 100 percent, and 120 percent of production capacity. If the plant is operating one month at 120 percent of rated capacity, it will be expected to adhere to the 120 percent budget. Next month, operation may be at 100 percent capacity. In this manner, smooth, continuous budgetary control is assured even during times of varying production. Figure 17-3 presents an example of a flexible budget for manufacturing expenses.

	Operating Capacity				
Account	*80%*	*90%*	*100%*	*110%*	*120%*
Clerical	$7,000	$7,200	$8,000	$8,200	$9,000
Watchmen	3,200	3,200	3,200	3,200	3,200
Maintenance	7,000	7,500	8,000	8,500	9,000
Power, light & heat	3,700	3,900	4,100	4,300	4,500
Gas	210	220	220	220	220
Water	1,100	1,150	1,200	1,250	1,300
Rent	12,000	12,000	12,000	12,000	12,000
Depreciation	12,900	12,900	12,900	12,900	12,900
Compensation insurance	2,800	3,300	3,800	4,300	4,800
Fire insurance	1,200	1,200	1,200	1,200	1,200
Property taxes	5,200	5,200	5,200	5,200	5,200
Supervision	14,500	19,800	19,800	19,800	22,300
Total	$70,810	$77,570	$79,620	$81,070	$85,620

Figure 17-3. Flexible budget for manufacturing expenses.

Breakeven Charts

Examining the breakdown of costs that appears on a flexible budget, one finds certain costs, such as rent, taxes, and insurance, that are constant even as production varies. Other cost items, such as wages and materials, vary as production varies. These differences in the basic nature of production costs suggest the construction and use of breakeven charts. A breakeven chart shows the cost of production at various levels of output as well as the income from sales at the same output levels. It must be assumed that all goods produced are sold, or else the chart has little meaning. With this assumption, a typical chart will show total income at various output levels (see Figure 17-4). Where the two lines cross is the breakeven point, for if the plant produces at that level it won't lose any money, but on the other hand it won't make any money either. Output above the breakeven point will result in a profit and output below will result in a loss—the amounts of which can be determined by reading the appropriate points on the graph.

The breakeven chart in Figure 17-4 is designed largely for illustrative purposes; it is doubtful whether any firm has a breakeven chart as simple as this one. Instead, practical breakeven charts are much more complex and as a result are much more difficult to construct. The main difficulty is that costs never break out as simply as this chart would imply. Fixed costs turn out to be straightforward, but variable costs have differing degrees of variability. The breakeven chart of Figure 17-4 shows all variable costs as being *directly* variable with production, and this is seldom the case. Some, like direct labor and direct material, may be directly variable, but many costs, like supervision, will vary in a manner other than directly. This has given rise to a classification of *semivariable costs,* which would include all costs that are both not fixed and not directly variable. Under this concept, it is possible to

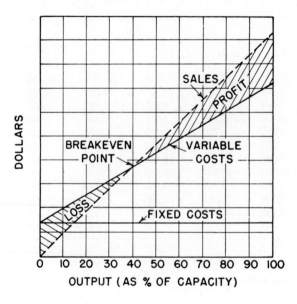

Figure 17-4. Simplified version of breakeven chart.

have more than one breakeven point, and a company might choose to produce at a point so as to maximize profit or to minimize loss. A feeling for this type of possibility comes by visualizing a production situation where expanded output would necessitate the opening of another wing of the plant but would not allow full utilization of all the additional area. Figure 17-5 shows a more realistic version of a breakeven chart, although it, too, is simplified.

Another bit of realism illustrated in Figure 17-5 as compared to the simplistic breakeven chart of Figure 17-4 is the curvature of both the income and total cost lines at or above 100% capacity. Anyone asked to recommend a point of operation on Figure 17-4 would suggest a point at the extreme right—even off the page— since it appears that the two lines diverge indefinitely. In actuality, one realizes that the selling price would decrease as the market becomes saturated, causing the sales income line to droop downward. Further, expanding output above design capacity would no doubt cause the total cost line to rise sharply, reflecting such extra costs as overtime and maintenance. In other words, realistic total cost and total income lines tend to converge as one exceeds plant design capacity levels of output and sales.

The reader should not get the impression that breakeven charts are easy to construct or that every company knows precisely what its breakeven point is. Companies attempt to determine their breakeven points in two ways. One is to build up basic cost and sales data much in the manner we have discussed in this chapter. The other is to accumulate historical cost and sales data for each accounting period and plot these on a set of axes. Of course, several accounting periods will be re-

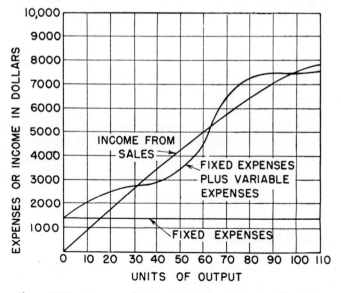

Figure 17-5. A more realistic breakeven chart. Note that (1) variable expenses are not all directly variable with production, (2) for this particular plant there is more than one area of unprofitable operation, and (3) the sales income line is not straight.

quired before a coherent chart is developed, but at least the company will have the satisfaction of knowing that the points represent actual operation rather than planned or hoped-for operation.

Profit Centers

Attempts are often made to apply the break-even chart technique to the company as a whole. If the company produces and sells but one product, such an attempt will be relatively successful. On the other hand, if a number of products are produced and sold, summary figures of sales and costs may not have too much meaning. Variations in product mix will cause variations in summary figures, which might in turn lead to erroneous conclusions. It makes much better sense to divide the organization into units or centers and to compute costs and profits for each of the various units.

A center could be a department, a machine, a group of machines, or a process. The only requirement is that the various activities or parts of the unit have a common interest so far as producing the product is concerned. Although many such centers are thought of strictly on a cost basis, certain centers, such as departments, can often be thought of as profit centers, for they produce a product or perform a service that is sold and thereby produces income.

Interpreting any center or unit as a profit center rather than a cost center has great value—psychological and otherwise. We have discussed earlier how standard costs are computed and actual costs compared with standard, with the result that everyone attempts to "control" actual costs to keep them in line with the standard. Such a system will work very well, but in many cases much more interest and enthusiasm is generated on the part of all concerned if profit rather than cost is used as a criterion of performance. To determine that costs have risen by 15 percent seems to have less meaning than to determine that profits have fallen by the same percent. Apparently "profits" sound closer to home than do "costs." This device will be especially useful if "income" to a department or unit can be easily determined. A more obvious extension of the profit-center idea is the evaluation of branch plants of a multi-plant company based upon profit produced. This would entail separate financial statements for each branch plant. Nonetheless, it is common practice to take such action.

Accounting and Management

In this chapter we have discussed the use of accounting, especially cost accounting, in the management of a manufacturing enterprise. Before ending the chapter it may be well to emphasize that cost accounting is a means to an end and not an end in itself. This familiar and overused phrase is particularly applicable in this case, for often we become overawed with the apparent accuracy of cost figures, with the possible result that the company is being operated for the convenience of the cost-accounting department. Cost accounting is a tool or an aid to good management, the same as many other functions are aids. All must be kept within the proper framework so that the company as a whole may prosper.

This is easier said than done, for it is desirable to have all who work in a staff capacity develop great enthusiasm for their particular activity. But in encouraging enthusiasm for staff activity, we may overshoot to the point where concern for the company is in second place rather than first.

In accounting work, people sometimes get the mistaken impression that the accounting staff "makes" the profits and that the cost accounting staff "determines" the costs. Both costs and profits are *determined* by the way management conducts the business. Accounting people simply keep records and compute results according to best accounting practices. By looking at past results and making use of engineering estimates, accountants can set budgets, standard costs, and other control devices—which again are designed to assist management in running the business. Of course, as accounting practices change, it may appear that accountants are manipulating costs and profits; but although some manipulation of accounts undoubtedly takes place in the business world, it is only the manipulation of figures and not the manipulation of the manner in which the business is operated. After operating results are reported by the accountants, whether they be short term or long term, some modification in the operation of the business may be called for. This is the true function of accounting and cost accounting, for in this way they assist in the management of the business.

QUESTIONS

1. What is the difference between cost accounting and cost control?
2. Explain the use of the four fundamental steps in control (see Chapter 11) in terms of the cost-control situation.
3. Why is the cost of producing a product only a guide in establishing the selling price? What other factors enter in?
4. Select some common product such as a desk, table, or chair and list all direct and indirect materials that were probably used in its manufacture. Do the same for direct and indirect labor.
5. If a company has "low overhead," will this mean lower prices to purchasers? Explain your answer.
6. What are some logical bases that could be used to apportion (a) sales expenses and (b) administrative expenses?
7. Explain how it is possible to predict overhead costs ahead of time.
8. List and briefly explain the three uses for budgets in manufacturing.
9. Why are flexible budgets used in industry?
10. The breakeven chart of Figure 17-4 suggests that this manufacturer should expand operations, for the greater the expansion the greater the spread between the cost and sales

lines and hence the greater the profit. Would this be true in an actual situation? Explain your line of reasoning.

11.   Distinguish between a cost center and a profit center. Explain the usefulness of each.

CASE PROBLEMS

Wimmert Machine Company

The Wimmert Machine Company operates a small but successful machine shop in northern Indiana. Two reasons for its success are the careful attention paid to cost information and the accurate estimating that precedes the acceptance of every order.

The general estimating procedure followed is to study the blueprints submitted and ascertain the amount of material required. The cost of this material is then determined with the aid of vendors' catalogs. Direct labor dollar cost is obtained by multiplying the estimated direct labor hours by the appropriate hourly rates. For all small jobs, overhead is charged at the rate of 210% of direct labor costs.

Last week the estimating department was told that the company could secure an order for 600 special pump parts from the Mattoon Refrigerator Company if the factory cost was no more than $15.50 per unit. If factory cost can be kept at or below this figure, the selling price not only will cover administrative and selling expenses but will yield a good profit. A study of the job revealed the following cost data per unit:

  Estimated direct material cost: $3.18 each
  Direct labor cost:
    10 minutes @ $4.10 per hour
    30 minutes @ $5.80 per hour
    50 minutes @ $5.00 per hour

Since this job would tie up the entire shop facilities for one month, last year's average monthly factory overhead of $3170 was selected to be used as a guide, instead of the usual rate of 210%.

Soon after the above cost estimates were completed, it was learned that an order for 600 units of the pump part per month for the next twelve months might be secured if the factory cost was no more than $11.50 each.

To undertake such an order, new equipment would be required, and the tool designers found that there were three possible tooling programs. Tooling A would cost $5760, tooling B would cost $3600, and tooling C would cost $1440. In addition, the following was determined:

  Tooling A production rate: 2 units/labor hr. @ $4.60/hr. labor rate
  Tooling B production rate: 2 units/labor hr. @ $5.80/hr. labor rate
  Tooling C production rate: 1.5 units/labor hr. @ $5.80/hr. labor rate

Since a large quantity of material was to be purchased, a 10% reduction in direct material costs could be obtained from the vendor. Overhead could be computed in the usual manner as 210% of direct labor cost, since the special tooling would release equipment for other orders.

Questions:

1.   Should the Wimmert Machine Company accept the initial order for 600 pump parts?
2.   Should the company accept the order for 600 pump parts per month?

3. Which tooling program do you recommend and why?
4. Evaluate the method of estimating overhead in the two cases.
5. If a 20% gross profit on sales is required, what would be the selling price of the initial order? (Use your computed factory cost.)

Lane-Patton, Inc.

Mr. John Willard, the general manager of Lane-Patton, Inc., was not convinced that the company was using the proper costing methods when it placed bids on jobs. Since the company operated strictly as a job shop producing machined steel parts, it was particularly important that each job be priced properly. Seldom did any order run over 100 or 200 pieces. Recently the company had lost some jobs because their prices were "out-of-line," and Mr. Willard wondered if these "out-of-line" prices might be due to improper allocation of overhead. Overhead for the entire shop was high, and its improper allocation to jobs could easily cause a price to be too high or too low.

In order to study the situation more closely, Mr. Willard asked the chief accountant to supply him with a series of data. The data are presented below and represent average monthly figures based on operations during the past year.

Direct material dollars:	$ 46,000 per month
Direct labor dollars:	$125,000 per month
Direct labor hours:	50,000 per month
Machine hours:	35,000 per month
Total factory cost:	$585,000 per month
Total factory area:	260,000 square feet

Mr. Willard soon realized that additional investigation would be necessary before he could establish proper overhead rates.

Questions:

1. With the information given, compute as many different overhead rates as feasible.
2. What would be the general requirements of any method of allocating overhead in this company?
3. What additional information could Mr. Willard use before making up his mind concerning overhead allocation?
4. Of the methods you used in Question 1, which would be easiest and least costly to put into use? Which would be most costly?

Murphy Machines, Inc.

Although trained as an engineer, Harry Townes had essentially become a cost expert during the 12 years he had been working for Murphy Machines. It all started when he joined the company and his boss thought that the courses he had taken in college relating to accounting and engineering economics would qualify him to make a number of cost analyses for the company's product line. Harry took well to the assignment, and now he and the company consider him to be a cost engineer.

Over the years Harry has become increasingly interested in breakeven charts and the part they could play in the operation of the business. He has devoted much time to collecting information that would yield a suitable chart not only for the company as a whole, but also for each of the major machines in the product line. No one else in the company had shown much interest until the day a good potential customer proposed a sizeable order for the company's Model 85A printer, but at a price considerably below the normal sale price.

A meeting was held of various concerned persons to try to settle the issue, and Harry was invited along with accounting and sales people, with the president presiding. As might be expected, the sales people were anxious to accept the order, but the accountants were against acceptance. The accountants pointed out that the fully absorbed cost of producing Model 85A was $250, while the price offered by the customer was $225 compared to the regular sale price of $285. "The numbers speak for themselves," said the chief accountant, "and we are foolish to even hold this meeting to consider the matter." The president withheld any comment at this point and called on Harry to state his views.

Harry started out by indicating that what had been said was certainly the truth, but he didn't feel it was the whole truth. He then proceeded to draw a breakeven chart on the board provided and talked as he drew. "Fully absorbed costs mean that the total cost includes fixed overhead as well as the directly variable costs such as material and labor," he explained, "and I can show these on my chart with a horizontal line for the fixed cost, on top of which I indicate a line sloping upward to represent the variable costs. The sloping line, then, is really total cost at any given level of output. That line of total cost can be described by a formula which in this case is $1287 + $186X$, where X is the volume of output. In other words, the fixed costs assigned to Model 85A are $1287 and the variable costs for one unit are $186."

"On top of this cost line," Harry continued, "I will draw another line representing income from the sale of Model 85A at our regular sale price of $285. Naturally, this income line starts from zero and slopes upward. Where the income line crosses the total cost line is the breakeven point for Model 85A and is a point where we don't make any profit, but we won't have any losses either. For the past eighteen months we have been producing and selling 20 units of Model 85A a month; so we are well above the breakeven point. This new order will add some 6 units a month to our production schedule, but the extra cost of producing these units will be only $186 rather than the $250 stated earlier. The $186 represents the variable costs, which are the only ones to be considered since above the breakeven point the fixed costs have been covered."

The chief accountant found all this a little hard to buy on such short notice but could only retaliate by asking the question, "But won't our customers who usually buy Model 85A for $285 also want to benefit from the reduced price of $225?"

Questions:

1. Draw Harry's breakeven chart, marking all lines and areas appropriately.
2. Compute the breakeven point to verify Harry's statement.
3. Should the president agree with Harry's reasoning and agree to the sale at the reduced price?
4. How can the reduced price to this new customer be justified to the older customers or to any new customers that come along?

18

PERSONNEL MANAGEMENT

In spite of modern technology and all the systems and computers coming into widespread use, *people* remain the most important factor in manufacturing. None of these techniques or management methods are effective unless they are administered and carried out by competent employees. Dynamic leadership must be applied at the top of an organization, and capable employees must exist throughout the organization in order for a company to operate, grow, and prosper. In other words, the human resources available at all levels in the organization will be the key to success.

The Role of People

The role of people in industry has been recognized to some extent since earliest recorded history, but its degree of importance seems to vary with the times. The history of early industrial development in the United States reveals there was little concern for workers as human beings. They seem to have been regarded as simply other machines. This attitude resulted in great dissatisfaction on the part of employees, which no doubt led to more rapid growth of unionism. Between World War I and World War II, however, there was increasing emphasis upon the importance of the human being and a great growth of personnel departments as well as interest in "human relations." In fact, attention to human relations became so fashionable that it was almost a cult. Currently, in some instances it might seem that the human relations angle may have overpowered the employee angle to the point that companies are more concerned with their employees' happiness than they are with their employees' output.

Employee dissatisfaction is very difficult to assess. Some years ago studies of employees on assembly lines emphasized dissatisfaction due to the repetitive and boring nature of the job. More recent studies indicate that workers feel threatened if they have to make decisions on the job and prefer the repetitive, one-operation, no-think type of job. Obviously it is difficult, if not impossible, to draw broad general conclusions about all industrial workers; and each company will need to concentrate on learning the attitudes and desires of its own employees rather than worry about employees in general.

Although there are many things that we do not know and understand about human behavior, we do know that employees like to be treated as individuals. On the other hand, a company planning and outlining a personnel program must set up fair policies and administer them consistently so as to avoid accusations of favoritism. Whether or not a company can successfully follow a path between individual treatment on the one hand and consistent policy on the other is seriously open to question. Obviously, some companies are better than others at this delicate balancing game, and all companies consistently attempt to improve their performance.

Although personnel and industrial relations departments are given the responsibility for administering much of a company's personnel program, personnel work as such goes on everywhere in the organization. Personnel relations are personal relations, and they affect all the people whose work must be directed and coordinated. In this sense, then, every supervisor and officer of the company is a personnel type and must act accordingly. The central personnel or human resources department acts as adviser and overall coordinator, in addition to maintaining records and providing certain services. The areas generally administered by such a department are (1) employment, (2) training, (3) health, (4) safety, (5) benefits, (6) services, (7) labor relations, and (8) wage administration. The first six of these items are discussed in the pages that follow in this chapter. The next chapter covers the subject of labor relations and Chapters 20 and 21 cover wage administration. Figure 18-1 outlines the duties usually assigned many industrial relations jobs.

Employment

The fundamental purpose of the employment section of the industrial relations department is to maintain an adequate supply of qualified workers. This is done by (1) maintaining adequate sources of recruits and (2) careful selection from those recruited.

The recruitment of potential employees refers to the contacting of qualified people who may be interested in working for the concern. A company wouldn't normally offer jobs to all those recruited, but the more people it recruits the more selective it can be in filling jobs. Sources of new employees to fill any particular job openings may be categorized as coming from either inside the organization or out-

Industrial Relations Jobs in Business Organizations

(This is a partial list to be augmented through further study)

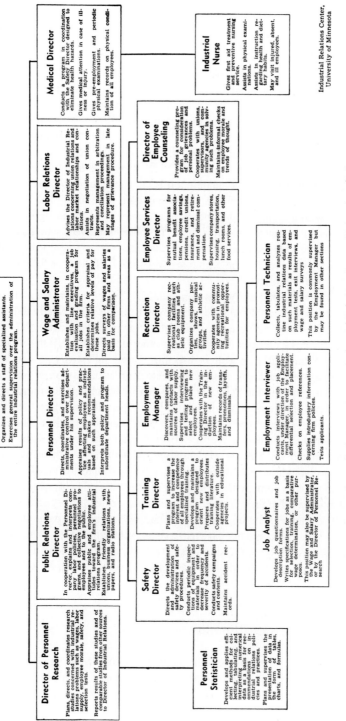

Figure 18-1. Jobs in industrial relations. (Courtesy Industrial Relations Center, University of Minnesota, Kriedt and Bendston, "Jobs in Industrial Relations.")

side the organization. The sources within the organization include transfers from some other department or job and promotions within the company. Some companies make it a policy to fill all jobs requiring any degree of skill from within the organization. Such a policy usually means better morale on the part of present employees, for they feel they will have an opportunity to get ahead.

Of particular interest in connection with filling job openings inside the organization are practices of "job bidding" and "bumping." The details of either practice vary according to company policy and union agreement. In general, however, job bidding or posting refers to the practice of posting a notice on company bulletin boards to the effect that a specific job is open and anyone interested in being placed on this job should so indicate within a certain time limit. The duties and pay connected with the job are also indicated. At the end of the designated time period the employment manager lists the names of those employees who have submitted their applications, and the final selection is then made by the supervisor of the department involved, who selects the employee who best qualifies for the job on the basis of ability and seniority.

Bumping practice varies tremendously, but the main idea is that one employee may claim or "bump" another employee from his job, usually only on the basis of seniority. Rules are usually established having to do with the skills involved, whether or not one can bump jobs in other departments in the plant, and whether one can bump uphill as well as downhill. Bumping usually gets started during periods of lay-offs and obviously can create a great disruption in jobs and personnel. Both bumping and job bidding may become headaches to the employment manager, since both practices create delays in getting people placed on their final job and in making clear what type of person or skill is needed from outside sources.

Outside sources of recruits cover a wide variety of possibilities. Among the more popular sources are (1) employment agencies, both private and public, (2) schools, including specialized trade schools as well as the public schools, (3) casual applicants who come to the employment office directly, (4) miscellaneous organizations such as churches, lodges, and veterans' groups, (5) special arrangements with other businesses whereby employees laid off in one company may be hired by another, and (6) recommendations from present employees. The alert employment manager will develop these sources to a fine degree so that in a relatively short time employees possessing the needed skills and abilities can be supplied to the company.

Employment Policies

Before an employment manager can begin hiring, he or she must be familiar with both written and unwritten employment policies imposed upon the department by the company. These policies not only influence the sources that might be pursued for recruits, but also are a basis for preliminary screening and final selection of employees. Detailed analyses of employment policies are beyond the scope of this book; however, increasing public attention is being given to the discriminatory practices of many organizations, and it is clear that it is important to a company that it have well-considered and defensible employment policies. Companies that have discriminated against applicants in the past owing to their religion, race, sex, physical handicaps, or other characteristics would do well to reconsider the background and reasons for such policies. This is true not only because of laws and enlightened social pressures, but because the broadening of one's point of view might uncover some heretofore untapped sources of employees. In other words, every company should be an "Equal Opportunity Employer."

Unfortunately, many companies appear to hire employees under the principle of "survival," i.e., the person hired is one who survives the many hurdles placed in his or her path. These hurdles include not only various tests and interviews that are administered, but also certain employment policies, which may in effect really discriminate against certain people. No one condemns an employment manager for attempting to protect the best interests of the company; however, it is proposed that the company's "best interest" might be served if a positive approach to recruiting and hiring is taken. Such an approach would be to determine carefully the skills and abilities required by a particular job and then to hire a person who best meets these requirements. By thus avoiding artificial barriers, the employer discriminates in favor of ability and against incompetence, instead of unrelated factors such as race and religion.

Steps of Selection Procedure

Recruitment was described as the process of getting potential employees willing to apply for a job with the company. If recruitment is successful, several will apply, and from these the more desirable applicants must be selected. The basis of selection will normally be outlined on a job specification form which will list the qualifications a person must possess before being assigned to any particular job. For an applicant to be selected, he or she will usually have to pass satisfactorily through several steps in the selection procedure.

Companies will often include either a preliminary interview or a preliminary application blank in their selection procedure. Such steps are designed to eliminate the applicant who is obviously unfit for the type of work offered. Lack of certain requirements in education or experience might determine unfitness.

A preliminary step offers advantages not only to the company, but to the applicant as well. If an applicant is eliminated in the early part of the selection procedure, the company is saved the expense of processing this person through the remaining steps of the procedure. The applicant is also saved the time and trouble of going through the same procedure.

Whether or not a preliminary application blank is used, there is almost always a step in the selection procedure calling for the applicant to supply detailed information on a complete application blank. A typical example is shown in Figure 18-2.

THE TRANE COMPANY FACTORY EMPLOYMENT APPLICATION
(PLEASE PRINT ANSWERS)
EXCLUDE ANY INFORMATION DEALING WITH RACE, COLOR,
RELIGION OR NATIONAL ORIGIN   20.04--(472)

NAME _____ SOC. SEC. NUMBER _____

ADDRESS _____   YEARS AT
                    STREET   CITY   STATE   THIS ADDRESS _____

TELEPHONE NO. _____ DO YOU OWN HOME ☐ RENT ☐ ROOM ☐ U.S. CITIZEN ☐ YES ☐ NO

MARITAL STATUS: MARRIED ☐ SINGLE ☐ DIVORCED ☐ WIDOWED ☐ NUMBER OF DEPENDENTS EXCLUDING YOURSELF _____

HAVE YOU BEEN CONVICTED OF AN OFFENSE OTHER THAN A MINOR TRAFFIC VIOLATION? YES ☐ NO ☐

                                    RELATED HOBBIES
POSITION APPLIED FOR _____ OR JOB INTEREST _____
NAMES OF RELATIVES   HAVE YOU EVER
AT TRANE _____ WORKED FOR TRANE? _____ WHEN? _____

DATE OF BIRTH*					PHYSICAL IMPAIRMENT, IF ANY:
MONTH	DAY	YEAR	HEIGHT	WEIGHT	

EDUCATION: NAME AND LOCATION OF SCHOOLS		DATES		GRADUATE		COURSE
		FROM	TO	YES	NO	OR DEGREE
GRAMMAR SCHOOL:						
HIGH SCHOOL:						
COLLEGE OR UNIVERSITY:						
COMMERCIAL, TECHNICAL TRADE OR CORRESPONDENCE:						

                                                TYPE OF
MILITARY SERVICE: FROM _____ TO _____ DUTY _____
BRANCH OF   RANK OR   TYPE OF   DISABILITY
SERVICE _____ RATING _____ DISCHARGE _____ RATING % _____
EVER HOSPITALIZED? _____ REASON _____
TECHNICAL OR
SPECIAL TRAINING _____

PREVIOUS EMPLOYMENT RECORD: START WITH LAST OR PRESENT EMPLOYER AND INCLUDE MILITARY SERVICE   20.04--(Back)--(472)

NAME AND ADDRESS OF EMPLOYER	LENGTH OF SERVICE				DUTIES	WHY DID YOU LEAVE
	FROM		TO			
	MO.	YR.	MO.	YR.		

PLEASE LIST THE NAMES AND ADDRESSES OF TWO PERSONAL REFERENCES:

NAME	ADDRESS	OCCUPATION

I certify that all answers given by me on this application are true. I also understand that any false statement will be reason for my immediate discharge. I further certify that I have not been, nor am I now, a member of any organization that advocates the forceful overthrow of the Government of the United States of America. I also release The Trane Company and any other firm from any liability in the release of information concerning me.
                    Date _____ Signed _____

*THE AGE DISCRIMINATION IN EMPLOYMENT ACT OF 1967 PROHIBITS DISCRIMINATION ON THE BASIS OF AGE WITH RESPECT TO INDIVIDUALS WHO ARE AT LEAST 40 BUT LESS THAN 65 YEARS OF AGE.

Figure 18-2. Application blank for factory workers. (Courtesy The Trane Company.)

The application blank should call for information that has a bearing on the fitness of the applicant for the job, but on the other hand, it should be as simple as possible. Questions having no bearing on suitability for the job should be eliminated, and other questions calling for long or complex answers might better be asked and answered during an interview.

Employment tests are often used in selection procedures. However, they should be considered simply a step and not a replacement for other phases of the procedure. The real value of tests frequently lies more in eliminating those applicants who have very little chance of job success than in selecting those applicants who will definitely be successful on a job.

There are several types of tests that are used in selection procedures, among which are performance tests, aptitude tests, intelligence tests, dexterity tests, interest tests, and personality tests.

Performance tests are designed to measure what individuals know about a particular job or their degree of proficiency in performing certain tasks. They are probably most useful in hiring employees at the lower levels, for one can easily discover the ability of a prospective typist or welder by simply having them perform the task involved.

Aptitude tests attempt to measure a person's capacity to learn the skills required in a particular area. Examples would be a clerical aptitude test or a mechanical-relationships test. These tests usually determine specific aptitudes, although tests have been designed for measuring a whole group of aptitudes at the same time.

Intelligence tests are designed to measure the individual's ability to deal with abstract symbols, ideas, words, numbers, and so forth. The intelligence test was the first type of test to be used in personnel work, and it is probably still the most popular. Although the majority of questions asked are practical and job-oriented, there are many that are abstract. The whole point of any question used on such a test is whether or not it consistently helps to select the employee who will be successful in the future.

Dexterity tests are used to discover people's cleverness with their hands. Many jobs require the skillful use of one's hands and body, and standardized dexterity tests can simplify the selection of persons to fill these jobs.

Interest tests are designed to measure an individual's preferences for certain activities of either a vocational or avocational nature. These tests usually have been used for vocational counseling, although they have some application in personnel selection, especially for sales jobs or other jobs requiring contact with other people.

Personality tests are undoubtedly the least useful of all those mentioned simply because of their lack of validity. Many personality tests have been devised for the purpose of measuring such characteristics as emotional adjustment, self-confidence, originality, and other "traits." But until more is known about personality, it is doubtful whether most of these tests can be of much value in the selection process. There are a number of these tests available on the market today. Although many may possess high validity and reliability under certain conditions, these same results cannot always be duplicated under different conditions. For this reason, the generally preferred procedure is to have industrial psychologists develop tests that take into account the particular needs of the company. Even then, the tests should not be considered a cure-all. They might be expected to improve the percentage of successful employees selected, but they can't be expected to raise that percentage to 100.

Application blanks and tests provide much valuable information about applicants, but normally not enough to decide whether or not to hire them. Additional information that can be learned only through personal contact is required. An interview gives the company an opportunity to learn of special abilities, interests, and desires or personal characteristics possessed by the applicant that might not otherwise be revealed. The interview also gives the applicant a chance to ask questions about the company, the job, and future prospects. In other words, a more complete understanding should result from the interview.

The success of the employment interview will depend to a large extent on the conditions surrounding it and on the abilities of the interviewer. Some good principles of interviewing are (1) conduct the interview in private, (2) make the applicant feel at ease, (3) give the applicant your full attention, (4) discount your own personal prejudice, (5) keep control of the interview, and (6) arrive at a conclusion—not necessarily about offering or not offering a job, but about what comes next in the procedure or what action needs to be taken.

Many persons do not regard references as an important determinant in employment procedures, because information received from previous employers of the applicant or from his personal acquaintances may not reveal enough—one way or another. This has been true particularly when the reference check was carried on by mail. Personal interviews or telephone calls are more helpful and are used when checking on applicants for higher-bracket jobs. Some companies still use reference checks on hourly employees simply to verify the facts concerning previous employment. Such facts would include time employed and jobs held. Figure 18-3 illustrates one type of reference form.

The use of physical examinations as a step in an employment procedure serves three purposes. First, it is a genuine selection device. A company generally wishes to hire only people who are in good physical condition and are free of communicable diseases. The company may have health standards as well as intelligence test standards or skill standards. Secondly, the physical examination assists in placing employees on specific jobs. An applicant may pass general health standards but be better qualified to work on certain jobs from a physical point of view. Thirdly, the company's general health program is facilitated by this initial physical examination. Later physical checkups will indicate whether the employee's general health is improving or deteriorating.

On the basis of these selection steps, the employment department can arrive at a decision as to which applicants should be offered jobs. Inasmuch as the employ-

EASTMAN KODAK COMPANY
ROCHESTER 4, NEW YORK

Applicant Appraisal Form

AND ASSOCIATED DIVISIONS
including

TENNESSEE EASTMAN COMPANY
TEXAS EASTMAN COMPANY
EASTMAN CHEMICAL PRODUCTS, INC.
RECORDAK CORPORATION
DISTILLATION PRODUCTS INDUSTRIES

Kodak

To:

Applicant:

An application has been received from the individual whose name is given. We should appreciate your evaluation of this person's characteristics, ability, and potential by completing this form. In particular, we should appreciate any comments you can provide on the back of this form, as such information is especially valuable. Your evaluation and comments will be held confidential.

It is important that the completed form be returned promptly so we may proceed with our consideration. A self-addressed envelope is enclosed for this purpose. Your co-operation will be most helpful and very much appreciated.

Please use as a basis for rating, the comparison of this individual with all of the students with whom you have come in contact in your teaching (or working) career.

Yours very truly

Business & Technical Personnel Department

	NO BASIS FOR RATING	POOR	FAIR	AVERAGE	GOOD	SUPERIOR
1. GENERAL APPEARANCE — Neatness, grooming, posture, dress, physical appearance.						
2. SOCIAL IMPRESSION — Social ease, speech and expression, mannerisms.						
3. ABILITY TO GET ALONG WITH OTHERS — Patience, open-mindedness, adaptability, respect for others.						
4. COMPETENCY — Ability to learn easily, ability to apply knowledge and ideas readily, creativeness, ability to analyze and plan, accuracy, reliability.						
5. ABILITY IN MAJOR FIELD — Comprehension of material studied, depth of interest.						
6. DRIVE TO ACCOMPLISH — Perseverance, thoroughness, initiative, enthusiasm.						
7. MATURITY — Common sense, stability, self-confidence, realistic outlook.						
8. LEADERSHIP — Ability to inspire confidence, organizational ability, desire and capacity for responsibility, ability to initiate, ability to make decisions.						

KO 1537 KP♦ 41845D   (OVER)

Figure 18-3. Appraisal form for business and technical applicants. (Courtesy Eastman Kodak Company.)

ment department is a staff department, it is clear that this selection is not a final one but instead a recommended or preliminary one. The foreman or supervisor in the department where the job opening exists will usually make the final selection. Another way to look at this procedure is to say that the employment department selects for the company and the foreman selects for the department.

Training

The first task of the training department, as far as new employees are concerned, is to introduce them to their jobs and to the plant environment. Such introduction shouldn't be on a casual "they'll pick it up in time" basis, but instead, should be a planned, well-thought-out program. They must learn the locations of lockers, washrooms, and the cafeteria and must meet the people for and with whom they are to work. They must learn company policies on matters of immediate concern to them, and finally they will have many questions that must be answered as completely and accurately as possible. Their future success on the job will depend to a large extent on the manner in which they are introduced to their jobs and to the company.

The orientation of the new employee actually begins when he or she first hears about the company and begins to make inquiries about a job. The employment interview that follows covers many aspects of the company's operations, such as products, pay, working conditions, and other items of interest. However, once the person is hired, these facts need to be covered again so as to be certain that no misunderstanding has developed. Three approaches are usually followed. The first is a group meeting of all new employees conducted by a representative of the personnel department. The meeting may have speakers from other departments, such as medical services and the safety committee, whose presentations are directed toward getting the new employees started off on the right foot. Although questions may be answered during the group meeting, probably the best place for the new employee to get questions answered is during an individual conference with the immediate supervisor. This conference is the second step of orientation and on a person-to-person basis is probably the best opportunity for complete and thorough indoctrination. Thirdly, written orientation aids are used to contribute to the learning process. In general, these are handbooks or leaflets that contain facts, regulations, and policies of all types of interest to the new employee. It is unlikely that the new employee takes time to read and understand all the information presented in such a handbook, but at least it is available for future reference.

New employees with some past experience may be able to take over certain jobs with little or no training, but in spite of experience, some training is usually necessary for anyone beginning a new job. Training of hourly workers generally takes one of the following forms: on-the-job, classroom, cooperative, apprentice, or vestibule school.

On-the-job Training

Training factory workers on the job that they will eventually take over is a universal practice in industry. It is simple and inexpensive, and the actual training is performed by the employee's supervisor or by an experienced worker already familiar with the job. This method of training is entirely satisfactory under many conditions; however, it will not produce skilled workers in a short time nor will it produce workers uniformly skilled. Since on-the-job training tends to be administered and coordinated on a somewhat haphazard basis, these limitations are not surprising.

Nevertheless, on-the-job training is still one of the most effective and popular means of training in industry. Its flexibility allows a program to be started and stopped at will and to be adjusted to the individual concerned. The employee has firsthand experience with the job and learns by doing. With adequate supervision and guidance, correct performance can be immediately applauded, and wrong performance can be immediately corrected. Perhaps this direct contact with the job helps compensate for the lack of organization of material presented and the possibility that certain factors may be omitted.

Classroom Training

Classroom training is conducted in a room set aside for the purpose and makes use of procedures similar to those used in regular group discussions. Classroom training makes it possible to handle a maximum number of trainees with a minimum number of instructors and so is suitable for carrying out large-scale instruction. On the other hand, unless the groups are limited in size, there may be some hesitancy on the part of the individual participant to ask questions, and the effectiveness of this method of instruction may be limited.

A common failing of classroom instruction is for the instructor to depend entirely upon lectures as the medium of training. The lecture method by itself is seldom completely satisfactory, but its value can be enhanced by the use of audiovisual aids and by the use of some of the participative methods, such as role-playing and discussion sessions.

Apprentice Training

Apprentice training is really a variation of on-the-job training, but it has a different goal. In on-the-job training, the objective is to qualify the trainee to take over the job calling for a specific set of work patterns. In apprentice training, the trainee is being trained to take over a job requiring highly skilled work applied to varying work patterns. The training provided prospective machinists, electricians, or tool makers is commonly handled by means of an apprentice program.

As companies add more automatic equipment, apprentice programs are being directed toward the development of skilled mechanics who maintain such equipment. Mechanics to handle this type of job require a much broader apprentice-type training than has normally been provided in the past.

An apprentice program will usually last for a number of years, and during that time the trainees will carry out a planned sequence of jobs as well as spend a prescribed number of hours in the classroom. Pay will normally start at a relatively low rate and increase as the apprentice completes definite steps in the program. When the entire program is completed, the person is considered qualified to receive the minimum of the regular pay for a journeyman of his or her particular craft.

In recent years apprenticeship training programs have been influenced by federal and state legislation. Laws regulate such factors as the pay, number of hours worked, and amount of time devoted to schooling. Apprenticeship training usually entails arrangements involving the trainee, the employer, the union, and perhaps a vocational trades school.

Cooperative Training

Cooperative training is now made available by many high schools, colleges, and trade schools. In such training programs students spend part of their time in a practical job experience and part of their time as students in school. This division of time may be made each day, or perhaps during different parts of a school year. In any case, the students are compensated for the time spent at work, and their job experience is related to their academic work in the classroom. A student not only secures some income, but has some experience to indicate on an application blank when seeking permanent employment following the completion of his or her educational goal. The cooperating companies usually benefit from such an arrangement because they have made contact with prospective employees to be hired upon graduation.

Vestibule Schools

When large numbers of workers are to be trained in similar skills, and when it is desirable to have them trained quickly and uniformly, vestibule schools are usually the answer. Such a school is set up on the company property, and the equipment actually used on the production floor is duplicated as closely as possible. The trainees' slowness in learning or the mistakes they make while learning naturally have no effect on actual production. When the trainees become proficient in the school, they are transferred to the production floor, where they can take over a regular job with a minimum of delay. If the simulated work setup in the vestibule school is not exactly like the actual work setup, some on-the-job training still will be necessary; however, the time and effort required will be much reduced.

Vestibule schools are not without certain disadvantages. The cost of setting up such a school is such that not every company can afford it, and any company will need to study its long-run training needs very carefully before launching such a school. The school has maintenance costs that sometimes constitute a disadvantage. The space and the skilled instructors needed may also work a hardship on the organization.

Teaching Machines

The use of teaching machines in industrial training was inevitable despite the differences of opinion regarding learning theory and educational technique. Although training typically teaches a student only "what" to do, and education attempts to explain "why," developers of teaching machines claim that they are able to impart some of both to the student with the use of these devices.

Most teaching machines work on the principle that the learner is presented certain factual material, after which he is to indicate a response. Immediately upon making his response, he is informed whether or not this response was correct. A correct response allows him to go on to the next point, whereas an incorrect one forces him to go back and review what he has missed. This procedure reinforces his learning process and allows him to progress at his own rate.

Some electronic manufacturers are making use of combined tape recordings and slide projections to train workers in the assembly of electronic panels. Prerecorded tapes tell the operator what to do step by step, and the projected slide lets the operator compare the appearance of what he or she has done with the correct appearance. Both slide projection and the tape recording are under the control of the operator and may be repeated as often as found necessary (see Figure 18-4).

Figure 18-4   An audiovisual instruction system in use. (Courtesy Videosenic Systems Division, Hughes Aircraft Company.)

Some manufacturers have made use of the device described above in such a way as to eliminate training altogether for the assembly of certain panels. In other words, the operator is not expected to learn how to wire the panel, but instead is led through the wiring program step by step and repeats the program on the tape recording and slides for each panel he or she wires. In such a case a set of slides and a tape recording is checked out together with the raw materials necessary to do a job. Such a procedure seems highly desirable in a setup where only a few panels of any one type are made at any one time. In some cases the instructions on the tape recordings also serve to pace the operator through the job. In between instructions background music is heard, and in at least one instance, the persons on the job reported that they would prefer to listen to the background music on the tape recorder than to be free to talk with their neighbors.

Health

The health and safety of employees have been concerns of employers since the beginning of the factory system, as well they might be since only workers in good physical condition can work at their top level of efficiency. It is clear, however, that in the future employers will be giving even more attention to health and safety as a result of the passage of the Williams-Steiger Occupational Safety and Health Act of 1970.

The stated purpose of the Act (usually abbreviated OSHA) is "to assure so far as possible every working man and woman in the Nation safe and healthful working conditions and to preserve our human resources." To carry out the purpose of the Act, the Department of Labor, in cooperation with the various states, is authorized to establish safety and health standards for industries and jobs. In addition, inspectors are provided who are authorized to cite violations of the standards which could result in rather severe penalties for the employer. Since enactment of the Act, employers have been faced with increased record keeping and inspections by government agents in addition to increased efforts to provide safe and healthful working conditions. Health factors are discussed in this section, with the following section being devoted to a discussion of safety.

Physical Examination

The role of the physical examination as a part of the selection procedure and as a part of the general health program has already been mentioned. At this point let us re-emphasize the importance of maintaining adequate records of the physical deterioration of employees, particularly when such deterioration may be caused by the conditions under which the employee works. The effect of harsh chemicals, dust, fumes, oils, and excessively loud noise must be watched, for the company may be held responsible for any physical deterioration that occurs. Any effect on employee health from these conditions may be slow in manifesting itself, and careful records of periodic examinations may be the only way it can be detected.

General Treatment

It is not common practice for the company doctor or nurse to treat employees for their general ailments unless the condition has resulted from their jobs. The main service the company doctor renders in this connection is in early detection and in recommending that the employee consult his own family physician. Of course, there is no hard-and-fast line between those ailments the company doctor will and won't treat. Treatment of minor colds and general first aid are usually handled by the company hospital staff regardless of the origin of the ailment.

Treatment of all injuries that occur within the plant is the main purpose of the company hospital or dispensary. Every injury that occurs in the plant is a potential "accident" in the technical sense and must be given close attention. The problem in this connection is to get the injured employee to report to the hospital for treatment. One employee ignored a piece of rope fiber that became lodged in his finger. A week later he spent three days in the hospital with an infected finger, and a lost-time accident was chalked up against him and his department.

Being equipped and able to handle the more serious and emergency injuries is also one of the important phases of the work of the company hospital. Factories working around the clock have a special problem in this respect. If such a company has enough employees to warrant it, a nurse is kept on duty all night. Otherwise, a doctor or nurse is always on call. Training supervisory people and other employees in first aid will facilitate the handling of the emergency cases when they arise.

Health Programs

A preventive rather than corrective approach to health has encouraged many companies to inaugurate programs which encourage physical exercise and proper diets. Some companies sponsor membership in health clubs or even install suitable facilities on their own premises. More and more, recreation is having built into it an element of health as well as fun. Staying healthy shouldn't be a matter of just correcting things as they go wrong but preventing the problems from arising.

Safety

A consistently good safety record doesn't come about through chance alone. Companies that enjoy good safety records have had to spend much time and effort working toward that goal. This time and effort is coordinated by the safety director. Sometimes the coordinated effort is called a "safety program," and it will be referred to by that name here. The name, "program," however, should not imply that it has a beginning and an end. Safety programs never end. More or less emphasis may be placed on the program, but it must be continuous if a good safety record is to be achieved or maintained. Analysis of most successful safety programs will disclose that they contain the four "E's"—Engineering, Education, Enlistment, and Enforcement.

Mention has already been made of the importance of coordinating safety and "engineering" when it comes to the design and installation of new machines or equipment. If jobs can be *designed* so they are safe, a big forward step will have been made in any safety program.

The "education" of employees in safe practices and in being alert to hazardous conditions is another important part of the safety program. Normally workers do not instinctively follow methods that will protect them from injury. Instead, correct and safe methods must be taught thoroughly enough to become habitual.

The next "E" of a good safety program is "enlistment" and concerns the attitude of workers and management toward the program and its purposes. In spite of hazards that may exist on the job, it becomes necessary from time to time to inject into the minds of all concerned a greater interest in accident prevention and a certain safety-consciousness. This need is emphasized through safety meetings, safety posters, safety contests, safety films, safety committees, and numerous other devices.

"Enforcement" is the last "E" and in many respects can be the most important. A safety program must have the support of management, from the top levels on down to the foreman. However, management must not only observe safe practices and participate in the program, but must be willing to enforce adherence to safety rules and safe practices generally. A management that gives lip service to safety but winks at violations of sound, safe practices cannot expect a safety program to yield beneficial results beyond a bare minimum.

Costs of Accidents

There are definite costs associated with accidents. Some are direct and measurable; others are indirect and somewhat intangible but nevertheless real. Companies pay for the costs of accidents in three ways: (1) medical and hospital care that may be required by the injured employee, (2) weekly payments to the injured employee, computed as a percentage of regular weekly wages and continuing for as long as the employee is unable to work, and (3) increased rates of compensation insurance.

There are other costs connected with accidents. An accident may mean damage to tools, equipment, or materials, the cost of which can be computed. Some production time will be lost by the injured worker. Other workers will cease work in order to assist or investigate at the time of the accident. Even if they don't cease work altogether, a slackening of pace is almost sure to take place. Time will be spent by foremen, safety engineers, and company executives in investigating the accident. This time, however, cannot be considered entirely wasted if it is fruitful in preventing another accident. Of course, morale of employees throughout the plant will sag, and if a plant becomes known as one having frequent accidents, its reputation throughout the community suffers. This may have an effect on employee and public relations in general.

Evaluation of the Safety Program

The first problem in evaluation is the definition of an "accident." In general, an accident is any unforeseen event that causes personal injury or property damage. Although this definition covers both the cut finger and the broken leg, there may be a need to separate them statistically. A common way to categorize accidents follows.

Minor injuries. All injuries that can be adequately treated in the company hospital or dispensary are minor. This would usually include cut fingers, splinters, and sprained ankles.

Compensable injuries. Those injuries that require treatment beyond routine first aid and that do *not* result in the employee's losing time from his job are compensable. Injuries of this nature would be covered under the workers' compensation laws; a typical example would be a broken finger, which would require an X-ray and setting.

Lost-time accident. An injury that causes the employee to lose time from the job either immediately or sometime later is a lost-time injury. This requires interpretation, for all injuries result in some lost time for treatment if nothing else. If an employee is injured one day and as a result is off the rest of that day *but* returns to work the next day, the injury is not considered lost-time. The accident becomes lost-time if the worker fails to return the next day or some subsequent day.

The evaluations and comparisons of most safety records are based upon lost-time accidents. Obviously, these are the really serious ones and so warrant maximum attention. Studies of minor and compensable injuries are nevertheless worthwhile, for the record of these injuries may indicate trends or show opportunities to eliminate hazards. Contests or safety record comparisons based on minor injuries are to be avoided, for if employees become too worked up over the record, they may become reluctant to report their injuries. The same could be true of compensable injuries, although to a lesser degree.

Frequency rates are determined from the number of lost-time accidents per million man-hours worked. This ratio relates the number of lost-time accidents to the exposure to possible injury. For any particular time period, it can be computed using the formula

$$\text{Frequency rate} = \frac{\text{Number of lost-time accidents} \times 1,000,000}{\text{Number of man-hours worked}}$$

Obviously, this ratio will not tell the whole story, for some lost-time accidents are more serious than others. The severity rate takes this into account, measuring the total time lost in days per million man-hours of exposure. For any given time period, it can be computed by

$$\text{Severity rate} = \frac{\text{Total time lost in days} \times 1,000,000}{\text{Number of man-hours worked}}$$

It can be seen from these two formulas that a good safety record would call for both a low frequency rate and a low severity rate, and ''low'' can be considered only in a relative manner. One company's frequency rate may be low compared to the rest of the industry, or lower this year than last. As long as all computations are made on the same basis, the results are comparable.

It is customary for companies to compute frequency and severity rates both monthly and yearly. In addition, they will keep track of the number of man-hours worked since the last lost-time accident. A desirable goal for a plant to work toward is one million man-hours worked without a lost-time accident. It is not too uncommon for plants to reach this goal, and a few have managed to go considerably beyond it.

Accident Causes and Prevention

There is no single cause of accidents nor is there any sure way to prevent them. Many people are quick to point out that accidents don't just happen, but instead are caused by either an unsafe act or an unsafe condition.

The majority of accidents happen because of an unsafe act by the person concerned. Such an act may occur because of the employee's ignorance or forgetfulness, or because he or she deliberately took a chance. Experience shows that the employee may ''get away with it'' for a while, but eventually will have to pay the price. Operating a fork truck too fast, tying down safety switches, and failure to use personal safety devices are all examples of unsafe acts.

Unsafe conditions are those situations in our physical environment that *could* cause accidents. The broken safety guard, the leaking acid valve, and the protruding packing-case nail are all examples of unsafe conditions. Eliminating unsafe conditions is relatively easy—once they are identified.

Environmental Factors

In addition to providing facilities for training employees, an employer is responsible for providing a work environment that is reasonably free of conditions that might be detrimental to the physical well being of the employee. Besides correcting unsafe conditions that might cause an accident and providing hospital facilities for aid in treatment, companies must also attend to various environmental factors that may influence employees' health and safety.

Lighting has probably received more attention than any other factor of the work environment. Management has long realized that illumination affects not only health and safety, but also efficiency and morale as well. In planning for good illumination, consideration must be given to the distribution, intensity, and color of light.

Noise has been a controversial factor of the work environment largely because studies of the effect of noise have been inconclusive. People have different reactions to noise. Some find any type of noise distracting; others seem indifferent to it, and still others claim that noise facilitates their work. In spite of these contradictions, in recent years management has given increasing attention to the problems of noise, particularly since the courts have granted some compensation to employees based upon the claim of loss of hearing resulting from high noise levels.

Individual differences make it difficult to determine precise safe limits of noise. However, the possibility of permanent auditory damage exists at about 90 decibels, and at 120 decibels the probability of permanent damage to the hearing after long exposure is very high. Noise containing high frequencies is more damaging than that composed largely of low frequencies, and explosive noise is more damaging than continuous noise. Companies should make periodic surveys of noise levels in various parts of their plants and should also establish a hearing-testing program in order to detect any trend that may develop in loss of hearing owing to the work environment. A hearing-testing program would also help to protect the company in case of possible claims for worker's compensation.

Proper ventilation has received greater emphasis during recent years and in many companies is considered to be as important as lighting in its effect upon employees' health and safety as well as upon employee efficiency and morale.

Almost every manufacturing concern has some type of health hazard that should receive special attention as part of a health and safety program. Departments working with chemicals, radioactive materials, and similar toxic items should get special treatment. Excessive amounts of dust and odors from processes may constitute specific health hazards as well as detriments to employee efficiency and morale.

In addition to the environmental factors already mentioned, it is also important that work surroundings be attractive in physical appearance. Neatness and cleanliness in both plant and office areas are conducive to safe and efficient operation. Serving the personal needs of employees by providing clean washrooms and well-ventilated locker rooms as well as attractive eating facilities is an important part of an effective health and safety program.

Benefits

There is no clear-cut distinction between *benefits* and *services* that are offered employees by companies, but we have chosen to consider benefits as the "extras" that result in financial gain to the employee. Employees may or may not contribute to their support, but even if they do contribute, they receive a gain financially because they are employees. Group insurance plans would be an example. Most benefits could show up in the pay check, but for various reasons do not, and this becomes a tax advantage for the employee. The word "fringe" is often applied to benefits because they are outside the pay check.

Services are considered to be all those other extras that do not consist of a financial gain to the employee but do fulfill social, recreational, or cultural needs of the employees and at the same time make life easier because of sheer convenience. These will be discussed in the next section.

Pay for Not Working

In spite of the insistence of some employers that they will never pay someone for not working, almost every company does; and the tendency, if anything, seems to be increasing, largely in an effort to reduce job dissatisfaction, particularly on assembly line jobs. It shows up usually in three forms: rest periods, paid holidays, and paid vacations.

The rest period is usually divided into two parts for the two halves of a shift, each period being from 10 to 20 minutes in length. Each period usually provides an opportunity for the employees to smoke or procure food and drink. Although some research indicates that workers maintain their efficiency better throughout the day if allowed rest periods, for many plants this is not the determining factor. It is simply a matter of having time off. In very heavy and hot jobs, rest periods are a necessity and may total several hours in a day. An extension of the rest-period idea exists in some plants in the form of allowance for luncheon on company time. This practice is prevalent where continuous operations take place.

Ten paid holidays a year are common in industry. Employees are given straight-time pay for the holiday not worked. Should it be necessary for an employee to work on a paid holiday, he or she may receive double or triple pay, depending on the union agreement or company policy.

The length of paid vacations offered to employees usually varies with the length of service and the nature of the position. A typical pattern would be one week of vacation for less than five years' service, two weeks for five to 15 years' service, and three weeks for service over 15 years. Some companies have gone to 4 weeks' vacation for 20 or 25 years of service. Pay will usually be either at a straight-time rate or at an average rate if the employee has been working on incentive-pay jobs during the year.

With so many employees getting vacations, some companies have found it economical to shut down during the vacation period instead of trying to operate all summer long with many people missing. The shutdown period also offers an opportunity to perform large maintenance jobs on buildings and equipment.

Suggestion Systems

Suggestion systems are designed to tap the tremendous store of ideas that rest in the minds of employees. Some employees will volunteer ideas for improvements simply because of the satisfaction that comes from having made a suggestion. For the most part, however, employees will be reluctant to volunteer suggestions without some kind of system that makes it easy for them to do so and offers some reward. Two methods for computing remuneration are prevalent. One is a flat rate system such as $25–$50 per accepted suggestion. The other is a certain percentage of the first year's savings that result from application of the idea. Awards under the latter system have run into several thousand dollars.

A certain amount of "ballyhoo" seems to be necessary in order to make a suggestion system fully successful. The recipient should be given nonfinancial recognition as well as the cash award. Presentation dinners, newspaper stories and pictures, and appropriate notations on the employee's record card can all be made a part of the promotion campaign so as to encourage other employees to turn in their ideas too.

Health Benefits

Health benefits in general were discussed earlier. To the extent that the plant hospital will treat employees' ailments not directly connected with their jobs, this would be a true health benefit. Conceivably, much of the treatment received would have to be paid for on the outside if it were not available within the plant.

Insurance Plans

Workers' compensation is certainly a benefit offered by the employer, even though the employer is forced by law to provide it. Workers' compensation, however, gives no coverage for illness or injury that occurs outside the plant. To handle this contingency, companies provide disability, hospitalization, and surgical insurance for their employees. In some cases the employee pays the entire cost of the coverage, in others the company pays the premiums, and in still others the cost is shared. In any case, the cost of coverage is usually less than private individual coverage, because the coverage in the company plan is on a group basis.

Individual plans vary considerably in details, but the intent is usually the same and that is our main interest here. Disability coverage is intended to provide some income to employees during the time that illness prevents them from working. The income may be a flat amount or computed as a percentage of average earnings. Most disability plans will contain provisions stating that an employee must be under a physician's care during the period—as evidenced by a signed certificate—and that payment will be made only if the absence lasts a certain minimum length of time, usually a week. These provisions minimize the effect of one- or two-day absences caused by colds or by the fact that someone just didn't "feel" like coming to work. Hospitalization insurance pays specified amounts toward board and room charges and also toward any X-ray, operating room, or other hospital charges. Limits are usually placed on the total number of days per year a person can collect for the same ailment. Surgical insurance pays specified amounts toward the doctor's fee for performing surgery.

Group life insurance coverage for employees is probably the most common type of insurance in industry today. The cost of coverage is small because of the group feature, and although the face value is usually not large (commonly $10,000–$20,000), some protection is provided for the employees' families.

Retirement and Pension Plans

With the population becoming older and retirement being delayed to age 70,[1] it seems natural that employers would be offering pension plans either of their own volition, through pressure from unions, or by law. Under the Social Security Act, both employers and employees are required to make contributions toward a federal fund that provides benefits on retirement. Many companies supplement Social Security benefits by setting up a pension plan of their own, and the combination might provide a total monthly pension to a retired employee of $2000 or more. Some companies tie their profit-sharing and pension plans together. Instead of being distributed in cash, profits are held in a trust fund until retirement, at which time an annuity would be purchased for the employee. In cases like this, if profits have been good, the total pension might approach the employee's former monthly wages.

The most important aspect of any company's retirement plan is that it provides sufficient retirement income to insure that the employee suffers no fear for his security. However, a good retirement program should do two other things, namely, prepare the employee for retirement, and continue a relationship with the employee after employment is terminated. Preparation for retirement should preferably start two or three years before the actual retirement date. In this manner, the employee is helped to make the necessary social and psychological adjustments and is encouraged to develop ideas concerning hobbies, additional jobs, community services, or business pursuits in which he or she would like to engage sometime in the future.

---

[1]As of this writing some 19 states have passed laws prohibiting any fixed retirement age, with the prospect that other states will soon follow suit. There is some attempt for a federal law along this line, too. The impact of these state laws does not seem to be great, since most older workers do not want to work longer that perhaps age 65 or 70, and of course some companies give employees some extra incentives in the way of bonuses to voluntarily retire early.

Many employees are reluctant to think of these things ahead of time, for on their own initiative they are unable to visualize a future life in which the pressures, worries, and companionships of their current jobs are no longer present. A preparation-for-retirement program need not be elaborate. Many successful programs are maintained by companies in which employees about ready to retire are provided an opportunity to meet together and discuss the problems they share.

An equally important part of any retirement program is its role in maintaining contact between the company and the employee after retirement. Employees who have worked many years for a company have developed a loyalty and feeling of attachment toward the organization, which, wisely, should be fostered and continued as assurance of security and goodwill in the minds of the retirees. Many companies make certain that the names of the retirees are kept on the mailing list to receive the company's newsletter and other literature. Retired employees are also invited to company social activities and given certain other privileges and services that active employees are entitled to. A retired employees' club is another way to allow the retiree to keep in touch with the company as well as his former associates.

To make themselves generally "leaner" and to get rid of some of their higher paid employees, some companies have followed a rather common practice of offering incentives for some of the senior employees to take early retirement. This is done in a variety of ways, such as increasing the company pension entitlements, providing a generous terminal pay arrangement, paying equivalent Social Security benefits until such time that the employee is entitled to receive them from the government, or some combination of incentives. When a middle-sized life insurance company offered a package option to 140 of its older employees, 80 chose to take early retirement.

Other Benefits

Guaranteed wages, guaranteed employment, profit-sharing, and stock-purchase plans are all commonly found in industry today. These will be discussed in the chapters on wage administration.

Services

All the items just discussed as benefits were included under that head because they provide some element of financial return to employees. *Services,* on the other hand, are provided by the company in order to fill some particular need of some or all of the employee group. Some services may be more necessary than others in any particular situation; some are simply conveniences and may not be "necessary" at all. Companies provide services in order to instill a feeling of group solidarity and general loyalty to the company. Pleasant "off-job" relationships probably make for more efficient "on-job" relationships. It is not our purpose to cover all possible services that a company might offer. Instead, some of the more common and more important ones will be discussed, with emphasis being placed on how they fit into the total industrial relations picture.

Communications

The general problem of communications in a manufacturing concern is much too complex to attempt to cover here, but one of the aspects of this problem is getting information to employees. Two common methods of accomplishing this are the bulletin board and the company magazine or newspaper. Both of these usually come under the jurisdiction of the personnel department, which accounts for their inclusion under employee services.

The bulletin board is usually reserved for official notices on company or union affairs. Some companies provide a true employees' bulletin board where anyone can post a notice signifying his desire to sell a car, buy a boat, or give away a spare kitten. The company newspaper or magazine may contain some official information, but it is more apt to include material of general interest to employees. General news items concerning fellow employees, standings of the company softball team, and a feature article concerning Joe's vacation trip to Alaska will all be of interest.

Social Programs

Social programs vary in extent all the way from the annual company picnic to the employees' social club offering all varieties of social activities throughout the year. Parties, dances, and general get-togethers are designed in such a manner that every employee will find some feature enjoyable. Games and contests are arranged for all ages, with appropriate prizes being awarded the winners. Families become an important part of these affairs, as well as the employees themselves.

An overall employees' social and recreational club may oversee the entire social program, or there may be small clubs appealing to people with specialized interests. Garden clubs, stamp clubs, rifle clubs, and drama clubs are only a few of the possibilities. Such clubs would be separately organized, each carrying on its own program in its own field of interest. The nature of the club to which any one employee belongs would usually be determined by his hobby interests.

Musical activities are receiving increasing attention as part of social programs. Choral groups and orchestra groups provide enjoyment not only for the actual participants, but also for other employees who enjoy listening.

Athletic Programs

For those who desire active physical exertion, athletic programs are offered by many companies. Bowling and softball are the two of the more popular sports since they do not require the specialized skill of basketball or football. Competition is maintained between departments within a plant and also between plants. Industrial leagues for both bowling and softball are quite active in many communities.

Although the major sports may receive most of the attention and publicity, there is still a lot of room in the industrial recreation program for minor sports. Some, such as tennis, horseshoes, ping pong, and badminton, have a special appeal, for often they can be enjoyed during the noon hour and do not require after-hours arrangements. Other sports, such as swimming, hockey, and golf, have their appeal to those interested, but they require facilities and are definitely after-hours or week-end activities.

While the athletic programs mentioned will provide physical exercise for the participants, it is fairly common today for companies to have exercise programs and even provide the necessary facilities. These programs exist not only for recreation but for health reasons.

Eating Facilities

Companies situated in isolated areas or operating around the clock find it almost mandatory to offer restaurant or cafeteria services to their employees. To expect everyone to carry their lunch is too much in these days of emphasis on hot meals and good nutrition. Even without any special set of circumstances, companies provide eating facilities simply as a convenience. Less time is consumed in obtaining and eating the meal, and oftentimes the prices are less than in commercial establishments since the cafeteria is operated on a non-profit basis. There is never any compulsion to buy food in the company cafeteria, although all are invited to eat there even though they bring their lunches from home.

A·variation of the company cafeteria is the lunch wagon that circulates throughout the plant as a convenience to those employees who must eat on the job. Such wagons also provide the coffee and doughnuts for the daily rest period. This service eliminates the necessity of employees rushing to the neighborhood coffee shop and back.

The vending machine has had a phenomenal growth as a factor in food service and may replace both the lunch wagon and the cafeteria. Vending machines are now able to provide both hot and cold foods, and to the extent that their operators can provide good food at reasonable prices and keep the machines from breaking down, the vending machine may be the answer to the in-plant eating facility problem.

Professional Services

Of course, the medical service discussed earlier is a professional service, but there are a few others commonly provided. Legal advice is one of these and can be a real service, since employees seldom know what to do when faced with legal difficulties. Company legal departments do not carry out court actions, but simply make recommendations and perhaps help in selecting competent legal counsel to carry out the court action.

Another professional service sometimes offered is personnel counseling. The counselor might be anyone from a white-haired grandfather to a trained psychologist or ordained minister. The point is that someone is available to hear the employee's story and maybe offer a little advice. Experience has shown that a good listener can often be of more value to an employee who has a personal problem than an expert who gives advice freely.

Credit Union

It can hardly be said that a company offers a credit union to its employees, although a company may permit and cooperate in the formation of a credit union by the employees themselves. The credit union is really a small bank, licensed by a government agency and operated by employees for their own benefit. Employees can deposit money in the credit union and receive interest on it. In addition, loans can be obtained at rates less than those charged by private loan companies. Companies cooperate with the credit union and will make deductions from pay checks for the purpose of deposits or to pay off a loan. In this way, much of the bookwork is eliminated.

Policies Regarding Benefits and Services

Companies that adopt many of the benefits and services discussed in this chapter do so to gain certain returns—be they tangible or intangible. The maximum return will be obtained only if proper policies are followed in the installation and operation of the various benefits and services. There is no set of policies that will meet every situation; however, the following principles will be worthy of consideration in any situation.

No Substitute for Wages

There is *no substitute* for a sound wage structure, and this structure should stand on its own feet without help from any benefit and service program. Employees who feel they are not paid fair wages, that their hours are too long, or that working conditions are inadequate will not respond to the fringe offerings of the employer. Any doubts concerning employee reaction to wages, hours, and working conditions should be removed before benefit and service plans are seriously considered.

Fulfilling Need

In their more philanthropic moments, employers sometimes decide that their employees need a particular benefit or service. The decision may be correct in some cases, but, in general, such a method of determining need is unsound. Such an approach was used many years ago only to fail miserably and to be labeled "paternalism." The label continues to be applied in certain instances, even against the employer with the purest of intentions.

A more successful approach is to fulfill a request from employees for certain benefits or services. A recreation club will be much more successful if set up at the request of a group of employees than if set up because the employer feels the employees "need" it. Of course, an employer can and perhaps should do what he or she can to stimulate interest and in that way assist in the creation of a need. Hints dropped at the right time and place may grow to such an extent that everyone becomes convinced that the idea came from the employees themselves.

Competing Services

Closely related to the establishment of a need is the point that company benefits and services should not be set up in competition with benefits and services already adequately established in the community. There is no need to start a new hospitalization plan if coverage is already adequately provided by some community plan. By the same token, if the union has an active social program under way, there may be little need for a similar program sponsored by the company.

Financial Support

By their very nature, *benefits* will tend to have the complete financial support of the company. Employees may contribute to a certain extent, such as in contributory pension plans or in profit-sharing or stock-purchase plans that are tied in with employee savings. Following the collective bargaining history of any one company, however, one usually finds that year by year the employer pays a larger percentage of the benefit bill.

Services are a little different. These in particular should be established after employee request, and employees should be made to demonstrate their interest by contributing time, effort, and even money. Such contributions will make people work harder for the success of the endeavor and, of course, make employees feel that it is really *their* organization or activity.

A satisfactory way for service organizations to obtain financial support is through the proceeds of vending machines. Vending machines appear to be quite necessary in our plants today, and since companies never want to "make money" from their employees, contributing the profits to employee service organizations works out fine for all concerned.

Complete Coverage

One of the knotty problems concerning the establishment of service activities in a plant is the danger that the activities will serve only a few. Each clique or group satisfies its particular desire and worries little about the others. Coverage of service activities should be broad enough that everyone finds something of interest, even if only as a spectator. This is easier said than done, but it deserves consideration.

Sincerity

Our last and probably most important point is that the employer should enter into each benefit or service with complete sincerity and with a genuine desire to see it benefit the employees. If a plan is regarded as a "gimmick" to "keep 'em happy for a while" or to "keep out of the union," the plan as well as employer–employee relationships are doomed to failure. There is more to good industrial relations than a recreational building, a profit-sharing program, or a softball club. The substitute for a genuine interest in one's fellow human being—whether this be an employee or a neighbor—has yet to be found.

QUESTIONS

1. List several specific sources of employees in a community with which you are familiar. Briefly discuss the work of each source.
2. Comment on the role of each of the selection steps in hiring a floor sweeper. Do the same for hiring a welder.
3. Distinguish between on-the-job training and apprentice training.
4. Outline a training situation in a company where the use of a vestibule school would definitely pay off.
5. Why should a company concern itself with the general health of its employees?
6. List and explain the four "E's" of a good safety program.
7. Discuss the necessity of some arbitrary definition of accidents.
8. For what reasons would employees demand and employers grant fringe benefits such as insurance, pensions, and health programs instead of simply increasing wage rates?
9. Some companies have been accused of hiring new employees based on their ability to play basketball, bowl, or perform in other sports so as to strengthen the company team. Would you call this a good or a poor practice? Give your reasons.
10. Should a company store or cafeteria be operated on a profit basis? State your reasons either way.
11. How can an employer be certain that a new benefit or service fulfills a need?
12. Personnel management activities as described in this chapter have to be considered as overhead costs (see Chapter 17). Explain how a manager could and should "control" these costs.

CASE PROBLEMS

Lucas Products, Inc.

For the past ten years Mr. Paul Millis, the industrial relations director of Lucas Products, Inc., has been computing employee turnover according to the formula

$$\frac{\text{Number of replacements}}{\text{Average number on payroll}} \times 100$$

The computation was made on a monthly basis, and the average number of employees on the payroll was determined by averaging the number on the payroll the first day of the month with the number on the payroll the last day of the month.

Mr. Millis felt that this formula for employee turnover gave him a reliable indication of the overall efficiency and performance of industrial relations in the Lucas organization. He took pride each month in showing the general manager the current employee turnover figure and comparing it with the results of the last several years. And the record did look good. During the ten-year period, employee turnover had never exceeded 10% and in recent months had been running about 5%. Mr. Millis was careful to point out each month that he claimed no personal credit for this record but that the efforts of everyone, in particular the foremen and supervisors, made the record possible.

Yesterday a clerk gave Mr. Millis the turnover figure for last month and it showed a sharp rise to 9.6% from 4.3% for the previous month. Needless to say, Mr. Millis was shocked and immediately went to work to determine the causes. He knew he would have to do a lot of explaining when he next saw the general manager.

Questions:

1. In searching for causes for the sharp rise, what types of things should Mr. Millis look for?
2. Should Mr. Millis feel on the defensive concerning the sharp rise in employee turnover? Explain.
3. Was Mr. Millis correct in placing so much faith in this computation of employee turnover as a measure of overall efficiency and performance of industrial relations? Explain.
4. Can you think of any improvements in the calculation so it would more closely accomplish what Mr. Millis expected?
5. Would you agree that the turnover record of Lucas Products as described was a good one? Explain.

The Sieber Pen Company

The Sieber Pen Company has a plant located in a city of 10,000 population in eastern Kansas. For the past 25 years the company has been the principal employer in the community, and at present it employs about 1500 people. Approximately one-half of these are women, many of whom are under 21 years of age.

Sieber Pen Company has a reputation in the community as being a good place to work. The relations between the employees and the employer have always been congenial, and to date no serious attempt has been made to unionize the plant.

In an attempt to provide sound recreational facilities for its employees, the company built an employee recreation club containing a gym, squash courts, bowling alleys, billiard tables, shower rooms, a dining room and guest rooms, as well as a number of other facilities. All of the facilities, except the dining room and guest rooms, may be used by any employee without any dues or charge.

When the recreation club was first built, a considerable number of employees made use of its facilities; however, very few people have availed themselves of this privilege during recent years. The management has in part justified the existence of the club by using it as headquarters for dealers attending company training schools.

Within the past few months, word has reached top management that a number of workers have expressed a desire for an increase in the number of bowling alleys in the club so that an intra-plant bowling league may be organized. Also, inasmuch as the plant does not have a cafeteria, several employees have asked to have a cafeteria installed in the club so they can eat their lunch there. Employees can eat lunch in the dining room of the club, but the general feeling is that the dining room is too elegant for employees to use when attired in work clothes.

Questions:

1. Should the Sieber Pen Co. go ahead and install the requested extra facilities? How should they go about arriving at their decision?
2. What can be done to stimulate greater usage of the club's facilities?
3. How can the company evaluate the value of the club to the company and to the employees?
4. What recommendations can you make regarding the company's policies in regard to employee services?

Yeager and Bradshaw

In the mind of Charlie Yeager, President of Yeager and Bradshaw, the company had a terrible safety record. He met regularly with presidents of other companies in the Midwestern city where his plant was located, and it was clear to him from what the others told him that his company had one of the poorer records on safety.

One day about six months ago Charlie called in the company's safety director, Jim Sullivan, and explained his concern. He also pointed out the previous month's accident frequency rate of 21.8 and compared it with the record for the previous two years. In just glancing at the data, it appeared that last month's record was about the same as the company had experienced during the entire two years. In other words, there was no improvement, but fortunately it hadn't gone much higher either. Severity rates seemed to follow a similar pattern.

The meeting ended with Charlie charging Jim with the duty of coming up with a positive safety program that would have a real impact on the company's safety record. The firm implication to Jim was that he had better have a good program and show some results, or else Charlie would find someone that could produce some results.

Jim understood his situation thoroughly and so went to work with a program making use of the four "E's" of safety. He worked night and day on the assignment and secured much more cooperation from others in the company than he expected; so he was certain that improvements would show up in the data quite soon.

He computed the average of the frequency rates for the past two years, and it did turn out to be the 21.8 predicted earlier by inspection. The first month after inauguration of the program showed an increase to 21.9 and the second month a further increase to 22.4. However, the third month showed the rate to be down to 20.7, and Jim jumped for joy since here was clear evidence of significant improvement.

Jim promptly took the new data to Charlie's office and wasted no time in gloating over his accomplishment. Charlie listened to it all with apparent pleasure and made it a point to compliment Jim on all the various aspects of his safety program that he saw in evidence around the plant. In the end, however, he puzzled Jim greatly by asking the question, "Quite clearly, last month's frequency rate is less than the previous month's and even less than the average for the past two years, but is it significantly less? Maybe it is within the range of normal variations that we have been experiencing in frequency rates over the years."

Jim left the office almost more puzzled than normal. It sounded like Charlie knew something about significance that he didn't know, but he knew he would have to find out.

Questions:

1. Is 20.7 significantly less than 21.9?
2. What kind of information would one have to have in order to determine any significant difference between the two numbers?
3. Is it possible to "control" safety performance the same as one controls quality performance? (See Chapter 15.)
4. If one were to set up a control chart for accident frequency rates and found a point out of control on the low side, what corrective action would be called for?

19

LABOR RELATIONS

The total personnel program contains many facets. This chapter deals with the area generally known as labor relations and is concerned with the conditions of employment as arranged between the employer and groups of employees. The process of arranging for these conditions of employment is generally referred to as "collective bargaining," as contrasted to "individual bargaining." We usually think of collective bargaining taking place when a union is present. However, companies without a union representing their employees must still give considerable attention to the collective reactions of employees to the work conditions established.

Influence of Unions

Strangely enough, unions do not represent the bulk of workers. It is estimated that less than a quarter of the total labor force in the United States are members of trade unions. If agricultural workers are eliminated, organized labor consist of less than one-third of the work force. Furthermore, the labor unions have experienced some difficulty in recent years in increasing their membership on a percentage basis. Organized labor has consisted of not more than one-third of the non-agricultural work force for many years, and a 1984 survey indicated that the percentage had dropped to 27.2.

There are a number of reasons for this leveling off in the growth of labor union membership, but one particularly important reason is the changing nature of the American work force. With the advent of automation and the growth of service industries generally, the work force has tended to become more of the white collar type rather than blue collar, and white collar workers have generally resisted the organization drives of labor unions. Some success has been achieved among nurses, school teachers, college professors, and, in particular, persons working in the public sector. With changes in the organizing tactics of labor unions, perhaps more white collar types will become members. On the other hand, companies may become more successful in persuading their employees to identify themselves more with the company than with a trade union, and thereby reduce the role played by the union. The improvement of personnel programs by management has undoubtedly had its effect on the slowing down of the labor union movement; nonetheless, the presence of a union or the threat of a proposed union has made companies extremely interested in the subject of labor relations. Since all companies must abide by the law, whether or not a union is present, the law in connection with the work force is of particular interest.

Certainly, a company's success is dependent to a large extent upon the mutual understanding that can be developed between the management and workers as represented by the union. It is important, therefore, that management have some familiarity with union objectives, policies, and organization, as well as with the problems confronting the leaders of these unions. The following topics considered in this chapter will provide background information concerning unions, their operations, and the law that applies to both the company and the unions.

1. The union movement
2. The history of American unions
3. Independent unions
4. Union organization and operation
5. Union security
6. Economic weapons of the union
7. Labor law
8. Relations with the union

The Union Movement

Attempts have been made to trace the lineal descent of the trade-union movement of the nineteenth and twentieth centuries from the guilds of the Middle Ages; but trade unionism as we know it was clearly the creation of modern industrial conditions. It owes its birth to the capital system, and, viewed after more than a century of growth, it is seen as a sort of self-protection of workers against the complex economic changes that they may fail to understand. Labor unions were and are a defensive and offensive method for maintaining and improving working conditions. In recent years, however, they have become much more than simply that, for they are now an integral part of the machinery of industrial life. In addition, labor unions have become a significant part of our social and political lives as well.

The attitude of American law toward unions has been derived naturally from the English common law. There was a time when, by common law of England, combinations of working people were, with minor exceptions, regarded as illegal. They were considered to be contrary to public policy and fell into the category of "conspiracies in restraint of trade." Membership in such a body was punishable by fine and imprisonment, and although the common law applied to combinations of both masters and workers, it was against the workers that the law was later developed and directed. From the time of Edward I to the end of the first quarter of the nineteenth century there were more than thirty legal enactments that enforced and extended the common law in connection with labor unions, and all of these measures were designed to prohibit and prevent labor organizations.

Although unionism in America can be traced to colonial days, developments in the movement were generally several years behind English developments. American courts tended to hold the same view of unions as did English courts and ruled that unions were conspiracies until 1842. The decision of the Supreme Court in the *Commonwealth v. Hunt* case removed the conspiracy label from labor unions and opened the way to the growth of such bodies. Changes in public attitudes regarding unionism began to follow, and during the quarter century until the Civil War unionism grew gradually, together with many radical and utopian offshoots.

One such offshoot organization, called the Knights of Labor, was organized in 1869 as a secret group. It appeared in the open in 1880 as a union of all workers, skilled and unskilled, manual, clerical, and professional, and even of the small businessman. By 1886 the Knights had a membership close to one million and an influence far exceeding its size. But it had neither the financial resources nor the staff to carry out its basic objective, the organization of all workers.

Support for the Knights of Labor came largely from a spontaneous uprising of workers, and when strikes ended in failure and strikers lost their jobs, the inability of the Knights to provide assistance made it exceedingly difficult to arouse enthusiasm for the organization. Much of the attention and energy of the officers of the organization was dissipated in carrying out the various economic programs of the Knights, which dealt with everything from central trade union action to schemes for reorganization of the currency and banking system of the country. The Knights ran into further trouble when they attempted to take over the jurisdiction of the various craft unions that existed in the country at that time.

Probably the main contribution of the Knights of Labor to the union movement in this country was that their mistakes later served as guidelines to the founders of the American Federation of Labor.

The History of American Unions

The direct forerunner of the American Federation of Labor (hereafter referred to as AFL) was the Federation of Organized Trades and Labor Unions, begun in 1881. The AFL appeared on the scene in 1886 under the leadership of Samuel Gompers and his associates. Mr. Gompers was elected its first president and is considered the "father of the American labor movement."

Previously, the Knights sought to absorb the existing craft unions, to remove their autonomy, and to involve them in industrial disputes in which their own interests were apparently not at stake. The AFL benefited from the mistakes of the Knights and organized a loose federation of the various craft unions, which remained for half a century the sole unifying agency of the American labor movement. The AFL followed a policy of "business unionism," and made it a point to keep out of political entanglements other than using votes for "rewarding friends." Union leaders devoted their efforts to improving wages, hours, and working conditions.

The national and international unions within the AFL were originally composed mainly of skilled crafts workers. Futhermore, most of these unions were opposed to the addition of industrial workers or unskilled workers into the AFL ranks. Much of this opposition was due to the fear of the crafts groups that their status would be weakened by bringing in the less skilled workers from the mass production industries. Nevertheless, there was considerable interest in the many thousands of workers in the mass production industries, which were then unorganized, and in 1935 John L. Lewis, president of the mineworkers, together with the presidents of seven other unions, formed a Committee for Industrial Organizations within the AFL structure.

The Committee was organized as a protest against the failure of the AFL organizing campaign and its unwillingness to grant full jurisdictional rights to the new unions in mass production industries. It hoped to demonstrate the feasibility of organizing non-union industries and to protect the young industrial unions from attacks from the older craft unions. There was no intent to do this outside the AFL, but later events indicated otherwise.

A few months after its formation the CIO undertook its first campaign and met with great success. The AFL still refused to recognize the organization of the CIO despite its organizing success and declared that its activities were outside the lawful rights of its constituent unions. The Committee was ordered to disband under the threat of suspension and eventual expulsion if it failed to comply. When the CIO unions defied this order in 1938, they all were expelled. Shortly thereafter, the expelled unions, along with some other unions, set up a rival federation of labor and challenged the jurisdiction of the AFL in all industries and occupations. In November 1938, it held its first constitutional convention and changed its name to the Congress of Industrial Organizations. By 1939 the CIO claimed at least fifty affiliated national unions and more than four million members.

During the ensuing years competition for members caused bitter jurisdictional clashes between the AFL and CIO union groups. By tradition, the AFL was thought of as a craft union organization and the CIO as an industrial union organization, but their organizational clashes soon broke down these traditional barriers, since the main concern of each was to gain additional members. The CIO made a particular effort to gain the support of minority groups by trying to avoid racial and religious discrimination. It also encouraged political activity by unions at all levels. Although political activity on the part of unions was curbed somewhat by the Taft-Hartley Act in 1947, unions still participated in political campaigns by endorsing candidates sympathetic to labor and attempting to persuade their members to vote for these candidates.

Rivalries between the AFL and CIO did much to mar the public image of the American labor movement, and there was considerable public pressure to merge the two groups. After a number of faltering efforts, the two groups were reunited in 1955 into a single AFL-CIO organization. The merger at the top, however, did not solve all the problems throughout the organization. Competition between unions and individual labor leaders created many problems, and some of these remain to this day in spite of the settlement of the jurisdictional and "no raiding" disputes among the affiliates.

Independent Unions

Although the majority of national labor unions are affiliated with the AFL-CIO organization, a number of them remain independent and unaffiliated. The most outstanding examples are the teamsters and the railway unions. Other unions go in and out of the AFL-CIO organization owing to differences in policies, accusations of being Communist-dominated, and various other reasons. This makes it difficult to keep an accurate count as to the number of affiliated and unaffiliated unions.

Another type of independent union is commonly referred to as a "company" union. In past years the term company union referred to one accused of being a company-dominated union. The domination of a union by a company is now illegal under federal labor law, and so a company union is now, technically, a union whose membership is limited to the employees of a particular company. Many such unions exist and are just as vigorous in representing their members as any other union. Needless to say, an AFL-CIO organizer would disagree with this statement, for he would argue that affiliation with the larger labor organization brings considerably more pressure to bear upon the employer concerned. On the other hand, many members of such company unions like their present arrangement inasmuch as they do not have to contribute dues to the national organization and they can pursue their particular interests and local concerns without interference from a national representative.

Union Organization and Operation

Except for those unions that are local in scope, a union organization typically consists of a parent organization known as the national or international union and a group of affiliated unions. Groups having locals in Canada refer to themselves as international unions. Local unions are the basic units within the national unions and have considerable strength by virtue of the united efforts that they can exert through the national union.

The national union is the primary source of authority and control within the union organization, and its constitution provides the rules and conditions that must be met before the local unions can be admitted to the national organization. Further regulations are often imposed upon the local in regard to the collection of dues, the admission of members, and the need to bargain with employers for standard provisions in the labor contract. National unions also provide many services and forms of assistance to the locals. These may be in the form of technical assistance and contract negotiation and administration, financial assistance during periods of organizing drives or strikes, and education and publicity guidance.

The local union is the organizational unit that has direct contact with employers and workers, and to both groups is probably "the union." The officers of the local union are workers within the company or plant involved and are well known to the company management. Management and the union bargaining committee negotiate the labor contract, although the union may receive outside help from representatives of the national union. The local union has its own charter, and its bylaws must be written in accordance with the national organization's constitution. In smaller unions the officers hold full-time jobs and often perform their union duties without pay. In larger unions the major officers may be full-time employees of the union.

Two union officials worthy of special mention are the business agent and the union steward. These are the union officials with whom employers have the most frequent and direct contact, and their attitude and behavior can be an important factor in the degree of cooperation and harmony between the company and the union. The business agent is elected by the members of the local and is employed full time to administer the business affairs of the local union. Usually she has worked her way up within the local organization and has held other offices. She may exercise a stronger influence within the local than any of the other officers because of her experience and background. Her duties include not only seeing that the labor contract is followed by the employer, but helping to prepare for and conduct negotiations for new contracts. She processes members' grievances in many cases and serves as general administrator for the union office. In other words, she frequently serves as "all things to all persons" within the union.

The union steward or "shop steward" is technically a union representative rather than an officer of the union. He represents the union in his designated area of the plant and becomes the union counterpart of his foreman in that particular area. He is responsible for seeing that the rights of the members whom he represents are protected, and that the grievances of these members are processed properly. In so doing, most of his relationships are with the foremen of the departments involved. The steward is generally elected by the members within the area that he represents, and this area may vary depending upon the number of members working in a plant. Many plants have a number of stewards, in which case a chief steward is usually designated to coordinate the activities of the various shop stewards. Obviously, the steward has a key role to play in the union organization. However, some unions have found it difficult to get capable members to accept the added responsibility and problems of this position. Shop stewards usually serve without pay, although most labor contracts allow them time to handle union business at company expense.

Union Security

Every union wishes to gain maximum recognition and security in its relation with employers. The degree of recognition and security achieved by unions is an important factor in determining their ability to bargain for further concessions from an employer and to enforce demands when these bargaining efforts fail. The degree of security also affects a union's ability to withstand similar bargaining and economic pressures that the employer may exert.

Below are listed and briefly discussed the many forms of union security that are in existence today. The following discussions are general, and many contracts may introduce a great number of variations in any particular form of union security. Also, we refer to security for the union as an organization only, and security for the individual worker or union member is a different matter. The nine items are listed roughly in order of increasing degree of union security.

1. Closed non-union shop. Strictly speaking, this item does not belong on the list since it offers no union security and is, in fact, just the reverse of union security. In this situation the employer runs the shop in such a manner that anyone belonging to a union either is not hired or is fired should they join a union after being employed. The employer, thus, clearly discriminates against union members. This employment situation has been illegal since 1935. Obviously, if union discrimination is a violation of the law, unions are in a stronger position to press for one of the true forms of union security.

2. Open shop. The open shop is an employment situation wherein employees of the company are able to join or not to join a union as they wish. The company does not discriminate against union members, and by the same token individual members can bargain directly with the employer. Several states have passed what are known as "right to work" laws, which forbid any employee from being forced to join a union in order to hold his job. In those states, therefore, a form of open shop is mandatory.

3. Dues checkoff. The dues checkoff is an arrangement whereby an employee authorizes the company to deduct union dues from his or her paycheck and turn it over to the union directly. Under the Taft-Hartley Act, a union cannot compel its members to pay its dues in this manner. However, most members usually authorize the employer to make the deduction if such an arrangement is available. The checkoff is a considerable advantage to the union inasmuch as it assures the union an income and reduces the work of collecting dues individually from each member. Employers are generally cooperative in making these dues deductions, for they benefit by eliminating the need for soliciting dues by union members, frequently done on company time, and by eliminating the need to discharge any employee because of failure to pay dues. Such a discharge requirement would exist only if one of the other higher forms of union security were in effect. The dues checkoff usually occurs fairly early in union–management relationships and remains throughout such relationships. In other words, although the dues checkoff is listed as number three in order of increasing union security, it continues to exist throughout the remaining other forms in most instances.

4. Bargaining for members only.   This type of shop arrangement involves only limited recognition for a union, for the presence of the union is simply acknowledged by the management. Although technically the union has a right to bargain for those employees who are members only, it is difficult to visualize a concession being made to union members and being withheld from non-union members in today's industrial environment.

5. Exclusive bargaining shop.   As the name implies, this arrangement is such that the union is not only recognized as the bargaining agent for its members, but acts as the bargaining agent for all employees whether or not they are members of the union. This arrangement does not force employees to join the union, nor does it force the employer to give union members any special treatment. It does require the employer to bargain exclusively with the union in regard to all employment conditions.

6. Maintenance of membership shop.   Under this arrangement an employer may hire whomever he wishes, and employees are not required to join the union as a condition of employment. However, a cutoff date is provided after which those employees who are union members must retain their membership in the union during the life of the contract or suffer loss of their jobs. Such a provision protects the union against having empolyees drop their membership while the contract is in effect.

7. Agency shop.   The agency shop does not require employees to be members of the union as a condition of employment, but it does require them to pay equivalent dues to the union. The reasoning behind such an arrangement is that the union, acting as bargaining agent for all employees, has been able to secure certain benefits that are enjoyed by non-union members as well as union members. The cost of securing these benefits, therefore, should not be borne alone by the union members, but by the non-union employees as well. Payment of equivalent dues to the union then provides support for the bargaining efforts without forcing the employee to become a member of the union. The agency shop has come into use only during recent years and is undoubtedly the union's answer to the view that no employee should be forced to join a union as a condition of employment; however, unions will always press for the union shop.

8. Union shop.   A union shop clause in a contract would specify that all employees in a bargaining unit must become members within a certain period of time after employment. According to the Taft-Hartley Act, this can be no less than thirty days. Under today's federal law the union shop arrangement gives a union the highest degree of union security that is legal. Certainly, in a situation where all employees must become members of the union eventually, the union has considerable strength and is able to maintain control and discipline among its members. True, in this situation employees have been required to join a union as a condition of employment, and to many people such an arrangement not only gives the union too much power but is not consistent with concepts of American freedom. On the other hand, many employers prefer a union shop arrangement, since it eliminates certain difficulties that otherwise exist when a union is forced to fight for its status.

9. Closed shop.   Under a closed shop arrangement an employer can hire only union members for his employees. Although made illegal by the passage of the Taft-Hartley Act in 1947, in actuality many closed shop arrangements still exist throughout the country today. While probably no union contract exists that specifically enumerates a closed shop arrangement, the practical workings between union and management result in a closed shop. This is particularly true in what may be called the "casual trades," or those situations where employees do not enjoy any form of tenure for long periods of time. The employer finds it much easier to call the union and ask it to send over the number of workers desired than to recruit workers from the general market. Both the employer and the union benefit from the arrangement, so there are few complaints. The persons who suffer from the arrangement are workers who would like to get good jobs in a trade but are unable to do so inasmuch as the union will not admit them as members.

Another illegal arrangement that sometimes occurs is referred to as a "preferential shop." This is an arrangement whereby union members are given preferential treatment in various phases of their employment. Such treatment might occur in the hiring of new personnel, promotions, or priority in layoffs and rehirings. The arrangement provides a certain degree of security for the union involved and might appropriately be listed in our hierarchy of types of security between numbers four and five. As mentioned, the arrangement is illegal, since under the law employers cannot discriminate in favor of a union member any more than they can discriminate against a union member.

Economic Weapons of the Union

On the whole, employers and unions settle their differences through peaceful and voluntary means. However, in certain circumstances one side or the other may bring economic pressure to bear in an attempt to force the other to concede. Unions bring economic pressure upon employers by (1) striking against them, (2) picketing them, or (3) boycotting their products and encouraging others to do so. These forms of union economic pressure are discussed briefly in the following paragraphs. Employers can bring economic pressure on unions by shutting down operations and laying off employees. This is commonly termed a "lockout" and is rarely used, although the threat of a lockout perhaps is always present. It has been used most commonly by employers within an association to support one of its members that has been struck by a union.

Like the strike, the lockout is really a sort of tool for negotiating while fully expecting to get back into operation at some later date and continuing business as before. Sometimes, however, economic conditions (and poor management) force the company to the brink, and they feel compelled to go to employees with what is essentially a demand for a sizeable reduction in wages or else close down the plant. (Frequently, this is referred to as concessionary bargaining.) Many employees (and their unions) have accepted such demands, feeling that this saves their jobs, and that perhaps later they can gain back what they lost. A classic case is the Chrysler Corporation situation. In other cases, such as National Homes Corporation, employees (and their unions) turned down the demand, only to have the plant closed.

Simply defined, a strike is the refusal of employees to perform their jobs. Strikes may be held informally by any group of employees, or in a more organized fashion, by a union. Success of the strike depends upon the ability of the strikers to keep the employer from continuing to operate. The general trend has been toward a reduction in the number of strikes. If the employer continues to operate through the use of supervisory personnel or by hiring other employees, obviously much of the impact of the strike is lost.

Picketing is almost a standard practice when a union strikes an employer. Persons are placed at the entrances of the employer's plant to give notice of the dispute and to discourage others from entering or leaving the premises. Many times the striking employees represent only a small portion of the total employees of the plant, but the non-striking employees will often refuse to cross the picket line, thereby helping to exert pressure upon the employer. Even more pressure is brought to bear upon the employer when the employees of other companies refuse to cross the picket line as they made deliveries or pick up goods from the employer. Obviously, refusal to cross the picket line is a basic tenet of the union movement, and most union members are generally receptive to the practice of supporting other unions. This is not always the case, however, as when rival unions are involved, or when individuals are involved who consider it more important to work than to simply respect a union principle.

Peaceful picketing is generally regarded by the courts as a form of free speech, but sometimes picketing is not peaceful. Employees who attempt to cross the line may be subjected to insults or even physical violence. Mass picketing has been employed whereby the pickets become so numerous that the path of anyone attempting to enter the plant is blocked physically. Pickets are usually union members, but sometimes unions employ outsiders to picket for them and are known to select them particularly for their physical attributes of size and strength. Such practices usually result in court action and also do much to arouse unfavorable public opinion against the union and its activities.

Boycotting is another economic weapon employed by unions that may adversely affect an employer. A manufacturer who is able to continue operating during a strike by hiring non-union workers might find his market considerably reduced if the striking union members were to refuse to buy the product of the manufacturer and were successful in influencing other onion members to do the same. Such a practice on the part of unions is technically termed a primary boycott and is considered legal. Should the union go further, however, and boycott other employers with whom it does not have a labor dispute in an effort to force them not to patronize a second employer with whom the union does have a dispute, the appropriate term would be a *secondary boycott;* this is declared illegal under the Taft-Hartley Act.

Labor Law

Like other forms of jurisprudence in this country, labor law developed through the common law, or that body of law that came through custom or through the precedence of previous court decisions. Our early common law in turn derived largely from the English common law, and in the case of labor unions tended to favor employers and not unions. The efforts of employees to form unions to bargain collectively with employers were interpreted as being criminal acts of conspiracy until the *Commonwealth v. Hunt* decision in 1842. That decision, along with growing union strength and an apparent change in public attitude, meant the beginning of a body of statutory law that tended to give recognition to unions and establish their right to bargain collectively with employers. For the most part, the federal government led the way in the field of labor legislation, with the states playing a secondary role. The federal government has exercised control over labor relations by virtue of two authorities: the regulation of interstate commerce and the control the federal government has over public contracts.

Perhaps the most important legal victory for the union movement came in 1887 when the Interstate Commerce Act was passed. This gave the federal government the right to settle labor disputes in the railroad industry. Specific railway legislation was passed later which will be discussed in the next section. As time went on, however, the Supreme Court interpreted the federal government's authority in interstate commerce to cover a broader and broader area, and it is undoubtedly these interpretations which allow the federal government to be predominant in the labor legislation area.

The second method by which the federal government influences labor relations is through its control over the conditions of employment in public contracts. These are contracts with the federal government to supply materials or to perform construction work. It is logical that the federal government should have the right to specify the terms of these contracts and the employment conditions to be observed by the successful bidder. The conditions of employment covered by these contracts are generally more restrictive than those specified in the broader federal labor laws. Contractors must therefore choose between keeping their work on the public contract separate from their other work, or simply meeting the stricter conditions for all employees, regardless of what contract they are fulfilling. An example would be overtime pay for a workday longer than eight hours. The general labor law on wages and hours specifies that overtime will be paid for work longer than 40 hours per week, but the public contract acts specify that overtime pay shall be paid for work either over 40 hours per week, or over 8 hours per day. Obviously, most employers follow the more restrictive public contract proviso. (There has been some movement in Congress, however, to change the public contract laws—particularly the overtime provisions.) The various acts dealing with public contracts are discussed in Chapter 20.

Railway Labor Legislation

The Arbitration Act of 1888 was the first federal labor legislation. It requested that disputes in railway and other transportation industries be resolved by submitting them to an arbitration board, provided that such action was agreeable to both parties. If the voluntary arbitration was not agreeable, the law gave the President the power to appoint a commission to investigate the dispute. The arbitration provisions were never exercised, but a commission was appointed in 1894 to investigate the Pullman strike, and that commission report led to the replacement of the Arbitration Act with the Erdman Act in 1898. The Erdman Act set up a permanent mediation and conciliation commission to handle the voluntary arbitration of railway labor disputes. It provided for a cooling-off period in the event of a dispute and permitted court enforcement of the arbitration awards. It also had a provision forbidding the use of yellow dog contracts, which employees were sometimes required to sign, whereby they agreed not to join the labor union. This clause was later declared unconstitutional by the Supreme Court, but its inclusion in the Erdman Act is significant in the development of labor law.

A number of laws dealing with railway labor problems were enacted in 1913 and 1916, but these were all finally consolidated into the Railway Labor Act of 1926. As well as providing for the peaceful settlement of disputes, this act also included specific provisions guaranteeing railway employees the right to organize and bargain collectively through their representatives. Railroads were forbidden to interfere with union organization or to require their employees to sign yellow dog contracts. The act was therefore an important piece of labor legislation, for it was the first to provide for the protection of employee bargaining rights. It was amended in 1934, after which the protection of bargaining rights was assigned to a new national mediation board, and a national railway adjustment board was created to handle grievances and labor disputes. For many years the Railway Labor Act was cited as a model act for maintaining labor peace. However, the nationwide railway strike in 1946, as well as many railway disputes since, have shown that this act is not the panacea for solving union–management difficulties as had been thought previously. In fact, labor disputes in other national welfare areas, such as those involving dock workers and teamsters, have generated considerable interest in the development of special procedures to provide settlement without damaging the economy so severely.

Background of Federal Labor Law

The current law governing union–management relations is the outgrowth of earlier antitrust legislation as well as labor legislation. Some of the more important legislative acts that provide this background are the (1) Sherman Antitrust Act of 1890, (2) Clayton Act of 1914, (3) Norris-LaGuardia Act of 1932, and (4) National Industrial Recovery Act of 1933. It is ironical that one of the first laws to affect the activities of labor unions was one aimed primarily at controlling business monopolies. There is some controversy as to whether Congress intended the Sherman Antitrust Act of 1890 to apply to labor unions. However, in 1908 the Supreme Court ruled that labor unions were subject to its provisions. The Court's historic decision in the Danbury Hatters case gave the company $252,000 in compensation for losses suffered as the result of a boycott undertaken by the union. This decision naturally reduced the bargaining power of labor unions by nullifying one of their economic weapons, the boycott.

After these developments unions waged a vigorous campaign to be exempted from the provisions of the Sherman Antitrust Act, and their efforts were rewarded by the inclusion of certain key sections in the passage of the Clayton Act of 1914. These sections exempted labor from antitrust prosecution, curbed the power of the federal courts to issue injunctions against unions, and granted the right of a jury trial to persons who were charged with contempt of court for violating a court injunction. While passage of the Clayton Act was first hailed as an outstanding victory for labor, later Supreme Court decisions ruled that the act did not give labor unions complete exemption from antitrust prosecution. The Supreme Court ruled that certain activities of the unions, such as the boycott, which were proved to be in restraint of trade, were still subject to both injunctions and prosecution. It was not until 1932 that organized labor obtained the protection from injunctions that it had hoped to gain from the Clayton Act.

The Norris-LaGuardia Act

The Norris-LaGuardia Act of 1932 was the first of a number of legislative enactments that improved considerably the status of unions during the thirties. The passage of this act, and the fact that it was later upheld by the Supreme Court, finally gave the unions protection from injunctions, which they had long sought. During earlier years, the injunction was the main device used by employers to fight unions, for injunctions were easily obtained from judges who were prone to protect property rights and who felt that strikes and boycotts interfered with these rights. The Norris-LaGuardia Act does not prohibit federal courts from issuing injunctions, but it did establish such rigid requirements in regard to their use that the injunction ceased to be a threat.

The Norris-LaGuardia Act also contained a clause long sought by labor unions, namely, the banning of the yellow dog contract. When it upheld this provision of the act, the Supreme Court reversed itself from earlier decisions.

The National Industrial Recovery Act

The National Industrial Recovery Act of 1933 was one of the first pieces of legislation passed in the Roosevelt Administration and was an attempt by the federal government to promote economic recovery by permitting industries to establish regulatory codes concerning their operation. Organized labor was recognized in the famous Section 7-A of the act. This section endorsed the concept of collective bargaining and the right of employees to join organizations without employer interference. It established a national labor board to help settle disputes and to handle employee representation problems as well as cases of violation under the act. The National Industrial Recovery Act was later declared unconstitutional in its entirety, but in 1935 the section dealing with labor was lifted and passed as the Wagner Act, which remains the law of the land today. The Wagner Act goes considerably beyond the NIRA provision, but the basic philosophy is the same.

The Wagner Act

The primary aim of the National Labor Relations Act (Wagner Act) was to place the support of the federal government behind the efforts of workers to organize and bargain collectively. In addition, the act was designed to curtail some of the weapons employers used to resist the efforts of their employees to form unions and bargain collectively. The one-sided nature of the act simply reflected the sympathetic attitudes toward organized labor at the time.

The most important feature of the act was the guarantee that it gave to employees in exercising their right of collective bargaining. The following quotation is taken from Section 7 of the act: ''Employees shall have the right to self organization, to form, join, or assist labor organizations to bargain collectively through representatives of their own choosing, and to engage in concerted activities, for the purpose of collective bargaining or other mutual aid or protection . . .''

Section 8 of the act attempted to make this guarantee more specific and listed five employer activities that were considered to be in violation of the bargaining rights of employees. These were defined as unfair labor practices and include the following: (1) to interfere with, restrain, or coerce employees in the exercise of the rights guaranteed in Section 7; (2) to dominate or interfere with the formation or administration of any labor organization or contribute financial or other support to it; (3) to encourage or discourage membership in any labor organization by discrimination in regard to hiring or tenure of employment or any term or condition of employment; (4) to discharge or otherwise discriminate against an employee because he or she has filed charges or given testimony under this act; (5) to refuse to bargain collectively with the duly chosen representatives of employees.

The Wagner Act also established a national labor relations board whose functions remain about the same under the Taft-Hartley Act as they were with the Wagner Act, namely, (1) determination of bargaining units, (2) elections for representation, and (3) unfair labor practices.

Taft-Hartley Act

The Wagner Act and its interpretations by the National Labor Relations Board were so one-sided in favor of labor that by 1947 the Act was amended by the Labor-Management Relations Act, more commonly referred to as the Taft-Hartley Act, in an attempt to make the labor law of the land fair to both sides. All of the provisions of the Wagner Act remained in effect under the Taft-Hartley Act, but certain provisions have been added that give additional rights to employees, employers, and unions, and protection for the public. Brief statements of some of these provisions are listed below:

Provisions giving employees rights in addition to above:

1. Closed shop is outlawed.
2. Checkoff permissible only after authorization by the employee.
3. Excessive union initiation fees prohibited.
4. Employee can process grievances alone or through union.
5. Employee can be dismissed in a union shop only after nonpayment of initiation fees and dues.
6. Union members entitled to annual union financial reports.
7. Employee welfare funds must be administered through joint employer union board.

Rights of employer:

1. Can express self on union matters as long as no threat or coercion to union members is implied.
2. Can discharge employees who engage in illegal strikes.
3. Can ask N.L.R.B. for vote to determine bargaining agent.
4. Can insist that unions also bargain in good faith.
5. Can sue unions in federal court.
6. Is free from rules requiring that pay be given for work not done.
7. May refuse to bargain with unions representing supervisors.

Rights to unions under proper conditions:

1. Can ask N.L.R.B. for recognition election.
2. Can require employer to bargain in good faith.
3. Represent all employees eligible to vote.
4. Maintain status for one year without fear of jurisdictional dispute.
5. Represent employees in processing grievances.
6. File charges with N.L.R.B. against unfair labor practices.
7. Call strikes.

Protection provided for the public:
Strikes affecting public health and safety can be delayed for 80 days while a special board investigates and reports.

Figure 19-1 outlines the processing of unfair labor charges through the National Labor Relations Board.

Labor Reform Act

The only significant addition to labor law since passage of the Taft-Hartley Act of 1947 has been passage of the Labor–Management Reporting and Disclosure Act of 1959, more commonly known as the Labor Reform Act. This act resulted from findings of congressional investigations regarding the activities of union leaders. Many instances of theft or embezzlement of union funds were uncovered, and it was felt that union members needed protection from their own leaders. The main provisions of the law govern the handling of union funds and regulate the activities of union officers in positions of trust. The principal technique employed is disclosure. Every union must file annually with the Secretary of Labor a detailed financial report. In addition, it must make the information contained in the report available to each of its members. Another provision is that the union officers and employees must file annual reports of all conflict of interest transactions in which they or their wives or children have engaged. Theft or embezzlement of union funds is expressly made a crime, punishable by fine and imprisonment.

Relations with the Union

Normal relations with unions usually entail (1) negotiating labor contracts, (2) processing grievances, (3) day-to-day relations with employees and union officials.

In some companies negotiation of labor union contracts can be a full-time job in itself. No sooner is a contract signed than it is time to begin thinking about the next bargaining session. In fact, in companies having very successful union–management relationships, bargaining is essentially a continuous operation, with the

BASIC PROCEDURES IN CASES INVOLVING
CHARGES OF UNFAIR LABOR PRACTICES

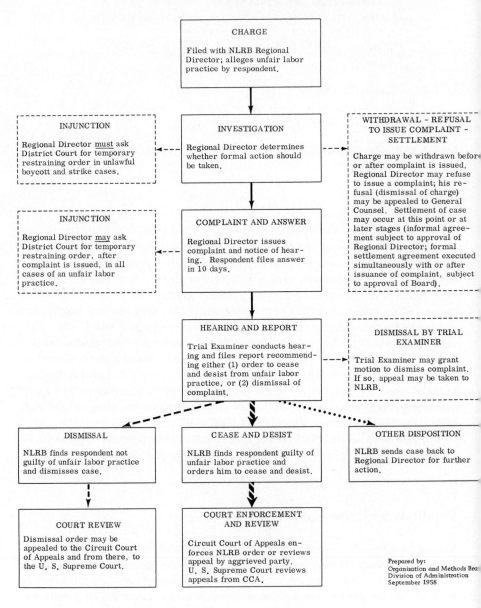

CHARGE

Filed with NLRB Regional
Director; alleges unfair labor
practice by respondent.

INJUNCTION

Regional Director <u>must</u> ask
District Court for temporary
restraining order in unlawful
boycott and strike cases.

INVESTIGATION

Regional Director determines
whether formal action should
be taken.

**WITHDRAWAL - REFUSAL
TO ISSUE COMPLAINT -
SETTLEMENT**

Charge may be withdrawn before
or after complaint is issued.
Regional Director may refuse
to issue a complaint; his refusal (dismissal of charge)
may be appealed to General
Counsel. Settlement of case
may occur at this point or at
later stages (informal agreement subject to approval of
Regional Director; formal
settlement agreement executed
simultaneously with or after
issuance of complaint, subject
to approval of Board).

INJUNCTION

Regional Director <u>may</u> ask
District Court for temporary
restraining order, after
complaint is issued, in all
cases of an unfair labor
practice.

COMPLAINT AND ANSWER

Regional Director issues
complaint and notice of hearing. Respondent files answer
in 10 days.

HEARING AND REPORT

Trial Examiner conducts hearing and files report recommending either (1) order to cease
and desist from unfair labor
practice, or (2) dismissal of
complaint.

**DISMISSAL BY TRIAL
EXAMINER**

Trial Examiner may grant
motion to dismiss complaint.
If so, appeal may be taken to
NLRB.

DISMISSAL

NLRB finds respondent not
guilty of unfair labor practice
and dismisses case.

CEASE AND DESIST

NLRB finds respondent guilty of
unfair labor practice and
orders him to cease and desist.

OTHER DISPOSITION

NLRB sends case back to
Regional Director for further
action.

COURT REVIEW

Dismissal order may be
appealed to the Circuit Court
of Appeals and from there, to
the U. S. Supreme Court.

**COURT ENFORCEMENT
AND REVIEW**

Circuit Court of Appeals en-
forces NLRB order or reviews
appeal by aggrieved party.
U. S. Supreme Court reviews
appeals from CCA.

Prepared by:
Organization and Methods Bran
Division of Administration
September 1958

Figure 19–1. Processing of unfair labor charges through the NLRB.

formal signing of a contract taking place at periodic intervals. Figure 19-2 contains the table of contents from a typical union contract. From this list, one can see the range of matters that are considered bargainable under modern labor relations, and the list expands yearly.

One section of most labor contracts usually deals with the matter of grievances. A "grievance" is an official complaint filed by an employee or by the union in regard to an action taken by management or to an interpretation of the labor contract. Basically, a grievance can be considered a difference of opinion between the company and the union on some matter. Of course such differences occur all the time, but when they become "official" differences of opinion, a grievance procedure is specified in order to settle the issue. Figure 19-3 outlines a typical grievance procedure. Final settlement will take place under a procedure such as this, since in the last step the issue is placed before an impartial arbitrator who must make a decision. If the parties do not like the arbitrator's decision, they are free to negotiate over the item at the next contract-signing time. In the meantime, however, both parties are committed to abide by the arbitrator's decision. Both parties are usually anxious to settle any issue before it reaches the arbitration step and will spend a great deal of time investigating and discussing the issues during each of the preceding steps in the grievance procedure. One can see that if there are many grievances active at any one time, union officials and company officials alike will be spending considerable time processing them and attempting to get them settled.

There is indeed more to labor relations than negotiating for signed labor contracts and processing grievances. In addition to these rather formal aspects, day-to-day matters arise that must be handled with labor union officials or with employees directly. This type of work usually entails interpreting the labor contract, or arriving at a mutually agreeable solution to a problem in the absence of a clear-cut method for handling it in the contract. The way in which these daily contacts and daily compromises are handled makes the difference between strictly formal labor relations conducted at "arm's length" and the sincere, informal "let's get our problem solved" type. Examples of both types appear in the news practically every day. Some companies and unions always seem to be at odds with one another, with strikes, shutdowns, and controversy being the usual thing. Other relationships seem to go on year after year without these outward evidences of internal strife. There is no known sure answer for the achievement of "labor peace," but experience seems to indicate that a genuine and sincere attempt, day by day, to work with department stewards and union officials in the handling of mutual problems will do much to achieve that nebulous goal. This cooperative effort seems to be on the increase in recent years, probably brought about by the harsher economic times or possibly by a more sincere interest in labor peace.

This is not to imply that a company *must* have its employees represented by a labor union in order that good relations exist between management and workers. Many companies have been and still are operating with no labor union involved—and doing so successfully as far as good relations are concerned. Some large

Article I. Bargaining Unit, Recognition and Union Membership
    Section 1—Bargaining Unit
    Section 2—Recognition
    Section 3—Union membership

Article II. Employees' *Definitions*
    Section 1—"Employee" *defined*
    Section 2—"Regular employee" *defined*
    Section 3—"Temporary employee" *defined*

Article III. Wages
    Section 1—Wage scales
    Section 2—Incentive pay
    Section 3—Off-standard work, down time, and waiting time
    Section 4—Rates for new machines
    Section 5—Report-in pay
    Section 6—Pay on temporarily assigned jobs
    Section 7—Shift differentials
    Section 8—Rest periods
    Section 9—Holiday pay

Article IV. Check-Off

Article V. Hours of Work
    Section 1—Normal workday
    Section 2—Normal work week
    Section 3—Scheduling and division of overtime

Article VI. Standards
    Section 1—Standards now in effect
    Section 2—Standards for new jobs
    Section 3—Review of standards

Article VII. Vacations
    Section 1—Eligibility
    Section 2—Vacation pay
    Section 3—Vacation period

Article VIII. Seniority
    Section 1—Seniority list
    Section 2—Temporary employees
    Section 3—Layoff
    Section 4—Available jobs
    Section 5—Transfers to and from supervision
    Section 6—New jobs and vacancies
    Section 7—Seniority after leave of absence
    Section 8—Union officers seniority
    Section 9—Incapacitated employees
    Section 10—Job elimination
    Section 11—Employees in armed forces

Article IX. Management of Plant
    Section 1—Management in charge of employer
    Section 2—"Proper cause for reduction, suspension, and discharge" *defined*
    Section 3—Absenteeism

Figure 19–2. Table of contents of typical union contract.

Article X. Adjustment of Grievances
Section 1—Local committees
Section 2—Procedure
Section 3—Time limit for filing grievances

Article XI. No-Strike Clause
Section 1—Use of grievance procedure
Section 2—No strikes or lockouts
Section 3—Limitation of union
Section 4—Discharge of wildcat strikers

Article XII. General Provisions
Section 1—Clock punching
Section 2—Leaving department
Section 3—Union bulletin boards
Section 4—Pensions and insurance
Section 5—Safety and sanitation

Article XIII. Duration

Figure 19–2. (continued)

companies with scattered plants will have some plants organized by labor unions and others not—again with apparent success. Why unions get started in one plant and not in another is beyond the scope of this treatment. Let us simply point out that successful management–worker relations seem to hinge not solely on whether or not unions are present, but on the kind of treatment given workers by management. Unions may serve as protective agencies in some cases, but apparently, in many plants and companies no protection is necessary.

As a matter of policy, both state and federal governments attempt to stay out of any labor dispute. However, since labor disputes can have a very serious effect on the economy and on the general welfare of the populace, governments often offer assistance. The Federal Mediation and Conciliation Service is an outstanding example. This service never settles disputes, but will offer assistance in getting the parties together so they can settle the dispute themselves. Many states offer a similar service.

Step Number	Union Representative	Employer Representative
1.	Employee or steward, or both	Foreman
2.	Chief plant steward	Superintendent of department
3.	Plant grievance committee	Plant manager
4.	National union representative	President of company
5.	Arbitration	

Figure 19–3. Steps of a grievance procedure.

QUESTIONS

1. How does a typical grievance procedure operate?
2. Differentiate between a "grievance" and a "complaint."
3. From an employer's point of view, what are the advantages of dealing with a union representing employees?
4. Under the law, are foremen and supervisors prohibited from joining a union? Explain.
5. On what basis did Congress pass a law prohibiting closed shop employment agreements?
6. What authority is possessed by the National Labor Relations Board when it comes to handling charges of unfair labor practices.
7. Does industry-wide bargaining appear to be in violation of the antitrust laws?
8. Distinguish between mediation, conciliation, and arbitration.
9. Why do some employees object to and even refuse to join unions?
10. What influence will the use of computers and automation generally have on labor unions and their growth?
11. What would happen to the collective bargaining process if *all* workers were members of one huge union?
12. How is the general public protected in labor disputes?

CASE PROBLEMS

Munson Mills

Munson Mills had been a textile plant in a large Vermont city for as long as anyone could remember. It had been started by "Jep" Munson, who ran the company with an iron hand, but who had a reputation of taking good care of all his employees. The tradition was carried on by his son, by his grandson, and by his great grandson. In other words, for four generations the company was run by members of the same family, all of whom followed the same patterns and traditions.

Generally speaking, the Munsons had all been very progressive and very aggressive. As a result, the business had grown and prospered. The company possessed one of the more modern textile mills in the country and was able to compete with all the other mills that had moved South, while at the same time paying the relatively high wages of the North.

There was one difficulty, however: the Munsons were violently opposed to unions in any form and to any degree. Over the years there had been many attempts to organize the employees, gain union recognition, throw up picket lines, and call strikes. These had been only partially successful, for the Munson in power had always held firm. The Federal Government tried to nudge the company toward union recognition during World War II, and there were some court battles; but the war ended, and with it, the power of the government agencies causing the trouble.

A month ago the last Munson, Charlie, died suddenly in his sleep of a heart attack. Since he was only 55 and thought he had many more years of control ahead of him, he had failed to make any provision for his successor in the company. He had no sons and only one daughter, who had married John Spencer, a very competent superintendent in one of the mills.

John has just been informed that the family has decided to place him in charge of the company as president. He is pleased and flattered. However, he stipulates that he will do so only on condition that he be allowed to cooperate with unions rather than fight them. He feels that the battle with unions was responsible for his father-in-law's premature death.

Questions:

1. Can an employer such as Munson Mills be forced to bargain with a union?
2. Can John Spencer legally decide to recognize a union of his choice and have them represent his employees?
3. What would be the result of any attempt of Spencer's to kill the union with kindness rather than with threats?
4. Why would well paid employees like Munson's wish a union to represent them?

The Tower Corporation

Ben Been and Charlie Walters got along together very well—so well, in fact, that they often fished together, in addition to bowling on the same team. The relationship seemed unusual to many, inasmuch as Ben was the plant manager of Tower's midwestern plant of 1200 employees and Charlie Walters was the president of the union representing those employees.

Charlie had been elected for a two-year term, and from the beginning the two men hit it off. There were some heated discussions at bargaining sessions, but two contracts had been signed during Charlie's term, which added substantially to employee benefits. At the same time, Charlie demonstrated his concern for company success and prosperity, saying that without a prosperous company there would be no jobs and no union. Naturally, this attitude endeared him to Ben Been, particularly as contrasted to that of earlier union presidents.

Since things were going so well, Charlie assumed that his re-election would be almost automatic. A month before the election, however, a rival for his job began a vigorous campaign asserting that Charlie was a tool of management and did not really have the welfare of the union and its members at heart. Charlie lost the election by a small margin. Although this was a blow to Charlie's pride, both he and Ben Been feared what would happen to labor relations at the plant in the future.

Questions:

1. Comment on Charlie Walter's attitude and approach toward labor relations.
2. Why did Charlie Walters lose the election?
3. Would it have helped the situation if the friendship between the two men had been less obvious?
4. What difference would there be in such a situation as this between an independent union and one affiliated with the AFL-CIO?
5. What was Charlie Walters' responsibility to the union as compared to his responsibility to the employees? Did he fail one or the other?

Peerless Electric

Peerless Electric has been the dominant electric installation and repair firm in the western state where it is located. Its domination of the business came about not only because of the excellence of its work, but because it ran a strictly union type of operation. Unions have been strong in this state and have tended to influence the state government considerably; so Peerless has always been given very careful consideration in decisions to grant electrical contracts for state projects.

This mode of operation has gone on for some 40 years, but during the past 10 years there have been some significant developments. Unions are simply not as influential in the state as they have been, and although the right-to-work movement hasn't succeeded in getting their ideas across to the legislature, they are expected to win within the next few years. In the light of economic difficulties, companies are standing up to the unions more, and some have simply closed down rather than accede to union demands. Union membership has decreased considerably, and with all the people unemployed, there seems to be plenty of opportunities to hire non-union types for construction work. In fact, many construction outfits have gone non-union. These trends are noticeable throughout the nation as well as within Peerless' area.

Peerless has felt the trend in more ways than one. First, they see the effect in the lower bids the non-union competition is able to submit on some jobs. Peerless feels that the firm has lost six good jobs during the last year to lower bidding competitors. Further, many of Peerless' workers are becoming somewhat restless about the union and in particular about the increased assessments to which they have been subjected. With the general loss of membership, the union has seen fit to assess members an extra $55 a month on top of their regular dues of $79 a month. To many of the members, this seems merely to be a method to maintain the jobs of the union business officers rather than benefit the members in any way.

Basically, George Peerless still runs the company after having started from scratch almost 50 years ago, although he is grooming his son, Henry, to take over in due time. George has never fought the unions over the years, nor has he given them any benefit. He has been dedicated to doing what is best for the company and clearly his son has some of the same attitudes and values.

In recent weeks George and Henry have discussed this problem almost daily. They have concluded that, if the present trend continues, they are soon going to have to go non-union in order to be able to compete with other non-union outfits. On the other hand, there is the possibility of losing some of their clout with the state when they make the move. They are trying to monitor the situation very closely, and part of the monitoring is to be as close to their employees as possible in order to know their moods.

Questions:

1. Are unions and union influence on the decline throughout the country and world today?

2. What benefits do unions offer their members that should be a factor in the Peerless situation?

3. The Peerless electrical union is part of a national union with headquarters located in Washington, D.C. Would there be a benefit to the Peerless workers if they retained a union at the local level only and severed their connection with the national group?

4. If Peerless were to suddenly go non-union, would or should they immediately lower the wages paid to present employees? If not, how would they save money in the long run?

20

WAGE AND SALARY ADMINISTRATION— POLICY CONSIDERATIONS

One of the major problems that confronts the management of every company is the determination of a satisfactory wage structure. The problem is complicated by the fact that it has become accepted practice for the business to provide its employees with group insurance, retirement, recreational, and other benefits—all of which become forms of indirect wage payment. But the present concept of "wages" involves other factors. In our society, employees' wages tend to determine their standard of living and their social position. Consequently, there are tremendous psychological implications associated with the individual's wage.

Wage and salary administration is that function of management that is concerned with the determination of how much the employees are to be paid, based upon thorough analysis of all factors affecting such remuneration. The many factors entering into this determination make it a very complex problem. It is confused by internal as well as external considerations, many of which we shall discuss in later sections of this chapter and in a chapter on job evaluation and employee appraisal.

Wages vs. Salaries

Broadly, "wages" covers all forms of compensation paid to the employees of a business. These include salaries, bonuses, commissions, or any other form of monetary payment. Based upon popular usage, the term "wages" is frequently used to refer to the cash compensation given to hourly paid employees who are employed on nonsupervisory jobs. On the other hand, ''salaries'' are sometimes distinguished from ''wages'' and are considered the sums paid non-hourly rated employees. This distinction has become a widely accepted one as a result of a wage and hour regulation contained in the Fair Labor Standards Act, which exempts certain employees, including supervisors, managers, and salesmen, from premium pay for overtime.

Wages—A Motivating Factor

If an organization is willing to pay high wages, it can usually attract well-qualified employees. There are many motivating factors—security, job status, opportunities for advancement, recognition, and good working conditions—that influence a person's feelings about a job, but pay is still one of the foremost considerations. If one's earnings are at an acceptable level, based upon an evaluation of one's own worth, the other factors will become less important. If earnings are inadequate, then there is strong possibility one will become dissatisfied.

Basis for Paying for Jobs

At the outset of considering an equitable basis for paying employees, management is confronted with a number of questions:

1. Should pay be on a basis of worker needs, or on the value of the job to the company?
2. How can the conflicting interests of the owners, the workers, and the customers best be reconciled?
3. How can the worth of jobs be determined?
4. What are the economic elements in wages?

In this country, it has been accepted practice that a worker be paid on the basis of what the job is worth, and not on the basis of personal needs. Thus, a single man and a married man of equal competence and years of service would usually receive the same pay. Likewise, based on the provisions of the Equal Pay Act (See Figure 20-1), there can be no discrimination in the wages paid employees on the basis of sex. Thus, men and women of equal merit, working on jobs which have equal skill, effort, and responsibility requirements and under the same working conditions, must be paid equal wages.

The conflicting interests of the owners, workers, and customers are sometimes difficult to reconcile because they tend to oppose each other. The workers are anxious to receive high wages because their wages are their livelihood; the owners are anxious to receive a good return on their investment and may frown on the payment of exorbitant wages; and the customer will buy from the company only if the price and quality are right. It is management's problem to keep each of these groups

Name of Law	Provisions Pertaining to Wages and Hours
Davis-Bacon Act of 1931	Provided for payment of prevailing wage rates (for similar job classifications on similar projects) on Federal construction projects in excess of $2000 and established an eight-hour working day, except for certain emergency contracts.
Social Security Act of 1935	Provided for payroll withholding from employees and for employer contributions to cover a system of old-age and survivors insurance and unemployment insurance.
Walsh-Healey Public Contracts Act of 1936	Established certain standards of work done on U.S. Government contracts exceeding $10,000, specifically, payment of time and one-half for all hours worked in excess of eight in one day or 40 in one week. It also permitted the fixing of prevailing minimum wages in those industries performing contracts.
Fair Labor Standards Act (Wage and Hour Law) of 1938	Provided for minimum hourly wages and time and one-half the employee's regular rate for overtime over 40 hours per week for employees engaged in interstate commerce, including those in any closely related process or occupation directly essential to such production. The statute set forth what was meant by minimum wages, stated conditions under which overtime provisions might be exceeded, exempted certain employees—executives, administrators, professionals, and outside salesmen—from coverage, and prohibited the employment of children under 16 (18 for hazardous occupations) in commerce or in the production of goods for commerce. The Act has been amended several times, and the minimum rate has steadily increased.
Equal Pay Act of 1963	Amended the Fair Labor Standards Act to provide that both sexes should receive equal pay for work demanding equal skill, effort, and responsibility. Made provision for wage differentials based on merit, seniority, and wage incentives.

Figure 20–1. Principal provisions of federal labor legislation affecting wages and salaries.

happy by (1) paying the workers a fair wage so that they will remain a satisfied, productive group; (2) operating the business at a profit so that adequate dividends can be declared for the stockholders; and (3) maintaining costs and quality at such a level that the company will be in a good competitive position.

One of the difficult aspects of wage and salary administration is that of determining the worth of jobs. In considering this problem, management must recognize that (1) its salary structure should be at the level required to attract the type of workers it wants to hire and retain; (2) the variations in wages and salaries paid for the different jobs within the company are just as important as the level of wages; (3) employees' feelings about their wages are relative to what others receive; and (4) employees expect wages to increase as the degree of responsibility and authority increases. At its best, the basis for paying for jobs is quite arbitrary. But in recent years industry has attempted to bring about a more systematic approach to this problem through the use of job evaluation, which will be discussed in detail in Chapter 21.

There are no economic laws that stipulate exactly how much a company should pay in wages. Many theories have been offered, but to date there are no formulas that can be used in determining wages, and it is probable that the variables are so great that no stipulation in purely economic terms is possible. Hence, the company is subjected to the realistic situation of paying the wage that the various economic factors in the labor market force it to pay.

In competing for workers' services, the company is confronted with much the same problem that is encountered in a commodity market. If there is a shortage of a particular skill, it becomes possible for the workers in that field to demand and get a higher wage; if there is an oversupply of labor, the result may be lower wages, unemployment, or both. In any one labor market, however, the wages paid the employees will reflect the wage policies of the employers. For the most part, the most profitable firms will pay the highest wages and less successful firms the lowest. Obviously, those companies that are able to pay the highest wages find themselves in a highly advantageous position in attracting good employees.

Organization for Wage and Salary Administration

The position of wage and salary administration in the organization varies from company to company. In the larger companies there is usually a staff department of wage and salary administration, which is responsible for advising and aiding the entire organization on wage problems. Because the setting of wages and salaries plays such an important role in manpower management, this department is most commonly found in the human resources, industrial relations, or personnel department.

In smaller organizations, the wage and salary function may be assigned to the controller, treasurer, or some other administrator whose responsibilities include other fields. Where this is done, it is important that the attention given this function not be subordinated to the other duties of the administrator.

Whatever the position of wage and salary administration in the organization, top management should insure that it be given adequate attention and should adhere to sound wage policy. Although it is difficult to state a wage policy that will have universal application to all companies, the following factors are usually considered important:

1. The company's wage policy should be consistent with its stated personnel policy. The company's wage level should be at least equal to the prevailing wages for similar jobs in the labor market.
2. A consistent basis for determining the relative worth of the jobs within the company should be established and adhered to. As a part of this, the job content should be reviewed periodically.
3. Provision should be made for periodic review of wages and a sound basis for merit increases established.
4. Consideration should be given to the establishment of individual or group incentives wherever applicable in order to reward additional effort of the employees.
5. Standards of performance should be established at reasonable levels consistent with the policy of a "fair day's pay for a fair day's work," and these standards should be maintained at this level.
6. Complaints arising from any phase of wage administration should be given prompt attention and settled in accordance with the facts of the case.
7. Complete information on all phases of the wage program should be expressed in writing and disseminated to all employees, and management should be willing to discuss any phase of the program whenever requested.

Factors Influencing Wages

In considering the proper compensation for the employees of a company, many complex factors enter. It isn't as simple as determining that each employee should be paid at the rate of so much per hour or per piece. Workers may also receive paid sick leave, paid vacation and holidays, and premium pay for overtime and holidays. These and other forms of indirect remunerations are commonly referred to as "fringe benefits."[1] In addition, a few companies have profit-sharing arrangements in which the employees receive some of their compensation through participation in the profits of the company. Closely related to profit-sharing plans are stock-ownership plans designed to encourage employees to purchase company stock.

Labor legislation. Several federal laws have had a marked influence on minimum wages, working hours, and payroll withholding. Chief among these are the Davis-Bacon Act of 1931, the Social Security Act of 1935, the Walsh-Healey Public Contracts Act of 1936, the Fair Labor Standards Act of 1938, and the Equal

---

[1]The term "fringe benefits" is commonly used to refer to group life and hospitalization insurance, unemployment compensation, retirement programs, Social Security benefits, paid vacations, paid holidays, severance pay, and similar employer expenses that compose indirect forms of remuneration (see Chapter 18).

Pay Act of 1963. The principal provisions of these five laws are presented in summary form in Figure 20-1.

Collective bargaining.   For those employees who are members of unions, one of the major factors influencing their wages will be the union scale, which results from collective bargaining. The labor agreement usually provides a pay scale for various job classes which will be in effect during the life of the agreement. It may also stipulate the minimum earning potential available under incentive systems.

The effect of collective bargaining in a labor market will be felt even by non-unionized companies. Some employers may desire to equal or exceed the union scale in order to avoid the unionization of their employees.

Over the years, the collective bargaining in several major industries has had considerable influence on other companies. There has been a tendency to use one large company as a lever against another company, and this has had tremendous impact on the wage picture in both large and small firms. Also, the union's demands for some type of guaranteed employment plan and other fringe benefits have added considerable indirect payment to the workers.

Starting in the early 1980's there was a deceleration in wage gains, falling from annual pay hikes of about 9 percent to about 4 percent. Some of this was the result of increased foreign competition and the recession years of 1981 and 1982. Surprisingly, the workers who fared the worst were the union members, and it was not unusual to read that the employees had accepted a wage freeze or a reduction in wage rates (oftentimes as a result of concessionary bargaining).

There appeared to be a new sense of realism and urgency in the collective bargaining process, and labor and management were able to communicate on the effects of competition and the long-term stability of the company. One offshoot of this atmosphere was the initiation of a two-tier wage system in some companies in which new employees were paid at a lower rate than veteran workers; cuts ranged from 5 to 50 percent and averaged 15 percent. As examples of how the cuts operate, in the Packard Division of General Motors, those newly hired get 55 percent of the wages of veterans on the production line and must work 10 years to catch up; in USAir, new flight attendents get 22 percent less than veteran employees and will have to work six years to catch up; and the Teamsters Union and major trucking companies set up a wage scale paying new employees 30 percent less than veteran workers, and the new employees will have to work three years to catch up.

One of the goals that management personnel of many companies have sought is to offset wage increases with increases in productivity. As a move in this direction, they have asked for changes in work rules that lead to rigid job classifications and inflated staff levels. In one airline pact with the International Association of Machinists, scheduled wage increases were linked to specified productivity levels.

Another element of management's strategy is to reduce the number of full-time workers with seniority who do all of the jobs. Companies are relying more than ever on part-time and temporary workers, who get lower wages and fewer benefits than full-time employees. Among the industries most aggressively moving in this direction are airlines, electronics, trucking, and retail food.

The labor market.   In a labor market the supply and demand for a particular type of labor will tend to seek a balance. Seldom, however, will it attain an absolute balance, wide differences will usually prevail in the hourly rates paid by various employers for equivalent labor on similar jobs. Owing to the immobility of labor, surpluses of some skills may exist in one area while shortages exist in others.

The shortage of qualified workers for certain jobs may have considerable influence on the wages demanded by persons possessing those skills. From time to time, this has been the situation for engineers. The frequent shortage of engineers has had considerable influence on the starting pay offered young engineers.

Geographic location.   Wage differentials have always existed among different geographical areas. Some jobs are rated higher in a large city than in a smaller community, or higher in the North than in the South (although the South is catching up). The common explanation for this difference is that the cost of living is less in one area than in another.

Cost of living.   During periods of rising prices, the cost of living becomes an item of major importance in wage determination. It frequently may be one of the foremost items posed by the unions in collective bargaining sessions and has led to "escalator" clauses being incorporated into many union agreements. Based upon the provisions of these clauses, the wages of the employees are adjusted upward or downward periodically, depending upon the rise or fall of a cost-of-living index (the one prepared by the Bureau of Labor Statistics, United States Department of Labor). One of the recent bargaining strategies that a number of companies have adopted is that of trying to discontinue cost-of-living adjustments (COLAS). In 1982, the United Automobile Workers Union traded the COLA (which had become essentially a 3 percent annual pay hike) for profit sharing.

Tying wages into the cost of living may prove to be a troublesome consideration for management, because sales, income, and profits may not coincide with the retail prices used in calculating the cost-of-living index.

Comparable worth.   One of the questions that a number of women's organization have raised in recent years is "Why should there be a wage gap between men and women, and why should women earn only about 72 cents for every dollar earned by men?" This has led to much disputation (including strikes) and to a concept referred to as *comparable worth*. Comparable worth is a controversial theory that jobs have an intrinsic, measurable value that should dictate the wages paid. Federal law states clearly that workers performing the same job cannot be paid differently because of their sex or race. Nonetheless, the advocates of comparable worth would take these guarantees a step further: employees in such traditionally male jobs as accountant, construction worker, and truck driver would no longer make 30 to 40 percent more than the holders of traditionally female jobs like nurse and secretary.

An analysis of the wage gap between men and women reveals that it is a complex phenomenon. In general, women work at different jobs from men, with fully half of all women concentrated in three occupations: clerical, sales, and professional. These occupations command salaries in the labor market commensurate with the supply and demand of people able and willing to do the work. Thus, many people question the need to make comparable worth the law of the land.

It is of interest to note that Australia has had a variation of comparable worth since 1972. Within five years after the law was passed, female unemployment in Australia rose, the number of women working part time increased, and the growth of female participation in the labor force slowed.

Ability to pay. "Ability to pay" has been used frequently by employers to counter a demand for wages that they feel are excessive. One of the best illustrations of this usage arose in the General Motors negotiations several years ago where both the company and the union (United Auto Workers) made claims and counter-claims as to the company's breakeven point, costs, and profit picture. In other cases the employer has used this argument to request a reduction in wages on the grounds that the present wage level would jeopardize the future of the company. As an example of this, the employees in Anchor Glass Container agreed to take a pay cut if the company would continue to operate its ten plants. For the most part, however, employers have argued that the ability to pay has nothing to do with wages.

Over the long run, a company's wage policy must reflect its ability to pay. The company cannot afford to pay wages at an exorbitant level at the expense of its customers or owners. At the same time, it must pay wages at the level necessary to maintain the desired caliber of the workforce. If wages were cut because the company was operating at a loss, some of the employees would leave to work elsewhere.

Wage level. The wage level maintained in a company is influenced by the company's wage policy and by the "going rates" for jobs in the labor market. If the policy of the company is to pay at least as well as other industries in that area, then its pay scale will be based upon the community wage level as determined from wage surveys. This will be discussed in greater detail in Chapter 21.

Compensation of Supervisors and Executives

The compensation of supervisors and executives presents a special problem. There are few, if any, good bench marks to use as a guide in paying these employees. Local wage surveys usually do not include these jobs, and there are no "going rates" for the positions of president, vice president, plant superintendent, or foreman. Moreover, even with data that are available from wage surveys, the duties and responsibilities inherent in the different positions vary so much that such rates may be of little value.

Determining equitable compensation for production supervisors presents a difficult problem because of the relationship between their pay and that of persons they supervise. It is generally assumed that the supervisor should earn 10 to 20 percent more than those he supervises. But this differential, which is usually based upon the worker's normal weekly earnings, will be eliminated when the workers put in overtime and receive 50 percent more pay per hour or when some of the employees working on incentive plans are able to make a 10 to 25 percent bonus. As a counter to this problem, some companies have placed their supervisors on a bonus plan, making it possible for them to receive increased pay for increased productivity.

The pay scale for executives is determined on a basis that is even more arbitrary than that used for the production workers. Although a number of executive surveys have been undertaken by the National Industrial Conference Board and a few consulting firms, these surveys are difficult to make because of the many variations in compensation of executives. Consequently, the determination of an executive's pay tends to be based on what subordinates and superiors receive, on survey data, or on the amount required to hire and keep the executives. A few companies have attempted to do something about this situation by attempting to evaluate the worth of executives' jobs and affixing salary boundaries for the various position classifications.

In the mid-80's the salaries paid to top executives attracted extensive media coverage, most of it critical. Many people questioned whether the highest paid executives should continue to get big pay boosts and to receive annual total compensation (annual salary, bonus, and deferred long-term compensation) that averaged $1.1 million in 1984. A few management experts contend that over the years chief executives' pay increased only slightly in relation to the average industrial worker's wages. Some of these experts go even further and contend that the leaders of huge corporations are underpaid—particularly when their compensation is compared to the incomes of star athletes, entertainers, movie stars, and television personalities.

One criticism often leveled at chief executive officers and directors is that compensation has had only a modest connection with performance. Some companies are trying to change that, primarily through long-term programs that attempt to tie compensation to the fate of company shareholders.

Methods of Compensation

One of the policy decisions that every company must make is that of determining the method of compensating its employees. In general, the methods of wage payment may be grouped into three major classes: those based on some unit of time, those based on some unit of output or accomplishment, and those based on some form of gainsharing. Each of these will be discussed later.

In selecting an appropriate method of wage payment, we must keep in mind that it should adhere to the company's overall wage policy and be appropriate for the type of work being performed. For example, it is unheard of to pay the chief engineer of a company on an hourly basis. He is usually paid an annual salary at so much per month and accepts this as being a satisfactory method of wage payment. In the same way, a worker on an assembly line probably would consider an hourly rate of so much per hour and payment once a week as an acceptable form of wage payment. Among the considerations that must be taken into account in selecting a suitable method of compensation are:

1. Does it provide proper incentive to get the job done?
2. Does it facilitate managerial controls?
3. Is it easy to administer?
4. Does it keep the employees satisfied?
5. Is it appropriate for the type of work being performed?
6. Is it based upon a sound system of job evaluation?

Wage Payment Based on Time

The most common form of wage payment is that based on some unit of time, for example, $8.00 per hour for a worker in the plant, $250 per week for a clerk in an office, $1,400 per month for a foreman in a plant, or $25,000 per academic year for a schoolteacher. In the case of hourly wages, the employees receiving them are usually paid at weekly or biweekly intervals. Persons receiving higher salaries are usually paid on a monthly basis.

A number of advantages may be cited for the time wage-payment plan: it is simple to compute and to understand, it requires no calculation of incentive bonuses, the payroll remains fairly stable and payroll accounting is simplified, it is favored by many unions, and quality is not sacrificed because there is no attempt to stimulate high production.

On the other side, there are a number of disadvantages to this form of wage payment: there is no strong motivation to maintain high production, no monetary recognition is given for increased worker effort and performance, and unit costs are more difficult to compute than under systems requiring time standards.

The adoption of a time wage-payment plan is generally advisable under the following conditions:

1. Time standards for the job are very difficult to set and maintain.
2. Output is beyond the control of the individual and subject to considerable fluctuation.
3. The worker is paced by a machine or other item of equipment such as a conveyor.

4. The job requires concentration, creative thought, or decision-making (e.g., engineering design, research, supervision).
5. Employees and unions insist upon its use.
6. Quality of workmanship is more important than quantity.

Wage Payment Based on Output

Wage-payment plans based on output or accomplishment vary a great deal in complexity but are commonplace for a variety of jobs. Salesmen frequently receive their compensation in the form of commissions on sales; executives may be paid bonuses based upon the earnings of the company; and production workers may be paid an amount for each unit they produce. It is evident that the primary reason for paying employees on the basis of output is to motivate them to perform above some minimal level. The method of compensating production workers for goods produced is commonly referred to as an "incentive system" of wage payment, and it is to this system that we shall devote most of the discussion in this section.

Much controversy exists about the use of wage incentive plans for the payment of production workers. Even though many companies have chosen not to use them, such a form of wage payment is still common in such industries as apparel, textiles, footwear, and some metalworking. It is estimated that about 25 to 30 percent of workers in manufacturing are paid through some form of incentive payment. In general, wage incentive plans probably work out best where labor cost is a large percent of total cost, where the competition is high, and where units of output are easily measured. Clothing manufacturers are good examples of those firms that meet these requirements.

As was pointed out in Chapter 8, work measurement provides the basis for most production-type wage incentive plans. Herein lies the source of many problems that arise from wage incentive plans. If the time standards for operations are set accurately, and if the workers are able to earn reasonable bonuses on the basis of reasonable effort, then probably everybody will be happy and the plan will work well. On the other hand, if the time standards are too "tight" and allow the workers to make too small or no bonuses, then they may submit grievances, slow down, or both. By the same token, if the time standards are too "loose" then the workers may make excessive bonuses on the basis of too little effort and management will be unhappy because of exorbitant costs. In the latter type of situation companies may get locked into bad standards through union agreements. This has led a number of companies to eliminate their wage incentive plans.

One of the most widely used incentive plans has been piecework, in which the individual is paid a fixed rate for each part produced. The monetary rate per piece is determined by dividing the operator's hourly base rate of pay by the number of pieces to be produced per hour (based on the standard time established by work measurement). It is of interest to note that the minimum hourly rate (established by the Wage and Hour Law) must be guaranteed and that some companies establish lower base rates of pay for incentive applications than they would for non-incentive operations. This differential was made legal by the Equal Pay Act of 1963. The formula for the computation of the wage under the piecework plan is

$$W = N \times R_p$$

where N = Number of pieces produced

R_p = Rate per piece in dollars

W = Wages earned

Many companies have preferred to establish an incentive system known as a "standard hour" plan instead of using piecework. As may be seen in Figure 20-2, the earnings for these two are the same, but the "standard hour" plan has a decided administrative advantage in that a change in the worker's hourly rate doesn't necessitate other changes, whereas when using the piecerate plan it would require changing the price per piece. The formula for this plan is

$$W = H_s R$$

where W = Wage

H_s = Standard hours of work produced

R = Rate of pay per hour

The scope of this chapter doesn't permit discussing the many plans that have been adopted by industry. However, a study of these plans would divulge that some offer a constant incentive, others a high initial incentive and then diminishing returns, and still others an ever increasing incentive as the worker's output increases.

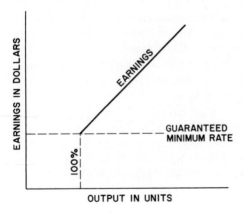

Figure 20–2. Earnings from piecework and standard hour incentive plans.

Among the advantages that are commonly associated with wage incentive plans are that they provide strong monetary motivation and are a means of maintaining high production, they reward the individual for increased effort and performance, they reduce the degree of supervision required, and they provide a useful basis for cost control purposes. On the other hand, some disadvantages of wage incentive plans commonly cited are that earnings may be difficult to calculate, the plans require additional administrative overhead in the form of clerks, they are frowned upon by many unions, quality may be sacrificed in an effort to get high production, and malpractice has led to "speeding up" the workers.

A number of characteristics, expressed in the following rules, are usually associated with a good wage incentive system:

1. The plan should be simple and easily understood by the employees.
2. The plan should reward employees in direct proportion to increased output.
3. Hourly base rates should be established by job evaluation.
4. The task imposed for the incentive plan should allow sufficient earning potential so that the worker can make at least 20 percent above the hourly base rate.
5. Time standards should be established by a sound system of work measurement and should be guaranteed against any change except where there has been a definite change in methods, tools, equipment, specifications, or materials.
6. Shop procedures involving production control, materials control, and other items should be standardized.
7. Time standards should be based on definite quality standards.
8. Provision should be made for handling production and other delays that are beyond the control of the operator.
9. The plan should be applied to as many direct and indirect workers as possible.
10. The plan should be rigidly maintained.

Gainsharing

As pointed out earlier in this chapter, a number of companies are trying to offset wage increases by increases in productivity. Over the years, a number of plans have been designed and implemented to try to achieve this end. Among the best known of these are the Scanlon, Rucker, and Improshare plans. Sharing productivity gains is simple in both concept and practice. A total labor cost base per unit(s) to make is established for a plant as a whole, and when costs are reduced through employee participation, the gains are shared with all employees. In the Improshare plan, the productivity base is the average productivity over a past period.

The Scanlon Plan[2] is one of the most interesting approaches to sharing the gains of employee participation. Although the plan has not been widely adopted, modifications of it have proven to be highly successful in plants like Donnelly Mirrors, Inc. in Holland, Michigan. The plan consists of establishing a wage formula or incentive, and production and screening committees that consider suggestions for increasing productivity and cost reduction.

The wage formula is designed to share the gains of increased productivity proportionaily among all the employees in the company. The formula can be tailored to each company's needs; but it usually involves a determination of the labor cost and the establishment of a ratio between this cost and the sales value of goods produced. For each percent increase in production value (increase in productivity), a 1 percent participating bonus will be paid to each employee working under the plan. The procedure for paying the gainsharing bonuses is subject to variation, but it is common to distribute them monthly. In the original plan, 100 percent of the gain was shared in the bonuses, but in later plans this was reduced to 75 percent.

As a means of increasing productivity, the Scanlon plan has met with varied success. The Donnelly Company experienced great success, and productivity per person more than doubled between 1952 and 1977.[3] It appears as though the plan is most successful in small companies where both the employees and management are able to make substantive changes in their patterns of behavior and where good internal communications exist.

Profit Sharing

One of the methods used to augment the compensation of employees is through the sharing of the profits of the enterprise. Profit sharing has had a long history. Although there has been no pronounced trend toward the adoption of profit-sharing plans, the Bureau of Labor Statistics estimates that over 2 million workers are covered by such plans. A nationwide Council of Profit Sharing Industries was established several years ago, and this council has urged many companies to develop programs.

Profit-sharing plans differ markedly in coverage and in their methods of distributing the profits. In some companies they are limited to executives, whereas in others they have universal coverage. In general, they provide a system of distributing net profits, after dividends have been set aside, on some predetermined basis at the end of an annual or other stipulated period.

In some profit-sharing plans, the payments may be made on a deferred basis,

---

[2]Adapted from George Strauss and Leonard R. Sayles, *Personnel: The Human Problems of Management;* Englewood Cliffs, New Jersey: Prentice-Hall, Inc., 1972, p. 644.

[3]See Frank McCann, "The Donnelly Management System for Increased Production," *Ninth SDCE International Die Casting Exposition and Congress,* Society of Die Casting Engineers, Milwaukee, Wisconsin, June 1977, p. 1.

which may provide a source of funds for retirement programs, disability payments, separation payments, or loans. Payments made on this basis can greatly supplement the benefits of a company's regular pension plan. If the plan meets the requirements of the Internal Revenue Service, the employer can contribute up to a maximum of 15 percent of the total payroll. This provides a definite, long-term income advantage for employees.

The method of distributing the profits to the employees differs from firm to firm. Some organizations apportion the payments among the employees on the basis of their years of service with the firm, others pay them a fixed percentage of their total wages during a stipulated period, and still others prefer to pay on the basis of the merit ratings of the individuals. In companies having excellent records of earnings, the payments may be sizable and, in such notable companies as the Lincoln Electric Company in Cleveland, may actually equal or exceed the individual's annual wage.

The proponents of profit sharing claim a number of benefits from their programs. Among these are increased productivity, reduced labor turnover and greater loyalty on the part of the workers, better cooperation among the employees, and improved employee attitudes towards their jobs and the company. But profits cannot be shared unless the business has a successful record of earnings, and this poses one of the problems associated with such programs. The workers come to expect some form of profit distribution and if the sum is lower than anticipated, they may be disappointed and disgruntled. The long-term nature of the profit-sharing period provides little day-to-day motivation, and many of the most successful programs have been accompanied by direct wage incentive systems. Also, the most successful programs appear to have been those companies that stressed sound managerial practice and placed considerable emphasis on maintaining an excellent personnel management program.

Guaranteed Annual Wage

The guarantee of an annual wage or annual employment has long been the desire of the worker, but it has only been in recent years that this subject has created national interest. The successful attempt of the United Auto Workers Union to secure a partial wage guarantee from the major automotive companies lent great strength to this movement.

A number of firms, including the Procter and Gamble Company, Nunn-Bush Company, Armstrong Cork Company, and Sears, Roebuck and Company, are widely recognized for their contributions to wage stabilization, and have had a long history of successful operation of their programs. Although the plan in each of these companies differs somewhat from the others, the net effect is to guarantee the employee a minimum number of weeks of work each year. In some of the more recent programs, the employment guarantee has been tied in with the unemployment compensation benefits provided through Social Security.

For the most part, companies that have established wage stabilization programs have been in the consumer-good industries. The employees usually become eligible after a fixed period of service and may be guaranteed all or a stipulated proportion of weekly wages for a certain number of weeks. The costs of operating such a program vary widely and have been estimated to be as high as 20 percent of the annual payroll. It is obvious that it is not easy to stabilize employment in businesses subject to seasonal fluctuations in sales, and this poses a real problem for management. Extensive consideration must be given to market research, business forecasting, diversification of the product, new markets, and manpower control in order to maintain production at a stable level.

QUESTIONS

1. A worker is employed on a job in a plant that pays her $20 a week less than her best friend receives for similar work in a different company. What psychological implications may this have for her?

2. The supervisor of Department A in a company works about 45 to 50 hours per week with no overtime pay because he is exempted by the Wage and Hour Law. On the other hand, the workers in his department get overtime pay for all hours worked in excess of 40. Is this a good situation? Discuss.

3. The ABC Company makes it a policy always to pay at least the prevailing wage for all its jobs. Is this a good policy? Why?

4. Why have many incentive plans for factory workers failed?

5. To what extent has labor legislation influenced the wages paid by industry?

6. To what extent has collective bargaining influenced the wages paid by industry?

7. Are geographic wage differentials as large as they used to be? Why?

8. Do you think that company presidents are worth as much as they get paid? Why?

9. The Peerless Products Company employs 150 production workers on a large number of precision machining operations. The company's costs have been rising and it has been suggested that they install a wage incentive plan. What problems might the company encounter in such an installation?

10. Would a profit-sharing plan be a desirable program to install in a company that is trying to increase the productivity of its workers? Why?

11. Do the advocates of comparable worth have a sound basis for their claims? Discuss.

12. Why haven't more companies installed gainsharing plans?

CASE PROBLEMS

Steelcraft Metal Products Company

The Steelcraft Metal Products Company is a small metal stamping company located in an industrial city of about 600,000 population. The company has been operating for 40 years, and now employs about 400 non-union men and women production workers. During the past few months the company has received numerous complaints on its wage system, and the president has asked the chief industrial engineer to submit a report on the company's wage program and to make recommendations for improving it. The principal provisions of the wage program were found to be the following:

1. No employees working on incentive are allowed to earn more than 20% in excess of their base rate.
2. Time standards are subject to change at management's discretion.
3. Time study sheets and time standards are not available to employees.
4. Women receive the same pay as men employed on the same job.
5. The standard hour wage incentive plan is used on nearly all production jobs. The base rate is guaranteed by management.
6. Indirect workers are not on incentive.
7. Employees on incentive are paid their base rate during all non-productive periods, e.g., downtime, vacations, and holidays.
8. All employees participate semiannually in the profits of the company. All shop employees receive the same amount of bonus. Executives' bonuses are based upon a different system determined by the president.
9. Wages and salaries are adjusted annually as management deems desirable. Management attempts to keep all wage rates on a par with similar jobs performed in the community.
10. Wage increases are granted individuals on the basis of merit, and all wages are reviewed at least once each year.

Questions:

1. Based upon the above information, analyze each of the ten items included in the wage policy and give your reasons for retaining, discarding, or correcting it.
2. In order to analyze the wage program completely, what additional information should be obtained?
3. What additional policies should be adhered to?

Richard V. Owen and Associates

Richard V. Owen and Associates is a Cleveland-based management consulting firm that specializes in manufacturing data base systems. Richard Owen, a former professor of industrial engineering at a midwestern university, started the firm in 1975, and it has enjoyed great success. By 1983, the company had grown to 80 employees, most of whom were engineers, computer and software specialists, statisticians, and other professionals.

One of the secrets of Richard V. Owen and Associates' success was the outstanding personnel policy that was established at the outset. Richard Owen is a brilliant, personable engineer and provides an outstanding role model for his associates. He feels very strongly that his fellow employees should perform their jobs well, and in return they should have good offices, adequate clerical and computer support, and liberal salaries. In addition, he insured that the company had a well structured benefits package, including health insurance, term life insurance, travel accident insurance, illness/injury pay, a bonus plan, and paid vacations of up to four weeks (after six years of employment).

By 1983, one void in the benefit program was the lack of a retirement program. After several months of study and consultation with outside consultants, the company decided to introduce a profit-sharing plan for all employees who had a year of eligible service and were 21 years of age or greater. The annual profit sharing declared by the Board of Trustees would be invested in each individual's account in a large bank, under the supervision of the bank's trust officer. The normal retirement age would be 65, but provisions were made for early retirement at age 55 and completion of 20 years of service. Partial vesting of each employee's account would take place after four years, and full vesting would take place after 10 years of service. The proposed program meets all of the federal requirements for retirement plans.

Questions:

1. Comment on Owen and Associates' benefit package.
2. Why do you think the company chose a retirement program based on profit sharing? Was it a sound decision?
3. Do both a profit-sharing plan and a cash bonus plan (paid annually) appear to be compatible?
4. Based on going rates of interest, estimate how much a 25-year-old engineer currently earning $30,000 per year might expect to accumulate in his account by age 65 if he averages 8% annual pay increases and 7% in profit sharing.

21

WAGE AND SALARY ADMINISTRATION—JOB EVALUATION AND EMPLOYEE APPRAISAL

In the preceding chapter, we noted many of the problems that arise in the field of wage and salary administration. Few of these are more complex than that of determining the worth of jobs. This is particularly difficult because employees have their own methods of evaluating jobs. It behooves the employer, then, to use a systematic approach to job evaluation rather than "hit-or-miss," "rule-of-thumb" techniques.

Closely related to the problem of determining the worth of a job is that of determining the worth of the employees performing that job. If a wage-rate range exists for the job, there should be some way of determining whether one worker is worth more than another. It is for the purpose of answering this question that industry has established formal systems of employee appraisal.

This chapter will be devoted to a discussion of the above two areas.

Job Evaluation

Examination of any organization will reveal it to contain a number of jobs, and someone will have established a wage rate for each of these jobs. Some companies' wage rates will have been established by managerial intuition, others by "rule-of-thumb" techniques, and still others by a formal system of job evaluation. It is with the formal system of job evaluation that we shall be concerned in this chapter.

Job evaluation is a systematic procedure for determining the relative worth of jobs within an organization and for establishing an adequate wage structure. This function has been commonly performed by the wage and salary administration department or by one of the industrial engineering groups.

The usual objectives of a job evaluation program are as follows:

1. To eliminate wage inequities.
2. To establish sound wage differentials among the jobs.
3. To provide a sound wage base for incentive and bonus plans.
4. To establish a sound wage structure.
5. To facilitate the maintenance of a consistent wage policy.

The methods used in evaluating jobs will frequently consist of the following major steps:

1. Determining the jobs to be evaluated.
2. Analyzing each job.
3. Evaluating each job.
4. Fitting the jobs into the wage structure.

Range of Jobs to Be Evaluated

In planning a job evaluation program, one of the first questions that needs to be answered is, "What jobs should be covered by the evaluation?" This question needs to be given consideration because of the inherent differences that exist between the jobs performed in the shop and in the office. Thus, it is common practice to select those jobs which are somewhat homogeneous (e.g., shop operations) and to tailor a job evaluation program to best fit only those jobs. In the same manner, a different program might be selected to cover either office or managerial jobs.

Since job evaluation is for the purpose of studying *jobs* and not people, it is important that we recognize what a job is. A job is a grouping of work tasks, duties, and responsibilities. On the basis of this definition, an office might have jobs entitled stenographer, clerk typist, secretary, typist, and mail clerk. Further, it is evident that several people may be performing the same job (e.g., five typists) and that the number of employees filling the jobs may exceed the number of jobs.

Job Analysis

The basis for job evaluation, as well as for certain other personnel department activities, is provided by job analysis. The purpose of job analysis is to collect complete information on all requirements of the job. Among the items of information collected will be (1) complete identification of the job, (2) the duties performed on the job, (3) the responsibilities required by the job, (4) the working conditions under which the job is performed, and (5) the personal qualifications required by the job. The job analyst may secure this information by questioning the person working on the job, from the worker's supervisor, from others familiar with the job, or from actual observation.

It is common practice to use one or more forms in performing the job analysis, but the most frequently used form is the *job description*. Such forms are usually similar to that illustrated in Figure 21–1.

Evaluating the Jobs

Following the analysis of the jobs, the next step will be to evaluate them in non-financial terms. This evaluation assumes that the jobs can be weighed objectively by means of factors or definitions arbitrarily assigned. The most frequently used methods for performing the evaluation are the ranking method, job classification method, point method, factor comparison method, and job component method. Each of these will be described briefly in the sections that follow.

Ranking method.   The ranking method is the simplest of the job evaluation methods. It consists of having supervisors or other persons compare the overall job contents (usually without the aid of a job description) of the various jobs and then arrange them in a job hierarchy. Oftentimes the names of the jobs are placed on cards and the persons doing the evaluating arrange the cards in the order of importance in which they feel the jobs should be ranked. A common method of accomplishing this is to pick out the most important and least important jobs first and then several other key jobs somewhere in between. The other jobs to be evaluated are then placed in the proper place among the jobs first selected. When the persons doing the evaluating have agreed on the relative positions of the jobs, then the jobs may be grouped into job classes for affixing the wage rate.

The "paired comparison" method of ranking jobs has been devised in an attempt to improve the reliability of ratings and is a better method of ranking jobs. It consists of comparing every job with every other job by pairs. The jobs are randomly paired, and the job most often considered most valuable is rated as the top job, the one picked next most often becomes the second job, and so forth. A convenient device for performing this comparison is a table such as that illustrated in Figure 21–2. Using such a table, the rater is asked to check the higher of the two jobs indicated by each of the cells of the table. The job receiving the most checks is ranked first, the next highest is ranked second, and so forth. The reader will no doubt note that the comparisons repeat themselves and that only the upper or lower half of the table needs to be used.

The ranking method of job evaluation has several obvious disadvantages: it is difficult to use except where the number of jobs is small, it requires several raters who are familiar with the jobs and it may be difficult to find qualified raters, the

JOB DESCRIPTION

Department ....   Standard Code ....
Subdivision ....   Standard Title ....
Branch of Plant ....   Plant Title ....
Date ....   Plant Code ....

Summary of Duties

Detailed Statement of Work Performed

Source of Supervision

Tools and Equipment

Materials

Responsibility (For safety of others, company funds or property, for performance of
             work without supervision, etc.)

Qualifications Required:

  Special Knowledge:

  Previous Experience:

  Physical:

Working Conditions:

  Surroundings:

  Hazards:

Relation to Other Jobs

  Promotion from:

  Promotion to:

Job Analyst.......................................
Approved By ....   Date ....

Figure 21–1. Job description form.

	Stenographer	Clerk Typist	Secretary	Mail Clerk	Typist
Stenographer	—				
Clerk typist		—			
Secretary			—		
Mail clerk				—	
Typist					—

Figure 21–2. Paired comparison table.

biases of the raters will tend to influence their evaluations of the jobs, it is difficult to defend the individual ratings, and it assumes equal spacing between ranks. On the other hand, it is simple and may prove to be a very satisfactory method in small plants having a small number of jobs.

Job classification method. The job classification (or job grade) method has become well known through extensive use for evaluating United States Civil Service jobs. Although it has been in common use in government circles for many years, it has found only limited use in industry.

The job classification method consists of setting forth broad definitions or descriptions describing the level of work of several job classes, which are arranged in order of importance. An example of such descriptions is illustrated in Figure 21–3. New jobs to be evaluated are then compared to these descriptions, and the jobs are placed in those classes most closely identifying them. A class, then, includes all jobs considered to be of the same grade without any detailed analysis of the job.

The principal disadvantages that arise in using this method are the problem of writing grade descriptions in terms such that jobs can be compared to them and the difficulty of placing a borderline job in the correct class.

Point method. The point method of evaluating jobs is by far the most widely used in industry. It consists of a "yardstick" containing various factors such as skill, education, and responsibility that are inherent in the jobs and that vary in importance. The degree of importance of each factor is determined by arbitrary decision, and a suitable point value is specified for each. As an aid, each factor is described by a suitable definition, and appropriate benchmark jobs may be selected for comparison purposes. One of the most widely used plans of this type is that put out by the National Electrical Manufacturers Association (same plan used by National Metal Trades Association), whose evaluation form is illustrated in Figure 21–4.

Grade 1.   Performs simple routine tasks under close supervision and following standard or established procedures. Work is light manual, requiring only minor degree of mental alertness such as sorting or arranging in alphabetical, numerical, or chronological order—counting, stamping, delivering messages, and mailing.

Grade 2.   Performs routine tasks under close supervision involving minor degrees of skill and easily learned, elemental business and office procedures such as posting, filing, and simple calculations and limited use of typewriter, address-ograph, duplicating machine, and other office equipment. Has no business contact with others and any errors in workmanship and judgment have little consequence.

Grade 3.   Performs, with normal degree of supervision, semi-routine tasks involving good working knowledge and understanding of business and office procedures, the ability to think out simple problems, and the expanded use of office equip-ment. Independent action permitted within prescribed limits with irregularities referred to supervisor. Has business contacts only with employees in related fields and exercises limited supervision over personnel in lower grades.

Grade 4.   Performs non-routine work with limited supervision, involving considerable knowledge of a specific area of work, the ability to handle special calculations and problems in the specific area, and an understanding of the operations of office equipment. Has the ability to investigate irregularities and ordinary discrepancies; takes responsibility for monies and confidential matters. Has considerable contacts with public and fellow employees, exercising supervision over employees in lower grades.

Grade 5.   Performs, with little or no supervision, tasks of high-grade clerical nature, requiring an intimate knowledge of the operational functions of the organi-zation, with ability to assemble designated information and to prepare a com-prehensive report. Maintains and advises superior on daily schedules, planned activities, and reports. Supervises employees in lower grades. Makes both employee and public contacts.

Figure 21–3.   Grade descriptions of clerical positions. (Source: Charles W. Brennan, *Wage Administration*; Homewood, Ill.: Richard D. Irwin, 1963, p. 123. Reprinted by permission.)

An idea of the content of the definitions for each of the factors used in this plan may be obtained from the definition for the Education Factor contained in Fig-ure 21–5.

Under the plan, in the evaluation of any particular job, the job description is compared to the job factors on the evaluation form and those degrees most appropri-ate are assigned. The total points for all the factors then determine the relative posi-tion of that job among other jobs. Of course, the point values must be converted into money values; we shall discuss this in a later section of this chapter.

The point system has become the most popular method of job evaluation be-cause it possesses a number of advantages over the non-quantitative methods. By using graphic or other rating scales, it is possible to attain consistency among the raters. The factors and point values may be agreed upon in advance by the employer and the union. Moreover, the raters do not have to be thoroughly familiar with the jobs in order to do an accurate job of rating. Also, the system tends to minimize the effects of personal bias of the raters. The total point values that arise from the use of this method make it easy to group the point values into job classes.

Factors	Degrees and Points				
	1st degree	*2nd degree*	*3rd degree*	*4th degree*	*5th degree*
SKILL					
1. Education...................	14	28	42	56	70
2. Experience	22	44	66	88	110
3. Initiative and ingenuity	14	28	42	56	70
EFFORT					
4. Physical demand	10	20	30	40	50
5. Mental and/or visual demand ..	5	10	15	20	25
RESPONSIBILITY					
6. Equipment or process	5	10	15	20	25
7. Material or product	5	10	15	20	25
8. Safety of others	5	10	15	20	25
9. Work of others	5	10	15	20	25
JOB CONDITIONS					
10. Working conditions	10	20	30	40	50
11. Hazards	5	10	15	20	25

Figure 21–4. Degrees and points assigned to job factors. (Courtesy National Electric Manufacturers Association.)

Education or Trade Knowledge

This factor measures the job requirements in terms of the mental development needed to think in terms of, and understand, the work being performed. Such mental development or technical knowledge may be acquired either by formal schooling, night school, or through equivalent experience.

Trades or vocational training is considered as a form of education and should be evaluated under this factor.

1ST DEGREE

Requires the ability to read and write, add and subtract whole numbers.

2ND DEGREE

Requires the use of simple arithmetic such as addition and subtraction of decimals and fractions, together with simple drawings and some measuring instruments such as caliper, scale.

3RD DEGREE

Requires the use of fairly complicated drawings, advanced shop mathematics, handbook formulas, variety of precision measuring instruments; some trade knowledge in a specialized field or process.

4TH DEGREE

Requires the use of complicated drawings and specifications, advanced shop mathematics, wide variety of precision measuring instruments, broad shop trade knowledge.

5TH DEGREE

Requires a basic technical knowledge sufficient to deal with complicated and involved mechanical, electrical, or other engineering problems.

Figure 21–5. Definition of education factor. (Courtesy National Electric Manufacturers Association.)

One of the disadvantages of this system is the problem of constructing it so that proper factors are selected and proper weightings are assigned them. In addition, the system may be difficult to explain to the employees and is time-consuming and costly.

The factor comparison method.   The factor comparison method is favored by many wage and salary administrators because it is tailored to fit each company. It is like the point system in that it makes use of arbitrarily selected factors, but it differs by making use of key or benchmark jobs as the basic yardstick. These key jobs are selected by a committee as being representative of the job hierarchy of the company both in their content and in the wage rate being paid for them. The committee arbitrarily selects several factors, such as skill, physical requirements, responsibility, working conditions, and mental requirements, for which they feel the company should pay. Then they rank each key job in order for each of the factors, as illustrated in Figure 21–6.

Using these ranks as a guide, the committee members then divide the present hourly rate being paid each key job among the five factors in accordance with their judgments as to how the money should be distributed among the factors. When they have agreed on this distribution, a table such as that illustrated in Figure 21–7 may be prepared.

	Average Rank				
Job	*Mental Require-ments*	*Physical Require-ments*	*Skill Require-ments*	*Responsi-bility*	*Working Con-ditions*
Gager	2	13	2	3	15
Pattern maker	1	12	1	1	16
Common laborer	16	1	16	16	1
Power shear opr.	11	11	9	5	4
Plater	10	6	6	12	9
Riveter	12	3	12	14	8
Blacksmith	13	2	8	13	7
Punch press opr.	14	4	13	15	5
Automatic screw machine opr.	4	8	3	2	13
Casting inspector	3	7	4	4	10
Millwright	9	10	5	6	11
Tool crib attendant	7	16	14	10	14
Arc welder	8	9	7	9	3
Electric truck operator	6	15	11	8	12
Crane operator	5	14	10	7	6
Watchman	15	5	15	11	2

Figure 21–6. Average ranks of 16 tentative key jobs as assigned by committee. (Source: David W. Belcher, *Wage and Salary Administration*; Englewood Cliffs, N.J.: Prentice-Hall, Inc., 1962, p. 264. Reprinted by permission.)

Job	Average Cents per Hour Assigned					
	Mental	Physical	Skill	Responsi-bility	Working Conditions	Present Rate
Gager	2.90	1.41	4.00	1.89	.88	11.08
Pattern maker	3.24	1.44	4.24	2.22	.86	12.00
Common laborer	.67	2.22	.79	.52	1.88	6.08
Power shear opr.	1.54	1.59	1.91	1.82	1.19	8.05
Plater	1.65	1.89	2.36	1.11	1.24	8.25
Riveter	1.32	2.07	1.41	.96	1.24	7.00
Blacksmith	1.40	2.28	1.98	1.06	1.80	8.52
Punch press opr.	.90	2.00	1.13	.85	1.58	6.46
Automatic screw machine opr.	2.32	1.80	3.45	1.85	1.09	10.51
Casting inspector	2.36	1.80	2.90	1.85	1.09	10.00
Millwright	1.80	1.67	3.38	1.74	1.02	9.61
Tool crib attendant	1.98	.96	1.09	1.29	.90	6.22
Arc welder	1.82	1.70	1.99	1.30	1.20	8.01
Electric truck opr.	2.13	1.18	1.65	1.41	.98	7.35
Crane operator	2.25	1.25	1.80	1.55	1.35	8.20
Watchman	.75	1.96	.86	1.18	1.69	6.44

Figure 21–7. Average distribution of present wages. (Adapted from David W. Belcher, *Wage and Salary Administration*, p. 265, by permission.)

After the job-rating scale has been established as indicated in Figure 21–7, all other jobs can be evaluated against this yardstick. Each job is broken down into the five factors and compared factor by factor against the rating scale. Thus, if the job contains approximately the same degree of skill as a punch press operator, it would be assigned that amount for that factor. The total of the five values assigned the job becomes its evaluated rate.

The factor comparison method possesses a number of advantages not found in other methods of job evaluation. It is not difficult to set up a job comparison scale, and this scale is tailored to fit the company's jobs. In using the scale to evaluate jobs, the jobs are compared to other jobs and evaluated in terms of their monetary worth. It is unnecessary to convert from points or job classes into money.

The major disadvantage of the factor comparison method involves the design of the rating scale. If the going rates of the key jobs and the monetary values assigned each factor for each key job are incorrect, then new jobs will be evaluated at incorrect rates. An additional disadvantage may be the complexity of the method and the difficulty of explaining it to the employees.

The job component method.   The traditional methods of job evaluation are usually based on information contained in job descriptions and knowledge which the evaluators have about the jobs. In recent years, there have been attempts to evaluate jobs directly from structured job analysis questionnaire information, thereby bypassing the need for evaluations based on judgment. Such procedures have been referred to as the job component method of job evaluation. For example, in evaluating clerical jobs, Miles[1] developed a clerical task inventory consisting of 139 tasks that are performed in clerical and other office-type jobs. These tasks have been rated in relative monetary worth, through an appropriate procedure. Each job to be evaluated is analyzed in terms of both the tasks and the worth for each task. The total of the tasks selected is then determined and becomes the rated value for the job.

Miles' work has been extended by McCormick and others to incorporate a broader range of jobs, including managerial and professional positions.[2]

Evaluation of Office, Professional, and Executive Positions

Much of the material previously covered will apply equally well to office positions. The principal difference between job evaluation in the office and in the shop is that direct classification of whole jobs is still commonly used in the office.

Many companies have adopted job evaluation plans for use in their offices, and there appears to be a trend in this direction. Of the plans in effect, there is much more widespread usage of the ranking and job classification methods than in the shop. Also, where the point or factor comparison methods are employed, separate plans will be used and will include factors more pertinent to office jobs. Some use has been made of the job component method, but it has not become very popular.

Owing to the nature of many scientific-professional positions in industry, limited application of job evaluation has taken place for these positions. In attempting to evaluate engineering positions, for example, it is difficult to measure the creativity that may enter into a designer's or researcher's work. However, this has not prevented some plans from being designed and put into effect with a high degree of success.

Limited use has been made of job evaluation for supervisory and executive positions. The principal reason for this limited use is that it is difficult to analyze the complex and varied characteristics that compose supervisory and executive positions. We need but think about the many activities performed by supervisors and executives to realize the problem of isolating and evaluating the activities that are required on these jobs. However, this has not prevented some companies from installing salary evaluation plans that apply to their supervisors and middle executives. Among the companies that have installed such plans are Westinghouse Electric Company, S.C. Johnson Company, General Foods Corporation, and the General Electric Company.

---

[1]M. C. Miles, "Studies in Job Evaluation: Validity of a Check List for Evaluating Office Jobs," *Journal of Applied Psychology*, Vol. 36, 1953, pp. 97–101.

[2]Ernest J. McCormick, P. R. Jeaneret, and Robert C. Mecham, "The Development and Background of the Position Analysis Questionnaire (PAQ)," West Lafayette, Indiana: Occupational Research Center, 1969. See also Gavriel Salvendy, *Handbook of Industrial Engineering*, p. 5.3.11.

Pricing the Jobs

Inasmuch as it would be far too unwieldy to try to fit every job separately into the wage structure, it is common practice to categorize jobs by job classes and to pay jobs of equal or approximately equal difficulty the same rate or in the same rate range. The wage structure that results from pricing the job classes is most frequently shown graphically in the form of a wage curve.

Wage curve. The wage curve is merely a graphical method of showing the relationship between wage rates (present, community, and collective bargaining) and number of points, job classes, or evaluated rates. Most employers are interested in knowing how their wage rates compare with similar jobs in other companies in their community, and this information is usually obtained from a community wage survey. The manner in which this survey is conducted will vary from area to area. It may be performed by telephone calls, questionnaires, or other means. The data may be used for establishing community wage curves for the jobs with which the company is concerned.

The position of the company wage curve with regard to the community level will depend upon management policy and the demands of the union. If it is the policy of the company to pay wages above the going rate for the community then its wage curve must be above the community curve.

Establishing the wage structure. A number of decisions must be made before a company can establish its wage structure. Among the questions that must be answered are (1) Is provision to be made for merit increases? (2) Are jobs to be grouped into job classes? (3) Are the wage rates for job classes to overlap? If so, how much? and (4) How should borderline jobs be treated?

The practice in most companies is to use a wage range in pricing jobs and job classes. The wage range usually consists of a minimum or starting rate and a maximum rate, and enough money spread between the two to make it possible to grant several wage increases. Figure 21–8 illustrates the wage structure for a point method of job evaluation in which the hourly rate is plotted against point values. Note that in this curve each job class has a range of 50 points and that job classes overlap.

The procedure for pricing the job structure will vary somewhat depending upon the method of job evaluation used. When the point plan is used, the rates for certain key jobs can be plotted against their point values and a best-fitting line determined. This line will represent the average wage paid by the company and may be compared with the "going rates" for the community. When the company's wage curve has been determined and necessary adjustments made in it, the rates for job classes will be established. Also, a decision will have to be made as to how the current rates above and below the wage curve are to be handled (see page 449).

For the other methods of job evaluation, the company's wage curve may be compared with the "going rates" for the community for key jobs and then any nec-

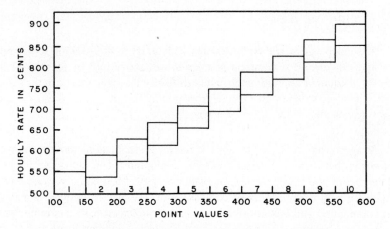

Figure 21–8. Wage structure with overlapping rate ranges.

essary adjustments made in the wage curve. Following this, the present rates may be compared to the evaluated rates and necessary adjustments made in the job rates. After the wage rates have been assigned, jobs are usually grouped into classes or grades. The purpose of this is to reduce the administrative problem associated with many different wage rates.

Administration of Job Evaluation

In administering the job evaluation program, the wage and salary administrators are confronted with many problems and issues. In those companies having unions, one of the foremost of these is the relationship with the unions. The attitude of the various national or international unions ranges from complete opposition to job evaluation to full participation in the installation and administration of programs. Examples of two unions that typify the opposing viewpoints are the International Association of Machinists, which is against such programs, and the United Steel Workers of America, which has worked cooperatively with the basic steel industry in establishing and administering the Cooperative Wage Study Plan. It is necessary for management to decide at the outset, then, the extent to which the union is to be involved in the program. Another far-reaching decision that must be made pertains to the job evaluation committee. Considerable thought should be given to insure that this committee contains persons sufficiently high in the company to be able to accomplish its objectives.

During the process of designing the method of job evaluation to be used, many questions arise that must be answered. For example, if a point plan is to be used, how many factors should be used in the plan, and what weighting should be assigned to these factors? Many point plans are subject to criticism because they involve too many factors and improper weightings of factors. Another question that must be resolved is, How are the employees to be informed of the system so that they will understand it?

Many day-to-day problems will arise to confront the administrators. Some of these are:

1. How can job descriptions be kept current?
2. How should out-of-line jobs be treated?
3. How should borderline jobs be evaluated?
4. At what rate should transferees be paid?
5. How can the influence of supply and demand be taken into account?

In the paragraphs that follow, we shall discuss briefly preferable practice on each of these issues.

It is very difficult to keep job descriptions current unless the complete cooperation of the supervisors and others familiar with job content can be secured. A plan should be devised for having them report all job changes, and, in addition, periodic reviews should be initiated to provide a check on all jobs.

One of the touchiest aspects of job evaluation is that of establishing a policy on the method of pricing out-of-line jobs. For example, based on the wage structure illustrated in Figure 21–8, what should be done about those jobs that fall above or below the rate range in any job class? It is usual practice to guarantee the employees that their wage rates will not be reduced because of the job evaluation program, and yet, the aim of job evaluation should be to get the wage rates in line with the evaluated rates. The jobs priced too low present no real problem and are merely raised (sometimes gradually) to the evaluated rate. The jobs priced too high cannot be handled this easily, and it is common practice to let the present job holders retain their old rates permanently or for some fixed period. On the other hand, new persons hired on these jobs are paid at the evaluated rate.

It is difficult to devise a sound approach to the treatment of "borderline" jobs. These are the jobs on the fringe area between two adjacent job classes, and there is little choice but to make an arbitrary decision as to the class in which each one best fits. The use of overlapping point values for adjacent grades is one technique that has been used as a means of minimizing friction, but even this does not solve the problem.

Employees transferred from one job to another present no problem if their new job pays the same or a higher wage rate than their old job. However, they will resent taking a pay cut if demoted to a lower-paid job. If the worker has had experience on the new job to which he or she is being demoted, it is common to pay the maximum rate for the new job. Other companies will pay this person the maximum on the new job if it is anticipated that he or she is capable of performing the job even with no previous experience on it. In still other cases where individuals have had no previous experience and their performance may be questionable, they may be started at the midpoint of the range.

The influence of supply and demand is one of the complex problems encountered in job evaluation programs. In a number of cases, a shortage of qualified persons may make it necessary for a company to exceed the evaluated rate in order to hire the employee needed. Where this happens, immediate consideration should be given to alleviating the situation by initiating a training program or by adding additional responsibilities to the job to upgrade it to a higher job class. Certainly, deviation from the wage structure should not be considered the only solution.

Based on our discussion of the many aspects of job evaluation, it should be self-evident that job evaluation is not a scientific method of determining job rates, but is merely a systematic approach to a difficult problem. It is subject to the forces of collective bargaining, supply and demand, and other external factors. Like all programs involving human judgment, it is not infallible. However, its many virtues so completely outweigh its shortcomings as to make it a *must* in well-managed companies.

Employee Appraisal

Many situations arise in the workaday world in which employees have to be judged for wage increases, promotions, or other matters. Often seniority becomes a major factor in making such decisions, and many organizations (e.g., the military services) have even built "years of service" into their pay structures. Likewise, the unions have been staunch supporters of the use of seniority as a basis for promotions and layoffs. On the other hand, there is another point of view that ascribes to the use of some systematic type of employee appraisal to determine the basis for such things as pay increases, promotions, and other functions. In the sections that follow, we shall be discussing this area of supervisory activity.

Merit Rating

In every work situation, supervisors are observing and forming impressions of how their subordinates are performing on their jobs. In many organizations, this may be done on an informal basis. However, most large and many small organizations have developed formal plans for evaluating employees. These plans may go by a variety of labels (e.g., "merit" rating, "performance" rating, "personnel" rating, "service" rating). The term *merit rating* has been a traditional term that has been associated with rating plans for hourly paid workers, and we have chosen to use that term in the sections that follow.

In contrast to the impersonal nature of job evaluation, *merit rating* is concerned with employee appraisal. It is a systematic and (so far as possible) impartial procedure for determining the excellence with which an individual is performing a job. Merit rating programs are usually installed in an attempt to eliminate the many different approaches to employee rating that may be exercised by the supervisors in a business. As a result, employees are evaluated by means of a standardized system, and the ratings are more consistent, fair, and impartial.

Merit rating programs should be tailored for the employees they are to cover and should take into account those factors that are important in performing the jobs on which the individuals are employed. The rating should cover those items for which the company is willing to pay and may include such factors as experience, skill, judgment, dependability, adaptability, and other matters that have a bearing on job performance. It is common practice to use one rating scale or method for production workers, another for office workers, and still another for salesmen, engineers, or other groups.

Purpose of Merit Rating

The information obtained from merit rating may be used for a number of purposes, including the following:

1. As a basis for pay increases.
2. As a basis for promotions, transfers, or layoffs.
3. To determine the proportion of profit-sharing bonuses to be paid to employees.
4. As a basis for counseling employees.
5. To provide information for employee placement.
6. As a criterion for the evaluation of personnel programs such as personnel testing.
7. As a means of uncovering special talents and abilities.

In addition, merit rating probably forces closer and better supervision, in that the supervisors must observe the employees closely if they are to rate them accurately.

Methods of Rating

The rating of employees is one of the oldest and most universal practices of management, but it is only in recent years that systematic merit rating programs have been installed in industry. In establishing these programs, a great variety of methods have been devised for rating the employees. Among these are person-to-person, paired comparison, forced choice, checklists, critical incident, and graphical scales. The use of a graphical scale such as that illustrated in Figure 21–9 has proved to be one of the most popular methods of rating. Considerable care must be taken in designing these scales to insure that they contain suitable traits, a limited number of degrees of each factor, adequate descriptions of factors, and sound weightings of factors.

FCA 7-6

EMPLOYEE APPRAISAL

Employee's Name _____ Classification _____

Bank _____ Department _____ Division _____

Rating Supervisor _____ Section _____

This form is designed to help you appraise accurately the value of employees to the organization. You are asked to rate the employee on each of the several traits or qualities listed here. After each trait there is a line representing various degrees of the trait. The descriptive phrases beneath the line indicate the amounts or degrees of the trait represented by five points along the line. They are guide-posts. You rate the employee by checking at any place along the line that represents your judgement of him.

In view of the importance of these ratings, you are asked to study and observe the rules printed on the other side of the sheet.

QUALITY OF WORK

| Doubtful that quality is satisfactory. | While not unsatisfactory, quality is not quite up to standard. | Quality is quite satisfactory. | Quality of work is superior to that of general run of employees. | Exceptionally high quality. | No chance to observe. |

VOLUME OF WORK

| Unusually high output. | Turns out more work than general run of comparable employees. | Average, satisfactory output. | Inclined to be slow. | Insufficient output. | No chance to observe. |

CAPACITY TO DEVELOP

| Future growth doubtful. | Moderate development ahead. | Shows promise. | Very promising promotional material. | Great future growth probable; should go far | No chance to observe. |

Figure 21–9. Portion of a simple personnel rating scale using descriptive phrases. (From W. G. Ireson and E.L. Grant, *Handbook of Industrial Engineering and Management*; Englewood Cliffs, N.J.: Prentice-Hall, Inc., 1955. Reprinted by permission.)

Administration of Program

Anything that may influence employees' pay is of utmost importance to them and may lead to considerable friction if not properly administered. Therefore, management should give a great deal of attention to the design, installation, and maintenance of the merit rating program. Many of the problems that might otherwise be encountered in a merit rating program can be prevented through proper planning and installation. A suitable plan must be selected, the employees must be thoroughly acquainted with the program, competent raters must be selected, and the raters must be trained in the use of the system. It is common practice to perform the rating either every six months or annually, and then to discuss the ratings with the employees. This provides an effective basis for counseling employees and lets them know "how they stand" in the eyes of their boss.

For the most part, the rating is done by the employee's immediate supervisor, but it is not uncommon to have a general foreman, plant superintendent, or other executive rate the individual. Whenever possible, it is desirable to have more than one person rate the ratee, taking care that every rater has sufficient opportunity to observe the ratee and is competent to perform this important function.

In any rating system a number of deficiencies will appear that must be taken into account. The administrators of the program must provide a continuous check on the system's validity (does it measure what it is supposed to?) and reliability (does it measure consistently?). Also, they must guard against the common rating errors of the *halo effect*—the tendency of the rater to rate the ratee too high or too low on every trait because of some bias; the *leniency effect*—the tendency to rate the individual higher than he or she should be; and *central tendency*—the tendency to avoid the extremes of the scale in rating the employees. By and large, these rating errors can be reduced to a minimum through proper design of the rating scale (or other method) to be used, and then by thoroughly training the raters in its use.

Like job evaluation, merit rating is subject to the shortcomings of any program involving human judgment. However, employees must be rated, and merit rating provides a means for placing employee evaluation on a systematic basis. Thus, it, too, has come to be accepted as an indispensable tool of well-managed companies.

QUESTIONS

1. Will a job evaluation program remove all wage inequities? Why?
2. The Jackson Manufacturing Company, which employs about 350 production workers in the manufacture of metal office desks, is considering the installation of a job evaluation system. It has been proposed that all employees of the company (workers, clerks, supervisors, and others) be covered by the same plan. Would this be desirable? Why?
3. What is the relationship between job evaluation and wage incentive plans?
4. Why is it desirable to analyze jobs before attempting to evaluate them?

5. Would the job classification method of evaluating jobs be a good method for evaluating factory jobs? Why?

6. The point system of job evaluation is by far the most popular method of job evaluation. How do you account for this?

7. Would the factor comparison method of job evaluation be a desirable method to use in a company having only 40 jobs? Why?

8. What factors would be particularly important in a point system for evaluating top management jobs?

9. What problems might be encountered in trying to secure data to establish a community wage curve?

10. Some companies have used the practice of bringing out-of-line jobs that are above the wage curve back into line by keeping such jobs at their present levels and then letting the wage curve catch up to them through subsequent annual wage increases. Comment on this practice.

CASE PROBLEMS

Blodgett Company

The Blodgett Company has been in the woodworking business for eight years and during that time has experienced rapid growth. It now employs 400 employees on one shift.

Wage rates have developed in a rather haphazard manner over the years, and Roger Smith, the general manager, now realizes the need for a more scientific method of wage determination.

As a result, a point system of evaluation has been developed by the industrial engineering department and all jobs have been evaluated under this system. A comparison of the points assigned each job and base rates *presently* paid on each job follows:

Job #	Points	Present Rate	Job #	Points	Present Rate	Job #	Points	Present Rate
1	150	$6.70	11	700	$6.98	21	800	$7.45
2	120	6.65	12	400	7.00	22	740	7.52
3	180	6.68	13	305	7.18	23	710	7.30
4	290	6.78	14	450	7.02	24	760	7.45
5	220	6.88	15	480	7.10	25	725	7.35
6	220	6.78	16	450	6.98	26	750	7.35
7	120	6.58	17	650	7.18	27	900	7.50
8	250	6.62	18	525	7.15	28	880	7.60
9	200	6.68	19	600	7.30	29	905	7.60
10	510	7.05	20	575	7.30	30	930	7.65

Questions:

1. Assume that you are the industrial engineer and you decide to plot a scatter diagram of the above data using evaluation points as the abscissa. Draw the straight line of best fit (by eye).

2. After viewing the chart drawn above, Roger Smith feels that the general level of wages drawn by your line is about right. However, some jobs are out of line. He decides that about 10 pay grades should be set up, with all jobs in the same pay grade being paid on the same basis. Draw appropriate pay grade division lines on your diagram.
3. List the rate ranges and the point ranges that go with each pay grade. (No overlapping rate ranges.)
4. Do you advise the use of a rate range for each pay grade, or the adoption of a single rate for each pay grade? Briefly state your reasons.
5. What steps do you suggest to get those jobs that are out of line back into line?

Dolores Simpson

Dolores Simpson, 63, has been employed as a group secretary for three members of the Engineering Department in Acme Plastic Company for the past five years. Dolores has had an impressive work history, and one of her former bosses says, "She was the finest secretary I ever had." During the past year, however, the young engineers for whom Dolores works have expressed frequent complaints to Jack Tichenor, the Manager of Engineering, about her growing incompetence. Jack hasn't been surprised, because he has observed that she increasingly spends her time on trivia.

Like many companies, Acme Plastics requires its managers to sit down periodically with each of his or her subordinates to discuss performance. The annual employee appraisal report is usually used as a springboard for such discussions. Following the completion of Dolores's annual report, Jack Tichenor called Dolores into his office. After several moments of pleasantries, Jack asked her if she was aware that there had been complaints about her work and tried to acquaint her with ways in which she had been slipping and the reasons for her minimal wage increase. Dolores immediately became emotional and began to defend her actions, asking, "Who says I am not doing my job? I have been working my tail off for those young son-of-a-guns." Jack Tichenor was overwhelmed by her outburst and tried to console her. He said, "Dolores, you know that you and I are the same age, and I feel myself slowing down a bit these days. Is it possible that you are, too?" This statement set her off even more, and she stalked out of Tichenor's office. Her performance improved only slightly in the next three months, and she would hardly speak to Jack Tichenor.

Questions:

1. If you were Jack Tichenor, what strategy would you have used in meeting with Dolores?
2. In recent years, a number of companies have become discouraged with the use of evaluation interviews because of the discomfort that it creates. As one supervisor said, "I dread the day when I have to give Mary and John their annual ratings." If there is so much objection to appraisal interviews, what are the arguments for using them?
3. In considering Dolores's situation, it is evident that she is near the normal retirement age of 65 and already is eligible for Social Security payments. Should this enter into trying to decide what to do about her? What action do you recommend?

22

RESEARCH, DEVELOPMENT, AND ENGINEERING

This chapter is concerned with the development of new products and processes and the improvement of old products and processes. For a company to prosper and grow, it must do more than keep up with its competitors—it must get ahead of them whenever possible. "Getting ahead" almost invariably hinges upon research, development, and engineering activities. In considering the subjects of research, development, and engineering, this chapter will attempt to give meanings to these terms individually, but of more importance, it will attempt to show the interrelationships and need for coordination among these functions within a manufacturing concern.

Research seeks to make basic discoveries and uncover new principles. Some of this work is "pure," i.e., it has no foreseeable practical application; and other work is "applied," meaning that it is directed toward the solution of some particular practical problem. These concepts will be developed later, but we should bear in mind that both types of research make use of the basic sciences, the distinction between them usually being that of the end use.

Development usually follows applied research and often is concerned with the construction of pilot plants to show that a process is feasible, or with the construction of models to demonstrate the basic ideas incorporated in the new product.

The work of the research and development groups must next be transformed into commercial benefit. This means achieving a workable process on a production basis, or a product capable of economical manufacture, or both. Such transformation is the work of engineering.

Undoubtedly, many successful companies spend little effort or money on the three functions just mentioned. Many such companies depend on the designs of their customers and simply supply materials, parts, and components for use in the products of their customers. Other companies make it a practice to appropriate the designs and ideas of their competitors. Although this does not enable them to get ahead of their competitors, it does reduce their cost of research, development, and engineering.

To some degree, engineering will be required even in these last two categories of companies mentioned. Designing processes probably has a higher priority than designing products. However, some companies even avoid much of their process engineering work by using the services of equipment suppliers. There are many small concerns with only one engineer on the payroll, and this person may perform many duties other than strict engineering work.

Our concern here is primarily with the company that does perform an appreciable amount of research, development, and engineering work. Such a company is aware that tomorrow's profit depends to a large extent upon today's research, but it is also aware that dollars invested now in research and development probably will produce no income for a number of years to come. Without the research and development effort, however, there may not be a future for the company.

Companies have a tendency to expand their research and development effort in good times, but during poor economic times it is one of the first things to be cut. A forward-looking company will resist such a tendency or maybe even reverse it.

Types of Research

In the general sense, "research" is simply a systematic search for as yet unknown facts and principles. However, "research" is such a popular word in the present age that its use has been extended to cover many varied types of activities. For example, some companies have research departments that are largely concerned with uncovering knowledge of a type that is known by someone, although not by this particular company. Research of this sort consists largely of searching the literature and various reports published by institutions of one type or another. Although such activity is necessary in any company, it does not constitute a true research activity in the strict sense.

In this section we are going to identify and briefly discuss some of the commonest areas of research in the broad sense. It must be remembered that companies frequently identify subdivisions of research activity, largely for the purpose of more clearly organizing and controlling their total research effort.

Pure Research

Pure research, sometimes referred to as "fundamental research," refers to investigations undertaken primarily for the sake of knowledge itself. In this type of research activity there is no consideration of commercial possibilities, and the effort is directed primarily toward learning nature's laws simply for the sake of knowing nature's laws. A study of why grass is green is often cited as a classic example of pure research. Other examples would be an examination of the behavior of silicon crystals and studies of molecular particles. The direction of any pure research activity is usually not specified in advance, but is determined as the work progresses and promising avenues for further investigation identify themselves.

With a few outstanding exceptions, pure research is normally not indulged in by the industrial concern. Instead, such work is usually performed by universities, by special projects financed by the federal government, or by independent research agencies. The expense is too great and the return too small and nebulous for most industrial concerns to get very far into pure research. Nonetheless, some of the larger concerns that maintain elaborate research facilities have made real contributions to the scientific knowledge of the country. And certain projects started on a pure research basis have turned out to have very practical applications. An example is the development of nylon by du Pont. Other companies conducting pure research are Eastman Kodak, General Motors, A.T.& T., and General Electric.

Applied Research

As its name implies, applied research is normally directed toward solving some specific problem, or has a definite practical purpose. Applied research frequently finds uses for results of pure research. Examples would be the development of the transistor, robot applications, and the development of videotape recorders. In any case, a vast store of pure research findings or a vast store of knowledge concerning nature's laws must be available in order for applied research efforts to be successful. It is possible to succeed in solving a practical problem simply by chance alone, but in research effort, whether pure or applied, there is emphasis upon a systematic search for solutions.

Applied research has more appeal to the industrial concern, for it can see the prospects for quicker return for the investment made. In this type of research the basic sciences are adapted to industrial processes, materials, or products. The hope is to improve the present product by making it cheaper by using a better material, improving the container, adding a new customer appeal, or improving its appearance. In addition, the company might hope to improve the operating efficiency of the plant or even develop a totally new product. It follows that most industrial research is applied research, for in most industrial projects the goals are rather specific, and practical applications are expected from the results.

Product Research

Probably all types of research could be classified as either pure or applied, but it is common and also helpful to further break down and identify the research areas.

One common category is product research, which, as the name suggests, attempts to insure continued prosperity of the company by uncovering new product ideas that will meet the requirements of current and prospective customers.

In expanding product research, particular effort may be directed toward altogether new and different products, new and original uses for present products, or the utilization of a by-product. It is obvious that the stimulation for product research can come from many sources, including the results of some pure research effort, some ideas from customers, the need to utilize some particular technical skills possessed by the company, or simply the desire to expand the product line in whatever direction seems most feasible. In any case, emphasis is placed upon discovering a useful and saleable product.

Manufacturing Research

The discovery of new products is one path toward improved prosperity of a company, but the improvement of manufacturing processes and the resultant reduction in costs is another equally good path. For this reason, more and more companies are performing research efforts in the manufacturing area and with good results. Disk-controlled machines are a case in point, as are a number of developments of machines made by A. T. & T. Technologies that assemble parts and solder connections. In fact A. T. & T. Technologies operates a special manufacturing research division in Princeton, New Jersey.

Manufacturing research is usually directed toward the development of tools and equipment, handling devices, and methods of manufacture, all of which tend to reduce costs and increase productivity. In many cases, however, manufacturing research must be carried on at the same time as product research, for a product research idea may be feasible only if a feasible manufacturing method can be devised. In other words, product research and manufacturing research can be carried on as separate and distinct activities, but in some cases they may have to join forces in order to achieve the best overall results.

With the introduction of microcomputers and robots into industry, interest in manufacturing research has grown considerably in recent years. These new hardware components, along with new concepts such as just-in-time manufacturing, have fueled great interest and research effort in manufacturing systems. Chapters 5 and 6 discuss recent developments in manufacturing systems.

Materials Research

Materials research is basically linked with both product research and manufacturing research, for the discovery and improvement of materials often makes possible new products or new processes that were impossible prior to that time. The jet and missile age has placed great emphasis on materials research, and the success of many of the space programs was made possible only after the development of materials that could withstand the stresses imposed. In recent years, materials research has brought about significant improvements in almost any material one can name.

Market Research

Market research is more thoroughly discussed in Chapter 25, but needs to be mentioned here as another type of research activity. The principal aim of market research is to learn the needs and desires of customers. With this information, a company can carry out the technical phases of a research project with greater assurance of customer acceptance later on, and the company is also in a better position to plan its sales promotion campaign, pricing schedules, and sales effort generally. Undoubtedly, many manufacturers have produced products and placed them on the market with no idea in advance as to the possible customer acceptance of that product. The prudent manufacturer in today's world of high costs and high risks, however, attempts by means of market research effort to learn the reaction of his customers to the product before tooling up to produce that product.

Operations Research

Operations research has been referred to throughout this book, but perhaps this is the one place where we should attempt to give it a definition. This is extremely difficult to do, for there appear to be as many definitions of operations research as there are operations researchers. It seems safe to say, however, that operations research is the organized application of the methods and techniques of science to the study of operating problems in business, government, or military activities. In practice, the word "science" in the sentence above turns out to be essentially mathematics. In other words, generally speaking, operations research usually involves quantifying a problem and developing mathematical models that help explain actual events in an enterprise and that will permit experiments of a theoretical nature. This results in factual data that are used as an aid in arriving at management decisions.

Although operations research has been very helpful to many companies and has reportedly enabled these companies to save considerable sums of money, it should not be considered a cure-all for poor management. Perhaps its greatest difficulty is the need to quantify all of the facts relating to a particular situation under study. This requires some assumptions to be made in most cases, which in turn cast some doubts upon the the validity of the results. The results of any operations research effort can only be as good as the input data, which causes us to emphasize once again that operations research is simply an aid to decision-making. The executive responsible for the ultimate decision not only must consider the evidence produced by the operations research work, but must have knowledge of the input data and arrive at a decision after taking into consideration many other factors, which perhaps were not included in the model used. Some of these factors might be the financial position of the company, long-range goals of the company, special public relations considerations, and varying human factors. These, as well as many others, defy quantification but are highly important in any managerial decision.

Development

The distinction between research and development sometimes becomes rather fine. *Research*, whether pure or applied, attempts to discover or uncover facts or principles heretofore unknown or unrecognized. *Development* concerns the most economically feasible method for applying the facts or principles identified. It follows that development work many times is carried on after the applied research has been completed, and that applied research many times follows the completion of pure research.

The chemical industry presents an outstanding example of the use of development work as well as research work. Chemical research for the most part is conducted in laboratories, making use of the test tubes and other equipment of small size which can be easily handled on a bench or table. With such arrangements, many new facts, principles, and reactions are discovered. And these discoveries, if properly exploited, may have great use and application for industry if they can be adapted to large-scale manufacture. This is where the development people come into the picture with the construction of a pilot plant.

A discovery that was made in a laboratory using small equipment may be perfectly valid. But will the discovery prove valid with large-scale production equipment? The pilot plant is an intermediate step between the laboratory and the plant production equipment and is designed to provide at least a partial answer without too much expense. The pilot plant uses relatively small equipment for the purpose of studying and perfecting the chemical engineering aspects of the discovery. If the pilot plant proves successful, a full-scale plant can be constructed with some assurance that it, too, will work out satisfactorily.

Process Development

Development is generally concerned with putting new scientific discoveries into practice. Some of these discoveries may be incorporated into products and others into manufacturing processes. For the most part, development work is the work of engineers rather than researchers, although in many cases both groups must work together.

Process development has to do with machines, tooling, methods, plant layout, and the design of any special device or combination of devices needed to manufacture products. Although basic process discoveries have been made in an earlier research effort, it is the job of the development engineers to reduce the discoveries to practice and to make certain the ultimate designs will hold up under repeated use and possible abuse. As just described, process development comes very close to manufacturing engineering, which is discussed in a later section of this chapter, and not every company separates one function from the other. When separated, however, process development would probably concern itself most with the development and design of individual components, whereas manufacturing engineering would be more concerned with the installation and integration of the various components.

CAD/CAM, discussed in Chapter 5, is an excellent example of process development which requires the abilities and efforts of many types of engineers in order to achieve a successful application.

Product Development

Like process development, product development is a bridge between research work and engineering work. Typically, the work of product development groups consists of making several product designs and then testing and evaluating these designs. Through testing such designs not only in the market but in terms of performance in the laboratory or on the customer's premises, the group hopes eventually to come up with one best design.

Another possible activity of a product development group, usually carried on in cooperation with process development, would be the making of one or more pilot runs of the new product. Such runs would provide some actual products for testing as mentioned above, as well as give an opportunity to examine the process being used and to work out any flaws that might turn up. In addition to revealing the need for minor changes in product design, tooling, and methods of work, such runs also reveal some cost information that would be useful in price setting.

Organization for Research and Development

Ideally, the director of research and development should report directly to the president. In this way the research activity will receive the attention it requires, and coordination with the other activities will be facilitated. The importance of coordination of research effort needs to be emphasized.

Research directors are frequently in a position where they must ask for continually increasing appropriations while being able to show only prospective gains to balance the department budget. Their requests must be adequately supported and explained to those who are responsible for budgets and financing. The role of the engineering department must also be worked out, clearly defined, and coordinated. The engineers may be responsible for development as previously defined, or they may come into the picture only when production equipment is ready to be installed and maintained. In any case, close liaison is a prime requirement.

Coordinating research with sales and production is another point worthy of consideration. Such coordination is a prime necessity when research is of the applied variety, for the goal is the discovery of practical applications. In this case research people must have a keen understanding of and appreciation for the requirements of the markets. In addition, they must keep in mind the present production facilities and the adaptability of the facilities to new uses or new products. Coordination of this type is usually obtained by the use of a new-products committee composed of representatives of all the interested groups in the organization.

The internal organization of a research department varies in the same way that companies vary one from another. In a small concern it is no particular problem, for the director heads up whatever technicians and research workers there are. In a large company with a large research department the problem of internal organization becomes acute, for one must make certain that the researchers are divided into effective and efficient units. There are three common methods of division.

One way research activities may be divided is according to *plants or manufacturing departments*. Each plant or department in such a case would be engaged in making a product more or less distinct from that of the other plants, so research problems would also be distinct. Of course, if there is no valid distinction, then this method of dividing research activities would have its drawbacks because it would mean a duplication of personnel, effort, and equipment at each of the plants.

The second common division of research activities is made on the basis of *specific purposes*. Under this arrangement, one research laboratory serves all plants in the company, but is broken down into groups of specialists for each problem or process on which the company is working. For example, one unit may specialize in "pumping" problems and another may specialize in "power plant" work.

The third method of division is according to *research techniques*. Thus, there might be a group of organic chemists as one unit, nuclear physicists as another, and so on. This may seem the most natural division of activities, but it places a great premium on collaboration among the groups.

Very large companies make use of a combination of these methods, at the same time maintaining flexibility in their organization structure. Should a particularly urgent project come along, the organization structure of research may be rearranged so as to get the right people with just the right skills to work on the project. When that project is complete, some other type of organization structure is set up to handle the next project.

It was mentioned earlier that small companies have no particular problems with the internal organization of their research departments. But they do have a problem in carrying out research, because their funds usually are limited. One company has solved this problem by setting up a "research advisory committee" as part of its external organization structure for research. The committee is made up of outside scientists who are employed elsewhere (mostly at universities) full time and who consult with the company on research projects. In this way the company receives the advice of experts in the field without the expense of a large full-time research staff or elaborate facilities. Other companies have made extensive use of private research facilities such as Battelle Memorial Institute, Midwest Research Institute, and Armour Research Institute. Still other companies have financed continuing research projects in the universities.

Engineering

In considering the role of engineering in an industrial concern, we should keep in mind that this discussion refers to functions to be performed, and not to people or departments that may be responsible in any one company for performing the function. Figure 22–1 shows the functional relationship between research and development and the normal engineering activities carried on in a plant.

Although engineering skill and practice enter almost all phases of manufacturing activity, in general, engineering functions are considered to fall into three categories: product engineering, manufacturing engineering, and plant engineering. Engineers with various kinds of professional training, such as electrical engineering, industrial engineering, or mechanical engineering, may receive various assignments to perform any of the three functions.

Product Engineering

Product engineering as a function is mainly concerned with product design, that is, design of the product for manufacturing. Research and development have also been concerned with design, but largely of the laboratory type. Product engineering will design for commercial usefulness or application.

Design of components.   The ideas or models conceived through research and development must be further developed into specific practical designs. This will entail considerable design work which must be performed in close liaison with the research and development people, assuming that different persons are involved. Those responsible for design of the various components must have specialized training, background, and experience, but can be assisted greatly by currently available computer-aided design techniques and three-dimensional graphics packages. Knowledge of basic principles, manufacturing methods, and market demands can result in a product design that will make a sizable contribution to the success of the business.

Preparation of specifications.   Once the product design has been settled, the next step is to prepare product specifications for production departments. Such specifications will outline in some detail the finishes required and, to some extent, the processes to be used. Bills of material, which list all the materials and parts needed and in what quantities, must also be prepared. These will be used by the

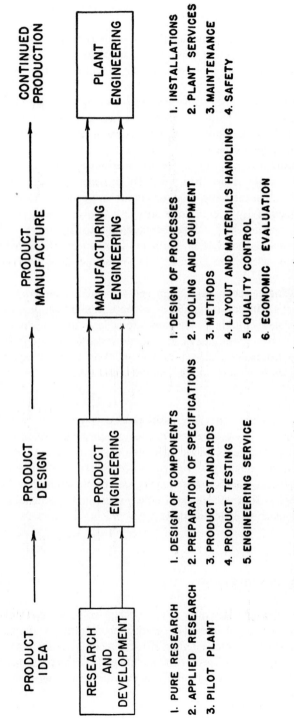

PRODUCT
IDEA

PRODUCT
DESIGN

PRODUCT
MANUFACTURE

CONTINUED
PRODUCTION

RESEARCH
AND
DEVELOPMENT

PRODUCT
ENGINEERING

MANUFACTURING
ENGINEERING

PLANT
ENGINEERING

1. PURE RESEARCH
2. APPLIED RESEARCH
3. PILOT PLANT

1. DESIGN OF COMPONENTS
2. PREPARATION OF SPECIFICATIONS
3. PRODUCT STANDARDS
4. PRODUCT TESTING
5. ENGINEERING SERVICE

1. DESIGN OF PROCESSES
2. TOOLING AND EQUIPMENT
3. METHODS
4. LAYOUT AND MATERIALS HANDLING
5. QUALITY CONTROL
6. ECONOMIC EVALUATION

1. INSTALLATIONS
2. PLANT SERVICES
3. MAINTENANCE
4. SAFETY

Figure 22–1. Three groupings of the engineering functions in manufacturing.

465

purchasing department to order from suppliers, as well as by the production departments. Engineering drawings will naturally be supplied to all interested departments, together with any other production details essential for the desired result.

Product standards. The quality of materials going into the product, as well as standards of performance of the completed product, are the concern of product engineering. Materials going into the product must be of sufficiently high quality to insure successful product performance, but not so high as to increase costs unreasonably. By the same token, product performance must meet customer requirements, but need not do more than this. To provide a product design and specifications that will meet these requirements is a big order. However, every product engineering activity is constantly striving to do just that.

Product engineering has another opportunity to keep costs down: by standardizing as much as possible on parts and components. Close coordination among design personnel will do much to achieve this desirable goal.

Product testing. Specifying design and standards is oftentimes not good enough, for product engineering will also be concerned with final product performance. This is particularly true in the manufacture of large units such as steam turbines or jet engines. Each unit must be thoroughly tested to be certain it meets the specifications of performance and has no defects. With complex equipment, the testing operations are more than routine; so the work is assigned to qualified test engineers.

Engineering service. In many cases product engineering may be called upon to perform service activities for both the manufacturing and sales departments. To aid sales, product engineers may confer with customers about complex problems, particularly if the company isn't large enough to have sales engineers. In addition, product engineers may be called in on certain manufacturing problems, particularly when there is some discrepancy between product specifications and the capabilities of the machine being used.

Manufacturing Engineering

Figure 22–1 shows the next step after product design to be product manufacture. Actual manufacture will be performed by production departments; however, engineering plays a considerable role in getting efficient manufacturing processes set up and operating properly. This function is frequently called *manufacturing engineering,* and much of the work is done by individuals with training in industrial and/or mechanical engineering.

Design of processes. As the name implies, product engineering is mainly concerned with the *product* and getting it ready for production. Manufacturing engineering as a function will be more concerned with the *process,* with the means and methods used to produce the product. Design of a suitable process is the main subdivision of manufacturing engineering activity. Frequently this work must be closely coordinated with product engineering, since the design of a suitable product may depend to a large extent on the design of a suitable process. Chapter 5 covered in some detail the design of manufacturing processes.

Tooling and equipment. Basic production equipment (such as milling machines or draw presses) may be available for the manufacture of a new product, but must be tooled or adapted for the new job to be done. New dies may have to be designed, new inspection devices worked out, or automatic controls rearranged. All this is included in manufacturing engineering and was covered more completely in the chapter on industrial equipment (Chapter 6).

Methods. Another problem for manufacturing engineering is the analysis of methods of using processes, machines, and equipment. The study of methods may entail modification or addition of equipment, but the main emphasis will be on the work pattern to be followed by the workers as they use the machines and equipment (Chapter 7).

Layout and materials handling. Closely allied with methods will be the layout of machines and equipment and the means of transporting materials between the machines. These two considerations go together; the layout used determines to a large extent the type of materials handling problems that must be met. These topics were discussed in Chapters 9 and 10.

Quality control. Setting product standards, one of the phases of product engineering discussed earlier, includes setting both quality limits and performance standards. A problem in production is the maintenance of certain quality limits throughout the manufacturing process, and it is the function of manufacturing engineering to set up controls for doing just that. Usually manufacturing engineering will work closely with product engineering in setting the original quality specifications. This is necessary so that quality limits will not be called for that are beyond the basic capabilities of the machines and processes available. Quality control was discussed in Chapter 15.

Economic evaluation. Manufacturing engineering must be cost-conscious throughout the fulfillment of all its functions; so economic evaluation is performed by almost everyone involved at every step. A manufactured product must be satisfactory not only in quantity, quality, delivery, and function, but also in cost. Manufacturing engineering makes one of its greatest contributions by constantly devising ways and means to reduce costs. The control of costs was treated in more detail in Chapter 17.

Plant Engineering

The final engineering function in manufacturing shown in Figure 22–1 is plant engineering. For the most part, plant engineering will be responsible for continued production after the facilities are designed and laid out. Other activities such as plant services and safety are in many cases also made the responsibility of plant engineering because of the close tie with maintenance work generally.

Installation

With manufacturing engineering having accomplished the design and layout of processes, it is usually the lot of plant engineering to perform the installation work. This comes about quite naturally. Plant engineering departments usually have the skilled mechanics under their direction, and these mechanics may do maintenance work as well as installation work. In the large plant there may be two sets of mechanics—one set working exclusively on new installations and another set working exclusively on repair and maintenance.

Plant Services

Plant engineering departments traditionally operate all central services—for example, the supplying of power, steam, air, and water in a factory. Elevators also fall into this category so far as direct responsibility for maintenance is concerned. If services are purchased from outside suppliers, the plant engineering department arranges for such purchases, checks equipment, checks usages, and generally coordinates the activities of the operating departments with the outside suppliers.

The care of buildings and grounds can be included too. This work is of such broad nature that it is best handled by plant engineering. Some plant engineering departments are also responsible for the company fleet of cars and trucks.

Maintenance

Probably the most important responsibility of plant engineering is that of maintaining the plant facilities and equipment. Only if equipment is adequately maintained can it be expected to operate properly and thereby yield a product of high quality at reasonable cost. Maintenance as a manufacturing activity was discussed in considerable detail in Chapter 16.

Safety

As a function that gives concern to management, safety is more completely covered in the chapter on personnel management (Chapter 18). However, since engineering departments frequently have some responsibility for safety work in a plant, it is well to discuss some aspects of safety here.

Although this section is included under plant engineering, the engineering aspects of safety are just as applicable to manufacturing engineering. Safety begins on the drawing board and continues through every step of the design and construction of a machine, workplace, or plant. A safety-minded designer or engineer should be certain that every possible precaution is taken to prevent human injury. Many times it is just as easy to design a machine so that it is safe to operate as it is to ignore the problem. The only difference is whether or not the designer is safety-conscious.

Plant engineering may be given a sort of overall responsibility for plant housekeeping. It would not be required to take any direct action, but more probably would inspect for poor housekeeping conditions and make appropriate reports. Housekeeping has a direct effect on equipment maintenance, on safety and health, and on fire hazards. Since plant engineering is directly concerned with these things, it thereby becomes concerned with good housekeeping throughout the plant.

Product Development Cycle

The development of a new product or the improvement of an old one commonly goes through the following seven steps before the product is ready for the customer to purchase:

1. Obtaining ideas.
2. Screening ideas.
3. Technical evaluation.
4. Market evaluation.
5. Final decision.
6. Getting into production.
7. Introduction to the market.

These steps aren't always separate and distinct, for in many cases it is desirable to carry on two or more steps at the same time. The point is that all are carried out—either knowingly or unknowingly—in the development of any new product.

Obtaining ideas.   Any new product comes from someone's ideas. A company wanting to develop and introduce new products must provide some means to obtain new product ideas. There are many possibilities. The job of some research people is to dream up new ideas. Employees, customers, and suppliers often have ideas worthy of consideration. Some companies even advertise for people to send in their ideas for new products. An aggressive concern should assure that all sources are investigated so that no possible ideas will be overlooked.[1]

Screening ideas.   After having collected a series of new product ideas, a company must screen them to separate the foolish ideas from those having real merit. This is naturally much easier said than done. There are any number of cases on record where a company thought it was rejecting a foolish idea only to have someone else accept and achieve considerable success with it.

Preliminary screening is usually handled by the director of research and development or by someone under his or her direction whose task is to consider new ideas. Those ideas having any merit at all are passed along to a committee made up usually of the research director, the sales manager, the production manager, and the president, plus others who may be concerned with the new idea. This committee has final say as to whether the idea is to be investigated further or else forgotten. By virtue of their position, experience, and knowledge of the business and its policies, the members of the committee are supposedly qualified to make such a decision.

Technical evaluation.   Should the committee decide to investigate the new idea further, one aspect of such an investigation would be a technical evaluation. Such an evaluation might attempt to answer such questions as method of manufacture, cost of manufacture, performance characteristics, and labor and machine requirements. Even before these questions are answered, some applied research may be necessary. In this or some other way, an investigation might get out of hand in regard to spending time and money. To forestall this possibility, the committee may authorize the expenditure of a fixed number of dollars in time and equipment to investigate any one idea. When the money is spent, the research director must report back to the committee stating the results to date and making recommendations. Then, more money may be authorized, or the idea may be dropped completely. One company spent $500,000 investigating an idea only to drop it at last, but during the process of technical investigation complete control was maintained by the simple expedient of regulating the money to be spent.

Market evaluation.   Concurrently with the technical evaluation is the need for a market evaluation. Again, some controls over the evaluation must be estab-

---

[1]The popular Post-It note pads came from a 3M scientist who sang in a church choir and was annoyed that the notes he used to mark the hymns kept falling out of the book. He yearned for an adhesive that would cause the notes to stick, but not stick permanently. An answer was found and test marketed in Boise, Idaho. Its success there led to national distribution and great success throughout the world.

lished and this is also done in terms of money allotted. Perhaps the first evaluation will be simply a cursory survey by salesmen. If the idea still looks promising, later on enough money might be appropriated to make a nationwide scientific survey of the market.

Final decision. Suppose we have gathered all the information possible (within reason) on both the technical aspects and the marketing aspects of a new product idea. A final decision is now necessary. Are we going to go ahead and make the product, or shall we shelve the whole idea, as did the company mentioned earlier which had already poured in $500,000? This decision will undoubtedly be made by the executive committee of the company or by the board of directors, based upon the recommendations of the new-product committee.

Getting into production. Assuming we have decided to go ahead, the next step is to transform the idea into a saleable product. From our technical evaluation, we know pretty much the steps required in terms of design work, machines to be ordered or constructed, workers to be trained, materials to be ordered, and control systems to be established. If the product is to be mass produced, the problems of getting into production are greater than if the product is to be made on a job-lot basis. In any case, there are many decisions to be made and problems to be solved—many of which are discussed throughout this book.

Introduction to the market. Perhaps even while we are getting into production, plans are being considered for introducing the product to the market. From the market evaluation, the size, location, and characteristics of the market are known, and now ways and means must be devised to impress this market favorably with the new product. This is normally the work of the sales and advertising departments. Problems dealing with packaging, channels of distribution, prices, discounts, guarantees, and service must all be worked out as part of this step.

Product Protection

To conduct a great deal of research and development work and introduce a new product only to have some competitor start making the same product soon thereafter is, to say the least, heartbreaking. Not only that, it may be financially disastrous. If this happened often, few companies would be interested in performing research and development work. Our federal laws are designed to prevent this situation, for they provide that inventors may patent their inventions, thereby keeping others from using them without permission. Patents are issued by the Patent Office in Washington, D.C., and may be secured either for new products or processes or for improvements on old products or processes.

In applying for and securing a patent, a full description of the product or process must be made. The wording of the patent itself must be very carefully devised or else the patent's value may be restricted because its coverage is restricted. Of course, the Patent Office will not grant the patent unless it feels that it does not infringe on some other patent, and this again places great importance on wording and description. A company will want to have on hand copies of all patents relating to its field (available from the Patent Office), not only to avoid applying for a patent that infringes on someone else's, but to be certain that its own patents are not being infringed on.

Patents run for seventeen years and are not renewable. After that time they are in the public domain, and anyone who wishes to is free to use the ideas. The government has simply granted seventeen years of protection in return for the inventor's divulging the idea so that after seventeen years all can use it. Sometimes the effective life of a patent can be extended by patenting improvements. In such a case competitors may use the basic patent but may not use the improvement patent without permission.

A patent in itself is no *absolute* guarantee of exclusive right for seventeen years. In spite of the best patent attorneys a company may hire, and despite the fact that the Patent Office won't issue a patent unless the officials feel it does not infringe on any other patent, holders of patents may have to fight for their rights and get them established in a court of law. If Company A starts to make a product covered by a patent held by Company B, then it is up to B to sue and establish in the courts the validity of the patent. The Patent Office in this case is an innocent bystander.

Frequently, products will appear with "Patent Applied For" or "Patent Pending" imprinted on them. These are simply used in an attempt to prevent prospective competitors from entering the field.

Since patents give protection for only seventeen years, and since they sometimes have to be fought for in the courts, some companies attempt to keep their ideas secret rather than apply for patents. In this case the protection lasts indefinitely so long as someone doesn't discover the secret. If the secret is discovered, there is nothing the company can do to prevent its use. Keeping a secret is very difficult, particularly with *products,* that is, if the products are sold to customers. *Processes* are easier to keep secret, for the people who come in contact with the process can be carefully selected and their number restricted. In one company where the process is a secret, only a handful of people are permitted access to the process room. The finished product comes out of the room through a slot in the wall.

Simplification, Diversification, and Standardization

The process of adding new products to a line or adding more varieties and sizes of a product is known as *diversification*. We have emphasized the need for a company to add new products to a line in order to prosper and grow. Sales departments in particular are anxious to have a diversified product line so that they can meet almost any objection or requirement that a customer might pose.

Of course, the idea of diversification can be carried too far. There can become so many types, styles, colors, and varieties of products that many are sold at a loss rather than a profit. It then becomes necessary to reduce or eliminate many of the marginal lines of products; this process is called *simplification*. Companies sometimes have to adopt elaborate programs of simplification because over the years their product line has been gradually expanded in order to supply the various needs of customers. The process has been so gradual that it is not noticed until someone thinks to raise the question. One company making electrical equipment found they were offering over 9000 different varieties of products. By redesigning products, talking with customers about their needs, and simply dropping some products, the company was able to reduce the line to about 300 varieties with no appreciable loss in business.

A third term frequently used is *standardization*. In a narrow and somewhat technical sense, standardization refers to the setting up of exact specifications or precise measurements. For example, there is the standardization of light sockets or the standardization of the lengths of measure.

There is undoubtedly a use for this narrow concept of standardization, but for the most part and for our purposes in this book there is little practical difference between standardization and simplification. Companies like to standardize on certain parts that are used in their products. This reduces the inventory problem and simplifies maintenance and repair. But this standardizing of the line, if it involves reducing variety, is equivalent to simplification.

Much standardization (simplification) has been accomplished on an industry-wide basis under the guidance of the Department of Commerce, the Bureau of Standards, the American Standards Association, the A.S.M.E., and others. Light sockets have been mentioned, but much standardization has also been carried out in bottles, nuts and bolts, flashlights, and hundreds of other items ranging from adhesive plaster to yarn. Such standardization works very well until competition becomes keen, and then someone comes out with something different in spite of standardization.

The optimum point between diversification and standardization has to be worked out for each company. There is much to be said for the application of standardization in the strict sense when applied to parts and small components. But when considering the product itself, even Henry Ford had to give in and offer cars in colors other than black. To go too far in varieties, however, may mean a considerable inventory and manufacturing problem with no gain in net profit. Every new product or variety of product should fill a need and justify its existence.

A company considering the question of diversification or expansion of its product line should ask the following questions: (1) Can some proprietary right be established for the new product? In other words, if a patent is secured on the product, or if a part of the process could be kept a secret, would the new product have a greater chance of payoff? (2) Will the new product complete a line of products, or make possible some sales that have heretofore been lost? (3) Can the product be marketed through our present sales organization and sales contacts? If the present sales staff does not possess the necessary know-how about the new product, or if another sales organization and distribution channel must be established, a company is essentially launching a new business rather than expanding a present one. (4) Are the research, development, and engineering technologies involved in the new product similar to those we already possess? (5) Is the manufacturing technology required by the new product in line with those technologies we already possess? Having to learn new technologies is not undesirable, but one should recognize the time, cost, and risks involved if such learning is necessary in order to diversify a product line. (6) Can raw materials for the new product be purchased at some particular advantage to us? (7) Can some by-product be utilized in the new product development?

Technical Management

Earlier in Chapter 3 we discussed management requirements generally and implied that the principles involved had applications in all management situations. While this is still true, it is desirable to briefly discuss some of the ramifications of management when dealing with the technical areas of research, development, and engineering.

Almost by definition, these technical areas consist of personnel with much higher levels of education than the general run of employees in a manufacturing organization. These education levels are necessary in order to get the required work performed, but this in turn calls for some special handling on the part of the manager. Generally, there is a greater need for democratic methods or even free-rein methods in dealing with a group of Ph. D.'s than there is in dealing with factory workers. The creative nature of research, development, and engineering requires that the manager set up and maintain an environment conducive to such creativity, perhaps even at the cost of certain company regulations and rules. The flexible-time concept would seem to have special application in the technical work-place.

The manager of any technical function has undoubtedly been trained in this technical function himself and probably has had very little training or exposure to management concepts. Anyone promoted to a management position from a technical position must devote considerable effort to learning the requirements. One of the more important concepts to learn is the fact that the higher the level of management, the less time is spent on technical matters and the more on management concepts and human relations matters. There is also the necessity to develop a leadership style, but in dealing with the technical function this style must be as flexible as possible in order to accommodate the variety of problems and situations that inevitably develop. This flexibility is called the *contingency theory of leadership* and enjoys considerable popularity today.

Owens[2] has indicated the value of technical managers regarding themselves as facilitators even though they have the word "manager" in their job titles. The

---

[2]James Owens, "R&D Managers as Facilitators," *Mechanical Engineering*, January 1985, p. 72.

facilitator provides support and leadership to the group but refrains from much advice or solutions to problems since the individuals in the group probably know more about their specific areas than does the facilitator. In other words, there is less likelihood of the usual superior–subordinate relationship in the technical areas than in many of the other areas of the manufacturing organization.

QUESTIONS

1. Outline a suitable management philosophy in regard to research and development—assuming the company wishes to prosper and grow.
2. Getting a man on the moon required the efforts of thousands of persons engaged in research, development, and engineering. Discuss the problems in each of these three areas in regard to the moon project.
3. What role could a pilot plant play in a company that manufactures products made from plastic?
4. Make a clear distinction between the technical evaluation of a new product idea and the market evaluation of that idea.
5. How could the work of a research advisory committee, made up of people outside the company, be coordinated with the work of a new-products committee, made up of people inside the company?
6. What "rights" does a patent give the owner of that patent?
7. Through what process is the validity of a patent fully established?
8. Suggest some bases that might be used to determine when to eliminate an item in a product line.
9. Describe the functional relationships between the various engineering activities carried on in a manufacturing plant.
10. What contributions could a trained engineer make in a research and development department?
11. Distinguish between product design and process design. In what types of situations would they be closely allied?
12. What role in safety work is played by product engineering? By manufacturing engineering? By plant engineering?

CASE PROBLEMS

Tudor Electric Company

The complete line of the Tudor Electric Company included over 900 items, all of which were manufactured in the company's Milwaukee plant. The company could supply any need in the way of small electrical equipment with the exception of wire, which it did not make. Its heaviest sales were in relays, switches, and sockets, which were produced in a variety of types and sizes.

An active and aggressive research and development department had been responsible to a great extent for the expansion of the company's line of products. During the past year 17 new products had been developed and turned over to the engineering department.

Getting the new products into production proved to be a long and difficult process in almost every case. Ed Belcher, the manufacturing manager, had experienced so much trouble along this line that he learned to dread any new product developments. He was increasingly confronted with recurring complaints from foremen that "designs don't work" or that "Engineering expects us to do the impossible." When Mr. Belcher investigated specific complaints, however, he found that few were really justified. Unfortunately, there had been two instances during the past year when the R & D department had actually requested the "impossible," and the engineering department, in working out the specifications, had not caught the error. In talking over these two cases with the director of research and the chief engineer, Mr. Belcher emphasized the general need for closer coordination. Both men assured him of their willingness to cooperate in any scheme that would reduce friction and eliminate such costly errors.

Questions:

1. What coordination plan can you suggest for this company?
2. Would you say that coordination is the only problem facing Mr. Belcher?

Atlantic Chain Company

The Atlantic Chain Company manufactures millions of feet of roller bearing chain annually. Until recently, 130 different chain styles were made, stored, and sold. The differences among the chains were minute and resulted from slight variations in dimensions and in other minor respects. Since the volume of sales on 50 of the styles was very low, a start at simplification was made by eliminating the 50 low-volume styles. Inasmuch as the company had been losing money on the 50 styles eliminated, profits were expected to increase, even if the customers who had purchased one or more of these 50 styles should fail to switch to one of the remaining 80 styles.

An analysis of costs and sales seemed to indicate that the company was making money on each of the remaining styles, but common sense told the management that there was no reason why 80 styles were needed.

Questions:

1. What steps could the company take so that further simplification of the chain styles could be effected?
2. Would there be any objections to simply eliminating those styles that contribute the least profit? Why?

Black Brothers Company

Dennis Black had just returned to his office full of enthusiasm and gusto after attending a technical meeting in St. Louis. He could hardly contain himself until he had a chance to visit with his brother Perry to discuss his ideas. Dennis and Perry were the owners of Black Brothers Company, and they divided responsibilities by Dennis covering all technical matters and Perry covering all sales and general office matters. The brothers were very close, however, and made it a practice to discuss almost any and all problems or questions with each other.

Dennis's enthusiasm after returning from the meeting centered around the use of the computer. The company had used a computer for many years for payroll and inventory purposes, and the engineering section had made extensive use of it for computational purposes; so most people, including the brothers themselves, felt very comfortable with the computer and its power. For some months Dennis had heard and read about such things as CAD/CAM and even CAE (computer-aided engineering), but he felt skeptical until he attended some sessions at the technical meeting. These sessions were demonstrations of CAD/CAM and CAE concepts in real-world situations, and they served to make a believer out of Dennis. Dennis in turn wanted to make a believer out of his brother before making any moves in this direction.

At their first meeting after Dennis's return, Perry urged caution. He said he didn't doubt what Dennis told him, but he reminded Dennis of the time he had returned from a technical meeting all pumped up about the value of operations research and wanted to set up an OR department right away. Perry had urged caution, with the result that in due time they were able to put operations research in the proper perspective within the company. They had also exercised caution in regard to other computer applications, and so far they didn't feel they had made any mistakes. Dennis, on the other hand, felt that the company could save so much money on the development of designs and in planning for manufacture that he wanted to call in a consultant and get started right away.

As usual, the brothers were so close that when they saw a difference of opinion they both backed off somewhat and made an extra effort to understand the point of view of the other. Both launched programs to learn more about CAD/CAM and CAE as well as about the applications to their particular company. They both felt that this development, like all others adopted in the past, should be made use of only if it were to improve operations and save some money.

Questions:

1. What is the proper perspective regarding operations research in companies today?
2. What could CAD/CAM do for a manufacturing company today?
3. What is CAE as compared to CAD/CAM?
4. Is the suggested criterion of justifying the installations of an innovation by money saving proper, or should one install new things because they are new and "we should get there first"?

23

FORMS OF OWNERSHIP

Basically, every industrial enterprise is in business to make a profit. It does this by producing goods or services for sale in a market. There appear to be many other purposes of modern business—for example, to provide income and security for employees, aid the government in defense, aid in the performance of certain public services, or even bring entertainment such as television shows to viewers. Regardless of how worthy each of these purposes may seem, we must return in the end to the realization that the enterprise would not be possible if someone were not willing to invest money in it. Being human, such investors do so only because they hope or expect to receive some profit.

In return for this investment, the owners enjoy certain rights and privileges. They decide what goods or services are to be offered to the market. They set basic policies on how the business will be managed. They decide how much money is needed, how it will be obtained, and how it will be spent. They reserve the right to change the general nature of the business or even dissolve it if it suits their pleasure. These rights and many others that could be enumerated go automatically to those who by virtue of investing their money have become owners.

The owners use various frameworks of business organization in exercising their rights and accomplishing their objectives. Several forms of ownership are available, and the owners will select the one that best meets their needs. Among these are (1) the individual proprietorship, (2) the general partnership, (3) the limited partnership, (4) the cooperative, and (5) the corporation.

Individual Proprietorship

A business owned by one person is an *individual proprietorship*. This is the oldest and simplest form of ownership, and although in many types of business it is outmoded, it still plays an important role in the present-day economic structure. Individual proprietorships are particularly important in agriculture, retail trade, and service industries. In manufacturing, the individual proprietorship seems over the years to have decreased in importance. This has come about because of the capital required in many kinds of manufacturing; however, manufacturing that can be conducted on a small scale is adaptable to the individual proprietorship form. Examples are the clothing and canning industries.

The greatest advantage of the individual proprietorship is its ease of formation. Another advantage is the complete control the owner can exercise in operating the business. She may change at will the type of business in which she engages, and, with the possible exception of special licenses, she pays no special organization or franchise taxes. Any profits made by the business belong to her, and she doesn't have to share any special trade or business secrets with others unless she chooses to do so. But all is not ideal with the proprietorship. There are some disadvantages too.

It was stated above that the proprietor can keep the profits for herself. Unfortunately, the same goes for losses. And the right to run the business as she sees fit, which seems to be an advantage, can work as a disadvantage. Not every proprietor is qualified to handle all the many problems of finance, production, and sales. She may hire assistants, but must know how to pick people, or losses may result.

A further disadvantage of the average individual proprietorship is the difficulty in raising large amounts of capital. The reason is the unstable nature of such a form of ownership. Should anything happen to the proprietor, the business as such no longer exists. So the proprietor has nothing but her personal credit position to aid her in securing loans.

The owner is liable for all the debts of the business, even though those debts may exceed the amount of the investment. This means that in the event the business should fail, the creditors could take her personal property as well as her business property in order to settle their claims. The owner of an individual proprietorship thus enjoys unlimited rights to profits and to the control of the business at the price of unlimited liability of debts and losses.

General Partnership

The *general partnership* overcomes some of the disadvantages of the individual proprietorship and has an important place in our economic system. A general partnership is an association of two *or more* persons to carry on a legal business as co-owners for profit. Sometimes there is confusion about how many persons can be partners in a partnership; strictly speaking, there can be any number, despite the common impression that the limit is two.

A partnership may be formed by means of a written agreement, or it may be simply an oral understanding among the people concerned. In either case a partnership exists in the eyes of the law. In a general partnership each partner has full agency powers and may bind the partnership by any act. In a sense, each partner may act as though he were an individual proprietor—the difference being that his actions affect not only himself but his partners as well.

The general partnership keeps many of the advantages of the individual proprietorship. It is, in the first place, easy and inexpensive to form. There are no organization taxes, and two or more people can form a partnership by nothing more than a verbal agreement. The partners then have direct control of the business and, of course, have full rights to all profits.

Two additional advantages, however, distinguish the general partnership from the individual proprietorship. First, since there are more owners, there may be more capital available. There are, at any rate, more people to be held responsible for the business, and more credit will be available to the firm. The second advantage is that more talent is available for running the business. It was mentioned earlier that rarely does one person possess all the abilities needed to operate a business successfully. A number of people, each with different skills and abilities, might form a partnership and as a group operate a very successful business, whereas any one of them going it alone might be likely to end up in bankruptcy.

There are certain disadvantages to the general partnership. The most serious is the fact that *each* partner has unlimited liability for the debts of the firm. If one partner commits the firm to the payment of large sums of money, the other partners are also held responsible and can be made to pay even to the extent of having their personal property attached.

The second disadvantage to a partnership, almost as important as the first, is the premium it places on the partners' ability to get along with one another. Since all partners can act as general agents, there is a great need for complete agreement as to who will do what. Usually these things are worked out thoroughly ahead of time— preferably by means of a written agreement. But even with a written agreement, there can be times of misunderstanding, disagreement, or mistrust that may lead to catastrophe for the enterprise.

There are other disadvantages to the partnership. Like the individual proprietorship, it lacks permanence and stability. Should a partner die (or become mentally unfit), the partnership as such no longer exists; all activity of the business is stopped, books are closed, and the deceased's estate is allocated its share of the assets. Then, if desirable, a new business is started, which may or may not be another partnership.

And, although the partnership enjoys a better credit rating and better access to capital than the individual proprietorship, there are still serious limitations on both. Many investors hesitate to invest money in a firm when they must take on personal liability for the firm's debts. Lenders hesitate to lend money because of a firm's lack of stability. Further, a partnership compares unfavorably with an individual proprietorship in that profits must be shared, keeping business affairs secret is more difficult, and there is a risk of choosing incompetent or dishonest partners.

Limited Partnership

In order to overcome the main disadvantage of the general partnership, namely, the unlimited liability of each partner, many states have statutes that permit the formation of a limited partnership. The limited partnership is an association of one or more general partners who manage the business and one or more limited partners whose liability is limited to the capital they have invested in the business. The limited partners must be genuine part owners rather than moneylenders, and they receive a share of the profits rather than interest on their invested money. The limited partner has limited liability only so long as he or she does not share in the control or the management of the business or attempt to interfere with the general partners' management of the business. In other words, the limited partner, in order to protect his or her limited liability status, must be a ''silent'' partner.

It must be borne in mind that under this arrangement there must be at least one general partner who manages the business and therefore is subject to unlimited liability. The limited partnership is applicable only in the state in which it is organized and will probably be treated as a general partnership in any other state unless it is also organized under the laws of that state. Obviously, its chief advantage is its ability to attract risk capital from those persons who would not enter a general partnership because of its unlimited liability features.

Cooperative

Strictly speaking, the cooperative can hardly be considered a form of ownership available to an individual who wishes to start a business. However, it is a form of private ownership, and it contains features of the partnership as well as some features of the corporation. The principal intent of the cooperative is to eliminate profit and thereby provide goods and services to the members of the cooperative at cost. Special laws deal with the formation and taxation of cooperative associations; so they enjoy separate and distinct status as a form of ownership.

There are shareholders in cooperatives in addition to a board of directors and elected officers, similar to the corporation. Members buy shares and pay fees to the association, and profits, or rebates, are distributed to its members periodically. The concentration of control in a few members is avoided by the stipulation that each member has only one vote.

For the most part, cooperatives exist in two forms: consumers' cooperatives, which deal in retail trade and services, and producer cooperatives, which are organized for group buying and selling of items such as fruits, grain, or livestock. Cooperatives are a much more popular form of organization in Europe than they are in the United States and do not appear to be particularly active in manufacturing operations. This has changed somewhat in recent years and gives promise of changing more in the future, as the line of demarcation between agriculture and business becomes less distinct. "Agri-business" is becoming a popular concept, and even now some consumers' cooperatives manufacture some of the products that they sell to their members.

Corporation

There are many reasons for the popularity of the *corporation* as a form of ownership. One is the recognition of its creation by the state in which it is organized. The laws surrounding the formation and operation of a corporation are fairly clear-cut, and the owners have a good idea of how they stand. Of course, this works a hardship too, for it means that the corporation is subject to many controls, regulations, and taxes.

Another reason for the popularity of the corporation is the limited liability of the owners or stockholders. Usually the liability of the stockholder is limited to the amount of his or her investment, although there have been exceptions to this in cases where workers had been unpaid for their services.

The corporation is recognized by the state as an "artificial person." This artificial person can hold property, sue, and be sued. The shares of stock that are evidence of ownership can be transferred without affecting the company; this means that the corporation can enjoy stability and long life.

The owners or stockholders of the corporation elect a board of directors which is charged with the responsibility of running the business. The board of directors then elects the officers who make the day-to-day decisions necessary for successful operations. The profits of the business are paid out to the stockholders from time to time in the form of dividends as the board of directors sees fit.

Stability, long life, legal sanction, transferability of shares, and limited liability all mean that the investor can invest without fear of jeopardizing other holdings and with some assurance that the worth of the investment will increase as the years go by. This has made it possible for the corporation to raise capital with relative ease.

There are some disadvantages to the corporation. Its being subject to various taxes, controls, and reports has already been mentioned. Another disadvantage is the usual lack of interest on the part of the stockholders. A great many stockholders look only for their yearly dividend and take little or no interest in the affairs of the business.

A final disadvantage is that the corporation's income is taxed twice. It is taxed first as income to the corporation. Then, as profits are paid out, they are taxed as personal income to the individual stockholders. This has led some corporations to hold back on dividend payments until those years when income tax rates are low.

Where to Incorporate

On first thought, one might assume that a corporation would incorporate in the state where it anticipated doing the major portion of its business. Closer examination will show that this is not necessarily so. Many considerations may make it desirable to incorporate in one state and do business in another.

The general corporation laws of the states vary considerably. Some are considered more liberal than others. Some states have a reputation for being tough on corporations; others enjoy a reputation of being fair and equitable. When a state's incorporation laws *are* liberal, it doesn't necessarily follow, from the point of view of the stockholder, that it would be desirable to incorporate in that state. Liberal laws may not sufficiently restrict operations to protect the investors' interests. States sometimes both liberalize their laws and lower their tax rates in order to attract businesses into locating there as well as incorporating there.

To incorporate in one state is not automatically to gain license to do business in other states. The incorporating state can give its own permission to the corporation to do business in other states; but to the other states the corporation is a "foreign" corporation, and they are not required to admit it. As a matter of practice the states do admit "foreign" corporations, but the "foreign" corporation must meet certain requirements. These requirements may be the payment of certain taxes and fees and the filing of annual reports. The reports are usually more or less routine, but the taxes and fees might be a real burden. Penalties for failure to comply with the laws pertaining to "foreign" corporations may be even more burdensome. Such penalties may be fines or perhaps the refusal of the state courts to enforce the contracts of the corporation.

Small and Large Corporations

It is difficult to draw a sharp line between small and large corporations because there is no clear agreement on their definitions. However, some distinction between the two should be made in order to clarify previous points and to introduce a few new ones in regard to the corporate organization.

It should be kept in mind that the corporation is first and foremost a form of ownership, and there is no requirement that a company must be of a certain size before it qualifies for the corporate form. It therefore follows that many very small businesses are organized as corporations and may perhaps have only one or a few stockholders. On the other hand, there is no reason why a proprietorship or partnership should not become a very large company in terms of number of employees or dollars of assets, although this seems highly unlikely because of the unlimited liability feature of these forms of ownership. If a business having only one or two owners should reach such large size, the owners would undoubtedly incorporate in order to protect their personal holdings. For many years the Ford Motor Corporation was owned entirely by the Ford family even though it was one of our country's largest manufacturing concerns.

Of course, most of our very large corporations have large numbers of stock-holders, sometimes up into the hundreds of thousands. In many of these corporations, no one person owns as much as one percent of the stock, and such situations lend credibility to the observation that stockholders sometimes lack interest in the affairs of the corporation. In some cases it has been demonstrated that stockholders do not even know the products of the corporation in which they own an interest, or know the kind of business involved. This is because of the ease with which shares of stock can be traded and the fact that many people buy and sell shares of stock in the hope of making a profit rather than with the intent of becoming part owner of a business concern.

When one person owns all or at least 51 percent of the stock in a corporation, control of a corporation is obviously no problem. This person undoubtedly selects a board of directors of his or her choice which in turn can be expected to elect officers of the choice of the major stockholder. It follows that in a very small corporation the owner of the stock is also a member of the board of directors and probably president of the corporation. In some states there is a specified minimum number of members of the board of directors; in such a case the sole owner of the stock may have to get one or two of his or her close friends or family members to serve on the board of directors. The sole owner nevertheless wields complete control over the corporation according to personal judgment.

Control of a corporation becomes a different matter when no one person or group of persons owns 51 percent or more of the stock. Particularly interesting is the problem of control in the corporation mentioned earlier wherein no one person owns as much as one percent of the outstanding shares. In cases such as this, the current management of the corporation sends out proxy solicitations to the stockholders. The proxy is simply a form on which the stockholder may, by signing and returning it, authorize the management of the corporation to vote his or her stock as it sees fit at the forthcoming stockholders' meeting. If there are important issues to be dis-cussed at the meeting, the proxy solicitation may offer the stockholders an opportu-nity to indicate how they wish their stock voted on these issues. On specified issues the management is obligated to vote the stock as indicated by the stockholders. On other issues the management is free to vote the stock as it sees fit if the stockholders sign and return their proxies in time.

Thus, through the proxy system, the management of many large corporations perpetuate themselves in office even though they personally own a very small frac-tion of the outstanding shares. So long as they conduct the business in a manner satisfactory to the stockholders, the stockholders almost automatically sign and re-turn the proxies without question. There have been a number of outstanding cases, however, when stockholders became unhappy with the way the corporation was be-ing run and managed successfully to overthrow the current management and vote in another management more acceptable to them. It is possible for others to solicit proxies in the manner described above, and there have been a number of very interesting proxy fights in a few companies during recent years. The very threat of such action may be a potent factor in keeping the management of a corporation on its toes. It is well for everyone to keep in mind that management personnel are employees just as are other personnel in the corporation and serve at the pleasure of the owners of the corporation.

Charter and Bylaws

The activities of a corporation are controlled by three things: (1) the statutes in the state where it is formed, (2) the corporation charter or articles of incorporation, and (3) the corporation bylaws. The statutes vary somewhat from state to state, but in every state the incorporators are required to draw up a petition outlining certain facts about the proposed corporation. This petition is called the charter, or the articles of incorporation, and is addressed to the proper state official, usually the secretary of state or a commissioner of corporations; and when the appropriate state official approves it, it becomes the corporate charter or articles of incorporation. At the time of approval, the official will ordinarily issue another certificate, signifying approval of the application, and the corporation automatically comes into being. Approval of the charter by the state official usually has the additional meaning that the law of the state is considered part of the charter. This has the effect of notifying the corporate officers that they should become familiar with the state law and comply with it.

Since the incorporators make out the charter, they can place anything in it they wish so long as it meets the requirements of the state law. As a result, charters or articles of incorporation often confer very broad powers on the corporation, for certainly it is better to have powers unused than to lack powers later necessary.

Although the charter gives many details about the general nature and administration of the corporation, it does not give all of them. The bylaws are for the purpose of guiding the officers of the corporation in the management of the company, and for the sake of completeness the bylaws will often contain the same information given in the charter. Some common provisions of corporate bylaws are the following:

1. Date and place of annual stockholders' meeting.
2. Date and place of meetings of board of directors.
3. List of officers of corporation, including their duties, terms of office, and method of appointment.
4. Number, term of office, powers, and compensation of directors.
5. Method of amending the bylaws.
6. Types of proposals that must be submitted to the stockholders for approval.

The stockholders have the power to make and amend the bylaws, although they may delegate this power to the board of directors. Practically speaking, the stockholders have very little control over the activities of the corporation officers or the board of directors. They must exercise control by the broad measures or controls set up in the bylaws. The bylaws outline the fundamental policies of the corporation, and it is up to the board of directors to see that they are carried out.

Stock and Stockholders

There are many varieties of stock in existence, but for the most part all varieties can be classed into two groups: *preferred* and *common*. In either case, the holder of a share is a part owner of the corporation itself; but the share of stock does represent a pro rata interest in the assets.

Preferred stock, as the name implies, is a stock that in some manner is preferred over common stock—usually in terms of dividends or assets or both. Preference as to assets means that in case the corporation is dissolved the preferred stockholder has claim to the assets ahead of the common stockholder. Of course, all creditors and bond holders must be paid off before even the preferred stockholder has any claim. The amount paid the preferred stockholder in such a case is the par value of the stock, or, if the stock has no par value, an amount stated either on the stock certificate or in the charter.

Preferred stock may also take precedence in dividends. The percentage dividend paid to preferred stockholders is usually fixed at the time of issue—for example, 7 percent. The 7 percent dividend to preferred stockholders would have to be paid before any dividend could be paid the common stockholders, and the 7 percent would be computed based on original selling price, usually $100. If the preferred stock is cumulative, dividends not paid in any year cumulate, and the total must be paid the preferred stockholder before any are paid the common stockholder. If the preferred stock is non-cumulative, a dividend skipped in any one year is not made up in any subsequent year.

The attraction of preferred stock can be seen from the above discussion. It confers certain privileges as to dividends and assets, and its rate of return is usually constant. However, if the corporation should have very high profits, the preferred stockholder might receive no more than the usual fixed return. In such a case the stock is called *non-participating*. If the stock is *participating*, the preferred stock is paid its dividend first; then the common stock is paid its dividend up to a rate equalling that paid the preferred stock; and finally, both participate at equal rates in any further dividend.

Preferred stock may also be made redeemable, which means that such stock may be purchased back by and at the option of the company under the conditions and terms specified in the certificate. The stock may also be made convertible at the option of the holder into other securities as specified in the certificate. In some instances the preferred stockholder is denied the right to vote except, perhaps, on certain issues or under certain conditions such as the skipping of a dividend. In one company the preferred shareholder has one and one-half votes per share as compared to one vote per share of common stock. Obviously, preferred stock issues vary considerably, and the corporation that issues them offers enough features to make the stock attractive to the market at the time.

Common stock is the simplest form of corporate ownership. The holders of such stock enjoy all the rights of stockholders, but without any of the special privileges discussed above. Corporations normally prefer to have their ownership entirely in the hands of common stockholders, not wishing to grant special privileges to the preferred stockholder. The pattern in issuing stock is oftentimes one of issuing common stock when the corporation is first formed; then, sometime later, when times become a little difficult and the company needs more capital, it may issue preferred stock. In difficult times common stock may not sell well, so in order to raise capital, some special attraction is necessary.

Although common stock does not offer the security of preferred stock, it does have speculative value. If profits are high, common stockholders may receive high returns. On the other hand, if profits are low, they may receive nothing. Common stock in some of the so-called blue chip companies has paid regular dividends for a number of years and so has become almost as secure as preferred stock. This status is made possible by good management of both the financial and the productive aspects of the business.

Not all stock carries voting rights at the stockholders' meetings. Although the practice of issuing non-voting stock is frowned upon, some nevertheless is current. Non-voting stock is sometimes issued to raise capital while leaving control in the hands of the original incorporators. Some preferred stock has no voting right unless dividends are skipped.

Reference has been made to the *par value* of stock. This is usually a somewhat arbitrary original value assigned to a share of stock. The actual selling price may be more or less than this amount. Selling price will usually reflect the earning power of and the assets behind the stock, and so the par value of a share is often meaningless. Therefore, it is common practice to issue common stock with no par value.

Stockholders are the true owners of the corporation, and as such, they have certain rights both individually and collectively. As individuals, stockholders have a right to their dividends when declared, to vote in stockholders' meetings, to share in the assets in case of dissolution, to sell their stock, to inspect the records of the corporation, and to participate in additional issues of stock. Collectively, the rights of stockholders are much broader and include the power to

1. Adopt and amend the bylaws.
2. Elect the directors.
3. Sell the assets of the corporation.
4. Amend the charter with the consent of the state.
5. Dissolve the corporation.

Bonds and Bondholders

Bonds are quite different from stocks. Stocks represent shares in the owner-ship of a corporation, and money invested in them becomes a permanent part of the capitalization. Bonds, on the other hand, are corporate credit obligations, and the holders of the bonds are creditors. It is expected that the money received from the sale of bonds will be returned on the date of maturity. Throughout the bond's life the corporation must pay interest on it, just as if it had borrowed from a bank.

Bonds are bought and sold just like stocks, and the interest is paid to whom-ever holds the bond on the day of payment. The investment risk in a bond is less than that in either preferred or common stock. The interest rate on bonds is fixed; the money paid out as interest is a cost of doing business. In case of liquidation, the bondholders have prior right to assets ahead of all stockholders.

So long as the corporation pays the interest due on the bonds and can pay them off at maturity, the bondholder has nothing to worry about. Should the corporation default in its payments, the bondholder can exercise certain rights as set forth in the charter, bylaws, and trust indenture. Basically, the rights of bondholders in such a case are similar to those of any creditor—the right to take over the property con-cerned. Since bonds, like stocks, are usually widely held, it would be extremely difficult for the bondholders to be sure the corporation was always living up to its obligations. Consequently, at the time of issue, a *trustee* is appointed to look out for the rights of the bondholders, and the trust indenture will specify the action to be taken in case of interest default. In the end the trustee may foreclose, take posses-sion, and sell the property for the benefit of the bondholders—a procedure similar to the one followed in case of default by individuals on car or house payments.

A corporation may retire an outstanding bond issue in a number of ways. First, it can pay off the bonds at maturity, usually 20 years or more after issue. Second, it can call in its bonds for payment prior to maturity if it has reserved that right. Third, it can purchase its own bonds in the securities market. Finally, at the option of the bondholder, the bond may be converted into preferred or common stock. Sometimes too, bonds are paid off at maturity by the process of "re-funding." In this case, a new issue of bonds is sold in order to raise money to pay off the old issue. A corporation might use this procedure if it continued to need the capital.

Board of Directors

Except in those matters that are reserved for the consideration of the stock-holders, the board of directors has final authority in all corporate matters. The num-ber of directors varies, but state laws usually set a minimum. Variations from three to 20 are not uncommon. The term of office is usually one to three years, but it is common for directors to be re-elected, with the result that many serve for long peri-ods.

Specific powers usually exercised by the board of directors are:

1. Election of officers.
2. Making contracts in the name of the corporation.
3. Declaring dividends.
4. Issuing corporate stock.
5. Determining corporate policies.

Of the specific duties listed above, the more important ones are the decisions on company policies and the making of contracts in the name of the corporation. In carrying out these duties, the board exercises control over the expenditure of large sums of money and gives its approval to plans to exploit new markets. It is common for the corporate officers to formulate policies and plans for the board's approval, for usually the officers are more familiar with details than are the directors; but the officers must "sell" the plan to the directors. Should the plan fail, the directors will no doubt be more careful in approving the next plan and may even start looking for new officers.

Directors acting as a group may make serious mistakes that cost the corporation dearly. If they have acted in good faith and have exercised reasonable caution, they are not held liable. However, should they have been negligent in the conduct of corporation affairs, they may be held personally liable for the resultant losses. If any one director feels that the action taken by the board as a whole is not to the best interests of the corporation, he can protect himself against liability by stating his disapproval and having his statement duly recorded in the minutes of the meeting at which the action was taken.

The makeup of the board of directors varies considerably among American corporations. One school of thought holds that members of the board for the most part should *not* be employees of the company, and many corporations, following this practice, make certain that a majority of the board members are not employees. In such cases, the only employees who are board members are probably the duly elected officers of the corporation. A second school of thought believes that board members *should* be employees, and although such an arrangement is quite common in a very small organization with only a few members on the board, it is also followed by a few of our very large corporations. The advantage of having directors who are also employees is that they are more familiar with the affairs of the company and perhaps would be in a better position to make decisions or contribute to the making of important decisions. On the other hand, one of the more significant functions of a director is to ask discerning questions, an activity that does not depend upon an extensive knowledge of the affairs of a business. The ability to ask perceptive questions comes from experience in decision-making in a variety of business situations, and such persons often develop an intuitive feeling about business problems and considerations and are almost instinctively able to ask the kinds of questions that should be asked before a new venture is launched. The purpose of the questions is not to place management on the spot but to be certain that all facts are considered, that all facets of the problem have been explored, and that the alternative courses of action have been properly rejected. It seems reasonable to assume that if management had to present their proposals to a board made up of persons able to ask this discerning type of question they would do their utmost to anticipate the questions and to exercise considerable care in preparing and presenting any proposal. By such a process, both board and management contribute toward the future growth and success of the organization.

Corporate Officers

The bylaws of a corporation usually provide for the election of four officers, though there may be more. The four are president, vice president, secretary, and treasurer.

The *president* is usually the chief executive officer and has responsibility and authority to carry out the policies adopted by the board of directors. He or she provides guidance to the other executives and keeps the board of directors informed on the progress of the various phases of the business. Although the office of *vice president* was created originally in order to have someone to take over should the office of president become vacant, it currently denotes the head of an executive function such as sales or manufacturing. The person designated to take over in the absence of the president is frequently called the *executive vice president*.

In many corporations, e.g., General Motors, Chrysler, and Brunswick, the chairman of the board of directors is the chief executive officer rather than the president. In such cases the president is designated the chief operating officer. The division of duties between the two positions varies from corporation to corporation.

The *secretary* has a number of legal duties to perform, such as filing reports with state officials, maintaining stockholder lists, handling stock transfers, and sending out notices of stockholder and director meetings. The *treasurer* is in charge of the receipt and disbursement of all corporate funds and will render reports from time to time accounting for the money entrusted to his or her care. Figure 23-1 shows the basic organization of a corporation. See Chapter 4 to relate the corporate organization to the operating organization.

Government Regulation

Having been created through the authority of the state, the corporation finds itself very much regulated by the laws of the state. Laws requiring corporations to file various forms and reports have already been mentioned.

There are state laws that tax the corporation's income and that regulate the sale of its securities. The federal government likewise has laws that control many phases of the corporation's work if it is engaged in interstate commerce. And, of

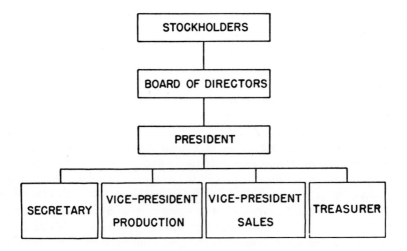

Figure 23-1 Basic organization of a corporation.

course, whether or not the corporation is doing business across state lines, it is subject to the federal tax on income.

Each of the states has its own laws that attempt to protect the public from buying fraudulent securities. Usually such laws require the corporation to file a statement qualifying it to sell the proposed securities. The corporation can then proceed only after approval by the state authorities. In the meantime, investigations can be made as to the truth of statements and claims. In general, statements are approved if there is no untruth stated or implied in them. The government doesn't assume the responsibility of saying whether or not a security is a good buy; but it does want the whole truth put before the investor before the investor buys.

The depression of the early thirties, in which many people lost millions of dollars in worthless securities, led to the passage of federal laws regulating the issuance and sale of securities. The main laws were the Securities Act of 1933, the Securities Exchange Act of 1934, the Public Utility Holding Company Act of 1935, and the Investment Company Act of 1939.

The Securities Act of 1933 followed the principle of getting all the facts about the issue before the public. A registration statement giving all the essential facts must be filed with the Securities and Exchange Commission if the issue is to be offered publicly in interstate commerce. A waiting period is provided between the filing of the statement and the issuing of the securities, so that the stated facts may be investigated. The commission is given effective powers to force observance of the law.

The Securities Exchange Act of 1934 provided for supervision of the stock exchanges and of the activities of the security markets. The Holding Company Act of 1935 gave the Securities and Exchange Commission powers over the financing of public utilities and broke up some of the holding companies in the public utility field. Investment companies and investment advisers were placed under control by the Investment Company Act of 1939.

Ownership Combinations

Combining businesses is a continuous process taking place in order to effect operating economies or increase profits. In the early days companies combined in an effort to increase profits through monopoly and restraint of trade. Today, companies combine in one manner or another to increase profits through diversification or to provide an outlet for some technical skill or marketing ability.

In 1890, all business combinations designed to restrain trade were prohibited by the passage of the Sherman Antitrust Act. This act applies to all businesses engaged in interstate commerce. It may be of historical interest to indicate what a trust was prior to 1890, since this is what the Sherman Antitrust Act specifically prohibited. Strictly speaking, the trust was a "voting trust," which was an arrangement whereby the holders of stock in competing companies turned their shares over to trustees, who would then vote all of the stock and thus control the policies of the several corporations. Trust certificates were issued in place of the shares turned over to the trustees. There were leading trusts formed in the oil, whiskey, sugar, lead, and cotton oil industries.

The Sherman Antitrust Act made the above form of business combination illegal and was the first of a series of federal acts designed to protect trade and commerce against unlawful restraints of trade and monopolies. The Clayton Act was passed in 1914 to correct some abuses that had not been affected by the Sherman Act, and in the same year the Federal Trade Commission Act, which prohibited unfair methods of competition, was passed. The Clayton Act was amended in 1936 by the Robinson-Patman Anti-price Discrimination Act; the Tydings-Miller Act was passed in 1937, amending the Sherman Act; and in 1938 the Federal Trade Commission Act was amended by the Wheeler-Lea Act. Whereas the Sherman Act made illegal the existence of monopolies, the later acts and amendments were generally designed to prevent tendencies toward monopolies. In spite of all such legislation, one only has to read current reports of antitrust suits to recognize there is a certain amount of inconsistency in public policy regarding the definition of monopolies and tendencies toward them.

A consolidation of two or more corporations takes place when the existing corporations are fused into a single new one. The plan of consolidation must necessarily meet the legal requirements of the state in which it is formed, but generally speaking, upon the approval of the specified percentage of the outstanding shares and the filing of the contract of agreement as to the fusion of the various corporations, the actual exchange of the stock certificates of the old companies for that of the new can take place, and the original companies no longer exist.

A merger is slightly different from a consolidation in that one or more corporations are absorbed into another corporation. Again, agreements are worked out whereby the stock of the corporation that is to remain active is exchanged in some ratio for the stock of the corporation that is to be absorbed. When approved by the required number of stockholders, the exchange is made and the merger takes place, with the result that the absorbed company ceases to exist.

Consolidations and mergers seem to take place in cycles in this country. In the 1950's and 1960's many so called conglomerates were formed as companies such as I. T. & T. and Litton bought up many companies in order to expand their business and improve their earnings ratio. The trend became so pronounced that Congress considered laws to prohibit many takeovers. The 1980's have produced another cycle of takeovers and threatened takeovers, many involving billions of dollars. Oil companies in particular seem to be targets for takeovers. Ironically, earlier conglomerates have been selling some of the companies they previously took over.

Effective combination of corporations can take place through either the sale of assets or the lease of assets. One corporation could sell its assets to another and continue to exist as a corporation, although if it ceased to exist, the combination would simply be a merger. The leasing of assets is also commonly practiced, and some of these leases endure for a hundred years, thereby having about the same effect as a sale.

We commonly think of a holding company as one that holds stock in other corporations but performs no operations itself. This may be true in the strict sense, although many corporations today conduct operations of their own as well as hold stock in other corporations. In some cases the stock held constitutes a large proportion of the outstanding shares, and the "held" company may be operated as a separate division. In such a case, one company is usually referred to as the parent company and the other as the subsidiary.

QUESTIONS

1. Compare the means by which owners exercise their rights in a partnership with the means to this end in a corporation.
2. Some thought has been given to putting government-operated business on a profit basis. Is this a desirable step? Explain your answer.
3. Distinguish between the words "company" and "corporation." Are they ever interchangeable?
4. Corporations have often been called "monsters with no soul." Explain the justification for such a statement.
5. Explain the double taxation of a corporation's income.
6. What is the distinction between the corporation charter and the corporation bylaws?
7. Distinguish between "par value" and market value" of a share of stock.
8. An issue of preferred stock is cumulative and participating and also takes precedence

in dividends and distribution of assets. Explain in some detail the basic features of this issue.

9. How can someone own less than 51 percent of the shares of a corporation and still control it?

10. What are the rights of bondholders in a corporation?

11. What is the source of the authority of the board of directors?

12. Would it be possible in a corporation for the officers, the board of directors, and the stockholders to be the same group of people? Explain.

13. If the Securities and Exchange Commission approves an issue of stock, does this mean that the stock is a good buy? Explain.

14. Investigate and report on (a) a company that has recently acquired another company and (b) a company that has recently sold one of its businesses to another company.

CASE PROBLEMS

J.J. McCormick, Inc.

The board of directors of J.J. McCormick, Inc., has given final approval of a plan to expand production facilities over 100%. The approval was voted with the proviso that a satisfactory proposal for raising the necessary capital be submitted by the treasurer of the company. The money to be raised would more than double the company's present capitalization of $200,000.

In appraising the various possibilities for raising capital, the treasurer notes that the company is in good financial position and has paid regular dividends on the common stock since incorporating 25 years ago. He also notes that the present board of directors as a group owns over 50% of the common stock.

Questions:

1. List factors both for and against a recommendation that the expansion be financed by the sale of
    (a) common stock.
    (b) preferred stock.
    (c) bonds.

2. Based on your listings in Question 1, what method would you recommend? Outline any assumptions made.

3. Would a decision be easier to reach if the board as a group owned only 5% of the common stock?

Riverside Investment Club

The Riverside Investment Club had turned out to be a very remarkable organization. It was formed 17 years ago by 15 local business people in a Midwestern city for the purpose of making investments in the stock market on a mutual basis. The so-called dues to the club were $100 a month per member, and at their monthly meeting the members decided how to invest their money. There was a new investment each month, but at the meeting they also considered and made decisions regarding possible changes in earlier investments.

The club was remarkable for two reasons. First, it had done extremely well in the stock market. In fact, one of the engineering members made an economic analysis over the life of the organization and determined that members had obtained a 28.4 percent return on their money on an annual basis. The second remarkable feature was that the same 15 people had stayed together in the club all these years. They had all remained rather tight-lipped about their results in the club, so that there were no requests for others to join the club in order to benefit from their success. In other words, they were a very close-knit group, all of whom liked and trusted one another.

Since all the members were local business people, they were very interested in a new small manufacturing company that had been started in their community a couple of years ago. The interest stemmed from both what seemed to be a wonderful product and the owner, who possessed remarkable technical know-how. After two years, however, the owner found himself in financial difficulty even though his product was enjoying considerable success in the marketplace. Jerry Knapp, who was this year's president of the club, had been having many discussions with the owner of the new business and learned that he was quite willing to sell out and stay on as an employee.

Jerry had immediately suggested to his fellow club members that they should consider taking over this business, for the opportunities were tremendous and the club could easily raise the resources required by either selling some of its holdings or using the holdings as security for bank loans.

Since all the club members were fairly familiar with the overall situation, Jerry's suggestion won general acceptance fairly easily and quickly. Today's meeting, however, dealt with the matter of the best form of ownership. The present owner was operating as a proprietorship, and certainly no one in the club wanted to enter into the arrangement as a general partnership because of liability problems. The general assumption had been that they would form a corporation, but at today's meeting a dissenting voice on the matter was heard.

"My business is organized as a limited partnership," said Don Hand, who ran a local machining and plating business. "There are about 25 people who own shares in the company and who are silent partners, while I am the general partner. As general partner, I run the business and accept all the liability. It operates essentially like a corporation, but was much less costly to set up than a corporation and avoids all the monkey business of having to deal with the state."

"But, who among us wants to be the general partner?" asked Jerry. "We all have our own separate interests and obligations."

"Why not make the present owner the general partner?" answered Don. "We could adjust the purchase price so he could retain some ownership as a partner and then retain him as the general manager and general partner. We could be the silent partners."

After an hour of further discussion, it was decided to contact a local attorney and have her come to a special meeting the following week to point out the advantages and disadvantages of each type of ownership arrangement.

Questions:

1. Make a table comparing all the advantages and disadvantages of the corporate form of ownership to the limited partnership form of ownership as they would be applied in your state. Recognize that these will probably be different in some other state.

2. Can a manufacturing business expect to produce a rate of return equal to the 28.4 percent which the investment club has produced over the years?

3. On the basis of your above answer, would you recommend that the club make the investment?

4. Knowing the involvement of the club members in the local community and their interest in this business, do you think they could remain silent and thereby retain their limited liability status if they formed a limited partnership?

5. What is your final recommendation as to the best form of ownership should the club decide to go ahead?

24

FINANCIAL MANAGEMENT

Someone has said, "It takes money to make money." Though not always true, this statement does contain a large element of truth when applied to a business or industrial establishment.

Capital is the lifeblood of a business. Regardless of how good an idea one has, money will be required to turn that idea into profits. There must be sufficient capital to organize the business, to provide necessary buildings, machines, and equipment, to buy raw materials, to meet advertising and sales expenses, to meet payrolls, and to take care of a host of other expenses incurred in getting established . Enough capital must also be available to carry the business until it shows more income than outgo.

Kinds of Capital

In using the word "capital" the businessperson usually lumps together all of the elements that will be needed to start an enterprise, namely, land, buildings, machinery, tools, and materials. In the technical sense, land should be distinguished from the other means of production because the latter are reproducible and land is not. However, this distinction is rarely made. Furthermore, capital is most often thought of in money terms, for promoting a new enterprise or expanding a present one is largely a financial operation. Money and credit are the chief means for acquiring the elements of production just mentioned, including the land, so it seems logical to employ the word capital in this purely financial sense. For our purposes, then, capital will mean the cash money and credit required to start and operate a business. Money and credit should not be regarded as simply that, however, but should be considered with a special view to their source, time required to acquire and/or repay, and intended use. Failure to make these distinctions has led many businesses, large and small, into financial difficulties.

Equity Capital and Borrowed Capital

Equity capital is that money put into the business by the owners of the business and may be in the form of land, buildings, machinery, or materials, as well as cash itself. Borrowed capital, obviously, is that money obtained from some outside source with a promise to repay at some future date. This is almost always in the form of cash. The difference between these two kinds of capital is highly significant for the beginning or expanding business. Of necessity, the borrowed capital contains a commitment to repay at some specific future time, as well as an obligation to pay interest during the intervening time. The equity capital contains no such firm promise, although there is naturally an expectation and a moral obligation to pay dividends if profits should be forthcoming. The difference between these two types of obligation is particularly significant during a period of depressed business conditions. A company highly dependent upon borrowed capital may find itself forced out of business by its creditors, whereas a company more dependent upon equity capital could delay dividends to its stockholders until a time that profits would justify such payments. Lack of profits does not cancel a company's obligations to its creditors, or to its sources of borrowed funds.

Short-Term, Intermediate-Term, and Long-Term Capital

As regards capital funds that are borrowed, another important distinction is made according to the time period for which the loans are made. Business loans are usually made by banks, although insurance companies do sometimes make the longer-term loans to manufacturing concerns. Short-term capital refers to loans made for periods of one year or less. Thirty-day loans are not uncommon and are generally made for the purpose of paying for material, labor, or other items for the production of goods which will be completed and sold in the very near future. Money borrowed as intermediate capital would be for a period of a few years, rarely exceeding five, and would be for the purpose of purchasing tools, machinery, and other equipment having a life of several years and therefore likely to have an appreciable effect upon costs and profits during that time. Long-term capital would be that money borrowed for repayment in ten, twenty, or even fifty years. This money would normally be for the purpose of financing the purchase of land, erection of buildings, and purchase of basic machinery having a long life. Since pay-off of this kind of investment could not be expected for a number of years, one would logically prefer to arrange for long-term capital rather than short-term or intermediate-term capital.

The distinctions regarding the time periods of borrowed capital are not always clear and simple, and there is likely to be much overlapping. For example, the borrower of intermediate capital may obtain the benefit of long-term capital through successive renewals of his loan. Likewise, the borrower of long-term capital may gain some of the advantages of intermediate-term capital by having the privilege of paying off the loan before it matures. The three classes, however, do represent three different types of capital funds and become important, not only because they show the different financial needs of a business, but because they identify different sources of funds.

Fixed and Working Capital

This final classification of capital refers to the use made of the money. The typical industrial enterprise has land, buildings, machinery, tools, and equipment. Assets of this type are intended for use over and over again for a long period of time and are commonly called fixed capital. In addition, an enterprise needs funds to cover its cost of operating. The latter includes purchase of materials, payment of wages, storage costs, advertising, maintenance, and shipping. Moreover, there is a need for money to carry the enterprise during the time lag between the sale of its products and the payment for them. Funds to cover these costs are commonly called working capital.

The relationship between the needs of capital and its sources should be fairly obvious. Money for basic facilities such as land and buildings should normally and preferably come from equity sources, but if borrowed capital must be used, it should be of the long-term variety. Short-term loans could supply some of the working capital, with the possibility of intermediate capital being used for the same purpose. Clearly, sound financial management depends upon the proper balance of the sources of capital, methods of raising capital, time elements involved, and uses that are to be made of the capital.

Sources of Capital

Where does one get money to start a business or to breathe new life into it after it is started? The main sources of capital are savings, loans, sale of securities, trade credits, and profit plowback. Which source one taps will depend upon many factors. Some are appropriate when the business is getting started, some are more appropriate later on, and some are appropriate at any time. We will discuss each in turn, indicating desirable and undesirable features.

Savings

Fundamentally, all capital for investment in business and industry comes from savings. People, rich or poor, save their money, or, more explicitly, save what money they have left over after paying their bills. With this money, they buy shares in building and loan concerns, they purchase life insurance, they buy stocks and bonds, or they put cash in the bank for a "rainy day." In any of these events the money is made available for further use and investment. If people did not save or did not have some money left over after their bills were paid, much of the money used for capital expansion would no longer be available. The Japanese seem to save more of their earnings than do Americans, and the Scandinavians save less than Americans. Probably the differences have some relationship to the extent the respective governments provide a "welfare" state.

Although the general concept of savings is important to the future growth and expansion of our economy, it is the problem of financing an individual business we wish to pursue here. If we think in these narrower terms, we might ask where Joe Jones gets the money to start a machine shop in his basement. Chances are he gets the money from savings—his own personal savings, for this is the way that many such businesses get their start. The great advantage of the use of personal savings is the freedom from outside interference it gives the founder. In addition, the founder is probably more careful since he is risking *his* money and not someone else's. Personal savings may not be enough, and other sources may have to be tapped, but except for a few clever promoters, most founders of businesses must make some personal contribution toward the initial capitalization.

With the introduction of the progressive income tax in our country, the savings of individuals cannot play the role that they once did in financing and making possible industrial expansion. It is extremely difficult for a person to accumulate a fortune by savings alone. In spite of this, people do save, and they do invest either in their own businesses or the businesses of others. Even high taxation cannot kill the American spirit of competition. Everyone hopes that his mousetrap or his can opener is the one that will revolutionize the industry.

Loans

To consider loans as a source of capital is to see a multitude of possibilities open. The first possibility is to borrow from friends or relatives. These personal loans are frequently made to get small businesses started, and although they can be handled as formally as a bank loan, they oftentimes are not. There may not be any definite rate of interest or time for repayment. Under such circumstances they are more favors than loans.

Of course, there are many institutions in the country that are strictly in the lending business. They are not just doing a businessman a favor by lending him money; they are in business to lend money, and they make money doing it.

Banks come to mind first when lending institutions are mentioned. Commercial banks and savings banks collect the savings of individuals and in turn make them available for financing. In addition, we have savings and loan associations, insurance companies, finance companies, foundations, and other institutions that have funds they wish to invest for a good return.

These lending institutions are all privately owned and controlled, although they must abide by certain government regulations. The federal government has been and is in the lending business also. For many years the Reconstruction Finance Corporation made loans to private businesses either to get them started or, later, to refinance them. The RFC was abolished in 1953 and replaced by the Small Business Administration, whose main purpose is still to lend money to businesses in need—but supposedly only to those small businesses that cannot obtain funds from some private source.

Borrowing money to start or finance a business saddles the business with a fixed obligation that must be met. Interest must be paid on time and the loan itself must be paid back at the agreed-upon date. Such repayment may not be possible or desirable, and further borrowing or refinancing may be necessary.

On the other hand, borrowing allows the founder or owner to retain ownership rights in the business and thereby control over it. Many founders have lost control of their enterprises when financial interests have manipulated the voting stock. If financing can be performed adequately and successfully by loans, avoiding the sale of stock, then the founder need not fear loss of control.

Sale of Securities

Financing a business by the sale of securities means that the founders have decided upon the corporate form of ownership. Of course, using the sale of securities as a method of financing could be a strong reason for forming a corporation in the first place, or it could be a reason for changing from one of the other forms of ownership to a corporate form.

A corporation just starting will finance itself though the sale of common stock. Later on, should extra funds be required and the market for common stock appear not too favorable, the corporation might issue and sell preferred stock. By so doing, it may find money available that otherwise would not be forthcoming. Another way of obtaining additional funds after a corporation has begun operation is by the sale of bonds. This is usually possible only after the corporation is old enough to have established its credit and earning power. Since the sale of bonds is essentially the borrowing of money, the lender will require security for the loan. This security may be in the form of a mortgage on some of the assets of the corporation, but in addition, the bondholder, or the trustee acting for him, will want to be certain the business is stable enough and strong enough to make the interest payments when they are due.

If complete freedom of choice is theirs, many businessmen will normally finance their corporations entirely by means of common stock—both in the initial financing and in the financing of expansion. By so doing, they avoid assuming the burden of the fixed charge of interest that bonds impose. Preferred stock commits the corporation to a stipulated dividend and of course means that the corporation has granted certain special privileges to the owners of these certificates. The use of only common stock puts all stockholders on the same basis. On the other hand, financing through the sale of more and more common stock in many cases dilutes the ownership. In closely held corporations, this may mean that the original owner loses control. In addition, the owner may expect large profits from his operations and may wish to retain them for himself. A stated dividend on preferred stock or stated interest rates on bonds permit the owner (common stockholders) to retain the extra profits.

Obviously, businessmen must weigh all methods of financing and decide which ones are best for them. Experience shows that most business concerns have their profitable years and their lean years. And so the selection among methods of financing through the sale of securities often becomes a matter of expediency: the corporation *must* sell the kind of securities that the public will buy.

Securities Exchanges

Contrary to the belief of many, the various security exchanges do not buy or sell stocks and bonds, and they are not lending institutions. Instead, they fulfill the function of providing a market or trading place for those people who wish to buy and sell stocks and bonds. Various brokerage firms are members of the exchanges, and the representatives of these firms do the actual buying and selling for their clients. For example, an individual who wishes to buy ABC Corporation stock, which is listed on one of the exchanges, contacts his broker. The broker's representative on the exchange floor offers to buy ABC Corporation stock, and after so doing, she learns that some other broker's representative has some ABC Corporation stock to sell. Assuming that the two representatives can agree on price, the deal is closed. In this manner, someone in New York could easily sell his or her stock to someone else in California without either of the two individuals knowing it—and this could all be done in a matter of minutes!

The security exchange also provides a certain amount of protection for investors. An exchange won't ''list'' a security until the company meets certain requirements. Requirements vary with exchanges, but typically, to be listed, a corporation must have a certain minimum number of stockholders, so many millions of shares outstanding, net tangible assets above a certain figure, and the ability to earn a minimum figure of profit after taxes. In addition, the exchange will probably refuse to list a stock that does not carry voting rights. These requirements provide the investor with a higher degree of confidence in any ''listed'' security that he might purchase as compared to an ''unlisted'' issue. It is possible for a corporation to sell a stock or bond issue worth several million dollars all over the United States in a matter of days. The exchanges and their member brokers, who in turn have contacts with thousands of investing individuals and institutions, provide a market. Strange as it may seem, there is always someone willing to buy a ''good'' security at a ''good'' price. If there can be agreement on the definition of the word ''good,'' then a corporation can easily raise capital through the sale of securities.

Profit Plowback

Obviously, at the outset, a new business cannot be financed through the plowback of profits; nevertheless, profit plowback is a method of financing commonly used by established companies. This means that instead of all the profits being paid out to the stockholders or owners as dividends, they are retained in the business and used to finance expansion. By so doing, the present stockholders finance the expansion, whether they want to or not. Of course, they can always sell their stock or voice their objections at the stockholders' meetings. But theoretically they haven't lost anything by the plowback, because the value of their stock is supposed to have gone up. If the expansion is successful, the value of a share of stock will increase beyond the value of the dividends that were originally retained.

Some companies make it a practice to finance expansion in this manner. They avoid any long-term debt and do not dilute the ownership by the sale of voting stock. Here is what happened when one company financed expansion in this manner:

A share of stock sold for $100 when the company was first incorporated. A person buying one share at that time and holding it over the years would have had to invest another $890 in order to exercise the various rights that were issued and buy up odd shares of stock that resulted from stock splits. So our hypothetical person would have had to make a total investment of $990 over a period of 70 years. However, at the end of the 70 years she would own 1680 shares of common stock worth a market value of $134,400. In the meantime, she would have received approximately $40,980 in dividends. This illustrates the growth that is possible through the wise plowing back of profits to expand a business. Of course, profit plowback was not the only contributing factor. Certainly the management was of high caliber, for otherwise the profits would not have been there to plow back.

Trade Credits

We normally don't think of trade credits as a method of financing a business enterprise. But when one stops to consider, trade credits are one of our main methods of financing—particularly in the small enterprise. Some businesses, during their early life or during difficult periods, depend upon trade credits to finance machinery, materials, and miscellaneous equipment. Just as a farmer borrows on a future wheat crop, through trade credits a manufacturer borrows on a future "crop" of production.

Of course, one cannot recommend this method of financing as the one for a business to be entirely dependent upon. Trade credit has a way of disappearing sometimes when it is needed most. But it is a source that can be useful and one that plays an important role in short-term financing.

Financial Statements

The preparation of financial statements is a necessary part of every business, no matter what the form of ownership or the type of business activity. Because these statements show the financial status and progress of the company, they are of interest to the managers, the owners, the lenders, the employees, the creditors, and almost anyone who has any interest in or concern for the business. In most businesses, two financial statements are prepared: the *balance sheet* and the *profit-and-loss statement*. Manufacturing enterprises have need for a third statement, the *manufacturing cost statement*.

These three statements are usually made up by the controller or by the division of the business which deals with financial matters. It is not our purpose to delve into the techniques and problems of accounting, but we do feel it necessary for the reader to achieve a basic understanding of these financial reports. Many business decisions are made only after consulting balance sheets and profit-and-loss statements or after *financially* justifying the move.

The preparation of the balance sheet and of the profit-and-loss statement is normally referred to as a job of "financial accounting." The manufacturing cost statement is usually the work of "cost accounting." Cost accounting and cost control work in general have been treated in Chapter 17. The manufacturing cost statement is included at this point simply to complete the financial status picture.

The Balance Sheet

The balance sheet is a statement showing the financial status of the company at any given time. The statement itself is divided into three parts: (1) *assets,* which are what the company owns; (2) *liabilities,* which are what the company owes; and (3) *net worth,* or capital, which is the amount by which the assets exceed the liabilities. In formula form this would be ASSETS = LIABILITIES + NET WORTH. Note that this relationship holds true on the sample balance sheet shown in Figure 24-1.

Assets have been defined as what the company owns. There is considerable variation in the manner in which assets are listed on balance sheets, but common practice would include the following groups:

Current assets
Investments
Fixed assets
Intangible assets
Deferred charges

Current assets include those items that the company expects to "turn over" during the following accounting period, or else those items that can be quickly turned into cash. Typical items would be cash (naturally), accounts receivable, notes receivable, and inventories.

Investments include stock and bonds of other companies, or other property that the company has purchased with the expectation of a financial return. United States government bonds and United States Treasury notes are also common investments of industrial concerns.

Fixed assets are those items that are more or less permanently used in the business and are not for sale. Such items would include buildings, land on which the plant buildings are situated, machinery, tools and other production and office equipment.

Intangible assets include such items as copyrights, patents, goodwill, and franchises. As the name implies, it is difficult to attach a fair value to these items. We know, for example, that the General Foods Corporation enjoys a large amount of goodwill throughout the country, but how much stated in dollars? The same line of reasoning holds for the other items. The result is that most companies follow the conservative practice of listing these items at a very low valuation—unless the items have been purchased from some other company, in which case they would be listed at the purchase price.

Deferred charges are sometimes referred to as "prepaid expenses" and include those items that have been paid for in advance. An unexpired insurance premium or taxes paid in advance would be good examples.

The method of listing liabilities also varies, but commonly liabilities are shown as "current" and "other." "Current" liabilities include those items that must be paid within the next accounting period. These would typically be accounts payable, notes payable, and expense items such as taxes and wages. "Other" liabilities for the most part include only long-term debts, such as a long-term loan from a bank or an outstanding bond issue.

While net worth is the difference between total assets and total liabilities, it also represents the worth of the ownership of the company. In the case of the proprietorship or the partnership, the net worth represents the amount of money the owners have invested in the business. As profits are made, they are either removed by the owners or allowed to stay in the business, in the latter case the net worth is increased just as if the owners had invested more money.

THE ABC COMPANY, INC.

Balance Sheet, December 31, 19......

Assets		
Current assets:		
Cash	$ 42,650	
Accounts receivable	44,931	
Notes receivable	10,744	
Inventories	160,734	
Total current assets		$259,059
Investments:		
U. S. Government bonds	$ 4,717	
Other marketable securities	16,360	
Total investments		$ 21,077
Fixed assets:		
Land	$ 11,638	
Buildings and equipment	391,382	
Total	$403,020	
Less accumulated depreciation	138,589	
Fixed assets, net		$264,431
Goodwill, patents, and licenses		2,519
Deferred charges		7,026
Total		$554,112

Liabilities		
Current liabilities:		
Bank loans	$ 9,000	
Accounts payable	69,002	
Accrued taxes	20,984	
Total current liabilities		$ 98,986
Long-term debt		31,525
Total liabilities		$130,511
Net Worth		
Preferred shares		$ 2,250
Common shares		48,844
Earned surplus		372,507
Total net worth		$423,601
Total liabilities and net worth		$554,112

Figure 24-1. Balance sheet of a corporation.

In the case of the corporation, the net worth acccount is divided into two parts. One is the *capital stock* account, which indicates what the original shares of stock were sold for. The second part is called *surplus*. As profits are earned, they are shown in the surplus account and are then available to be distributed to the stockholders in the form of dividends, or to be used to finance expansion of the business, or to be kept for that inevitable "rainy day"—as the board of directors sees fit.

The preparation of a balance sheet can be likened to the snapping of a photograph. Both the photograph and the balance sheet give you a picture that represents a single instant; the next instant the view may be different. In order to appraise a business properly, one needs to take a financial picture from time to time. Oftentimes, after the picture is taken, certain ratios are computed to aid in financial appraisal, as, for example,

$$\text{Current ratio} = \frac{\text{Total current assets}}{\text{Total current liabilities}}$$

A desirable current ratio is usually considered to be 2:1. This means that every dollar of current liabilities is covered by two dollars of current assets. In a similar manner,

$$\text{Proprietary ratio} = \frac{\text{Total net worth}}{\text{Total liabilities and net worth}}$$

Proprietary ratio indicates the degree of dependency of a company on its creditors for capital funds.

One must keep in mind that these ratios, as well as others that can be computed, do not show much by themselves. They are of value only when compared with other ratios—either ratios computed for the same company from year to year or similar ratios computed for other companies. An analysis of trends is of great importance when it comes to studying the financial status of a company.

Profit-and-Loss Statement

While the balance sheet shows the financial status of the company at one instant of time, the profit-and-loss statement summarizes the operations of the company for a period of time. This is done in terms of a profit realized or a loss suffered during the period. To show this effect, the statement starts with a report of the income for the period, from which are deducted all the costs incurred as a result of operations. The net figure is the profit or loss for the period. In the case of a corporation it is customary to divide the profit for the period by the total number of shares outstanding so as to arrive at the earnings per share of stock.

As shown in Figure 24-2, companies often have income from sources other

THE ABC COMPANY, INC.

Profit and Loss Statement
Year Ended December 31, 19......

Net sales	$1,038,290
Cost of goods sold	663,096
Gross profit	$ 375,194
Marketing and administrative expense	254,092
Profit from operations	121,102
Interest on investments	1,462
Other income	310
Other expense (deducted)	1,944
Profit before income taxes	120,930
Federal income taxes	54,240
Other income taxes	7,372
Total taxes on income	61,612
Net profit	$ 59,318
Profit per share of common stock outstanding	3.05

Figure 24-2. Profit-and-loss statement for a corporation.

than the sale of manufactured goods. For example, there might be income from stocks or other investments. By the same token, a company might have expenses other than those connected with the manufacture of goods. There might, for example, be interest charges on debts or notes. Both these items of "other" income and "other" expenses are shown separately on the profit-and-loss statement, enabling the reader to appraise the results of the manufacturing operations apart from "other" operations.

The main point of interest in the profit-and-loss statement on the part of stockholders—or of anyone interested in the business—is naturally the amount of profit made. However, just as with the balance sheet, it is possible to work out some ratios that will allow a better financial evaluation. Using figures from both the balance sheet and the profit-and-loss statement, typical ratios would be

$$\text{Net profit ratio} = \frac{\text{Net profit}}{\text{Net sales}}$$

which shows percentage of profit for each dollar of sales, and

$$\text{Rate of return on investment} = \frac{\text{Net profit}}{\text{Net worth}}$$

which shows the earnings rate of the company for each dollar invested by the stockholders, as well as

Rate of earnings on total capital employed

$$= \frac{\text{Net profit}}{\text{Total liabilities and net worth}}$$

which shows the percentage return for every dollar of liabilities and net worth employed.

Many other ratios might be computed, but we have illustrated the principle. Again, we must keep in mind that the ratio has meaning only if it is computed the same way for a number of years and therefore shows trends. Bankers considering a loan of money to industrial concerns will be very interested in many of these ratios and in their trends over the years. In this way a better appraisal of the financial position of the company can be made.

Manufacturing Cost Statement

In examining the profit-and-loss statement in Figure 24-2, one will notice the listing of income followed by a list of expenses, as is typical. The first item of expense listed, however, is the cost of goods sold, which in this case alone accounts for about 64 percent of the net sales. Since this percentage is so large, it seems desirable to break down the cost of goods sold in greater detail. Sometimes this is done right on the profit-and-loss statement, but it is probably more common to submit a separate statement called the *manufacturing cost statement.*

The statement in Figure 24-3 is a typical manufacturing cost statement. In general, it will show the dollars spent for direct labor, materials, and manufacturing expenses. ''Manufacturing expenses'' include all the miscellaneous items necessary for the manufacturing operation, such as repairs, heat, light, and taxes.

To summarize the manufacturing cost statement, it lists and outlines all the costs of manufacturing products during the period covered by the profit-and-loss statement. The methods used to arrive at and control these manufacturing costs were explained in the chapter on cost control (Chapter 17).

Risk and Insurance

Practically everything we do involves a certain amount of risk. When we carry on economic activities, however, it is a special problem to be *aware* of all the risks involved. The farmer is well aware of his risks and of what might happen to his crops because of weather, insects, diseases, or even market price. He does all that he can to avoid these hazards or at least minimize their effects. Manufacturers are no different from farmers in this respect. They must recognize their risks and do all that they can to avoid them or minimize their effects.

THE ABC COMPANY, INC.

Manufacturing Cost Statement
Year Ended December 31, 19......

Materials consumed:
Inventory raw materials Jan. 1, 19 .... $ 9,645
Add purchases of raw materials 326,148

Total raw materials handled .... $ 335,793
Less inventory raw materials December 31, 19.. 13,954

Material consumed .... $ 321,839
Direct labor 248,031
Manufacturing expenses:
Indirect labor .... $ 45,328
Indirect materials 8,967
Power and light 5,627
Repairs 11,411
Miscellaneous expenses 3,018
Property taxes 14,842
Depreciation of buildings and equipment 23,618
Insurance 2,180

Total manufacturing expenses .... $ 114,991

Manufacturing charges for the period .... $ 684,861
Add inventory goods in process, January 1, 19 81,131

Total goods in process handled .... $ 765,992
Deduct inventory goods in process, December 31, 19................ 94,320

Cost of goods manufactured .... $ 671,672
Add inventory finished goods, January 1, 19 43,884

Total cost finished goods available for sale .... $ 715,556
Deduct inventory finished goods, December 31, 19 52,460

Cost of goods sold .... $ 663,096

Figure 24-3. Manufacturing cost statement for a corporation.

First, the manufacturer must contend with economic variations. The business cycle may take a dip just when he can least afford it. Or perhaps there is a long-term trend taking place wherein people are changing their habits and needs. Both of these economic fluctuations might cause loss, and both are extremely difficult to guard against. But the astute businessman can watch economic trends and business forecasts, thereby minimizing the guesswork about the future. Over and above being familiar with general business and market conditions, the manufacturer can reduce his own economic risk by being in close touch with his own particular market. This he does by studying his customers, their needs, and their desires. In this way he can be more nearly certain that what he produces will meet his customers' needs, and that his customers will buy his products. This is the job of *marketing research,* which is treated in more detail in the next chapter.

The manufacturer also faces property risk. There are possibilities of fire, flood, storm, or earthquake. This type of risk can best be minimized by proper plant location and by proper selection and installation of equipment, both of the productive type and of the protective type. Productive equipment must be non-hazardous; the protective equipment, such as sprinklers and fire extinguishers, must be able to do the job when called upon. A certain amount of property risk can be shifted to others by the purchase of insurance. But this is never completely satisfactory in case of a loss. For example, even if the plant were fully insured, a fire might cause the additional loss of several months of production.

A company places a great deal of confidence and trust in its top executives. But what if one or more of these executives makes poor decisions, embezzles the company's money, or dies? What happens to the business then? This is an administrative risk that must be borne. Such risks are usually minimized by proper organization, making for the best decisions and minimizing the possibility of collusion. Independent auditors hired by the board of directors keep tab on the financial status. By good organizational planning, companies provide for replacements in case something should happen to one of their top people. Finally, many companies take out life insurance on their top executives. Although the company may have a replacement being groomed for the job, some disruption still is likely when a new executive takes over, and the life insurance policy will protect the profit account during that period.

Risks other than those discussed above exist for the manufacturer. Manufacturers run risks that their employees will be injured while on the job. This risk is partially covered by worker's compensation. People coming into the plant may fall or otherwise injure themselves. This possibility can be covered by liability insurance. Finally, the manufacturer runs the risk that someone else will develop and market a better product or will develop an improved and cheaper method of manufacturing the present one. Either might have a very serious effect on the future welfare of the business. The manufacturer, then, must be certain that he keeps up to date on new developments and techniques.

Budgets and Financial Control

Budgets and their use in control have been discussed briefly in the chapter on cost control (see Chapter 17). We bring up the topic again at this point to indicate the role of budgets in the overall financial control of the business enterprise.

A complete budget is a coordinated financial plan for a business enterprise, including estimates of sales, production, purchases, labor costs, miscellaneous expenses, and financial operations. Its purpose is to facilitate the planning, coordinating, and controlling of the various departments, divisions, and activities of the business. The total budget will be broken down into various departmental budgets, which will show the requirements for the departments for the period ahead. Most budget estimates are naturally stated in dollars and cents; however, in some cases supplementary estimates must be prepared in other terms. Estimates of sales and production are usually made in terms of units of product, which in turn may be broken down into various styles and sizes. Purchases must be estimated not only in dollars but in units of material required. The labor budget should indicate not only the dollars of cost but the number of workers involved and possibly the skill level required of those workers.

Costs of operation and production are naturally an important aspect of the total budgeting problem. However, the complete budget must provide for the possible expansion of plant facilities and the procurement of funds through bank loans or other sources in order to make the expansion plans possible. In addition, cash may be required to finance research activities and operations until such time as payment is received for the goods produced and sold during the budget period. There is need, therefore, for a strictly financial budget, which usually comes under the jurisdiction of the treasurer or controller, and which is concerned largely with the flow of cash during the budget period and with the possible need to raise additional cash on the outside to meet requirements.

Budget Preparation

One person is usually designated as chief budget officer and is responsible for the preparation of the complete budget. This person is likely to be the controller or someone connected with the accounting office because of his or her knowledge of the activities of the company and of the dollar figures of income and expenses that are associated with those activities. The chief budget officer usually does not have power to approve or disapprove a requested budget item, but serves only as coordinator and adviser to the other executives and department heads as they put together their financial requirements for the budget period ahead.

The submission of any budget figures must be preceded by a study of past performance combined with an analysis of the prospects and plans for the following year. A department head must have this information at her fingertips before she can adequately prepare proposals. The chief budget officer will probably transmit information to her from the sales forecast and production budget, as her department is influenced by these items, and this information, in addition to her own knowledge of past costs, allows her to make plans for future operations. These plans are then transmitted to the chief budget officer, who then compares them with the plans and budget estimates of all the other department heads. Obviously, the various estimates must dovetail with each other, and seeing that they do is the primary responsibility of the budget officer. Performance in one department may depend completely upon the performance of another department, and both must be allowed for in the budget plans. It is likely that the original budget proposals submitted by the department heads will need to be revised and resubmitted, perhaps a number of times, before a complete and coordinated plan of operation for the following year is evolved. If a company genuinely considers the budget to be an operating and controlling device, the preparation of the budget becomes a very careful operation and may require a great deal of time on the part of department heads and their staffs.

The most common budget period is one year in advance. Financial budgets including plans for the financing of plant expansion are usually made for a much longer period, perhaps ten years or more. Operational budgets, while projected for the year ahead, are usually broken down further into quarters and perhaps even months. Some companies project their budgets twelve months in advance on a continuous basis. At the end of each month, the current month is dropped from the estimates and the corresponding month of the following year is added. This enables each department to make plans and commitments on a continuous basis rather than in steps. The step approach is used by companies that set up a budget for one year or six months at a time and provide little or no opportunity to change the plans during the period in question. Smooth operation is somewhat inhibited under such a system, unless the budget is a flexible one rather than one that is fixed. A flexible budget allows for different levels of output and provides better control over expenditures for the manufacturing operation in those plants where frequent variations in volume of production occur.

While the budget is a considerable aid in planning, coordination, and control, it should not be regarded as a straitjacket, as it might limit the exercise of good business judgment during the budget period. On the other hand, if the budget has too much ''flexibility'' in it, control can easily be lost. The point is simply this: in these days of professional management, no manager can afford to sit back and wait to see how things come out at the end of the year. Instead, he or she must make certain that they will come out in the manner desired, and the budget is a way of achieving this. A budget, however, is simply a plan, an estimate, and a prediction, which may not allow for all eventualities; so, realizing this, astute managers provide all the flexibility they can in the design of budgets without losing control.

Subsidiary Budgets

Figure 24-4 is an abridged breakdown of the total budget, showing how it would be built from a sales forecast and would end in an estimated profit-and-loss statement and estimated balance sheet. Although this is an abbreviated picture of the budgeting process, it is designed to indicate the division of production costs into the components of labor, material, and overhead. These headings are much too broad to be meaningful in an actual budget preparation, and it should be obvious that much more detailed breakdowns are normally necessary. For example, the use of a purchases budget is common, and such a budget would estimate the purchases to be made during the coming year, taking into account the inventories of materials on hand and the established reorder points. In addition, certain purchases may have to be made in order to handle the maintenance budget, which would normally be considered a part of the overhead budget. So the maintenance budget not only has in it material requirements but a certain amount of labor requirements for various catego-

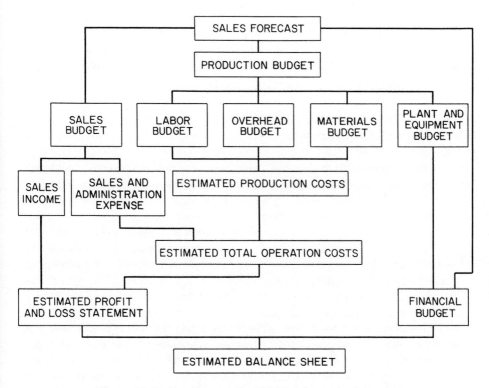

Figure 24-4. Development of total budget from sales forecast.

ries of repair work and preventive maintenance. These examples should illustrate the complexity possible in budget preparation and the need for a coordinator of this work if the budget is to have any meaning.

The plant and equipment budget shows projected changes in the investment in fixed or capital assets. Such changes would be dependent upon the requirements of the production budget and would include both the scrapping of obsolete equipment as well as the purchase of new equipment. The role of the financial budget is that of providing the necessary cash to operate the plant during the period in question as well as providing the necessary new equipment. Research expenditures would also be considered a part of the financial budget inasmuch as they relate to long-term investments rather than short-term operating expenses.

Budget Operation

The preparation of the budget is only the first step in the total program, for the success of budgeting requires follow-up and control. The accounting department should prepare monthly or periodic reports, which show the budgeted amount for each item of income or expense and which compare this amount to the actual amount of income and expense to date. Variations will be evident, and operating people should be asked to explain significant variations. The purpose is not to put anyone "on the spot," but to improve operations. In the long run, an operating official should be able to outline accurately his or her plans for the future and then be able to carry out those plans as outlined.

Capital Budgeting

The previous discussion has dealt largely with the matter of budgeting operating expenses, although some mention was made of the necessity of having plant and equipment items shown in the operating budget because of their close relationship. In general, however, operating budgets are considered separately from capital budgets because of the differences in the sources of funds, as indicated in the first part of this chapter. Since funds for the investment in capital assets are usually limited in any given period of time, many companies are turning to the concept of capital budgeting or capital rationing in dealing with their expansion programs. Let us assume, for example, that the XYZ Company has a hundred thousand dollars available next year for investment in capital assets. It is likely that this company has a number of proposals for capital expenditures during the year to follow, and it is also likely that the total cost of these proposals is probably several times more than the hundred thousand dollars available. The capital rationing concept would then have the company list these proposed projects in order of decreasing prospective rate of return on the investment. One would then simply go down the list as far as the hundred thousand dollars available would permit and install those projects that had the highest prospective rate of return. The process is more simply said than done, but the principle is sound inasmuch as one should be certain that money is invested in projects having relatively high rates of return.

QUESTIONS

1. Outline the various channels through which the personal savings of the people living in your community might eventually be used to finance the expansion of one of your local industries.

2. List the advantages to a corporation of financing expansion (a) by borrowing, and (b) by sale of stock.

3. Could a stockholder have any particular reasons for desiring the corporation to expand by plowing back profit?

4. What is the essential difference between the balance sheet and the profit-and-loss statement in connection with the date shown on each?

5. What is the main method of financing expansion employed by the ABC Company? (See Figure 24-1.)

6. What makes intangible assets intangible?

7. Someone mentions that a particular company made 12 percent profit last year based on

sales. Would you say this was high or low? What would you need to know in order to give a completely adequate answer?

8. What is the need for a manufacturing cost statement if you already have a profit-and-loss statement for the period in question?

9. Make a list of all the possible risks that a manufacturer takes, and, after each, indicate how that risk can be minimized.

10. Does the corporate form of ownership involve fewer risks than the proprietorship and the partnership? Explain.

CASE PROBLEMS

The ABC Company

Financial statements for the ABC Company are shown in this chapter (see Figures 24-1 and 24-2). Referring to the information on these statements, answer the questions indicated below:

Questions:

1. What is the current ratio?
2. What is the proprietary ratio?
3. What is the net profit based on sales?
4. What is the net profit based on total capital employed?
5. What is the net profit based on total investment of stockholders?
6. Would you say the profit percentages computed in Questions 3, 4, and 5 are high or low? Explain your answer.
7. What is the book value of a share of common stock?
8. What factors will influence the market value of a share of this stock?
9. Are corporate dividends paid out of the "earned surplus" account or the "cash" account? Explain.

Walker Metal Parts Company

The issue was clear to the management of the Walker Metal Parts Co.: unless new and improved machinery could be installed within the next two years, competition would drive them into bankruptcy. Slow and inefficient equipment simply cost too much to operate and maintain. Unfortunately, however, the company did not have the $100,000 necessary to make the needed purchases.

The company was considered to be in good financial condition. It had never missed paying a dividend since incorporation, some 40 years before this crisis. Total capitalization was $500,000 when the company was formed and consisted entirely of common stock. There is currently less than $5,000 surplus shown on the company's books as a result of a rather liberal dividend policy over the years.

Questions:

1. What would be the best method of raising the $100,000?
2. Would you suggest any modification in future dividend policy? In equipment replacement policy?

University Bookstore, Inc.

Alice Dernford, manager of the University Bookstore at the local university, received the following letter in the mail this morning:

Dear Ms. Dernford:

   I have been reviewing the financial statement for the bookstore for the past year and have noticed that the store has over a million dollars in earned surplus. It seems to me quite illogical for the bookstore to retain this kind of money, which would be much better invested by offering it to students in the form of scholarships.

   I would like to suggest that you and the board of directors give consideration to my suggestion in the near future.

Sincerely,
Paul Conover, student

In abbreviated form, the financial statement the student has reviewed looked like the following:

Assets		Liabilities & Net Worth	
Cash	$ 5,000	Accounts payable	$3,500
Inventory	602,000	Ownership:	
Equipment	452,000	Stock	10,000
		Earned surplus	1,045,500
	$1,059,000		$1,059,000

Questions:

1. In what manner has the University Bookstore financed their operations in the past?
2. What would the bookstore have to do in order to use the earned surplus for student scholarships?
3. Formulate a suitable reply for Alice to send to the student in a letter.

25

Marketing Management

Most of this book is about manufacturing a product. Certain chapters deal with setting up, financing, and organizing the business. Others deal with the physical facilities that a company must provide and maintain. Another group is concerned with control of the various manufacturing functions, and still others consider the employees who actually produce the product. All of these activities are necessary and worth-while, but it must be emphasized that they would all be useless without the ultimate sale of the product to a customer. The customer may be a consumer who enjoys and ultimately "consumes" the product, or the customer may be another manufacturer who makes use of the product to make still another product. Basically, all of these manufacturing activities are carried out only because the company assumes that someone has need for its product and therefore will buy it. This belief or hope that someone will buy a product cannot be left to chance. Too much is at stake for a business enterprise to concentrate entirely on manufacturing and not to concern itself with marketing. Hence the growth of the field of marketing.

We shall consider the problem of marketing particularly as applied to manufacturing. In so doing, we shall begin by noting the general nature of markets and the common channels of distribution. Following this, we will examine the five basic marketing functions performed by most manufacturing concerns.

Classification of Goods to Be Sold

Goods that must be marketed by manufacturers can be classed into two groups: consumer goods and industrial goods. Consumer goods are those items that will be used ultimately by the household consumer. Examples are foods, refrigerators, and rugs. Industrial goods, on the other hand, are those items that are used to produce other goods. Examples are machine tools, fork trucks, and overhead cranes.

Such a classification helps us to understand marketing patterns and to appreciate the different marketing techniques used. For example, one could hardly conceive of advertising machine tools, an industrial good, by means of television. On the other hand, televison may be a very appropriate means of advertising soft drinks, a consumer good.

Consumer Goods Market

The consumer goods market can be further broken down into classifications of durable goods and non-durable goods. As the name implies, non-durable goods are those that last a short length of time or that are destroyed by use or after use. Examples would be food, facial tissues, and soap. Durable goods are those items that last for some time or wear out slowly. Examples would be automobiles, household appliances, and furniture. Drawing the line between these two is often difficult. Inability to draw a definite line often leads to a classification called semidurable goods. A typical example is clothing.

These various classifications of consumer goods create some inconsistencies when it comes to describing the characteristics of the market, but the characteristics are so decidedly different from those of the industrial goods market that confusion seldom results. Some of the important characteristics of a consumer goods market are the following:

1. It is a nationwide or worldwide market, although a company can concentrate on the market in a particular area or region. It exists wherever people live and can be no greater than the demands of these people. Certain differences in the needs and desires of people depend on the section of the country or world in which they live (snow skis do not sell well in Florida). For consumer goods markets, one must look to where people live, work, or play.

2. Most consumer goods are produced before orders are placed, rather than after, as is often the case with industrial goods. Bathing suits are made during the winter in anticipation of a summer demand. There is obviously a certain element of risk in producing goods ahead of the demand; however, this risk can be minimized by thorough knowledge of the market.

3. Buyers of consumer goods are generally not very skilled at buying as compared to buyers of industrial goods. Inflation has certainly caused consumers to sharpen their buying skills in recent years, but consumers are still more likely to

make purchases without much thought to efficiency, economic values, or long-run costs. Of course, such factors may not be critical in many cases because of the next characteristic of the consumer goods market.

4. Most consumer goods have a small dollar value attached to them. This, of course, doesn't hold true for durable goods; however, for non-durable goods the average item costs very little. This may account for the consumers' lack of skill in buying. Development of buying skill seems to some to be hardly worth the trouble when so few dollars are involved.

5. The final characteristic of consumer goods market is that many items are sold through mass-distribution channels. Such items as food and drugs are well adapted to this type of distribution, as our supermarkets have discovered. In the past many specialty items have not been mass-distributed, but more and more we see consumer items, both durable and non-durable, marketed in this fashion. The growth of supermarkets and discount houses in recent years has disturbed classical distribution methods, with the result that distribution costs and prices to consumers are generally lower. As an example of the changing methods of distributing consumer goods, we note that one department store has offered for sale "his" and "hers" airplanes. (We have no information, however, concerning the number of sales!)

Industrial Goods Market

Like consumer goods, industrial goods can also be classified as either durable or non-durable; however, it turns out that our general concept of industrial goods leaves little that is non-durable. "Supplies" are about the only industrial goods in the non-durable category. Other items, such as equipment, both major and accessory, parts, tools, and materials used in production, are certainly durable.

Some characteristics of the industrial market are the following:

1. Demand tends to fluctuate widely as business conditions fluctuate. When times are bad, users of machine tools, for example, make the old machine last a while longer instead of buying a new one. When times are good, machines are replaced and the demand is often more than the manufacturer can supply.

2. The number of prospective customers is limited, depending somewhat on the type of product. A particular machine will probably have application in a limited number of plants, although some machines or industrial items (for example, conveyors) can be adapted to many plants. Certainly, the industrial market is smaller than the consumer market in number of customers, although not necessarily in number of dollars.

3. Buyers of industrial goods are generally skilled at their work. Purchasing agents enjoy a certain amount of professional stature and are tending more and more to leave personal prejudice or emotion behind when buying industrial goods. Instead, they are carefully studying costs of operation, effect on safety, and productiv-

ity before signing a purchase order. They usually ask the advice of many people within their companies before deciding on purchases.

4. Although some industrial items (lubricants and standard cutting tools, for example) are produced in anticipation of demand, many are made to order. The specialized or the very large machine may have many "standard" parts, but it is usually built to meet the customer's specifications. This generally means production after the order is signed.

5. The last characteristic of the industrial market we shall mention here is the role of the engineer or technical specialist in this field. Because so many items in the industrial field are special or must be engineered to meet technical requirements, engineers play an important role. As sales engineers, they not only sell the products to the customers but also render engineering service before, during, and after installation. To be only a salesperson is often not enough in industrial sales work.

Distribution Channels

Getting a product into the hands of the ultimate consumer is one of the manufacturer's problems. It is not so much a physical problem as it is organizational. The physical movement of products is a concern of the traffic department and is not considered here. To speak of a "channel of distribution" is to refer to the exchange of ownership of the product until it finally reaches its user. Manufacturers commonly make use of the following channels of distribution:

1. Directly to the user, who may be an individual, a company, or another manufacturer.
2. Through wholesalers or jobbers, who in turn sell to retailers or to other manufacturers.
3. Through agent middlemen to other manufacturers or users.

Selling directly to users is a popular method in the marketing of industrial goods. The more specialized or technical the product, the more chance there is of selling it directly. By so doing, the manufacturer can be certain that he or she understands the customer's problem and is delivering what the customer desires. Another factor is that many industrial items require follow-up and service that can be better provided by the manufacturer than by a middleman. Without doubt, direct selling gives the manufacturer maximum control over selling practices and policies, while the use of other channels tends to reduce that control.

Some consumer goods are sold directly, but with consumer markets being so broad and with many items being small in value, this method of distribution becomes rather inefficient. Industrial purchases in many cases run into the tens of thousands of dollars each, while consumer purchases average no more than a dollar or two per item. Although we often try to "eliminate the middleman," it becomes obvious that such elimination won't always bring reduced prices.

The classic distribution channel for consumer goods is through wholesalers or jobbers to retailers and then to consumers. Some industrial goods, such as supplies, are handled this way, particularly when no one customer purchases very much at a time. This becomes an efficient channel for consumer goods because one jobber or wholesaler can handle and deliver the products of many manufacturers to one retailer in the small quantities required. A toothpaste manufacturer could hardly sell one case of toothpaste to the local drugstore at any kind of a reasonable price. A wholesaler, on the other hand, can afford to buy toothpaste by the truckload and deliver one case to the local drugstore if at the same time he can deliver small quantities of candy, cosmetics, first aid supplies, and other items.

Agent middlemen are of three types: brokers, manufacturers' agents, and selling agents. One of the distinctions between the agent middleman and the wholesaler or jobber is in the matter of title to the products handled. Wholesalers and jobbers usually buy the products handled and store them until sold to their customers. Agent middlemen, on the other hand, seldom purchase the products they handle. Instead, they arrange the sale of the product and then collect a commission based on the amount of the sale.

Fundamentally, *brokers* find buyers and/or sellers for their clients and negotiate with them on price and terms of sale. Their greatest use is in the marketing of standardized goods, where price is the predominant factor in determining a sale. Hides, cotton, and steel are typical products marketed through brokers.

A *manufacturers' agent* sells the products of a number of non-competing manufacturers in his particular territory of operations. He will usually handle industrial goods of fairly standard types. By selling non-competing lines for several manufacturers, he can offer more complete lines to his customers and more closely meet his customers' needs. Such an agent might offer a complete line of materials handling equipment by representing a company making fork trucks, another making conveyors, a third making cranes, and so on.

The *selling agent,* sometimes also known as a selling house or commission house, assumes full responsibility for the sale of the manufacturer's product in a territory or in all markets. In a sense, the selling agent is a sales department not under the control of the manufacturer. This, of course, can become a bad feature of the selling-agent method of distribution, as the manufacturer may find himself with little control over selling policies and practices. On the other hand, a small manufacturer who has limited financial resources but requires wide distribution may find the selling agent the best answer to this marketing problem.

Manufacturers who are particularly concerned about having control over the price, terms, and method of sale of their products will practice *consignment selling.* Under this arrangement, title to the goods remains with the manufacturer until the goods are resold to consumers, and the retailer will make payment to the manufacturer or wholesaler after the sale is made. Many retailers and wholesalers favor consignment selling because they have no capital invested in the merchandise and are able to handle it without responsibility for the goods. The manufacturer, on the other hand, can prevent price cutting, which is often thought to be destructive to product prestige.

Cost of Distribution

Several possible channels of distribution and their application have been discussed. Obviously, manufacturers consider many different angles in selecting the channel of distribution that is best for them. One factor, however, that must always be considered is the matter of cost. In the long run a manufacturer will usually employ the channel that allows distribution of the product at the least cost to him. If he doesn't do this, eventually he may be out of business.

The determination of distribution costs is not an easy matter, and it is for this reason that cost analysts have tended to concentrate on manufacturing costs and bypass distribution costs. Changes are taking place, for companies more and more are realizing the need for analyzing distribution costs. Figure 25-1 shows an analysis of distribution costs of two products. Such analysis has been very enlightening to companies who thought they were making a profit on a product only to find they were actually suffering a loss.

	Product A	Product B
Warehousing and handling	.63%	8.20%
Delivery	.06	.87
Office	.93	2.33
Selling	2.50	2.50
Administrative	2.00	2.00
	6.12%	15.90%

Figure 25-1. Distribution costs for two products.

Marketing Functions

The broad functions of marketing management consist of (1) marketing research, (2) product planning, (3) advertising, (4) sales, and (5) product service. Although these operations constitute the main areas of marketing management and serve as units of discussion to follow, we must recognize that there are a number of other miscellaneous operations—dealing with the total marketing problem—that must be performed and that are often assigned to a marketing department. Most of these activities are discussed in other chapters of this book, as appropriate; however, when applicable to marketing situations, they are simply adapted to meet the requirements of marketing problems. They include, for example, such functions as warehousing the product, control of finished goods inventory, coordination with production scheduling, order servicing, organization of the total marketing function including the various sales units, and the recruiting, selecting, training, placement, and development of personnel throughout the marketing department.

Marketing Research

The purpose of marketing research is to determine who and where the customers are; what they need, want, and will buy; where and how they will buy; and how much they will pay. We apply the scientific method in learning answers to these questions so as to maximize the service rendered and the net profits earned.

Some years ago manufacturers considered hunches and trial-and-error experience to be completely adequate in managing the marketing phase of their businesses. If manufacturers carried on research activities at all, they were of the technical variety such as are discussed in Chapter 22 under the heading of Research, Development, and Engineering. This early philosophy ruled out the possibility of research in the marketing field.

Today, the picture is different. Marketing research has come to be a very important part of the marketing function. When properly conducted, marketing research is just as valuable to the manufacturer as is technical research. However, we must quickly point out that the state of the art is not as advanced. Management will seldom know as much about the performance of the marketing function as about the manufacturing phases of the business.

Tremendous progress has been made during recent years in developing marketing research techniques, and we have every reason to believe that such progress will continue. But one can appreciate the difficulties of marketing research when the intangible factors become evident. Determining how many times a refrigerator door can be opened and closed before it fails is relatively easy, but determining why a housewife buys one kind of refrigerator in preference to another is a different kind of problem.

Types of Marketing Research Activity

Essentially, all marketing research activity consists of the gathering, analyzing, and interpreting of facts and opinions that concern marketing, and doing so early enough to insure sound decisions in all aspects of the marketing process. Actually, it would be easy for a company to determine the success of a particular product by producing and selling it and then measuring the number of units that were sold. If very few were sold, it could be concluded that the product was a failure; if a great number were sold, it could be assumed that the product was a success. This is an expensive process, however, and few companies can afford it. A more prudent practice would be to make some studies regarding the proposed product ahead of time in order to form a basis of prediction as to its probable success and its influence upon the company's profit-and-loss position.

For this reason, marketing research personnel conduct a number of various types of studies in order to provide the type of answers needed by all of the various marketing functions. These studies can generally be grouped into four areas outlined below, although one should realize that in an actual research program there might be considerable overlap among the four areas, depending upon the nature of the problem.

Research relating to product or service. This area of research is concerned with customer reaction to a product. In other words, what does he or she think or feel about the product? In durability tests a certain brand of refrigerator may be the best one on the market, but if potential purchasers don't like it for some reason and therefore won't buy it, then it matters little how long the refrigerator will last. Product research in marketing attempts to uncover customer likes and dislikes for products and to do so before the product is placed on the market. Typical studies under this heading might concern new product development (non-engineering), improvement of present products, new uses for old products, the competitive position of the company's products, packaging, pre-testing of new products, customer preferences, product elimination or simplification of lines, and naming of products.

Research relating to markets. This type of research attempts to learn all aspects of the market for a product. In general, it will attempt to measure the size of a market, its location, and any peculiarities concerning it that may be helpful in planning a sales program. More specific types of studies would include analysis of consumer markets (including industrial markets), analysis of wholesale markets, analysis of relative profitableness of markets, analysis and interpretation of general market data, estimate of potential sales, estimate of demand for new products, market analysis by customer, market analysis by areas, establishment of sales territories, establishment of sales quotas, analysis of competitive conditions in markets, general business forecasting, analysis of potential new market areas, and analysis of potential of old market areas.

Research relating to sales methods. Studies of sales methods relate largely to the problems of distribution and advertising. In the study of distribution, we are attempting to select a method of distribution that will result in the lowest cost. In advertising studies, we are attempting to determine the value and influence of advertising. The two main concerns in advertising research are (1) what advertising messages have greatest appeal (copy research), and (2) where messages should be placed (media research). More specific studies include those of advertising practices in relation to competitors, distribution costs, sales devices, choice of advertising copy, choice of advertising media, selection of distributive channels, sales performance tests, and sales training.

Research relating to policy.   This area of research is concerned with general company policies and not specific policies regarding new products. Success of a marketing activity may depend to a large extent on how problems are handled when they involve price structure, sales methods, advertising policy, cancellations, returned goods, credit, discounts, public relations, dealer relations, transportation, sales compensation, wholesale and dealer margins, premiums, raw materials, price changes, and inventory.

The Methods of Marketing Research

There are three different kinds of basic research data, namely, (1) historical data, (2) survey data, and (3) experimental data.

The routine operations of the business enterprise frequently are recorded, and these records, often extending back through the years, provide a valuable source of information. Sales data classified by territory, product, class of customer, salesperson, and so on are frequently available from routine records without any special research effort. Also, it is possible to get, from other sources, a great deal of information concerning the characteristics of the various groups that constitute the consumers and potential consumers of any product. Various government bodies have such data available, and many local chambers of commerce and trade associations may have data concerning special segments of the population. The statistical analysis of the sales data of an individual enterprise and of the relationship of these data to other variables such as income or population is known as "sales analysis." Such analysis is probably more widely used than any other method of research as a basis for marketing decisions, inasmuch as the data are usually available without any large expenditure of energy or money and can be made to yield suggestive hypotheses concerning the consequences of alternative marketing decisions.

Statistics provided by government bodies have been mentioned as a valuable source of information for marketing research. An example of this is information regarding the baby boom recorded in the late 50's and early 60's as the U. S. birth rate greatly increased following World War II. These baby boomers have been closely watched in the marketplace and their needs anticipated by many companies. In 1978, 4.3 million births took place, the greatest number recorded in any one year. It would appear that in the late 80's the children of the baby boomers are causing some special needs in the marketplace which, in turn, should present some opportunities for companies who are alert to the possibilities.

The second major source of information for marketing research work is the survey. The survey attempts to reach a representative group of the population under study (for example, consumers or dealers), in order to learn directly from them particular information of interest. Such information might include a reaction to a product or an intention to buy the product within the next year.

There are two types of surveys: a single communication with a segment of the population under study, and a repeated contact or panel-type survey. The one-time communication is usually made through a personal interview, a telephone interview, a mailed questionnaire, or a questionnaire included with the product. The interview, whether in person or by telephone, solicits answers from the respondents concerning their reactions to a product. The questions may refer to the product's design, package, or usefulness, depending upon the purpose of the study. The questionnaire does the same thing by mail but places an extra premium on careful construction of the questions, since a confusing question may bring confusing answers. The panel is simply a group of cooperative respondents who agree to give repeated reactions to new products, new designs, or new packages. The people or family chosen for the panel are supposed to be "representative" of the buying public.

The third major type of data that can be used as evidence of the probable effects of alternative marketing decisions is data arising from experiments. In this context, an experiment is a process created or conditioned by an investigator so that observations can be made that will yield meaningful conclusions concerning the relationships between the observed variables. For example, different methods of shelf display may be instituted in a number of self-service retail stores in order to observe the sales resulting from each method. Such experiments are frequently called sales tests. Manufacturers often make other sales tests on a new product by producing it in limited quantities and offering it for sale in selected outlets under rather carefully controlled conditions. The selected outlets would be in cities that have age and income distributions that match the nation's as closely as possible. Such experiments provide useful data in predicting customer acceptance of the product.

What Marketing Research Does for a Business

Generally speaking, marketing research contributes in four ways:

1. It keeps the business in touch with its markets.
2. It uncovers new product ideas.
3. It assists in sales management.
4. It measures market potential.

Keeping in touch with the market reveals such things as overall market size for any specific product and the portion of the market *our* company has or can secure. Learning the likes and dislikes of the market is important and must be done on a continuing basis, for customers, whether industrial or consumer, change their tastes from time to time.

Uncovering new product ideas includes ideas for the improvement of old products as well as ideas for totally new products. A company anxious to grow and maintain its position in the market must have many good sources of new product ideas. Marketing research provides one of the better sources.

Sales management is frequently faced with problems of setting up territories, measuring territorial potential, and setting standards for salespersons' performance. Marketing research can provide a basis for answers to these problems as well as help in the making of overall sales forecasts for the company.

Product Planning

Product planning is the function that makes certain that new products are added, old ones are discontinued, and questionable ones changed at the right time. It involves setting up clear-cut objectives for the complete line of products and adopting policies in line with these objectives. Furthermore, it is usually charged with developing the sales forecast for each product and for each territory for specific periods of time in the future. Obviously, then, the operations of product planning may be aided considerably by the results of various marketing research studies.

During periods of prosperity, when industrial goods are in demand, a manufacturer tends to neglect thinking of the future. When she receives more orders than she can fill, her attention is directed almost entirely to the problems of production, but when the cycle of business reverses and she awakens to the fact that orders are no longer running the plant at capacity, she turns her attention to the cultivation of old customers and the development of new ones. By then, however, it may be too late. The wise manufacturer does not wait for a period of recession or depression before taking corrective action. Through a combination of marketing research and product planning, she is in touch with the market and has planned her product line so as to meet the needs of the customers and thus maintain a higher level of manufacturing activity.

Product planning is a necessary activity for the long-run success of the business and must be carried out regardless of whether a buyer's market exists or a seller's market exists. Constant attention must be paid to the various product lines to be certain they are meeting the requirements of the customer in regard to performance, appearance, pricing, and service. Product simplification and component standardization are also important aspects of meeting customer needs, as well as reducing costs of manufacture.

The sales forecast has an important role in the operation of a business and must be made with the greatest care. Production schedules will be set up based upon the forecast, and errors on either the high side or the low side could be very costly to operations in general. Usually, the forecast is projected for a year and then is broken down into quarters, months, or even weeks. The forecast represents a commitment on the part of the sales department and each of its divisions, and it becomes a goal against which the effectiveness of the department will be measured. It becomes clearer, therefore, that the sales force should actively participate in the determination of the sales forecast so that they will be motivated to put forth their best efforts.

Advertising

A good argument can be started at almost any kind of gathering by asking, "Why do companies spend so much money on advertising?" The argument occurs because some people regard all advertising as a waste of money and others look upon it as an absolute buying guide. Probably, neither view is correct. Instead, advertising plays a role somewhere between these two extremes.

In general, consumers and buyers regard advertising as an informative device. Through advertising, one learns of bargains at the local department store, or of the introduction of a new-model automobile. Often the potential buyer gains all or much of the following information:

1. The fact that a product exists.
2. Where it can be procured.
3. What it will do.
4. The price.
5. How to care for it.
6. How to use it.
7. Probable length of life.

The seller, on the other hand, looks at advertising as a means of reducing selling costs. Any product can be sold to a degree through the use of personal selling or salespeople. But can you imagine getting wide distribution of chewing gum solely by means of salespeople and with no advertising? It undoubtedly could be done, but the costs would be tremendous. The gum would be so expensive that few of us could afford to chew it. The same line of reasoning can be applied to almost any product. Mass production can be supported only by mass distribution, which is made possible by mass advertising. A manufacturer may use personal selling, but he will usually depend upon advertising to reduce the selling job required of his salespeople.

Types of Advertising

Advertising can be divided into two principal types:

1. Advertising that promotes a product.
2. Advertising that promotes an idea or the name of a company.

The first type is perhaps the more common, the one that first enters our minds when someone mentions advertising. Newspapers and magazines are full of advertisements of this type—all designed to get the customers to come and buy a particular item. The approach is direct, with the hope of obtaining immediate action.

Advertising that promotes an idea is a little more subtle in its approach. It is commonly known as goodwill or institutional advertising and is usually employed by a company in order to keep the company's name before the eyes of the public. Companies sponsoring symphony broadcasts or running special ''art'' paintings in magazines under the company name are using this type of advertising.

Advertising Media

The advertising medium may be thought of as the carrier of the advertising message. Basically the problem is one of communications, for in some way the manufacturer must communicate with customers, both potential and actual. Common media used by manufacturers are:

1. Newspapers.
2. Magazines.
   a. General magazines.
   b. Trade journals.
   c. Sports and hobby magazines.
   d. Farm magazines.
   e. Technical and professional journals.
   f. Men's or women's magazines.
3. Radio and television.
4. Direct mail.
5. Outdoor transportation.
6. Exhibits and displays at trade shows.
7. Merchandising aids.
8. Motion pictures.

Probably no one manufacturer uses all of these, but instead will select those most likely to reach the market for his or her product. This means a careful analysis of markets so that advertising dollars can be most efficiently utilized.

Producers of consumer goods will usually employ media that give wide contact with the buying public. Popular magazines, radio, and television are widely used for this purpose. Manufacturers of producer goods, on the other hand, will be much more selective in deciding upon media. A manufacturer of machine tools, for example, will probably use direct mail, trade journals, and exhibits. Even these will be used on a restricted basis after careful analysis of what constitutes the market.

The Advertising Agency

From the preceding section, one can see that the selection of media for advertisements is a specialized problem that can be answered only after careful research. To aid them in doing this work, manufacturers frequently employ advertising agencies. In addition to rendering advice on media, these agencies present ideas and themes for advertising programs and prepare the separate advertisements. This means that the advertising agency is simply an outside consultant; but it does not mean that the manufacturer can regard it the same as other outside consultants, because the advertising agency is paid for its services in a unique way.

The usual charge for the services rendered by the advertising agency is 15 percent of the media cost. The advertiser is billed for the full rate, and the agency takes out its 15 percent and remits the balance to the media. In other words, the 15 percent is not an additional charge; it is deducted from the money the media would normally receive. The manufacturer pays no more for advertising whether or not she uses the services of an advertising agency. By using the agent, she saves the expense of employing a staff of advertising specialists. In addition, if the manufacturer should become dissatisfied with the work of the agency, it is much easier to change to another agency than it is to reorganize an advertising department.

Just because the advertising agency offers so many advantages to a manufacturer doesn't mean that she will not have an advertising department as part of her organization. Such a department, however, will usually act largely as a coordinating group between the company and the agency. The advertising department will supply necessary information, product samples, and records and give approval to the campaigns laid out by the agency.

Coordination of Sales and Advertising

We have been speaking of sales and advertising largely as separate and distinct functions in a business enterprise. Although they may be organized in this manner and shown thus on the organization chart, special emphasis needs to be placed on the need for close coordination between the two. Neither can go its own separate way without causing ultimate harm to the business.

Some companies have one person heading up both the sales and advertising functions. On paper this appears to insure close coordination, but it doesn't necessarily follow. Instead, true coordination comes through close contact among the people concerned with the two functions. For example, here are some kinds of coordination that benefit a business:

1.   Advertising should pave the way for salespersons' calls. First calling the customer's attention to a new product through advertising will make a sale easier.
2.   Advertising can secure leads for salespeople. Inquiries that result from advertising should be passed on to salespersons for follow-up.
3.   Advertising should "contact" buyers between the salespeople's calls. This will tend to maintain interest.
4.   Advertising can be used to relieve salespeople of unprofitable

accounts. Rather than lose small accounts altogether, advertising could solicit what business there is.

5. Salespeople should report on customer reaction to advertising copy. In this way copy can be improved constantly.
6. Salespeople can lend assistance in planning advertising campaigns. Their knowledge of customers and territories will be of considerable aid.

Selling

In one sense, all activities of the marketing department may be considered selling; however, here we refer in particular to the work of the salesperson. Salespeople and sales offices are often required to perform many of the other activities mentioned under the various headings of marketing, and certainly the sales force should participate in many of these activities—sales forecasts, for example—although they may not be given direct responsibility for these areas. We are choosing to regard selling as a separate and distinct function because of its extreme importance to the success of the whole manufacturing activity.

Once the plans and policies for the manufacture and distribution of products have been established and the advertising material has been distributed through various media, it becomes the responsibility of salespeople and the various branch sales offices to make personal contact with the customers and to secure the orders. This personal approach seems to have no substitute that is fully adequate, for many customers make their choice of products in terms of their likes and dislikes of the salesperson. This is particularly true in those market areas that have many competing products available. Maintaining personal contact with customers presents quite a challenge to a selling activity, particularly if the sales area involved covers a large geographical area. For this reason, many companies restrict their overall marketing area in order to give better contact and service to those territories that they do attempt to cover.

There are some special considerations to be borne in mind when setting up and administering the selling function. The problems involved are different from those of a typical manufacturing department, and it is important that these differences be clearly recognized.

1. The importance of the salesperson and the fact that he or she represents the culmination of all prior planning and effort in the entire manufacturing enterprise should be recognized. If he or she should fail the job, the entire effort has been for nothing.
2. Salespeople represent the company and speak for the company. Whatever they say or do will reflect on the company in some manner and will perhaps have a definite influence on present or future business relationships.

3. Salespeople perform their duties alone. They must often make spot
    decisions whether or not they are qualified, or have the knowledge to
    do so. Unlike someone performing a job in the plant, a salesman
    cannot go ask his boss what to do about a particular situation or
    problem.
4. The performance of selling is a costly one in which it is extremely
    difficult to measure the benefits of money expended. One should make
    every effort to keep these costs low; however, the influence of
    personal contact with customers may be considerable, and one must
    guard against cutting costs to the point where accounts are not
    properly serviced.

It is difficult to overemphasize the importance of proper selection, training,
and development of the sales force.

Product Service

Product service is the function that makes certain that all moral and legal responsibilities connected with product performance are properly fulfilled so that customer
satisfaction and repeat business are obtained. More and more, such service is becoming an essential part of the sale itself, and a service guarantee accompanies the
product. A manufacturer of production machinery finds it essential to see that his
products are properly installed. He does this not only as a service to his customers
but as a protection against possible complaint or general dissatisfaction. Once the
equipment is installed, the manufacturer may instruct the maintenance crew of the
customer in its proper care. Of course he may charge a fee for maintenance service,
but this presents an additional problem inasmuch as he must then be able to provide
complete and rapid service through a network of branch offices.

Sometimes the salesperson is also responsible for product service, and, depending upon the complexity of the product involved, the salesperson may have to
be a trained engineer in order to provide the service required. Some companies employ engineers as salespeople, not only to render service after the sale, but to facilitate the sale in the first place. This practice is common in companies that produce
specialized items that are highly technical in nature and require close cooperation
with the customer's engineers before specifications are drawn up and the item ordered. There are many fine opportunities in industry for trained engineers who enjoy
contact with customers and the challenge of solving customer problems.

Whether the manufacturer employs a combined salesperson and product service person or sets up his product service group separately from his selling group is
of no particular importance for our discussion. He will follow one method or the
other, depending upon the problems he faces and his ability to work out solutions.
The important thing for our purposes is that the concept of product service must not
be overlooked if the long-run success of the business is to be assured.

QUESTIONS

1. Discuss the role of marketing in a manufacturing organization.
2. How would the sales organization of a manufacturer of consumer goods differ from that of a manufacturer of industrial goods?
3. From the basic characteristics of consumer and industrial markets, outline desirable qualifications of salespeople for each of these markets.
4. What features distinguish the three basic channels of distribution?
5. How could a distribution cost analysis cause a manufacturer to change the basic price structure of the products he or she sells?
6. Describe the role of advertising in today's economy.
7. The advertising agency performs what functions for the manufacturer?
8. What are some important factors to be considered in the selection of a suitable advertising medium?
9. Make a clear distinction between product research and market research.
10. Describe the function of marketing research in a manufacturing concern.

CASE PROBLEMS

Canary Appliance Corporation

At its plant in Cleveland, Ohio, the Canary Appliance Corporation manufactures a complete line of small electrical appliances, including an electric iron, broiler, fry pan, blender, toaster, coffee maker, deep fat fryer, mixer, and roaster. An annual volume of sixty million dollars is sold through a variety of outlets such as appliance wholesalers, chain stores, mail-order houses, hardware jobbers, variety stores, and auto-accessory distributors. Sales to these various outlets are handled by a group of 25 salespeople who have been assigned territories throughout the country.

The manufacture of small appliances created some painting problems, and Mr. Lester Frey, who was chief engineer for the company, had spent considerable time on these problems. Two years ago he and some of his assistants developed a new paint-spraying process that cut the cost of painting in half and reduced the scrap caused by poor painting to almost nothing. In addition, the process was adaptable to the use of different colors, which is in line with current trends away from the traditional white.

At the time the process first showed promise of success, the company applied for a patent on it in Mr. Frey's name. After the patent was issued, Mr. Frey suggested that the company manufacture the various key parts of the spray-painting system and sell them to other manufacturers. He visualized a tremendous market and predicted there would be several thousands of dollars added to net profit the first year. He argued that the patent protection would minimize competition and that the company's experience in developing and using the process would enable them to manufacture it for sale to others with very little extra trouble.

Questions:

1. Should Canary Appliance Corp. put their spray-painting process on the market?
2. If they do, what channels of distribution should be used?
3. What problems do you visualize if the new process is marketed?
4. Outline how the company could determine the size of the market for the new paint-spraying process.

David's Dilemma

Larry David had finally concluded that he really was riding a dead horse, or at least one that had a terminal disease. As president of David Drafting, Inc., he was responsible not only for the business as a whole, but since it was largely owned by members of the David family, he felt a special responsibility to all his dozens of cousins and shirttail relatives who owned stock. The company had been founded by his great grandfather 125 years ago and had enjoyed much success over the years largely because management had always been centralized in the hands of one person in spite of the fact that ownership had been disbursed in the hands of many family members. Larry himself owned only 2 percent of the outstanding stock.

The company produces and sells many items useful to drafting and engineering work for their customers, but such work isn't being done the way it used to be. Slide rules used to be a big business for David, but that simply died with the advent of the electronic calculator. Other items in the product line may be going in the same direction with the introduction of computer-aided design and computer-aided manufacturing. Larry reasoned that there will probably always be need for some hand work on the part of all companies, but not enough to constitute a growing business for David, and maybe not enough to constitute a sustaining business.

Larry woke up one morning with the sudden realization that his responsibility in his job was not so much to preserve the drafting business but to preserve the assets of the company. He had always conceived the business as drafting and had developed interests and had expanded into only those items that were related to drafting. Now he decided that this was the "dead or dying horse." He simply had to find another horse, or at least develop some different concepts of business philosophy.

As a prolific reader of trade publications, Larry was familiar with all the things that were reportedly businesses of the future, and in fact, he had been accumulating a file of articles relating to these ideas and success stories. The file included many stories about success (and failure) in the computer business and various specialties in that area, but it also contained articles about hospitals, nursing homes, day care centers and health care generally, and articles about the baby boom and the fact that the baby boomers are now having babies, which might present a good market.

On the surface, none of the ideas in Larry's file struck his fancy as the answer to his prayer, but he continued to search and talk with everyone possible about what would present some attractive possibilities for the future of David Drafting. He recognized that in any area that was examined and found to be calling for action he could either try to develop a business from scratch or buy out an already established business.

Questions:

1. What is the role of the chief executive officer in any company? Answer in the light of David's dilemma.

2. If preservation of assets is so important, as Larry seems to think, why not simply sell out and use the money to buy CD's?

3. Outline a method of approach and action for Larry to analyze the opportunities and possibilities of any particular business area in which he might have interest.

4. What are the relative advantages and disadvantages of starting a new business from scratch compared to purchasing one that is already established?

5. What general advice would you have for Larry in trying to solve his dilemma?

INDEX